THE **Public Debate** OVER
CONTROVERSIAL
SUPREME COURT DECISIONS

THE Public Debate OVER CONTROVERSIAL SUPREME COURT DECISIONS

Edited by Melvin I. Urofsky
Virginia Commonwealth University

CQ PRESS

A Division of Congressional Quarterly Inc.
Washington, D.C.

11-30-2005
ww
₱/20

CQ Press
1255 22nd Street, NW, Suite 400
Washington, DC 20037

Phone: 202-729-1900; toll-free, 1-866-427-7737 (1-866-4CQ-PRESS)

Web: www.cqpress.com

CQ Press gratefully acknowledges the permission granted by National Review, Inc. to reprint two excerpts that appear in chapter 32. The first, on page 303, is excerpted from "The Abortion Front: The End of the 'Phony War,'" *National Review,* March 2, 1973, 249–250, © 1973 by National Review, Inc., 215 Lexington Avenue, New York, NY 10016. The second, on pages 303–304, is excerpted from "Raw Judicial Power," by John T. Noonan Jr., *National Review,* March 2, 1973, 260–264, © 1973 by National Review, Inc., 215 Lexington Avenue, New York, NY 10016.

Cover design: Jeffrey Miles Hall, ION Graphic Design Works

Cover photo: R. Michael Jenkins, Congressional Quarterly

∞ The paper used in this publication exceeds the requirements of the American National Standard for Information Sciences—Permanence of Paper for Printed Library Materials, ANSI Z39.48-1992.

Printed and bound in the United States of America

09   08   07   06   05   1   2   3   4   5

Cataloging-in-Publication Data is available from the Library of Congress

ISBN 1-56802-937-3

For

Mr. Justice Michael McHugh

and

Alison Stenmark, S.C.

who helped make our visits down under truly delightful

CONTENTS

CASES ARRANGED ALPHABETICALLY

ABOUT THE EDITOR

Melvin I. Urofsky is professor of public policy and law at the L. Douglas Wilder School of Government and Public Affairs at Virginia Commonwealth University. He is the author or editor of more than two dozen books on constitutional law, Supreme Court history, and religious freedom. His other publications with CQ Press include *The Legal Philosophies and Influences of Supreme Court Justices: A Biographical Encyclopedia* (2006); *100 Americans Making Constitutional History* (2004); and *Landmark Decisions of the United States Supreme Court*, with Paul Finkelman (2003).

ABOUT THE CONTRIBUTORS

Howard Ball is professor emeritus at the University of Vermont, where he was also dean of arts and sciences. He is the author of more than three dozen articles in political science, public administration, and law journals and more than two dozen books, including biographies of Thurgood Marshall, Hugo L. Black, and William O. Douglas. He has written texts for students of the U.S. Supreme Court as well as books about the international criminal court. His most recent publications are *The Supreme Court in the Intimate Lives of Americans*, 2d ed. (2004); *Murder in Mississippi* (2004); and *War Crimes and Justice* (2002).

B. Keith Crew is professor of sociology at the University of Northern Iowa. He has researched and published on the impact of race and gender on criminal sentences, public opinion on appropriate punishments for convicted criminals, and the social context and impact of the *Miranda* and *Furman* cases.

Lyle Denniston is the senior reporter in the Supreme Court's press corps. Having covered the Court since 1958, he has reported on one-quarter of the justices in its entire history. Currently, he covers the Court for an Internet-based clearinghouse of information about the Supreme Court's work—the Web log known as "SCOTUS-blog"—and for radio station WBUR in Boston. He is the author of *The Reporter and the Law: Techniques of Covering the Courts* (1992) and a contributor to *100 Americans Making Constitutional History* (CQ Press, 2004).

Bruce J. Dierenfield is Peter Canisius Distinguished Teaching Professor of Modern American History and director of the African American Experience at Canisius College. He is the author or coauthor of three books, including *The Civil Rights Movement* (2004); *Keeper of the Rules: Congressman Howard W. Smith of Virginia* (1987); and *The Federal Role and Activities in Energy Research and Development, 1946–1980: An Historical Summary* (1983). His essays and articles on school prayer have appeared in many publications, including CQ Press's *100 Hundred Americans Making Constitutional History* (2004). His forthcoming book is *A Godless Nation? The School Prayer Case of* Engel v. Vitale.

Paul Finkelman is Chapman Distinguished Professor at the University of Tulsa College of Law. He is the author, coauthor, or editor of more than twenty books, including *Landmark Decisions of the United States Supreme Court*, with Melvin I. Urofsky (CQ Press, 2003); *A March of Liberty: A Constitutional History of the United States*, rev. ed. (2002), with Melvin I. Urofsky; and *Slavery and the Founders: Race and Liberty in the Age of Jefferson*, 2d ed. (2001).

Louis Fisher is senior specialist in separation of powers at the Congressional Research Service of the Library of Congress. His books include *American Constitutional Law*, 6th ed. (2005); *Military Tribunals and Presidential Power* (2005); *Nazi Saboteurs on Trial*, 2d ed. (2005); and *Presidential War Power*, 2d ed. (2004).

Tim Alan Garrison is associate professor of history and director of Native American Studies at Portland State University. He is the author of *The Legal Ideology of Removal: The Southern Judiciary and the Sovereignty of Native American Nations* (2002).

Robert Justin Goldstein is professor of political science at Oakland University and research associate at the Center for Russian and Eastern European Studies at the University of Michigan. He is the author of ten books, including *Flag Burning and Free Speech: The Case of* Texas v. Johnson (2000) and *Burning the Flag: The Great 1989–1990 American Flag Desecration Controversy* (1996).

Sarah Barringer Gordon is professor of law and history at the University of Pennsylvania and teaches in the areas of church and state, property, and legal history in the law school and American religious and constitutional history in the Department of History. She is the author of *The Mormon Question: Polygamy and Constitutional Conflict in Nineteenth-Century America* (2002), which won a 2003 Best Book Award from the Mormon History Association and the Utah Historical Society. She is currently working on a new book about religion and litigation in the twentieth century, titled *The Spirit of the Law*.

Vivien Hart is research professor of American studies at the University of Sussex, in Brighton, England. She is author of *Bound by Our Constitution: Women, Workers, and the Minimum Wage* (1994) and articles and chapters on gender politics and historical and contemporary constitutionalism. She is the editor with Alexandra Dobrowolsky of *Women Making Constitutions: New Politics and Comparative Perspectives* (2003).

Gregg Ivers is professor of government at American University. He is the author of *American Constitutional Law: Power and Politics,* Volumes 1 and 2 (2001) and *To Build a Wall: American Jews and the Separation of Church and State* (1995) and coeditor of *Creating Constitutional Change: Clashes over Power and Liberty in the Supreme Court* (2004). His research interests include American constitutional development, interest group use of the courts, and comparative U.S.-Canadian judicial process.

John W. Johnson is professor of history at the University of Northern Iowa. He is the author of several books, articles, and essays on legal topics, including Griswold v. Connecticut: *Birth Control and the Constitutional Right of Privacy* (2005) and *The Struggle for Student Rights:* Tinker v. Des Moines *and the 1960s* (1997), and is the editor of *Historic U.S. Court Cases: An Encyclopedia* (2001).

Paul Kens is professor of political science and history at Texas State University–San Marcos. He is the author of Lochner v. New York: *Economic Regulation on Trial* (1998) and *Justice Stephen Field: Shaping Liberty from the Gold Rush to the Gilded Age* (1997).

Mark R. Killenbeck is Wylie H. Davis Distinguished Professor of Law at the University of Arkansas. He teaches constitutional law and legal history and has written widely on American constitutional history with a special emphasis on questions regarding federal-state relations during the first fifty years of the nation's history. He is currently completing the volume *M'Culloch, Securing a Nation:* M'Culloch v. Maryland.

John W. Lemza is a retiree from the U.S. Army, having served for more than twenty years. He graduated from Virginia Commonwealth University in 2005 with a master's degree in history. He teaches history at John Tyler Community College and also works as a historical researcher.

Carolyn Long is associate professor of political science and director of the Program in Political Affairs at Washington State University. In addition to her book *Religious Freedom and Indian Rights: The Case of* Oregon v. Smith (2000), she has written a number of articles and book chapters on civil liberties issues. She is working on a book about *Mapp v. Ohio* and the exclusionary rule.

Erin K. Mooney is an honors graduate of Virginia Polytechnic Institute and State University.

David M. O'Brien is Spicer Professor of Politics at the University of Virginia and author or editor of nineteen books, including *Storm Center: The Supreme Court in American Politics,* 7th ed. (2005), which received the ABA's Silver Gavel Award, and *Animal Sacrifice and Religious Freedom* (2004).

David Ray Papke is professor of law at Marquette University, where he teaches family law, property law, and American legal history. His most recent book is *The Pullman Case: The Clash of Labor and Capital in Industrial America* (1999). He is a contributing editor to the forthcoming *Law & Pop Culture: A Textbook.*

Ellen Holmes Pearson is assistant professor of history at University of North Carolina, Asheville. She is completing a book on legal scholars and the construction of identity in early America. Her recent publications include essays on the legal rights of free people of color in antebellum New Orleans and Connecticut and constitutionalism in the early national period.

Shawn Francis Peters has taught writing and rhetoric at the University of New Hampshire, the University of Iowa, and the University of Wisconsin. He is the author of two books on religion and law, *The Yoder Case: Religious Freedom, Education, and Parental Rights* (2003) and *Judging Jehovah's Witnesses: Religious Persecution and the Dawn of the Rights Revolution* (2000).

Peter G. Renstrom is professor of political science at Western Michigan University. He teaches courses in constitutional law, civil liberties and rights, and judicial process. He is the author or coauthor of fifteen books, including *Constitutional Rights Sourcebook* (1999) and *Constitutional Law and Young Adults,* 2d ed. (1996). He recently served as the editor of a fourteen-volume series on the Supreme Court.

Harvey Rishikof is chair of the national security law department and professor of law and national security studies at the National War College in Washington, D.C. He specializes in the areas of national security, national security law, military theory, civil liberties, civilian and military relations, and constitutional law.

Arthur J. Sabin is professor emeritus of The John Marshall Law School. His books include *In Calmer Times: The Supreme Court and Red Monday* (1999) and *Red Scare in Court: New York Versus the International Workers Order* (1993).

James Z. Schwartz is lecturer in history at the University of Dearborn–Michigan. His specialty is early American history and, in particular, Michigan history.

Brooks Simpson is professor of history at Arizona State University. He has written widely about nineteenth-century American politics, especially during the Civil War and Reconstruction. His books include *Ulysses S. Grant: Triumph over Adversity, 1822–1865* (2000); *The Reconstruction Presidents* (1998); *America's Civil War* (1996); *The Political Education of Henry Adams* (1996); and *Let Us Have Peace: Ulysses S. Grant and the Politics of War and Reconstruction, 1861–1868* (1991).

Bartholomew H. Sparrow is associate professor of government at the University of Texas at Austin. He is the author of *Emergence of Empire: The Insular Cases and the Territorial Expansion of the United States* (forthcoming), *Uncertain Guardians: The News Media as Political Institution* (1999), and *From the Outside In: World War II and the American States* (1996). His research interests include federalism and territorial expansion, the political development of the American state, and U.S. media politics.

Robert Stanley is professor of political science at California State University, Chico, and author of *Dimensions of Law in the Service of Order: Origins of the Federal Income Tax, 1861–1913* (1993), and related essays.

Peter Wallenstein is professor of history at Virginia Polytechnic Institute and State University. His books include *Blue Laws and Black Codes: Conflict, Courts, and Law in Twentieth-Century Virginia* (2004) and *Tell the Court I Love My Wife: Race, Marriage, and Law—An American History* (2002). His research interests emphasize the history of the U.S. South, including the desegregation of higher education.

Stephen J. Wermiel is associate director of the Marshall-Brennan Constitutional Literacy Project and adjunct professor at American University Washington College of Law. He has published numerous law review articles about judicial selection, news media coverage of the Supreme Court, and the legacy of the late Supreme Court Justice William J. Brennan Jr., whose biography he is writing.

Jason E. Whitehead is a doctoral candidate in political science at the University of Southern California. He has published journal articles in the areas of critical legal theory, jurisprudence, criminal procedure, and antitrust law. He currently teaches courses in constitutional law, judicial process, jurisprudence, criminal procedure, political theory, and American politics.

Nancy Woloch teaches history and American studies at Barnard College, Columbia University. Her books include *Women and the American Experience,* 4th ed. (2006) and Muller v. Oregon: *A Brief History with Documents* (1996).

Christine M. Yantis Hargrove is a master of divinity candidate at Harvard Divinity School, where she studies women in religion.

PREFACE

The U.S. Supreme Court is nonpartisan, and its nine justices are supposedly accountable only to their own values and interpretations of the law, but in fact the Court is a highly political institution. As the third branch of a government of separated functions and divided powers, the Supreme Court is embedded in a political process. The Court, however, in the words of Alexander Hamilton, "has no influence over either the sword or the purse" to enforce its decisions, be they mundane or controversial. Instead, the Court must rely on the cooperation of the other branches as well as the willingness of the public at large to abide by its decisions.

Over two centuries the Supreme Court has built up a great reservoir of influence, and we Americans accept the vast majority of its decisions, which affect how we live and vote, how we are treated, and how our property is protected, as definitive rulings on the meaning of the Constitution and federal law. But the Court still must lead by moral suasion. Contrary to the usual result, sometimes Supreme Court decisions inspire anger, condemnation, and defiance from citizens, statesmen, public opinion journals, and newspaper editors. This book provides a lively, balanced look at the public response to some of the most controversial cases handed down by the Court.

As the country has grown more politically polarized, the Court's decisions seem to strike at core values held by one side or the other. The 2003 decision *Lawrence v. Texas,* on the hot-button issue of gay rights, demonstrates how public reaction can greatly magnify the importance of a decision. The Court, as we are constantly told, does matter.

This influence is not, however, a new phenomenon. From the Court's earliest days, its decisions exerted a powerful effect on our development as a people and as a nation. Cases such as *McCulloch v. Maryland, Pollock v. Farmers' Loan & Trust I and II* (the Income Tax Cases), the Insular Cases, and *Schechter Poultry Corp. v. United States* and *Butler v. United States* (two of the New Deal cases) had an impact on government institutions, on what powers the federal government could or could not exercise.

Many controversial cases arose from complaints by individuals claiming rights and privileges under the Constitution. Dred Scott (*Dred Scott v. Sandford*) wanted to be freed from slavery, Lillian Gobitas (*Minersville School District v. Gobitis*) did not want to salute the flag, and Linda Brown (*Brown v. Board of Education*) did not want to go to a segregated school. But these cases went far beyond their impact on the individual plaintiffs, or even the groups to which they belonged. In some ways, Dred Scott's case helped trigger a civil war; the flag salute case made manifest what the free exercise clause meant, even in wartime; and *Brown v. Board of Education* began the great civil rights revolution.

These cases did not pass unnoticed at the time. Contemporaries understood their meaning and recognized that they would affect how we lived as a people and as a nation. Depending on their point of view, they applauded or condemned the Court and its decisions. They wrote letters to the press or to their representatives in Congress, and in some instances to the justices themselves; newspapers ran editorials praising or reviling the Court and its decisions; politicians, reflecting the views of their constituents, joined in the chorus; while law professors and legal historians analyzed the decisions in scholarly journals. Samples of these and other kinds of reaction are included in the chapters in this book.

The book follows two other CQ Press reference works that provide students and other general interest readers with knowledge and understanding about the Supreme Court and its decisions. The first volume,

Landmark Decisions of the United States Supreme Court (2003), by Paul Finkelman and Melvin I. Urofsky, provides synopses of the 1,000 most important decisions that the Court had handed down. The volume *100 Americans Making Constitutional History: A Biographical History* (2004), edited by Melvin I. Urofsky, profiles many of the people at the heart of the most important Supreme Court cases—the men, women, and children who were willing to fight their legal battles up to the Supreme Court. This book, *The Public Debate over Controversial Supreme Court Decisions,* shows how the public reacted to some of those decisions.

In most instances, these reactions are contemporary to the decision and reflect current passions about what happened. In others, the impact of the ruling had long-range results, and reactions might occur years or decades later. In the Japanese Internment Cases, for example, we see not only the wartime response to the Court's approval of the relocation program of Japanese Americans, but also the shift in public opinion that took place within a few years, and then the playing out of the drama for several decades until Congress issued a formal apology. In the case of George Reynolds (*Reynolds v. United States*), most nineteenth-century Americans applauded the Court for refusing to allow Mormons to practice polygamy. But over the years there has been a continuing discussion on whether the case had been properly decided, and the discussion continues to this day.

Each of the forty entries in this book begins with an overview that presents the facts of the case, the Court's ruling and its importance, and a brief synopsis of the scope and magnitude of public debate. This background information is followed by a selection of public responses from a wide range of sources, including daily, business, and labor newspapers; political journals; law reviews; speeches; letters to the president; congressional floor debate; international governments and presses; and the litigants themselves. Care has been taken to ensure that these sources of reaction present, to the extent possible, diverse viewpoints. Each example is presented in its original wording, spelling, and punctuation.

The entries in this volume are not meant to be definitive: after all, tomes have been written about some of the cases and even about some of the participants. The sampling of reactions in this volume are just that—samplings—and readers who want to know more can use these entries to start their research. But many of those interested in the Court will find that the entries provide not only interesting but also ample information about how the public has reacted to important Court decisions. They will also gain insight into how the specific legal issues and justifications have evolved into political controversies that continue to impact American democracy.

Acknowledgments

Books like this take a great deal of work on the part of many people. My thanks go to the contributors, who were able to take mountains of material and condense them into usable and readable form. At CQ Press, it has been a pleasure working with Douglas Goldenberg-Hart, who helped fashion the concept and parameters of the book; January Layman-Wood, who oversaw the mechanics of taking a concept and making it into the volume you hold in your hands; Carolyn Goldinger, editor *par excellence,* who worked her usual magic to make all of us look good; Joan Gossett, who handled production duties with diligence and grace; and Timothy Arnquist, whose support work helped us put finishing touches on the book.

The dedication is to friends in Australia who have made our trips "down under" such pleasant voyages.

Melvin I. Urofsky
Virginia Commonwealth University

McCulloch v. Maryland

Mark R. Killenbeck

McCulloch v. Maryland
17 U.S. 316 (4 Wheat. 316) (1819)

DECIDED: March 6, 1819
VOTE
CONCURRING: 6 (John Marshall, Bushrod Washington, William Johnson, Henry B. Livingston, Gabriel Duvall, Joseph Story)
DISSENTING: 0
OPINION OF THE COURT: Marshall
DID NOT PARTICIPATE: Thomas Todd

McCulloch v. Maryland was part of a protracted debate about the respective rights of the nation and the states in the new system of government created by the Constitution. One of the major concerns about the Constitution was that it would create a new federal government with too much power over the states. The opposing sides in that debate became known as Federalists and Anti-Federalists. One important part of the Anti-Federalist creed was the doctrine of states rights, founded on the belief that the states were sovereign entities and that, as such, each enjoyed all the attributes of a nation.

The Federalists arguably won the debate, at least to the extent that the Constitution was in fact ratified. But approval of the document did not end the dispute. If anything, it intensified during the first decades of the nation's history as Congress began to exercise its powers in ways that seemed to confirm anti-Federalist fears that the federal government was acting against the needs and interests of the states. One of those measures was Alexander Hamilton's proposal to create the First Bank of the United States, which was approved in 1791. That measure was opposed by states rights advocates, in particular by Thomas Jefferson and his allies, who believed that both the spirit and the letter of the Constitution were being violated. Indeed, the dispute between Hamilton and Jefferson on these matters became one of the important factors in the eventual development of an "opposition" party (the Democratic Republican Party, eventually the Republicans, albeit not the same group that bears that name today) that would contest the general approach toward government and many of the specific proposals of the Federalists, who were the party in power for the first twelve years of the nation's history.

By the time *McCulloch* came before the Court, the First Bank of the United States had been succeeded by the Second Bank of the United States, an institution that many saw as the exemplar of an overreaching federal government. The Second Bank had actually been championed by many Republicans and signed into law by James Madison, a Republican president. But a strong and vocal group of states rights advocates, including Jefferson, believed that Congress did not have the authority to create a bank. In particular, they believed that the power of the bank to establish branch offices in the states represented an unprecedented extension of federal authority, forcing states to accept a federal presence in their midst without their consent. Many also believed that the bank was evil; it was both a federal institution that they could not control and, as a bank, an institution they believed to be a means by which the privileged few exploited the people. One of the ways they chose to fight back was to enact various state constitutional provisions and state statutes that would force the bank to close its branch offices.

The case arose when the state of Maryland attempted to levy a tax on banknotes issued by James M'Culloh, cashier of the Baltimore branch of the Second Bank of the United States.[1] An action of debt (a legal proceeding claiming that money was owed) was brought against the bank, and the Baltimore County Court found that the bank should be required to pay the tax, a judgment that was affirmed by the

Maryland Court of Appeals. The Supreme Court issued a writ of error, indicating its belief that the lower court's decision might be wrong and should be reviewed, and set the case for argument in its February 1819 term. Oral arguments began on Monday, February 22, 1819, and lasted nine days, with Chief Justice Marshall announcing the decision of a unanimous Court on Saturday, March 6, 1819.

The Court held that Congress had the authority to create the bank. The fact that such a power was not specifically mentioned in the Constitution did not matter. The powers of the national government were both express and implied, and the test an arguably simple one, according to the chief justice: "Let the end be legitimate, let it be within the scope of the constitution, and all means which are appropriate, which are plainly adapted to that end, which are not prohibited, but consist with the letter and spirit of the constitution, are constitutional." Maryland, in turn, could not interfere with the bank's activities. Because "the power to tax involves the power to destroy," a state's exercise of that sovereign prerogative must necessarily yield in the face of a congressional judgment that a national bank was both necessary and proper. "Such a tax," Marshall concluded, "must be unconstitutional."

The general consensus is that *McCulloch* is one of, if not *the*, most important decisions in the Court's history. It came at a crucial juncture in the nation's history and was a central part of the Marshall Court's vision of a strong national government that could meet the exigencies of changing times and changing circumstances. The implied powers doctrine provides the foundation for much of what the federal government does today. The belief that in most instances judgments about what is constitutionally "necessary and proper" are best left to Congress, free of any potential second guessing by the courts, is a central part of the modern theory of judicial review. *McCulloch*'s assumptions about the nature of federal power and the relative role of the states lie at the heart of the Court's current reassessment of these matters in a string of important decisions that since the 1990s have reshaped our understanding of the nature and scope of the commerce power and the Eleventh Amendment.

INITIAL RESPONSES

The reaction to the decision in *McCulloch* was immediate and intense. Part of that response reflected the long-standing dispute between the Federalists, who favored a strong national government, and the Republicans, who were dedicated to protecting the sovereignty of the states. The implied powers doctrine was especially anathema to states rights advocates, who believed that it would serve as the license for all manner of federal abuses. The notion that implied powers existed had been sharply contested during the Constitution's framing and ratification, and states rights proponents believed it had been settled—and rejected—by the Tenth Amendment, which reads: "The powers not delegated to the United States by the Constitution, nor prohibited by it to the States, are reserved to the States respectively, or to the people." Moreover, in 1819 Congress began discussing the admission of Missouri to the Union as a slave state, and the South harbored deep concerns about Congress's ability to condition admission of a new state on an end to slavery within it and to bar slavery from national territories. Neither power was mentioned in the Constitution, but both would, presumably, fall within the scope of any expansive reading of the text, in particular one sanctioning the existence of implied powers and the notion that such matters were best left to the political process. *McCulloch* accordingly struck fear into the hearts of the proslavery factions.

In addition to suspicion about abolition, many people were opposed to banks and banking, which they viewed as tools of the rich and powerful. Moreover, the Second Bank of the United States had an unfortunate record because of its role in creating and intensifying the economic problems that became known as the Panic of 1819. And, even as *McCulloch* was argued and decided, information about the mismanagement of the bank and the criminal activities of some of its officials was emerging—information that would lead to the dismissal of M'Culloh in May 1819 and his subsequent prosecution by the state of Maryland.

The importance of the decision was obvious to everyone, especially the members of the Court. Justice Story wrote to his wife, Sarah:

Despite the Supreme Court's decision in *McCulloch v. Maryland* (1819), the Bank of the United States remained under attack. This cartoon depicts the bank as a monster and President Andrew Jackson taking it on with his veto stick. Vice President Martin Van Buren, center, helps kill the creature, whose heads represent Nicholas Biddle, bank president, and directors of the state banks. —Library of Congress

We have decided the great question as to the right of the States to tax the Bank of the United States, and have declared that they have no such power. This decision excites great interest, and in a political view is of the deepest consequence to the nation. It goes to establish the Constitution upon its greatest principles. You, perhaps, from your retired life, may hardly think it possible that such should be the case, but if you mingled with the busy circle of politics, or took an interest in the objects of governments and states-men, you would readily admit its fundamental importance to the existence of government.[2]

The newspapers, in turn, printed the full text of the decision and, depending on their political inclinations, either applauded or condemned it. The Federalist press was, for example, pleased at both the affirmation of federal power and the restrictions imposed on the states. The Washington, D.C., *National Intelligencer*, declared:

The Supreme Judicial authority of the Nation has rarely, if ever, pronounced an opinion more interesting in its views, or more important as to its operation, than that recently given, as to the right of a state of the Union to tax the National Bank. We have therefore taken some pains to procure a copy of this interesting and elaborate opinion for publication, and have the pleasure today of presenting it to our readers. At no previous term of the Supreme Court have more important questions of constitutional law been settled and decided.[3]

An editorial in the *Boston Daily Advertiser* said: "It is one of the most able judgments, I will venture to say, ever delivered in this Court, and when read it will satisfy all minds."[4]

And the *Kentucky Gazette* declared:

> This interesting decision cannot be too highly appreciated, and it will furnish a happy lesson to local politicians against their right to infringe upon the National Constitution or the laws of Congress. We hope to see no more interference by State Legislators.[5]

But the Republican press saw the decision as both a betrayal of the Constitution and a blow to states rights, and their condemnation was lengthy and bitter. The influential *Niles Weekly Register* charged:

> An insidious dilapidation or violent dismemberment of the American union, together with a consolidation of the reserved rights and powers of the states, is the darling hope that the enemies of liberty, at home and abroad, have hugged to their heart with demonic fervor and consistency. They have hated and still hate the freedom of the people of the United States, on the principles with which Satan regarded the happy condition of our first parents in the garden of Eden—their own perverse dispositions not being fitted to participate in an equality of rights, or their inordinate pride rejecting every measure calculated to do away distinctions among men, save in virtue and usefulness. . . . A deadly blow has been struck at the *sovereignty of the states,* and from a quarter so far removed from the people as to be hardly accessible to public opinion. . . . We are yet unacquainted with the grounds of this alarming decision, but of this we are resolved—that nothing but the tongue of an angel can convince us of its compatibility with the constitution of the United States, in which a power to grant acts of incorporation is not delegated, and all powers not delegated are retained.[6]

Another Republican paper, the *Argus of Western Kentucky,* warned:

> The principles assumed in this decision must raise alarm throughout our widely extended empire. They strike at the root of states rights and state sovereignty. The people must rouse from the lap of Delilah and prepare to meet the Philistines. The national government is again encroaching on the rights of the states and the people. There must be a fixed, a determined resistance to these encroachments, not of arms, but of the moral energy of a free people. The power of Congress to establish a national Bank is alarming; but no mind can compass the extent of encroachments upon state and individual rights which may take place under the principles of this decision.[7]

Two sequences of commentary in the newspapers were of special interest. The first was a series of eleven articles condemning the decision and the Court, written by Amos Kendall, the part owner and editor of the *Argus of Western America.* The columns were in important respects prophetic, for Kendall later became a trusted adviser to the bank's greatest nemesis, Andrew Jackson. In the second column, Kendall wrote:

> There was a party in the convention and the country who were favorable to a more energetic system of government than that which was adopted. The proposition to give congress the power to establish corporations and many others of a similar nature, were a part of their system. But every attempt to destroy the sovereignty of the states and establish a more energetic government, was met and defeated by those who better understood

the true and permanent interests of the American people. Thwarted in the convention they carried their principles into the administration of the government and attempted to effect by the aid of congress, that which they could not accomplish with the consent of the people. At an early period of our government, they obtained an ascendency in every department, and commenced the execution of their plans with confidence and zeal. Hence the original bank, the alien and sedition laws, a standing army, unnecessary taxes, and all the arbitrary measures of the "reign of terror." But they advanced with too rapid strides. The people were alarmed; and driving them from power, intrusted the administration to those who interpreted the constitution, according to the intentions of the parties to that compact. . . . The Judiciary could not be so easily and so speedily reformed. The principles of the energy system had taken deep root in that department where they still continue to flourish with unabated vigor. Hence the United State Courts have sanctioned every encroachment which congress have made. . . .[8]

In column IV, Kendall asked:

Had the constitutionalists in the conventions of New York, Pennsylvania, Virginia or any other state, declared boldly, that Congress would possess the right to exercise implied powers which could neither be defined nor imagined, does any man believe that the federal constitution would ever have been ratified?[9]

Column V contrasted the views of Patrick Henry, a strong states rights advocate, and those of Chief Justice Marshall:

But the difference between the two men was this: Henry wished the state sovereignties preserved—Marshall wished them destroyed; Henry boldly and frankly declared his position—Marshall was silent; Henry opposed the constitution because he believed Congress might exercise implied powers—Marshall advocated it having the same opinion, although he did not declare it; he heard what he must have believed a false construction put upon this section by its friends, and he would not open their eyes—he wished to see the people deluded and subsequently to take advantage of that delusion.[10]

Kendall continued: "The creature is clothed with greater powers than the creator, and the states must bow in silence to the authority of the bank in cases where they might rightfully withstand the usurpations of the government."[11] And he ended with a recommendation to amend the Constitution:

It is difficult to distinguish between bankers whose business is regulated by the states and those whose business is regulated by the Union. *Banking* is still *their business,* and private gain *their end*. . . . *Disunion* and *consolidation* are the *Scylla* and *Charybdis* which it should be equally our care to observe and avoid. . . . But as the attempt by congress has been sanctioned by judicial authority, we now have no remedy but a peaceful acquiescence & a speedy amendment to the constitution.[12]

MARSHALL VERSUS BROCKENBROUGH AND ROANE

The second major series of articles was a sharp exchange of views between Marshall and two of his principal opponents, William Brockenbrough and Spencer Roane, two Virginia state court judges who were vocal states rights advocates. Marshall perceived a threat to the Court and felt duty-bound to respond. As Marshall explained to his like-minded colleague, Justice Story:

Our opinion in the bank case has roused the sleeping spirit of Virginia—if indeed it ever sleeps. It will I understand be attacked in the papers with some asperity; and as those who favor it never write for the publick, it will remain undefended & of course be considered as *damnably heretical.*[13]

To Justice Washington, the chief justice wrote similar observations:

Great dissatisfaction has been given to the politicians of Virginia by our opinion on the bank question. They have no objection to a decision in favor of the bank, since the good patriots who administer the government wished it, & would probably have been seriously offended with us had we dared to decide otherwise, but they require an obsequious, silent opinion without reasons. That would have been satisfactory, but our heretical reasoning is pronounced most damnable. We shall be denounced bitterly in the papers & as not a word will be said on the other side we shall undoubtedly be condemned as a pack of consolidating aristocrats. The legislature & executive have enacted the law but who have power & places to bestow will escape with impunity, while the poor court who have nothing to give & of whom nobody is afraid, bears all the obloquy of the measure.[14]

Brockenbrough's criticism, written under the pen name "Amphictyon," the mythical founder of a representative assembly of the states of ancient Greece, began appearing March 30, 1819. They were introduced by Thomas Ritchie, the editor of the newspaper, who stressed:

We cannot too earnestly press upon our readers, the following exposition of the alarming errors of the Supreme Court of the United States in their late interpretation of the Constitution. We conceive those errors to be most alarming, and this exposition most satisfactory. Whenever state rights are threatened or invaded, Virginia will not be the last to sound the tocsin.[15]

In the essay proper, Brockenbrough declared:

There are two principles advocated and decided on by the supreme court, which appear to me to endanger the very existence of state rights. The first is the denial that the powers of the federal government were delegated by the states; and the second is, that the grant of powers to the government, and particularly the grant of powers "necessary and proper" to carry the other powers into effect, ought to be construed in a liberal, rather than a restricted sense. Both of these principles tend directly to the consolidation of the states, and to strip them of some of the most important attributes of their sovereignty. If the Congress of the United States should think proper to legislate to the full extent, upon the principles now adjudicated by the supreme court, it is difficult to say how small would be the remnant of power left in the hands of state authorities. . . . I do humbly conceive that the states never could have committed an act of such egregious folly as to agree that their umpire should be altogether appointed and paid by the other party. The supreme court may be a perfectly impartial tribunal to decide between two states, but cannot be considered in that point of view when the contest lies between the United States, and one of its members.[16]

The second "Amphictyon" piece appeared a few days later:

The danger arising from the implied powers has always been seen and felt by the people of the states. . . . I cannot exclusively rely on my confidence in our representatives: if that were a sufficient guarantee for the preservation of our state rights, then there would be no necessity for a specific enumeration of granted powers.[17]

In an unusual step, the chief justice responded. Writing as "A Friend to the Union," Marshall published his letters in a Philadelphia newspaper:

> If Amphyctyon means to assert, as I suppose he does, that the powers of the general government were delegated by the state legislatures, then I say his assertion is contradicted by the words of the constitution, and by the fact; and is not supported, even by that report, on which he so confidently relies.[18]

In another letter, "A Friend to the Union" wrote:

> If the rule contended for would not absolutely arrest the progress of the government, it would certainly deny to those who administer it the means of executing its acknowledged powers in the manner most advantageous to those for whose benefit they were conferred. . . . It would be tedious to go through all the examples put by the supreme court. They are all of the same character, and show, conclusively, that the principles maintained by the counsel for the state of Maryland, and by Amphyctyon, would essentially change the constitution, render the government of the Union incompetent to the objects for which it was instituted, and place all its powers under the control of the state legislatures. It would, in a great measure, reinstate the old confederation.[19]

Roane then picked up the attack, writing as "Hampden," a British parliamentarian known for his stand against the tyranny of the king.

> None of [my fellow citizens] can be prepared to give a Carte Blanche to our federal rulers, and to obliterate the state governments, forever, from our political system. . . . That legislative power which is every where extending the sphere of its activity and drawing all power into its impetuous vortex, has blinked even the strong words of [the Tenth Amendment]. . . . [T]hat court had no power to adjudicate away the *reserved* rights of a sovereign member of the confederacy, and vest them in the general government.[20]

"Hampden" then wrote:

> The constitution of the United States was not adopted by the people of the United States, as one people. It was adopted by the several states, in their highest sovereign character, that is, by the people of the said states, respectively; such people being competent, and *they* only competent, to alter the pre-existing governments in the said states. . . . [T]he *parties* themselves must be the rightful judges, whether the compact has been violated, and that, in this respect, there can be no tribunal above their authority. . . . The supreme court is but one department of the general government. A department is not competent to do that to which the whole government is inadequate. The general government cannot decide this controversy and much less can one of its departments. They cannot do it unless we tread under foot the principle which forbids a party to decide his own cause.[21]

Again Marshall responded. In a letter to Washington, he explained:

> The storm which has been for some time threatening the Judges has at length burst on their heads & a most serious hurricane it is. . . . I find myself more stimulated on this subject than on any other because I believe the design to be to injure the Judges & inpair

the constitution. I have therefore thought of answering these essays & sending my pieces to you for publication in the Alexandria paper.[22]

To the public, Marshall, now writing as "A Friend of the Constitution," declared:

> I gladly take leave of the bitter invectives which compose the first number of Hampden, and proceed to a less irksome task—the examination of his argument. . . . The power to do a thing, and the power to carry that thing into execution, are, I humbly conceive, the same power, and the one cannot be termed with propriety "additional" or "incidental" to the other. Under the confederation congress could do scarcely any thing.[23]

> In no single instance does the court admit the unlimited power of congress to adopt any means whatever, and thus to pass the limits prescribed by the constitution. Not only is the discretion claimed for the legislature in the selection of its means, always limited in terms, to such as are appropriate, but the court expressly says, "should congress under the pretext of executing it powers, pass laws for the accomplishment of objects, not entrusted to the government, it would become the painful duty of this tribunal, should a case requiring such a decision come before it, to say that such an act was not the law of the land."[24]

> The reasoning on which this objection seems to be founded, proceeds from the fundamental error, that our constitution is a mere league, or compact, between the several state governments, and the general government. . . . This government has all the departments, and all the capacities for performing its various functions, which a free people is accustomed to bestow on its government. It is not then, in any point of view, a league. As little does it resemble a compact between itself and its members.[25]

> To whom more safely than to the judges are judicial questions to be referred? They are selected from the great body of the people for the purpose of deciding them. To secure impartiality, they are made perfectly independent. They have no personal interest in aggrandizing the legislative power. Their paramount interest is the public prosperity, in which is involved their own and that of their families. *No* tribunal can be less liable to be swayed by unworthy motives from a conscientious performance of duty. It is not then the party sitting in its own cause. It is the application to individuals by one department of the acts of another department of government. The people are the authors of it all; the departments are their agents; and if the judge be perfectly disinterested, he is exempt from any political interest that might influence his opinion, as imperfect human institutions can make him. . . . Let Hampden succeed, and that instrument will be radically changed. The government of the whole will be prostrated at the feet of its members; and that grand effort of wisdom, virtue, and patriotism, which produced it, will be totally defeated.[26]

THE VIEWS OF MADISON AND JEFFERSON

The decision also provoked two influential individuals who had played major roles in the debate about the constitutionality of the First Bank of the United States. James Madison and Thomas Jefferson were troubled by the decision, but for different reasons. Madison wrote to Roane:

> But what is of most importance is the high sanction given to a latitude of expounding the Constitution which seems to break down the landmarks intended to by a specifica-

tion of the Powers of Congress, and to substitute for a definitive connection between the means and ends, a Legislative discretion as to the former to which no practical limit can be assigned. In the great system of Political Economy having for its general object the national welfare, everything is related immediately or remotely to every other thing; and consequently a Power over any one thing, if not limited by some obvious and precise affinity, may amount to a Power over every other. . . . Does not the Court also relinquish by their doctrine, all controul on the Legislative exercise of unconstitutional powers? According to that doctrine, the expediency and constitutionality of means for carrying into effect a specified Power are convertible terms; and Congress are admitted to be Judges of the expediency. The Court certainly cannot be so; a question, the moment it assumes the character of mere expediency or policy, being evidently beyond the reach of Judicial cognizance.[27]

Jefferson had opposed the bank from the time Hamilton had first proposed it during the Washington administration. Jefferson wrote approvingly to Roane:

I have read in the Enquirer, and with great approbation, the pieces signed Hampden. . . . They contain the true principles of the revolution of 1800, for that was as real a revolution in the principles of our government as that of 1776 was in its form. . . . The Constitution, on this hypothesis, is a mere thing of wax in the hands of the judiciary, which they may twist and shape into any form they please. . . . My construction of the Constitution is very different from that you quote. It is that each department is truly independent of the others, and has an equal right to decide for itself what is the meaning of the Constitution in the cases submitted for its action; and especially, where it is to act ultimately and without appeal.[28]

Two years later, on reading a book attacking Marshall's expansive interpretation of the Constitution, Jefferson told Roane:

I have read Colonel Taylor's book of "Constructions Construed," with great satisfaction, and I will say, with edification; for I acknowledge it corrected some errors of opinion into which I had slidden without sufficient examination. It is the most logical retraction of our governments to the original and true principles of the Constitution creating them, which has appeared since the adoption of that instrument. I may not perhaps concur in all its opinions, great and small; for no two men ever thought alike on so many points. But on all its important questions, it contains the true political faith, to which every catholic republican should steadfastly hold.[29]

The book to which Jefferson referred was by John Taylor, an ardent states rights advocate and prolific spokesman for that position. In *Construction Construed and Constitutions Vindicated* Taylor attacked the Court and the bank decision at length and expressly made the connection between *McCulloch* and the slavery question:

Which can do most harm to mankind, constructive treasons or constructive powers? The first takes away the life of an individual, the second destroys the liberty of a nation. The machine called inference can act as extensively in one case as in the other. . . .

As ends may be made to beget means, so means may be made to beget ends, until the co-habitation shall rear a progeny of unconstitutional bastards, which were not begotten by the people; and their rights being no longer secured by fixed principles, will be hazarded upon a game at shuttlecock with ends and means, between the general and the state governments. To prevent this, means as well as ends are subjected by our constitution to a double restraint. The first is special. In many instances, the means for executing the powers bestowed, are defined, and by that definition, limited. The other is general, and arises necessarily from the division of powers; as it was never intended that powers given to one department, or one government, should be impaired or destroyed, by the means used for the execution of powers given to another. Otherwise, the indefinite word "means" might defeat all labour expended upon definition by our constitution.

One portion of the union is afflicted by negro slavery; therefore, make it tributary to capitalists. Cultivation by slaves is unprofitable; therefore, make it tributary to capitalists. The freedom of labour deprives it of the benefit of being directed by intelligence; therefore, subject it to capitalists. Taxation is preferable to economy; therefore, enhance it for the nourishment of capitalists, and the gratification of avarice.

Let us recite the succession of events. The great pecuniary favour granted by congress to certificate-holders, begat banking; banking begat bounties to manufacturing capitalists; bounties to manufacturing capitalists begat an oppressive pension list; these particularities united to beget the Missouri project; that project begat the idea of using slavery as an instrument for effecting a balance of power; when it is put in operation, it will beget new usurpations of internal powers over persons and property, and those will beget a dissolution of the union.[30]

FURTHER CHALLENGES TO *McCULLOCH*

The challenges to *McCulloch* were not simply rhetorical. There was also a concerted effort to defy the ruling and overturn it. In Ohio this effort took the form of an attempt to levy an annual tax of $50,000 on the bank, a measure that was passed on February 8, 1819, less than a month before the Court's decision. In the fall an Ohio newspaper wrote:

> If a case decided, an agreed case,—in which this State is not a party, can be considered binding upon this State, if such a decision is to suspend the force and operation of our laws legally, regularly and constitutionally enacted, what are our boasted privileges? . . . We complain that in the case of *McCulloch v. Maryland,* matters have been conceded by the latter, or rather, many of the strongest grounds were relinquished or not brought into view, on which this State meant to reply. The State of Ohio does not admit that a case between two parties, collusively or ignorantly agreed upon, is or ought to be binding on any other party.[31]

As the committee of the Ohio legislature that reported the bill noted on December 12, 1820:

> And upon the promulgation of [*McCulloch*] it is maintained that it became the duty of the state and its officers to acquiesce, and to treat the act of the legislature as a dead letter. The committee have considered this position, and are not satisfied that it is a correct one.[32]

Ralph Osborn, Ohio's auditor, ordered the assets of the bank to be seized to pay the tax. The resulting litigation ended at the Supreme Court in *Osborn v. Bank of the United States* (1824). The Court reiterated its adherence to the principles enunciated in *McCulloch*:

> A revision of [*McCulloch*] has been requested; and many considerations combine to induce a review of it. . . . [T]he Court adheres to its decision in [that] case . . . and is of

the opinion, that the act of the State of Ohio, which is certainly more objectionable than that of the State of Maryland, is repugnant to a law of the United States, made in pursuance of the constitution, and, therefore, void.

The feeling of the bank's opponents about the Court's decisions were perhaps best captured by William Gouge in an essay published in 1833: "The Bank was saved and the people were ruined."[33]

The bank eventually perished at the hands of Andrew Jackson, whose long-standing hostility to the national bank and banking was well known. "You know my op[in]ion as to the Banks," Jackson declared, "that is, that the Constitution of our State, as well as the Constitution of the united States, prohibited the establishment of Banks in any state."[34] Jackson's hostility found its fullest expression in his veto of a measure that would have extended the bank's charter, a veto whose primary author was Amos Kendall, former editor of the *Argus of Western America*:

> A bank of the United States is in many respects convenient for the Government and useful to the people. . . . Mere precedent is a dangerous source of authority, and should not be regarded as deciding questions of constitutional power except where the acquiescence of the people and the States can be considered as well settled. . . . The Congress, the Executive, and the Court must each for itself be guided by its own opinion of the Constitution. . . . The opinion of the judges has no more authority over Congress than the opinion of Congress has over the judges, and on that point the President is independent of both. . . . There is nothing in its legitimate functions which makes it [the bank] necessary or proper. Whatever interest or influence, whether public or private, has given birth to this act, it can not be found either in the wishes or necessities of the executive department, by which present action is deemed premature, and the powers conferred upon its agent not only unnecessary, but dangerous to the Government and the country. . . . Nor is our government to be maintained or our Union preserved by invasions of the rights and powers of the several States.[35]

One final aspect of the case is worth noting: the fall and eventual rebirth of James M'Culloh. John Quincy Adams wrote in his diary:

> May 30, 1819. . . . [Baltimore branch president James A.] Buchanan and McCulloh have used the funds of the Bank as if they were their own. . . . Mr. Cheves, the new President of the bank, pursued the research, and found there were immense debts of the President and Cashier not secured. He obtained such security as he could, and then the Board of Directors at Philadelphia removed McCulloh, the Cashier at Baltimore. For a day or two there was great blustering in the Baltimore newspapers, as if the grossest injustice had been done to McCulloh; but the mine was blown up. Buchanan . . . resigned, and a debt of nine hundred thousand dollars appears against the connection, little more than one-half of which is even supposed to be effectually secured.[36]

Anna Boyd, a woman living in Baltimore, wrote in despair to a friend:

> I think John, one of the most provoking parts of the business is, that these destroyers of widows, and orphans, affect to consider themselves as persecuted men. McCulloh for example struts about in all the pride and gaiety belonging to an honest heart, and unspotted name boasting as it were; that he is stript of his feathers, that they have determined to bring him down and have succeeded.[37]

Adams was wrong about the extent of the damage to the bank. Fraudulent transactions by M'Culloh and his business partners, Buchanan and George Williams, actually cost the bank more than $1.5 million.

The state indicted the three men for conspiracy to defraud. Ultimately, they were acquitted, a verdict that was more an indictment of the bank than a vindication of their conduct or acceptance of their defense, in which they cast themselves as the true victims. General Winder, M'Culloh and Buchanan's lawyer, admitted that:

> the conduct of the Traversers was indiscreet; that they relied too strongly upon the hopes and calculations in which the whole community indulged; but the failure of their stock speculations was rather to be pitied as a misfortune, than condemned as a crime. Those who were now the most eager in prosecuting his clients, were, in 1817, the first to praise the course of conduct for which they were indicted; and those who now believed them guilty of a conspiracy to defraud, were then their most strenuous supporters. . . .
>
> Adverse circumstances had depressed stock, when, if it had risen, the defendants would have been looked upon as nobles, as the architects of their fortunes, by the very men who now prosecuted them, and lauded to the skies as possessing spirits fraught with enterprize. . . . Did the Bank afterwards pursue the proper course to heal the wounds. Its strange administration was an *incubus* upon it, and was another cause of depreciations of its Stock, so that, in fact, the Bank itself occasioned the losses upon which the present indictment was founded.[38]

NOTES

1. One of the legacies of the case is the question of how one should spell the name of the individual who was the nominal party in the dispute before the Court and, for that matter, how one should spell the case name itself. The official report of the decision adopts the form "M'Culloch," and other writers use "McCulloh." But the common usage is McCulloch, and that is the spelling used here. The name of the cashier of the Baltimore branch of the bank was, however, James William M'Culloh, a fact verified by a substantial number of official documents and reports published when the case was litigated and decided. Accordingly, that is the spelling used here when describing the person, rather than the case.

2. Joseph Story to Sarah Story, March 7, 1819, in *The Life and Letters of Joseph Story*, ed. William W. Story, 2 vols. (Boston: Little and Brown, 1851), 1:28–29.

3. *Washington, D.C., National Intelligencer*, March 13, 1819.

4. *Boston Daily Advertiser*, March 13, 1819.

5. *Kentucky Gazette*, March 19, 1819.

6. *Niles Weekly Register*, March 13, 1819.

7. *Argus of Western Kentucky*, April 2, 1819.

8. "State Rights II," *Argus of Western America*, May 14, 1819.

9. "State Rights IV," ibid., May 28, 1819.

10. "State Rights V," ibid., June 4, 1819.

11. "State Rights IX," ibid., July 2, 1819.

12. "State Rights XI," ibid., July 23, 1819.

13. John Marshall to Joseph Story, March 24, 1819, in *The Papers of John Marshall*, 11 vols., ed. Charles F. Hobson (Chapel Hill: University of North Carolina Press, 1974–), 8:280.

14. John Marshall to Bushrod Washington, March 27, 1819, ibid., 281.

15. Thomas Ritchie, *Richmond Enquirer*, March 30, 1819.

16. William Brockenbrough, "I Amphictyon," *Richmond Enquirer, March 30, 1819.*

17. *"II Amphictyon,"* ibid., April 2, 1819.

18. John Marshall, "I A Friend to the Union," *Philadelphia Union*, April 24, 1819.

19. "II A Friend to the Union," ibid., April 28, 1819.

20. Spencer Roane, "I Hampden," *Richmond Enquirer*, June 11, 1819.

21. Roane, "IV Hampden," ibid., June 22, 1819.

22. Marshall to Bushrod Washington, June 17, 1819, *The Papers of John Marshall*, 8:316–317.

23. Marshall, "II A Friend of the Constitution," *Alexandria Gazette*, July 1, 1819.

24. Marshall, "V A Friend of the Constitution," ibid., July 5, 1819.

25. Marshall, "VIII A Friend of the Constitution," ibid., July 14, 1819.

26. Marshall, "IX A Friend of the Constitution," ibid., July 15, 1819.

27. James Madison to Spencer Roane, September 2, 1819, in *The Writings of James Madison,* 9 vols., ed. Gaillard Hunt (New York: G. P. Putnam's Sons, 1908), 8:447–453.

28. Thomas Jefferson to Spencer Roane, September 6, 1819, *The Writings of Thomas Jefferson,* 20 vols., ed. Andrew A. Lipscomb and Albert Ellery Bergh (Washington, D.C.: Thomas Jefferson Memorial Association, 1903–1904), 15:212–216.

29. Thomas Jefferson to Spencer Roane, June 27, 1821, ibid., 15:326–329.

30. John Taylor, *Construction Construed and Constitutions Vindicated* (Richmond: Shepherd and Pollard, 1820), 22–23, 84, 257, 298.

31. *Steubenville Herald,* quoted in *Niles Weekly Register,* October 30, 1819.

32. *Report of the Joint Committee of Both Houses of the General Assembly, on the Communication of the Auditor of State Upon the subject and proceedings of the Bank of the United States, against The Officers of the State in the United States' Circuit Court,* Columbus: Printed at the Office of the *Columbus Gazette,* P. H. Olmsted), 14.

33. William M. Gouge, *The Curse of Paper-Money and Banking* (Philadelphia: T. W. Ustick, 1833), 73.

34. Andrew Jackson to William Berkeley Lewis, July 16, 1820, in *The Papers of Andrew Jackson, 1816–1820,* 6 vols., ed. Harold Moser, David R. Roth, and George H. Hoemann (Knoxville: University of Tennessee Press, 1994), 4:378.

35. President Andrew Jackson, Veto Message, July 10, 1832, in *The Messages and Papers of the Presidents,* 10 vols., ed. James D. Richardson (Washington, D.C.: Bureau of National Literature and Art, 1909) 2:576–591.

36. Charles Francis Adams, ed., *Memoirs of John Quincy Adams, comprising a portion of his diary from 1795 to 1848* (Philadelphia: J. B. Lippincott, 1874), 382–383.

37. Anna Boyd to John McHenry, August 6, 1819, McHenry Papers, Maryland Historical Society, Baltimore.

38. Robert Goodloe Harper, *A Report of the Conspiracy Cases, Tried at Hartford County Court in Maryland* (Baltimore: Thomas Murphy, 1823), 113, 170.

The Cherokee Cases

Tim Alan Garrison

Cherokee Nation v. Georgia

30 U.S. 1 (5 Pet. 1) (1831)

DECIDED: March 18, 1831
VOTE
  CONCURRING: 4 (John Marshall, William Johnson, John McLean, Henry Baldwin)
  DISSENTING: 2 (Joseph Story, Smith Thompson)
OPINION OF THE COURT: Marshall
CONCURRING OPINION: Johnson
CONCURRING OPINION: Baldwin
DISSENTING OPINION: Thompson (Story)
DID NOT PARTICIPATE: Duvall

Worcester v. Georgia

31 U.S. 515 (6 Pet. 515) (1832)

DECIDED: March 3, 1832
VOTE
  CONCURRING: 5 (John Marshall, Gabriel Duvall, Joseph Story, Smith Thompson, John McLean)
  DISSENTING: 1 (Henry Baldwin)
OPINION OF THE COURT: Marshall
CONCURRING OPINION: McLean
DISSENTING OPINION: Baldwin
DID NOT PARTICIPATE: Johnson

The Cherokee cases resulted from Georgia's effort to expel the Cherokee Indians from the state. In 1802 Georgia surrendered its territory west of the Chattahoochee River in exchange for a promise from the federal government that it would eliminate Indian land claims in the state as soon as the titles could be acquired "peaceably" and "on reasonable terms." At the time, the Cherokees and the Creeks possessed much of what is now central and western Georgia. After the War of 1812 Georgia began calling on the national government to fulfill its promise and remove the Cherokees and the Creeks (who ceded their remaining territory in the state in 1826) from its borders.

The Removal Crisis escalated in July 1827 when the Cherokee Nation drafted and ratified a republican constitution and declared itself an independent nation. The Cherokee declaration enraged removal proponents, who maintained that the Cherokees residing in Georgia were subjects of the state. In December the Georgia legislature began passing laws that extended the jurisdiction of the state over the Cherokee Nation's territory and that purported to abolish the tribe's government, laws, and courts. Alabama, Mississippi, and Tennessee soon joined Georgia's campaign in Congress to relocate the Indian tribes from the Southeast across the Mississippi River into the territory the United States had acquired in the Louisiana Purchase. The major tribes subject to these pressures—the Creeks, the Choctaws, the Chickasaws, the Cherokees, and the Seminoles—adamantly refused to leave.

In 1828 Andrew Jackson was elected president of the United States, and he made the removal of the Indian nations a primary objective for his administration. By 1830 he had persuaded Congress to pass the Indian Removal Act, which gave Jackson authority to conclude removal treaties with the tribes in the East.

Georgia then sent surveyors into the Cherokee Nation pursuant to a plan to seize the tribe's land and disperse it to white citizens of the state. The state also created a paramilitary force called the Georgia Guard to enforce state law in the Cherokee Nation and seize control of gold deposits recently discovered on Cherokee land.

When John Ross, the principal chief of the Cherokees, appealed to the federal government for assistance to protect his people from Georgia's attacks, Jackson and his representatives advised the Cherokees to either remove to the West or fall under the jurisdiction of the state. The Cherokee government then decided to take its grievances to the federal judiciary. On December 27, 1830, the Cherokee Nation filed a suit with the U.S. Supreme Court under its original jurisdiction. The suit declared that the Cherokee Nation was a sovereign nation holding legal dominion over its territory and deserving of standing under Article III of the Constitution, which provides the Court with jurisdiction to hear controversies "between a State . . . and foreign States, Citizens or Subjects." The Cherokee Nation's petition added that the United States had recognized its legal and political rights in treaties dating back to the Treaty of Hopewell in 1785. Georgia had not only violated the tribe's national rights by its actions, the Cherokee Nation argued, but also had encroached on the federal government's exclusive treaty power, as set out in Article VI of the Constitution, to conduct relations with the Indian tribes. The Cherokees asked the Court to strike down Georgia's extension legislation and enjoin the state from enforcing its laws in the Cherokee Nation. Georgia refused to respond to the petition and did not appear at the oral arguments.

The Court heard the Cherokee Nation's argument on March 11, 12, and 14, 1831, and issued its decision less than a week later. The Court was divided into three factions. Chief Justice Marshall, writing for himself and Justice McLean, declared that the Cherokee Nation was not a "foreign state" that could be granted standing before the Court under Article III. In attempting to define the true nature of the Cherokee polity, Marshall wrote that the Cherokee Nation was a people "capable of managing its own affairs and governing itself." However, he added, the tribe had agreed by treaty to place itself under the protection of the United States and was therefore not "foreign" to the United States. Marshall suggested that the Cherokees comprised a "domestic, dependent nation," a conception he devised in an effort to describe the anomalous status of the Indian tribes residing within U.S. borders. He added that the Cherokees were a people in a "state of pupilage" and that their unique relationship with the United States "resemble[d] that of a ward to his guardian." Marshall noted that he was sympathetic to the Cherokees' troubles; however, he had determined that the Cherokee petition asked for remedies that could be provided only by the executive or legislative branches of the U.S. government.

Justices Baldwin and Johnson agreed with the decision to deny standing, but they pointedly rejected the assertion that the tribe possessed attributes of nationhood. They maintained that the native peoples were simply subjects of the states in which they lived. Justices Thompson and Story disagreed with Marshall's disposition of the case. Their opinion, penned by Thompson, argued that the Cherokee Nation was a "foreign state" as envisioned by the Framers under Article III and that the Court should have issued an order enjoining Georgia's encroachments on Cherokee rights. In other words, four of the six justices who heard the case (Justice Duvall was absent due to illness) agreed that the Court could not hear the merits of the dispute because, in their opinion, the Cherokee Nation did not deserve standing as a foreign state. Ironically, if they had agreed to hear the merits of the case, four of the six likely would have acknowledged that the Cherokee Nation possessed distinct sovereign powers and would have voted to sustain its request for an injunction.

RESPONSES TO THE 1831 CASE

The Philadelphia *National Gazette,* one of the first newspapers to react to the decision, expressed concern for the future of the Cherokee people:

With regard to the unfortunate Cherokees, it is doubtful what effect this result of their application to the Supreme Court will have upon them. We apprehend, while we sincerely deprecate, some ultimate violence—a melancholy and fruitless struggle. The Indians experience a fate like that of Niobe's children—they seem destined to perish all, by inevitable causes visible or invisible. From one source or other, fatal shafts are constantly sped, by which they are immediately destroyed, or driven into some field of gradual extermination. . . .

When they appeal to the immutable principles of right and the obligations of treaty, they find no umpirage by which their claims may be regularly adjudged, nor impartial power by which their humble fortunes may be shielded. They have surrendered the greater part of their original possessions, their best opportunities of defence and vengeance, under the forms of artificial law and diplomacy: When they seek some security and protection, in reference to the relics of their territory and independence, they discover that all the solemn stipulations were but a mockery,—that law and diplomacy can be used to defeat all their hopes and endeavors. . . . For whatever degree of national delinquency, or unlawful gain, may exist in this matter, there will be assuredly, Divine vengeance in some shape, or at some period.[1]

Newspapers in Georgia described the decision as a total victory for the state. One local paper reported, "[T]he Supreme Court has decided entirely in favor of the State of Georgia. . . . Thus, the views of the State, with regard to her entire jurisdiction over the Indians within her limits, are fully sustained in the last resort, and the Cherokees, therefore, must either submit altogether to our laws or emigrate to the West of the Mississippi."[2]

George R. Gilmer, the Jacksonian governor of Georgia at the time of *Cherokee Nation v. Georgia,* was pleased with the Court's decision to deny standing. He complained, however, that some of the justices had expressed concern for the Cherokees' plight and acknowledged that the Cherokee Nation possessed sovereign powers and title over its territory. He also suggested that the leaders of the Cherokee sovereignty movement were not, in fact, Indians:

The Court affirms, that no case could be better calculated to excite its sympathy than the conduct of Georgia to the Cherokees. . . .

What wrong has Georgia done to its Indian people to call for this extraordinary sympathy of the Court? They are in the peaceable possession of their occupant rights. Intruders have been removed from among them by severe penal laws. None of the burdens of Government have been imposed upon them. Instead of being reduced to a remnant of the land not more than sufficient for their comfortable subsistence, they are in the possession of near five millions of acres in this State alone, of which the Aborigines do not cultivate more than five thousand. . . .

It is difficult to conceive of any proposition tending to more absurd consequences than that laid down by the Court, that any Indian tribe with which the United States form contracts to which the term Treaty may be affixed, becomes a nation capable of governing itself, and entitled to the recognition of the courts as states. It would bring into being hundreds of states utterly incapable of self-defence, or exercising one attribute of national sovereignty. . . . But whatever obligations the United States may have incurred by its contracts with the Cherokees, it has no constitutional authority to limit, or in any manner alter the territorial rights which belonged to this State when it became a member of the Union.

Upon no subject has there been more misrepresentation than in relation to the government of the Cherokees, and the civilization of the people of that tribe. Upon examination, it will be found that the Aboriginal people are as ignorant, thoughtless, and improvident, as formerly; without any of the spirit and character which distinguished them when war was their employment, and their support derived from the forest: that none of them in this State, with the exception of one family, have acquired property, or been at all benefitted by the improvements which have been made by others among them; that the chief, the president of the council, the judges, marshal and sheriffs, and most other persons concerned in the administration of the Government, are the descendants of Europeans, and many of them citizens of this and the adjoining States; and that the Indians, instead of living under their own simple usages and customs, have been compelled to submit to a system of laws and police wholly unsuited to their condition.[3]

Cherokee leaders were angered by the suggestion that the decision was a victory for Georgia. On April 16, 1831, Elias Boudinot, the editor of the *Cherokee Phoenix* newspaper, explained the decision to his readers. His disturbance at how public figures and newspapers in Georgia were claiming victory for the state is clear:

[W]e perceive that an effort is insuing to mislead the public—to produce the impression that the case has not only been dismissed, but the pretensions of Georgia & the views of the Executive have been sustained by the Court. . . .

It is true the Court says that it cannot protect the Cherokees *as a nation,* but does it say that they are not entitled to the protection of the Gen. Government? The opinion plainly intimates that it is the duty of the Executive and Congress of the United States to redress the wrongs, and to guard the rights of the Cherokees if they are oppressed. The whole responsibility is thus thrown, by a judicial decision, upon those branches of the Government. The rights of the Cherokees are as plain, as sacred, as they have been, and the duty of the [federal] Government to secure those rights is as binding as ever. What will the Cherokees do under such circumstances? What else can they do but remain peaceably where they are and continue to call *upon* the *people* of the United States to fulfill their engagements, their solemn promises which have been repeatedly made and which have always been regarded until the commencement of [secretary of war] Mr. Eaton's "new era." We see nothing to alter their determination to remain and to maintain their rights by all suitable measures. The land is theirs—their right to it is "unquestionable," and it cannot be taken away from them without great injustice to them and everlasting infamy to the United States. They stand upon a perfectly safe ground as regards themselves—if they suffer, they will suffer unrighteously—if their rights and their property are forceably taken away from them the responsibility will not be upon them, but upon their treacherous "guardians."[4]

John Ross, the principal chief, reported to the Cherokee people on the meaning of the decision with his typical optimism:

[T]he court has admitted the Cherokees to be "a distinct political society, separated from others, capable of managing its own affairs and governing itself; and that the acts of the United States Government plainly recognizes the Cherokee Nation as *a State* & the courts are bound by these acts." Thus it will be perceived that the denial of the injunction has no bearing whatever upon the true merits of our cause, but owing to the limited powers of the Supreme Court; & so far as the opinion has been expressed in regard to the rights recognized & secured to the Cherokee Nation by the acts of the General Government, they are maintained by the Court & will be sustained whenever a case between proper parties may be brought before it. Moreover the Court viewed the features of [the] Bill presented, as calling upon it to exercise an authority rather of a political character, which more properly belongs to another tribunal. It now falls upon our political Father to exercise his authority & afford us the protection Solemnly guaranteed by Treaties with the United States; and whether the opinion of the Court will influence him or not on this occasion, it is our duty & our interest still to hold fast by the hand, cling to his skirts & cry aloud for justice & protection, until it shall be extended, or our feeble hand be shaken loose from its grip by the power of the General Government. . . .

The busy tattlers and intriguers who are ever ready to prey upon our vitals by false insinuations, will, no doubt, endeavour to persuade you to believe that there is no hope left for you on this side of the Mississippi: nay, the coarse voice is even now beginning to be heard rustling from the "forked tongue" o'er the plains, hills & mountains throughout the land, therefore beware & suffer not yourselves to be deluded by them. You have for the time past met oppression & injustice with fortitude & forbearance and I trust you will persevere in this prudent course; as it will not fail in due time to lead you to a safe deliverance from all the troubles you are experiencing under the cruel & unjust measures pursued by the state of Georgia & the President towards us. . . .

Our cause will ultimately triumph. It is the cause of humanity and justice. It involves a question of great magnitude & one of the most extraordinary character that has ever been agitated in the United States, and it will necessarily consume time to bring it to a final issue; but if the President will sustain the opinion of the court, as he ought to do, the question is already settled and our troubles would cease. And if he will not change his policy to sustain the opinion of the court, the next Congress will, in all probability, put an end to this grievous controversy. It becomes our duty, therefore, to maintain our ground, until it is finally settled.[5]

Chief Justice Marshall was no more satisfied with his own work than were the Cherokees. He admitted that the Court had rushed its deliberations to complete the term. "The judge who pronounced that opinion had not time to consider the case in its various bearings," he wrote.[6]

Justice Story, who supported the Cherokees' claims of sovereignty, was pleased that the Court's reporter, Richard Peters, was planning to publish the justices' opinions and other materials related to the controversy: "The publication will do a great deal of good—the subject unites the *moral* sense of all New England—It comes home to the religious feelings of our people. It touches their sensibilities, and sinks to the very bottom of their sense of Justice—Depend on it there is a depth of degradation in our national conduct, which will irresistibly lead to better things."[7]

Unfortunately for the Cherokees, Story's expectations were mistaken.

RESPONSES TO THE 1832 CASE

In *Cherokee Nation v. Georgia*, Chief Justice Marshall had suggested that the Cherokees' grievances might "be decided by this court in a proper case with proper parties." The state of Georgia provided the Cherokees with that opportunity within weeks of the decision. Removal proponents in the Georgia government had long believed, with good reason, that missionaries from the Northeast were encouraging the Cherokees to resist the state's pressures to leave their lands. In 1830 the Georgia legislature enacted a law prohibiting "white persons" from residing in the Cherokee Nation without permission from the state. Missionaries had until March 1, 1831, either to leave or to secure a license of residency from the governor.

In *Cherokee Nation v. Georgia* (1831) and *Worcester v. Georgia* (1832), the Supreme Court addressed the sovereignty of the Cherokee Nation and the state of Georgia's attempt to confiscate the Cherokees' land. The latter opinion declared the Cherokees to be sovereign, but did little else. Both decisions helped set in motion the chain of events that led to the 1838–1839 forced migration known as the Trail of Tears, during which 4,000 Cherokee died of cold, hunger, and disease on their way to western lands. —Woolaroc Ranch, Museum, and Wildlife Preserve

Those who sought such a license were required to take an oath to "support and defend the constitution and laws of the state of Georgia."

On July 7, 1831, Georgia arrested Samuel A. Worcester, Elizur Butler, and several other missionaries and agents of the American Board of Commissioners for Foreign Missions, a Congregationalist organization based in Massachusetts, for violating the license law by refusing to leave Cherokee territory. Worcester, the leader and most outspoken of the missionaries, had been living in the Cherokee capital of New Echota (located in the area now claimed by Georgia) and working with Boudinot to translate the Bible and other spiritual readings into the Cherokee language, using the syllabary invented by Sequoyah. Worcester became intimate with leaders of the Cherokee government and did indeed encourage them to resist the removal pressures.

Ross instructed the Cherokee Nation's lawyers to assist in the missionaries' defense. On September 15 a trial court in Gwinnett County convicted Worcester, Butler, and the other missionaries of violating the oath and license law. The court sentenced them to four years at hard labor in the state penitentiary. The missionaries appealed their convictions to the U.S. Supreme Court on the grounds that Georgia did not possess jurisdiction over residents of the Cherokee Nation or acts committed therein. They argued that the state's extension law scheme violated the Cherokee Nation's rights as a sovereign nation and unlawfully encroached upon the federal government's authority over relationships with the tribes. Georgia, again, refused to appear before the Court.

The Court announced its decision on March 3, 1832. Chief Justice Marshall, writing for the majority, first acknowledged that the Court held jurisdiction pursuant to its right to review state laws and actions that conflicted with the Constitution. Marshall then declared Georgia's extension laws "repugnant to the constitution, laws, and treaties of the United States" and ordered the state to release the missionaries. He added that "the Indian nations had always been considered distinct, independent political communities retaining their original natural rights, as the undisputed possessors of the soil, from time immemorial." He noted that the United States had repeatedly recognized this fact in a series of treaties and had promised in those agreements to protect the land rights and sovereignty of the Cherokee Nation. He also pointed out that Georgia had, even in the Compact of 1802, given "her acquiescence" to this "universal conviction." Marshall noted that the Cherokees had surrendered specific national powers in those treaties, but he concluded that the Cherokee Nation remained a distinct, sovereign nation that possessed legal right to, and dominion over, its territory.

Boudinot was in the American Board's office when he heard about the Court's decision. He expressed his joy in a letter to his brother, Stand Watie:

> It is glorious news—the laws of the state are declared by the highest judicial tribunal in the country null and void. It is a great triumph on the part of the Cherokees so far as the question of their rights were concerned. . . . The question is forever settled as to who is right & who is wrong & this controversy is exactly where it ought to be. . . . It is not now before the great state of Georgia & the poor Cherokees, but between the friend of the judiciary, and the *enemies* of the judiciary.[8]

The *Cherokee Phoenix* subsequently offered another statement of vindication:

> The question of our rights is not longer a matter to be debated—it is settled—the general and State Governments can operate against them now, only, by power, dictated by expediency & c. whilest the Cherokees will cling to them by virtue of the supreme law of the land, founded on justice—but should the President and Georgia regardless of honor, humanity and justice, exercise power to remove us by force, and such a removal bring ruin and destruction upon our nation, the accountability must rest upon those who ought to be our friends, guardians & protectors.[9]

Ross noted in a letter, "Our adversaries are generally down in the mouth—there are rejoicings throughout the Nation on the decision of the Supreme Court upon the Cherokee case. Traitors and internal enemies are seeking places where to hide their heads."[10]

Justice Story worried that President Jackson would not enforce the Court's decision:

> Georgia is full of anger and violence. What she will do, it is difficult to say. Probably she will resist the execution of our judgment, and if she does, I do not believe the President will interfere, unless public opinion among the religious of the Eastern and Western and Middle States, should be brought to bear strong upon him. The rumor is, that he had told the Georgians he will do nothing.[11]

George Troup, a former governor of Georgia and a prominent removal advocate, was indeed outraged by Marshall's decision against his state. He warned that those in the North and in the national government who wanted to protect the rights of Indians also envisioned abolishing slavery in the South:

> The people of Georgia will receive with indignant feelings, as they ought, the recent decision of the supreme court, so flagrantly violative of their sovereign rights. . . . The jurisdiction claimed over one portion of our population may very soon be asserted over another; and in both cases they will be sustained by the fanatics of the North. Very soon, therefore, things must come to their worst; and if in the last resort we need defenders; we

will find them every where among the honest men of the country; whom a just and wise conduct will rally to our banner.[12]

Wilson Lumpkin, a member of the Union Democrat Party, was the newly elected governor of Georgia. He complained that the decision violated the sovereign powers of the state:

> Our conflicts with Federal usurpation are not yet at end. The events of the past year have afforded us new cause for distrust and dissatisfaction. Contrary to the enlightened opinions and just expectations of this and every other State in the Union, a majority of the judges of the Supreme Court of the United States have not only assumed jurisdiction in the cases of Worcester and Butler, but have, by their decision, attempted to overthrow that essential jurisdiction of the State, in criminal cases, which has been vested by our Constitution in the Superior Courts of our own State. In conformity with their decision, a mandate was issued to our court, ordering a reversal of the decree under which those persons are imprisoned, thereby attempting and intending to prostrate the sovereignty of this State in the exercise of its constitutional criminal jurisdiction. . . . I have, however, been prepared to meet this usurpation of Federal power with the most prompt and determined resistence, in whatever form its enforcement might have been attempted by any branch of the Federal Government. . . .
>
> The ingenuity of man might be challenged to show a single sentence in the Constitution of the United States giving power, either direct or implied, to the general government, or any of its departments, to nullify the laws of a State, enacted for the government of its own population, or coerce obedience, by force, to the mandates of the Judiciary of the Union. On the contrary, the journals and proceedings of the convention that framed the Federal Constitution abundantly evince that various attempts were made to effect that object, all of which were rejected. This proves that the States of this Union never did, and never will, permit their political rights to be suspended upon the breath of the agents or trustees to whom they have delegated limited powers to perform certain definite acts. I, however, deem it unnecessary for me, at this time, to animadvert on this decision of the Supreme Court. Its fallacy, its inconsistency with former decisions, and its obvious tendency to intermeddle with the political rights of the States, and to change our Federal system into one consolidated mass, has been so often exposed by the most able jurists and statesmen that a large majority of the people of this Union are confirmed in the conviction of the fallibility, infirmities, and errors of this Supreme tribunal.[13]

The Augusta, Georgia, *Chronicle* reacted to the *Worcester* decision by linking the states' rights issues of Indian removal and nullification:

> One good at least, will grow out of the decision, inasmuch as it must tend to unite the southern states more closely, and show them that they have common cause of self-protection and self-defence against federal usurpation and oppression. . . . [S]hould a federal force ever be marched against Georgia, our life upon it, that it would never pass through Carolina, but over the prostrate lifeless bodies of all her patriot sons.[14]

The *Alabama Journal* also noted the connection between Indian removal and nullification:

> By this decision, the Court declares the States have not the right of jurisdiction over the Indian tribes. This is the most important decision ever yet made by that Court. It involves the great principle of States Rights and will now test the efficacy of Nullifica-

tion. Will Georgia submit to this decision? She cannot, and will not! What, then, will be the consequence? Nullification.[15]

The Newark, New Jersey, *Advertiser* responded to the threats published in southern newspapers:

> Much as we would regret the necessity of sustaining the supremacy of the laws, by an appeal to arms, still we have no doubt, that every State in the Union, would promptly furnish the Executive of the nation its requisite portion of patriotic freemen, to aid him in upholding the judiciary, and preserving the integrity of the Union.[16]

The Washington, D.C., *National Intelligencer* called for restraint in the press by attempting to explain the process that the Cherokee Nation would have to pursue to enforce the Court's decision:

> At length we have received the opinions of several journals in the state of Georgia, and no doubt remains on our mind, from their tone, that the mandate of the Supreme Court in that case will be *disregarded,* however it might have been hoped otherwise. . . .
>
> The very respectable editor of the Political Arena (at Fredricksburgh, Virginia) speculating on this subject in his last number, says "We have arrived at a crisis—an undoubted and momentous crisis. A few days will decide the question of the further duration of the Union!"
>
> We fully concur in the opinion expressed in the first of the above sentences, while we dissent in part from that conveyed in the second. We trust that the Union will *endure* for many centuries, though more than one state shall rise against it. At any rate, so far as it may be directly affected by the action of Georgia in the case before us, we are under the impression that it will be more than a few days before the question will be decided. . . .
>
> The mandate of the Supreme Court is directed to the Superior Court for the county of Gwinnet, in the state of Georgia; and it requires of that court that it do release the missionaries, who are confined at hard labor in the penitentiary. . . .
>
> If the court *obey* the mandate, it is well, and no more is to be said or done.
>
> If the court *does not obey* the mandate, application will, we suppose, be made to the Supreme Court, at its next term. . . .
>
> If, finally, process issuing from the Supreme Court, and which must be granted as a matter of course, shall be resisted, it will be the duty of the marshal of the United States for that district to summon a *posse comitatus,* and of the president of the United States, if necessary, to place the army and militia of the United States at the service of the civil authority.
>
> In any event, it will be seen that the danger from this source is not so immediate as supposed by our friend at Fredericksburgh.[17]

In fact, Georgia did refuse to obey the directive of the Court, and President Jackson did not feel inclined to force the state to abide by the Court's decision. In the 1860s, when Horace Greeley published a history of the United States, he reported that Jackson's reaction to *Worcester v. Georgia* was, "John Marshall has made his decision, now let him enforce it." Although scholars have found no written evidence of that statement, it is certain that Jackson declared in a letter soon after the decision, "The decision of the supreme court has fell still born and they find that they cannot coerce Georgia to yield to its mandate."[18]

THE IMPACT OF THE CHEROKEE CASES

Jackson's inaction proved to be the death blow to Cherokee hopes to remain in their southeastern homeland. When the leaders of the Cherokee Nation planned their legal challenge to Georgia's extension laws, they hoped that a decision supporting their declaration of sovereignty would persuade Congress, and perhaps even Jackson, to restrain Georgia and forestall the removal pressures being brought to bear against their people. When this did not follow, Ross lost the support of several prominent Cherokees. Boudinot and Major Ridge, a respected member of the Cherokee National Council, urged the chief to negotiate the best terms he could and lead the tribe to the West. When Ross refused, a minority faction of Cherokees, led by Boudinot and Ridge, signed a removal treaty at New Echota in 1835. Ross and the majority of Cherokees protested that the treaty was illegal and continued to oppose removal until 1838, when President Martin Van Buren ordered the U.S. Army to round up the Cherokees into temporary stockades and prepare them for relocation. In the winter of 1838–1839 the Cherokees migrated to their new home in the Indian Territory (now Oklahoma). Perhaps as many as 4,000 Cherokees, roughly one-fourth of the nation's population, died on the removal paths that came to be known as the Trail of Tears.

Public criticism of Georgia's incarceration of the missionaries persuaded Governor Lumpkin to work for their release. He asked the state legislature to repeal the law used to convict them and worked doggedly to convince Worcester and his imprisoned allies to apologize and accept a pardon. Worcester and the others were freed from prison in January 1833 after serving more than a year. Worcester joined the Cherokees in their exile and continued his work among them until he died.

Although *Worcester v. Georgia* did not protect the Cherokees from removal as Ross and the Cherokee National Council had hoped, the decision became the legal foundation for the modern conception of tribal sovereignty. In several decisions in the latter half of the twentieth century, the Supreme Court revived Marshall's assertion that the Native American tribes possess an inherent form of national sovereignty and the right of self-determination. Long after its failure to deliver the Cherokees from Georgia's attacks, *Worcester v. Georgia* served as the Indian nations' most powerful weapon against state and local encroachments on their tribal powers; and the Cherokee Cases, as they came to be called, became the authorities that defined the relationships between the states, the federal government, and the tribal nations.

NOTES

1. *National Gazette,* March 21, 1831.
2. Reprinted in the *Cherokee Phoenix,* April 9, 1831.
3. George R. Gilmer, *First Settlers of Upper Georgia* (New York: D. Appleton, 1855), 294–296.
4. *Cherokee Phoenix,* April 16, 1831.
5. John Ross, "To the Cherokees," April 14, 1831, in *The Papers of Chief John Ross,* 2 vols., ed. Gary E. Moulton (Norman: University of Oklahoma Press, 1984), 1:215–219.
6. John Marshall to Richard Peters, May 19, 1831, in Peters Papers, Pennsylvania Historical Society, quoted in Joseph C. Burke, "The Cherokee Cases: A Study in Law, Politics, and Morality," *Stanford Law Review* 21 (1969): 518.
7. Joseph Story to Richard Peters, June 24, 1831, Peters Papers, quoted in Burke, "The Cherokee Cases," ibid.
8. Elias Boudinot to Stand Watie, March 7, 1832, Cherokee Nation Papers, Western History Collections, University of Oklahoma, Norman, Oklahoma, quoted in Henry Thompson Malone, *Cherokees of the Old South: A People in Transition* (Athens: University of Georgia Press, 1956), 178.
9. *Cherokee Phoenix,* May 26, 1832.
10. John Ross to the Cherokee Delegates, March 30, 1832, *The Papers of Chief John Ross,* 1:241.
11. Joseph Story to George Ticknor, March 8, 1832, in *The Life and Letters of Joseph Story,* 2 vols., ed. William W. Story (Boston: Charles C. Little and James Brown, 1851), 2:83.
12. *Georgia Journal,* March 15, 1832.
13. Wilson Lumpkin, "Annual Message, 1832," *The Removal of the Cherokee Indians from Georgia* (New York: Arno Press and the New York Times,1969), 103–105.
14. *Augusta Chronicle,* no available date, republished in the *Adams Sentinel* (Gettysburg, Pa.), April 4, 1832.
15. *Alabama Journal,* March 17, 1832.
16. *Newark Advertiser,* no available date, republished in the *Adams Sentinel,* April 4, 1832.
17. The Washington, D.C., *National Intelligencer,* no available date, republished in *The Clarion* (Sandusky, Ohio), April 4, 1832.
18. Andrew Jackson to John Coffee, April 7, 1832, in *Correspondence of Andrew Jackson,* 7 vols., ed. John S. Bassett (Washington, D.C.: Carnegie Institute, 1926–1935), 4:430.

Dred Scott v. Sandford

Paul Finkelman

Dred Scott v. Sandford
60 U.S. 393 (19 How. 393) (1857)

DECIDED: March 6, 1857

VOTE

CONCURRING: 7 (Roger B. Taney, James M. Wayne, John Catron, Peter V. Daniel, Samuel Nelson, Robert C. Grier, John A. Campbell)

DISSENTING: 2 (John McLean, Benjamin R. Curtis)

OPINION OF THE COURT: Taney

CONCURRING OPINION: Wayne

CONCURRING OPINION: Nelson (Grier)

CONCURRING OPINION: Grier

CONCURRING OPINION: Daniel

CONCURRING OPINION: Campbell

CONCURRING OPINION: Catron

DISSENTING OPINION: McLean

DISSENTING OPINION: Curtis

Dred Scott's case and his story are often misunderstood by scholars and the public. Scott was not a fugitive slave, as many people believe; rather, he was a slave who attempted to use the legal system to gain his freedom. His case helped shape the political debate of the late last few years before the American Civil War. Ultimately, the case helped lead to the Fourteenth Amendment to the U.S. Constitution, which made all people born in the United States—including African Americans—citizens of the nation. The memory of the case in both law and political culture remains strong, even if many Americans are unaware of what it was actually about or how it turned out.

Scott was born in slavery around 1800. His owner, a Virginian named Peter Blow, moved him to Alabama in 1818 and to St. Louis in 1830. Blow died in 1832, and Scott was sold to Dr. John Emerson, a U.S. Army surgeon. Captain Emerson took Scott with him to military posts in Illinois and the part of the Wisconsin Territory that is now Minnesota. From 1836 to 1838 Scott lived at Fort Snelling, in what is today St. Paul, where he married Harriet Robinson. Before her marriage, Robinson was the slave of Maj. Lawrence Taliaferro, the fort's resident Indian agent. Taliaferro was also a justice of the peace, and in that capacity he performed a wedding service for the couple. The marriage became a significant factor in Scott's claim to freedom because slaves could never be legally married. Scott's lawyers would later argue that he must have been free at the time he was married by a justice of the peace.

Emerson died in 1843, and the Scott family, which now included two daughters, passed into the hands of Emerson's widow, Irene. She hired Scott out, and for a few years he worked in Texas. In 1846 Scott was back in St. Louis, where he tried to buy his freedom from Irene Emerson, but she rejected his offer. Scott then sued for his freedom, based on his residence in the free state of Illinois and the free territory of Wisconsin. As early as 1772 the Court of Kings Bench, in England, had ruled in *Somerset v. Stewart* that a slave became free the moment he set foot in a nonslave jurisdiction. This decision was based on the idea that slavery could exist only by "positive law"—that is, statutory law—and without a law creating slavery, no one could be enslaved.

In 1787 Congress, under the Articles of Confederation, had passed the Northwest Ordinance, which prohibited slavery north and west of the Ohio River. This territory included the future state of Illinois and part of what became Minnesota. After the Constitution was adopted, the new Congress reaffirmed the provisions of the ordinance. Illinois came into the Union as a free state in 1819. A year later, in the Missouri Compromise, Congress banned slavery north and west of the new state of Missouri. Finally, in 1836, just before Scott was taken to Fort Snelling, Congress passed the Wisconsin Enabling Act, which reaffirmed the provision of the Northwest Ordinance and also applied all of the existing laws of the Michigan Territory to the Minnesota area. One of those laws banned slavery.

DRED SCOTT'S LEGAL ODYSSEY BEGINS

On the basis of pre-Revolutionary English precedent, Illinois law, and a myriad of federal laws, Scott claimed to be free. His claim was strengthened, he argued, by his marriage before a justice of the peace, which was a de facto recognition by his master of his free status. Finally, he claimed freedom under Missouri precedents. Although it was a slave state, Missouri had long accepted the *Somerset* principle that a slave taken to a free state became free. The Missouri Supreme Court had taken this position in *Winney v. Whitesides* (1824) and reaffirmed it in a number of subsequent cases. Based on these precedents, in 1850 a St. Louis court declared Scott free. In *Scott v. Emerson* (1852), however, the Missouri Supreme Court reversed this decision, declaring that it would no longer follow the 1824 precedent. The court's decision was blatantly political. The opinion stated:

> Times are not now as they were when the former decisions on this subject were made. Since then, not only individuals but States have been possessed with a dark and fell spirit in relation to slavery, whose gratification is sought in the pursuit of measures, whose inevitable consequence must be the overthrow and destruction of our Government. Under such circumstances, it does not behoove the State of Missouri to show the least countenance to any measure which might gratify this spirit. She is willing to assume her full responsibility for the existence of slavery within her limits, nor does she seek to share or divide it with others.[1]

The case might have ended here, but about this time Irene Emerson moved to Springfield, Massachusetts, where she married Dr. Calvin C. Chaffee, an active opponent of slavery, who later served two terms in the U.S. House of Representatives, 1855–1859, first as a member of the American Party and then as a Republican. Before marrying Chaffee, Irene transferred ownership of the Scotts to her brother, John F. A. Sanford. (His name was misspelled as Sandford when the case reached the U.S. Supreme Court.) Sanford lived in New York City but had business interests in Missouri. Scott sued Sanford in federal court, under diversity jurisdiction. Scott argued that he was a citizen of Missouri and therefore could sue Sanford, a citizen of New York, in federal court

In response, Sanford presented a plea in abatement—a plea to end the suit—arguing that Scott could not sue in federal court because, in language later picked up by the U.S. Supreme Court, Dred Scott "is not a citizen of the State of Missouri, as alleged in his declaration, because he is a negro of African descent; his ancestors were of pure African blood, and were brought into this country and sold as negro slaves."[2] Sanford, in effect, argued that blacks could not be considered citizens for purposes of diversity jurisdiction. Judge Robert W. Wells of the U.S. district court rejected this plea. Wells concluded that *if* Scott were free, he had the right to sue in federal court as a citizen of Missouri. This statement did not mean that Wells thought free blacks were full-fledged citizens, but he did think free blacks ought to be able to defend their rights in federal courts. The ruling against Sanford's plea allowed the suit to proceed.

Once he heard the case, however, Wells determined that Missouri law was binding, and, because the state supreme court had ruled against Scott's freedom claim, he must remain a slave. Wells decided the case on the basis of the Missouri Supreme Court's earlier ruling, in effect asserting that each state has the right to determine the status of people within its jurisdiction. Scott claimed he was free because he had lived in

Illinois, and Wells reasoned correctly, based on Supreme Court precedent, that Missouri was free to accept or reject the law of Illinois. Both states were "equal," and therefore one state could not dictate to another what the status of its residents should be. By analogy, Wells applied the same logic to Scott's residence at Fort Snelling: the Wisconsin Territory could not dictate to Missouri how it should treat people within its borders.

Judge Wells's analysis was generally consistent with nineteenth-century constitutional thought and theory. In reaching this conclusion, however, Wells ignored the federal aspect of the case. Illinois and Missouri were coequal partners in the Union, but the laws of both states were subordinate to the U.S. Constitution and to the acts of Congress implementing the Constitution. Article VI says, "This Constitution, and the Laws of the United States which shall be made in Pursuance thereof . . . shall be the supreme Law of the Land; and the Judges in every State shall be bound thereby, any Thing in the Constitution or Laws of any State to the Contrary notwithstanding." Although he did not explicitly say so, Wells in effect held that Missouri had the right to overturn or at least ignore a series of federal laws, including the Missouri Compromise and the Wisconsin Enabling Act, which made slavery illegal where Scott had lived and presumably made him free.

Had Sanford lost ownership of Scott, he probably would have appealed the ruling on the plea in abatement, but, because he retained his property, he had no reason to appeal any part of the lower court decision. Scott won on the issue of the plea in abatement, and he naturally did not appeal that part of Judge Wells's decision. He did, however, appeal the ruling that he was not free under the Missouri Compromise.

U.S. SUPREME COURT DECISION

The appeal reached the Court in late 1854, but it could not be placed on the docket until the following term, which began in December 1855. The Court heard arguments in February 1856 but did not give a decision at that time. Instead, it scheduled reargument for the December 1856 term. Abraham Lincoln and other Republicans would later claim that the delay was part of a deliberate conspiracy to overturn the Missouri Compromise, force slavery into the territories, and elect Democrat James Buchanan president. During his campaign for the Senate in 1858, Lincoln suggested that the Court did not dare strike down the Missouri Compromise before the 1856 presidential election and delayed by scheduling reargument in order to decide the case after the election. On March 6, 1857, two days after Buchanan was inaugurated as president, Chief Justice Taney announced the opinion of the Court. Speaking for a 7–2 majority, Taney rejected Scott's suit. Even though the issue of the plea in abatement was not technically before the Court, the Supreme Court decision focused on both the plea in abatement—that is, the right of blacks to sue in federal court—and the constitutionality of the Missouri Compromise. The Court asked two questions. First, did Scott, or any black, have the right to sue in federal court as a citizen of a state? Second, did Congress have the power to prohibit slavery in the territories and thereby emancipate slaves brought into the territories?

Chief Justice Taney held that Congress had no power to pass general laws to regulate the territories. He also held that the Missouri Compromise unconstitutionally deprived southerners of their property in slaves without due process of law or just compensation, in violation of the Fifth Amendment. By implication, this also meant that no territorial legislature could ban slavery in a federal territory. This part of the ruling undermined the concept of "popular sovereignty" that the leading northern Democrat, Sen. Stephen A. Douglas of Illinois, had developed as a way of solving the problem of slavery in the western territories. Under *Dred Scott,* slavery would be legal in all the federal territories and could be prohibited only at statehood. This aspect of the decision shocked northerners, who had long seen the Missouri Compromise as a central piece of legislation for organizing the settlement of the West and for accommodating differing sectional interests. It also shocked many northern Democrats, who had supported opening up the Kansas and Nebraska territories to slavery under popular sovereignty.

Taney also denied that blacks could ever be citizens of the United States, declaring:

> The question is simply this: Can a negro, whose ancestors were imported into this country, and sold as slaves, become a member of the political community formed and brought into existence by the Constitution of the United States, and as such become entitled to all the rights, and privileges, and immunities, guarantied by that instrument to the citizen? One of which rights is the privilege of suing in a court of the United States in the cases specified in the Constitution.[3]

Ignoring the fact that free black men in most of the northern states, as well as North Carolina, could vote at the time of the ratification of the Constitution, Taney declared that blacks

> are not included, and were not intended to be included, under the word "citizens" in the Constitution, and can therefore claim none of the rights and privileges which the instrument provides and secures to citizens of the United States. On the contrary, they were at that time considered as a subordinate and inferior class of beings who had been subjugated by the dominant race, and, whether emancipated or not, yet remained subject to their authority, and had no rights or privileges but such as those who held the power and Government might choose to grant them.[4]

According to Taney, blacks were "so far inferior, that they had no rights which the white man was bound to respect."

Justices McLean and Curtis wrote lengthy dissents, disputing Taney's conclusions point by point. They stressed black participation in the Revolution and black voting at the time of the adoption of the Constitution. They reminded the Court that the first Congress had readopted the Northwest Ordinance, which implied that the Framers of the Constitution believed Congress had the power to prohibit slavery from the territories.

RESPONSES TO THE DECISION

The public responses to the decision were tied to the politics of the 1850s. Before 1850 slavery was not allowed in the territories west and north of Missouri. Congress had not yet decided the status of slavery in the territories acquired from Mexico after the 1846–1847 war. The Compromise of 1850 allowed slavery in these newly acquired territories, while admitting California into the Union as a free state. Meanwhile, the Whig Party was soundly beaten in the 1852 election and virtually disappeared. In 1854 the Democrats, firmly in control of Congress and the White House, passed the Kansas-Nebraska Act, which allowed slavery into the territory immediately west of Missouri. This law was designed to placate the southern wing of the party, which insisted that slaveholders have access to new territories in the West. According to the Kansas-Nebraska Act, the settlers of the territories would decide for themselves, under a theory called popular sovereignty, whether slavery would be legal in a particular territory. At first glance, popular sovereignty seemed to be the essence of democracy because it allowed settlers to decide if they wanted slavery. But northerners argued that southerners, with their numerous slaves, would present unfair competition to free labor. Furthermore, many northerners argued that the Missouri Compromise was a fundamental, almost sacred, compact for the preservation of sectional harmony, and it was morally and politically wrong to repeal it.

The primary engineer of the Kansas-Nebraska Act was Senator Douglas, who claimed that he did not care whether slavery was voted up or down; he only was interested in allowing the settlers to decide the matter. His real goal was to build a railroad from Chicago to California, and the best way to do that was through Missouri and Kansas. He therefore wanted Kansas opened to settlement, and he wanted southern support for his railroad. In the North the reaction to the Kansas-Nebraska Act led to the formation of the

THE POLITICAL QUADRILLE
Music by Dred Scott

This parody of the 1860 presidential contest highlights the impact of *Dred Scott v. Sandford* (1857), in which the Court ruled that neither the federal government nor territorial governments could prohibit slavery in the territories. Here the four candidates dance with partners representing their supporters, while Scott, a former slave, plays the fiddle. Clockwise, starting at the upper left, Southern Democrat John C. Breckinridge dances with Democratic incumbent James Buchanan, depicted as a goat or (as he was nicknamed) "Buck"; Republican Abraham Lincoln prances arm-in-arm with a black woman, a reference to his abolitionist supporters; Constitutional Union party candidate John Bell dances with an Indian brave, perhaps an allusion to Bell's Native American interests; and Stephen A. Douglas dances with an Irishman. —Library of Congress.

Republican Party, which was dedicated to stopping the spread of slavery into the West. In 1856 this brand-new party nearly won the presidency, but the victory went to James Buchanan, a Pennsylvania "doughface" Democrat. (The doughfaces were northerners who consistently voted with the South on issues involving slavery.)

Even before the decision in *Dred Scott* was announced, Buchanan and other Democrats were laying the groundwork for supporting it. At his inauguration Buchanan and Taney had a brief conversation—in full view of the audience—just before Buchanan gave his inaugural address. In that address, delivered just two days before Taney announced his opinion, Buchanan said that the issue of slavery in the territories was "a judicial question, which legitimately belongs to the Supreme Court of the United States," one, he noted, that would "be speedily and finally settled." Buchanan pledged to "cheerfully submit" to this decision, as he believed "all good citizens" would.

Many Republicans would later charge that in that brief conversation Taney violated Court ethics by telling Buchanan what the Court would decide, so that the pro-slavery Buchanan could support the decision in his inaugural address. There is no record of what Taney said to Buchanan in that whispered conversation on the podium, but it is clear that Buchanan already knew what the decision would be. Well before the inauguration, Justice Robert Grier, another Pennsylvania doughface, told president-elect Buchanan how the Court would rule. Buchanan, therefore, could safely endorse the forthcoming decision in his inaugural address.[5]

Southerners and conservative northern Democrats rallied to the *Dred Scott* decision. Since 1854 northern Democrats had faced fierce competition from the Republican Party, whose main platform was opposition to new slave states and to slavery in the territories. Taney's opinion, holding that Congress could not ban slavery in the territories, undermined the whole purpose of this party. Democrats cheered the decision as providing a constitutional argument against the Republicans. Democrats also hoped the decision would end all discussion of slavery in the territories and move politics away from this divisive issue.

Not surprisingly, the southern press praised the decision. The New Orleans *Daily Picayune,* a Whig paper, gleefully noted that the decision was the cause for "bitter comment in the anti-slavery journals" because it marked "the overthrow" of the "favorite theories and upset their political plans." The paper said the decision "gives the sanction of established law, and the guarantees of the constitution" to the South while being "a heavy blow to Black Republicanism."[6] The more states rights–oriented Richmond *Enquirer* declared that with this decision, "The *nation* has achieved a triumph, *sectionalism* has been rebuked, and abolitionism has been staggered and stunned."[7] The Charleston *Mercury* noted that the Supreme Court had never been "the special guardian of State Rights and the interests of the South," and therefore it felt the *Dred Scott* decision was greeted with "exaggerated effect of surprise." The paper approved the decision, but correctly predicted that it would "precipitate rather than retard" what would be "the final conflict between Slavery and Abolitionism." The *Mercury* was not as sanguine as other papers supporting the decision, per-haps because sentiment in South Carolina was already deeply hostile to the Union. Moreover, the paper doubted that northerners, especially Republicans and abolitionists (and the paper made no distinction between the two) would accept the decision.[8]

Most northern Democratic papers were delighted with the decision. The *Pittsburgh Post,* for example, declared that the Republicans were "very busy in hunting up an issue on which to contend with the Democrats in the next election" because the *Dred Scott* decision had taken away their main platform plank. This Democratic paper believed that "nothing can be made out of it [the decision] as a political issue. It is law, and cannot be reversed by any other tribunal."[9] On March 11, 1857, the New York *Journal of Com-merce* told its readers that the issues in the case were "now decided on authority which admits no appeal or question." A day later the paper declared that "the so called Republican Party is only another name for Rev-olution and anarchy."

The *Washington Union,* which was closely tied to the Buchanan administration, was delighted with the result. The paper, like other Democratic papers, believed the decision would cripple the Republicans by taking their main issue—slavery in the territories—out of the political debate. The *Union* declared its belief "that this decision will meet a proper reception from the great mass of our intelligent countrymen; that it will be regarded with soberness and not with passion; and that it will thereby exert a mighty influ-ence in diffusing sound opinions and restoring harmony and fraternal concord throughout the country." The paper reported that the Court had "settled the vexed constitutional question as to the power of Con-gress over Territories [by concluding that the power] is entirely independent of the legislative branch of the government. It is elevated above the schemes of party politics, and shielded alike from the effects of sudden passion and of popular prejudice."[10]

Northern Democrats, like their papers, hoped the decision would end the debate over slavery in the territories and destroy the new Republican Party. While running for reelection to the U.S. Senate in 1858, Stephen Douglas asserted, "The right and province of expounding the Constitution, and construing the law, is vested in the judiciary established by the Constitution." Unlike his opponent, Abraham Lincoln, Douglas declared, he had "no warfare to make on the Supreme Court." Douglas was also happy to endorse the Court's holding that free blacks could never be citizens of the United States. On July 9 he asserted:

I am opposed to negro equality. I repeat that this nation is a white people—a people composed of European descendants—a people that have established this government for themselves and their posterity, and I am in favor of preserving not only the purity of the blood but the purity of the government from any mixture or amalgamation with inferior races.[11]

Not surprisingly, most northern papers—all that were not tied to the Buchanan administration—were hostile to the decision. The *New York Tribune,* the nation's leading Republican paper, responded to the decision with outrage, calling Taney's opinion "wicked," "atrocious," and "abominable" and a "collation of false statements and shallow sophistries." Editor Horace Greeley thought Taney's decision had no more validity than the opinions which might be expressed in any "Washington bar-room."[12] He even published a pamphlet edition of Taney's opinion and the Curtis dissent to help the Republican cause. The *Chicago Tribune* declared that Taney's statements on black citizenship were "inhuman dicta."[13]

Republican politicians launched unrelenting attacks on Taney's opinion. Many focused on the brief conversation that Taney had with Buchanan at the inauguration. Republicans publicly speculated that in this conversation Taney had told Buchanan what the Court was about to decide. Sen. William Henry Seward, R-N.Y., later claimed that the "whisperings" between Taney and Buchanan were part of a conspiracy to hang "the millstone of slavery" on the western territories.[14] Only a few minutes after the exchange, Buchanan urged the nation to accept and support the forthcoming decision in *Dred Scott.* Seward, Lincoln, and other Republicans insisted that Taney had told Buchanan how the Court would decide the case.

The most famous, and effective, attack on the decision came from Lincoln, who on June 16, 1858, launched his 1858 Senate bid with the now-famous "House Divided" speech, saying, "I believe this government cannot endure permanently, half slave and half free." He claimed that the *Dred Scott* decision was part of a long-term conspiracy to force slavery on the North and warned that continued Democratic rule would soon lead to a nationalization of slavery. Lincoln told his fellow Republicans, "We shall *lie down* pleasantly dreaming that the people of *Missouri* are on the verge of making their state *free;* and we shall *awake* to the *reality,* instead that the *Supreme* Court has made *Illinois* a *slave* state." Lincoln was convinced that the "logical conclusion" of *Dred Scott* was "What one master might lawfully do with Dred Scott, in the free state of Illinois, every master might lawfully do with any other *one,* or *one thousand* slaves in Illinois, or in any other free state."[15] Lincoln lost the election, but not the cause. In an 1859 speech he warned that some future Supreme Court case would be like a "second Dred Scott decision" and would make "slavery lawful in all the States."[16]

Lincoln was not alone in articulating this fear. In 1859 Gov. Salmon P. Chase, R-Ohio, who would become chief justice after Taney's death, predicted that if the Democrats won the presidency in 1860 there would be a new decision, allowing slavery in the North "just as after the election of Mr. Buchanan, the Dred Scott." Chase asked, "What will the decision be?"

It will be just as they claim, that they can take their slaves into New York over the railroads of New Jersey, through Pennsylvania and through Ohio, Indiana, Illinois . . . to any state of the North, and that they can hold them there during all the time that it is convenient for them to be passing through. In other words, it is a decision in favor, not of the African slave trade, but of the American slave trade, to be carried on in the free states.[17]

The Springfield, Massachusetts, *Republican* asked, "If slavery is a national institution, recognized, protected, and carried into the territories, why does not the same authority recognize, protect, and carry it into all the several states?"[18]

Perhaps the most interesting critique of the decision came from the black abolitionist Frederick Douglass. Earlier in his career Douglass had refused to vote and denounced politics. But by 1857 he was actively involved in antislavery politics and at least sympathetic to the Republican Party. In 1860 he would grudgingly vote for Lincoln and in 1864 enthusiastically endorse him.

For Douglass, the opinion was both an outrage and a call to increase efforts to end slavery. In an 1857 speech he argued that this "judicial incarnation of wolfishness" made his hopes "brighter" than ever before. He argued that this "open, glaring, and scandalous tissue of lies" found in the decision would serve the cause of liberty in the long run. He declared that "we, the abolitionists and colored people, should meet this decision, unlooked for and monstrous as it appears, in a cheerful spirit. This very attempt to blot out forever the hopes of an enslaved people may be one necessary link in the chain of events preparatory to the downfall and complete overthrow of the whole slave system."[19] He used the decision to denounce the followers of the abolitionist William Lloyd Garrison, who argued that the Constitution was proslavery and therefore abolitionists should reject political action. Garrisonians argued for northerners to secede from the Union. To the contrary, Douglass argued that the Constitution was not proslavery and that Taney's opinion was wrong and should be overturned by a combination of political action and appeals to God and conscience.

> Such a decision cannot stand. God will be true though every man be a liar. We can appeal from this hell-black judgment of the Supreme Court, to the court of common sense and common humanity. We can appeal from man to God. If there is no justice on earth, there is yet justice in heaven. You may close your Supreme Court against the black man's cry for justice, but you cannot, thank God, close against him the ear of a sympathizing world, nor shut up the Court of Heaven. All that is merciful and just, on earth and in Heaven, will execrate and despise this edict of Taney.[20]

Douglass's rhetoric may seem overblown, but his predictions proved to be remarkably accurate. In less than four years Lincoln was elected president on a platform that promised to reject Taney's conclusions and guarantee that slavery would be excluded from the territories. Southern secession and civil war followed, and that in turn ended slavery.

IN THE COURT OF HISTORY

Frederick Douglass had found a reason for hope in the decision. He understood that the decision would push the nation closer to brink of disaster, which he believed would end slavery. He displayed remarkable optimism. He told a New York audience: "You will readily ask me how I am affected by this devilish decision—this judicial incarnation of wolfishness! My answer is, and no thanks to the slaveholding wing of the Supreme Court, my hopes were never brighter than now." Douglass believed that the decision would raise "the National Conscience." Moreover, he saw in the decision the beginning of the great cataclysm that could destroy slavery:

> The Supreme Court of the United States is not the only power in this world. It is very great, but the Supreme Court of the Almighty is greater. Judge Taney can do many things, but he cannot perform impossibilities. He cannot bale out the ocean, annihilate this firm old earth, or pluck the silvery star of liberty from our Northern sky. He may decide and decide again; but he cannot reverse the decision of the Most High. He cannot change the essential nature of things—making evil good, and good, evil.[21]

The change Douglass called for came more quickly than he could have imagined. On June 19, 1862, President Abraham Lincoln signed legislation ending slavery in the territories. Despite Taney's assertions that Congress could not take this action, Congress and the president did so. Congress also outlawed slavery in the District of Columbia. On January 1, 1863, Lincoln issued the Emancipation Proclamation, which led to slavery's demise in most of the Confederacy. Slavery no longer had a special constitutional protection;

indeed, it had almost no protection at all, as U.S. soldiers had already ended it for many thousands. In addition, before the war was over, more than 200,000 black men had served in the army and navy. Too old to serve himself, Douglass personally recruited more than 100 blacks in upstate New York, including his two sons. In his newspaper, Douglass "issued a stirring call, 'Men of Color, to Arms!' " People who were written out of the Constitution in 1857 helped rewrite the constitutional arrangements only a few years later. In early 1865 Congress passed, and sent to the states, the Thirteenth Amendment, which says: "Neither slavery nor involuntary servitude . . . shall exist within the United States." A year later Congress passed the Fourteenth Amendment. Ratified in 1868, the amendment made all people born in the United States citizens of the state in which they lived as well as citizens of the nation. *Dred Scott v. Sandford* was now a dead letter.

Although Scott did not live to see the demise of the case that bore his name, he did attain freedom. Shortly after the decision, the sons of his first owner, Peter Blow, purchased Scott and his family and emancipated them. Scott remained a free man, and something of a celebrity from May 26, 1857, until his death on February 17, 1858.

Chief Justice Taney died on October 12, 1864, without seeing the undoing of his judicial handiwork. By then he surely understood the depth of his failure in *Dred Scott*. His decision had put in motion forces that ended the controversy over slavery in the territories, but not in the way he wanted.

In February 1865 the Senate debated a bill to appropriate money to honor Taney. The Senate bill would have provided money for a bust of the late chief justice to be placed with busts of all other deceased justices. This honor was considered pro forma: no justice had ever been denied his place in the pantheon of American jurists.

But no other justice was like Roger B. Taney, who, at the time of his death, was denounced and vilified. Sen. Charles Sumner, R-Mass., opposed having a bust of Taney placed alongside the other departed justices. Sumner argued, "If a man has done evil during his life he must not be complimented in marble." Sumner noted that England had never honored the hated Chief Justice Jeffries, "famous for his talents as for his crimes." Like Jeffries, Taney had been "the tool of unjust power." Neither deserved honor. Taney had "administered his last justice wickedly, and degraded the judiciary of the country, and degraded the age." He was not to be remembered by a marble bust; rather, Taney was to be dealt with in the works of scholars. There, Sumner confidentially predicted "the name of Taney is to be hooted down the page of history."[22]

In the years since Sumner gave this speech, Chief Justice Taney's reputation has fluctuated. He was on the Court for nearly thirty years and wrote many important opinions. Much of his jurisprudence on economic issues is highly regarded by many scholars. But, in the end, his reputation, and that of the antebellum Court, turns on *Dred Scott v. Sandford*.

NOTES

1. *Scott v. Emerson*, 15 Mo. 576, at 586 (1852).

2. *Dred Scott v. Sandford*, 60 U.S. 393 (19 How. 393), at 394 (1857).

3. Ibid., at 403.

4. Ibid., at 405–406.

5. Don E. Fehrenbacher, *The Dred Scott Case: Its Significance in American Law and Politics* (New York: Oxford University Press, 1978), 473 passim. See also Paul Finkelman, *Dred Scott v. Sandford: A Brief History with Documents* (Boston: Bedford Books, 1997), 46–47.

6. New Orleans *Daily Picayune*, March 21, 1857.

7. *Richmond Enquirer*, March 21, 1857.

8. Charleston *Mercury*, April 2, 1857.

9. *Pittsburgh Post*, March 17, 1857.

10. *Washington Union*, March 12, 1857.

11. Quoted in Paul M. Angle, *Created Equal? The Complete Lincoln-Douglas Debates of 1858* (Chicago: University of Chicago Press, 1958), 24 (as quoted in Finkelman, *Dred Scott v. Sandford*, 201.

12. *New York Tribune,* March 7, 1857.

13. *Chicago Tribune,* March 12, 1857, as quoted in Fehrenbacher, *Dred Scott Case,* 417.

14. *Congressional Globe,* 35th Cong., 1st sess., 941, quoted in Fehrenbacher, *Dred Scott Case,* 473.

15. Quoted in Angle, *Created Equal?* 1–9.

16. "Speech at Columbus, Ohio," Collected Works, 9 vols., ed. Roy P. Basler (New Brunswick: Rutgers University Press, 1953–1955) 3:404.

17. *New York Evening Post,* August 31, 1859.

18. *Springfield Republican,* October 12, 1857.

19. Frederick Douglass, Speech to American Abolition Society, May 11, 1857, in Finkelman, *Dred Scott v. Sandford,* 169–181.

20. Ibid.

21. Ibid.

22. *Congressional Globe,* 38th Cong., 2d sess., February 23, 1865, 1012–3.

Ex parte Milligan

Brooks Simpson

Ex parte Milligan
71 U.S. 2 (4 Wall. 2) (1866)

DECIDED: April 3, 1866
VOTE

CONCURRING: 9 (Salmon P. Chase, James M. Wayne, Samuel Nelson, Robert C. Grier, Nathan
Clifford, Noah H. Swayne, Samuel F. Miller, David Davis, Stephen J. Field)
DISSENTING: 0

OPINION OF THE COURT: Davis
CONCURRING OPINION: Chase (Wayne, Swayne, Miller)

Ex parte Milligan is best known today as a shield protecting the civil liberties of civilians from military
authorities in time of war. Its attack on military commissions in areas where civil courts were in operation, phrased in the passionate rhetoric of Justice Davis, remains a celebrated statement on behalf of the
rule of law and the supremacy of civil over military authority. But the opinion sparked an uproar when it
was published in large part because many Republicans feared its impact on the federal government's ability
to use the military to protect the civil rights and liberties of black Americans, their white allies, and military personnel in the South during the early years of postwar Reconstruction. Critics charged that the
opinion was merely the first sign of the Court's willingness to overthrow Congress's Reconstruction initiatives; they worried that it presaged the forging of an alliance between the Court and President Andrew
Johnson to ensure that white supremacy and disloyalty prevailed in the occupied South, endangering the
fruits of Union victory secured after four years of bloody war. There were even calls to reform or curb the
Supreme Court. Oddly enough, neither critics nor supporters of the decision expended much time or
energy discussing the fate of Lambdin P. Milligan and his fellow Indiana Democrats; rather, it was the
effect of the decision on Reconstruction policy that stirred emotions and inspired debate.

Within weeks of the commencement of the Civil War in 1861, President Abraham Lincoln suspended
the writ of *habeas corpus* (issued to determine if a person held in custody is being unlawfully detained) in
response to secessionist activity in eastern Maryland; in September 1862 he suspended the writ in all cases
where military authorities had arrested civilians in the North and provided that they should be tried and
punished by military commissions. Although Chief Justice Roger B. Taney had challenged Lincoln's assertion that the president could suspend the writ, his protest in *Ex parte Merryman* (1861) was ignored by
Lincoln. Democrats charged that the Lincoln administration's policy of arbitrary arrests and trials
smacked of despotic tyranny; Congress in the Habeas Corpus Act of 1863 chose to delineate procedures for
detained prisoners. But the debate over what constituted legitimate dissent and the powers of the federal
government to use the military to subdue what it believed to be illegitimate dissent proved to be a controversial issue through the war and beyond.

In such circumstances, the line between legitimate partisan debate and disloyalty was sometimes hard
to define, and nowhere was this more evident than in Indiana, where the fury of partisan politics was particularly intense. When the Democrats secured control of the state legislature in the elections of 1862,
Republican governor Oliver P. Morton, a fierce partisan who had already alleged that disloyal elements had
infiltrated Democratic ranks, preferred to allow the state legislature to shut down when a boycott of sessions by Republican members made it impossible to secure a quorum. Deprived of appropriated funds to
run the state, Morton secured other sources of money and credit. A year later he stood for reelection, por-
traying the opposition Democrats as treasonous.[1]

Although Morton may have been prone to exaggeration, he was not altogether wrong. Some Indiana Democrats, the so-called Copperheads, engaged in activities that were highly questionable, and there is little doubt that in some cases their activities crossed the line. Gen. Alvin P. Hovey, who headed the Military District of Indiana, agreed. Investigators had uncovered a plot whereby disloyal Democrats, known as the Sons of Liberty, would raid several federal arsenals in the Midwest and use the weapons to free and arm Confederate prisoners of war. Hovey arrested several men associated with the plot, including Milligan, a lawyer who had unsuccessfully sought the Democratic gubernatorial nomination that year. Although those arrested could have been prosecuted through civil courts, Hovey, supported by Morton, preferred to try them by military commission. Eventually, that commission found Milligan, Stephen Horsey, and William A. Bowles guilty of conspiring against the government of the United States, offering aid and comfort to enemies of the United States, inciting insurrection, disloyal actions, and violations of the laws of war. The commission sentenced them to death.

Doubts about the men's guilt and questions about the conduct of their trial led President Johnson to commute their sentences to life imprisonment. In the meantime Milligan filed for a writ of *habeas corpus* with the U.S. Circuit Court sitting in Indianapolis. Milligan based his request upon a reading of the Habeas Corpus Act of 1863, which directed the secretaries of state and war to inform federal judges promptly of all persons held in custody. Furthermore, the law provided that should a grand jury be convened after an arrest and if it failed to indict the prisoner, the prisoner should be released from military custody. As a grand jury had indeed met and adjourned without indicting Milligan, it appeared he might be entitled to relief; moreover, because the law also provided for the release of the accused should the cabinet officers in question fail to tell the judges who had been incarcerated, the accused should be freed.[2]

Under such circumstances, Milligan might have secured his release. That result, however, would not have touched upon the legality of the military commission or the actions of military authority in the case, which was what Justice Davis, sitting in the federal circuit court at Indianapolis, wanted to test, and he wanted the Supreme Court to confront those questions. During the war the Court had passed up a chance to rule on the legality of military commissions when it declined to take up the case of Clement L. Vallandigham, an Ohio Democrat who was a virulent critic of the Lincoln administration's policies. Military authorities arrested Vallandigham in May 1863 on the grounds that he had offered aid and comfort to the enemy by delivering a particularly vehement speech. Tried by a military commission, Vallandigham sought a writ of *habeas corpus.* The Court ruled that it had no appellate jurisdiction over military commissions and would not review the decision.[3] On the face of it, Milligan's case was not much different, except for the fact that, by directing his appeal for *habeas corpus* to the federal circuit court, he had followed a path that would allow the Supreme Court to rule. Moreover, he was fortunate in that Justice Davis, who was staunchly opposed to military commissions, happened to be sitting on the circuit court in question. Negotiating an agreement with his fellow federal judge, Thomas Drummond, Davis was able to ensure that Milligan's case would come before the Supreme Court in such a way that it would be able to issue a ruling on the merits of the case.

Ex parte Milligan brought three questions before the Court. First, ought a writ of *habeas corpus* be issued in this instance? Second, ought Milligan be released from custody? Third, did the military commission in question have legal jurisdiction to try and sentence Milligan? Oral argument began March 5, 1866. Milligan was represented by three prominent lawyers: Jeremiah S. Black, who had served in President James Buchanan's cabinet as secretary of state and attorney general; David Dudley Field, Justice Field's brother; and Rep. James A. Garfield, R-Ohio. For the government, Attorney General James Speed was supported by Henry Stanbery and Benjamin F. Butler, who had been nicknamed the "Beast" for his harsh treatment of rebels in New Orleans. Oral argument lasted for seven days, ending on March 13. Three weeks later, the Court issued its finding: the writ should be issued; the prisoners should be released; and the military commission lacked jurisdiction. The Court, however, delayed publishing the full opinions until the December 1866 term.

At first glance it might appear that the mere announcement of the Court's decision would draw little comment pending the publication of opinions, but President Johnson had been waiting for word of what the Court might do. That was understandable, but what Secretary of the Navy Gideon Welles recorded in his diary about a conversation on April 2 is somewhat more revealing. The president, he reported, "said the Court was nearly tied, but that judgment would probably be rendered tomorrow, at all events within a day or two." How Johnson came to obtain this information Welles did not say. Sometime later that day, for reasons not made explicit, Johnson issued a proclamation declaring the war virtually at an end everywhere but Texas. There had been no prior consultation with the cabinet about such a proclamation; even Secretary of State William H. Seward was unaware of it until late on the afternoon of April 2. "A sudden determination seems to have influenced the President," Welles reflected.[4]

Perhaps, but it seems curious that a president privy to inside information about the deliberations of the Court would suddenly take it upon himself to issue a peace proclamation the evening before the Court announced its decision. Welles, for one, made the connection immediately. On April 4 he conferred with Johnson about the fate of one Rafael Semmes, who was to be tried by a mixed military and naval commission for alleged violations of the laws of war. Welles, who initially had shown some enthusiasm for the case, now preferred to drop the matter. "Peace having been declared in all the States and the decision of the Supreme Court in the Indiana cases . . . being adverse to military commissions," he noted, it was perhaps best to act now. Johnson agreed, and before long Semmes was released from custody.[5] On May 1, 1866, Johnson issued General Order No. 26, which directed that henceforth military authorities should employ the civil courts, not military commissions, to try civilian offenses; two months later he ordered the release of any civilians who had served at least six months of a sentence imposed by a military court or commission. Weeks later Justice Nelson further challenged the jurisdiction of military commissions when he ordered the release of a man named Egan who had been found guilty of murdering a black youngster in Lexington, South Carolina, in 1865. Nelson ruled that "the moment the rebellion was suppressed" and civil government had been reorganized, civil courts resumed jurisdiction.[6]

Not everyone took the Court's decision as eliminating the possibility of erecting military commissions in the reconstructing South, however. Thwarted in its first effort to refashion the Freedmen's Bureau by presidential veto, Congress crafted a new bill in the spring of 1866, making explicit provision for using military jurisdiction to offer equal protection under the law in cases where "the ordinary course of judicial proceedings has been interrupted by the rebellion, and until the same should be fully restored, and until such State shall have been restored in its constitutional relations to the Government, and shall be duly represented in the Congress of the United States."[7] Johnson did not agree. In his veto message he insisted that civil courts had been reestablished in the South "and are now in full practical operation." He made no reference to *Milligan*.[8] In the same month, however, general-in-chief Ulysses S. Grant issued an order authorizing military authorities to arrest alleged violators of law in cases where a civil court had failed to act and to hold them in military confinement "until such time as a proper judicial tribunal may be ready and willing to try them."[9]

On August 20, 1866, Johnson rendered the situation murkier still by proclaiming that the war was at an end. This time there was no qualifying or wavering language to leave readers uncertain as to the president's intended meaning. It placed Grant's orders in limbo; as Gen. Phil Sheridan observed, "If civil authorities are to be looked to for justice, I fear that the condition of affairs will become alarming."[10] That Sheridan's fears were justified became evident in October, when a judge ordered the release of four men convicted by a military commission in April 1866 of murdering three Union soldiers on the grounds that civil government existed in South Carolina.[11]

Concerned about the content of the Court's forthcoming opinion and the impact it might have on wartime and postwar legislation, some congressional Republicans rushed to shore up their defenses. A week before the release of the written opinion, Rep. John A. Bingham, R-Ohio, introduced a bill that would have declared valid all presidential proclamations relating to the war and its immediate aftermath issued between the day Lincoln took office and December 1, 1865. Bingham's bill would have prevented civil courts from undoing proceedings based on these proclamations and would have protected people from civil prosecution for acts done in compliance with them. Similar bills had been introduced before that offered retroactive protections.[12]

On December 17, 1866, the Court issued the majority and concurring opinions in *Ex parte Milligan*. All nine justices agreed that Milligan, Bowles, and Horsey were entitled to *habeas corpus,* that they should be released, and that the military commission in question lacked jurisdiction. Where the justices parted company was the reason the military commission lacked jurisdiction. Noting that the court had been established under executive mandate, Davis argued that the executive had no authority to establish military commissions in areas where civil courts were open and functioning: "Martial rule can never exist where the courts are open, and in the proper and unobstructed exercise of their jurisdiction. It is also confined to the locality of actual war."[13] Neither Congress nor the president could act otherwise: neither could establish military commissions. Chase's opinion was limited to arguing that Congress could indeed establish military commissions (as, for example, it had in the Freedmen's Bureau Act of July 1866).

In short, the Court was unanimous in declaring that it rejected the use of military commissions to try civilians in areas where the civil courts were in operation. Whether one could resort to such commissions in areas where the civil courts were not functioning was another question; a minority of the Court did not agree with the majority's willingness to strike at Congress as well as president as having no authority to make provision for such courts. Although the decision sparked immediate discussion, it was not until the opinions were released for publication on January 1, 1867, that the debate got underway in earnest: the Court had directed that there be no transcriptions of the decisions as read in the courtroom.[14]

Lamdin P. Milligan, a Southern sympathizer, tried to persuade men not to join the Union army and was accused of conspiring to free Confederate prisoners. He was charged with treason and tried by military authorities. In a decision that stirred debate about Reconstruction policies, the Supreme Court in *ex parte Milligan* (1866) held that constitutional protections against unlawful imprisonment do not disappear in wartime and that neither the president nor Congress may authorize military courts to conduct trials of civilians in areas where civilian courts are operating. —Indiana Historical Society

INITIAL REACTIONS IN THE PRESS

Very little of the ensuing debate was devoted to Milligan's personal fate, although Democratic papers cheered that the decision vindicated their protests about executive tyranny during the war. Some observers asserted that it rendered illegal the military commission that tried the conspirators in the Lincoln assassination, and, indeed, before long Dr. Samuel A. Mudd, convicted for his alleged involvement in the assassination because he set John Wilkes Booth's broken leg hours after Booth had shot Lincoln, made application for a writ of *habeas corpus* (which proved unsuccessful).[15] Most commentary emphasized the impact of the decision upon current congressional Republican attempts to frame new measures concerned with restoring civil governments while protecting the freedmen and their allies. In light of Davis's opinion, could Congress establish military commissions in the South under present circumstances? Did a state of complete peace obtain, despite Congress's decision not to seat the representatives of ten former Confederate states? Were the civil courts in the South truly functioning if they failed to protect the freedmen, their allies, or federal personnel? To be sure, no war was being waged; yet to assert that civil governments in the South were in full operation strained credulity in the wake of the Memphis and New Orleans riots of 1866, in which civil governments either failed to prevent violence or actively took part in violence against freedmen. Davis's opinion had spoken of civil courts as "open and functioning," but were southern civil courts truly functioning when it came to protecting the rights of the freedmen? Had the Court overreached itself in ruling on a question not before it, much as it had in *Dred Scott v. Sandford*? (See page 24.)

As one might expect, Democratic papers celebrated *Milligan*. "The whole Copperhead press exults over the decision," grumbled the *New York Times*.[16] The *New York World* demonstrated the truth of the *Times*'s claim by cheering a decision that was "both a triumphant vindication of the Democratic party and a happy augury of the future."[17] The *Brooklyn Daily Eagle* declared that the decision was "a vindication of free government."[18] Most southern newspapers were especially pleased. "If the authority of the Constitution shall be vindicated, the South is safe and the end of her troubles approaches," the *Richmond Enquirer* declared.[19] Aside from such pronouncements, however, the papers presented little analysis of the specific import of the decision for Reconstruction policy. At best, some issued vague warnings: the pro-Johnson Washington, D.C., *National Intelligencer* said it believed that in time the Court "will extend its broad aegis over the violated commonwealths of the South."[20]

Most Republican journals attacked the decision. *Harper's Weekly* held that the decision "is not a judicial opinion—it is a political act"; it added that "the Indiana decision operates to deprive the freedmen in the late rebel States, whose laws grievously outrage them, of the protection of the Freedmen [Bureau] courts." The issue was clear: "The question in regard to the Supreme Court need not be misunderstood. It is not whether in a time of peace in loyal states the civil courts should be supreme, which nobody questions. It is whether loyal men or rebels shall reorganize the Union." No wonder it headlined its editorial "The New Dred Scott."[21] If the *Milligan* decision applied to the South," the *New York Times* observed, "martial law could no longer be enforced there."[22] The *Chicago Tribune* deftly handled this question. Asserting that Davis's opinion discussed matters not before the Court, it suggested that one could ignore its possible broader application and insist that it failed to touch the military commissions established under the Freedmen's Bureau Act of 1866: "It unsettles nothing."[23] Other critics were not so confident. The *Washington* (D.C.) *Chronicle* argued, "Time and reflection have only served to strengthen the conviction of the partisan character of the decision and the apprehension that it is the precursor of other decisions in the interest of unrepentant treason in the support of an apostate President."[24]

In many instances criticism of the Court's decision became criticism of the Court itself. "The court is made the object of the most violent abuse," noted *The Nation*, "and the agreement of the judges on a point of law of unusual clearness is denounced unsparingly as a 'judicial conspiracy,' and movements are even talked of for putting the judges on . . . trial for it."[25] Several comments were particularly pointed. "The Supreme Court, we regret to find, throws the great weight of its influence into the scale of those who assailed the Union, and step after step impugned the constitutionality of nearly every thing that was done to uphold it," declared the *New York Times*.[26] The *New York Herald* found Davis's opinion "utterly preposterous" and "constitutional twaddle." The Court was "a relic of the past, nine old superior pettifoggers, old marplots, a formidable barrier to the consummation of the great revolution."[27]

Other papers joined in the attack. The *Washington Chronicle* announced, "The hearts of traitors will be glad that treason, vanquished upon the battlefield and hunted from every other retreat, has at last found a secure shelter in the bosom of the Supreme Court"; the *Independent* growled that Davis's opinion was "a sorry attempt of five not very distinguished persons to exhibit themselves as profound jurists."[28] In several instances the attacks went to extremes: as James Garfield noted, "the papers are insanely calling for the abolition of the court." [29] *The Nation* deplored the "very wild and absurd talk" that accompanied some of the criticism.[30]

Davis's willingness to go beyond the case at hand to hold forth on larger principles in ways that threatened black rights reminded many observers of Taney's opinion nine years earlier in *Dred Scott*. It was this form of judicial activism that brought forth the most severe commentary. Even calmer heads wondered why the Court would engage in such risky behavior. "The chief duty of the court, as we conceive, in dealing with the tremendous questions which will be brought before it, is to confine itself strictly to the matter at hand, to decide the precise points before it, and to abstain rigidly from the slightest discussion of political questions not necessarily involved," *The Nation* wrote. Agreeing, the *American Law Review* observed that had the Court restricted itself to the case at hand, and offered its unanimous opinion "simply and directly, it would have established for ever a solid principle of law, on which, in all troublous times, the country would have relied." But, as in *Dred Scott,* some members of the Court went further in ruling on matters not before the Court, embroiling the nation in yet another debate about the proper place and role of the Supreme Court. "They have seemed to forget how all-important it is for the preservation of their influence that they should confine themselves to their duties as judges between the parties in a particular case," the *Review* said; this was especially true in cases where the "political aspect" of a case was apparent.[31]

OFFICIALS' REACTIONS TO *MILLIGAN*

It did not take long for Andrew Johnson to invoke the *Milligan* ruling. In Rockbridge County, Virginia, James L. Watson, a white physician, learned that a black man, William Medley, had driven a carriage that collided with another carriage in which Watson's wife and daughter were passengers. Watson sought out Medley and shot and killed him. Admitting his act, Watson willingly turned himself over to local authorities in Lexington, only to be released when the examining board, by a vote of 3 to 2, refused to indict him. This incident appeared to offer a prime example of the failure of southern civil legal institutions to protect the rights of blacks: both the Civil Rights Act of 1866 and Grant's General Order No. 44 appeared to authorize federal intervention in the matter. So believed Gen. John M. Schofield, who decided to arrest Watson and try him in front of a military commission—a decision made in part to test the authority of military commissions in such matters. Arrested on December 4, 1867, nearly two weeks before the Court issued its opinions in *Milligan,* Watson was set to be tried in Richmond several weeks later when word came from Washington that President Johnson wanted the commission dissolved and Watson released. Attorney General Stanbery had advised the president that the newly available *Milligan* opinion applied: as Virginia was at peace and civil courts were open, military commissions were unconstitutional. Several southern newspapers celebrated Johnson's application of the *Milligan* case. Northern observers shook their heads. "Courts such as now exist in the South are no more protection to the freedmen than if they did not exist," concluded *The Nation,* "and we cannot and ought not to suffer so large a proportion of our population to remain without the protection of law of some kind." [32]

Johnson's decision in Watson's case confirmed Republican fears of how the president would use *Milligan.* As one Michigan newspaper noted, "It is certain that no punishment will be administered by the civil courts. Mr. Johnson has taken care that none shall be administered in any other way." [33] Another newspaper reported Johnson's conversation with a member of the South Carolina state legislature, in which he reportedly said that he had good reason to believe that the Supreme Court would not sustain the Fourteenth Amendment.[34] That the Court appeared to be hostile to congressional Reconstruction initiatives became even more evident when it released its opinions in several other cases involving test oaths, setting aside a favorite Republican device to limit the participation of former Confederates in the reconstructed political order. Newspapers reported that Secretary of War Edwin M. Stanton argued that *Milligan* might strip the military and the Freedmen's Bureau of their ability to protect the freedmen.[35]

Rep. Thaddeus Stevens, R-Pa., a leader of his party's radical wing, which sought to protect the rights of freedmen by exercising stern congressional oversight over the reestablishment of southern state governments, recognized the threat *Milligan* posed. On January 3, 1867, Stevens shared his concerns with his fellow representatives. "That decision, although in terms perhaps not as infamous as the Dred Scott decision, is yet far more dangerous in its operation upon the lives and liberties of the loyal men of this country," he declared. "That decision has taken away every protection in every one of these rebel States from every loyal man, black or white, who resides there." *Milligan* "has rendered immediate action by Congress upon the question of the establishment of governments in the rebel States absolutely indispensable." One needed to look only at the results of the Watson case for the possible impact of "this most injurious and iniquitous decision."[36]

Rep. James F. Wilson, R-Iowa, joined the attack on *Milligan;* in advocating Representative Bingham's December 1866 proposal to his colleagues, he characterized Davis's opinion as "a piece of judicial impertinence" that overreached in addressing Congress's powers, an issue not before the Court in the case at hand.[37] Other Republicans simply denied *Milligan*'s relevance to Reconstruction. As the 39th Congress drew to a close, Sen. Lyman Trumbull, R-Ill., proclaimed: "There has been no decision that you cannot try a person by military commission. The decision was that a particular military commission in a certain State, under the peculiar circumstances of that case, was not authorized to try the party, but military commissions in the disloyal States have never been pronounced to be illegal."[38]

The justices may have been aware of the importance of their decision, but not all of them were content with how it was being applied to the issue of Reconstruction. A newspaper correspondent reported that one justice, "a personal friend of Mr. Lincoln," was particularly unhappy with the ensuing controversy. "He shudders as he sees the cruelties that are to be perpetuated all over the South under his decision but it is too late. If a case could properly come before the Court, it would be found that a majority do not hold that military tribunals are unconstitutional in the rebellious States, for Congress holds that they are still in a belligerent condition."[39] Another newspaper reported that at least one justice was "nervous over the use the President is making of it at the South."[40]

Justice Davis was justifiably proud of his opinion, but he was also puzzled at how Republicans interpreted it as a threat to Reconstruction. In private correspondence he pointed out that the opinion did not mention Reconstruction and that the power to erect military commissions "is conceded in insurrectionary states." He resented Republican comparisons of the decision to *Dred Scott v. Sandford* and freely assailed his critics; yet because the wording of the opinion left it open to such debate suggests that, in going beyond the facts before the Court (a decision he defended as necessary given the nature of his argument), Davis may not have gone far enough to make explicit in the opinion what he declared in private.[41]

Republicans in Congress remained determined to use the military to oversee the implementation of its policy for reconstructing southern state governments in a process in which the freedmen would play an active role. In late February Congress passed the first of what became known as the Reconstruction Acts. The initial legislation divided the ten former Confederate states not represented in Congress into five military districts, each managed by a general, who would oversee the registration of voters and maintain law and order; in so doing the generals were authorized to organize military commissions if in their judgment the existing civil courts were operating in an unsatisfactory manner.[42] In vetoing that legislation on March 2, 1867, Johnson made specific reference to *Milligan.* Arguing that peace had been restored and that the civil courts were in full operation, Johnson quoted from the majority and concurring opinions to assert that the preconditions for the establishment of military courts and martial law did not exist in the South. Congress overrode Johnson's veto: once more it would be left to the courts to determine whether military commissions could operate in the reconstructing South—and indeed whether the Reconstruction Acts could survive a legal challenge.[43]

Within a short time of the legislation's passage, it faced its first court tests. In *Mississippi v. Johnson* (1867), the Supreme Court rejected an effort to enjoin the president from executing the Reconstruction

Acts on the grounds the acts were unconstitutional. A second case was immediately filed against Stanton, Grant, and military authorities; the suit sought injunctions preventing them from administering the Reconstruction Acts, specifically citing *Milligan,* but the Court dismissed the suit by saying it lacked jurisdiction. When a divided Court refused to hear a variant on the second case, it appeared that perhaps the crisis had subsided. But that was not to be.[44]

It did not take long for the issues in dispute to reach the Supreme Court once more. Acting under the authority vested in him by the Reconstruction Act of March 2, 1867, Maj. Gen. Edward O. C. Ord, in charge of the Fourth Military District (Mississippi and Arkansas), ordered the arrest on November 8, 1867, of William McCardle, editor of the *Vicksburg Times,* on the grounds that a series of his editorials against the Reconstruction Acts were incendiary and encouraged violence, and others advocated obstructing implementation of the acts. McCardle's attorney immediately sought a writ of *habeas corpus;* when that was denied, he filed an appeal under a federal act of February 5, 1867, which authorized an appeal to the Supreme Court in cases where judges had ruled on cases of *habeas corpus.* McCardle's brief made it clear that he would assail the use of military commissions as set forth in the Reconstruction Act. Two of McCardle's attorneys, Jeremiah Black and William L. Sharkey, cited *Milligan* as reason to strike down the use of military commissions under the Reconstruction Act, as did their fellow counsel David Field, who characterized *Milligan* as "a judgment which had given the Court a new title to the respect of the world, and which will stand forever as one of the bulwarks of constitutional freedom." For the government, Matthew A. Carpenter sought to set *Milligan* aside as having "no bearing whatever on this discussion."[45]

Black and Field offered the appealingly simple logic that if the Court upheld *Milligan,* it must strike down the Reconstruction Acts; and Carpenter attempted to decouple the two cases. The Court might have applied *Milligan* to the use of military commissions in the First Reconstruction Act, only to limit its ruling to that aspect of the legislation while leaving the larger edifice intact. But the Court never ruled on the issue, because congressional Republicans moved quickly to repeal the portion of the February 1867 statute upon which McCardle based his appeal, overcoming a presidential veto. What might have been an excellent court test of congressional Reconstruction devolved into a test of Congress's ability to shape the Court's appellate jurisdiction: the Court ruled that it no longer possessed such jurisdiction in this particular case. In 1869, however, Chase privately expressed the opinion that "had the merits of the McCardle case been decided the court would doubtless have held that his imprisonment for trial before a military commission was illegal."[46]

Chase's Court would have yet another chance to rule upon the use of military commissions as part of Reconstruction. In June 1869 Edward M. Yerger of Mississippi killed the army officer serving as mayor of Jackson, Mississippi. When a military commission took charge of the case, Yerger's attorneys challenged the commission's jurisdiction. As anticipated, an application for a writ of *habeas corpus* was made to the Supreme Court, first to Justice Swayne, who turned it down, and then to Chief Justice Chase, who advised that Yerger file his appeal with the federal circuit court first. If the circuit court failed to grant relief, Yerger could apply to the Supreme Court for a writ of certiorari. A similar case from Texas also made its way to the Court's docket. The Court claimed it indeed had jurisdiction in this case (a claim that appeared to run counter to *McCardle*); however, with the restoration of civil government in Mississippi expected shortly, Attorney General Ebenezer R. Hoar cut a deal with Yerger's counsel: Yerger's lawyer would not press for a hearing, and the attorney general would turn Yerger over to the civil courts once Mississippi was readmitted to the Union. That deal removed yet another opportunity for the Court to rule on the constitutionality of the Reconstruction Acts; it also cut short yet another flurry of proposals to curtail the Court's powers with regard to acts of Congress. Whether the Court would have ruled adversely remains a matter of scholarly controversy. Surprisingly, Justice Field, long believed to be sympathetic to criticisms of Reconstruction, reflected in his autobiography, "It came to be generally believed that it was the purpose of the Court, if an opportunity offered, to declare invalid most of the legislation relating to the Southern States which had been enacted during the war and immediately afterwards. Nothing could have been more unjust and unfounded."[47]

In the twentieth century most scholars, judges, and others celebrated *Ex parte Milligan* as a bulwark of the defense of American civil liberties during wartime. Scholars of a contrarian disposition, notably Mark E. Neely Jr., claim that the decision's fame was primarily the production of constitutional textbooks. In Neely's words, "The decision itself had little effect on history."[48] If one believes Field and Neely as well as Davis's comments that *Milligan* did not concern Reconstruction, one might conclude that indeed there was much ado about very little. But that was not how it appeared to President Johnson, Secretary of War Stanton, General Grant, Republicans and Democrats in Congress, and the partisan press at large. The broad and sweeping language of Davis's opinion may today sound like a ringing defense of civil liberties, but at the time it also appeared to many readers to sound a death knell for protecting the rights of the freedmen and their allies against the pernicious neglect of southern civil courts controlled by white supremacists determined to thwart the promise of emancipation.

NOTES

1. Alan T. Nolan, "Ex Parte Milligan: A Curb of Executive and Military Power," in Patrick J. Furlong et al., *We the People: Indiana and the United States Constitution* (Indianapolis: Indiana Historical Society, 1987), 34–39, offers a succinct summary of these events.
2. Ibid., 37–42.
3. Ibid., 31–33.
4. Howard K. Beale, ed., *The Diary of Gideon Welles,* 3 vols. (New York: W. W. Norton, 1960), 2:471–474.
5. Ibid., 2:474–477.
6. Edward McPherson, *The Political History of the United States of America During the Period of Reconstruction* (New York: Negro Universities Press, 1969 [1875]), 17; Brooks D. Simpson, *Let Us Have Peace: Ulysses S. Grant and the Politics of War and Reconstruction, 1861–1868* (Chapel Hill: University of North Carolina Press, 1991), 138–139; Charles Fairman, *Reconstruction and Reunion, 1864–88,* 2 vols. (New York: Macmillan, 1971), 1:148–149. One may rightly ask in the case of Egan whether civil government had been restored in South Carolina as of September 1865.
7. McPherson, *Political History,* 151.
8. Andrew Johnson, Veto Message of July 16, 1866, in ibid., 147–149.
9. General Orders No. 44, July 6, 1866, in ibid., 124
10. Simpson, *Let Us Have Peace,* 145–146.
11. *Harper's Weekly,* January 19, 1867; Fairman, *Reconstruction and Reunion,* 1:148–149.
12. *Congressional Globe,* 39th Cong., 2d sess. (December 10, 1866), 47.
13. Fairman, *Reconstruction and Reunion,* 1:208.
14. Ibid., 1:214.
15. Ibid., 1:238–239.
16. *New York Times,* January 3, 1867.
17. Charles Warren, *The Supreme Court in United States History,* 2 vols. (Boston: Little, Brown, 1937), 2:437.
18. *Brooklyn Daily Eagle,* January 2, 1867.
19. Warren, *Supreme Court,* 2:439.
20. Ibid., 2:435.
21. *Harper's Weekly,* January 19, 1867.
22. *New York Times,* January 3, 1867.
23. *Chicago Tribune,* January 4, 1867. The *Springfield Republican* agreed. See Warren, *Supreme Court,* 2:437.
24. Warren, *Supreme Court,* 2:434.
25. *The Nation,* January 17, 1867.
26. *New York Times,* January 3, 1867.
27. Quoted in Samuel Klaus, ed., *The Milligan Case* (New York: DaCapo Press, 1970 [1921]), 48.

28. Quoted in Willard L. King, *Lincoln's Manager, David Davis* (Chicago: University of Chicago Press, 1976 [1960]), 256.

29. James A. Garfield to Burke A. Hinsdale, January 1, 1867, in *Garfield-Hinsdale Letters: Correspondence between James Abram Garfield and Burke Aaron Hinsdale,* ed. Mary L. Hinsdale (Ann Arbor: University of Michigan Press, 1949), 88.

30. *The Nation,* January 17, 1867.

31. Ibid., January 10, 1867; *American Law Review* 1 (April 1867): 572, quoted in Warren, *Supreme Court,* 2:441–442.

32. See Robert J. Kaczorowski, *The Politics of Judicial Interpretation: The Federal Courts, Department of Justice and Civil Rights, 1866–1876* (New York: Oceana Publications, 1985), 42–43; Fairman, *Reconstruction and Reunion,* 1:215; *The Nation,* December 12, 1866.

33. *Jackson* (Michigan) *Citizen,* January 1, 1867, quoted in Fairman, *Reconstruction and Reunion,* 1:215.

34. *New York Times,* December 27, 1866; *Harper's Weekly,* January 19, 1867.

35. Warren, *Supreme Court,* 2:443n2, 445.

36. *Congressional Globe,* 39th Cong., 2d sess., January 3, 1867, 251.

37. Ibid., February 22, 1867, 1484.

38. Ibid., March 2, 1867,1962.

39. *Cleveland Herald,* quoting the *Detroit Tribune,* January 2, 1867, in Warren, *Supreme Court,* 2:444–445.

40. *Springfield Republican,* December 29, 1866, quoted in *ibid,* 2:445 n1.

41. David Davis to Julius Rockwell, February 24, 1867, David Davis Papers, Illinois State Historical Society.

42. McPherson, *Political History,* 191–192.

43. Andrew Johnson to the House of Representatives, March 2, 1867, *Journal of the House of Representatives,* 39th Cong., 64:564, 567–568.

44. Warren, *Supreme Court,* 2:455–464; Philip B. Kurland and Gerhard Casper, eds., *Landmark Briefs and Arguments of the Supreme Court of the United States* (Washington, D.C.: University Publications of America, 1975–), 5:59, 148.

45. Fairman, *Reconstruction and Reunion,* 1:452–455; Kurland and Casper, *Landmark Briefs,* 5:160, 162–163, 239, 285.

46. Salmon P. Chase to Robert A. Hill, May 1, 1869, in *The Salmon P. Chase Papers,* 5 vols., ed. John Niven (Kent, Ohio: Kent State University Press, 1998), 5:302.

47. Fairman, *Reconstruction and Reunion,* 1:564–585; Field quoted in Stanley I. Kutler, *Judicial Power and Reconstruction Politics* (Chicago: University of Chicago Press, 1968), 113.

48. Mark E. Neely Jr., *The Fate of Liberty: Abraham Lincoln and Civil Liberties* (New York: Oxford University Press, 1991), 184.

Bradwell v. Illinois

Christine Yantis Hargrove

Bradwell v. Illinois
83 U.S. 130 (16 Wall. 130) (1873)

> DECIDED: April 15, 1873
> VOTE
>> CONCURRING: 8 (Nathan Clifford, Noah H. Swayne, Samuel F. Miller, David Davis, Stephen J. Field, William Strong, Joseph P. Bradley, Ward Hunt)
>> DISSENTING: 1 (Salmon P. Chase)
> OPINION OF THE COURT: Miller
> CONCURRING OPINION: Bradley (Swayne, Field)
> DISSENTING WITHOUT OPINION: Chase

Myra Colby Bradwell, after reading in law, applied to practice in the state of Illinois. As a lawyer, she would be bound by the express and/or implied contracts the law created between a client and an attorney. As a married woman, however, she would be unable to hold herself wholly accountable to these contracts. At the time, a married woman could not enter into contractual agreements alone. She existed as a *feme covert,* a woman whose legal identity was wholly defined as her husband's, making her a dependent legal nonentity, a poor status for a lawyer. Common law defined a married woman as subject to her husband, and normally she could not conduct business on her own.

Bradwell had earlier encountered these limitations as the founder, chief editor, and head of the *Chicago Legal News,* a well known Midwest legal publication. So important was this publication to lawyers and judges, and so esteemed was its editor, that the state of Illinois had previously granted her a special charter to conduct the legal aspects of her own business. But when she applied for admission to the Illinois bar in 1869, the state denied her application on the grounds that no married woman could lawfully enter into a contract in her own name.

Bradwell decided to take the case to court, where she argued that married women had a right to enter into contracts in Illinois because of their newfound rights to own property through passage of the Illinois Married Woman's Property Act in 1861 and the Earnings Act of 1869, legislation she had helped to write. Moreover, another married woman, Arabella Mansfield, had been admitted to the Iowa bar earlier that year. Although the judges of the Illinois Supreme Court seemed sympathetic, they claimed that the legislation surrounding admittance to the bar had not been written with the possibility of women's applications.

The court had no personal objection to her; in fact, the judges knew her quite well and respected her mind and her character. But state law prohibited all women, married or single, from practicing law. Charles B. Lawrence, chief justice of the Illinois Supreme Court, made it clear that the court had "no doubt" as to her qualifications, but it was "the sex of the applicant . . . [that was] a sufficient reason for not granting the license." The Illinois legislature, Lawrence claimed, in establishing the criteria and procedures for licensing lawyers had never contemplated allowing women to become part of the profession. It was an "axiomatic truth" to the court that "God designed the sexes to occupy different spheres of action, and that it belonged to men to make, apply and execute laws." By basing its decision on her sex rather than her marital status, the court avoided addressing the question Bradwell had raised in her argument, namely, whether married women could make binding contracts in their own name.

Bradwell then acquired the legal services of Sen. Matthew Hale Carpenter, R-Wis., and appealed her case to the U.S. Supreme Court, providing the Court with its first opportunity to interpret the privileges and immunities section of the newly ratified Fourteenth Amendment. Bradwell knew that female suffrage, or "the woman question," was highly contested and that as a married woman she had little state or federal legal precedent to enter into independent contracts. Because of the Married Woman's Property Act and the Earnings Act, however, married women had gained control over their personal earnings and property in much the same way that single women controlled their own money. Her financial rights at this point were nearly identical to any male citizen's in Illinois, an important victory for a businesswoman. But the state was unwilling to draft additional privileges into law and grant them to all citizens because of "inherent differences" between the sexes, differences that supposedly disqualified married women from business activity apart from their husbands. Many people believed that women were "naturally" relegated to the private sphere and that men "naturally" were able to mingle in both the public and private spheres. To have a woman work so prominently in the public sphere was an assertion that she *could* exist independently of her husband and a challenge to the very definition of woman as subsumed by her husband.

THE SUPREME COURT'S DECISION

Knowing the vehemence of these traditional arguments and the angry sentiment behind them, Bradwell and Carpenter chose, instead, to argue on behalf of federalization and federal citizens' rights in an attempt to curtail the Illinois decision. During the oral argument, Carpenter asked, "Can this court say that when the Fourteenth Amendment declared 'the privileges of no citizen shall be abridged,' it meant that the privileges of no male citizen or unmarried female citizen shall be abridged?"

He went on to link the fate of married women to that of African American men:

> If this provision does not open to all the professions, all the avocations, all the methods . . . to the colored as well as the white man, then the Legislatures of the State may exclude colored as well as the white man, then the Legislatures of the State may exclude colored men from all the honorable pursuits of life, and compel them to support their existence in a condition of servitude.[1]

The Supreme Court agreed that specific immunities and privileges belonging to U.S. citizens could not be abridged by states. It did not, however, consider the right of admission to practice law in state courts to be one of these specific privileges and immunities, which made irrelevant Bradwell's claim of her rights as a U.S. citizen. The granting of licenses to practice law in state courts was a matter to be determined by the states themselves. At least for the present, Myra Colby Bradwell would be unable to practice law in Illinois.

Within the Court, the question of gender was not entirely overlooked. Even though the majority opinion did not address Bradwell's "womanhood," the concurring opinion by Justice Bradley denied that women enjoyed the same rights as men to pursue an occupation.

> The civil law, as well as nature herself, has always recognized a wide difference in the respective spheres and destinies of man and woman. Man is, or should be, woman's protector and defender. The natural and proper timidity and delicacy which belongs to the female sex evidently unfits it for many of the occupations of civil life. The constitution of the family organization, which is founded in the divine ordinance, as well as in the nature of things, indicates the domestic sphere as that which properly belongs to the domain and functions of womanhood. The harmony, not to say identity, of interests and views which belong, or should belong, to the family institution is repugnant to the idea of a woman adopting a distinct and independent career from that of her husband. So firmly fixed was this sentiment in the founders of the common law that it became a maxim of that system of jurisprudence that a woman had no legal existence separate

45

from her husband, who was regarded as her head and representative in the social state. . . .

It is true that many women are unmarried and not affected by any of the duties, complications, and incapacities arising out of the married state, but these are exceptions to the general rule. The paramount destiny and mission of woman are to fulfill the noble and benign offices of wife and mother. This is the law of the Creator. And the rules of civil society must be adapted to the general constitution of things, and cannot be based upon exceptional cases.[2]

Bradley's statement was widely publicized and still serves as the banner argument of this case. It succinctly encapsulated the depth of sexism against which Bradwell was fighting as well as the privilege enjoyed by the male judges to allow their personal imaginations concerning women's place to overtake legal discussion and logical reasoning. Only Chief Justice Chase dissented and sided with Bradwell, but no evidence of a written dissent has been found.

RESPONSES TO THE OPINION

Bradwell's case against the state of Illinois was situated within many layers of controversy over women's rights, female suffrage, and federalism versus states rights. In some ways she and her case functioned as a blank slate onto which opinions and commentary could be placed; she represented what journalists either desired for society or feared. Newspapers from all over the country picked up the story. As Jane Friedman noted in her biography of Bradwell:

The *New York World,* in listing the "follies" that were currently seeking protection under the Fourteenth Amendment, included the "preposterous" claim of a Chicago "she-attorney" that the amendment granted her the right to practice law. Likewise, the *Nation* called Myra's constitutional claim "ridiculous" and "interesting as showing the effect produced by legal study on the female mind." It concluded by surmising that Myra "must have known the Court would decide against her, unless she either supposed that they were likely to be influenced by personal solicitation and clamor, or else that they were all gone crazy."

Among the news media, the *Rockford Register* and the *St. Louis Republic* seem to have stood virtually alone in condemning the state of Illinois and the United States Supreme Court for their combined rejection of Myra's application.[3]

The *Rockford Register* went so far as to accuse the Court of resisting rational equality and liberal progress. Bradwell's case, in the eyes of the news media, had become a partisan issue much in the way that abolition had been a partisan issue years before. When it was addressed, it was an opportunity for each side to sling mud at the other side without debating the social and professional implications of married women's opportunity to practice law or engage in other forms of contractual business independent of their husbands. Opponents of women's rights tended to treat Myra Bradwell as an amusing, albeit successful, woman who misunderstood her place as a married woman in society. Her influence through the *Chicago Legal News,* which had become the most prominent law weekly in Illinois as well as nationally known, was conveniently ignored. Bradwell's status as a woman superseded her status as a businessperson in the public eye even as she maintained her status within the legal community as a powerhouse. Her status as a *married* woman increased her honorability or character in the public eye, but this was confounded by the fact that she aimed to practice business independently of her husband, thereby specifically *not* behaving in a feminine, domestic, fitting way for a wife. Her power in the city of Chicago and beyond set her above other members of society, the very same people who limited her professional mobility.

It was impossible for journalists to pin Bradwell down, to paint her onto the page in a sensible way. She continually and forcefully defied convention even as she vocally upheld societal ideals. She could not be caricatured; therefore she became important simply for what she represented to the national media rather than who she was as a person and suffragist.

Bradwell had been involved with organizing for women's suffrage, but she divided her efforts between the vote for women and women's rights. She worked hard for suffrage, but she favored rights. She knew the suffragists, particularly Susan B. Anthony and Elizabeth Cady Stanton, fairly well and considered herself allied with them even though she approached the "woman" problem—the lack of voting and other rights— from a different angle. Many of the suffragists pushed specifically for women's right to vote as they took on the male-dominated system of government. They cheered for her in her efforts to become a lawyer as well as her success as a businesswoman and editor, but they did not enjoy a sense of camaraderie with her or her tactics. They hoped to use Bradwell's defeat, shocking because of her honorable reputation and sway in Chicago and Illinois law circles, as evidence of blatant discrimination. Few judges could deem Bradwell unworthy as a legal mind or object to her character. The fact that her rejection rested solely on her sex and nothing else called into question many other forms of discrimination that had been blamed on some "deficiency" of the women who challenged them. Bradwell proved that simply being overqualified was not enough to overcome sexism.

The *Woman's Journal*, a prominent newsletter for suffragists and other progressive women,

Myra Bradwell, a women's rights activist and a legal-professional insider, was denied the right to practice law because she was a married woman. In *Bradwell v. Illinois* (1873), the Court upheld a state's refusal to allow a woman to practice law, ruling that the Fourteenth Amendment did not affect a state's authority to regulate admission to the Bar. —Library of Congress

frequently addressed the question of single women's right to practice law, but only one issue addressed Bradwell's fight:

> If Mrs. Myra Bradwell, of Chicago, persists in her resolution to practice law—as, being a woman and opposed, it is pretty safe to assume she will—the Chicago *Post* doubts whether it is in the boots of any old fogies, on the bench or elsewhere to prevent her. It seems that, after the State Supreme Court so ungallantly denied Mrs. B's application for a license, the Legislature of the State took it in hand by passing a little act, the first section of which runs as follows: "Be it enacted by the people of the State of Illinois, represented in the General Assembly, that no person shall be precluded or debarred from any occupation, profession or employment (except military) on account of sex; provided that this act shall not be construed to affect the eligibility of any person to an elective office." That seems to be very much to the point; and, whenever Mrs. Bradwell

returns to the charge, we shall look to see the Illinois Supreme Court come down from
its lofty perch of masculine dignity a good deal more nimbly than it climbed up.[4]

Although Bradwell was a fellow journalist, this contributor chose to dwell on the *Chicago Post*'s opinion
of her rather than state the *Woman's Journal*'s point of view. The piece also displayed a shallow view of
Bradwell as a worker for women's rights by assuming that Bradwell would limit herself to practicing law
or agitating for women's inclusion in the legal profession.

BRADWELL'S RESPONSE TO HER LOSS

Bradwell continued her work at the *Chicago Legal News* and made it essential to everyone in the legal
profession. The 2002 *Enterprising Women* exhibit, a traveling exhibit highlighting important entrepreneur-
ial women in American History, goes so far as to state that the *Chicago Legal News* became the " 'Bible' for
lawyers."[5] Bradwell agitated and created change by her scathing weekly editorials even as she specifically
flattered the judges who had been the most discriminatory against her. She appealed to their consciences
while ridiculing the decision they *must* have made in error or through misunderstanding woman's true
abilities. The *Chicago Legal News* also provided editorial support to women around the country seeking to
obtain law licenses in their own states, and she used her financial prowess to build the *News* from a small
weekly into an essential publication.

Bradwell argued for her causes using social morality and character references rather than religion. Her
method was notable because the judges' decisions against her had been based on ideas they identified as
"natural" or "biblical." Choosing not to engage in Scriptural banter, she confined her argument to the
social and moral accountability of all those involved in the legal profession, proving herself to be an exceptional legal and practical mind even as she was excluded from outright participation in the profession. In
her weekly column, "Law Relating to Women," she addressed issues of equality, property rights, law school
admissions for women, and women's service on juries. "Insisting that equality for women was not a partisan issue, she exhorted state officials of both parties to end discrimination against women in employment
and allow women greater control over their property. The *Chicago Legal News* also provided editorial support to women around the country seeking to obtain law licenses in their own states."[6]

Bradwell also wrote about her defeat in the courts. Ever positive, she continued to champion women's
rights and emphasized other important changes for women's rights that had occurred since her initial
attempts at bar admittance:

> Although we have not succeeded in obtaining an opinion as we hoped, which should
> affect the rights of women throughout the nation, we are more than compensated for all
> our trouble in seeing, as the result of the agitation, statutes passed in several of the
> States, including our own, admitting women upon the same terms as men. Women have
> since been admitted in Wyoming, Utah, the District of Columbia, Iowa, Missouri, Ohio
> and other States. [7]

She noticeably did not address whether these women were married; in fact, "woman lawyers" had been a
constant topic of editorials and news bits in suffrage papers as well as more common newspapers.

The division for Bradwell between married women and unmarried women became a moot point.
Even while the Supreme Court was deciding her case, the Illinois legislature had passed an act giving all
persons, regardless of sex, freedom in selecting an occupation. Although she did not receive her law license
until 1890, she had succeeded in agitating the "woman question" to the point that the legislature had been
forced to take action on it. She had proven to all that she was a capable and important member of the business world, and her case for admittance to the bar association of Illinois brought into stark contrast the
possibility of women's participation with the blatant discrimination in practice.

BRADWELL'S PLACE AMONG SUFFRAGISTS

In 1893, three leading suffrage and women's rights leaders put together a compendium of portraits of "Leading American Women." Of Myra Bradwell they wrote:

> She was the first woman in the America to ask for admission to the bar, and it was refused because she was a married woman. She immediately set to work, with the aid of her husband, to have this legal disability removed, and the success of their undertaking is a matter of congratulation for all women. Mrs. Bradwell declared that she should never again apply for admission to the bar, but, to her surprise, she one day received a certificate upon the original application from the court that had refused her years before.[8]

Following the Court decision, Myra Bradwell virtually disappeared from journalists' eyes until her death in 1894. After a battle with cancer, she was remembered fondly in print media. In an ironic twist, the *American Law Review* in a long obituary tribute called her "one of the most remarkable women of her generation," and the Illinois State Bar Association declared, "No more powerful and convincing argument in favor of the admission of women to a participation in the administration of government was ever made, than can be found in her character, conduct, and achievements."[9] The *Woman's Journal* devoted nearly an entire page to an obituary remembering their friend Myra, who had grown in importance as she continued in age and in the women's rights movement. The most moving passage recalled her enterprising and ingenious spirit:

> In the early days of the women's rights movement when the shafts of ridicule were hurled at all who were working for the emancipation of women Mrs. Bradwell was roundly abused for daring to believe it appropriate for a married woman to practice law. But no one who ever knew Mrs. Bradwell ridiculed her. So sweet, so gentle a soul, with such a charming personality, such a quiet, unobtrusive, courteous manner, such exquisite tact, could not fail to win and turn a detractor into an admirer. Like the lamented Lucy Stone, mild but firm, Myra Bradwell was a rare combination of sweetness and strength. Of a daring, progressive nature, which scorned to be hampered by the prevalent narrow notion of woman's sphere, firm in her convictions, and tenacious of purpose, she never lost an opportunity to work for the cause which was so dear to her heart. Never antagonistic or aggressive, many were the converts she made by her gentleness and grace. Earnest, tender and womanly, full of that poetic inspiration which is so commonly, but mistakenly considered the exclusive prerogative of youth, she lived a beautiful life and never grew old. Death came to her just when she was beginning to see the fruition of her life work the dawn of a better day for women—for humanity.[10]

To be compared to Lucy Stone in a favorable manner was honor indeed, but this passage depicts her as an approachable, lovable person even as she enjoyed the power and prestige she had earned. Bradwell had become more than another court case or businesswoman; she was essential to the women's rights movement for everything she overcame and who she was.

Within the last century, however, Bradwell has been looked upon as the "first woman lawyer" who conveniently was deemed unable to practice law by the U.S. Supreme Court. She has been painted as a pioneer woman in the legal field. This portrayal is correct but does not address her life accurately or deeply enough. She was a pioneer in the legal field not because she took her case to the Supreme Court, lost, and then continued to practice law. She was a pioneer in law through her artful demonstration of practical knowledge in the *Chicago Legal News*. As women's rights became *en vogue* in the 1960s and 1970s, Myra Bradwell became a common name in legal history. She is frequently mentioned as part of the civil rights movement of the nineteenth century, or what is commonly called the "first wave" of feminism. In Chicago, there is a Myra Bradwell Communication Arts and Science Academy, named in 1895. The Minnesota Women Lawyers association presents an award in her name each year. The Chicago Tribute, an organization that commemorates notable Chicagoans by marking the places they lived or worked, has included the Bradwell home on Michigan Avenue for this honor.[11] The Women Lawyers Association of Los Angeles also bestows a Myra Bradwell award. She was inducted into the National Women's Hall of Fame in 1994. She was featured in the *Enterprising Women* traveling exhibit, which is organized by the Schlesinger Library of the Radcliffe Institute for Advanced Study at Harvard University and travels all over the United States in an effort to educate people on women's contributions to American history and economic life.

Many feminist Web sites note her as a true, early feminist, one who did not expect women to go into "womanly" careers and who pushed for a more complete set of career options. These Web sites, similar to the earliest accounts of *Bradwell v. Illinois,* address Myra Bradwell as someone who represents the spirit of liberation and freedom. A site entitled "Capitalist Chicks" writes of her initial defeat,

> Myra decided it was time to get organized. She joined a group of women and men who successfully lobbied the Illinois General Assembly to pass a law in 1872 barring employers from discriminating on the basis of sex. This was the first such law in the nation. . . . It took Myra Bradwell 21 years from the time she passed her exam to become a practicing lawyer. Twenty-one years of determination and lobbying to break down the barrier wall and pave the way. Yet another road made easier to travel today by the Steamrollers of long ago.[12]

For this Web site, Myra Bradwell exists as a woman whom we might know, respect, and support even today. She remains relevant through her message of independence and perseverance, even as a maverick among feminists.

NOTES

1. Elizabeth Frost-Knappman and Kathryn Cullen-DuPont, *Women's Rights on Trial: 101 Historic Trials from Anne Hutchinson to the Virginia Military Institute Cadets* (Detroit: Gale, 1997), 102.
2. *Bradwell v. Illinois,* 83 U.S. 130 (1873).
3. Jane M. Friedman, *America's First Woman Lawyer: The Biography of Myra Bradwell* (Buffalo: Prometheus Books, 1993), 27.
4. Unknown contributor, *Woman's Journal,* April 26, 1873.
5. Radcliffe Institute of Advanced Study, Schlesinger Library, Harvard University, *Enterprising Women Exhibit,* 2002, http://www.enterprisingwomenexhibit.org/publish/bradwell.html.
6. *American National Biography* computer software. (Published by Oxford University Press under the auspices of the American Council of Learned Societies, 2000).
7. Myra Bradwell, *Chicago Legal News,* April 19, 1873, 354.
8. Frances Willard, Mary A. Livermore, and Charles Wells Moulton, eds., *A Woman of the Century: Fourteen Hundred-Seventy Biographical Sketches Accompanied by Portraits of Leading American Women in all Walks of Life* (1893), http://www.law.stanford.edu/library/wlhbp/archives/bradwell_myra1893.pdf.
9. Edward T. James et al., eds, *Notable American Women, 1607–1950: A Biographical Dictionary,* 3 vols. (Cambridge: Harvard University Press, 1971) 1:225.
10. *Woman's Journal,* March 17, 1894.
11. Chicago Tribute, "Myra Bradwell," http://www.chicagotribune.org/Markers/Bradwell.htm.
12. Capitalist Chicks, http://www.capitalistchicks.com/html/features-printpage-23.html.

Reynolds v. United States

Sarah Barringer Gordon

Reynolds v. United States
98 U.S. 145 (1879)

DECIDED: January 6, 1879
VOTE
CONCURRING: 9 (Morrison R. Waite, Nathan Clifford, Noah H. Swayne, Samuel F. Miller, Stephen J. Field, William Strong, Joseph P. Bradley, Ward Hunt, John Marshall Harlan)
DISSENTING: 0
OPINION OF THE COURT: Waite
CONCURRING OPINION: Field

R*eynolds v. United States* was the first test in the Supreme Court of the First Amendment's religion clauses. George Reynolds, a member of the Church of Jesus Christ of Latter-day Saints, a group commonly called "Mormons," was convicted in Utah Territory of polygamy, a crime under federal law. The Court sustained his conviction in an opinion that was broadly popular outside Utah when it was decided. Indeed, for most of its history and in the view of most commentators, the case was rightly decided. Vocal minorities, mostly from Utah in the nineteenth century and among civil libertarians in the late twentieth century and into the twenty-first, have criticized the holding for, among other things, its restriction of sexual practices among consenting adults. But *Reynolds* has survived as good law, even growing in importance and stature as the religion clauses acquired central status in constitutional jurisprudence over the course of the twentieth century. In this way, the *Reynolds* case should be distinguished from many nineteenth-century opinions on political and civil liberties, such as *Plessy v. Ferguson* (1896) (see page 75), that have either been overruled or marginalized in subsequent eras.

To appreciate the importance of the case and the controversy that has surrounded the opinion and its holding, it is necessary to understand the background of Reynolds's prosecution as well as the legal and political status of the Church of Jesus Christ of Latter-day Saints. When Joseph Smith, prophet and first president of the Mormon Church, founded the new faith in upstate New York in 1830, he was an obscure and impoverished young man. By the time of his martyrdom in 1844 at the hands of an anti-Mormon mob in Illinois, his church had grown exponentially, and its followers had braved many privations and endured persecution and violence at levels unprecedented in the relatively peaceful history of religious conflict in America. Three years after Smith's lynching, the church's new president and prophet, Brigham Young, led the faithful westward into the arid Great Basin region, where in the late 1840s he established the new state of Deseret, now known as Utah.

Although much of the oppression suffered by Mormons can be laid at the door of sheer prejudice, it is also undeniable that the new church espoused many doctrines that were deeply disturbing to those outside the faith. Two aspects of Mormonism are crucial for purposes of this study: first, the embrace of theocracy and, second, the commitment to polygamy. Both doctrines were vital to early Mormon success in attracting and keeping converts, and both were essential to the eventual dismantling of the Mormon system of self-governance in the late nineteenth century. *Reynolds* was the beginning of the end of this early period in the history of the faith. The case also marks a turning point in American jurisprudence, as the Supreme

Note: Thanks go to Kristen Jensen of Brigham Young University and Brad Kramer of the University of Utah for their valuable and timely assistance in researching this essay.

Court took its first step onto a road that has since proven long and often hard. *Reynolds* was the Court's inaugural attempt to create a sustainable and coherent constitutional law of religion.

In some respects, the problems presented to the Court (and the rest of the country) by Mormonism were familiar: theocracy was a well known and much feared concept in America. By the middle of the nineteenth century, even the dyspeptic religious establishments that had survived the revolutionary period had been dismantled in all of the states. Virginia was the first, enacting in 1785 Thomas Jefferson's Bill for the Establishment of Religious Freedom, which ended the state's official support for the Anglican Church. Other states either never had an established church or followed Virginia's lead more or less promptly. Massachusetts was the last to disestablish when the state finally amended its constitution in 1833, but orthodox Congregationalists had distrusted the motives of state officials for more than a decade, ever since the Supreme Judicial Court of Massachusetts held in 1820 that ministers could be chosen by a town's voters in an open election, rather than screened for religious orthodoxy. Many churchmen as well as laypeople concluded that establishment was inimical to democracy and in turn destructive to truly voluntary religious commitment. For the most part, the shift to disestablishment happened so peacefully and with such popular support that most Americans today assume that "religious freedom" has always meant the absence of an established church.

Joseph Smith and his followers, however, had a starkly different view of the religious and political landscape. Mormons admired the Constitution and believed that it had been divinely inspired. Instead of envisioning a country where multiple faiths flourished in equal regard under law, however, they argued for their right to be different. Especially, they claimed that they had a right to build the Kingdom of God on earth, the only truly righteous government, that would pave the way for the Second Coming of Jesus and the onset of the Millennium. They blended political and religious leadership, with Joseph Smith crowned as "king" even as he declared himself a candidate for the U.S. presidency in 1844. The reunion of church and state in Mormon doctrine was called "theodemocracy" by nineteenth-century church leaders, a concept that blended obedience to God's law with respect for human agency. Each person, in this perspective, would have the option to obey divine law, or to apostatize in rebellion against truth and revelation.

Among the most vital means of building the new kingdom was "celestial" or "plural" marriage, according to a direct revelation from God received by Joseph Smith in 1843. According to this new doctrine, marriages celebrated in the proper manner endured not only during the lives of husband and wife, but also throughout eternity. Only those married according to the new revelation could be "exalted" and reach the highest tiers of salvation. The revelation also proclaimed that the "law of Abraham" meant that men who were called upon to do so by faith and church authority were "justified" in marrying more than one woman. Refusal to enter into such marriages if the circumstances called for it would result in destruction and damnation. Within Mormonism, polygamy was practiced by virtually every leader for more than half a century. The practice of "plural marriage," as it was called within the faith, was both difficult and rewarding. Many diaries record unhappy struggles to adjust to such a radically different family structure, and Mormons spoke often of the demands of "living the Principle" of polygamy. Divisions and apostasy over polygamy tore families apart, especially during the early years of its practice. Yet plural marriage also helped knit together diverse and even disparate groups, creating complex family networks in an extraordinarily short time. Living the Principle gave faithful Mormons a profound sense of accomplishment through sacrifice.

Even as it strengthened and reinforced the commitment of followers, however, polygamy created new vulnerabilities for the young Mormon religion. Polygamy was wildly unpopular outside the faith. Critics called the practice barbaric and cruel, especially to women and the children born into such relationships. Many reformers compared polygamy to slavery, arguing that the two were fundamental violations of human rights and dignity. For many opponents of Mormonism, the practice of polygamy was evidence that the new faith was not even Christian. Polygamy seemed to represent all that was despicable about

Mormonism, according to its enemies: it united theocratic control with the oppression of women and the sexual self-indulgence of men who called themselves "priests."

WHAT THE COURT DECIDED

When George Reynolds was indicted in 1874, the prosecutors and the defendant understood that his was to be a test case. A Republican-dominated Congress had outlawed polygamy in all U.S. territories in 1862. Because Utah was a territory, Republicans argued that the national government should have the right to control the laws that governed even internal relations such as marriage. But no Mormon had been successfully prosecuted under the law; despite the existence of a criminal statute outlawing plural marriage, no Mormon jury would convict a respected leader. Thanks to a new statute that allowed federal prosecutors a more active role in selecting jurors, the U.S. attorney for Utah arrested George Q. Cannon, one of the highest Mormon officials and Utah's delegate to Congress. Cannon, in turn, agreed that it was time to test the constitutionality of the antipolygamy law and suggested that Reynolds, his protégé, would be a suitable defendant. Reynolds agreed to provide the information that would form the basis of his own indictment, and the test case was born. By the time the case arrived at the Supreme Court, both sides were convinced that the other was deceitful and devious. Whatever amity had existed at the outset was replaced by a deep distrust that characterized relations between Mormon leaders and territorial officials for the next decade at least.

The central argument of Reynolds's lawyers was that Congress had no jurisdiction over "domestic relations" in the territories. Any other position, they said, would reduce territories to the status of colonies. This argument was bolstered by language in *Dred Scott v. Sandford,* the infamous slavery opinion written by Chief Justice Roger B. Taney in 1857 (see page 24). When *Reynolds* was argued over two days in 1878, however, much had changed politically, and the Court had a new, Republican chief justice. Polygamy fared far differently at the Supreme Court than slavery had two decades earlier.

This time, Chief Justice Waite wrote an opinion that skipped over how much power the central government had over territories and focused instead on whether or not a criminal defendant should have the power to evade conviction because he was obeying a religious obligation when he committed the crime. By placing religion front and center, Waite raised the question of precisely what the religion clauses of the First Amendment meant. To answer this question, he turned to the writings of Thomas Jefferson, a passionate advocate for separation of church and state and influential in the enactment of the Bill of Rights. According to the Court's analysis, Jefferson's Virginia was the model to follow when interpreting the religion clauses, and Jefferson himself was the foremost authority on what the Constitution protected. Waite pointed out that three years after it banned state support for the Anglican Church, Virginia enacted a statute that imposed the death penalty for bigamy and polygamy. Moreover, in 1802 President Jefferson had said in the now famous "Letter to the Danbury Baptists" that the religion clauses had erected a "wall of separation" between church and state, that religious "opinions" were absolutely protected, and government could "*reach actions only.*" [1]

Applied to the *Reynolds* case, such historical precedents and analysis meant that Mormons were free to believe in polygamy, but if they acted on it, they could be punished. This distinction between belief, which was protected by the Constitution, and actions, which exposed the believer to law, was well recognized in state law across the country, even though Waite drew only on Virginia. This is not to say that any and all actions were illegal if only a legislature chose to forbid them. Jefferson stressed that actions, even those based on principle, were punishable if, and only if, they transgressed "peace and good order." Polygamy was just such a transgression, the Court concluded. Quoting Prof. Francis Lieber, a leading intellectual and writer on the law and democracy, Waite described a political regime that tolerated polygamy as one that would inevitably become mired in "stationary despotism," a phrase that reformers and liberal politicians had long used to describe slavery. Marriage, in this view, so deeply affected society that civilized countries

In this 1885 portrait, a Mormon man stands among the multiple wives he took, a practice the Supreme Court had ruled against several years earlier. In a celebrated test case concerning the religion clauses of the First Amendment, the Court decided in *Reynolds v. United States* (1879) that Mormons were free to believe in polygamy but could be punished if they practiced it. --Library of Congress

always regulated it in the interests of social advancement. The argument made by Reynolds, by contrast, flew in the face of progress, even as it also violated the "direct and serious prohibition of polygamy . . . in our law [based] on the precepts of Christianity, and the laws of our social nature, supported by the sense and practice of civilized nations."

With law, civilization, and Christianity all lined up against Mormon polygamy, the Court held that the practice easily satisfied the standard of an action that must violate "good order" to be punishable. Otherwise, Reynolds's "professed doctrines of religious belief" would undermine the power of law and eventually destroy government itself. Reynolds went to jail, celebrated in Utah as a "prisoner for conscience' sake," but a condemned criminal in the eyes of the law.[2] From the Mormons' perspective, the test case that had begun with the arrest of George Cannon had gone horribly wrong. To those outside the faith, the case marked an important moment in the antipolygamy movement. Most newspaper accounts of the case praised the Court's opinion.

REACTIONS

The *New York Times,* for example, agreed with many antipolygamists when it wrote that Mormon arguments that plural marriage was divinely sanctioned were on the same moral ground as claims that "incest, infanticide or murder was a divinely appointed ordinance." In the story "A Blow against Polygamy," the *Times* was pleased that the "courts have made short work of George Reynolds and his celebrated test case," and Mormons' defense of "this last of 'the twin relics of barbarism.' " "This degrading practice cannot be very long-lived," the story predicted.[3] Other papers made similar points, and several noted that enforcement of the law was now the order of the day. Some cautioned that overly zealous law enforcement could work hardship on Mormon families, but none doubted that *Reynolds* spelled the beginning of the end for polygamy in Utah.

In the territory itself, the reaction was far different. "I will not desert my wives and my children and disobey the commandments of God for the sake of accommodating the public clamor of a nation steeped in sin and ripened for the damnation of hell," thundered Wilford Woodruff in June 1879.[4] One after another, outraged Mormon patriarchs railed against the opinion, calling it the product of fanatical anti-Mormonism, pandering to public opinion, and even cowardice. They swore undying resistance.

Cannon, whose arrest five years earlier had started the whole process, was especially vociferous. No doubt he felt responsible for Reynolds's fate; in addition, he was the representative of his people and territory in Washington, a public spokesman whose mission was to appeal to the rest of the country. Cannon wrote a lengthy and learned pamphlet, "A Review of the Decision of the Supreme Court of the United States."[5] He attacked the *Reynolds* opinion and the judges who signed on to it on many different levels. First, Cannon charged, the Court was hardly infallible, given its support for slavery before the Civil War: "It requires no great age, no venerable experience, to remind citizens of this fact; men of middle age have but to contrast the present with the past, which they can recollect, to convince themselves of it." From a fallible Court, Cannon argued, came a flawed opinion: "It is superficial, careless and immature. It reads more like the plea of an advocate than the well-considered, thoroughly weighed and ripe decision of great judges upon an important and long agitated constitutional question."[6]

Cannon attacked not only the Court's reliance on history, which he characterized as hopelessly one-sided, but also its distinction between belief and action. Blackstone, the venerable English legal commentator, wrote that when the laws of God conflict with the laws of man, the former must always prevail. Cannon pointed out that for religion truly to be freely exercised, as the Constitution dictates, then practice must be part of the equation, particularly in a case, as with Mormon plural marriage, when God's explicit law required the practice of polygamy. "Liberty, then, not of mere opinion alone, but religious liberty of practice, is my natural and indefeasible right, and with this neither the legislature nor any branch of the civil power can legitimately interfere." Cannon also countered the claim that Mormon marital practices violated peace and good order: "Our actions do not injure others. We do not trespass on private right or the public peace." Cannon asked rhetorically, "Because human sacrifice is wrong, does it necessarily follow that human propagation [through plural marriage] is wrong?"[7]

This was precisely the question in dispute—was polygamy as practiced in Mormon Utah akin to slavery or even murder, a violation of the rights and dignity of women? Cannon argued that women were protected by plural marriage and treated with greater respect in Utah than elsewhere. He even appealed to Shakers and Roman Catholics, both of whom practiced celibacy of varying degrees, arguing that if the Supreme Court could get away with punishing Mormons, then other faiths would be next. Do not let the widespread unpopularity of this group, he begged, obscure the fact that the Court had sustained a law that interfered with the most sacred obligations of Latter-day faith. "It happens to be the Latter-day Saints against which the late decision is hurled; but the precedent once established, and what security has any unpopular sect for religious liberty?"[8]

Cannon's plea fell on deaf ears outside Mormon circles. Instead of provoking protest, the *Reynolds* opinion unleashed a new wave of antipolygamy sentiment. Politicians, editors, clerics, lecturers, and others called on the government to enforce the law. Cannon was right about one of his main points: the unpopular Mormons became the focus of intense national scrutiny and indignation, yet few of their attackers thought about what precedent *Reynolds* set for the treatment of religion in the courts. Instead, they called for the eradication of the "twin relic of barbarism." Even those few who defended the Mormons, typically southerners who argued against national power in the territories, made it clear that they did not condone polygamy; rather, they condemned the centralization of power that antipolygamy legislation (and cases such as *Reynolds*) represented.

Cannon and others like him who argued against the extension of federal power into Utah fought a losing battle. In the end, the Mormon Church was forced to capitulate, as hundreds of men went to jail, families were broken up, and church property was declared forfeit. In 1890 Woodruff, who only eleven years earlier had declared his intention to defy the *Reynolds* holding and now president of the entire LDS Church, assured the U.S. government that he would counsel followers to obey the law. Although it took a generation for many Mormons to adjust completely to the accommodationist approach, and some renegades have never abandoned "the Principle," the church and its members are now rigorously monogamous. Today Mormons are considered to be among the most family-oriented of all Americans. They cooperate frequently with other conservative Christian groups, despite a lively memory of the persecutions and suffering that forged them into a "peculiar people."

For much of the twentieth century, polygamy—and the furor it caused in the nineteenth century—seemed like an obscure and atypical episode in American history. *Reynolds,* although it remained on the books, and was cited from time to time, was neither widely discussed nor remembered. The Supreme Court did not decide religion cases, and Utah had been an exception, because of its status as a territory, rather than a state.

THE IMPACT OF *REYNOLDS*

Until the 1940s it seemed that *Reynolds* would molder indefinitely. In two cases during that decade, however, the Court "incorporated" the free exercise and establishment clauses, ruling for the first time that states would be held to the same constitutional standard that applied to the federal government. With these decisions, the Court stepped onto a path that has entailed many twists and turns and more or less constant controversy; the law of religion is one of the most contentious and least predictable of all areas of constitutional jurisprudence. *Reynolds* has roared back to life in case law and commentary.

Some modern legal scholars reject the premise underlying the *Reynolds* decision. They dismiss as misguided the campaign to eradicate the practice that gave rise to the case, while also dismissing the Mormon claims that divine law makes all the difference between plural marriage and garden variety bigamy. They do not accept the argument that marriage is integrally related to political structure and that some forms of the relationship are inconsistent with the survival of democracy and the flourishing of women. They see marriage as a private "lifestyle" choice based only on the consent of the parties to the arrangement. This view is a shallower understanding of marriage than nineteenth-century theorists on either side of the polygamy divide would have accepted. *Reynolds,* after all, was grounded on the idea that marriage—and the private relations it legalized and contained—was vitally important politically as well as personally.

Consensus on the role of marriage in public life has been eroded by civil libertarianism, the belief that government has no business inquiring into the private lives of citizens. Civil libertarians, although never a majority of scholars or judges, have had profound influence on the public's thinking about law and what matters are considered "private." Today, arguments over whether marriage is a private affair have again taken center stage, this time in debates over whether governments should be allowed to prohibit same-sex marriage. This new and deeply divisive argument over marriage influences how *Reynolds* and its importance in life and law are seen.

The critique of *Reynolds* from the bench began with a lone dissent by Justice Frank Murphy in 1946. In *Cleveland v. United States,* Murphy argued strenuously that a Mormon polygamist should not be punished under the "White Slave Act" of 1910, a federal statute that prohibited taking women across state lines for "illicit purposes"—that is, for prostitution. Murphy argued that polygamy was simply another form of marriage, as legitimate if not as morally laudable as monogamy. Certainly, Murphy claimed, Mormon plural marriage was a far cry from the sexual enslavement targeted by the statute. The majority opinion, written by Justice William O. Douglas, conceded no such thing. Douglas, a believer in the analogy of polygamy to slavery, relied on *Reynolds* to uphold the conviction.

In 1964 Mormon legal scholar Orma Linford published the first full description of all the polygamy cases and attacked the Supreme Court for "neither balance nor measurement" in its treatment of Mormonism.[9] Gradually, yet with increasing conviction, scholars treated *Reynolds* as an example of anti-Mormonism, rather than a case about marital structure and its political importance. Women, it seemed, had fallen out of the picture.

In 1972 the criticism of *Reynolds* was bolstered by the Court's decision in *Wisconsin v. Yoder,* holding that Old Order Amish parents could withdraw their children from school at age fourteen on religious grounds (see page 275). Justice Douglas, in partial dissent from the majority opinion, said that *Yoder* covertly overruled *Reynolds,* implying that it was only a matter of time before polygamy would reappear in America. Scholars picked up on his statement, arguing that the sexual revolution had rendered the prohibition of polygamy ridiculous. Harvard law professor Laurence Tribe, for example, predicted in the 1980s that *Reynolds* would soon be overturned.[10] Mormon scholars Edwin Firmage and Richard Mangrum argued that the prosecution of Mormon polygamists had chilled the freedoms and slowed the advance of all Americans, degrading the oppressive government as well as violating the rights of citizens: "Imposing conformity on a group of sincerely dedicated dissenters almost inevitably requires a level of force that debases the oppressor. In a sorry cycle, resistance breeds repression that calls forth yet more resistance, and yet more savage repression. In the case of polygamy, it may be questioned whether the prize was worth the price."[11]

In 1990, however, the Supreme Court defied the predictions. In *Employment Division v. Smith,* a case involving a religious freedom claim by drug users, Justice Antonin Scalia drew explicitly on *Reynolds.* (See page 341.) Resurrecting the distinction between the freedom to believe and the validity of punishing actions, Scalia placed *Reynolds* once again at the heart of religion clause jurisprudence. Leading scholars condemned the decision, but to no avail. The belief-action distinction, first made part of constitutional law in *Reynolds,* is back and so far has survived.

Although plural marriage is rarely discussed in public today by Mormon leaders, some scholars and commentators have begun a new line of argument, this time in favor of *Reynolds* and the prohibition of polygamy. One recent article celebrates the abandonment of polygamy and the integration of Mormons into the broader American culture as a "victory." Another tackles libertarian arguments head on, claiming that "legalizing polygamy would signal a deterioration of traditional values."[12] Whatever others may say about "lifestyle" choices, the Latter-day Saints are deeply committed monogamists and view heterosexual marriage as vitally important politically as well as personally and especially spiritually. Mormons today are commonly known as vigorous opponents of feminism, gay rights—and polygamy.

Reynolds, therefore, has a long and tangled history. It has been marked by controversy, but it would be overly simplistic to dismiss this case as a violation of civil rights by a harsh and narrow-minded nineteenth-century Court. Instead, once again Americans are learning that debates over marriage and its relationship to government involve profound questions of humanity, politics, and culture. In this light, *Reynolds* stands for the proposition that marriage is indeed important to the state. It is also undeniable, however, that much of the analysis used in *Reynolds* does not hold up well under a twenty-first century microscope. Professor Lieber's condemnation of polygamy no longer seems "striking and profound," despite Waite's praise. Jefferson's "Letter to the Danbury Baptists," moreover, which the Court used not only in *Reynolds* but in many subsequent establishment clause cases, has been roundly criticized as an authoritative source for interpreting the First Amendment. Like the gnarled veteran it is, *Reynolds* has survived a century and more of critique, manipulation, and exploitation. Never an easy or uncomplicated opinion, it is tarnished now.

But because marriage and religion are so central to American life, the old case remains vital. The questions about faith, marriage, and law that galvanized the country in the nineteenth century have come back in new and divisive ways in the twenty-first. *Reynolds* stands in part for the proposition that local differences in marital structure cannot survive federal attack. Yet *Reynolds* was also premised on the fact that Utah was a territory, without the full rights of states to govern itself. Much has changed in the interim, with states rights becoming a political football and jurisprudential battleground. The debates are inevitably relevant to the big new elephant in the room: same-sex marriage.

NOTES

1. Letter to the Danbury Baptist Association, quoted by Waite in *Reynolds v. United States,* emphasis added by Waite.

2. After Reynolds's request for a rehearing, the Court noted that the law did not require punishment at hard labor for the crime of polygamy. On May 5, 1879, the Court vacated its order for "the purpose of correcting" the error and remanded it with instructions to the lower court to amend the sentence.

3. *New York Times,* January 8, 1879, 4.

4. Quoted without further citation in Kimball Young, *Isn't One Wife Enough?* (New York: Holt, 1954), 354.

5. George Q. Cannon, "A Review of the Decision of the Supreme Court of the United States," Salt Lake City, 1879.

6. Ibid., 4.

7. Ibid., 20, 21, 35.

8. Ibid., 40.

9. Orma Linford, "The Mormons and the Law: The Polygamy Cases," *Utah Law Review* 9 (1964): 308–370, 543–591, 589. See also Harrop Freeman, "A Remonstrance for Conscience," *University of Pennsylvania Law Review* 106 (1959): 823.

10. Laurence Tribe, *American Constitutional Law,* 2d ed. (Mineola, N.Y.: Foundation Press, 1988), 521–528.

11. Edwin B. Firmage and Richard Collin Mangrum, *Zion in the Courts: A Legal History of the Church of Jesus Christ of Latter-day Saints, 1830–1900* (Urbana: University of Illinois Press, 1988), 130.

12. Douglas Parker, "Victory in Defeat—Polygamy and the Mormon Legal Encounter with the Federal Government," *Cardozo Law Review* 12 (1991): 805–819; Mark S. Lee, "Legislating Morality," *Sunstone* magazine, April 1985, 8–12.

The Income Tax Cases

Robert Stanley

Pollock v. Farmers' Loan & Trust Co. (I)

157 U.S. 429 (1895)

DECIDED: April 8, 1895

VOTE

    CONCURRING: 6 (Melville W. Fuller, Stephen J. Field, Horace Gray, David J. Brewer, Henry B. Brown, George Shiras Jr.)

    DISSENTING: 2 (John Marshall Harlan, Edward D. White)

OPINION OF THE COURT: Fuller

CONCURRING OPINION: Field

DISSENTING OPINION: White (Harlan)

DISSENTING OPINION: Harlan

Pollock v. Farmers' Loan & Trust Co. (II)

158 U.S. 601 (1895)

DECIDED: May 20, 1895

VOTE

    CONCURRING: 5 (Melville W. Fuller, Stephen J. Field, Horace Gray, David J. Brewer, George Shiras Jr.)

    DISSENTING: 4 (John Marshall Harlan, Henry B. Brown, Howell E. Jackson, Edward D. White)

OPINION OF THE COURT: Fuller

DISSENTING OPINION: Harlan

DISSENTING OPINION: Brown

DISSENTING OPINION: Jackson

DISSENTING OPINION: White

In the Income Tax Cases the Supreme Court for the first time invalidated a federal tax law, with rulings so disruptive to the political mainstream that the decision became only the third of four to be directly overturned by constitutional amendment. Yet unlike *Chisholm v. Georgia* (1793), *Dred Scott v. Sandford* (1857) (see page 24), and *Oregon v. Mitchell,* (1970), which were overturned by the Eleventh, Thirteenth and Fourteenth, and Twenty-sixth Amendments, respectively, contemporary comment on the case—although immediate and deeply polarized—soon faded, and nearly a generation passed before the Sixteenth Amendment was successfully proposed and ratified.

Today, the byzantine fiscal imperatives and economic implications of income taxation dominate the federal revenue system, and most would understand historian George Mowry's assessment in *The Era of Theodore Roosevelt* that the "modern democratic social service state, in fact, probably rests more upon the income tax than upon any other single legislative act."[1] But the contemporary responses to the *Pollock* case occurred within three critical contexts that are now generally unfamiliar: the fiercely debated protective tariff system that provided the bulk of the government's ordinary revenues; the Court's recent controversial decisions in *United States v. E. C. Knight Co.* (1895) and *In re Debs* (1895), which left intact one of the nation's largest trusts and broke a railroad strike; and the unprecedented social upheavals of the depression that began with the panic of 1893.

The income tax law invalidated in *Pollock* was only a small part of the massive tariff reform package on which the Democratic Party staked its future in 1894, and in form it fit squarely within prior federal and state practice. But within a year of the enthusiastic celebration that greeted the Wilson Tariff Bill in the House, the income tax had triggered profound anxieties and bitter conflict in the Court, the public, and scholarly presses.

THE COURT ABANDONS TRADITION

Providing for a 2 percent tax on income in excess of $4,000, the income tax law of 1894 was an unpromising candidate for judicial invalidation. Treasury officials expected it to reach less than 1 percent of the population and to bring in less than 4 percent of the ordinary revenues—a lighter impact than the federal income taxes first levied from 1861 through 1872, whose sponsors included the Lincoln administration and Senate Finance Committee chairmen Justin Morrill, R-Vt., and John Sherman, R-Ohio.[2]

Moreover, the Supreme Court until then had been entirely unwilling to limit congressional taxing authority. The Constitution expresses no limitations on the tax bases Congress might reach, but does qualify the manner of assessment. Article I, sections 2 and 9, require that "direct taxes" be apportioned according to the population of each state; section 8 provides that "duties, imposts, and excises" must be "uniform throughout the United States." Since 1796 the Court had upheld as excises, taxes on carriages, corporate receipts, state bank notes, and inheritances. Finally, in *Springer v. United States* (1881), the Court had unanimously upheld the constitutionality of the income tax law of 1864, ruling that it was an "excise or duty," and not an unapportioned direct tax.

Led by William D. Guthrie, Joseph H. Choate, and former senator George F. Edmunds, R-Vt., opponents of the tax sought at least one of three possible rulings from the Court: (1) that the income tax was in whole or part direct and not apportioned among the states, as the Constitution required; (2) that it was not uniform because of the $4,000 exemption; and (3) that if part of the law failed, the whole should be invalidated. One of the lengthiest and most contentious oral arguments in history ensued, with Attorney General Richard Olney, Assistant Attorney General Edward B. Whitney, and James C. Carter supporting the traditional character of income taxation. Choate stripped the tax of all historical and precedential context, contending that it was unconstitutionally direct, and particularly that the exemption was "communistic in its purposes and tendencies."[3]

The Court's two *Pollock* rulings held that the tax was in part direct and that the whole law must fall. Before a packed courtroom on April 8, 1895, Chief Justice Fuller held for himself and five colleagues, over dissents by Justices Harlan and White (Justice Jackson was ill during the first set of arguments), that the tax as applied to income from real estate was direct and not properly apportioned. Fuller began with a neo-Calhounian (after John C. Calhoun, a former vice president and senator) view of the Constitution as a compact between sovereign states for the delegation of limited powers to the federal government. The direct tax clauses were specifically designed to deny the government "the power of directly taxing persons and property within any state through a majority made up from other states." Taxes on land had always been understood as direct in nature; therefore taxes on rents or other income from land were also direct. If apportionment according to state population would create new inequalities, it "must be held to have been contemplated" by the Framers, Fuller said, and been designed to "prevent an attack upon accumulated property by mere force of numbers." On May 20, 1895, facing another standing-room throng, Fuller held for a 5–4 majority that taxes on income from personal property were also direct and unconstitutional. Considering the taxes remaining—on the income from professions, trades, employments, or vocations—the Court ruled that if allowed to stand, "what was intended as a tax upon capital would remain in substance a tax on occupations and labor." Striking down the rest of the law, Fuller said, "We cannot believe that such was the intention of Congress."[4]

The Court declined to rule independently on these occupation-related taxes. It exempted from taxation the income from state and municipal bonds and noted that "the states have power to lay income taxes." Most important, the Court expressly rejected Choate's argument against the $4,000 exemption. "There is certainly no want of uniformity, within the meaning of the constitution," Fuller said.[5] The Court soon upheld progressive state and federal inheritance taxes in *Magoun v. Illinois Trust & Savings Bank* (1898) and *Knowlton v. Moore* (1900).

The public reaction to *Pollock* would track the main themes raised by Fuller's majority opinions, Justice Field's views, and the dissents of Justices Harlan and White, who were joined in the second ruling by Justices Jackson and Brown.

Field agreed that the taxes on income from real property were direct, but contended that the rest of the taxes were void for lack of uniformity, which he defined along the equal protection lines offered by Choate. Field sought to annihilate the entire law, along with the principle of progression symbolized in the $4,000 exemption. This he characterized as "class legislation," and warned that "the present assault upon capital is but the beginning . . . our political contests will become a war of the poor against the rich, a war constantly growing in intensity and bitterness."[6]

While Field saw the income tax as a match to the tinder of rising class tension, White and Harlan saw explosive potential in the manner of its demise. White's dissents decried the Court's denial of congressional power "conceded to it by universal consensus for one hundred years," attacked its departure from "a long and settled practice sanctioned by the decisions of this court," and noted that the tariff itself was subject to the same objections that had defeated the income tax. "Teach the lesson that settled principles may be overthrown at any time," White warned, and ultimately "the rights of property, so far as the Federal Constitution is concerned, are of little worth."[7]

In *Pollock v. Farmers' Loan & Trust Co. I and II* (1895), known as the Income Tax Cases, the Court declared the income tax law of 1894 unconstitutional. Controversial in the beginning, the decision gradually lost professional and political support. It was overturned in 1913 with the ratification of the Sixteenth Amendment, which exempted income taxation from the Constitution's apportionment requirements — Library of Congress

Harlan brought still more passion to the traditionalist argument, contending that the foundation of American law lay in respecting interpretations of the Constitution that have been "long accepted and acted upon by other branches of government and by the public." He feared that "the decision now made may provoke a contest in this country from which the American people would have been spared," because the rulings had specifically shielded invested wealth. "The real friends of property," thundered Harlan, "are not those who would exempt the wealth of the country from bearing its fair share of the burden of taxation." Brown saw in the decision "nothing less than the surrender of the taxing power to the moneyed class," a course "fraught with immeasurable danger to the future of the country."[8]

What the judicial combatants so earnestly sought was stability and the protection of property. What each side feared was the possibility that depression-borne social turmoil might grow into anarchy or revolution fueled by their opponents' hopelessly misguided positions on the income tax. Looking out the door,

Fuller glimpsed the "mere force of numbers," and Field predicted a class war. Harlan foresaw a "contest" and wrote to his sons that he thought Field had "acted often like a mad man" during the case.[9] White minced no words in his second dissent, warning that if apportionment of income taxation were enforced "the red specter of revolution would shake our institutions to their foundation."[10]

WILSON TARIFF BILL

The issue of class anxiety had also split the Democratic leadership during acrimonious congressional debate over the law the year before. Sen. David B. Hill, D-N.Y., had portrayed the tax as the product of "little squads of anarchists, communists, and socialists," but in the House, Rep. Uriel Hall, D-Mo., had called the income tax "a measure to kill anarchy and keep down socialists." For Hall, the continued taxing of working people through the protective tariff was the real "argument in favor of demagogy and socialism." Rep. Benton McMillin, D-Tenn., was even more specific. The income tax law would "diminish the antipathies that now exist between the classes," he said, because "[i]n the end it will be found cheaper to pay low taxes on large estates than to hire private watchmen and private policemen to guard them."[11]

The Wilson Tariff Bill had passed the House of Representatives on February 1, 1894, before "the largest audience ever gathered in the House." The Democratic Party's most visible effort to reverse the panic of 1893 was witnessed by "a maelstrom of restless, pushing, impatient men and women," by members' families, and House guests, including Frederick Douglass. Flowers were placed on the desks of Speaker Charles F. Crisp, D-Ga., and Minority Leader Thomas Brackett Reed, R-Maine, at the conclusion of their opposing addresses. When Ways and Means chairman and tariff sponsor William L. Wilson, D-W.Va., finished, "the crowds in the galleries seemed beside themselves," according to one reporter. To "a tumult of applause," Wilson was carried off the floor on the shoulders of his colleagues, including William Jennings Bryan, author of the income tax proposal.[12]

On that day the leadership hardly suspected how precipitous the downhill slide would be. But in spring 1895 the continuing depression and rising public controversy over the income tax could not have presented a more dramatic contrast. Whether cast in the language of the party-affiliated newspapers of the day or the more scholarly terminology of economics and law, public opinion generally mirrored the fear and fervor expressed in Congress and more recently in the Court. To its admirers, *Pollock* had extinguished a dangerous flame. To its critics, *Pollock* had ignited one.

CELEBRATION AND CENSURE

Editorials in two Democratic newspapers cheered *Pollock*. Welcoming Fuller's state compact view of the Constitution, the *New York Times* argued that "the income tax provisions of the tariff law of 1894 . . . were not Democratic in theory or policy, and the method of constitutional interpretation that has guided the Supreme Court in destroying them is one of the fundamental doctrines of the Democratic Party." The *Brooklyn Eagle* declared that whether the *Pollock* decision "be the end or but the beginning of the war between civilization and loot[ing] in this country, welcome is the decision and ready are the friends of civilization to meet whatever is yet to come." Also approving the decision, the Republican *New York Tribune* found in *Pollock* a bulwark against "the fury of ignorant class hatred" and saw Fuller's reading of the direct tax clauses as proof that the "great compromises which made the Union possible still stand unshaken to prevent its overthrow by communistic revolution."[13]

Independent publications found fault with Justice Harlan. The *Boston Herald* complained that his "extraordinarily vehement manner" in reading his dissent "has awakened a suspicion in some quarters that he cherishes political aspirations," and that his views "seem to squint very strongly toward Populism."[14] But E. L. Godkin in the *Nation* went further, attacking "the heat with which Justice Harlan expounded the Marx gospel from the bench."[15]

Other pro-*Pollock* editorials also expressed relief that a legislative revolution, at least, had been averted. The independent *Baltimore Herald* contended that only "in the minds of a comparatively few Populists who die hard does it appear that a great wrong has been perpetrated. The majority of Americans, upon reflection, will approve the decision, and feel satisfied that the national revenues should be obtained without creating class distinctions." The *Cincinnati Enquirer,* a Democratic paper, congratulated the country "upon this deliverance from the serious blunder of a bewildered and bewildering Congress," and the independent *Detroit News* argued that the income tax might apply in Britain, where "one class had special privileges," but not in the United States, where "we have all started on the level and wish to remain so. . . . The tax decision is one of the great American cases." [16]

More succinctly, the Republican *Philadelphia Inquirer* said the decision "deals a fatal blow to an insidious form of communism." The *New Orleans Times-Democrat* was one of the few supporters of the decision with qualms: "The country is well rid of an evil law no matter how much weakness the supreme tribunal of the land has betrayed in reaching that conclusion, nor how much the people's confidence in that judicial body may have been impaired in the process." [17]

As the *Times-Democrat* implied, the Court was hit hard by editorials attacking the decision. The Democratic *New York World* bitterly complained that "Great and rich corporations" had won the case "by hiring the ablest lawyers in the land and fighting against a petty tax on superfluity as other men have fought for their liberties and their lives." The paper called for a renewed income tax law and remarked that "If the Supreme Court shall again stand in the way the people can elect a President who will appoint somebody besides corporation attorneys to the bench." Failing that, the *World* called for a constitutional amendment. The Republican *Boston Transcript* attacked the Court's "anti-legislative power," noting that its members "are, in fact, a higher and closer Senate, and with infinitely greater power upon legislation—a power superior, indeed, to that of the President himself." [18]

At the heart of the matter was the Court's treatment of wealth and poverty in the midst of social upheaval. In Philadelphia the *Journal* of the Knights of Labor contended that "when the people have made up their minds, as they have in the income-tax case, the most that the Court can do is to delay the final consummation of their will." The people, the *Journal* continued, "have demanded that a tax be placed upon the incomes of the rich in order to compel them to make some slight restitution of the enormous amount of stealings which they are every year taking from the earnings of honest toil." The independent *Springfield Republican* thought the tax had "proved to be perhaps the strongest feature of the tariff law," and called for a constitutional amendment because "the organic law of this nation cannot afford to set up the principle that taxation should be levied according to population rather than according to wealth. The justice of that proposition has been denied by every reputable economist who ever wrote a book." [19]

The Populist *Indianapolis Nonconformist* thought *Pollock* had been "trumped up in the interest of the moneyed classes," but that "perhaps something of the kind had to come as an accentuation of the pending social revolution and to force the people to realize the situation they are in." Two Democratic papers wanted legislative action. The *Augusta Chronicle* called for a new income tax law supported by a ballot-based "revolution in public sentiment," and the *St. Louis Republic* called for a constitutional amendment. The Republican *Salt Lake Tribune* found *Pollock* a "mighty disappointment." The decision "falls upon the fair-minded men of the country precisely as did the Dred-Scott decision forty years ago." The *Tribune* argued that "those who receive most of this world's goods and claim most protection from the Government ought to pay most of the Government's expenses." [20]

Finally, the Mormon *Salt Lake News* analyzed both sides of the bench:

> The majority of the Court insists that the income-tax division of the Wilson law was class legislation of an objectionable kind; while the minority insists that the defeat of the law is the establishment of a rule for class legislation of the most offensive character. One says the law was unjust to the few at the clamor of the many; the other that its defeat is favoring the wealthy few at the expense of the poorer masses. Summing these conclusions up, it would seem that the Court is practically unanimous on one point at least, looking from two sides, that in this country there is one law for the rich, and

another for the poor. This is the notable feature in which the opinions accord with the view, perhaps more bluntly expressed than in the Court's definitions, of a very large number of people.[21]

Economists and jurists articulated similar themes—sometimes in surprising ways. Since the 1870s, laissez-faire political economists had generally supported income taxation, based on a single rate and allowing at most a small exemption for necessities, as a desirable alternative to the market-destroying impact of taxes on goods that were imposed through the tariff and internal revenue systems. In the words of Yale sociologist William Graham Sumner, the tariff was a tool by which "government gives a license to certain interests to go out and encroach on others."[22] Appearing before a Senate committee in 1878, Sumner had said, "I am in favor of an income tax as a matter of public finance. If we had an income tax and could do away with tariff taxes, the result, I think, would be very beneficial to the whole community."[23] By contrast, Karl Marx himself opposed income taxation in prerevolutionary societies, because an "income tax presupposes various social classes, and hence capitalist society." Income taxation was not about production, but about the distribution of wealth after disaster had already occurred.[24]

By the 1880s many of the professionals associated with the new American Economic Association had begun to see income taxation as a useful but minor amelioration of the regressive implications of the tariff. Most important here were the views of E. R. A. Seligman, author of the influential *Economic Interpretation of History* and senior Columbia University colleague of Charles A. Beard.[25] During the controversy over the pending income tax law, Seligman had directly attacked critics who called the law "socialistic," writing that the tax would not replace, but simply "round out" the tariff system. "It seeks to correct the growing conviction among all masses of the population that our present tax system largely exempts those who are best able to pay."[26] In the wake of *Pollock,* legal scholars not only echoed the Court in debating the problem of rich and poor in a democracy but also added controversy over the role of the Court itself. Attorney Lafon Allen brought to the *American Law Review* a classic defense of judicial review predicated on the horrors of unlimited legislative power.[27] George F. Edmunds responded to an invitation in the *Forum* by contending that taxation could not "safely be left to the unlimited caprice or prejudice or selfishness of mere majorities represented in Congress."[28] In the *American Law Review* essay that had provoked Allen, Oregon governor Sylvester Pennoyer, elected as a Populist Democrat, called the *Pollock* decision "nullification, pure and simple." Pennoyer warmly supported progressive taxation and attacked the principle of judicial review, created by "the plausible sophistries of John Marshall."[29] In the *Forum,* Edward B. Whitney critiqued Chief Justice Fuller's antebellum view of the Constitution and concluded, "Unfortunately, there is a distinction between rich and poor which cannot be wiped out under our present civilization."[30]

TRADITION RESTORED

Despite the heat that *Pollock* had generated, by year's end the public controversy had faded, leaving the field to a small group of debating professionals. Forty-five different articles on income taxation appeared in the standard indexes of periodicals in 1895; the following year there were four; and over the next decade only thirteen articles were listed.[31] Deprived by the continuing depression of a campaign on the Wilson Tariff, and by the Court of the income tax issue, the Democratic Party went for Bryan and silver, losing Congress and the White House in the election of 1896. Not until the next economic crisis—in the wake of the panic of 1907—did public interest in the income tax revive. Both parties began to move toward the idea: Bryan continued his support; President Theodore Roosevelt was mentioning it by 1906; and in 1908 William Howard Taft carefully endorsed it while accepting the Republican presidential nomination.[32]

During this period, professional opinion moved decisively toward support for income taxation. Although some of the old fire lingered, most of the arguments were designed to defuse class anxieties. In 1906 Wayne MacVeagh, attorney general in the Garfield administration, supported Roosevelt, complaining that "capitalists exhibit a singular stupidity in resisting every attempt to impose upon them their proper share of the public burdens." There was no use, he said, "in pretending that the proposal to establish such a system of taxation is of a radical, much less of a revolutionary, character."[33] In 1907 Whitney weighed in again in the *Harvard Law Review,* providing several pathways for attacking *Pollock* directly, and supporting an amendment in the alternative.[34] In 1909 economist Delos Kinsman analyzed several state income tax initiatives, emphasizing their nonradical character and traditional high exemption-low rate form.[35]

In March 1909 President Taft called Congress into a special session on tariff revision, and by the summer a compromise package had been crafted. It included the Payne-Aldrich Tariff, a 1 percent corporate excise, and a constitutional amendment resolution that passed the House, 318–14, and the Senate, 77–0, with 15 abstentions.[36]

By this time, public opinion heavily favored the idea of the tax, and most of the invective was gone. From August 1909 through February 1913, of the thirty-five indexed articles expressing an opinion, twenty-two supported income taxation; and eight of the thirteen in opposition appeared in the *Outlook* or the *Nation,* both traditionally anti–income tax.[37]

The most influential professional supporter of the tax during the ratification years was Seligman, who resumed publishing on the subject in 1910 and the following year released his major work, *The Income Tax: A Study of the History, Theory, and Practice of Income Taxation at Home and Abroad.*[38] The book was the most significant to appear prior to ratification; it was heavily and favorably reviewed and was above all designed to deflate the 1890s notion that income taxation was radical. Even in opposition, the *Nation* reflected the new moderation, simply urging its readers to support a nondiscriminatory rate structure. In the *North American Review* in 1910, Sen. William E. Borah, R-Idaho, reminded readers that constitutions and statutes do not protect property in reality; that only an "intelligent, law-abiding and loyal" citizenship could do so, and that "every time wealth invades equal opportunity it is undermining its own stability."[39]

As formally ratified on February 3, 1913, the Sixteenth Amendment provides:

> The Congress shall have power to lay and collect taxes on incomes, from whatever source derived, without apportionment among the several States, and without regard to any census or enumeration.

Forty-two of the forty-eight states approved—six states above the constitutionally required minimum. The mean margin of support for the resolution in the thirty-nine approving states for which complete information is available was 94.9 percent in the houses and 89.4 percent in the senates.[40]

In the years between the Court's validation of the federal carriage tax in *Hylton v. United States* (1796) and the first law under the new amendment in 1913, *Pollock* represented only a brief departure from a historically rooted and broadly based constitutional understanding of congressional taxing authority: a deviation made dramatic because its nine opinions so aptly expressed the confusion and anxiety of its time. But by 1913 the "universal consensus" that Justice White had described in his first *Pollock* dissent had reasserted itself. Writing as Chief Justice for a unanimous Supreme Court in *Brushaber v. Union Pacific Ry. Co.* (1916), he flatly rejected multiple challenges to the constitutionality of the 1913 income tax law. White, who had supported the *Knight* and *Debs* rulings and is called by his biographer a "defender of the conservative faith," ruled that "there is no escape from the conclusion that the Amendment was drawn for the purpose of doing away for the future with the principle upon which the Pollock Case was decided. . . ."[41] By overturning *Pollock v. Farmers' Loan & Trust Co.,* the Sixteenth Amendment restored the traditional constitutional understanding.

NOTES

1. George Mowry, *The Era of Theodore Roosevelt, 1900–1912* (New York: Harper, 1958), 263.
2. Robert Stanley, *Dimensions of Law in the Service of Order: Origins of the Federal Income Tax, 1861–1913* (New York: Oxford University Press, 1993), Table 3-7, 133; 266.
3. *Pollock v. Farmers' Loan & Trust Co.* (I), 157 U.S. 429, at 532 (1895).

4. *Pollock (I)*, at 582, 583; *Pollock v. Farmers' Loan & Trust Co.* (II), 158 U.S. 601, at 637 (1895).

5. *Pollock (II)*, at 629–630, 693.

6. *Pollock (I)*, at 596, 607.

7. *Pollock (I)*, at 608, 637, 650–651.

8. *Pollock (II)*, at 663, 672, 676, 695.

9. Arnold M. Paul, *Conservative Crisis and the Rule of Law: Attitudes of Bar and Bench, 1887–1895* (Gloucester, Mass.: Peter Smith, 1976), 205, n.50, quoting David G. Farrelly, "Harlan's Dissent in the Pollock Case," *Southern California Law Review* 24 (February 1951): 179.

10. *Pollock (II)*, at 714.

11. David B. Hill, *Congressional Record*, 53d Cong., 2d sess., 3557–68; Uriel Hall, ibid., 1608–9; Benton McMillin, ibid., Appendix, Pt. 1, 415.

12. *New York Times*, February 2, 1894, 1, 6; *Washington Post*, February 2, 1894, 1.

13. Editorials collected in *Public Opinion* 18, May 23, 1895, 563; May 30 1895, 595.

14. *Public Opinion* 18, May 30, 1895, 593.

15. *Nation* 60, May 23, 1895, 394.

16. *Public Opinion* 18, May 30, 1895, 595, 596.

17. Ibid., 595.

18. *Public Opinion* 18, May 23, 1895, 563; May 30, 1895, 595.

19. *Public Opinion* 18, May 30, 1895, 596, 594.

20. Ibid., 594, 596, 595.

21. Ibid., 596.

22. William Graham Sumner, *Protectionism* (New York: Holt, 1888), vii.

23. House Misc. Doc 29 (45/3) S.S. 1863, 206.

24. Karl Marx, "Critique of the Gotha Programme," in *The Marx-Engels Reader*, ed. Robert C. Tucker (New York: Norton, 1972), 382, 394–396.

25. E. R. A. Seligman, *Economic Interpretation of History* (London: Macmillan, 1902).

26. E. R. A. Seligman, "The Income Tax," *Political Science Quarterly* 9 (1894): 610, 620.

27. Lafon Allen, "The Income Tax Decision: An Answer to Governor Pennoyer," *American Law Review* 29 (1895): 847.

28. George F. Edmunds, "Salutary Results of the Income-Tax Decision," *Forum* 19 (1895): 513.

29. Sylvester Pennoyer, "The Income Tax Decision and the Power of the Supreme Court to Nullify Acts of Congress," *American Law Review* 29 (1895): 550.

30. Edward B. Whitney, "Political Dangers of the Income-Tax Decision," *Forum* 19 (1895): 521.

31. Stanley, *Dimensions of Law in the Service of Order*, Table 5-1, 180.

32. Ibid., 186–187.

33. Wayne MacVeagh, "The Graduated Taxation of Incomes and Inheritances," *North American Review* 182 (1906): 824, 825.

34. Edward B. Whitney, "The Income Tax and the Constitution," *Harvard Law Review* 20 (1907): 280.

35. Delos Kinsman, "The Present Period of Income Tax Activity in the American States," *Quarterly Journal of Economics* 23 (1909): 296.

36. Stanley, *Dimensions of Law in the Service of Order*, 198-199.

37. Ibid., 180. Calculated from data collected for Table 5-1.

38. E. R. A. Seligman, *The Income Tax: A Study of the History, Theory, and Practice of Income Taxation at Home and Abroad* (New York: Macmillan, 1911).

39. William E. Borah, "The Income Tax Amendment," *North American Review* 191 (1910): 755, 763–764.

40. *Dimensions of Law in the Service of Order*, Table 5-5, 212.

41. 240 U.S. 1, at 18. Robert B. Highsaw, *Edward Douglass White, Defender of the Conservative Faith* (Baton Rouge: Louisiana State University Press, 1981).

In re Debs

David Ray Papke

In re Debs
158 U.S. 564 (1895)

DECIDED: May 27, 1895
VOTE

CONCURRING: 9 (Melville W. Fuller, Stephen J. Field, John Marshall Harlan, Horace Gray, David J. Brewer, Henry B. Brown, George Shiras Jr., Howell E. Jackson, Edward D. White)

DISSENTING: 0

OPINION OF THE COURT: Brewer

The litigation and appeals in this case grew out of a workers' strike against the Pullman Palace Car Company and a supportive boycott of Pullman cars by the American Railway Union. The strike began in May 1894 in Pullman, Illinois, a company town that had been developed by millionaire industrialist George Pullman. Workers walked off their jobs when the company reduced wages without reducing rents for company-owned housing and while continuing to pay dividends to shareholders. The union, led by former railroad worker Eugene V. Debs, refused to move any train that included Pullman cars. More generalized railroad worker discontent and confrontational actions by the General Managers' Association, a coalition of twenty-four railroads with terminals in Chicago, led to violence and brought railroad traffic to a halt in the western half of the country. Federal troops were sent to Chicago and elsewhere, and the government obtained an injunction ordering the union to cease hindering the railroads. When the strike and boycott continued, Debs and his fellow union officers were found in contempt of court and sentenced to prison. Debs's lawyers petitioned the Supreme Court for a writ of *habeas corpus*, arguing that he had been improperly imprisoned and should have his liberty restored.

Writing for a unanimous Supreme Court, Justice Brewer addressed what he took to be the two most important issues in the controversy. The first involved the federal government's authority to prevent obstructions of interstate commerce and the transmission of the mails. Brewer insisted that the federal government had this authority, which could be exercised through the enactment of legislation, through actions in the federal courts, and—if necessary—through the deployment of federal troops. The second issue concerned the power of a federal court acting through its equity jurisdiction—deciding with an eye to fairness rather than technical legal rules—to issue an injunction against a strike or boycott. Such a power not only exists, Brewer ruled, but it is also "more to the praise than the blame of the government, that, instead of determining for itself questions of right and wrong on the part of these petitioners and their associates and enforcing that determination by the club of its policemen and the bayonet of the soldier, it submitted all these questions to the peaceful determination of judicial trials." Because the court could issue the injunction, a violator of the injunction could be held in contempt, and, furthermore, the sentencing of that person to prison for contempt in a civil proceeding did not constitute a denial of the right to trial by jury.

The petition for a writ of *habeas corpus* having been denied and the powers of the federal court clarified, Brewer also proffered a few words on law and a respect for it. He took umbrage with a statement that the strikers and boycotters should be thought of as self-sacrificing heroes. "It is a lesson which cannot be learned too soon or too thoroughly under this government of and by the people," Brewer said, "that the means of redress of all wrongs are through the courts and at the ballot-box, and that no wrong, real or fancied, carries with it legal warrant to invite as a means of redress the cooperation of a mob, with its accompanying acts of violence."

With the use of federal troops, the issuance of the injunction, and the arrest of the union leaders, the strike and boycott ended long before the Supreme Court ruled, but the decision in *In re Debs* had significant ramifications for the participants in the case and for labor and capital under American law. Pullman, who believed his company town and his relations with the workers were progressive, was deplored by many as a reactionary. Debs served his term in prison and not long after his release announced he had become a Socialist. He ran five times as the presidential candidate of the Socialist Party of America, garnering 6 percent of the national vote in 1912. With the Supreme Court's stamp of approval, meanwhile, the labor injunction supplanted the conspiracy prosecution as the most important way to stop strikes and boycotts. Labor injunctions in the early decades of the twentieth century numbered in the thousands, and the federal courts in particular became the institution through which capital could seek to control rambunctious, discontented workers. Indeed, labor injunctions remained a powerful weapon for American business until precluded by the Norris-LaGuardia Act of 1932, and it is revealing that this change came not from the Supreme Court but rather from the legislative and executive branches of the federal government struggling to counter the Great Depression.

PRESS RESPONSES

The Pullman controversy affected Chicago more than any other city, and Chicago's half-dozen daily newspapers reported extensively on the strike and boycott. Debs called the *Chicago Tribune* "the intensest foe I have," and, not surprisingly, the newspaper's editorial page strongly endorsed the Supreme Court decision.

> This decision is more than the mere relegation of Debs to jail. . . . It is a notice to all Anarchists and other disturbers of the public peace that the hands of the General Government are not fettered when it is dealing with questions which are under its exclusive control. It is a notification that when inter-State commerce, for instance, is interfered with the government can go into one of its courts and get an injunction warning offenders to desist. . . .
>
> The result of this will be that whatever else may be interfered with there will be no more attempts except on the part of train robbers to stop the transportation of the mails or to tie up inter-State commerce. There will be no more insurrections like that of last July. No so-called "labor leaders" will endeavor to block the wheels of commerce in order to bring pressure to bear on some private corporation. For they will know that if they attempt it the national courts will enjoin them from violating the law; that if they defy the courts they will either be arrested by its officers or the armed forces of the National Government will be called out to suppress them.[1]

The *Inter Ocean* was another important Chicago newspaper. As the following editorial suggests, the *Tribune* was not alone in its hostility toward Debs.

> This simply is a judicial affirmation of the doctrine of the inviolable right of a majority. If a minority, whether of railway laborers or of railway owners, of bankers or of farmers, of merchants or of clerks, can lay violent hands upon interstate traffic then there is an end of those peaceful conditions under which alone trade and commerce can thrive. If a minority of 20,000 or of 1,000,000 can coerce a majority of 60,000,000, then by parity of reason, a minority of one or two, if well armed and muscular, can coerce a majority of seven or eight, and housebreaking and highway robbery become legitimate trades.
>
> The Debs movement was the most absurd as well as the most iniquitous that ever was devised by the unwit of man. Had it been legalised into a precedent no class would have

been doomed to such suffering as that which would have fallen upon the wage-earners. In its last analysis, the Debs plan was that of organized anarchy.[2]

An editorial from the *New York Times* suggests that the mainstream press outside Chicago also praised the Supreme Court decision.

> The Supreme Court has decided unanimously that the action of the inferior court by which Eugene V. Debs was sentenced to imprisonment was within the Constitution and legal. This is a very important decision in many ways. It is the first instance in which the Supreme Court has been called upon to consider, first, the full scope of the powers of Congress with reference to the vast transportation system of the country by virtue of its relations to the Postal Service and inter-State commerce, and, second, the procedure by injunction and sentence for contempt of court in disobeying an injunction.... Both questions are fully met and definitely determined by the Supreme Court. Considering the membership of the court as to parties and as to sectional distribution, the unanimous decision of the Justices is of the highest importance....
>
> At the time of the Debs conspiracy and practical insurrection in Chicago, we called attention explicitly to the very great scope of the powers then exercised and for the exercise of which there was no distinct precedent. We expressed the opinion that the action of the lower court and that of the Federal Executive would be sustained by the Supreme Court. We had not ventured to think that the decision of the Supreme Court would be at once so complete and unqualified and be unanimous. That it is so marks a radical change, not in the legal powers of the General Government, but in its exercise of those powers with absolute and undisputed authority. Henceforth whenever the General Government, acting under a Constitutional law, applies for and receives an order of a United States court to enjoin resistance to that law, the whole power of the Nation is made available to enforce that order.[3]

LAWYERS' REACTIONS

Three lawyers made oral arguments on each side in *In re Debs*. Stephen Gregory, Lyman Trumbull, and Clarence Darrow argued for Debs. Darrow had resigned a position with the Chicago & Northwestern Railroad and was beginning to refine the skills and develop the political beliefs that would make him the nation's leading defender of underdogs during the early decades of the twentieth century. He thought the decision would severely harm the labor movement and that it showed the political preferences of the Supreme Court.

> Labor organizations might just as well go out of existence altogether if this decision is to stand all along the line. To my mind it means an end to all labor organizations. The only appeal now left to President Debs and his associates is to the people. They have fought their case all through the courts of the land and have lost. The railroad men, however, and especially those who will have to go to jail, are not the only ones who will feel the effects of the decision. In future it may be made to fit the cases of others who may engage in a struggle for better pay or better conditions, and thus it will affect all trades. A week ago that august body the Supreme court, decided against the income tax. To-day it follows suit against Mr. Debs and his colleagues. Such action shows how the land lies, and is pretty plain notice to the people on which side the Supreme court stands.[4]

KING DEBS.

This cartoon by W. A. Rogers critically depicts American Railway Union president and Pullman strike leader Eugene V. Debs as a king with the power to halt rail traffic. When Debs disregarded a federal court injunction to cease hindering the railroads, he and fellow officers were found in contempt of court and sentenced to prison. The Supreme Court upheld his conviction in *In re Debs* (1895). —Library of Congress

Darrow continued to denigrate the decision thirty-seven years later in his autobiography. He also spoke of his great admiration for Debs.

> The Supreme Court took the matter under consideration and in due time decided against Mr. Debs. This opinion strengthened the arm of arbitrary power. It left the law so that, in cases involving strikes, at least, a man could be sent to prison for crime without a trial by jury. The opinion of the Supreme Court was unanimous. Justice Holmes and Justice Brandeis were not then members.
>
> So Eugene Debs was sent to jail in Woodstock, Ill., for trying to help his fellow man. He really got off easy. No other offense has ever been visited with such severe penalties as

seeking to help the oppressed. When the idealist has tried hard enough and labored long enough it is always easy to lodge a specific charge against him. . . .

Eugene V. Debs has always been one of my heroes. And as he must figure further in this story I may as well complete what I have to say of "Gene" whether in the natural sequence or not. There may have lived some time, some where, a kindlier, gentler, more generous man than Eugene V. Debs, but I have never known him. Nor have I ever read or heard of another. Mr. Debs at once became the head of the Socialist Party of America. I never followed him politically. I never could believe that man was so constructed as to make Socialism possible; but I watched him and his cause with great interest. He was not only all that I have said, but he was the bravest man I ever knew. He never felt fear. He had the courage of the babe who had no conception of the word or its meaning.[5]

The lawyers making oral arguments for the government were Richard Olney, the attorney general; Edward B. Whitney, an assistant attorney general; and Edwin Walker, a special assistant U.S. attorney. Walker had obtained the injunction and contempt citation in the Chicago federal courts, and Olney invited him to Washington, D.C., when Debs's attorneys appealed. Walker reduced the Court's decision to a simple thought:

All that was contended for by the government was the supremacy of the law. I care nothing for the disposition of the other cases. I am satisfied with the result secured.[6]

Olney argued before the Supreme Court only twice during his tenure as attorney general, and one of those times was in *Debs*. A prominent railroad lawyer from Boston, Olney received assurances from President Grover Cleveland that he could continue his private practice while serving as attorney general. He dropped a note to his secretary on the day the decision was handed down, sharing the news of the victory and immodestly crediting himself with the Court's reasoning: "Nothing new—except that the Supreme Court to-day decided Debs case in my favor on all points—in fact took my argument and turned it into an opinion."[7]

Judge William A. Woods presided in the federal trial court in Chicago that had issued the omnibus injunction against hindering, obstructing, or stopping railroad traffic. Woods also ruled that Debs and other officers were in contempt of court for violating the injunction and should therefore serve time in prison. He saw the Supreme Court decision as an endorsement of his work.

It is highly gratifying to me and should be to any judge to learn his opinion has met with the sanction of the Supreme Court. Especially in this instance do I feel more than the usual gratification. I believed that I was right in issuing the injunction last summer against the officers of the American Railway Union, and, being right in the law, I sought to punish the men for contempt following as a natural sequence. . . . I sought to review the law in an exhaustive opinion handing down the judgment of the court. I spent six weeks in the preparation of those 27,000 words, and cannot add to them. The only adverse comment I saw was in the organ of the American Railway Union, which somebody sent me. I have read Mr. Debs' speeches about the matter, and they have amused me somewhat.[8]

Two years later Judge Woods reflected again on the Supreme Court decision, this time in the pages of a prominent law review. He attempted to explain why the Supreme Court had relied on general equitable principles rather than the Sherman Antitrust Act, as he had done. He also defended his contempt citation, which the officers of the American Railway Union continued to criticize.

The opinion in the Circuit Court was designed to show that the jurisdiction exercised was justifiable both upon general equitable principles and by the Act of Congress of July 2, 1890, known as the Anti-Trust Law. For reasons stated the decision was based upon the statute, though if the hearing had been in a court of last resort the broad equity ground would have been preferred, as it was by the Supreme Court, though that court was careful to say that it must not be understood that they dissented from the conclusions of the Circuit Court in reference to the scope of the Act of Congress. . . . In the contempt case it was held, or, perhaps it would be more accurate to say, it was assumed, that the contracts, combinations and conspiracies which under the statute might be enjoined were such as would be deemed to be unlawful irrespective of the act; but by this decision the Supreme Court goes much further, holding that every contract, combination or conspiracy, which in fact is in restraint of interstate commerce, being expressly declared unlawful, is hereby brought within the scope of the act. The distinction manifestly is one of very great significance.

Nobody in his right mind believes that there has been usurpation of power by the courts, or that the power exercised is the source or beginning of peril to individual or collective rights. Out of all that has been done by the courts since the Government was founded there can be deduced no sound reason for depriving them of their accustomed and well-understood power to enforce respect and order in their presence, and to compel obedience to their writs and commands wherever lawfully sent.[9]

OFFICIALS' RESPONSE

President Cleveland also had reason to be pleased with the Supreme Court decision. He had not only sent federal troops to Chicago but also accepted Attorney General Olney's suggestion that the federal courts enjoin strike-related activities.

> On the twenty-seventh day of May, 1895, the court rendered its decision, upholding on the broadest grounds the proceedings of the Circuit Court and confirming its adjudication and the commitment to jail of the petitioners thereupon. . . . Thus the Supreme Court of the United States has written the closing words of this history, tragical in many of its details, and in every line provoking sober reflection. As we gratefully turn its concluding page, those who were most nearly related by executive responsibility to the troublous days whose story is told may well especially congratulate themselves on the part which fell to them in marking out the way and clearing the path, now unchangeably established, which shall hereafter guide our nation safely and surely in the exercise of the important functions which represent the people's trust.[10]

During the Pullman strike and boycott in 1894, Gov. John P. Altgeld, D-Ill., had ordered the state militia to quell rioting and clear the way for trains. Thinking that order had been restored, he was upset when President Cleveland sent federal troops into Chicago. Altgeld later criticized the Supreme Court decision sanctioning the injunction and contempt citation:

> The remanding of Debs to jail is in itself a matter of small consequence compared with the principle established, which is of transcendent importance. This decision marks a turning point in our history, for it establishes a new form of government never before heard of among men, that is government by injunction. Under this procedure a federal judge sitting in a rear room can on motion of some corporation lawyer issue a release which he calls an injunction forbidding anything he chooses to and which the law does

not forbid. . . . In other words he can legislate for himself, and having done so can then turn around and arrest and imprison as many people as he pleases; not for violating any law but on the mere pretext that they had disregarded his injunction, and, mark you, they are not tried by a jury according to the forms of law, but the same judge who issued the release and who claims that his dignity was offended himself tries the case. . . .

The provision of the Constitution "That no man shall be deprived of his liberty without a trial by an impartial jury" is practically wiped out by this decision of the United States Supreme Court and the theory that ours was exclusively a government of law is now at an end, for every community is now subject to obey any whim or caprice which any federal judge may promulgate. And if federal judges can do this then it will not be long until State judges will follow this example. The Constitution declares that our government has three departments, the legislative, judicial and executive, and that no one shall tread on the other, but under this new order of things a federal judge becomes at once a legislator, court and executioner.[11]

George Pullman maintained a low profile during the Supreme Court proceedings and after the decision. He survived two assassination attempts in fall 1895 and died of a massive heart attack two years later. The General Managers' Association had actively tried to undermine the boycott and supported the petition for an injunction in the Chicago courts. George R. Peck, chairman of the association's legal committee, wired Attorney General Olney on the day of the decision to offer his compliments: "I congratulate you with all my heart on the Debs Decision. The Supreme Court seems to agree with you that 'the soil of Illinois is the soil of the United States.' "[12]

DEBS'S RESPONSE

By the time of the Supreme Court decision, the strike and boycott had ended, and, as a labor leader, Debs had reason to worry about the future of his American Railway Union. He linked the decision with one the Court had handed down just the month before. In *Pollock v. Farmers' Loan & Trust Co.* (see page 59) the Court found the income tax unconstitutional. Debs concluded that corporate interests had come to dominate the Court. Of his case, he wrote:

It appears the case was not decided upon its merits, but that it was found that the Circuit Court having final jurisdiction, its act was not reviewable by the Supreme Court and therefore the writ was denied. . . . After the decision by that tribunal upon the income tax bill I am not at all surprised to see the decision of the lower court affirmed in our case. Both decisions are absolutely in the interest of the corporations, syndicates, and trusts which dominate every department of the Federal Government, including the Supreme Court.

Jefferson's prophecy is being literally fulfilled. The "sappers and miners," as he denominated them, are at work undermining the Federal fabric. . . . Every Federal Judge is now made a Czar. The decision of the Supreme Court has crowned them and given them autocratic sway. They can now issue any kind of injunction restraining any man from doing anything, and then deprive him of his liberty after simply going through the farce of a hearing before the same Judge issuing the injunction. Railroad corporations may now reduce wages and enforce any kind of condition upon their employes without fear of resistance. If employes see fit to quit they can be put in jail for exercising this prerogative. And this infamous outrage has now the judicial sanction of the Supreme Court of the United States. . . . I shall abide by the decision with perfect composure, confidently believing that it will hasten the day of the public ownership, not only of the railroads, but of all other public utilities. I view it as the death knell of the wage system. In the long run this decision will prove a blessing to the country.[13]

Debs served a sentence of six months for contempt of court in a prison in Woodstock, Illinois. Upon his release he returned to his home in Terre Haute, Indiana, and in a speech delivered there on November 23, 1895, his outrage with the Supreme Court remained evident. The whole federal court system, Debs was sure, was in the pocket of the corporations.

> And how does it happen and why does it happen that corporations are never restrained? Are they absolutely law-abiding? Are they always right? Do they never transgress the law or is it because the federal judges are their creatures? Certain it is that the united voice of labor in this country would be insufficient to name a federal judge. If all the common people united and asked for the appointment of a federal judge their voice would not be heeded any more than if it were the chirp of a cricket. Money talks. Yes, money talks. And I have no hesitancy in declaring that money has even invaded . . . the Supreme Court and left that august tribunal reeking with more stench than Coleridge discovered in Cologne and left all the people wondering how it was ever to be deodorized.
>
> There is something wrong in this country; the judicial nets are so adjusted as to catch the minnows and let the whales slip through and the federal judge is as far removed from the common people as if he inhabited another planet.[14]

In the decades following the *Debs* case and especially after the enactment of new federal laws during the Great Depression of the 1930s, pointed political positions and class analyses gradually disappeared from disputes between labor and capital. Labor focused its attention on limited goals such as job security, higher wages, and improved working conditions rather than public ownership of the railroads and assorted means of production. Capital, meanwhile, felt less need to police and control the working class and instead took itself to be simply one economic interest among many. Laws and legal institutions remained important in workers' relations with their employers, but their importance related to specific complaints and controversies. Unlike the days of the *Debs* case, few in the present hope or fear that a fundamental change in American capitalism is in the offing.

NOTES

1. "Debs Insurrection Unlawful," *Chicago Tribune,* May 28, 1895, 6.
2. "The End of the Debs Case," *Inter Ocean* (Chicago), May 28, 1895, 6.
3. "The Debs Decision," *New York Times,* May 28, 1895, 4.
4. Clarence Darrow, quoted in "Persons Interested in the Debs Case Discuss the Decisions," *Chicago Record,* May 28, 1895, 6.
5. Clarence Darrow, *The Story of My Life* (New York: Charles Scribner's Sons, 1932), 67–69.
6. Edwin Walker, quoted in "Debs to Go to Jail," *Chicago Tribune,* March 28, 1895, 3.
7. Richard Olney to his secretary, May 27, 1895, quoted in *Richard Olney: Evolution of a Statesman,* ed. Gerald G. Eggert (University Park: Penn State University Press, 1974), 168.
8. William A. Woods, quoted in "How the News Was Received," *Inter Ocean,* May 28, 1895, 7.
9. William A. Woods, "Injunction in the Federal Courts," *Yale Law Journal* 6 (April 1897): 245, 248–251.
10. Grover Cleveland, *Presidential Problems* (New York: The Century Company, 1904), 117.
11. John P. Altgeld, *Live Questions* (Chicago: published by the author, 1899), 450.
12. George R. Peck to Richard Olney, May 27, 1875, quoted in *Clarence Darrow: A Sentimental Rebel,* ed. Arthur and Lila Weinberg (New York: G. P. Putnam's Sons, 1980), 59.
13. Eugene V. Debs, quoted in "What Debs Has to Say About It," *Chicago Tribune,* May 28, 1895, 3.
14. "The Role of the Courts," in Jean Y. Tussey, ed., *Eugene V. Debs Speaks* (New York: Pathfinder Press, 1970), 52.

Plessy v. Ferguson

Ellen Holmes Pearson

Plessy v. Ferguson
163 U.S. 537 (1896)

DECIDED: May 18, 1896
VOTE

CONCURRING: 7 (Melville W. Fuller, Stephen J. Field, Horace Gray, Henry B. Brown, George Shiras Jr., Edward D. White, Rufus W. Peckham)
DISSENTING: 1 (John Marshall Harlan)
OPINION OF THE COURT: Brown
DISSENTING OPINION: Harlan
DID NOT PARTICIPATE: Brewer

In 1890 Louisiana's legislature passed the Separate Car Law, which mandated the segregation of passenger trains traveling within the state of Louisiana. The law prohibited passengers, whether black or white, from occupying rail cars that were not assigned to their race. On June 7, 1892, a New Orleans shoemaker named Homer Plessy, who was one-eighth black, refused to move to the car reserved for blacks. Plessy was forcibly dragged from an East Louisiana Railroad train and charged with violating the "Jim Crow"—named after a black character in minstrel shows—car law. Judge John H. Ferguson of the New Orleans Parish Criminal District Court convicted Plessy of violating the law. Plessy appealed to the Louisiana Supreme Court, which upheld the legislation requiring "separate but equal accommodations." Plessy appealed to the Supreme Court, arguing that the Louisiana Separate Car Law violated the Thirteenth and Fourteenth Amendments of the U.S. Constitution.

On May 18, 1896, the Supreme Court upheld the Louisiana law by a 7 to 1 vote. Justice Brown delivered the majority opinion in *Plessy v. Ferguson*. Brown agreed that the purpose of the Fourteenth Amendment was to "enforce the absolute equality of the two races before the law," but it was not intended to "abolish distinctions based on color, or to enforce social, as distinguished from political equality, or a commingling of the two races upon terms unsatisfactory to the either." He insisted that separate facilities did not mean unequal facilities, and that, although the Fourteenth Amendment mandated legal equality, it did not legislate social equality. Therefore, if the two races should meet on terms of social equality, "it must be the result of voluntary consent of the individuals." Justice Harlan was the Court's lone dissenter. He wrote that the Louisiana law was "inconsistent with the personal liberty of citizens, white and black, in that state and hostile to both the spirit and letter of the Constitution of the United States." Harlan asserted, in a now-famous phrase, that the "Constitution is colorblind, and neither knows nor tolerates classes among citizens."

While the case was in Louisiana courts, Plessy and his crusade received considerable local publicity. The New Orleans *Times-Democrat* published an editorial lauding Judge Ferguson's decision to uphold the Separate Car Law in November 1892. The newspaper editors approved of the law as a

> move in the right direction, framed in the interest of the traveling public and intended to show the Negroes that while they lived side by side with the whites the line of distinction and separation between the races was to be forever kept up. . . . What [Judge Ferguson] says will have some effect on the silly Negroes who are trying to fight this law. The sooner they drop their so-called "crusade" against "the Jim Crow Car," and stop wasting their money in combating so well-established a principle—the right to separate the races in cars and elsewhere—the better for them.[1]

With the *Plessy v. Ferguson* decision, the Supreme Court opened a constitutional door for separating the races with more Jim Crow laws. The state legislatures did not, however, react with an immediate avalanche of statutes. In fact, many measures were not passed until several years later. Many states in the South had separate car laws on the books before *Plessy;* after the decision, South Carolina passed a similar law in 1898, North Carolina in 1899, and Virginia, Maryland, and Oklahoma followed in the early 1900s. By 1910, emboldened southern legislatures had passed laws segregating other public places, such as streetcars, public waiting rooms, restaurants, boardinghouses, theaters, water fountains, and public parks. Although the Supreme Court implied that facilities for whites and blacks had to be equal in quality, the separate schools, hospitals, and other public institutions designated for blacks were generally inferior. Jim Crow laws remained an accepted part of southern society until 1954, when the Supreme Court's decision in *Brown v. Board of Education* (see page 197) declared that racial segregation of facilities was unconstitutional.

The laws the Court sanctioned with the *Plessy* decision erased much of the progress black Americans had made since emancipation. It is curious, then, how little attention the mainstream press paid to the decision in 1896. Some publications registered opinions in favor of or opposing the decision, and the most prominent black social and literary figures contributed commentary. But, compared to many other landmark cases, *Plessy v. Ferguson* scarcely caused a ripple in newspapers or law journals. The most common response was a brief review of the decision; many took no notice at all. The *New York Times,* for example, placed the story on page three, in its weekly column on railway news.

The lack of attention from members of the national press should not be surprising. The Court's decision in *Plessy v. Ferguson* reflected prevailing ideas about race and racial intermixing. In the late nineteenth century, racial segregation was supported with a range of social, religious, and scientific arguments. In August 1896 Frederick L. Hoffman, a statistician for Prudential Insurance, published a statistical study of American blacks' behavior. The work appeared a few months after *Plessy* was announced. Although Hoffman did not mention the Supreme Court case in his study, the work illustrates the kinds of social and scientific data on which whites relied to support their efforts to segregate blacks. Based on his statistical analysis of religion, education, criminality, and illegitimate births among blacks, Hoffman concluded that the "charitable and philanthropic" involvement of the white race was not helping blacks to achieve equality in American society; in fact, whites' efforts to improve the black race seemed to be hurting blacks' progress. He predicted the demise of the Negro race because of its dilution with white blood. Hoffman believed that blacks, as a race, could be saved only if they changed their moral character and were segregated from whites:

> I have given the statistics of the general progress of the race in religion and education for the country at large, and have shown that in church and school the number of attending members or pupils is constantly increasing; but in the statistics of crime and the data of illegitimacy the proof is furnished that neither religion nor education has influenced to an appreciable degree the moral progress of *the race.* Whatever benefit the individual colored man may have gained from the extension of religious worship and educational process, *the race* as a whole has gone backwards rather than forwards. . . .
>
> . . . The downward tendencies of the colored race, therefore, can only be arrested by radical and far-reaching changes in their moral nature. Instead of clamoring for aid and assistance from the white race the Negro himself should sternly refuse every offer of direct interference in his own evolution. The more difficult his upward struggle, the more enduring will be the qualities developed. Most of all there must be a more general recognition of the institution of monogamic marriage and unqualified reprobation of those who violate the law of sexual morality. Intercourse with the white race must absolutely cease and race purity must be insisted upon in marriage as well as outside of it. Together with a higher morality will come a greater degree of economic efficiency,

and the predominating trait of the white race, the virtue of thrift, will follow as a natural consequence of the mastery by the colored race of its own conditions of life. The compensation of such an independent struggle will be a race of people who will gain a place among civilized mankind and will increase and multiply instead of dying out with loathsome diseases.[2]

REACTIONS IN THE PRESS AND LAW JOURNALS

Although direct reaction to *Plessy v. Ferguson* was limited, some publications did express opinions on the outcome. The newspapers were the first medium to react. Southern newspapers welcomed the decision. The New Orleans *Daily Picayune* lauded the decision, claiming that because similar laws existed in most southern states, the separation of cars would be enforced for long stretches throughout the South.

> Equality of rights does not mean community of rights. The laws must recognize and uphold this distinction; otherwise, if all the rights were common as well as equal, there would be practically no such thing as private property, private life, or social distinctions, but all would belong to everybody who might choose to use it.
>
> This would be absolute socialism, in which the individual would be extinguished in the vast mass of human beings, a condition repugnant to every principle of enlightened democracy.[3]

Likewise, the editors of the Richmond, Virginia, *Dispatch* wrote that the separation would provide a social buffer between whites and ill-behaved blacks.

> Some colored people make themselves so disagreeable on the cars that their conduct leads white men to ponder the question whether such a law as that of Louisiana is not needed in all the Southern States.[4]

Some northern media, particularly Republican newspapers, condemned the Supreme Court's decision. The black and Roman Catholic presses reacted with anger and expressed fears that the Court's sanction of segregation would not stop with laws segregating public transportation, nor would legal limitations be imposed on blacks alone. The Rochester *Democrat and Chronicle* praised Justice Harlan for his dissent and condemned the majority's opinion:

> Justice Harlan's vigorous dissent denouncing these laws as mischievous comes very much nearer the sentiment of the American people upon that question than the decision of the majority does. Justice Harlan says with entire truth that it would be just as reasonable for the states to pass laws requiring separate cars for Protestants and Catholics or for descendants of those of the Teutonic race and those of the Latin race.
>
> The announcement of this decision will be received by thoughtful and fair-minded people with disapproval and regret. It is not in harmony with the principles of this republic or with the spirit of our time. It is a concession to one of the lowest and meanest prejudices to which the human mind is liable, the prejudice which draws a line between citizens and discriminates against people of a specified race and color. It puts the official stamp of the highest court in the country upon the miserable doctrine that several millions of American citizens are of an inferior race and unfit to mingle with citizens of other races.
>
> The certain consequence of this decision will be to encourage Southern legislatures in passing other laws detrimental to the interests of the colored people of those states.[5]

The *A.M.E. Church Review* reminded readers of the equality of all people before God:

Briefly stated, the Court virtually takes the position that any law not involving the rights of the Negro to sit upon juries and to vote, is constitutional, on the ground that race conflicts will arise, if the prejudices of large numbers of the white race are thwarted.

Justice Harlan takes the ground that the intent and purpose of the constitution was to wipe out all official knowledge of race among citizens, by both State and nation, and that greater evils are in store by validating laws made in hate than can result from standing upon the broad grounds of right and humanity.

Which is the right position? Let the great American people answer as it answered once before when plausible sophistry had well-nigh obscured the plain teachings of Him who inspired the saying, "God is no respecter of persons;" "Of one blood hath God created all the nations of the earth;" for in Christ Jesus there is neither Jew nor Greek, bond nor free, Scythian nor Barbarian.[6]

An editor in southeast Kansas was outraged at the Court's behavior.

When such an august body stoops so low, then it is time to put an end to the existence of infernal, infamous bodies. If such an act as the Louisiana "Jim Crow" car law can be declared constitutional then it is time to make null and void all that tail end of the constitution; for it is certain that under such circumstances it is of no earthly use.[7]

Donahoe's Magazine pointed to a persistent American problem.

Events are shaping themselves strangely in this free land of late. With legislation against the Negro backed up by the highest tribunal in the country (just as if the *Dred Scott* decision had not passed into lasting infamy, and as if there had been no Civil War); with Congress passing restrictive immigration laws directed perceptibly and unfairly against special European nationalities; with religious prejudice organized into a conspiracy against the expressed pledges of the Constitution to American citizens, the United States presents to the world a sad spectacle of inconsistency and contradiction—a spectacle which reflects most significantly upon our boasted human freedom and brotherhood. Selfishness—individual, class, sectional and racial selfishness—is the great curse and danger of the American republic to-day.[8]

NEGRO EXPULSION FROM RAILWAY CAR, PHILADELPHIA.

This 1856 wood engraving depicts a black man being expelled from a railway car. Black community leaders in Louisiana mounted a constitutional challenge to racial segregation in *Plessy v. Ferguson* (1896), but the Court found "separate but equal" facilities for whites and blacks to be constitutional under the Thirteenth and Fourteenth Amendments. —Library of Congress

Most law journals, like most mainstream newspapers, took little note of *Plessy.* Law reviews at Yale and Harvard, for example, did not even mention the case. A few, such as the *Michigan Law Journal,* printed a paragraph that summarized the Supreme Court findings without editorial comment. A handful of law reviews, however, registered an opinion for or against the decision along with their summaries. The *American Law Review,* for example, predicted that one day Justice Harlan's view would prevail:

> In *Plessy v. Ferguson* the question before the Supreme Court of the United States was whether one of those statutes which have been generally enacted throughout the Southern States since the Supreme Court of the United States declared the Civil Rights Law unconstitutional, providing separate railway coaches for colored persons, and requiring the company to transport them in such coaches separately from white persons, was in contravention of the Thirteenth or the Fourteenth Amendment to the constitution of the United States. The court, affirming the Supreme Court of Louisiana, held that no such constitutional right was violated, although the person complaining was a citizen of the United States of mixed descent, seven-eighths Caucasian and one-eighth African blood, and although the mixture of colored blood was not discernible in him. The opinion of the court was written by Mr. Justice Brown, and he clearly shows that the conclusion of the court is in accordance with the analogies of other decisions both in the Federal and in the State tribunals. Mr. Justice Harlan delivered a strong dissenting opinion, which, whatever may be thought of it now, will do him honor in the estimation of future generations, who will study with curiosity these statutes, which will have become dead letters.[9]

The *Virginia Law Register* hailed the decision as following natural law:

> A like separation exists in churches, schools, theatres, hotels, etc. It will continue until the leopard changes his spots and the Ethiopian his skin. Nature has ordained it, and it is in vain that human legislation attempts to contravene the ordinance.[10]

REACTIONS FROM AFRICAN AMERICANS

Other reactions to *Plessy v. Ferguson* came from prominent members of the black community in the United States, who expressed emotions ranging from disappointment to outrage. Booker T. Washington, who was born a slave and rose to prominence as an educator, advocated a controversial strategy of accommodation for blacks to reach political and social equality. Although many blacks rejected his cautious approach, he was praised by white leaders. Washington reacted to the *Plessy* decision with disappointment:

> This separation may be good law, but it is not good common sense. The difference in the color of the skin is a matter for which nature is responsible. If the Supreme Court can say that it is lawful to compel all persons with black skins to ride in one car, and all with white skins to ride in another, why may it not say that it is lawful to put all yellow people in one car and all white people, whose skin is sun burnt, in another car. Nature has given both their color; or why cannot the courts go further and decide that all men with bald heads must ride in one car and all with red hair still in another. Nature is responsible for all these conditions.
>
> But the colored people do not complain so much of the separation, as of the fact that the accommodations, with almost no exceptions, are not equal, still the same price is charged the colored passengers as is charged the white people.
>
> . . . such an unjust law injures the white man, and inconveniences the negro. No race can wrong another race simply because it has the power to do so, without being ·

permanently injured in morals, and its ideas of justice. The Negro can endure the temporary inconvenience, but the injury to the white man is permanent. It is the one who inflicts the wrong that is hurt, rather than the one on whom the wrong is inflicted. It is for the white man to save himself from this degradation that I plead.

If a white man steals a negro's ballot, it is the white man who is permanently injured. Physical death comes to the Negro lynched—death of the morals—death of the soul—comes to the white man who perpetrates the lynching.[11]

Black scholar W. E. B. Du Bois was just beginning his academic career when the Supreme Court handed down *Plessy v. Ferguson*. Du Bois, the first African American to receive a Ph.D. from Harvard University, was a brilliant scholar, trained in history and the social sciences. He was the first black scholar whose work was widely published by universities, departments of the federal government, and influential national periodicals.

Despite his prominence in academic and political circles, Du Bois sometimes faced discrimination in his career and in his travels. In 1900, as a young professor of economics and history at Atlanta University, Du Bois instituted proceedings against a railroad. His case, *W. E. B. Du Bois v. Southern Railway Company*, was indefinitely postponed by the Interstate Commerce Commission in November 1905. In a letter written in March 1900, Du Bois explained the incident to a rail company official:

> On the evening of the 19th of February last I had occasion to go from Atlanta to Savannah on business for the Commissioners of the Paris Exposition. I boarded the Brunswick sleeper of the Cincinnati-Jacksonville train, leaving Atlanta at 10:45 P.M. On this train the sleeping car conductor, Mr. E. Davidson, declared that he could not furnish me a berth until the train conductor came through. The train conductor, Mr. J. A. Eikson (?), said that under orders issued by the Southern Railway, he could not give me a berth, as I was a Negro. I thereupon demanded separately both the Pullman conductor and the train Conductor to give me a berth and they both refused in the presence of W. B. Arwood, flagman of the train, and Booker Taylor, the porter of the car. There was plenty of room in the car—only four or five berths being made up, and I doubt if all of those were occupied. I thereupon left the car and was compelled to sit up all night—a matter which interfered with both my health and work, as I was then under the physician's care.[12]

Some of the more creative responses came from Charles W. Chesnutt, a prominent African American novelist who gained fame and garnered criticism by writing about some of society's most controversial issues, such as miscegenation and segregation. Chesnutt, like Homer Plessy, was light-skinned enough to "pass" for white, but he refused to do so. He illustrated blacks' reactions to separate car legislation, the *Plessy* decision, and the separate but equal doctrine in a variety of media. Chesnutt included stories of blacks' experiences on the "colored" cars in several different works. In an editorial published in the *Boston Evening Transcript*, he recounted his conversation with a Virginia conductor:

> "How long," I asked a Virginia conductor, "has this Jim Crow car system been in operation?"
>
> "Since 1st July," he answered.
>
> "Does it work alright?"
>
> "Oh yes."
>
> "Do the colored people object to it?"
>
> "No they don't mind it. Some of them kicked a little at first—a nigger likes to show off, you know, put on a little airs; but I told 'em it was the law, and they would have to

submit, as I had to. Personally I don't mean to take any chances: I've been hauled up in court once, or threatened with it, for not enforcing the law. I'd put a white man out of the colored car as quick as I'd put a nigger out of this one."

"Do you ever," I asked, "have any difficulty about classifying people who are very near the line?"

"Oh yes, often."

"What do you do in a case of that kind?"

"I give the passenger the benefit of the doubt."

"That is, you treat him as a white man?"

"Certainly."

"But suppose you should find in the colored car a man who had a white face, but insisted that his descent entitled him to ride in that car: what would you do then?"

"I'd let him stay there," replied the conductor, with unconcealed disgust, which seemed almost to include the questioner who could suppose such a case. "Anyone that is fool enough to rather be a nigger than a white man may have his choice. He could stay there till h-ll froze over for all I'd care." [13]

Chesnutt's reflections on the emotional impact of segregation were also incorporated into his fiction, including *The Marrow of Tradition,* published in 1901. The novel's protagonist, a black doctor named Miller, is forced to relocate to the colored car of a train traveling from Philadelphia into the South. Chesnutt's description of the incident illustrates the constant reminders of social isolation that the separate car laws engendered:

> The car was conspicuously labeled at either end with large cards, similar to those in the other car, except that they bore the word "Colored" in black letters upon a white background. The author of this piece of legislation had contrived, with an ingenuity worthy of a better cause, that not merely should the passengers be separated by the color line, but that the reason for this division should be kept constantly in mind. Lest a white man should forget that he was white—not a very likely contingency—these cards would keep him constantly admonished of the fact; should a colored person endeavor, for a moment, to lose sight of his disability, these staring signs would remind him continually that between him and the rest of mankind not of his own color, there was by law a great gulf fixed. [14]

Chesnutt described his reaction to the *Plessy* decision again in a speech, "The Courts and the Negro," originally written in 1908. In this speech, he traced the history of Supreme Court decisions with regard to blacks' rights in the United States, through a few landmark decisions. He characterized the *Plessy* decision as an act of violence, in which "the court stabbed in the back, and to death," the Fourteenth Amendment's

> ideal presentment of rights . . . and threw its bleeding corpse to the Negro, —the comprehensive Negro, black, brown, yellow and white—the plaintiff in that case, which involved the separate car law of Louisiana, was seven-eighths white and showed no sign of the darker blood. . . .
>
> . . . We are taught, and properly taught, to hold our courts in high respect. As a rule this is not difficult. But courts are made up of human beings. Under wigs and gowns and titles and deferential formulas, judges are simply men, and subject, as other men, to every human frailty. . . .
>
> . . . The [*Plessy*] opinion is a clear and definite approval of the recognition by State laws, of color distinctions, something which had theretofore been avoided in civil rights

cases. It establishes racial caste in the United States as firmly as though it were established by act of Congress. To the opinion Mr. Justice Harlan dissented with his usual vigor, and Justice Brewer did not hear the argument or participate in the decision.

... When it was suggested in the argument that to sustain such discriminating laws might justify separate cars for people with red hair or aliens, or require people to walk on different sides of the street, or require colored men's houses to be in separate blocks, the Court in the opinion said that such regulations must be reasonable. And the Court held: "In determining the question of reasonableness, it is at liberty to act with reference to the usages, customs and traditions of the people, with a view to the promotion of their comfort and the preservation of the public peace and good order."[15]

JUSTICE BROWN'S REFLECTIONS ON *PLESSY*

More than a decade after the Supreme Court's decision, retired justice Brown, one of the men whom Chesnutt accused of "murdering" the Fourteenth Amendment, expressed doubt about the majority opinion. In 1912 Brown published an article in the *American Law Review* about the dissenting opinions of Justice Harlan, who had died in October 1911. In his comments on Harlan's dissents in the *Civil Rights Cases* (1883) and *Plessy v. Ferguson,* Brown described his former colleague's belief that the Thirteenth and Fourteenth Amendments served to protect the rights of whites and blacks equally.

[T]here is still a lingering doubt whether ... the Constitution was not intended to secure the equality of the two races in all places affected with a public interest. It is somewhat remarkable that the only dissent emanated from the only Southern member of the Bench, all the others having been born in or appointed from the North.

[With regard to *Plessy v. Ferguson,*] Mr. Justice Harlan dissented upon the ground that the legislation was inconsistent, not only with the equality of rights that pertain to citizenship, but with the personal liberty enjoyed by everyone within the United States. He thought that the arbitrary separation of citizens on the basis of race, while they are on a public highway, was a badge of servitude wholly inconsistent with the civil freedom and equality before the law established by the Constitution, and could not be justified upon any legal grounds. He assumed what is probably the fact, that the statute had its origin in the purpose, not so much to exclude white persons from railroad cars occupied by blacks, as to exclude colored people from coaches occupied or assigned to white persons.[16]

NOTES

1. "The Separate Car Law," (New Orleans) *Times Democrat,* November 19, 1892.
2. Frederick L. Hoffman, F.S.S., *Race Traits and Tendencies of the American Negro* (New York: Published for the American Economic Association by the MacMillan Company, 1896), 310, 328.
3. "Equality, but not Socialism," (New Orleans) *Daily Picayune,* May 19, 1896.
4. "Separate Coaches," (Richmond) *Dispatch,* May 21, 1896.
5. "A Strange Decision," (Rochester, N.Y.) *Democrat and Chronicle,* May 20, 1896.
6. "Plausible Sophistry," *A.M.E. Church Review* 13 (1896), 156–162.
7. "A Damnable Outrage," (Parsons, Kansas) *Weekly Blade,* May 30, 1896.
8. "A Sad Spectacle," *Donahoe's Magazine* 36 (1896), 100–101.
9. *American Law Review* 30 (1896): 784–786.
10. *Virginia Law Register* 2 (1896): 347.
11. Booker T. Washington, "Who is Permanently Hurt?" *Our Day* 16 (June 1896), 311, in *The Booker T. Washington Papers,* 14 vols. 1895–1898, ed. Louis R. Harlan (Urbana, New York, and London: University of Illinois Press, 1975), 4:186–187.

12. W. E. B. Du Bois to Mr. S. H. Hardwick, March 15, 1900, in *The Correspondence of W. E. B. Du Bois,* vol. I, 1877–1934, ed. Herbert Aptheker (Boston: University of Massachusetts Press, 1973), 45–46.

13. Charles W. Chesnutt, "The White and the Black," in the *Boston Evening Transcript,* March 20, 1901, collected in *Essays and Speeches,* ed. Joseph R. McElrath, Robert C. Leitz, and Jesse S. Crisler (Stanford: Stanford University Press, 1999), 140–141.

14. Charles W. Chesnutt, *The Marrow of Tradition* (New York: Arno Press and the New York Times, 1969), 56.

15. Charles W. Chesnutt, "The Courts and the Negro," speech delivered c. 1908, collected in *Essays and Speeches,* 263, 266.

16. Henry Billings Brown, "Dissenting Opinions of Mr. Justice Harlan," *American Law Review* 46 (1912): 336, 338.

Insular Cases

Bartholomew H. Sparrow

DeLima v. Bidwell
182 U.S. 1 (1901)

> DECIDED: May 27, 1901
> VOTE
> > CONCURRING: 5 (Melville W. Fuller, John Marshall Harlan, David J. Brewer, Henry B. Brown, Rufus W. Peckham)
> > DISSENTING: 4 (Horace Gray, George Shiras Jr., Edward D. White, Joseph McKenna)
>
> OPINION OF THE COURT: Brown
> DISSENTING OPINION: McKenna (Shiras, White)
> DISSENTING OPINION: Gray

Downes v. Bidwell
182 U.S. 244 (1901)

> DECIDED: May 27, 1901
> VOTE
> > CONCURRING: 5 (Horace Gray, Henry B. Brown, George Shiras Jr., Edward D. White, Joseph McKenna)
> > DISSENTING: 4 (Melville W. Fuller, John Marshall Harlan, David J. Brewer, Rufus W. Peckham)
>
> OPINION OF THE COURT: Brown
> CONCURRING OPINION: White (Shiras, McKenna)
> CONCURRING OPINION: Gray
> DISSENTING OPINION: Fuller (Harlan, Brewer, Peckham)
> DISSENTING OPINION: Harlan

Opinions differ as to which decisions constitute the Insular Cases, but central to any list are *DeLima v. Bidwell* and *Downes v. Bidwell* (1901). Still important and included by most writers are *Dooley v. United States* (1901), *Fourteen Diamond Rings v. United States* (1901), *Hawaii v. Mankichi* (1903), *Dorr v. United States* (1904), *Rassmussen v. United States* (1905), and *Balzac v. Porto Rico* (1922).[1] Together, these decisions illuminated the Supreme Court's thinking at the turn of the twentieth century on the reach of constitutional protection to the inhabitants of U.S. territories overseas, in particular, Puerto Rico, the Philippines, and Hawaii.

In the Insular Cases, the Court established a new category of areas coming under the sovereignty of the United States. Added to the member states of the Union and the existing territories (and states to be) was territory "belonging to" the United States, but not a part of it. In his concurring opinion in *Downes v. Bidwell,* Justice White proposed the doctrine that territories were of two types. The first are "incorporated" territories or those fit to be states, and the second are "unincorporated" territories, which are the property of the United States. Congress could govern these latter territories as it wished, subject to "fundamental" protections under the Constitution, those protecting individual liberties rather than those granting political participation. A handful of the Insular Cases provoked the lion's share of popular and scholarly reaction.

In *DeLima v. Bidwell* the Supreme Court held that Puerto Rico was part of the United States for the purpose of the uniformity clause (Article I, section 8, clause 1) of the Constitution. The military, under orders from the White House, could not collect duties on imports from Puerto Rico because Puerto Rico had been annexed to the United States according to the terms of the 1899 peace treaty with Spain. In *Downes v. Bidwell*, however, which was decided the same day, the Court found that Congress could tax trade between Puerto Rico and the states. Puerto Rico was therefore *not* a part of the United States for tariff purposes—contrary to the uniformity clause. Chief Justice Fuller and Justice Harlan dissented vigorously on the grounds that once new territory was part of the United States, the Constitution applied in full.

Two cases were named *Dooley v. United States;* in the second one, decided in December 1901, a majority of the Court held that Congress could tax goods shipped from the states to Puerto Rico. Neither the uniformity clause nor the Constitution's prohibition of taxes on exports applied, once Congress acted under its authority under the territory clause ("Congress shall have Power to dispose of and make all needful Rules and Regulations respecting the Territory or other Property belonging to the United States," Article IV, section 3, clause 2). And in *Fourteen Diamond Rings* the Court ruled that Congress could not tax trade between the Philippines and the states because the Philippines were also annexed by the terms of the 1899 Treaty of Paris. All four cases of 1901 were five-to-four decisions.

In *Hawaii v. Mankichi,* the Court ruled that Hawaiian residents were not entitled to jury trial, even though the Newlands Resolution had annexed Hawaii shortly after hostilities had ended with Spain. And in *Dorr v. United States* the Court ruled Philippine residents, too, could be denied jury trial, despite the annexation and the fact that, as of July 1, 1902, the islands had an organized government. The Philippines were still "unincorporated." Alaska, however, *was* incorporated, despite Alaska's absence of a territorial government and minimal population (*Rassmussen v. United States*). Finally, the Supreme Court ruled unanimously in *Balzac v. Porto Rico* that Puerto Ricans, although they became U.S. citizens under the 1917 Jones Act and had a fully organized territorial government, were not guaranteed jury trial.

The U.S. government's plenary power over its territories had always been implicit by virtue of its authority to hold them as territories and to delay indefinitely their admission as states, to dispose of the land within the territories, and to set territorial boundaries. With the Insular Cases and with the U.S. acquisition of Puerto Rico, the Philippines, and Guam after the Spanish-American War—each densely populated by nonwhite inhabitants—the Court made Congress's power explicit. The U.S. Constitution did not operate *ex proprio vigore*—that is, by its own force.

REACTION IN THE PRESS

The Supreme Court's decisions of May 27, 1901, attracted the public's attention.

> The Court reached its decisions "after one of the most spirited discussions ever held within the sacred circle of the Supreme Court bench," the Associated Press reported.[2]

Many gathered to hear the rulings in the Court's small chamber in the Capitol.

> No such crowd either as to numbers or distinguished personnel has been seen in the Supreme Court room as that assembled there today. The hour for the Court to meet is noon, but long before that time arrived the little elliptical chamber was jammed with spectators representing every phase of life at the national capital, and long lines of eager people stretched in both directions from the doors down the gloomy corridors of the great Capitol Building. The colored bailiffs at the door had all they could do to hold the anxious throng on the outside in check, and thus protect the solemn dignity of the august tribunal from being rudely shocked. The bare rumor that the court would render its decision in the insular test suits was sufficient to create an interest among all sorts and conditions of people in Washington that sent them to the Capitol in a frenzy of excitement. They realized that no such momentous issues affecting the growth and progress of the nation are as likely again to come before the tribunal of last resort for arbitrament and every man who was fortunate enough to gain access to the chamber during the

delivery of the opinions appreciated that he was witnessing one of the most tremendous events in the nation's life.[3]

And once the Supreme Court announced its decisions, "Nothing else was talked of at the national capital to-day but the triumph of the government."[4]

OFFICIALS' REACTIONS

The "President and the Cabinet officers were elated over their victory, as though they have never doubted that the decision would be in favor of the government."[5] As former attorney general John Griggs, who had argued the cases for the government, stated, "It was a complete victory for the government, . . . I cannot think of any case ever before the Supreme Court involving larger interests than these cases, and in the larger sense, the government gained a complete victory." And as Solicitor General John Richards noted, "They sustain to the fullest extent, the so-called insular policy of the administration. The government now has the sanction of the Supreme Court for governing these islands as their needs require."[6]

Sen. Joseph Foraker, R-Ohio, the author of the legislation, explained:

> What the Court decided was that while we were occupying Porto Rico, prior to the ratification of the treaty of peace, it was foreign territory, and our occupation and government were military, and all that was done in the nature of a military necessity and valid on that account; that from and after the ratification of the treaty of peace it was no longer foreign, but domestic territory, within the meaning of our tariff laws, according to which tariff duties can be collected only on importations from foreign countries, and that, consequently, the duties collected on imports from Porto Rico after the ratification of the treaty of peace and prior to April 12, 1900, when Congress first legislated, were illegally collected, however, not because Congress was without constitutional power to impose such duties on importations from Porto Rico, but because during that period Congress had not so legislated. . . .
>
> The third proposition decided by the Court, and the one of supreme importance, was that Porto Rico, being a territory of the United States, is not a part of the United States, but only a territory belonging to the United States, and that it is therefore within the constitutional power of Congress to so legislate with respect to it, including the imposition of tariff duties, as it may see fit, and that Congress having so legislated on April 12, 1900, the provisions of that law are valid and to be upheld and enforced. In other words, the effect of the decision is that the constitution does not follow the flag and that Congress has plenary power under the constitution to govern our insular acquisitions according to their respective necessities. . . .
>
> The decision is a complete vindication of the position held by the Republican party with respect to the power of Congress to legislate for Porto Rico and the Philippines, and settles once and for all that the United States is the equal in sovereign power of any other independent government.[7]

In the House of Representatives, Charles Grosvenor, R-Ohio, "the recognized spokesman of the administration" as the *New York Tribune* described him, stated that "the insular test cases sustained all of the contentions and arguments of the Republican members of the House and Senate concerning all questions that were discussed and voted upon in Congress. Now there is nothing to do but to go ahead and legislate."[8] Joseph Cannon, R-Ill., chairman of the Committee on Appropriations, remarked: "It appears to me that the court did just the proper thing. If Congress has not the right to legislate for the territory acquired by the United States, then the United States has no right to acquire the territory."[9]

The architect of the insular policy, Secretary of War Elihu Root, agreed: "Unquestionably, the decision of the court sustains the contentions, theories and the policy adopted by the administration in conducting the affairs of the Spanish islands since the ratification of the Paris Treaty. The upholding of the Foraker act signifies that Congress had the power to legislate without being limited by the provisional contingencies of the constitution."[10]

THE QUESTION OF IMPERIALISM

William Randolph Hearst's *San Francisco Examiner,* however, saw the decisions as restrictive of presidential power, preventing "a President assuming the powers of a dictator":

> In ordering the return of the duties collected on Porto Rican products before the passage of the Foraker act, the court reduced the President once and for all to his proper position as the head of a republic government by written laws. By putting Porto Rico and the Philippines on the same footing with other territories, the decision deprived the Porto Ricans and the Filipinos of the feeling that they were discriminated against and treated as inferior races. At the same time, by conceding to Congress large discretionary powers in dealing with the territories, subject to the constitutional guarantees of civil liberty, the court made it possible to legislate for each new territory in accordance with its special needs, and so smoothed the way for expansion. . . .
>
> "EXPANSION WITHOUT IMPERIALISM has been the policy and the practice of the United States since the original thirteen states first set up housekeeping for themselves. . . . We must make our acquired territories what we have made of our acquired territories heretofore. We have met our race problems previously and some have proved difficult of solution, but not beyond the skill of the American mind to conquer. What we must avoid is ANY ATTEMPT AT IMPERIALISM. We want NO FOREIGN COLONIES to be plundered by a President's favorite; to be ruled by a statesman's incompetent sons. We want our new possessions to be TAUGHT TO GOVERN THEMSELVES. This is a continuation of the American policy which has won its way from Manhattan to the Klondike."

That was printed before a shot was fired in the Philippines and before we had incurred any of the troubles we have suffered from the attempt to apply an imperialistic

UNCLE SAM'S NEW CLASS IN THE ART OF SELF-GOVERNMENT.

This W. A. Rogers cartoon from 1898 depicts the United States' relationship with the overseas territories it acquired through the settlement of the Spanish-American War. Here, Uncle Sam tries to teach a class while students representing Cuba, Hawaii, and Puerto (Porto) Rico act obediently or unruly. The Supreme Court ruled on the legal status of the territories in the Insular Cases, a series of related decisions spanning two decades. —The Granger Collection, New York policy to our new possessions. . . . But the decision of the Supreme Court has cleared the last snags out of the road of expansion without imperialism.[11]

Others saw the Supreme Court's decisions as an endorsement of imperialism, including the well-qualified George S. Boutwell, R-Mass., a former member of Congress, secretary of the Treasury, and U.S. senator, as well as the first chairman of the Anti-Imperialist League (1898–1905). Boutwell remarked, "The opinion of the majority seems to justify the conclusion that *the power of acquiring territories is an indefinite power*. If this conclusion shall be justified by further reading of the opinion, there will then remain no legal obstacle to the transformation of this republic into an empire, with unlimited powers to acquire and with unlimited power to rule."[12]

The *New York Herald,* for its part, consistently opposed the policies of President William McKinley's administration:

> In the most important of the insular cases decided yesterday and the most momentous opinion rendered since the foundation of the government the United States Supreme Court by a bare majority of one holds that the constitution is supreme only in the States, and that million square miles, or one-fourth of the national domain, and ten million people are subject to no law but the will of Congress. . . .
>
> It can hardly be said that either the Court or the country is to be congratulated on a decision which four of its members say "overthrows the basis of our constitutional law and asserts that the States, and not the people, created the government."[13]

The next day the *Herald* wrote of the "lack of unanimity," "vulnerability," and "inherent weakness" of the Supreme Court's decision:

> No decision of more far reaching consequences has ever been rendered by the United States Supreme Court than in the *Downes case,* and no great constitutional opinion of that tribunal has rested on a basis more insecure. It is not only opposed by the largest minority of which the Court is capable, who declare through the Chief Justice that it "overthrows the basis of our constitutional law," but even the majority, while coinciding in the conclusion, could not agree in the reasoning by which it was reached. . . .
>
> In view of all these considerations and the fact that the majority that rendered the opinion may be turned into a minority by the accession of the next new member to the Bench, how long can the judgment withstand the onslaught which its own weakness will invite in the future?[14]

The *Denver Post* wrote that the "epoch making" *Downes* decision "at one fell swoop" was bringing the United States "into the ownership of colonies and putting us into the rank of the land-grabbing nations of Europe. We are now following the footsteps of England, not in planting colonies as it did in Australia, but in conquering and ruling unwilling alien races at it did in India and incidentally exploiting them." The *Post* concluded:

> No pronouncement of the supreme court since Chief Justice Taney's decision in the Dred Scott case is likely to provoke more widespread discussion, and none which has been rendered since the days of Marshall is likely to have a tithe of its wide reaching consequences. But colonies are now part of the possessions of the United States; they must go through a period of probation more or less, if not indefinitely, prolonged before they rise to the dignity of statehood or even reach the equivocal position of territories. . . .
>
> Therefore the question no longer is whether or not the constitution follows the flag,

whether we shall have colonies, but what methods congress shall adopt to govern them—only this and nothing more.[15]

Probably the best known response was that of Finley Peter Dunne writing as Mr. Dooley: "No matther whether th' Constitution follows th' flag or not, th' Supreme Coort follows th' iliction returns."[16] President McKinley, after all, had been reelected in a landslide against William Jennings Bryan in November 1900, just months before the Supreme Court issued its decisions.

CONTINUING CONTROVERSY

Subsequent public responses were just as divided. Eugene Stevenson, the outgoing president of the New Jersey Bar Association, endorsed Justice Brown's position. "The Constitution of the United States expresses the will and is maintained by the force of the inhabitants of the forty-five States of the Union," Stevenson argued, and "it neither expresses the will nor is it maintained by the force of the inhabitants of the District of Columbia or of the territories of New Mexico and Arizona, or of Alaska, Porto Rico, the Sandwich Islands or the Philippine Islands." Stevenson held that "all the territories of the United States, including the District of Columbia, occupy a position of absolute *political servitude* to the inhabitants of the forty-five States who compose the great body politic and who of themselves have the power to enact and re-enact and alter and amend from time to time the supreme law of the land which governs so much of the land as the lawgiver sees fit to include within the operation of his law."[17] Stevenson warned:

> If the minority of these learned Justices are right and no distinction can be drawn between Porto Rico on the one hand and the Philippine Islands and possible slices of China and Africa on the other, this would be the result: The treaty-making power composed of the President and Senate, could secretly effect the addition of fifty millions of Chinamen to the citizenship of the United States, all of whom would become voters upon establishing a residence in any State.[18]

Judge L. S. Rowe, a future president of the American Academy of Political and Social Science, favored Justice White's argument:

> His views give evidence of a desire to formulate a principle at once simple and readily intelligible. Whether we agree or disagree with his conclusions they furnish a clear and definite rule by which the political organs of the government may guide their conduct in dealing with newly acquired territory. The principle of interpretation as laid down gives to them complete power over such territory until, by express legislative enactment or by acquiescence in a rule contained in a treaty of cession, such acquired territory is made a part of the United States. Until such action is taken by Congress, the territory remains subject to the jurisdiction of the United States, but does not become a part thereof, and the only limitations upon the power of Congress are those prohibitions of the Constitution which go to the very root of the power of Congress.[19]

But Rep. Charles E. Littlefield, R-Maine, was less sanguine. "The Insular Cases, in the manner in which the results were reached, the incongruity of the results, and the variety of inconsistent views expressed by the different members of the court, are, I believe, without parallel in our judicial history," Littlefield wrote in the *Harvard Law Review*.[20] Political scientist John W. Burgess was similarly critical. "The judgment in the Downes case is . . . nothing but an arbitrary bit of patchwork," he wrote. "Its purpose is to satisfy a certain demand of fancied political expediency in the work of imperial expansion. It is based upon the narrowest possible view of that expediency."[21]

Nor did the cases settle matters, as several editors pointed out. "The decision . . . will probably emphasize and intensify rather than settle the political issues arising from the acquisition of our new possessions," wrote the *St. Louis Post-Dispatch* on May 28, 1901. The next day the *New York Herald* reported, "Amid the conflict and confusion of so many opinions it is not easy to define the limitations or the scope of what the Court has decided. But it is plain that vital issues are still unsettled and left to future discussion and determination." And the *Philadelphia Record* of May 28 cautioned, "The self-congratulations of the Imperialists" over the Court's decisions are "rather premature. What is clear is that a mutilated Constitution does follow the flag until Congress shall have determined to the contrary."

COMMENTS ON THE LATER RULINGS

On December 2, 1901, the Court issued its decisions in the two delayed cases, *Fourteen Diamond Rings v. United States* and *Dooley v. United States*. "Politically, and in respect to its broad measures of policy, the Executive Department of the Government is sustained by the decision of the court," the *New York Times* wrote. "It is not sustained in its contention, and it was not sustained in that contention in the Porto Rico cases, that it had power to levy and collect duties under military administration without the legislative authority of Congress. It made no difference that our occupation of Porto Rico was unresisted, while a great insurrection made our occupation of the Philippines costly and troublesome. For the purposes of this decision, cession and possession are held to be identical." The *Times* also pointed out, "The reasoning and decision are identical with those of the De Lima case . . . but it is plainly intimated by the Court that the principle of the Downes cases must control so soon as Congress authorizes the collection of duties on Philippine merchandise." At the same time, the *Dooley* decision "again confirms the constitutionality of the Foraker act and lays down once more the principle that our new territorial possessions are not a part of the United States within the revenue clause of the Constitution. The judicial branch of the Government has in all the insular cases sustained the policy of the Executive branch."[22]

The *Chicago Record-Herald* on December 3, 1901, commented more pointedly on the cases: "To-day Justice Brown was again the pivot in still another most important case—one of greater importance, so far as the future is concerned, than the Philippine case. This was the Dooley case, in which the constitutionality of the Foraker act was attacked, not upon the ground that Porto Rico was 'a part of the United States,' but on the ground that the tax levied at San Juan on goods going from the United States into Porto Rico was in violation of that clause of the Constitution declaring that 'no tax or duty shall be levied on articles exported from any state.' " The paper added, "But here Justice Brown joins forces with Justices Gray, Shiras, White, and McKenna, whom he could not agree with in the Philippine case, and forces the chief justice and his three colleagues to become again the dissenting minority. By another vote of 5 to 4 the court holds that such a tax is not an export tax and is therefore constitutional."

Chief Justice Fuller, his three colleagues, and Justice Brown "made short work" of the point that the status of the United States in the Philippines was different from that in Puerto Rico "because in the former an insurrection was still going on," the *Record-Herald* reported. The Court's decisions at once meant "a government defeat" in the Philippine tariff case and "a decided victory for the MCKINLEY administration" in *Dooley,* thanks to the "acrobatic Justice BROWN."[23]

Representative Grosvenor, however, believed that the Court's rulings in *Fourteen Diamond Rings* and *Dooley* fully resolved matters:

> The decisions taken together and added to the decisions of last spring, fully sustain all
> the points insisted upon by the Ways and Means Committee of the House of Represen
> tatives, and which became the position of the Republicans in Congress and the Adminis
> tration. The net result of the whole business is that by the treaty of Paris we acquired the
> islands without terms and with no stipulations controlling this Government in its rela
> tion to the new possessions. That while the treaty terminated the sovereignty of Spain

and made the territory the property of the United States, yet it placed no limitations upon the power of Congress to legislate on the new territory as it might deem wise and for the best interest of the islands. . . . The Supreme Court, after these great contests have ended, placed the court where Webster and Burton and Lincoln and the Republican platform of 1860 placed it.[24]

Sen. John Spooner, R-Wis., author of the Philippine resolution and a Senate leader, commented that the two decisions "certainly establish the proposition that Congress may levy a tariff for the benefit and support of the Philippine government upon articles going from the United States to the Philippines and coming from the Philippines to the United States. The decisions surely clear the way for intelligent action by Congress in devising a system of taxation which will provide for the support of the Philippine government, its schools, etc."[25]

The *Philadelphia Record,* which had a daily circulation of more than 180,000 in the nation's third largest city at the time, expressed a different view. It despaired of the Court's rulings: the "learned Justices of the Court . . . do not agree among themselves, and the people of the United States, while bowing to the determination of the Court, cannot be expected to understand the why and wheretofore."[26]

With both cases decided by "a bare majority of one" and with the bitter differences among politicians and the public over the nation's island territories, the outcome of any future insular case was thrown into doubt when Justice Gray announced his retirement. President Roosevelt wrote his friend, Sen. Henry Cabot Lodge, R-Mass., about appointing Oliver Wendell Holmes, Jr. to replace Gray:

> The majority of the Court, who have . . . upheld the policies of President McKinley and the Republican party in Congress, have rendered a great service to mankind and to this nation. The minority—a minority so large as to lack but one vote of being a majority—have stood for such reactionary folly as would have hampered well-nigh hopelessly this people in doing efficient and honorable work for the national welfare, and for the welfare of the islands themselves, in Porto Rico and the Philippines. No doubt they have possessed excellent motives and without doubt they are men of excellent personal character; but this no more excuses them than the same conditions excused the various upright and honorable men who took part in the wicked folly of secession in 1860 and 1861.
>
> Now I should like to know that Judge Holmes was in entire sympathy with our views, that is with our views and mine and Judge Gray's. . . . I should hold myself as guilty of an irreparable wrong to the nation if I should put in his place any man who was not absolutely sane and sound on the great national policies for which we stand in public life.[27]

Lodge promptly reassured the president that Holmes was safe on expansion and a good Republican. Then, in early 1903, Roosevelt appointed William Day to replace Justice Shiras, who he also made sure was sound on these issues.

Just a few months later, the Court issued its decision in *Hawaii v. Mankichi.* "The Constitution was not extended over Hawaii by the mere act of annexation," the *Philadelphia Inquirer* explained, "nor were local laws by that act suspended or abolished, or the Hawaiians would have been left without any kind of government."

> But what was the effect of the provision embodied in the Newlands resolution by which Hawaiian laws not contrary to the Constitution shall remain in force? Did that involve the elimination of all laws that were contrary to the Constitution? This is really the only question with which the court dealt, and it answered it in the negative upon the ground that it cannot reasonably be assumed that Congress intended a construction that

would have been attended by so much inconvenience. The legal logic of the conclusion is open to attack, but it accords with good common sense.[28]

On June 5, 1903, the *New York World* reacted more critically:

> By the usual vote of five to four the Supreme Court . . . has decided that the Constitution did not follow the flag to Hawaii, but waited to be shipped there by Congress along with the baggage of the territorial government. Again it is affirmed that the creature is greater than the creator. . . . It is as if a Council of Ministers appointed by the Czar of Russia should annex a territory and then decide whether or not the Czar's authority should have any standing in it.
>
> We owe all possible respect to the Supreme Court, but when the Supreme Court makes a decision by a majority of one, with the Chief-Justice and some his ablest associates in the minority, it is permissible to doubt whether the judgment is the final voice of inspired wisdom. . . .
>
> The minority dissenting from this decision is composed of Chief-Justice Fuller and Justices Harlan, Brewer and Peckham—beyond question four of the strongest justices on the bench. Of the majority—Justices Brown, White, McKenna, Holmes and Day—it is said that Justice McKenna is certainly not the strongest member of the court, that Justice Day was Secretary of State at the time the imperialist policy was adopted, and that he and Justice Holmes are the newest recruits to the bench.

A year later, the Supreme Court issued its decision in *Dorr v. United States.* According to the June 2, 1904, *Philadelphia Inquirer,* the Supreme Court

> decided that the Constitution does not of its own force penetrate into any country covered by the American flag. This is not a new doctrine. It was enunciated three years ago in the Philippine cases, where the tariff was solely in contention. . . . The doctrine that the Constitution is not for the States, but for all of the Federal territory, was originated by [John C.] Calhoun a little over fifty years ago, . . . [who] invented the theory in order to claim for slavery all of the public domain, and . . . the Supreme Court in the Dred Scott decision held that he was right. . . . That decision has been overturned not only by the courts, but by the trend of events. Ordinarily, we think that trial by jury is a right, and for most of us it is, but it is not a natural right, but only a guarantee given to those who live in the various States or specifically granted to inhabitants of some of the Territories. The Supreme Court has decided in accordance with the law and the facts of the case. Trial by jury is a boon granted by legislation, and not inherent in the flag.

In Buffalo, then eighth largest city in the United States, the *Buffalo Evening News and Telegraph* also supported the majority opinion. On June 1, 1904, the paper stated:

> The method of trial by jury, as established in England and America, is founded in common sense after long experience of ways of distributing justice. One of the conclusions formed after an experience of ages is that the system cannot be worked among the half-civilized races. The Supreme Court of the United States has just held that the jury system does not attach to our control of the Philippines until Congress establishes it by statute. That is so clearly the common sense view that one is constrained to wonder how there could be a contrary opinion in the Court.
>
> On the legal side of the prevailing opinion the Court shows a disposition to reach solid ground in the provisions of the Constitution that the Congress has power to make

rules and regulations for the territory of the United States without limit except within the ordinary guarantees of life, liberty and property secured by that instrument. The doctrine that the Constitution follows the flag is perfectly true, but only in the limited sense that Congress has power over territories as soon as the flag is raised in them permanently. The Supreme Court is slowly settling down to bedrock on territorial questions.

The *New York Herald* saw otherwise. "NO TRIAL BY JURY IN THE PHILIPPINES," read its news headline the same day, with successively smaller headlines running beneath: "Supreme Court Holds That Right Was Withheld by Congress on Account of Incapacity of the People"; "OPINION CALLED DANGEROUS"; and "Justice Harlan Says It Is an Amendment to the Constitution 'by Judicial Construction.'" As the *Herald* commented in its editorial:

> The constitutional doctrine affirmed by a bare majority of the court in this and the preceding insular cases is that the constitution does not apply to the nation's outlying possessions unless and until Congress expressly so declares. Of course authority to make such declaration carries authority to withhold it. This puts Congress above the constitution throughout a large part of the national domain. It concedes to that body supreme power to govern at will not only the present insular possessions but any that may be hereafter acquired. Congress under this ruling may, for example, abolish the jury system, as . . . in the Hawaiian case, and nullify all the other guarantees of personal rights and liberty. It may set up despotism in the administration of justice and even in the government itself.

Rep. David K. Watson, R-Ohio, who served one term, 1895–1897, wrote in the *American Law Review*, "The plain lesson of *Dorr* is that the Constitution applies to ceded territory which has been incorporated into the United States, but it does not apply to territory which has been annexed but not incorporated into the United States." In *Rassmussen v. United States*, Watson added, the issue "came before the Court for a last time"[29]

The *Rassmussen* decision attracted almost no public response, however, and neither did the last of the Insular Cases, *Balzac v. Porto Rico*. But as noted international lawyer Frederic Coudert wrote in 1926—he and his associates in Coudert Brothers had argued for the plaintiffs in *De Lima, Downes,* and *Hawaii v. Mankichi*—*Rassmussen* established that Alaska *was* incorporated, even though it had no organized territorial government; Alaskan citizens were therefore guaranteed jury trial. "It was not, however, until 1922, in *Balzac v. Porto Rico*," Coudert wrote, "that a unanimous court unequivocally adopted the incorporation doctrine as part of our constitutional law."[30]

Although the Insular Cases were highly controversial at the turn of the twentieth century—every bit as controversial as *Dred Scott v. Sandford* to some contemporary observers—interest in the cases faded away for most Americans. With a few notable exceptions, these cases have been absent from constitutional law casebooks.[31] And if the Insular Cases have attracted notice from the biographers of Chief Justice Fuller and Justices White and Harlan and from a handful of legal historians, few others have paid notice, even though the United States still governs territories—Puerto Rico, Guam, the U.S. Virgin Islands, the Northern Marianas, and American Samoa—that effectively have little voice in the U.S. federal government. They have no senators or members of Congress although they are still subject to the plenary power of the U.S. Congress, executive, and federal courts. Fortunately, recent works by Sanford Levinson, Efrén Rivera Ramos, Alexander Aleinikoff, Gerald Neuman, Rogers Smith, Sarah Cleveland, Christina Duffy Burnett, and the contributors to Christina Duffy Burnett and Burke Marshall's edited volume, *Domestic in a Foreign Sense,* have helped to put the Insular Cases back into the legal canon.[32]

NOTES

1. "Porto Rico" was the official spelling of Puerto Rico until 1923.
2. *Buffalo Evening News and Telegraph,* May 28, 1901.
3. *Denver Post,* May 28, 1901.
4. *Chicago Record-Herald,* May 28, 1901.
5. *Washington Post,* May 28, 1901.
6. *New York Daily Tribune,* May 28, 1901.
7. Ibid.
8. Ibid.
9. *San Francisco Examiner,* May 29, 1901.
10. *New York Daily Tribune,* May 28, 1901.
11. *San Francisco Examiner,* May 29, 1901.
12. *New York Daily Tribune,* May 29, 1901.
13. *New York Herald,* May 28, 1901.
14. Ibid., May 29, 1901.
15. *Denver Post,* May 28, 1901.
16. Finley Peter Dunne, *Mr. Dooley's Opinions* (New York: R. H. Russell, 1901), 26.
17. Eugene Stevenson, "The Relation of the Nation to Its Dependencies," *American Law Register* 36 (1902): 366, at 374, 375; emphasis in original.
18. Ibid., 385.
19. L. S. Rowe, "The Supreme Court and the Insular Cases," *Annals of the American Academy of Political and Social Science* 5 (1901): 226, 248–249.
20. Charles E. Littlefield, "The Insular Tariff Cases in the Supreme Court," *Harvard Law Review* 15 (1901): 168, 170.
21. John W. Burgess, "The Decisions of the Supreme Court in the Insular Cases," *Political Science Quarterly* 16 (1901): 486, 504.
22. *New York Times,* December 3, 1901.
23. *Chicago Record-Herald,* December 3, 1901.
24. *San Francisco Examiner,* December 4, 1901.
25. Ibid.
26. *Philadelphia Record,* December 3, 1901.
27. Theodore Roosevelt to Henry Cabot Lodge, July 10, 1902, in *Selections from the Correspondence of Theodore Roosevelt and Henry Cabot Lodge,* 2 vols., ed. Henry Cabot Lodge and Charles F. Redmond (New York: Da Capo Press, 1971), 1:518–519.
28. *Philadelphia Inquirer,* June 4, 1903.
29. David K. Watson, "Acquisition and Government of National Domain," *American Law Review* 41 (1907): 239, 253.
30. Frederic R. Coudert, "The Evolution of the Doctrine of Territorial Incorporation," *Columbia Law Review* 26 (1926): 823, 842–844, 847.
31. See Paul Brest, Sanford Levinson, J. M. Balkin, and Akhil Reed Amar, *Processes of Constitutional Decisionmaking,* 4th ed. (New York: Aspen Publishers, 2000).
32. Sanford Levinson, "Why the Canon Should be Expanded to Include The Insular Cases and the Saga of American Expansionism," *Constitutional Commentary* 17, no. 2 (2000): 241; Efréra Ramos, *The Legal Construction of Identity: The Judicial and Social Legacy of American Colonialism in Puerto Rico* (Washington, D.C.: American Psychological Association, 2001); T. Alexander Aleinikoff, *Semblances of Sovereignty* (Cambridge: Harvard University Press, 2002); Gerald L. Neuman, *Strangers to the Constitution* (Princeton: Princeton University Press, 1996); Rogers M. Smith, *Civic Ideals* (New Haven: Yale University Press, 1997); Sarah H. Cleveland, "Powers Inherent in Sovereignty: Indians, Aliens, Territories, and the Nineteenth Century Origins of Plenary Power over Foreign Affairs," *Texas Law Review* 81, no. 1 (2002): 1–284; Christina Duffy Burnett, "*Untied* States: American Expansion and Territorial Deannexation," *University of Chicago Law Review* 72, no. 3 (Summer 2005); Christina Duffy Burnett and Burke Marshall, eds., *Foreign in a Domestic Sense* (Durham: Duke University Press, 2001).

Lochner v. New York

Paul Kens

Lochner v. New York
198 U.S. 45 (1905)

DECIDED: April 17, 1905

VOTE

CONCURRING: 5 (Melville W. Fuller, David J. Brewer, Henry B. Brown, Rufus W. Peckham, Joseph McKenna)

DISSENTING: 4 (John Marshall Harlan, Edward D. White, Oliver Wendell Holmes Jr., William R. Day)

OPINION OF THE COURT: Peckham

DISSENTING OPINION: Harlan (White, Day)

DISSENTING OPINION: Holmes

In *Lochner v. New York* (1905) the U.S. Supreme Court overruled the Bakeshop Act, a New York law limiting the hours of work in bakeries to ten hours per day and sixty hours per week. The case began when Joseph Lochner, the owner of a Utica, New York, bakery, was fined $50 for violating the statute. After two state appellate courts upheld the conviction, Lochner appealed to the Supreme Court, which overturned his conviction and, by a vote of 5–4, held the Bakeshop Act unconstitutional.

Justice Peckham's opinion for the majority reflected a controversial constitutional theory that had been gaining ground during the 1880s and 1890s but had not yet been fully sanctioned by the Court. This theory was based upon the Fourteenth Amendment guarantee that no state shall deny any person life, liberty, or property without due process of law. It depended upon three interrelated concepts. The first was substantive due process. In contrast to the common view that "due process" was a guarantee of correct judicial procedure, this idea held that the *substance* of a law could deny a person life, liberty, or property. The second concept was liberty of contract—that the Fourteenth Amendment guarantee of liberty includes the freedom of two or more people to make any agreement they might desire. This liberty could not, however, be absolute. Consequently, the third concept, a narrow view of the police powers of the states, provided a counterweight for determining whether laws that limited the right of contract were legitimate.

Peckham's opinion defined the police power narrowly, saying that the workday limitations of the Bakeshop Act could be upheld only if it protected the public health. Moreover, Peckham placed the burden on the state to demonstrate that it did. A mere assertion that the law related to bakers' health was not enough, he ruled. The state had to prove that the law was reasonable. Taking "judicial notice" that baking was not an unhealthy trade, he then concluded that the state had failed to meet that presumption and the Bakeshop Act was, therefore, unconstitutional.

Dissenting, Justice Harlan agreed with the majority's underlying premise that a law mandating shorter hours might violate liberty of contract, but he argued that the burden should be on those challenging the law to prove "plainly, palpably, beyond all question" that the law was inconsistent with the Constitution. Justice Holmes also dissented, but he went much further. Attacking the majority's underlying premise, he argued that the Court had based its decision not on the Constitution, but on laissez-faire economic theory, which holds that an economic system functions best without government interference. As a result, he said, the Court had merely substituted its own judgment for that of the state legislature.

RESPONSES FROM THE PRESS

Critics' charged that the majority had rewritten, rather than followed, the Constitution, failed to pay deference to legislative decision making, and applied their own essentially subjective standards to *Lochner*. They have made *Lochner* a persistent symbol of judicial activism. Nevertheless, some early news reports expressed mild support for the outcome. Ten days after the Court announced the opinion, one New York newspaper borrowed heavily from Justice Peckham's opinion to write:

> The general right to make a contract in relation to his business was part of the liberty of the individual protected by the Fourteenth Amendment. The police powers of a State had not been exactly described or limited by the courts. They related to the safety, health, morals, and general welfare of the public. The Fourteenth Amendment was not designed to interfere with a reasonable and proper exercise of those powers. In many cases the Supreme Court had recognized the existence of the police power and upheld the exercise of it. . . . But there must be a limit to the valid exercise of this police power. In this case the limit has been reached and passed. As a labor law pure and simple the act was invalid, for there was no reasonable ground for interfering with liberty of persons or the right of free contract by determining the hours of labor for bakers, who were able to take care of themselves and were not wards of the state.[1]

The *New York Press* highlighted Peckham's emphasis on individual liberty.

> The State has no more right to fix the maximum time of a day's labor than it has to fix the maximum amount of a day's wage for the laborer. The decision of the Supreme Court is only another blast from the trumpet of liberty.[2]

RESPONSES FROM LABOR

Journeymen bakers were naturally disappointed with the Court's decision. To understand the depth of their disappointment, however, it is important to remember that late nineteenth-century workers knew nothing of minimum hourly wages or time-and-a-half for overtime. Workers were usually hired and paid by the week or, more commonly, by the day. The typical agreement might be for wages of two dollars a day and stipulate nothing about how many hours the employee was expected to work. At the turn of the century it was not unusual for journeymen bakers to work 100 hours a week. Moreover, most urban bakeshops were located in tenement house cellars, where bakers worked in abysmal conditions, exposed to flour dust, gas fumes, dampness, and extremes of heat and cold. The bitterness of their defeat in the high court shows through in the following excerpt from the union's newspaper.

> Again the Supreme Court of the United States has decided against the poor by a vote of five to four: actually one man has decided that the people of the great State of New York have not the right to protect the health of workingmen. Here's one-man government with a vengeance. . . .
>
> If Peckham's decision stands, every law upon the statute books of the states which are intended to regulate the hours of labor—of adults or minors—will be wiped out.
>
> Shrewd lawyers and pliant judges may, and doubtless will, make the decision apply to many of the other labor laws.[3]

Samuel Gompers, head of the American Federation of Labor, opposed using legislation to achieve labor's goals. He believed that lobbying was costly and time consuming, legislation was difficult to enforce, and laws were subject to being overturned in the courts. Gompers instead favored the direct method of collec-

Joseph Lochner, the owner of a Utica, New York, bakery, was convicted of violating a law limiting work hours to 10 a day and 60 a week. In *Lochner v. New York* (1905), the Court overturned Lochner's conviction, ruling in favor of liberty of contract between employer and worker over improved working conditions. Bakery workers and labor unions assailed the decision, fearing that it would lead to the overturning of other laws regulating labor. —Courtesy of the Collection of Joseph Lochner Jr. by Dante Tranquille

tive bargaining and strike. This opinion was reflected in his comments in the *New York Times* regarding the *Lochner* decision.

> I cannot restrain myself from saying if the majority of that court who signed the opinion had visited modern bakeries in this State and seen the conditions that prevail even under the ten-hour law they would have believed that it was within the police power of this State to regulate the hours and would have declared for the ten-hour law.

The article continued:

> "What are the bakers going to do?" asked Mr. Gompers. "Are they going to submit? I ask any gentleman here to put himself in their place, if you can imagine yourself in a bakery for ten hours a day. What would you do? I tell you what I would do. I'd strike, and strike hard, until I got the ten-hour day." [4]

The *New York Press* reported on April 18, 1905: "Eighty-five thousand bakers throughout the United States would go on strike as a result of the decision of the United States Supreme Court." The strike never took place.

The more radical elements within the labor movement attacked the decision as well. About a week after the Court announced its decision, the Journeymen Bakers' Association reprinted another attack on *Lochner*. Its author was Morris Hillquit, a Russian-born attorney who later joined the Social Democratic Party of Eugene V. Debs. Hillquit was among the most extreme of American Socialists, and his comments reflect some of the movement's zeal.

> The arguments . . . it will thus be seen are based entirely upon refined and casuistic reasoning and presuppose an imaginary state of facts. As a matter of fact, the liberty of "contract" does not exist for the large mass of workingmen. In the labor market, the seller of labor power is in almost all instances at a disadvantage before the purchaser of that power. "Contracts" between employer and workingmen are not as a rule made by a free and voluntary agreement on both sides: the terms of such contracts are dictated by economic necessity on one side, and by greed for profits on the other. The State has the right and duty to regulate the relations of its citizens with a view to the general welfare of the public. It has the right and the duty to curtail abuses practiced by one class of the population on the other, and to protect the weak against unscrupulous exploitation and maltreatment by the strong. All laws of civilized communities are based on that fundamental assumption.[5]

WEISMANN'S ROLE

Henry Weismann's part in the *Lochner* case gave it a twist that appealed to Americans' craving for sensationalism. In 1895 Weismann, then a leader of the Journeymen Bakers' Union, was a driving force behind passage of the Bakeshop Act. After a falling out with the union, Weismann opened several small bakeries and eventually became a lawyer. In this new role, he encouraged Joseph Lochner to appeal his case to the Supreme Court. Weismann brought in a more experienced lawyer named Frank Harvey Field, but he clearly participated in arguing the case before the nation's highest court. His story was told in several New York newspapers. For example, the *Times* ran the following:

> MADE THE 10-HOUR LAW, THEN HAD IT UNMADE

> The New York State law making ten hours a day's work and sixty hours a week's work in bakeries was declared unconstitutional by the Supreme Court of the United States as the result of arguments advanced by Henry Weismann, counsel for the master bakers of the State of New York.

> The same law was passed by reason of the labors of Henry Weismann, International Secretary of the Journeymen Bakers' Union of America.

> Henry Weismann, counsel of the master bakers, and Henry Weismann, International Secretary of the Journeymen Bakers' Union of America, are one and the same man.

> "When I was young—a journeyman baker and Secretary of their National organization—I thought labor was right in all things," said Weismann yesterday afternoon. "I was fiery and full of ideals. Later I became a master baker, and, undergoing an intellectual revolution, saw where the law which I had succeeded as a journeyman baker in having passed was unjust to employers. I withdrew from labor circles because I was unwilling to keep on saying 'Yes' and 'Amen' to measures which were manifestly wrong." [6]

RESPONSES FROM REFORMERS

In the political environment of 1890s New York, Weismann and his fellow journeymen bakers could not themselves have ushered the Bakeshop Act through the state legislature. Weismann's success would not have been possible without the active support of New York's mainstream reformers. Members of organizations such as the City Club of New York, City Reform Clubs, tenement house reform clubs, and good government clubs lined up behind the legislation. They tended to believe that radical adherence to either laissez-faire economics or socialism was an equally dangerous threat to the social order. They thought that moderate reforms designed to ameliorate the conditions of labor would release pressure, line up labor on the side of order, and avoid an upheaval. The *Lochner* decision was clearly a setback for mainstream reformers, whose concerns were reflected in an anonymous essay in the *Outlook,* a reform-minded publication.

> Unfortunately, the immediate effect of the decision, The Outlook fears, will be to increase the power of those labor leaders who are distrustful of the courts and who are prone to appeal to the strike as the effective weapon for securing justice. It may, too, give impulse to the Socialistic movement, since, if the people were to own the implements of labor and conduct the operation of industries, they would have, without question, control of the hours and conditions of labor. Those people of conservative tendencies who welcome this decision as a blow to Socialism and as a weakening of the power of labor unions will, we think, be disappointed.[7]

The same essay emphasized critics' belief that the Court's decision was entirely subjective.

> The fact that of the fourteen judges in the two courts which have passed upon the case seven are on one side and seven on the other alone gives to the dissent view great importance. The nature of this case, moreover, which involves a somewhat arbitrary ruling as to the limits of the police powers of the State, brings into greater prominence than usual the individual inclinations of the judges.[8]

Although the *Outlook*'s point was correct, its calculations were a little off the mark. Three appellate courts rendered opinions in the *Lochner* case. The Appellate Division of the New York Supreme Court upheld Lochner's conviction by a vote of 3 to 2. The New York Court of Appeals, the state's highest court, then upheld the conviction by a vote of 4 to 3. The vote in the U.S. Supreme Court was 5 to overrule and 4 to uphold the law. Counting all appellate judges, state and federal, voting on the case, eleven voted to uphold the law, and ten voted to overrule. If only the New York Court of Appeals and U.S. Supreme Court are counted, the vote is 8–8.

The subjectiveness of the majority opinion was a theme of the criticism in legal circles as well. After pointing out that the majority opinion rested on Justice Peckham's having taken "judicial notice" of the "common knowledge" that the baking trade is not so unsanitary that a compulsory limitation on the hours of labor can be looked upon as a measure reasonably necessary to preserve their health, law professor and social reformer Ernst Freund asked: "Has not the progress of sanitary science shown that common understanding is often equivalent to popular ignorance and fallacy?"

Freund then took up the theme of the proper role of the judiciary.

> The Court says, "This is not a question of substituting the judgment of the court for that of the legislature"; it thereby seems to admit that if it were, the court should yield its judgment to that of the legislature. But there is really no escape from the conclusion that this is an issue of judgment. It is either that, or an issue of common sense or of good faith. The dissent is based on the ground that there was an issue of judgment, and the New York courts had approved of the judgment of the legislature. And because it is believed that the choice between the comparative benefits of the public welfare and private liberty of action has, by the constitution, been committed to the legislature, it must also be believed that *Lochner v. New York* has been wrongly decided.[9]

Reformers complained that Justice Peckham's opinion in *Lochner* reflected a formal and abstract legal reasoning that had lost touch with the real world. Law professor Roscoe Pound called this "mechanical jurisprudence," which he defined as

> a condition of juristic thought and judicial action in which deductions from conceptions has produced a cloud of rules that obscure the principles from which they were drawn, in which conceptions are developed logically at the expense of practical results and in which the artificiality characteristic of legal reasoning is exaggerated.[10]

Pound proposed an alternative method of legal reasoning that he called "sociological jurisprudence."

> The modern teacher of law should be a student of sociology, economics, and politics as well. He should know not only what the courts decide and the principles by which they decide, but quite as much the circumstances and conditions, social and economic, to which these principles are to be applied; he should know the state of popular thought and feeling which makes the environment in which the principles must operate in practice. Legal monks who pass their lives in an atmosphere of pure law, from which every worldly and human element is excluded, cannot shape practical principles to be applied to a restless world of flesh and blood.[11]

In his famous speech in Osawatomie, Kansas, on August 31, 1910, former president Theodore Roosevelt introduced the political platform he called the "New Nationalism." His platform included an attack on the judiciary that specifically used the *Lochner* decision as an example of how courts had frustrated the public will. As he began an unsuccessful run to regain the presidency in 1912, Roosevelt introduced a plan of popular recall of state court decisions that invalidated legislation. This plan did not aim to recall judges; rather, it proposed a way to put a judicial decision before the electorate, which could approve or overrule it by popular vote. Although his plan was aimed only at state courts, Roosevelt's scorn was also directed at the U.S. Supreme Court. The excerpts below, from a 1912 article in the *Outlook* are typical of his comments.

> During the last twenty-five years the courts here in New York, helped, I am sorry to say, once or twice by the Supreme Court of the Nation, have thrown what at times have proved well-nigh or altogether insurmountable obstacles in the path of needed social reforms.
>
> I am not primarily concerned with the argument as to whether or not the philosophical system championed by the judges in question is mischievous—although I firmly believe it so to be. I am not primarily concerned as to whether we, you and I, are right, or whether the extreme apostles of the *laissez faire* system who disbelieve in any attempt by any form of law to make social conditions more even and better are right. But I insist, as a matter of fundamental and primary concern, that we, the people, have the constitutional as well as moral right to try these experiments if we soberly determine to try them. I believe we have the right to limit the hours of labor for women and children, to fix the closing hours for women, to pass mandatory laws in connection with safety appliances (which shall apply whether or not the beneficiaries contract to waive their advantage under them); that we have a right to say that men shall not labor under conditions that we regard as ruinous to their health, or for so many hours a day or so many days a week as to make it impossible that their lives shall not be stunted and warped by excessive toil and unhealthy surroundings. . . .
>
> I hold, not only, that the courts in these matters have usurped, or at least exercised in wholly wrong fashion, a power properly and clearly abiding in the people, but they have strained to the utmost (and, indeed, in my judgment, violated) the Constitution in order

to sustain a do-nothing philosophy which has everywhere completely broken down when applied to the actual conditions of modern life.[12]

SOCIAL JUSTICE AND THE COURT

Partially in response to Roosevelt, constitutional historian Charles Warren wrote several articles in which he sought to demonstrate that the Supreme Court was not as attached to *laissez-faire* economics as reformers claimed.

> The reformers who claim that the Court stands as an obstacle to "social justice" legislation, if asked to specify where they see the evil of which they complain and for which they propose radical remedies, always take refuge in the single case of *Lochner v. New York* decided by the United States Supreme Court in 1905, in which the Court held unconstitutional the bakers' 10-hour day law in New York.
>
> Yet a single case does not necessarily prove the existence of an evil.[13]

Warren counted 560 cases interpreting the due process and equal protection clauses of the Fourteenth Amendment and maintained that in only two instances did the Court overrule state statutes involving "social justice." He then continued:

> The National Supreme Court, so far from being reactionary, has been steady and consistent in upholding all State legislation of a progressive type. When this fact is once firmly grasped, it becomes clear that there is no necessity for the introduction of the new remedy—recall of judicial decisions—or for its application to decisions of State courts on questions involving "police power" or "social justice." For if any State court be found reactionary or inclined to deny constitutionality of State laws on social or economic matters, a very simple remedy is at hand—the enactment of a single change in the Federal Judiciary Act, a change urged by many lawyers and Bar Associations. The Supreme Court is now confined to passing only on those state statutes whose validity under the Federal Constitution a state court has upheld. If that Act shall be amended so as to provide that an appeal may be taken to the United States Supreme Court on a decision of a State highest court denying the constitutionality of a State statute, the people of this country can, by that very slight change enacted by Congress, be fully protected against any reactionary State court (if such exist); and practically every State statute involving great social or economic questions can then be quickly and finally passed upon by the Supreme Court of the Nation, whose progressiveness cannot be denied.[14]

Warren provided a detailed summary of cases to support his contention, but the themes of judicial overreaching, the subjectivity inherent in liberty of contract doctrine, its impact on the elected branches of government, and the clash with sociological jurisprudence persisted. In an address before the Chicago Bar Association on January 3, 1916, Louis D. Brandeis, a future Supreme Court justice, argued that the law had failed to keep pace with economic and social realities. He called for judges and lawyers to remedy this problem, and the injustices that had resulted, by adopting what he called "the living law." Brandeis's address reflected an emerging movement called legal realism.

> Political as well as economic and social science noted these revolutionary changes. But legal science—the unwritten or judge made laws as distinguished from legislation— was largely deaf and blind to them. Courts continued to ignore newly arisen social needs. They applied complacently 18th century conceptions of liberty of the individual

and of the sacredness of private property. Early 19th century half-truths like "The survival of the fittest," which translated into practice meant "The devil take the hindmost," were erected by judicial sanction into a moral law. Where statutes giving expression to the new social spirit were clearly constitutional, judges, imbued with the relentless spirit of individualism, often construed them away. Where any doubt as to the constitutionality of such statutes could find lodgment, courts all too frequently declared the acts void. Also in other countries the strain upon the law has been great during the last generation; because there also the period has been one of rapid transformation; and the law has everywhere a tendency to lag behind the facts of life. But in America, the strain became dangerous; because constitutional limitations were invoked to stop the natural vent of legislation. In the course of relatively few years hundreds of statutes which embodied attempts (often very crude) to adjust legal rights to the demands of social justice were nullified by courts, on the grounds that the statutes violated the constitutional guarantees of liberty or property. Small wonder that there arose a clamor for the recall of judges and of judicial decisions and that demand was made for the amendment of constitutions and even for their complete abolition. The assaults upon courts and constitutions culminated in 1912. They centered about two decisions: the *Lochner* case, in which a majority of the judges of the Supreme Court of the United States declared void a New York law limiting the hours of labor for bakers, and the *Ives* case [*Ives v. South Buffalo Ry. Co.* (1911)], in which the New York Court of Appeals had unanimously held void its accident compensation law.[15]

Lochner v. New York is one of the few cases ever to lend its name to an era of constitutional history. The period from 1905 to 1937 is commonly referred to as the *Lochner* era, and the doctrine of the time is often called laissez-faire constitutionalism. By 1937, however, that doctrine had come into conflict with Franklin D. Roosevelt's New Deal. Much of FDR's disagreement with the Supreme Court involved the justices' interpretations of the commerce clause that limited the federal government's power to regulate economic matters. When the Court changed direction in 1937, rejected the laissez-faire doctrine, and overruled earlier commerce clause decisions, *Lochner* went too. The Court overruled *Lochner* in *West Coast Hotel v. Parrish* (1937).

Nevertheless, the *Lochner* opinion has continued to serve as one of history's primary examples of judicial overreaching. To this day, lawyers, constitutional scholars, and even justices of the Supreme Court commonly call upon *Lochner* to condemn decisions with which they disagree. In the past several decades, however, some constitutional historians have challenged the idea that the *Lochner* case was based upon laissez-faire economic theory. Rather, they insist that the majority's opinion simply reflected long-held American beliefs in free labor, individual liberty, and limited government. Thus, more than one hundred years after it was decided, *Lochner* continues to be controversial.

NOTES

1. *Independent,* April 27, 1905, 917–918.
2. *New York Press,* April 19, 1905, 6.
3. *Bakers and Confectioners Journal,* May 6, 1905.
4. *New York Times,* April 18, 1905, 9.
5. *Bakers and Confectioners Journal,* May 13, 1905.
6. *New York Times,* April 19, 1905, 1.
7. *Outlook,* April 29, 1905, 1018–1019.
8. Ibid., 1017.
9. Ernst Freund, "Limitations of Hours of Labor and the Federal Supreme Court," *Green Bag* 17 (June 1905): 411–417, 415–416.

10. Roscoe Pound, "Liberty of Contract," *Yale Law Journal* 18 (1909): 454–487, 457.

11. Roscoe Pound, "The Need of a Sociological Jurisprudence," *Green Bag* 19 (1907): 607–615, 611–612.

12. Theodore Roosevelt, "Judges and Progress," *Outlook,* June 6, 1912, 42–44.

13. Charles Warren, "The Progressiveness of the United States Supreme Court," *Columbia Law Review* 13 (1913): 294.

14. Ibid., 295–296.

15. Louis D. Brandeis, "The Living Law," *Illinois Law Review* 10 (February 1916): 461–471, 463–464.

Muller v. Oregon

Nancy Woloch

Muller v. Oregon
208 U.S. 412 (1908)

DECIDED: February 24, 1908
VOTE

CONCURRING: 9 (Melville W. Fuller, John Marshall Harlan, David J. Brewer, Edward D. White, Rufus W. Peckham, Joseph McKenna, Oliver Wendell Holmes Jr., William R. Day, William H. Moody)

DISSENTING: 0

OPINION OF THE COURT: Brewer

On Labor Day 1905, an overseer at the Grand Laundry in Portland, Oregon, required a woman employee to work overtime in violation of an Oregon law of 1903. According to the law, no female could "be employed in any mechanical establishment, or factory, or laundry in this state for more than ten hours a day." The statute set penalties for transgressions. Two weeks later, the state of Oregon charged Curt Muller, the owner of the laundry, with defying the law. Convicted twice in state courts, Muller appealed to the U.S. Supreme Court, where he challenged the law's constitutionality. He argued that it violated his right to freedom of contract under the due process clause of the Fourth Amendment. Boston lawyer Louis D. Brandeis, who represented Oregon, claimed that the state could curb freedom of contract to protect the health and welfare of its people. In a 113-page brief, the innovative "Brandeis Brief," Brandeis presented a mass of citations from nonlegal authorities—doctors, factory inspectors, and other experts—to show the connections among long hours, worker health, and public welfare. Overwork, the brief contended, "is more disastrous to the health of women than of men, and entails among them more lasting injury"; "the deterioration is handed down to succeeding generations;" and "the overwork of future mothers thus directly attacks the welfare of the nation."

On February 24, 1908, the U.S. Supreme Court unanimously upheld the Oregon law. Speaking for the Court, Justice Brewer praised Brandeis's unusual brief and even mentioned the lawyer by name, a rare event in judicial opinions. Brewer also accepted the fundamental argument of the Brandeis brief: women's overwork injured the general welfare. Oregon's lawyer had shown that "women's physical structure and the performance of maternal functions places her at a disadvantage in the struggle for subsistence." Prolonged work on their feet had "injurious effects" on women's bodies, "and as healthy mothers are essential to vigorous offspring, the physical well-being of woman becomes an object of public interest and care in order to preserve the strength and vigor of the race." In addition, Brewer explained why women constituted a special class. Woman had always been dependent on man, he wrote. Even if legislation expanded her personal and contractual rights, "there is that in her disposition and habits of life which will operate against a full assertion of those rights. She will still be where some legislation to protect her seems necessary to secure a real equality of right." Woman was therefore properly placed "in a class by herself, and legislation for her protection may be sustained, even when like legislation is not necessary for men and could not be sustained." Indeed, such legislation was designed to compensate woman for "some of the burdens which rest upon her" and was necessary "to protect her from the greed as well as the passion of man." Most important, laws that protected woman by limiting her contractual powers were "not imposed solely for her benefit, but also largely for the benefit of all."

The *Muller* decision gratified progressive reformers, especially activists in the National Consumers' League (NCL), who had arranged for Brandeis's participation in the case on Oregon's behalf. Only three years before, the Supreme Court's decision in *Lochner v. New York,* which upset a ten-hour law for bakery workers, had threatened to cripple the reformers' campaign for worker protection. (See page 95.) The Oregon case, in contrast, legitimized it. By gaining acceptance for "sociological jurisprudence," or consideration by the courts of social and economic data, the Brandeis Brief offered a way to sustain further protective laws; by winning protection for women in industry, reformers made progress toward state protection for all workers. New Deal laws that provided maximum hours, minimum wages, and other regulations ultimately fulfilled the reformers' goals. A turning point in the movement toward modern labor standards, the *Muller* decision long enjoyed a high reputation.

But *Muller v. Oregon* also embedded in law a premise of female difference. Women as a class, said the Brewer opinion, could be treated differently from men. Supporters of women's rights criticized this aspect of the decision as soon as it was announced in 1908. Six decades later, the stream of rebuke became a torrent. Fired by feminist ideas of the 1960s, a new generation of women's rights advocates denounced *Muller:* it treated women as a separate class and thereby deprived them of equal rights. The decision not only endorsed protective laws that handicapped women workers, critics charged, but also served as a precedent for discrimination in other areas of law. The *Muller* decision suffered a great reversal of fortune. Once thought to compensate for women's disadvantages, it now seemed to impose them. Public response to the *Muller* decision underscores its dual roles in constitutional history: first, as a step forward toward state regulation of industry and, second, as a roadblock to sexual equality.

PRESS RESPONSE

The press of 1908 did not immediately recognize *Muller* as a major decision. Still, the newspapers that noticed *Muller* offered applause. To editorial writers, the decision seemed humane, fair, and civilized. Most saw it as a victory for women and sometimes for labor. "Labor had an inning yesterday in the United States Supreme Court's decision that the Oregon law limiting to ten the hours of labor for women in laundries in that state was valid," declared the *Washington Post,* under the headlines "Her Rights Greatest" and "Supreme Court Holds Woman Above Man in Law." [1] A Portland newspaper exulted with a five-part headline: "State May Limit Women's Work," "Oregon's Ten-Hour Labor Law Sustained," "Women Must Be Protected," "Difference Between Sexes Makes It Essential," and ending with "Safeguard Human Race." [2] To the press of 1908, women deserved the special protection of the law. An editorial in the *Chicago Daily Tribune* summed up the favorable response:

> The opinion of the court as stated by Justice Brewer calls attention to the fact that the rights of women can no more be infringed than those of men. But on many accounts women are entitled to greater protection than men. Whatever theories may be advanced in connection with women's rights, the facts remain that the sexes differ in structure of body, in physical strength, in the capacity for longer sustained labor, particularly that done standing. The difference is marked when there is consideration of the influence of vigorous health upon the future and well being of the race. . . .
>
> Because of these reasons the court declares that legislation in behalf of women may be sustained even if similar legislation is not required for men and could not be sustained. The difference in laws for men and women is justified by the inherent differences of sex. If some of the burdens which rest upon women are peculiarly heavy they ought to have compensation in other directions.
>
> There has long been recognition of the principle that child labor should have its own laws and should not be put upon the same plane as that of adults. This decision places the labor of women in a distinct category also. It does not deprive a state of the right to refuse to enact laws regulating woman labor, but it makes certain that state laws regulat-

When Oregon implemented a maximum work week of 60 hours for women, laundry owner Curt Muller (center, with arms folded) argued that the law violated his rights. In *Muller v. Oregon* (1908), the Court upheld the law, citing sociological arguments that overworking women injured the general welfare. Although the decision was supported by reformers who had been disappointed with the outcome of *Lochner v. New York* (1905), women's rights advocates denounced the ruling's paternalism. —Courtesy of Barbara and Bruce Whisnant

ing the labor of adult women which differ from those affecting adult males will not be set aside by the federal Supreme Court.

The reasons asserted by the court will be recognized everywhere as having great force. They will make their appeal to the better judgment of all. Whatever the theories advanced in favor of substantial equality of women and men in political, personal, and contractual rights, the fundamental differences of sex will continue to exist, and will be considered as important in shaping laws.[3]

The *New York Times* agreed:

That woman is a ward of the State, that she is set apart in a class by herself, and placed under the fostering care and special protection of the law, not because of consideration for her individual comfort and interests, but in the interest of the human race and of posterity, is a principle that has just been affirmed by the Supreme Court of the United States. . . .

[Treating women as a protected class under law] accords, also, with the policy of exemptions in favor of woman that prevails in all civilized countries, and largely, even, among primitive savages, exemptions, that is, from jury duty and military and constabulary service. It is in harmony with the laws that compel support of the wife by the husband, and provide for alimony when divorces are granted. [Such laws] do not spring from sentiment. They rest rather upon a maxim of the highest social policy. To the end that the race may be preserved, that the health, vigor, and soundness of posterity may be assured, that class of society charged with the chief functions of race preservation must be surrounded with peculiar safeguards.[4]

While some editorials, like that in the *Chicago Daily Tribune,* explained that woman's favored position under law was compensatory, others, such as that in the *New York Times,* stressed that the *Muller* decision sought primarily to benefit the rest of the human race. Justice Brewer, who had voiced both interpretations, reiterated the latter point in an article of 1908. The decision had meant no "disrespect" to women, Brewer contended. It had been "written with the utmost respect for them . . . and in the firm belief that there was something in [woman's] place and work in life which justified the legislature in forbidding her to contract for factory work beyond a limited time. The race needs her; her children need her, in a way that they do not need the other sex."[5]

To the NCL, which had championed the Oregon law and whose leaders had helped prepare the Brandeis brief, the *Muller* decision represented an overwhelming triumph. NCL leaders published Brewer's opinion, along with the Brandeis Brief, circulated it widely, and promoted it at every opportunity. Josephine Goldmark, head of the NCL's Publications Committee and Brandeis's sister-in-law, issued an exultant report to the NCL membership. Goldmark explained the nature of the NCL victory in *Muller,* the decision's benefits for women workers, and the need for further research on employee health:

> This decision is the most sweeping one ever promulgated by the Supreme Court of the United States in relation to working hours. It is not confined to a consideration of the ten-hours day or to a working day of any particular length. It leaves to the states liberty to determine what working hours are wholesome and reasonable. It goes far beyond the statute of issue, which dealt with the employment of women in factories and laundries, and looks forward toward the protection of women in other employments.
>
> The court's "judicial cognizance" of practical facts should act as a stimulus . . . the meagerness of the available American information on the social and medical effects of occupations was revealed in the course of preparing Mr. Brandeis's brief. . . . Not only the effect of long hours but the whole hygiene of occupations awaits adequate medical investigation.[6]

Florence Kelley, the NCL's general secretary, also touted the decision as "a service of incalculable value to wage-earning women in the United States."[7] Kelley claimed that the decision's impact would soon reach not only women workers but men as well:

> The ground taken by the Court is clear. It must be shown that a law restricting freedom to contract really protects the health of the person thus restricted. Henceforth both men and women need only show a clear relation between their working hours and their good or bad health in order to have statutory restrictions upon their working day sustained by the Supreme Court of the United States. . . .
>
> The only unsatisfactory thing about this decision is that women had no voice in enacting it in the state of Oregon, or in electing the men who did enact it, no voice in electing the judges who sustained it in Oregon, and will, except in four free states [that had already approved woman suffrage], have no share in enacting the beneficent legislation which will naturally follow upon the decision.[8]

SUFFRAGISTS' VIEWS FOR AND AGAINST *MULLER*

To what extent did suffragists share the enthusiasm of NCL activists? Leaders of the national woman suffrage movement in 1908 saw little link between Justice Brewer's treatment of women workers in *Muller* and the woman suffrage cause, except that the lack of the vote made protective laws necessary. Alice Stone Blackwell, editor of the suffragist *Woman's Journal,* referred to "some differences of opinion among suffragists" but denied any inconsistency between the *Muller* decision and the fight for women's enfranchisement:

> Some benighted opponents of equal suffrage are boasting over the decision as though there were something in it incompatible with political rights for women. Justice Brewer evidently does not think so, for he is an advocate of woman suffrage. And, in fact, where is the inconsistency in a man's believing that women should be protected against excessive and inhuman overwork, and at the same time believing that they should be protected against taxation without representation?[9]

But protests against Brewer's opinion also emerged in the suffragist press. A group of New York women, the Women's Henry George League of New York, voiced a series of grievances in a notice sent to suffragist publications. These women took an equal rights stance:

> Whereas, Woman is a human being just as much as man is, and therefore possesses an inalienable right to life, liberty, and the pursuit of happiness; and
>
> Whereas, Woman in a primitive state, unhampered by natural restrictions, not only fulfilled all of women's special functions, but also performed the heaviest labors of the tribe; and
>
> Whereas, For the successful propagation of the human species, fatherhood is as important as motherhood; and
>
> Whereas, No woman who is not free physically, mentally, morally, and economically, is fit for motherhood; and
>
> Whereas, The so-called protection afforded her by man-made laws has so far secured her nothing better than subjection; robbed her of the fruits of her labor; and even denied her the right to her own children; and
>
> Whereas, The recent decision of Justice Brewer is not in accordance with facts or with equity; therefore be it
>
> Resolved, That the Women's Henry George League of Manhattan protests against the said decision of Justice Brewer of the Supreme Court, as unjust and humiliating to women; as tending to sex slavery; as opposed to economic freedom; and as inimical to the best interests of present and future generations; and be it further
>
> Resolved, That a copy of these resolutions be sent to the newspapers.[10]

Western suffragists also expressed an equal rights stance. In Iowa, suffragist Louisa Dana Harding denounced the *Muller* decision in the official publication of the Iowa Woman Suffrage Association. To Harding, curtailing hours of work meant curtailing earnings. Moreover, state limits on hours in factories could easily lead to hours limits on women in other vocations and to yet further restrictions on women's activities. Finally, Harding argued, state regulation of hours was not necessarily for women's benefit; indeed, women would never benefit from laws passed only by men:

> Justice Brewer's decision that the state has the right to regulate the hours of work for women, is abominable. It is not proposed that any additional compensation shall be given for the loss of time thus sustained; this practically amounts to confiscation of whatever amount would have been earned during the forbidden hours. . . .

Furthermore, if women may only work a certain number of hours in factories, it is certainly permissible to limit the hours of work of women physicians, lawyers, and so on; and before long the state may be telling its wards how many hours to sleep at night, and what to eat; it has already prescribed a costume, and a most unsuitable and healthful one, at that. . . .

Whether an overworked drudge, or supervised by the state for its own selfish good (not hers at all), woman has not come out much ahead when she has taken legislation from the hands of other folk. When will those unrepresented in the government come to realize that no law is binding upon them which is made without their approval and assent, and that no present court has any jurisdiction in their case? One of these august tribunals recently decided that an American woman loses her citizenship when she marries a foreigner. It would be more sensible to recognize the fact that thus far she has not had any citizenship to lose.[11]

In the decades that followed, *Muller* provided the "entering wedge" for which reformers had hoped, a springboard to further curbs on employers' power. But the undercurrent of objection to the decision continued. Members of the National Woman's Party, formed in 1920, campaigned against single-sex laws and especially targeted the *Muller* precedent. Lawyer Blanche Crozier, an advocate of equal rights, assailed the *Muller* decision in an article of 1933:

But it is urged that women must be "protected" not only on account of their own physical delicacy and helplessness in the struggle for existence, but also "in order to preserve the strength and vigor of the race." It is stated in the *Muller* case and copied widely in other decisions, that the sexes differ greatly "in the influence of vigorous health upon the future well-being of the race." How can this be? In the transmission of all heritable disease or susceptibility to disease the two parents are on the same footing, and the potential mothers of the race play no different part from the potential fathers. . . .

Without involving heredity or the indefinite future, there is of course the possibility of direct injury to some one particular unborn child. Most obvious, perhaps, is the possibility of mechanical injury. Just as a man by some mishap fracture his leg or his skull, a woman may do the same. And if she is pregnant, the child may get hurt also. The home, however, is said to be the favorite place for such mishaps. . . .

The position of the proponents of "protective" laws is reactionary and not liberal. . . . This latter day "protection" is not very different from the method of the common law, which gave a woman's property to her husband in order to protect her. Certainly the conservative courts unhesitatingly recognized the old principle in spite of its new guise. . . . Mr. Justice Brewer, one of the staunchest of conservatives, wrote the court's opinion in *Muller v. Oregon*. Why not? It is certainly one of the most conservative opinions ever written. The philosophy which upholds "protective" legislation is nothing but the familiar attitude of the common law brought back for second blooming under the strange name of liberalism.[12]

MODERN VIEWS ON *MULLER*

Such equal rights assaults made little dent in *Muller*'s overwhelmingly favorable reputation, which reigned through the 1960s. Law texts, histories, and Brandeis biographies cited the decision as a milestone in the Supreme Court's retreat from the freedom of contract doctrine that had obstructed economic regulation. To political scientist and Brandeis biographer Alpheus Thomas Mason in 1964, *Muller v. Oregon* seemed "a judicial milestone unscarred by criticism."[13] Once the second wave of feminism erupted, however, new attacks on *Muller* revived the spirit of the earlier critiques and enlarged on them. Feminist lawyers, historians, and social scientists of the 1970s, 1980s, and 1990s assailed Brandeis's brief and Brewer's opinion. In 1978 political scientist Joan A. Baer fired an opening round at *Muller:*

> Brewer has weighed most of the distinguishing features of the situation of working women, and has chosen to emphasize those which are physical, and, in his view, unalterable in impact. He does not mention the economic conditions which might place women "at a disadvantage in the struggle for existence." He does discuss women's social and political disadvantages, but suggests that in the present case they are rather beside the point. He insists that even if these disabilities were removed, and the need for some kinds of special regulations perhaps eliminated thereby, women's physical and, perhaps, psychological nature . . . would still necessitate some special protection. Labor legislation based on women's physical characteristics is ruled permissible and advisable, not only now, but for all time. . . .
>
> If one believes that freedom of contract is a constitutional right, which workers actually enjoy, the limitation of this freedom for women can be defended only if one agrees that women should have less freedom under the Constitution than men. The opinion does not flinch from this necessity. It declares that women may be denied rights which men enjoy, both for what the state views as their benefit and in the interests of the larger society. [Brewer assumes] that the interests of women coincide nicely with societal interests. Fusion of these two sets of interests obscures the possibility of conflict between them. . . .
>
> As precedent, *Muller* was able to become even more controlling in the area of sex equality than in the area of economic regulation. For more than sixty years, courts upheld nearly all cases of sex discrimination, citing this case as binding precedent, following its lead in emphasizing permanent rather than temporary, physical rather than economic or social, aspects of women's condition. . . . The slavish following of the *Muller* precedent was to persist long after technological advances had ameliorated the conditions which had made restrictions necessary.[14]

In 1982 lawyer and legal historian Nancy S. Erickson added to the feminist charges:

> At the time *Muller* was seen as a victory for the friends of labor, because it eroded the *Lochner* rule that the legislature was not empowered to protect the health of the worker by maximum-hours laws. *Muller* is viewed in a somewhat different light today. From a modern feminist standpoint, the first justification for the holding in *Muller* is unacceptably paternalistic: it "protects" women, who are adult human beings equally capable to making their own decisions and looking out for their own interests as men are, even when women may prefer to risk a certain degree of harm in their pursuit of a desired goal. Additionally, even if the law truly helped all women workers and harmed none, [legislative classifications on the basis of gender carry the inherent risk of reinforcing sexual stereotypes]. The second justification is even more objectionable because it treats women as objects: as means rather than ends. That is, for the sake of "the race"—not even for the sake of a particular fetus that is already in existence—women's rights may be curtailed.[15]

Sociologist Lise Vogel similarly charged that the *Muller* decision enshrined an axiom of female difference, and she compared the decision to *Bradwell v. Illinois* (1873) (see page 44), which did the same:

With its opinion in *Muller,* the Supreme Court consolidated what may be seen as a modified version of the domestic code. As in its earlier decision in *Bradwell,* the Court declared that women are sufficiently different from men that they must come under different employment rules. At the same time, it recast the terms within which it thought about sexual difference and woman's place. In *Bradwell,* Justice Bradley projected distinctions between women and men to be all encompassing, eternally fixed, and divinely ordained. The court in *Muller* instead referred to evidence concerning physical and social differences between the sexes; scientific rationalism replaced religious belief as justification. Sexual differences were still viewed as fundamental and universal, but it now rested on what appeared to be a sound foundation of scientific documentation.

From the vantage point of the 1990s it is hard to imagine activists in the cause of women enthusiastically supporting the paternalistic verbiage generated by the *Muller* opinion. In the context of the period, however, protective legislation appeared to many to be the best bargain that could be struck to alleviate the burden of working-class women's double day and to defend them against their employers' greed. Not only would it provide a certain amount of immediate protection for women, it was also expected to set a precedent for a future campaign for sex-neutral labor policies.[16]

Lawyer Frances E. Olsen summed up the *Muller* decision's dual role and charged that it fostered sexual hierarchy:

Changed social conditions have made it easy in recent years simply to condemn *Muller* for its blatant sexism and offensive stereotyping, but at the time the case was decided, it was recognized that the case itself and the gender-based legislation it authorized had more complex and ambiguous implications. On the one hand, *Muller* was part of the attack upon the laissez-faire policies associated with *Lochner* and upon the *Lochner* case itself. *Muller* admitted what *Lochner* had tried to deny—that protective legislation can benefit workers and society. . . .

On the other hand, *Muller* undermined the struggles of women for equality and, paradoxically, even offered support for the *Lochner* free market principle by carving out a limited exception to it based on a view of women's frail physique and unique role in the family. . . . Indeed, associating the need for protective labor legislation with the frailty of women offered ideological support for the claim that legislative protection was unmanly. Moreover, protective legislation is effective only when its beneficiaries have no choice but to receive the protection; if individual workers or a whole group can waive the benefits, they can compete more effectively in the market. . . . Thus by restricting the protective legislation to women, *Muller* placed women at a competitive disadvantage. . . .

Muller illustrates another disadvantage of reforms that try to make the market responsive to human needs: the altruism they pose against market individualism is linked to hierarchy. *Muller* was based on the thesis that women differ from men in important ways, and although the case might have seemed to exalt women, it effectively degraded them by treating the asserted differences as evidence of women's inferiority.[17]

Critics of recent feminist commentary on *Muller* have charged that some commentators fail to take into account economic conditions of the early twentieth century, to consider the high level of support for the decision among women activists in 1908 and after, or to grasp the decision's crucial role in the campaign for protective laws for all workers. Other observers, too, make these points. "Fewer women were offended then than would be now offended by a comparable law," wrote attorney David P. Bryden in 1984. "Brandeis and his allies were trying to establish industrial ground rules that feminists today take for granted."[18] And as constitutional historians Melvin I. Urofsky and Paul Finkelman note, *Muller* did not suddenly make constitutional law sexist. "Discrimination based on gender had been firmly grounded in Anglo-American law for centuries before *Muller*. . . . Liberty of contract, that core ingredient of classical legal thought, belonged solely to adult males. The idea that women, especially married women, needed special protection had long been a staple of common law."[19]

Beginning in the 1970s the courts rejected the type of single-sex law that *Muller* had upheld and the rationale on which the decision had been based. Federal equal rights cases of the 1970s and later chipped away at the *Muller* precedent. Feminist objections to *Muller* were reflected in a 1991 Supreme Court decision, *Automobile Workers v. Johnson Controls*. Women employees at a battery manufacturing company had assailed the company's fetal protection policy as a violation of the federal Pregnancy Discrimination Act of 1978, and the Court endorsed the workers' position. In the majority opinion, Justice Harry A. Blackmun rejected the gist of *Muller v. Oregon*:

> Concern for a woman's existing or potential offspring historically has been the excuse for denying women equal employment opportunities. . . . It is no more appropriate for the courts than it is for individual employers to decide whether a woman's reproductive role is more important to herself and her family than her economic role. Congress has left this choice to woman as hers to make.[20]

NOTES

1. *Washington Post*, February 25, 1908, 1.
2. *Morning Oregonian*, February 25, 1908, 1.
3. "Women Workers," *Chicago Daily Tribune*, February 26, 1908, 8.
4. "The Position of Woman," *New York Times*, February 26, 1908, 6.
5. David J. Brewer, "The Legitimate Exercise of the Police Power in the Protection of Health," *Charities and the Commons* 21, November 7, 1908, 241.
6. "Report of the Publication Committee," *National Consumers' League Tenth Report* (New York: National Consumers' League, 1909), 42.
7. Ibid., 21.
8. Florence Kelley, "Justice Brewer's Decision," *Woman's Journal* 39, April 25, 1908, 68.
9. Alice Stone Blackwell, "An Important Decision," *Woman's Journal* 39, February 29, 1908, 33.
10. "Against Justice Brewer's Decision," *Woman's Journal* 39, March 21, 1908, 48, reprinted in the *Woman's Tribune* 5, May 9, 1908, 19.
11. Louisa Dana Harding, "Male Socialism," *Woman's Standard* 21, April 1, 1908, 2.
12. Blanche Crozier, "Constitutional Law—Regulation of Conditions of Employment of Women. A Critique of *Muller v. Oregon*," *Boston University Law Review* 13 (1933): 283–284, 290–291.
13. Alpheus Thomas Mason, "The Case of the Overworked Laundress," in *Quarrels That Have Shaped the Constitution*, 2d ed., ed. John A. Garraty (New York: Harper and Row, 1987), 193.
14. Joan A. Baer *The Chains of Protection: The Judicial Response to Women's Labor Legislation* (Westport, Conn.: Greenwood Press, 1978), 63–67.
15. Nancy S. Erickson, "Historical Background of 'Protective' Labor Legislation: Muller v. Oregon," in *Women and the Law: A Social Historical Perspective*, 2 vols., ed. D. Kelly Weisberg (Cambridge: Schenkman, 1982), 2:156–157.
16. Lise Vogel, *Mothers on the Job: Maternity Policy in the U.S. Workplace* (New Brunswick, N.J.: Rutgers University Press, 1993), 23–24.
17. Frances E. Olsen, "The Family and the Market: A Study of Ideology and Legal Reform," *Harvard Law Review* 96 (May 1983): 1497–1578.
18. David P. Bryden, "Brandeis's Facts," *Constitutional Commentary* 1 (Summer 1984): 297.
19. Melvin I. Urofsky and Paul Finkelman, *A March of Liberty*, 2d ed. (New York: Oxford University Press, 2002), 554.
20. *Automobile Workers v. Johnson Controls*, 499 U.S. 187, at 197 (1991).

Hammer v. Dagenhart

James Z. Schwartz

Hammer v. Dagenhart
247 U.S. 251 (1918)

DECIDED: June 3, 1918

VOTE

    CONCURRING: 5 (Edward D. White, William R. Day, Willis Van Devanter, Mahlon Pitney, James C. McReynolds)

    DISSENTING: 4 (Joseph McKenna, Oliver Wendell Holmes Jr., Louis D. Brandeis, John H. Clarke)

OPINION OF THE COURT: Day

DISSENTING OPINION: Holmes (McKenna, Brandeis, Clarke)

At the start of the twentieth century, a growing chorus of reformers urged the federal government to enact legislation to prevent children from working in factories and mines. Federal lawmakers responded by passing the Child Labor Act of 1916, which prohibited the interstate sale and transportation of goods produced by children who were under sixteen and who worked more than eight hours a day or six days a week. The legislation received widespread public support.

Some scholars view the act as a major constitutional turning point because it marked Congress's first attempt under the interstate commerce clause to regulate wages, working conditions, and other matters previously reserved to the states. On June 3, 1918, however, the U.S. Supreme Court struck down the Child Labor Act in *Hammer v. Dagenhart,* holding that by regulating labor hours in manufacturing, not interstate commerce, the law infringed on a matter reserved to state control. Writing for a 5–4 majority, Justice Day resurrected the distinction between manufacturing and commerce to rule the act unconstitutional, insisting that Congress could use the commerce clause only to regulate the production of goods that harmed consumers, but not to impede manufacturing that threatened workers' health. The government's real goal in this instance, Justice Day insisted, was to regulate child labor, which was a local concern and not subject to the commerce clause.

Congress had enacted the legislation because some, but not all, states had passed child labor laws. In making its case, the government claimed that the legislation aimed to protect manufacturers from competitors who had an unfair advantage because they operated in states that permitted them to use cheap child labor. Day rejected these claims, insisting that Congress had no power to determine how states controlled local trade and manufacturing. The Tenth Amendment, which the Court used to check federal control over commerce, ensured that such authority was reserved for the states.

Justice Holmes dissented. Although he acknowledged that Congress lacked the power to regulate factories, he asserted that the Constitution gave federal lawmakers the power to regulate interstate commerce, and that power could not be compromised by its influence on manufacturing. "The act does not meddle with anything belonging to the states," he asserted. "They may regulate their internal affairs and their domestic commerce as they like." But "when they seek to send their product across the state line, they are no longer within their rights." Holmes also took issue with Day's claim that goods produced by child labor posed no threat to the public's health. "If there is any matter upon which civilized countries have agreed," Holmes observed, "it is the evil of premature and excessive child labor."

EDITORIAL RESPONSES

The *New York Times*, on June 4, 1918, said the Court's ruling "caused the utmost surprise," noting that it was "received with much regret by those who worked for nearly fifteen years in Congress for the passage of the law." In overturning the Child Labor Law, the Court ruled that Congress had exceeded its authority under the interstate commerce clause.

The litigation began, the *Times* reported, when Roland H. Dagenhart went to court to obtain an injunction that would prevent the Fidelity Manufacturing Company's mill in Charlotte, North Carolina, from discharging his children, Roland Jr., Reuben, and John. The federal court for the Western District of North Carolina ruled that Dagenhart's "contention that the law was unconstitutional was well founded." The government appealed, and the U.S. Supreme Court upheld the lower court's decision.

Supporters of child labor laws, however, began efforts aimed at new legislation that, according to the *Times*, would "meet the Supreme Court's objections." In Congress, two "ardent supporters of the Child Labor Law," Rep. Edward Keating, D-Colo., and Sen. William R. Kenyon, R-Iowa, announced that they would launch a drive for a "new law," or for an "amendment to the Constitution, which would permit Congress to enact such a law." Keating suggested that Congress might tax goods from factories that employed children.

In its June 5 editorial, the *Times* applauded the Court's decision, arguing that the federal law invaded a "matter" that should be left to the states. The editors insisted, moreover, that a new child labor law was unnecessary because "every state" already had enacted a "law on the subject." Consequently, the *Times* contended, "Federal regulation" was "confusing." More important, the new law was "contrary to our political institutions," which were well "worth preserving."

The United States possessed "forty-eight varieties, more or less, of temperance laws and child labor laws," observed the *Times*. Such a "wide variance of opinion" existed that

> it would not be right for intolerant opinion on these subjects to impose its will upon others equally entitled to their opinions. There never could have been a United States without local control of local matters, and there is a national danger in forcing Federal regulation upon States in advance of public opinion in each of them.
>
> For those whose motives in opposing child labor are genuine—based on considerations of humanity, not merely on dislike of competition in the labor market—the decision opens the way rather than closes it. They can continue their movement in the States separately. Or they can produce a model statute, and seek to have it adopted by as many States as possible. There is no opposition to genuine reform regarding child labor in upholding the decision as supporting national interests. There is a real national danger in the antagonism sought to be created between State and national interests, and in seeking crosscuts to reforms of any sort in violation of constitutional safeguards of State or national rights. When sentiment is unanimous there is no difficulty in getting action. . . . But when sentiment is diverse in such high degree as upon prohibition and child labor and many social reforms, the tedious method of securing unity of sentiment in advance of unity of legislation is preferable.

The *Chicago Tribune*'s editorial of June 6, 1918, echoed these sentiments. Although the "decision displeases" those who focus on the "evil the law was designed to remedy, it pleases people who found in the method of remedy a cause of apprehension." The Court had earlier upheld a federal law that had used the interstate commerce clause to suppress the Louisiana lottery by "prohibiting the shipment of tickets, circulars, and other matters," the editors acknowledged. An important difference, however, existed between that case and *Hammer v. Dagenhart*. "Louisiana was corrupting the morals of the other states and its lottery could not exist unless it did so corrupt the other states."

In 1916 the Pennsylvania Child Labor Assocation, which supported child labor reforms, reproduced newspaper headlines announcing the effects of the Child Labor Act, which reduced the work hours of children and prohibited the interstate sale and transportation of goods produced by those under sixteen. The law was overturned in *Hammer v. Dagenhart* (1918) in which the Court ruled that Congress had no power to determine how states controlled local trade and manufacturing. —Library of Congress

It may be argued that a state employing child labor permits a cheap production which makes its competition unfair against a state not allowing this. There are methods of argument and distinctions which are unprofitably entered.

The method of federal regulation by indirection was bad in the beginning and remains bad. As an expedient in the lottery case it was not straightforward as an exercise of federal police power would have been. It was used as an expedient, and a plausible one, and the tendency has been growing to use the interstate commerce act for federal regulation of states in a fashion which is contrary to our system of government.

As federal regulation is extended by necessity it ought to be extended directly and straightforwardly. Many state functions retard nationalization. Others are valuable to it. The process of ruling states from Washington must be determined—if determined wisely—wisely, not by the evasive use of laws not intended for the purpose to which they are put.

Child labor is an evil. But more scrupulous attention must be given to the method of dealing with problems. Otherwise the method will develop a new set of evils itself.

Conservatives applauded the ruling as a victory for states' rights. Liberals and moderates, however, condemned the Court for its narrow construction of the commerce clause and for impeding the power of the federal government while the nation was fighting a world war.

In response, Congress passed the Child Labor Tax Act of 1919. Rather than using the commerce clause to regulate child labor, federal lawmakers employed their taxing power, levying high duties on items produced by children that crossed state lines. This strategy was based on the precedent set in cases such as *Veazie Bank v. Fenno* (1869) and *McCray v. United States* (1904), in which the Court recognized the breadth of Congress's taxing power.

The second child labor act, however, fared no better than the first. In *Bailey v. Drexel Furniture Co.* (1922), the Court struck down the law, claiming that it violated a function that belonged solely to the states. Writing for an 8–1 majority, Chief Justice William Howard Taft asserted that Congress was using the tax not to raise revenue, but to punish states that refused to regulate child labor. Justices Holmes and Brandeis joined the conservative majority because they agreed that Congress had overstepped its authority.

CONSERVATIVE VIEWS

Conservatives lauded the Court's rulings in both child labor law cases for limiting the power of the federal government. In the *Virginia Law Review,* two writers praised *Hammer* and *Bailey* for checking the growing power of the central government and for protecting the states' rights to control matters within their borders.

> It is satisfying to note that very recently the Supreme Court has, in Hammer v. Dagenhart, taken a long step towards establishing forever the right of a State to control its internal affairs without any outside intervention, in declaring unconstitutional the act of Congress entitled, "An act to prevent interstate commerce in the products of child labor." . . . The passage of this act was an attempt by the Federal Government to regulate conditions of labor within the State by providing that products of child labor could not be transported in interstate commerce. It was declared invalid because, although superficially an attempt to regulate interstate commerce, it was, in reality an attempt to regulate labor conditions within the State, and these conditions, being local in their nature, do not come within the regulative jurisdiction of Congress. Thus, it has been firmly established by our highest court that the power to regulate labor is inherently a State right and cannot be interfered with by Congress.[1]

Of *Bailey v. Drexel,* the second writer commented:

> The recent decision of the Supreme Court that the Child Labor Tax Law of 1919 is unconstitutional will probably stand out as one of the landmarks in our constitutional history. It brings to a halt the attempt to use the federal taxing power as a substitute for a general police power, an attempt which, if successful, would have revolutionized our constitutional system by practically wiping out the sovereignty of the States. This decision should go far toward clearing the air, so to speak, of the fogs that were fast obscuring some of the most fundamental principles of constitutional law. . . .
>
> [The Child Labor Law of 1916] provided a detailed regulation of child labor throughout the country by the device of prohibiting the interstate transportation of the products of establishments not conforming to these regulations. It having been settled in the Lottery Case [*Champion v. Ames,* 1903] and later cases that Congress could constitutionally exclude from interstate commerce articles of objectionable character aptly designated "outlaws of commerce," Congress attempted in the Child Labor Law to exclude unobjectionable commodities merely because [they were] not produced in accordance with regulations prescribed by Congress. This act ignored the clear, well-settled and important distinctions between production, which is a matter for State control, and marketing through the channels of interstate commerce, which is subject to regulation

by Congress. The admission of the principle involved in this statute would have taken from the States and given to Congress the control of productive industry of all kinds throughout United States. This revolutionary statute was held unconstitutional on the ground that it was not a proper exercise of the power to regulate interstate commerce, and also because it was an invasion of the police power to the States in the Tenth Amendment.[2]

CRITICAL VIEWS

Critics of the rulings questioned the Court's reading of both the Tenth Amendment and the commerce clause. Prof. Thomas Reed Powell of Columbia Law School attacked the majority's use of the Tenth Amendment to overturn the child labor laws, insisting that the justices gave it far more weight than it deserved.

> Constitutional law is not made by a machine or by any automatic logic. Into its composition there enters not a little of instinct or emotion or judgment of a political tinge. The Tenth Amendment may have some political significance over and above its command to Congress not to exercise powers not delegated. As a canon of political policy, it may carry a counsel of caution in deciding whether some proposed measure is really within or without the scope of national authority. The constitutional grants to Congress are for the most part so vague and indefinite that those who have to run the border lines can hardly escape the influence of a general preference for leaning to one side or the other. If government were a matter of precise mechanics, such a preference should operate only in deciding whether power possessed should in fact be exercised. It could play no legitimate part in drawing the line between power and usurpation. . . .

> It may well be that in the actual operation of our governmental enterprise, the Tenth Amendment has some influence in the official determination of what is an exercise of commerce power or of the taxing power. Whether such an influence is legitimate is another matter. In so far as it operates on the self-restraint of Congress, it is immune from criticism. Clearly, however, the Supreme Court should be cautious in allowing it to bear upon its judgments. It is a serious matter to declare invalid a law that the representatives of the nation have put upon the statute books. Courts should seek to keep clear the formal distinction between the existence of power and the wisdom of its exercise. They should bear in mind that the reservation to the states secured by the Tenth Amendment is a reservation of nothing more than of powers.[3]

Hammer's critics also questioned the Court's reading of the interstate commerce clause. The *Nation* noted that the Court had earlier approved Congress's use of the commerce clause to ban the sale of lottery tickets, alcoholic drinks, and impure foods across state lines. The *Nation* saw no valid distinction between these prohibitions and the one employed in the Child Labor Act of 1916 to ban the sales of goods produced by children across state lines.

> For the first time in its history the court holds [that] a prohibition of transportation across States lines is not a regulation of interstate commerce. Many times it has annulled State interferences with such transportation, branding them the exercise of a power which the Constitution by conferring upon Congress had denied to the States. Yet a law which regulates interstate commerce when passed by a state is now held not to regulate commerce when enacted by Congress. By such nimble metamorphosis the Supreme Court has created a vacuum in legislative power. It found no such vacuum when Congress forbade the transit across State lines of lottery tickets, alcoholic drinks,

and impure foods, and restrained men and women on interstate errands of vice. The barriers thus erected were held not to invade any reserved powers of the States. Justice Holmes paints the contrast when he says: "It is not for this court to pronounce when prohibition is necessary to regulation, if ever it may be necessary—to say that it is permissible as against strong drink, but not as against the product of ruined lives." . . .

The power of the producing state is no more interfered with by the Child Labor law than by the Pure Food law. Neither prohibits anything but interstate transportation. Both equally induce manufacturers from motives of gain to modify practices which they will not abandon from motives of humanity. But those who yield to inducement and voluntarily indulge in human decency do no more than they were free to do before Congress acted. . . . Manufacturing may go on as before. . . . But the goods which they wish to ship to other States must be made in factories which do no menace the health and strength of the future men and women of the nation.[4]

The *New Republic* placed the ruling in the context of America's recent entry into the world war, asserting that the *Hammer* decision impeded the power of the federal government at a time when it was urgently needed to lead the nation through a difficult period.

Even in these days of grave international concern, the decision of the United States Supreme Court in nullifying the Federal Child Labor Law demands national attention. As a result of this decision the United States, engaged in a world struggle, finds itself not a unity, not a nation capable of dealing with vital problems on a national scale, but forty-eight separate communities.

For the time being and we must devotedly hope only for a very brief time, the Supreme Court has destroyed a law enacted by Congress in response to a rudimentary national need. But the mischief wrought is greater and deeper than that. By this decision . . . the Supreme Court has occasioned more disquietude for the orderly working out of economic and social questions than by anything it has done in one term of Court since the Dred Scott case.

The world is in ferment and the problem of statesmanship is to guide the forces of unrest to new and stabler conditions of orderliness. That task will be gravely embarrassed and may well be rendered impossible if a judiciary immune not only from popular control but also from influence of those vital forces which govern and must govern the nation, should assert its obstructive veto against moderate and needful adjustments demanded by the changing facts of life. Fortunately such obstructions do not inhere in the Constitution. But if the interpretation of that document continues to rest with men who fail to exercise the vision of statesmanship, the nation will be forced to consider whether the dangers of entrusting to the fallibilities of a handful of judges the destinies of more than one hundred millions of people may not outweigh the value of the Court as the ultimate law giver.[5]

The *Harvard Law Review* echoed Holmes's dissent, asserting that child labor was just as harmful as prostitution, adulterated food, and any other product the Court allowed Congress to ban. In addition, the *Review* defended the Child Labor Act, noting that the legislation sought to create a more level playing field by protecting manufacturers in states with high standards from those in states with weaker regulations who benefited from cheap child labor.

The products of child labor are not harmless, and there is a definite evil in their very transportation across state lines. The evil is involved in the movement itself, and its effects are felt both in the state of production and in the state of destination. Transportation of child-made goods encourages the ruin of the lives of future citizens in the state of production. It directly aids this immorality as quite as much as the transportation across state lines of girls for the purpose of prostitution. Congress sought to remove this evil caused by the use of facilities over which it alone has control. It sought to remove it no further. Only that child labor was touched which depended upon the use of interstate commerce facilities for consummation of evil.

Moreover, the interstate transportation of child-made goods unfairly discriminates against citizens of the state of destination. It tends to lower their standards of child-labor protection. It is the same effect sought to be avoided by prohibition of importation of convict-made goods from foreign countries. . . .

The basis of federal action in the Child Labor Case . . . is . . . shown by the legislative history of the act. The situation which finally compelled Congressional action arose from the truly interstate character of the child-labor evil. . . . It appeared that the child-labor regulations of the states were not uniform and manufacturers in high standard states . . . felt at a disadvantage with competitors in states with low standards. The development of cotton manufacturing in the South . . . was said to be due to the employment of cheap child labor. The protest that the "unfair competition" of other states would be ruinous repeatedly defeated salutary measures proposed for the protection of children. Because the products met in competition in interstate commerce the states were powerless to protect themselves.[6]

William Carey Jones of the University of California-Berkeley condemned *Hammer* in the *California Law Review.* Jones emphasized the need for a Court that interpreted the commerce clause broadly. Without such flexibility, the nation would face numerous difficulties in the future. If the Court refused to embrace such a construction, an amendment would be needed to solve the problem.

As to interstate commerce, it is admitted that the power granted to Congress is not so broad as that over foreign commerce. But, it is to be remembered, the only limitations on the power over interstate commerce are such as are found in the Constitution itself, and these limitations are, upon investigation, found to be narrowed down to the general statement of principle contained in the Tenth Amendment, and to the more specific restriction of due process in the Fifth Amendment. . . .

The future of our constitutional government is largely dependent upon the spirit in which the Supreme Court construes and applies the commercial clause of the Constitution. If the construction be a liberal one, if the Constitution be interpreted in the spirit of Marshall, the instrument will be found flexible and sufficient to satisfy all the developing needs of society. If, on the other hand, the construction be narrow, if acts of Congress are nullified because of incidental conflict with reserved powers of the state, the country will be driven to amendment of the Constitution, or else fail in keeping in line with the progress of enlightened communities in the world. Now, every amendment in ordinary times is an evidence either of insufficiency of the Constitution itself or of lack of vision on the part of its interpreters.[7]

Prof. William A. Sutherland of Harvard Law School asserted that the Child Labor Act of 1916 was constitutional and should not have been overturned because it fell within the powers granted to Congress under the commerce clause. Sutherland, however, agreed with the Court that the 1919 child labor act was unconstitutional, because the tax that Congress imposed did not aim to raise revenue, but to regulate commerce.

The Child Labor Statute passed by Congress under the commerce power is constitutional. Even assuming that no part of its purpose or effect was to benefit commerce between the States, it is not a subterfuge. It is a real regulation of commerce. The states are sovereign and as such had power, before the adoption of the Constitution to regulate commerce from other states at will. It was proven under the Confederation that such a power in the states was destructive of union, and by the Constitution it was surrendered completely and without qualification to the federal government. . . . Such being the case, the only question that can arise when a statute prohibits the passage of certain goods in interstate commerce, is not whether it is within the scope of the general grant to Congress of power to regulate interstate commerce, but whether there are any other provisions of the Constitution with which the regulation conflicts. We have endeavored to show that the first Child Labor Law did not conflict with the due process clause or any other provisions of the Constitution. On the other hand, the second Child Labor Law is a subterfuge, pure and simple. It is not an exercise of power conferred or attempted to be conferred upon Congress. A tax is an imposition for the purpose of revenue, generally expressed in terms of money. It involves the idea of collecting as well as levying. And Congress is therefore without authority under the taxing clause to levy an imposition . . . which has for its sole purpose and effect, not the raising of revenue at all, but the regulation of intrastate business.

In the case of the taxing power the regulation is beyond its constitutional scope, whereas in the case of the commerce power the regulation is within its constitutional scope.[8]

In 1941 the Court in *United States v. Darby* finally upheld Congress's attempt to regulate working conditions, reversing *Hammer v. Dagenhart* and accepting a broad interpretation of the commerce clause.

NOTES

1. "Federal Taxation of Child Labor," *Virginia Law Review* 6 (November 1919): 115.

2. Joseph R. Long, "Federal Police Regulation by Taxation," *Virginia Law Review* 9 (December 1922): 81, 89–90.

3. Thomas Reed Powell, "Child Labor, Congress, and the Constitution," *North Carolina Law Review* 1 (November 1922): 61, 61–62.

4. Thomas Reed Powell, "The Child-Labor Decision," *Nation,* June 22, 1918.

5. "States' Rights vs. the Nation," *New Republic,* June 15, 1918.

6. Thurlow M. Gordon, "The Child Labor Law Case," *Harvard Law Review* 32 (November 1918): 45, 55, 63.

7. William Carey Jones, "The Child Labor Decision," *California Law Review* 6 (September 1918): 395, 403, 411.

8. William A. Sutherland, "The Child Labor Cases and the Constitution," *Cornell Law Quarterly* 8 (June 1923): 328, 358.

Adkins v. Children's Hospital

Vivien Hart

Adkins v. Children's Hospital
261 U.S. 525 (1923)

> DECIDED: April 9, 1923
> VOTE
> > CONCURRING: 5 (Joseph McKenna, Willis Van Devanter, James C. McReynolds, George Sutherland, Pierce Butler)
> > DISSENTING: 3 (William Howard Taft, Oliver Wendell Holmes Jr., Edward T. Sanford)
> OPINION OF THE COURT: Sutherland
> DISSENTING OPINION: Taft (Sanford)
> DISSENTING OPINION: Holmes
> DID NOT PARTICIPATE: Brandeis

*A*dkins was brought by an employer, Children's Hospital of the District of Columbia, together with a suit by an employee, Willie Lyons, a female elevator operator in a District hotel. *Adkins* challenged the 1918 federal minimum wage law for Washington, D.C. The statute established a board, chaired by District lawyer Jesse Adkins, to set minimum wages for women and children in industries in which wages were inadequate for the cost of living. A wage order covering workers in hotels and hospitals had been issued, and the hospital authorities and Lyons sought an injunction against enforcement of the law. They lost in the District Supreme Court (now the D.C. Court of Appeals) but won a reversal on a second appeal. Contested procedural maneuvers dragged the case out from 1920 until the final ruling by the U.S. Supreme Court on April 9, 1923.

The question before the high court was whether the minimum wage law "authorize[d] an unconstitutional interference with the freedom of contract included within the guaranties of the due process clause of the Fifth Amendment." By a 5–3 vote, the Court decided that it did. Writing for the majority, Justice Sutherland, one of three newly appointed justices, described the statute as "so clearly the product of a naked, arbitrary exercise of power that it cannot be allowed to stand under the Constitution of the United States." Chief Justice Taft and Justice Holmes wrote strong dissents. Justice Brandeis, a supporter of minimum wages, took no part because his daughter Elizabeth worked for the wage board.

Sutherland offered two main grounds for the decision, both controversial. The first concerned the status of women. He argued that gender inequality had diminished since 1908, when *Muller v. Oregon* had permitted legislation restricting the hours of work for women (see page 104). Indeed, given "the great—not to say revolutionary—changes which have taken place since that utterance, in the contractual, political, and civil status of women, culminating in the Nineteenth Amendment, it is not unreasonable to say that these differences have now come almost, if not quite, to the vanishing point," Sutherland wrote. The trend of recent legislation "by which woman is accorded emancipation from the old doctrine that she must be given special protection or be subjected to special restraint in her contractual and civil relationships" could not be ignored. Women, being now "legally as capable of contracting for themselves as men," must therefore enjoy the same freedom of contract as men.

The *Adkins* decision did not overturn *Muller*. But its second main point, on the wage bargain, distinguished and limited the reach of that case. Legislation based upon physical differences between the sexes might sometimes be acceptable. Hours of work were, however, a different matter from wages, which were "the heart of the contract." If hours were regulated, the employer could seek lower wages to compensate. But a wage statute made a "compulsory exaction" from the employer, "having no causal connection with his business, or the contract or the work the employee engages to do." The burden of supporting the poor belonged to society as a whole, not to employers alone. Due process in wage bargaining meant negotiation guided only by the "moral requirement implicit in every contract of employment" to agree upon a fair wage, where "the amount to be paid and the service to be rendered shall bear to each other some relation of just equivalence." On both gender and wage grounds, therefore, legislation restraining women's negotiation of their own wages was an unconstitutional breach of the due process guarantee of freedom of contract.

Reactions to Supreme Court decisions may be legal, political, or both, and *Adkins* met with a storm of criticism from both directions. Many lawyers were horrified that the decision pushed the doctrine of due process back toward the narrow, procedural definition that had stymied social legislation at the beginning of the twentieth century. Social reformers, especially women, were devastated. In an era when labor laws had been blocked by the assertion of men's constitutional right to freedom of contract, *Muller* had allowed minimal protection for women workers. Now two long decades of struggle for minimum wage laws seemed in vain. Women's wages in the District of Columbia fell when the board closed down, a dozen other state laws were sidelined, and campaigns elsewhere stopped. It was difficult to see how women workers could help themselves or be helped through state action or where they could turn for new constitutional validation.

Controversy began within the Court itself with two unusually strong dissents. Chief Justice Taft took issue with both of Sutherland's arguments, starting with the distinction between wages and hours:

> I regret to be at variance with the court as to the substance of this distinction. In absolute freedom of contract the one term is as important as the other, for both enter equally into the consideration given and received, a restriction as to one is not any greater in essence than the other and is of the same kind. One is the multiplier and the other the multiplicand.

Taft also dismissed the gender equality argument, declaring that the "Nineteenth Amendment did not change the physical strength or limitations of women upon which the decision in Muller v. Oregon rests."

Attacking Sutherland's "dogma" of liberty of contract, Justice Holmes was "absolutely free from doubt" that Congress had properly enacted this law. He agreed with Taft that wages and hours were two sides of the same coin and, as a party to the *Muller* decision, rejected Sutherland's reasoning on that, too:

> The bargain is equally affected whichever half you regulate. Muller v. Oregon, I take it, is as good law today as it was in 1908. It will need more than the Nineteenth Amendment to convince me that there are no differences between men and women, or that legislation cannot take those differences into account.

RESPONSES APPROVING *ADKINS*

Outside the Supreme Court, the business community roundly applauded the decision. The Chicago *Commercial and Financial Chronicle,* after reviewing the main arguments, went on to say:

> We may as well dismiss the technical side of the question. It is undeniable that the habit of bending old straight lines to fit present assumed emergencies is a confirmed one and that few seem to be taking thought whither that will carry us. . . . [T]he prevailing notion of liberty is that when the individual wants something he wants it, wants it now, and won't be satisfied till he gets it. . . . In terms, this decision applies only to the District and it is certainly not a final dispensation of the subject, since some fourteen states have minimum wage laws, to be attacked and defended. The fever for constitution tinkering will also burn with more heat. . . . Trying to make people virtuous, contented and happy

by legislation is miserable folly; the more we have of it the less satisfied they are, and the more they rush into blocs and clamor . . . some day it may decide us to stop the quackery and begin cutting the withes with which we have been tangling ourselves up and see whether liberty of individual action will not be better.[1]

The League for Industrial Rights, whose banner included the aims "To Secure legal responsibility and integrity of contract [and] Safeguard industrial liberty," wanted the Court to go even further and do away with the distinction between wages and hours, declaring all restrictions on the labor contract to be void:

> [It is] a question of importance and delicacy to determine whether the restriction imposed by a Minimum Wage Law for adult women in all occupations violates the constitutional guarantee or not. When people are compensated for their services according to what they can get, their failure to get enough to live on may present a question for public charity or public education. When, however, the law intervenes in the attempt to procure for them in wages what the law may determine that they need . . . [i]t is apparent that such an interference with the natural economic relation between wages and services may have a powerful effect upon the economic freedom of both employers and employes in making contracts for the sale and purchase of labor. . . .
>
> To deny that a real distinction exists between a maximum hour law and a minimum wage law seems to us like denying the distinction between a curfew law and a law which dictates how a member of the community shall spend his, or her, daylight hours. If the legal conception of liberty is to continue to include liberty of contract, the line must be drawn somewhere, and this [the *Adkins* decision] would seem to be a clearly distinctive place to draw it. Liberty of contract is certainly annihilated, and the advent of socialistic bureaucracy is at hand if the vast body of self-reliant women are to be told by the state that the terms under which they shall be allowed to sell their services shall be no other than those prescribed by law.[2]

Prof. Franklin Winton Ryan, who represented a small number of academics who endorsed the decision, declared that the Court had acted responsibly:

> There are certain economic laws which govern the making of a wage bargain. Society can set up rules in the form of statutes to govern such bargains but only up to a certain limit. If legislatures pass this limit, the statutes can operate only to obstruct and hinder the working out of the economic laws. So it comes to pass that any solutions of legal problems regarding wage bargains must recognize the fundamental principles of valuation agreements. Thus economics becomes part of jurisprudence and the jurist becomes an economist. . . .
>
> This decision seems to the writer not only to be correct but also to have unusual significance. In it the Court appears to have arrived at its solution of the problem by a resort to economic principles. It clearly recognizes that no statute can operate to nullify the economic laws of valuation as relating to the wage bargain. It brings out the seldom-recognized fact that within the bounds of jurisprudence is an inchoate evolving body of juristic economic theory apart from, but parallel to, the systems developed by economists.[3]

DEBATE OVER HOW TO RESPOND TO *ADKINS*

The most interesting responses were not public, but consisted primarily of a debate among supporters of minimum wage legislation over what could be done. Campaigning for minimum wage laws had involved an alliance between lawyers, led by Harvard Law School professor Felix Frankfurter, and reformers, led by the National Consumers' League (NCL) and its tireless general secretary, Florence Kelley. The "constitutional right to starve" was their view of the decision. Rollin Kirby's *New York Post* cartoon conveys their angry reaction.

The legal and political concerns were expressed by Justice Brandeis in a private letter to Frankfurter, that the "fundament vice . . . was the distortion of 'due process' 40 years ago," and from Charles Amidon, a liberal North Dakota judge, that employers were "preying upon the necessities of women."[4] Anger was succeeded by disagreement about the way forward. Many lawyers thought Sutherland had left a loophole with his assertion that a "fair wage" might be constitutional. Draft statutes including this language, court tests of the marginally different state laws still intact, a constitutional amendment permitting protective legislation, reform of the Supreme Court, and a mobilization of the female electorate were potential tactics that lawyers and reformers discussed.

Former secretary of war Newton D. Baker, in his role as NCL president, wrote, "The decision of the Supreme Court of the United States in the minimum wage case announced yesterday is, of course, most disheartening. In a day or two I assume I shall have the advance sheets of the opinion and be able to form some opinion of the wreckage. It looks to me as though President Harding had not appointed very progressive men to the Supreme Court."[5]

George Alger, another reformer and longtime supporter of minimum wage legislation, lamented to Kelley,

> It is simply a return to a problem which you and I had thought practically settled and settled right. The pendulum has come back. . . . It adds a new chapter—the right to work for less than a living wage—a political illusion in place of an economic reality. Most milestones of progress and reaction are judicial decisions. . . . We had every reason for believing that the *principle* of social legislation was accepted. . . .

Nation Wide Conference

called by

National Consumers' League

on the

Minimum Wage Decision

of the Supreme Court of the United States

CARTOON BY
ROLLIN KIRBY
BY COURTESY
N.Y. WORLD

This decision affirms your constitutional right to starve

As women campaigned for the right to vote, they also lobbied for the passage of minimum wage and maximum work hours laws. The Supreme Court ruled in *Adkins v. Children's Hospital* (1923) that such laws for women interfered with the liberty of contract guaranteed by the Fifth and Fourteenth Amendments. According to cartoonist Rollin Kirby, the decision affirmed women's "constitutional right to starve." — Library of Congress

But this sickening mess, the return to life of *Lochner vs. N. York* [see page 95]—from the limbo of the lost to disturb us once again, the whole reopening of the meaning of liberty and the revival of the economic crimes committed in her name means at least a temporary setback. It has hurt the Court seriously at a critical period in her history. It will suffer once more—from the foolish friends who will attempt to justify a wholly unjustifiable decision. I am for criticism on a broad scale, for a general protest which will put us back where we were, and which created an atmosphere in which social legislation for more than a decade progressed with judicial sanction. We are not in a period of reaction. The Court is wrong in thinking we are. I am reminded of a talk I had with [Theodore Roosevelt] when he was running his recall campaign. I was against it. We talked a long time and then finally he declared "Alger, there is one thing you wholly overlook—that is the capacity of the Courts and your noble profession for progress—*when well scared!* It seems too bad that the "scare" principle will have to be worked again.[6]

Adkins sought Frankfurter's advice on what they should do next, as most of the commissioners on the board, appointed by President Warren G. Harding, were unfriendly to the law to begin with and were therefore eager to accept the Court's decision and close the agency down. Adkins wrote:

> I should like very much indeed to know whether you think it is at all worth while to ask for a rehearing. Speed is rather important to us. . . . Personally I am not interested in the law if confined to minors. Practical operation would be very difficult and might do more harm than good. If we fixed a very low wage, employers would use that as an argument for reducing women's wages. If we fixed a high wage, the children would be unable to get work. . . . On the other hand I have some feeling of responsibility . . . I believe the law is constitutional as to minors and is separable as to them.[7]

Frankfurter's answer showed the problems facing the reformers and the fact that no clear solution existed that would meet Sutherland's objections to wage legislation.

> We simply must keep the issue alive in view of the terrible implications of the majority opinion. . . . What troubles me is whether we should make a direct attack in our litigation, or have the questions again appear in litigation coming up from one of the state laws. . . .
> From the foregoing, you will see—
> (1) That I am perfectly clear that an effort must be made to secure reconsideration of the wholly impossible grounds taken in the majority opinion. I am not clear whether we should do that by direct application for a re-hearing in our cases rather than to wait for a case . . . to reach the court. The grounds for my doubts are that the present application [for a rehearing] will surely be turned down, and therefore the chances of further consideration in independent litigation from the states will be practically nil. On the other hand, if we now lie low, we shall lose nothing and may possibly gain through the contingencies of time.
> (2) That I am perfectly clear that no effort should be left untried by you to keep alive the machinery and the functioning of your Board, on the theory that both the law is still in effect as to minors and is still in effect as to its fact-gathering machinery, although the penal enforcement for obedience is gone.[8]

Women had apparently lost the minimum wage because they had won the right to vote (although, ironically, at this time neither women nor men in the District of Columbia could vote for any office, federal or local). Kelley highlighted the limitations of this political equality: "Although the life, health and happiness of women and girls are at stake, no woman has participated in the minimum wage case at any of its stages ... the monopoly of jurisprudence by men, must, therefore, be replaced by just representation of women." [9]

To add insult to injury, in 1923 minimum wage supporters were embroiled in debate with former feminist allies, whose new definition of equality contradicted their own fight for equality of social condition. The National Woman's Party (NWP), led by Alice Paul, had started a fight for equality as a formal status in law; their goal was an equal rights amendment. Before joining the Supreme Court, Sutherland, who had enjoyed a reputation as a moderately progressive senator from Utah, had been an adviser to the NWP. His *Adkins* decision precisely echoed the NWP *amicus* brief in the case, rubbing salt into an open wound for Frankfurter and Kelley. The rift was clearly visible in the NWP's triumphal recollection of the meaning of the *Adkins* decision, as reflected in a brief it filed more than a decade later opposing a state minimum wage law:

> The Constitution of the United States is still supreme in the United States and ... the principles of constitutional liberty belong to women as well as to men. The Nineteenth Amendment gave them full political rights. The *Adkins* decision following closely thereafter gave them assurance that their fundamental liberties are recognized by the courts. It may be said that their *Magna Charta* is found in the words of Mr. Justice Sutherland. [10]

Frankfurter understood this, as he bitterly noted in a telegram to Kelley the day after the *Adkins* decision came down:

> Confidential. Most ominous part of the opinion is suggestion that Muller doctrine has been supplanted by nineteenth amendment stop Upshot would be adoption Alice Paul theory of constitutional law plus invalidity of legislation affecting industrial relations of either men or women stop Suggest vigorous pronouncement by League and aggressive campaign as to importance of dealing with peculiar position of women in industry. [11]

SEARCHING FOR A STRATEGY TO FIGHT *ADKINS*

Opponents of the *Adkins* decision made and contested plans to fight back, each struggling to control the definition of the problem that would determine future strategy. After a National Consumers' League conference of concerned parties, NCL staffer Molly Dewson wrote to Frankfurter:

> The conference was thoroughly unsatisfactory to me. The A.F. of L. [American Federation of Labor] was there in force to tell us what they wanted: help with a blanket amendment [to safeguard the rights of labor] and the organization of working women. Anything different they were prepared to kill. They did not bother to issue their ultimatum through the National Trade Union League [for Women], but spoke directly as the strategists for working women. They annexed the whole situation as a Labor question without admitting that the Public might hold it to be a health problem. Ethel Smith says the N.T.U.L. cannot buck the A.F of L. and must follow them.
>
> Besides Labor the Y.W.C.A. attended the conference in droves and talked at length. We all know that debate and generalities are their forte, and not "A STAND" or help in legislation. The latter are taboo to their Board.
>
> The rest of the conference was made up of lawyers, each one radically differing from the other with their usual independence of judgement, a few gently bleating ewe lambs, and the glum and gloomy from the National Consumers' League. [12]

Dewson had contributed 143 hours of overtime in three weeks on the huge compilation of sociological evidence that had accompanied Frankfurter's brief. Trying to console her for the Court's brusque rejection of her work, Frankfurter reminded her, "Molly, you must learn that if the United States Supreme Court says a red rose is green, it is green. That's final."[13]

But "that" was not "final." Over the next months, both feminist and legal strategies were advocated. Kelley argued that women had to take matters into their own hands:

> Since 1920, no woman can legitimately plead in excuse of our passive acceptance of judicial nullification as the natural lot of labor statutes for women and children, that we are innocent because we are powerless. Wherever we can, through our votes, acquire political power we are *particeps criminis* [an accessory to the crime] whenever a justice or a judge defeats the ends of health and labor legislation.
>
> . . . The time is past for resting content, after each new destructive decision, with years of struggle for new amendments to the federal constitution. It is too late to go on wasting precious years in work for more of these. . . . The time has come for the new voters to use our new powers for selecting modern minded judges wherever the judiciary is elective. And everywhere the need of the hour is a fresh affirmation of the constitutional right of free speech, applied respectfully but firmly to the need of a modernized Supreme Court of the United States.[14]

The *Nation,* one of the country's leading liberal journals, suggested that there still might be a legal means to reverse *Adkins.*

> We cannot escape the conclusion that the opinion of the court reveals an ignorance of the nature of the modern employment contract and of the facts which surround it which, in view of the court's pivotal position in determining the economic policy of the country, is nothing short of shocking. It assumes that there exists between employee and employer an equality of position which enables each to bargain with the other upon an equally advantageous footing. To suppose that such a situation exists in modern industrial society is indeed naive. The minority of the court clearly perceived this fatal weakness of Justice Sutherland's reasoning, and, recognizing the obvious fact that the class of employees at the bottom of the wage scale "are peculiarly subject to the overreaching of the harsh and greedy employer," held that the remedy proposed by Congress should not have been ruled out merely because the majority of the court thought that it was based upon unsound economic ground. . . . We cannot doubt that the Supreme Court by this decision has substituted its judgment of economic wisdom for the judgment of Congress and that as a result the people of the United States are without power, unless they amend the Constitution, to establish the principle of the minimum wage in any State or in Federal territory. That this is deplorable most progressive-minded people will agree. But that the highest judicial body in the land should thus assume to decide questions of economic policy is more deplorable still. The people ought to be entitled to decide such matters for themselves, free from the shadow of the potential veto of the odd justice of the Supreme Court. Until this power of judicial veto is limited or eliminated, the people of the United States will neither be wholly free nor will they have the opportunity to test the vital principles of government of, for, and by the people.[15]

Divisions soon deepened between the reformers and the lawyers. Kelley saw a problem of power and gender and sought both a binding constitutional amendment and radical structural change. "Women need votes, and *wage* statutes, *and* unions, *and* women judges."[16] But Frankfurter and most lawyers saw the problem as one of constitutional law, of redefining the principle of due process. They disliked the idea of an amendment, preferring to constrain the due process clause or circumvent it altogether. Harvard law professor Thomas Reed Powell pointed out how the elasticity of "due process" allowed the justices to impose their personal views, how the delayed hearing of the case meant that a sympathetic court in 1922 was replaced by the hostile majority of 1923 with three new justices. Powell then wrote one of the classic condemnations of the reactionary jurisprudence of the Court in the 1920s:

> The constitutional issue raised by such compulsory legislation is therefore whether an employer may be compelled to pay the cost of maintaining the employee whose full services he voluntarily uses in the conduct of his enterprise.
>
> This constitutional question finds no answer in the Constitution. While the legislation, like substantially all legislation and all law, involves a deprivation of liberty or property, such deprivation is constitutionally innocuous unless it is "without due process of law." The Constitution does not define due process of law. The task of definition is committed to the judges. They have recognized that definition is impossible. They have told us that instead of definition they will employ a process of "judicial inclusion and exclusion," and give us the reasons. These reasons can not come from the Constitution. They come from the judges. The law of constitutional due process is therefore as much judge-made law as any common law is judge-made law. . . . In cases of any considerable novelty, few reasons can be so compelling as to meet with universal acceptation. The determination of closely controverted constitutional issues depends, therefore, in large part upon the composition of the court of last resort at the particular time when the issue comes before it.
>
> Nowhere does this analysis find firmer confirmation than in the history of judicial decisions on the constitutionality of minimum-wage legislation. . . .
>
> Suffice it to say that minimum-wage legislation is now unconstitutional, not because the Constitution makes it so, not because its economic results or its economic propensities would move a majority of judges to think it so, but because it chanced not to come before a particular Supreme Court bench which could not muster a majority against it and chanced to be presented at the succeeding term when the requisite, but no more than requisite, majority was sitting. In the words of the poet, it was not the Constitution but "a measureless malfeasance which obscurely willed it thus"—the malfeasance of chance and the calendar. . . .
>
> As a flagrant instance of insufficient reasons and of a judgment widely regarded as an indefensible judgment, the minimum-wage decision has few if any rivals. While many may doubt the long-run wisdom of minimum-wage legislation, few have been heard to approve the authoritative declaration of its constitutional invalidity. The decision has evoked a more nearly unanimous chorus of disapproval than any other decision in years.[17]

Decrying *Adkins* as a "last skirmish with the fast-disappearing forces of logic and anachronistic formalism," a comment in the *Michigan Law Review* attacked the Court's formalism as well as its encroachment on the responsibilities of legislatures:

> [Past cases] viewed the problem from a mechanical, individualistic standpoint; that liberty, interpreted in the light of the nineteenth century doctrine of *laissez faire* by a strict process of logical deduction, should be conceived of as something static and absolute. . . . [W]ith the foregoing cases as a background, we come to the anomalous instant case.

> The court approaches the problem with what Dean [Roscoe] Pound aptly terms "assumed first principles," and proceeds by logical deductions of fixed and predetermined conceptions in disregard of actual facts. . . . [But] Liberty is not defined, nor can its limits be mapped and charted, by any absolute process of academic logic or classification. Restraints that were arbitrary yesterday may be necessary and rational today, else the law is static and fixed for all time to come. . . . [I]t is in the light of present day conditions and experience as revealed by accurate scientific data rather than the isolation of abstract economic and political philosophy that such statutory restrictions must be viewed. . . .
>
> It is submitted that the question of whether social and economic conditions warrant this type of legislation is not a question of law, as was first assumed; nor a question of fact simply, but really a question of opinion. It is not for the courts to settle, but must be left to the decision of the legislature. And unless it can be shown unmistakably that the opinion of the legislature as to the need for the social or economic legislation in question is unreasonable, judged in the light of actual conditions as revealed by scientific data, the legislative determination is conclusive upon the courts. Measured by this test . . . the instant decision is a step backward, to be retraced at the first opportunity.[18]

The solution, according to legal reformers, was to force the concept of due process out of the legal arena altogether or into a straitjacket that would restrain its use, by means of a bombardment of professional research, carefully worded statutes, and strategic cases that would channel the Court's thinking in the desired direction. Frankfurter wrote an unsigned *New Republic* editorial a year after *Adkins* was decided, when the use of the due process clause to void substantive legislation had become an issue in the presidential election.

> But there are two clauses of the Constitution which present very different problems of statecraft—the "due process" clause of the Fifth Amendment, a limitation upon the federal government, and the "due process of law," and the denial of the "equal protection of the laws" of the Fourteenth Amendment, limiting state action and subjecting every local act of every state to the scrutiny of the Supreme Court at Washington. . . . These are the clauses . . . which have brought forth the most abundant crop of judicial nullifications, and through which the most effective barrier has been raised against utilizing the inherent flexibilities of our Constitution for the adaptation of our traditional legal system to modern needs. The activity of our courts in bending the "conveniently vague" language of due process to the dominant service of vested property interests is a relatively recent tendency of our constitutional law. . . . And so we reach, for the present at least, the culmination of a long line of legislative fatalities in the decision striking down the District of Columbia minimum wage law for women. . . . It is this doctrine [freedom of contract] which the Supreme Court has used as a sword with which to slay most important social legislation and to deny the means of freedom to those least free. . . . The due process clauses ought to go.[19]

Frankfurter had taken Sutherland's hint that "fair wages" might meet a due process standard where "minimum" or "living" wages had not. Kelley pressed on with her constitutional amendment, only to be hurt by its eventual rejection even by friends and colleagues. Kelley's draft amendment would have safeguarded "legislation forbidding the employment of women and minors at wages less than sufficient to maintain them in health," or more ambitiously, as she altered the draft with her own pen, "the employment of any persons."[20]

Like most lawyers, Frankfurter opposed amending the Constitution except as a last resort. He clearly did not oppose the minimum wage, but feared that if liberals succeeded in getting their way through an amendment, in other times conservatives could wreak great harm in a similar manner. Better, he believed, to work slowly through the legal process. Frankfurter's instant rejection of an amendment strategy, and his insistence on working things out through a redefinition of due process, offended Kelley, and she responded angrily:

> The words *fair wages* are as incapable of standard definition as *due process.* . . . As to my impatience with further tinkering with legislation,—what have I done but tinker for forty-one years? My tragic error was failing to do both at once. I should have pushed a far-reaching Amendment from 1895 on, while promoting statutes and decisions. Far from being mutually exclusive both are necessary, now as then. . . . Why do you fancy that I think an Amendment can be quickly obtained? My father [Rep. William D. Kelley, R-Pa.] seconded Mr. Sargent's Joint Resolution for a Suffrage Amendment in 1875 and continued to introduce it after Mr. Sargent went to the Senate [Sen. Aaron Augustus Sargent, R-Calif.] until my father's death in 1889. My grandfather's aunt attended the first meeting (Seneca Falls) at which votes for women were proposed in this country. I have no illusions as to speed. . . . I am at a loss to understand wherein there is a conflict between your proposals . . . and the proposal for a simultaneous introduction of an amendment. There is no *logical* conflict. The federal Suffrage Amendment and the agitation for State laws were pushed simultaneously for many years, and each agitation helped the other.[21]

Frankfurter tried to calm her down and explain why he did not think the amendment route a good one to follow:

> There is no conflict *in logic* between pushing an adequate law for the District and pushing a constitutional amendment. For the moment I do not believe in the efficacy of the amendment movement because its realization is, for me, an extremely remote thing and I am confident that we can accomplish some important results by concentrating upon them. That is, I am anxious that the salvage of minimum wage legislation in the states wherein it is now administered and the passage of new legislation for the District be not treated as orphan children. If you and Miss Dewson go in heavily for the amendment, very, very little will be done in behalf of the requisite legislation. . . . And that, to my mind, would be a misfortune because even from the point of view of securing the amendment you are after, I think it essential to make one more try before the Court with a law that shall seek to avoid some of the foolish notions of Sutherland and yet accomplish in practice exactly what we are after. My prayer, therefore, is that we agree upon the Bill which we have drafted and that that Bill be pushed with all the pertinacity and capacity that you are capable of.[22]

Although Kelley continued to push for a constitutional amendment, within a few years Dewson and others in the NCL abandoned the amendment proposal and threw in their lot with the legal strategy. This was Kelley's political swansong. "I write in deep dismay from which I have not been able to recover since our annual meeting . . . not one vote or voice could be found for approving an amendment."[23]

Kelley died in 1932. The fight for new legislation and a new constitutional rationale continued, however, progressing fitfully through the early New Deal. In 1933 New York enacted a model law devised to bypass Sutherland's reasoning in *Adkins*. Despite its careful wording, the Court, by a narrow majority, struck it down in *Morehead v. New York ex rel. Tipaldo* (1936). But the legal tide, as Frankfurter had predicted, was turning. In a famous reversal, in *West Coast Hotel Co. v. Parrish* (1937), the Supreme Court effectively overruled *Adkins*. Only a year later, Frankfurter's entirely new rationale, relying on the commerce clause rather than the due process guarantee, framed the federal Fair Labor Standards Act of 1938 and its minimum wage for women and men. This nationwide law was duly upheld, in *U.S. v. Darby* (1941). Three days before this decision was handed down, Justice McReynolds, the last of the *Adkins* majority, retired.

It took nearly two decades and massive change in the political environment to resolve the dilemmas created by *Adkins*. It took both a persevering civil society and creative legal minds to clear the path for labor legislation for women and men. The response to *Adkins* demonstrates how many routes are open to those seeking constitutional change and how much time and persistence may be needed to succeed in any one of them.

NOTES

1. "The Supreme Court Passes upon Minimum Wage Laws," *Commercial and Financial Chronicle,* vol. 116, no. 3016, April 14, 1923, 1588–1589.
2. "Wage Fixing and Freedom of Contract," *Law and Labor* 5 (May 1923): 111–118.
3. Franklin Winton Ryan, "The Wage Bargain and the Minimum Wage Decision," *Harvard Business Review* 11 (January 1924): 207–218.
4. Louis D. Brandeis to Felix Frankfurter, April 11, 1923; letter, Charles F. Amidon to Frankfurter, April 12,1923, Felix Frankfurter Papers, Library of Congress.
5. Newton D. Baker to Florence Kelley, April 10 1923, National Consumers' League Papers, Library of Congress.
6. George W. Alger to Florence Kelley, undated [April 1923], Frankfurter Papers.
7. Jesse Adkins to Frankfurter, April 11, 1923, ibid.
8. Frankfurter to Adkins, April 16, 1923, ibid.
9. Florence Kelley, "The Minimum Wage—What Next?" typescript, May 1923, National Consumers' League Papers.
10. National Woman's Party, *Brief as Amicus Curiae on Behalf of the National Woman's Party, Morehead v. New York ex rel. Tipaldo,* 34.
11. Frankfurter to Kelley, April 10, 1923, Frankfurter Papers.
12. Molly W. Dewson to Frankfurter, May 25, 1923, ibid.
13. Molly Dewson to Isadore Lubin, April 16, 1957, Mary W. Dewson Papers, Franklin D. Roosevelt Library, Hyde Park, N.Y.
14. Florence Kelley, "Judicial Obstacles to Child Labor and Minimum Wage Legislation," *American Labor Legislation Review* 14 (September 1924): 224.
15. Editorial, *Nation,* vol. 116, April 25, 1923, 484–485.
16. Florence Kelley to Katherine Philips Edson, May 4, 1923, National Consumers' League Papers, C-3.
17. Thomas Reed Powell, "The Judiciality of Minimum-Wage Legislation," *Harvard Law Review* 37 (March 1924): 545–546, 552, 572.
18. F. M. P., "Constitutional Law—Minimum Wage Law for Women as a Violation of the Fifth Amendment," *Michigan Law Review* 21 (June 1923): 906–910.
19. "The Red Terror of Judicial Reform," *New Republic,* October 1, 1924, 111–112.
20. Florence Kelley, 1923, National Consumers' League Papers.
21. Florence Kelley to Felix Frankfurter, May 26, 1923, Frankfurter Papers.
22. Felix Frankfurter to Florence Kelley, May 31, 1923, ibid.
23. Florence Kelley to Katherine Philips Edson, December 2, 1925, National Consumers' League Papers.

Schechter Poultry Corp. v. United States and United States v. Butler

Lyle Denniston

Schechter Poultry Corp. v. United States
295 U.S. 495 (1935)

DECIDED: May 27, 1935

VOTE

CONCURRING: 9 (Charles Evans Hughes, Willis Van Devanter, James C. McReynolds, Louis D. Brandeis, George Sutherland, Pierce Butler, Harlan F. Stone, Owen J. Roberts, Benjamin N. Cardozo)

DISSENTING: 0

OPINION OF THE COURT: Hughes

CONCURRING OPINION: Cardozo (Stone)

United States v. Butler
297 U.S. 1 (1936)

DECIDED: January 6, 1936

VOTE

CONCURRING: 6 (Charles Evans Hughes, Willis Van Devanter, James C. McReynolds, George Sutherland, Pierce Butler, Owen J. Roberts)

DISSENTING: 3 (Louis D. Brandeis, Harlan F. Stone, Benjamin N. Cardozo)

OPINION OF THE COURT: Roberts

DISSENTING OPINION: Stone (Brandeis, Cardozo)

Deeply embedded in America's constitutional psyche is the understanding that however wrong the Supreme Court may be from time to time, it is more serious error for politicians to react by tampering with the Court's independence. Still, when the Court is on one of its streaks of boldness, the temptation to teach it a lesson in humility always seems to return. Those recurrent realities were never more vivid than during a fairly brief span of the 1930s.

On "Black Monday," May 27, 1935, and in the first week of the next year, January 6, 1936, the Supreme Court knocked over "the twin pillars on which the New Deal rested its hopes for recovery" from the Great Depression, in the words of historian Marian C. McKenna. Those felled pillars were the laws creating sweeping presidential authority to establish codes regulating industry and labor, the National Industrial Recovery Act (NIRA) and the expensive but widely popular program to rescue the nation's farmers from economic ruin, the Agricultural Adjustment Act (AAA). The two decisions that exhibited the Court at its boldest in response to the New Deal, the *Schechter Poultry Corp. v. United States* ruling in late May 1935 and *United States v. Butler* less than eight months later, can be understood and fully appreciated only in the context of their time. As matters turned out, they were quite temporary frustrations of the Roosevelt revolution. And, in the longer sweep of history, they have become mere relics, mentioned often in legal decisions but not followed. As curbs on big government, or as limitations on congressional and executive authority, they have become largely symbolic, rather than lasting, checks.

Put back into the time capsule of the mid-1930s, however, they regain their power. The two rulings, and the reactions they provoked, generated a constitutional crisis as serious, although not as dreadful in its outcome, as the crisis provoked by the *Dred Scott* decision in 1857 (see page 24). A self-confident Court

Note: Substantial research assistance was provided by Pamela Haughton-Denniston, a Washington, D.C., attorney.

and an equally, if not more, self-confident president each pushed against the limits of their authority and the limits of public tolerance.

President Franklin D. Roosevelt, newly in office, found Congress totally compliant with his wishes, perhaps contributing to an expectation that the Court would be, too. In the famous Hundred Days following Roosevelt's inauguration, Congress gave him not only the NIRA's "Blue Eagle" code program and the AAA, but also most of everything he sought in establishing the New Deal. Roosevelt expected these bold new experiments in industrial and agricultural governance to be tested in the Court, but the administration mistakenly believed that the atmosphere of acute crisis would provide as much legal as political cover.

The mood of the Court perhaps can be captured no better than in a brusque remark by Justice Brandeis, who was usually sympathetic to Roosevelt. Two White House aides who visited Brandeis on Black Monday recalled him saying, "The President has been living in a fool's paradise." Brandeis's colleagues would be equally emphatic, if more decorous in their choice of words. "Extraordinary conditions may call for extraordinary remedies," the Court would say, but then add, "Extraordinary conditions do not create or enlarge constitutional power."

DECISIONS IN *SCHECHTER* AND *BUTLER*

Those were the words of a unanimous Court, speaking through Chief Justice Hughes in what everyone felt was the main event in the arena of constitutional combat over the New Deal, *Schechter,* the so-called "sick chicken" case. The suit tested the NIRA's Live Poultry Code and, by implication, hundreds of other mandated controls in codes for other industries. The case against the NIRA was brought by the operators of two poultry slaughterhouses from Brooklyn, New York, who had been convicted of violating the poultry code. To many observers, it seemed that the entire New Deal was on trial.

The poultry "code of fair competition" and others like it under the act were industry-generated and presidentially approved measures designed to end "widespread unemployment and disorganization of industry." Freed of potential antitrust challenge, competitors could control mutual business conduct so as to "remove obstructions to the free flow" of commerce and improve labor conditions by, among other things, limiting the hours in the workweek and ensuring minimum pay scales. Fines of up to $500 per day would follow violations. The poultry code, officials said, would raise wages about 20 percent in the live poultry market in the New York City metropolitan area and increase jobs there by more than 19 percent.

The chief justice's opinion for the unanimous Court began with a swift and easy rejection of the president's claim of extraordinary powers to help industry to recover and government lawyers' claim that the codes were truly voluntary. The crisis did not erase constitutional limits on national power, the Court said. And, as to the poultry code, it added, the government was indulging in "the coercive exercise of the law-making power."

The Court then moved on to the two core constitutional questions. Making use again of a constitutional check it had used only once before, some five months earlier in *Panama Refining Co. v. Ryan* (1935), the first test case on New Deal legislation, the Court found the NIRA code provisions to be an unconstitutional transfer of Congress's legislative power to the president. And, borrowing a theory it had used in interpreting antitrust law, the Court said the codes in their attempt to control workers' hours and wages intruded upon the states' power to regulate business activity that was local in nature, not directly in interstate commerce.

Hughes's opinion conceded that Congress had flexibility in allowing other agencies of government to find specific ways to carry out congressional policy, but stressed that Congress had to retain for itself the definition of that policy and the standards it reflected. Section 3 of the NIRA, allowing creation of the competition codes, set only the vaguest standard, thus imposing next to no limits on presidential authority. "Congress cannot delegate legislative power to the President to exercise an unfettered discretion to make whatever laws he thinks may be needed or advisable for the rehabilitation and expansion of trade or industry," the Court ruled. "Such a sweeping delegation of legislative power finds no support in the decisions upon which the government especially relies."

Turning to the wage and hour restraints in the Live Poultry Code, the Court ruled that these provisions applied to activity that was purely intrastate. The poultry that slaughterhouse workers would process, it said, "had come to a permanent rest within the state," and therefore ceased to be in interstate commerce. "We hold the code provisions here in question to be invalid."

Justice Cardozo, in a concurring opinion joined by Justice Stone, reinforced the Court's ruling on the delegation of congressional power to the executive, calling it "delegation running riot. . . . Here in effect is a roving commission to inquire into evils and upon discovery correct them."

The Court's unanimity in *Schechter* would not hold when the *Butler* case arose on the constitutionality of the AAA, which Congress had passed shortly before it enacted the NIRA. *Butler* was decided by a 6–3 vote, the result of a sharp conflict within the Court over "judicial restraint," producing a dissenting statement on that subject that is quoted to this day. At the time, the outcome served mainly to deepen President Roosevelt's resolve to get a Court more to his liking. It also hardened the resistance among those who lost the benefits that AAA had bestowed.

Just as the NIRA had sought to resuscitate depressed companies and put money in the pockets of financially strapped workers, the AAA was intended to boost prices for basic farm commodities and enable farmers to buy more of the economy's other goods. The act had two principal parts: first, production of basic crops was to be reduced in order to boost prices, and in return farmers would get benefit payments in amounts needed to restore the purchasing power of their livelihood. Second, a system of taxes was to be levied on the processors of raw farm products to cover the cost of the benefit payments. The processors would be allowed to pass the taxes on to consumers through prices on finished or semifinished goods.

Cotton was one of the basic commodities covered by the AAA. When the government attempted to collect processing tax debts owed by the financially insolvent Hoosac Mills Corporation, a Massachusetts operator of several textile mills, the receivers for the company, including former senator William M. Butler, R-Mass., balked and successfully challenged the constitutionality of the tax.

Justice Roberts, writing for the Court majority, found that the receivers had a right to challenge the tax because it was not merely a revenue-raising measure (to which no individual taxpayer would be allowed to file a court challenge); rather, it was "the heart of the law," an indispensable part of the overall plan to regulate crop production, boost prices, and raise farmers' income. The act, Roberts said, "is one regulating agricultural production," and the tax "is a mere incident of such regulation."

The opinion then moved on to "the great and controlling question in the case," which was the power of Congress under the Constitution to spend the funds raised by the tax. Insisting that this review was not an exercise in controlling Congress's actions, but the customary judicial role of weighing constitutional questions, Roberts said that the only power it had as a court "is the power of judgment."

The Court declared that Congress may provide funds to promote "the general welfare," and thus is not confined to making appropriations solely to carry out its specifically enumerated legislative powers, a view it borrowed from Alexander Hamilton. But, it went on, the general welfare for which spending may be authorized—and taxes levied—is only that activity that would come within Congress's power to regulate. "The act invades the reserved rights of the states," Roberts wrote, because it is "a statutory plan to control agricultural production, a matter beyond the powers delegated to the federal government." The tax, the appropriation of the revenues raised, and the direction of their spending are "but means to an unconstitutional end," the Court concluded. The use of the spending power here, it said, was coercive, because it compelled needy farmers to take part in the production-reducing scheme of the act.

Justice Stone's dissent, joined by Brandeis and Cardozo, complained of "a tortured construction of the Constitution" and argued that Congress may use its spending power to persuade someone to take a desired action. The power of the purse, Stone wrote, presupposes the power to choose among different goals and to impose such conditions on the use of funds to make that choice effective. The dissent, in its most memorable passage, lectured the majority on what the dissenters perceived to be excessive judicial muscle-flexing: "While unconstitutional exercise of power by the executive and legislative branches of the government is subject to judicial restraint, the only check upon our own exercise of power is our own sense of self-restraint."

REACTIONS

In response, America gave the Court an earful of political complaint about judicial activism that has echoed ever since. It came from high and low.

A few days after Black Monday, President Roosevelt protested bitterly, "We have been relegated to the horse-and-buggy definition of interstate commerce." With reporters gathered around his White House desk, Roosevelt did not say what retaliation he was already contemplating, but Attorney General Homer Cummings had given voice to it in a private comment heard by Secretary of Labor Frances Perkins: "I tell you, Mr. President, they mean to destroy us. . . . We will have to find a way to get rid of the present membership of the Supreme Court."[1]

Months later, in rural America, the Court's rejection of the AAA crop-reduction subsidy drew a prompt and vivid retort. In Ames, Iowa, the news spread rapidly among more than 600 farmers who had gathered to plan their signups for AAA production allotments on corn and hogs. Before nightfall, a group of six men had bought twelve yards of black cloth and a half-dozen coat-hangers at a variety store in West Ames and fashioned, with crude cardboard faces, six effigies of the justices in the Court majority, hanging them on a billboard near the Iowa State College campus. The prank drew a scolding in an editorial, "This Sort of Thing Is Not Smart," in the *Des Moines Register* and a police investigation.[2]

That Court decisions would upset Americans was not entirely new. As historian Arthur M. Schlesinger Jr. has noted:

> The behavior of the Supreme Court in 1935 and 1936 exposed a familiar sensitivity in the American system. The traditional respect for the priesthood of the Constitution had always mingled in the popular mind with an instinctive skepticism about any men, especially lawyers, who claimed infallibility. Nearly every forceful President in American history had come at one time or another into a collision with the Court. When he did, his objections discovered a surprising resonance among the people.[3]

Did Americans of that time see the two decisions in those ultimate terms? Some did, but most apparently did not. Gauging the response to the two decisions, in government and outside, the critiques may be specific to one case or the other, but the public conversation that unfolded over the short interval between the two and after the second might be best understood as a continuing one, even though scattered and diffuse. It was a conversation made up, in nearly equal parts, of constitutional musing, political assessment, economic conjecture, and caustic judgment on presidential or judicial character. One aspect of the conversation was compelling: it showed a remarkably sophisticated awareness of the theory and substance of the New Deal itself, that amalgam of hastily crafted, bewilderingly complex, top-down, daredevil approaches to economic micromanagement.

One day after the NIRA decision, the *Indianapolis Star*, considered an independent newspaper, said editorially, "The decision undermines the foundation of most of the New Deal structures." The same day, the Democratic-leaning *Cleveland Plain Dealer* said it was "a blue Monday indeed for the New Deal. It is apparent that much of the work done in the direction of industrial control and to protect business from freely acknowledged abuses must be abandoned and others drastically revised." Added the *Los Angeles Times*, sympathetic to the Republican cause: "The ruling's devastatingly inclusive character is obvious. It

A. L. A. Schechter is lifted by his lawyers upon learning of the Supreme Court's decision in *Schechter Poultry Corp. v. United States* (1935). In what came to be known as the "sick chicken" case, the Court declared portions of the National Industrial Recovery Act unconstitutional, handing Schechter and his poultry business a victory and labor groups and President Franklin Roosevelt a defeat. — The Granger Collection, New York

makes abundantly clear that the days of a virtually uncontrolled one man dictatorship in the United States are at an end."

Shortly after the AAA decision, Frank R. Kent, political editor of the *Baltimore Sun,* in a column reprinted across the nation, kept up the practice of viewing the Court's work in this larger context. There should have been no surprise among "the New Dealers," Kent said, that the Court had placed "the AAA in the same unhallowed grave with the NRA [National Recovery Administration]. . . . Certainly there was nothing unexpected about it. It was the clear logic of the NRA decision. Prior to this last decision, it was almost impossible to find a lawyer of balance and standing, Democratic or Republican, who thought it possible for the court to sustain the administration." The *Washington Post* of January 7, 1936, was somewhat more temperate, but echoed the theme: "No event since the Roosevelt administration took office has produced repercussions as pronounced as may be expected from the Supreme Court decision invalidating the AAA. With this interpretation, the cloud of unconstitutionality seems to extend to a large part of the administration's 'recovery' legislation." Reporters for the Associated Press, seeking reaction to the AAA ruling in the hours after it came down, found some of the same gloomy expectations:

> A belief that much more of the New Deal is as good as dead gripped many of its strongest supporters today as they studied with dismay the 6-to-3 Supreme Court decision which wiped out AAA as completely as NRA. . . . Senator [James] Byrnes (D., S.C.), one of the highest in New Deal councils, expressed conviction that the court, as now constituted, would kill the vast social security program, pride of President Roosevelt.[4]

Roosevelt was in complete agreement. From the beginning—at least, from Black Monday and the downing of the Blue Eagle—the president suffered no doubt about what had happened and what he expected would continue to happen as the Court, case by case, reviewed his recovery plan. "The implications of this decision," he said at his "horse-and-buggy" news conference on May 31, 1935, "are much more important than almost certainly any decision of my lifetime or yours, more important than any decision probably since the Dred Scott case." Roosevelt had an agenda, at that point still largely hidden, that surely colored his judgment. But he was at least partly right in seeking to assess the ruling's comparative historical importance, as well as its short-term effect on his program to shore up the economy.

The president said the White House had received between 2,000 and 3,000 letters and telegrams so far, and he read excerpts from them to reporters. The public, according to the president, was talking of the woe that would befall the nation's economy and business without the NIRA. Most of the letters he quoted were from small businessmen or their trade groups, clearly a selection made to drive home his complaint that the true adversaries to the New Deal were the captains of industry and the American Liberty League, the organization the leaders of big business had created to undo his programs. And the president hinted at his ultimate plan of action in response by reciting part of a telegram from "a rather prominent lawyer in Atlanta who is also in business." The excerpt read:

> Respectfully call your attention to section of Constitution referring to appellate power: "The Supreme Court shall have appellate jurisdiction both as to law and fact, with such exceptions and under such regulations as Congress shall make." Suggest act establishing compulsory standard of labor relations and fair trade practices for all industries substantially affecting interstate commerce and creating special court with exclusive jurisdiction thereover and excluding appellate jurisdiction of the Supreme Court.[5]

Roosevelt also parsed the *Schechter* opinion point-by-point, again exhibiting his view that the Court was a continuing, not just a passing, adversary:

> [T]he implication of this opinion is that we have gone back, that the Supreme Court will no longer take into consideration anything that indirectly may affect interstate commerce. That hereafter they will decide the only thing in interstate commerce over which they can permit the exercise of Federal jurisdiction is goods in transit plus, perhaps, a very small number of transactions which would directly affect goods in transit. . . . It does bring up rather squarely as to the big issue in the country and as to how we are going to solve it. The big issue is this: Does this decision mean that the United States Government has no control over any national economic problem? . . . In some ways it may be the best thing that has happened to this country for a long time that such a decision has come from the Supreme Court, because it clarifies the issue.[6]

Some businessmen, too, thought what the Court had done was good for the country, but for entirely different reasons. The day after the *Schechter* ruling, Silas Strawn, a former president of the U.S. Chamber of Commerce, said, "The Supreme Court ruling is the best thing that has happened in this country since the administration took hold. It removes all the fear and apprehension which has been holding back business recovery. Business has been waiting for just this to go ahead."[7] Said a local Chicago meat retailer, Sol Westerfield: "I am quite happy over the decision, and I hope that it sends the death knell of attempted inequitable regulation of the small business man, by which he was given additional burdens and derived no additional benefits."[8]

Arthur Schlesinger, looking back, saw the initial response to *Schechter* as anything but clearly defined. "The public reaction to Black Monday was an indecipherable mixture of dismay, delight, and confusion.

There was no clear crystallization of popular sentiment . . . the one group unaffectedly angered by the decision was labor."[9]

Labor was indeed furious. "Return of Sweatshop Is Feared as Result of Supreme Court's Decision Voiding Recovery Act" blared a headline in the American Federation of Labor's *Weekly News Service* less than a week later:

> The Supreme Court decision . . . threw industrial America back into the jungle of wage slashing, lengthening of the work week, cut-throat competition, child labor, and all the other evils which are the legitimate products of unrestrained profit-seeking by subversive corporations and individual employers who are dead to human relations and know only the god of Mammon.[10]

A week later, an editorial in that publication sought to stir deep revulsion by predicting a dreadful fate for children:

> One of the most regrettable results of the edict of the Supreme Court invalidating the N.R.A. is the inevitable resumption of child labor exploitation by anti-social employers. . . . Freed from the "regimentation" of the N.R.A by the Supreme Court's edict, ruthless employers will again chain thousands of children to the wheels of industry and turn their tender bodies into interest coupons and dividend checks. . . .
>
> For the present, every child labor exploiter in the country can proceed in the ghoulish work of transforming the flesh and blood and mind of children into profits with the knowledge that this inhuman activity is under the protection of the Federal Constitution as interpreted by the Supreme Court.[11]

Not all of labor, however, was unhappy with the Court or the decision. Many black workers, it appears, thought the Court had gotten it right:

> The National Recovery Administration, or "NRA," a linchpin of Franklin Roosevelt's First Hundred Days, did not fare well in the African-American press. "Negro Removal Act," "Negroes Ruined Again," and "Negroes Robbed Again," were only a few of the epithets launched at what many blacks took to be a poisoned spoonful of alphabet soup. . . . When, on "Black Monday," the Supreme Court struck down the NIRA as unconstitutional, no one cheered more heartily than American blacks.[12]

It appears that much of the black protest of the NIRA was aimed at its favoritism of labor unions, from which blacks were then excluded, and the failure of the NIRA to provide wage protection for unskilled laborers.

The Supreme Court had other supporters who thought the justices had come to the nation's rescue. The *Philadelphia Inquirer* of May 28, 1935, was enthusiastic: "The Supreme Court here epitomizes representative government as it was envisioned by the founders. It establishes the truth that, no matter what wrecking crew attempts to destroy the vitality of American principles, it must eventually face the highest legal authority for ratification of its acts, so long as the Constitution is in force." The same day, the *St. Louis Globe Democrat* echoed, "The most encouraging impression is that the Constitution still lives and is still operative"; and the *Portland Oregonian* said, " 'Back to the Constitution' is no longer a forceful slogan. We are there."

Roosevelt, obviously, wanted the public to begin to see that the Supreme Court was the problem, but many believed he was the problem. A prominent Kansas editor, William Allen White, was emphatic about it in an editorial in the *Emporia Gazette*. Titled "The New Dred Scott," it said that Roosevelt's "problem is beginning to be deadly serious." It went on:

Until the Supreme Court decision destroyed the NRA as it stands, he could easily pull one trick after another out of the prestidigitator's plug hat without revealing his ultimate purpose, his final goal. Probably no one, not even his smartest brain trusters, ever knew exactly where Roosevelt is leading America. He has promised a gold pot at the foot of some rainbow. . . . Now the Supreme Court has declared in effect that Franklin Roosevelt is not a Messiah, that he must be circumscribed by the constitutional limits of the presidency. . . . He can no longer hide behind emergency legislation.[13]

Other editorial writers also took on Roosevelt. The *New York Herald-Tribune* started out in moderation, but quickly warmed to an attack:

The course of the President remains to be decided. If he is candid and has been sincere in his radical policies, he will seek the amendment of the Constitution to alter its basic structure and permit the socialization and regimentation of industry. Thereby would be raised an honest and straightforward issue which could be fought out on the merits. But the blow to the President's pride is heavy. The damage to his prestige is great. He is shown after two years, by the unanimous opinion of the Supreme Court, including all its most liberal and progressive members, to have been leading the country down a blind alley. No great leader was ever so completely mistaken. The test of the President goes to the heart of his character and conscience.[14]

Some modern observers of the period believe that Roosevelt's incendiary press conference after *Schechter* made him the issue. Marian McKenna writes:

In the press and over the radio, commentators expressed cool disapproval and even outrage over the ill-tempered attack on a revered institution. Newsmen upbraided FDR severely, took some of his remarks out of context, and portrayed him as rancorous—furious not only with the Court's decision, but with the nine men who rendered it. . . . [T]he course taken by the Court produced in FDR a feeling of almost personal injustice. The public reaction, far from being anti-Supreme Court, as he had expected, was in fact anti-Roosevelt.[15]

But those close to Roosevelt worked to maintain the president's insistence that the fault lay with the Court. Harvard law professor Felix Frankfurter, in a memo to Roosevelt two days after *Schechter,* listed other New Deal measures then pending in Congress and commented:

Let the Court strike down any or all of them . . . especially a divided Court. Then propose a constitutional amendment giving the national Government adequate power to cope with national economic and industrial problems.[16]

Arthur Krock, a *New York Times* columnist, seemed to share Frankfurter's insight on strategy, even as *Butler,* the AAA case, was working its way through lower courts in the wake of the NIRA decision. Attributing his assessment to "a high and shrewd administration quarter," Krock said that the White House wanted the Supreme Court to continue to nullify the New Deal, piece by piece. "The thought which fathers this wish is that only through a full set of judicial reverses can the people be induced to extend the Federal power sufficiently to make room for the New Deal." In fact, he suggested, the president and his lobbying aides were pushing bills through Congress knowing they were "of doubtful constitutionality," precisely to tempt the Supreme Court into more judicial nullifications.[17]

The test of that political perspective would come soon. In the term following the *Schechter* decision, the Court showed no sign of relenting. The most important of the decisions was *Butler,* which invalidated the AAA. Prof. William Lasser describes the political development that followed:

United States v. Butler had a profound effect on the developing showdown between liberals and conservatives. For one thing, unlike any New Deal program previously invalidated by the Court, the AAA was both popular and important. Unlike the *Schechter* case, which was applauded even by many who were friendly toward the administration, *Butler* was supported only by the anti-Roosevelt right. Farmers gave strong support to the agency, as did their representatives in Washington, for the simple reason that the program worked. A powerful grass-roots force was thus thrown into the anti-Court movement. More important, the Court's reasoning in *Butler* made it very clear that the judiciary's standing claim to be "above politics" was, in this instance at least, a sham. . . . Thus, it was *Butler* which inaugurated the six-month-long period in which attacks on the Court reached a peak, and in which constitutional amendments and statutory schemes to curb the Court were discussed with the most frequency.[18]

Political liberals, already deeply upset because of *Schechter,* could not contain their apoplexy over *Butler.* On January 15, 1936, the *Nation* magazine said:

> The nation's Lord High Executioners have again swung the ax. This time it is the Agricultural Adjustment Administration that has succumbed to the Supreme Court's kiss of death. Mr. Justice Roberts, speaking for the Court in the Hoosac case, in an almost incredibly mechanical and legalistic opinion, has ruled that the Administration's largely successful efforts to raise farm income are unconstitutional and must be undone. . . . The Hoosac case now takes its place in the sequence of retreat to an archaic conception of a national government with cruelly limited powers in a time of crisis. . . . After the crippling of the Congressional power over commerce through the Schechter decision, those who have wished to see the national power used for economic control have pinned all their hopes on the taxing and spending power of Congress under the "general-welfare" clause of the Constitution. . . . No use of the taxing power can henceforth be left constitutional under the general-welfare clause if it attempts Congressional regulation of agriculture or industry. . . . The common man, with his direct way of looking at governmental matters, will be unable to make any sense of it at all. . . . Now the Court proves definitely that it is the last bulwark of the vested interests.[19]

Out in the Farm Belt, the reaction was equally negative. The president of the American Farm Bureau Federation, Edward A. O'Neal declared:

> Those who believe the American farmer is going to stand idly by and watch the program for economic equality and parity, for which we fought more than a decade, swept into the discard, will be badly mistaken. . . . My greatest concern is to keep our people judiciously tempered from now on. That the decision will make the American farmer "see red" is a foregone conclusion. . . . If the Constitution in its present form makes it impossible for all groups to enjoy economic equality, steps will be taken immediately to amend the Constitution so that the rights of all citizens will no longer be jeopardized.[20]

The Court also had its supporters. In a January 7, 1936, editorial, the *New York Herald-Tribune* said:

> Unless the Constitution contains some such broad limitation upon the federal taxing power, it is difficult to see how the federal system, with its large faith in local powers, can possibly be preserved. . . . The last two years have shown it must always be to the Supreme Court that the people must look for an effective check upon an unauthorized

expansion of executive powers. The Supreme Court faces an inescapable duty which it has performed courageously. A real revival of confidence may well prove to be the result.

The American Liberty League, the target of Roosevelt's deepest animosity, also weighed in. Its president, Jouett Shouse, on February 6 made a speech to the Bondmen's Club of Chicago, titled "Shall We Plow Under the Supreme Court?" The aim was to try to force the president's hand on the question of amending the Constitution to get a Court more friendly to the New Deal. Said Shouse:

> I submit, gentlemen, that at no time in the prior history of this nation has there been such need as latterly and presently has existed for the preservation of the Supreme Court unimpaired and for the exercise under the Supreme Court of its solemn duty without ostentation, without prejudice, without acclaim, and without fear, to pass upon legislative enactments that may be presented to it, and for your protection to outlaw such enactments as do not conform to the basic and fundamental network of our law. . . . I am extremely anxious to know . . . what is the attitude of the President of the United States toward possible amendment of the Constitution.
> . . . We have plowed under the pigs, we have plowed under the cotton, we have plowed under the wheat, we have plowed under the tobacco, we have plowed under the peanuts, we were about to engage in the experiment of plowing under the potatoes. But far more serious than any of them is the question: Shall the Supreme Court be plowed under?[21]

Once more, Roosevelt's critics knew whom to blame. The *Baltimore Sun*'s Frank Kent, in his widely circulated column, argued:

> The final completeness with which the AAA has been killed, plus the knowledge that many other legislative acts are doomed, has vastly increased the confusion always the outstanding New Deal characteristic.
> Coming as it does on the threshold of Mr. Roosevelt's campaign for re-election, it is involved in the mists of presidential politics, and clear thinking upon the part of the people is not promoted by the immense face-saving efforts bound to be made, and the propaganda which is pouring out to cloak the collapse.
> Nevertheless, it does seem that, as he views the wreckage, one thought would permeate the mind of the average American who, charmed by the gay confidence of the president and pleased with the dramatic show he gave, has retained, despite apprehensions to the cost, [a] belief that Mr. Roosevelt's judgment was sound.
> That thought is the simple one that, pleasing as is his personality, he is an incompetent and unsafe leader, who, plunging ahead regardless of warnings and experience, has made a horrible mess of national affairs after three years of completely futile and terribly costly effort. . . .
> The supreme court needs no defense. It is above and beyond politics. Its members are not candidates for any office, have no part and no interest in campaigns or candidates. The great bulk of the people know and unshakeably believe this. The great bulk of them revere the supreme court as the most stable and detached, the least political and most disinterested of our institutions.
> The great bulk of them are resentful of the blatherskites who blame the supreme court for judgments which were inevitable. If blame is to be placed, the logical place for it is squarely upon Mr. Roosevelt.[22]

The Supreme Court term in which the AAA fell came to an end after seeming to erase any lingering shred of hope for the New Deal or for social legislation of the kind that Roosevelt deemed essential to rescue the nation's economy and its workers. The final thrust was a 5–4 decision on June 1, 1936, in *Morehead v. New York ex rel. Tipaldo.* The decision nullified a New York State law providing minimum wage guarantees for women and children. History professor John W. Johnson has called it "perhaps the most unpopular decision of the 1935–1936 Supreme Court term."[23]

The next day, Justice Stone, who had filed a bitterly worded dissent in *Tipaldo,* wrote to his sister, Helen Stone Willard:

> We finished the term of Court yesterday, I think in many ways one of the most disastrous in its history. At any rate it seems to me that the Court has been needlessly narrow and obscurantic in its outlook. I suppose no intelligent person likes very well the way the New Deal does things, but that ought not to make us forget that ours is a nation which should have the powers ordinarily possessed by governments, and that the framers of the Constitution intended that it should have. . . . [W]e seem to have tied Uncle Sam in a hard knot.[24]

ROOSEVELT'S PLAN TO "REORGANIZE" THE COURT

The presidential campaign then took center stage, with many political analysts convinced that the Supreme Court and its nullification of New Deal laws would be the dominant issue. Roosevelt, however, opted to aim his campaign, not at the Court, but at "economic royalists." In accepting the Democratic nomination on June 27, he accused "these economic royalists" of trying to "hide behind the Flag and the Constitution." The Republicans' campaign claim to be the defenders of the Constitution, their argument that Roosevelt would try to "pack" the Court if he won, was no match for Roosevelt. The voters responded, reelecting him by a margin of more than 11 million votes.

Continuing to hold behind his back his plan to "reorganize" the courts, Roosevelt waited even past his inauguration. On February 5, 1937, he announced his proposal to enlarge the Court. His idea was that for every justice who reached the age of seventy and refused to retire, the president could appoint another justice, up to six new members. The battle grew heated over the following months, until, on July 22, the "Court-packing" plan died in the Senate, a starkly obvious vindication of America's devotion to the Court's independence.

While that fight was going on, changes were already taking place at the Court, sometimes described as "the switch in time that saved nine." As history professor William E. Leuchtenburg put it, "Beginning in 1937, the Supreme Court upheld every New Deal statute that came before it."[25] Today, historians continue to debate why the Court switched. It is worth noting, however, that the Court has never explicitly overruled either *Schechter* or *Butler.* Neither side, then, in this jarring argument that so threatened the stability of the American constitutional order, would admit it was wrong. Yet history's judgment seems to be that such a confrontation should not be repeated.

THE EFFECTS OF *SCHECHTER* AND *BUTLER*

In addition to its immediate influence—cultural, social, or political—upon the affairs of its day, the historic stature of a Supreme Court decision can be measured by its enduring character. As sources of constitutional principle, the *Schechter* and *Butler* rulings, on their merits, have not been hardy precedents. *Schechter*'s view of the doctrine of congressional delegation was applied, fleetingly, some five months later in *Carter v. Carter Coal Co.* (1936), a decision striking down another New Deal program, the Guffey coal act, but has not controlled any decision since. The doctrine still enjoys some favor among some conservative theorists, who consider it not a dead letter, but a part of a "Constitution-in-exile." *Schechter*'s holding on the limits on congressional power to regulate commerce that seems local but has interstate effects was largely cast aside in ensuing decades, although it reappeared in the "New Federalism" decisions of the Court under Chief Justice William H. Rehnquist.

Butler's Hamiltonian understanding of spending to promote the general welfare retains its force, but not in the negative sense in which Justice Roberts used it. The Court has given Congress a wide berth, especially in recent years, to attach conditions to its spending allotments. Some vitality still exists in the doctrine that those conditions can become so onerous, at least to state governments, as to be coercive and arguably invalid. State governments have put that argument repeatedly before the modern Supreme Court, but have yet to attract its attention sufficiently to review a claim. *Butler* has not been used to nullify any federal statute under the spending clause. And Congress's power to tax has not diminished at all because of *Butler*.

Even so, *Schechter* and *Butler* continue to fascinate constitutional scholars and historians and seldom suffer from neglect in legal education. No self-respecting constitutional casebook would dare ignore them: they set the stage for an epic fight over presidential and judicial authority. If not the sole cause of President Roosevelt's attempt to "pack the Court," *Schechter* and *Butler* certainly were the greatest provocations. Some evidence exists that Roosevelt and his advisers had been thinking of remaking the federal courts well before New Deal reforms were tested in court. It cannot be doubted, however, that these two rulings, when they came down, galvanized Roosevelt's intentions. And, if Roosevelt had never been provoked into putting forth his plan, and had never seen it go down to defeat, would the Court as an institution be as securely independent today as it seems to be? When nothing else about the New Deal era is remembered, that crisis most assuredly will be. Each time, even today, that a disgruntled member of Congress introduces a bill to "correct" a Supreme Court decision, or to punish the justices for "activism," that crisis looms as a tall barrier to legislative enactment.

NOTES

1. Frances Perkins, quoted in Arthur M. Schlesinger Jr., *The Politics of Upheaval, 1935–1936,* Mariner Edition (Boston: Houghton Mifflin, 2003), 288.

2. *Des Moines Register,* January 7, 8, and 9, 1936.

3. Schlesinger, *The Politics of Upheaval,* 484.

4. Associated Press, datelined Washington, "Fear Most of New Deal Dead After Court Ruling," *Arkansas Democrat,* January 8, 1936, 1.

5. Press conference transcript, New Deal Network, http://newdeal.feri.org/court/fdr5_31_35.htm (last viewed March 2, 2005).

6. Ibid.

7. *Chicago Tribune,* May 28, 1935, 3.

8. Ibid., May 23, 1935, 3.

9. Schlesinger, *The Politics of Upheaval,* 283.

10. *Weekly News Service,* June 1, 1935.

11. Ibid., June 8, 1935.

12. Ken I. Kersch, "Blacks and Labor—The Untold Story," *Public Interest* (Summer 2002): 141.

13. *Emporia Gazette,* May 30,1935, signed "W.A.W."

14. *New York Herald-Tribune,* May 28, 1935.

15. Marian C. McKenna, *Franklin Roosevelt and the Great Constitutional War: The Court-Packing Crisis of 1937* (New York: Fordham University Press, 2002), 115.

16. Frankfurter Papers, Library of Congress, Box 98.

17. Arthur Krock, "In Washington," *New York Times,* July 18, 1935, 18.

18. William Lasser, *The Limits of Judicial Power: The Supreme Court in American Politics* (Chapel Hill: University of North Carolina Press, 2002), 139.

19. "The Supreme Court Swings the Ax," *Nation,* January 15, 1936.

20. Quoted in *Des Moines Register,* January 7, 1936, 1.
21. American Liberty League Document No. 101, on file with the Jouett Shouse Collection, University of Kentucky Libraries.
22. Frank R. Kent, "Roosevelt Is Place for Blame," *Des Moines Register,* January 11, 1936, 4.
23. *The Oxford Guide to United States Supreme Court Decisions,* ed. Kermit L. Hall (New York and Oxford: Oxford University Press, 1999), 201.
24. Alpheus T. Mason, *Harlan Fiske Stone, Pillar of the Law* (New York: Viking Press, 1956), 425–426.
25. William E. Leuchtenburg, *The Supreme Court Reborn: The Constitutional Revolution in the Age of Roosevelt* (New York and Oxford: Oxford University Press, 1995), 220.

Minersville School District v. Gobitis

Shawn Francis Peters

Minersville School District v. Gobitis
310 U.S. 586 (1940)

        DECIDED: June 3, 1940
        VOTE
        CONCURRING: 8 (Charles Evans Hughes, James C. McReynolds, Owen J. Roberts, Hugo L.
                                Black, Stanley F. Reed, Felix Frankfurter, William O. Douglas, Frank Murphy)
        DISSENTING: 1 (Stone)
        OPINION OF THE COURT: Frankfurter
        CONCURRING WITHOUT OPINION: McReynolds
        DISSENTING OPINION: Stone

M*inersville School District v. Gobitis* had its origins in a dispute between a trio of Jehovah's Witness schoolchildren and school authorities in a small town in eastern Pennsylvania. The Supreme Court's resolution of this clash—in a 1940 majority opinion written by Justice Frankfurter—helped catalyze the worst outbreak of religious persecution seen in the United States in the twentieth century.

In the mid-1930s Jehovah's Witnesses throughout the United States began to refrain from participating in flag salute exercises. Such ceremonies, they believed, were idolatrous and violated the teachings of the scriptures, especially those biblical passages proscribing the worship of "graven images" found in Exodus 20:4–5. Before long, the sect's position—which was interpreted by many as a sign of disloyalty to the United States—created conflicts for children who attended schools where participation in flag salute exercises was compulsory. Many were forced to make an agonizing choice: they could either follow their religious beliefs or adhere to the regulations enforced at their schools.

In 1935 Witness schoolchildren Edmund Wasliewski and Lillian and William Gobitas (their surname was later misspelled as "Gobitis" in the courts) balked at the patriotic exercises organized at their Minersville public school. At the time, the school had no regulation mandating that students participate in the flag salute, but, in response to the furor created by the young Witnesses' refusal to do so, the local school board quickly enacted one. The board then took action against the three Witness children, expelling them for violating the new measure. They were forced to attend a modest school operated by members of their faith.

With the support of the Witnesses' headquarters, which organized a full-scale legal campaign in the courts throughout the 1930s and 1940s, the Minersville Witnesses sued the local school board for violating their constitutionally protected freedoms of speech and religion. The Witnesses prevailed in the lower federal courts, which found that the enforcement of flag salute requirement encroached on the children's religious liberty. When the school district appealed to the U.S. Supreme Court, the Witnesses were supported by the American Civil Liberties Union (ACLU) and the American Bar Association's Committee on the Bill of Rights. In *amicus curiae* (friend of the court) briefs, both organizations stressed that the Witnesses' civil liberties would be violated if they were forced to salute the flag—and thereby repudiate one of the tenets of their religious faith—at school.

Justice Frankfurter maintained that the case had little to do with civil liberties. In his opinion for the Court's majority in *Gobitis,* which struck down the lower courts' rulings, he insisted that the Minersville dispute was largely a matter of determining when and how the courts could legitimately infringe on the "legislative judgment" normally exercised by lawmakers. Although civil liberties were precious, he maintained, the justices had to balance them against the legitimate interests of the state. "Conscientious scruples have not, in the long struggle for religious toleration, relieved the individual from obedience to a general law not aimed at the promotion or restriction of religious convictions," Frankfurter wrote, in upholding the school board's decision to expel the Witness schoolchildren. "The mere possession of religious convictions which contradict the relevant concerns of a political society does not relieve the citizen from the discharge of political responsibilities."

Only one member of the Court—Justice Stone—dissented from Frankfurter's opinion. In an impassioned defense of individual and minority rights, Stone noted, "History teaches us that there have been but few infringements of personal liberty by the state which have not been justified, as they are here, in the name of righteousness and the public good, and few which have not been directed, as they are now, at politically helpless minorities."

EDITORIAL RESPONSES

At first, the decision met with a smattering of praise. The *Washington Post,* for example, lauded it in an editorial:

> In periods of public excitement the fine line between liberty and license acquires a special significance. There is grave danger, on the one hand, that civil rights guaranteed by the Constitution will be recklessly suppressed as a means of promoting public safety. At the other extreme there is danger that complete freedom in the exercise of assumed rights may interfere with the effective functioning of democracy.
>
> A delicate line between these two positions was skillfully drawn by the Supreme Court yesterday in its decision that local authorities may require children attending public schools to salute the American flag. The opinion written by Justice Frankfurter did not [e]ndorse or condemn the practice of requiring pupils to salute the flag. Some regulations designed to stimulate a "common feeling for the common country," the court said, may seem harsh and others foolish. But the court insisted that the State Legislatures have a right to exercise their discretion in such matters without interference from the courts. . . .
>
> [I]t does not appear that the saluting requirement, arbitrary though it may be, violates any basic right. Obviously it has no connection with freedom of religion. If the United States supported a state church, a case could be made for refusal to salute the flag on religious grounds. But with our complete separation of church and state, there can be no religious or antireligious implications in a salute to the flag.
>
> Long ago the Supreme Court decided that freedom of worship does not give a sect a right to indulge in every practice which it may regard as part of its religion. Freedom of religion extends only to the realm of spiritual belief and ritualistic practice. It does not permit any group to interfere with legitimate functions of the state under the guise of practicing their religion.[1]

Such glowing assessments, however, were the exception rather than the rule. Other major newspapers, such as the *New York Times,* were ambivalent about—or even downright hostile to—the Court's ruling in *Gobitis.*

> All over the United States, on school days, children may be heard repeating the pledge to the flag: "I pledge allegiance to the flag of the United States of America, and to the Republic for which it stands, one nation, indivisible, with liberty and justice for all." With very few exceptions, they give the salute and repeat the words gladly and proudly. It is a ceremony which can be made to mean something beautiful. But the exceptions do

exist, and among them are the members of a sect known as Jehovah's Witnesses, who seem to regard the flag salute as a form of idolatry. Five years ago the school board of Minersville, Pa., expelled two children belonging to this denomination who refused to salute. The Supreme Court of the United States, in a decision written by a courageous friend of human liberty, Justice Felix Frankfurter, has now sustained the school board. Seven members of the court concurred. One, Justice Stone, dissented. . . .

Those of us who are unlearned in the law, and whose opinions do not become law, are probably not in disagreement with either the majority or the minority of the court in this case when we observe that the reverence for the ideals for which the flag stands is more important than any gesture. The salute will be easy if the reverence exists. The reverence will exist if teachers and other adults, especially those who hold public office, show in their own lives respect for the Bill of Rights. Even the members of Jehovah's Witnesses may well remember that among the principles for which the flag stands is their right to worship as they please, write as they please and speak as they please.[2]

In offering blunt criticism of the *Gobitis* opinion, several newspapers speculated that the Supreme Court seemed to have been influenced by mounting fears over the war in Europe and the possibility of subversion at home. The *St. Louis Post-Dispatch* made this point in an editorial condemning the Court's ruling in the flag salute case.

We think [the Court's] decision is a violation of American principle. We think it is a surrender to popular hysteria. If patriotism depends upon such things as this—upon violation of a fundamental right of religious freedom—then it becomes not a noble emotion of love for country, but something to be rammed down our throats by the law.[3]

In its own sly editorial the *Des Moines Register* made the same kind of connection between current events and the Court's reasoning.

Now, this may be heresy, but we just can't help wondering a little whether the Supreme Court's diminished enthusiasm [for protecting the civil liberties of Jehovah's Witnesses] is in any degree a by-product of the new circumstances that have developed in the world in the last month or two.[4]

For its part, the *Chicago Tribune*—a bastion of conservatism—blasted the Court for repudiating the liberal principles that its members purportedly espoused.

The decision offers additional evidence that the court as it is now constituted does not deserve to be called liberal. In a close case like this one the liberal will decide for the individual and against the government. He will resolve his doubts on the side of liberty. Mr. Roosevelt has created a court which resolves doubts against the citizen and for the coercive state. It is a Supreme Court which believes that the bureaucrats are almost always right and the individual is almost always wrong. The kind of court can be called socialist, but it should never be called liberal.[5]

CRITICISM FROM CIVIL LIBERTIES SUPPORTERS AND RELIGIOUS PUBLICATIONS

Not surprisingly, the decision in *Gobitis* appalled individuals, organizations, and publications that attempted to safeguard civil liberties. ACLU director Roger Baldwin expressed his dismay in a letter to Witness leader Joseph Rutherford.

It is something of a shock to find the court brushing aside the traditional right of religious conscience in favor of a compulsory conformity to a patriotic ritual. The language of the prevailing opinion unhappily reflects something of the intolerant temper of the moment.

It has always been our contention that where a conflict between duty to God and duty to the state arose, duty to God comes first where there is involved no interference with the rights of others or any practice contrary to the public peace and morality.[6]

Shortly after the opinion was handed down, another prominent member of the ACLU, clergyman John Haynes Holmes, published a moving defense of the Witnesses' beliefs. Holmes also argued that the Court's opinion had directly contributed to a succession of mob attacks upon members of the faith.

It is amazing, when you come to think of it, that [the Witnesses' reluctance to salute the flag] should be questioned or misunderstood, most of all derided and denied. Are not the Witnesses in the best tradition of the Christian spirit in refusing this salutation to the flag? What were the early Christians doing but this very thing when they refused to put their pinch of salt upon the altars of the Roman emperor? That was all the Roman authorities demanded—just this little pinch of salt as evidence of the loyalty of these Christians to the government! But the Christians insisted that the pinch of salt was a matter not of patriotism but of religion. If they made this gesture, they would be denying their sole allegiance on earth as in heaven, to God and to his Christ. And so they refused—and died! . . .

It is no accident that this long and violent succession of outrages against the Witnesses in recent weeks was coincident with the unfortunate decision of the Supreme Court refusing to interfere with the action of school authorities in demanding the salute.[7]

Numerous religious publications added their voices to the chorus of criticism that greeted the Court's decision in *Gobitis*. During the summer of 1940, the *Christian Century* devoted several editorials to picking apart the reasoning of Justice Frankfurter's majority opinion.

Loyalty to the nation and to its government is important. Saluting the flag is merely an arbitrary piece of ritual which is one way of expressing loyalty and teaching loyalty. Many of us like it. We love the flag. To us it is, in Justice Frankfurter's words, "the symbol of our national unity . . . the emblem of freedom . . . it signifies government resting on the consent of the governed, liberty regulated by law, the protection of the weak against the strong, security against the exercise of arbitrary power." Still, it is quite conceivable that there may be those to whom saluting a symbol seems equivalent to worshipping an image. This is, in our judgment, a foolish idea. But it is of the essence of liberty that there be room for harmless foolish ideas—or harmless ideas that seem foolish to the majority. Willingness to salute the flag is no criterion of loyalty. To make this particular ceremony a test is to make the flag quite different from what Justice Frankfurter says it means.[8]

Another *Christian Century* editorial struck a more ominous note.

Unpopular minorities are not always adequately protected by legislative bodies or appointed boards. The Constitution and the courts are their resource. But in the long run the rights of majorities also are at stake. . . . Courts that will not protect even the Jehovah's Witnesses will not long protect anybody.[9]

Many critics of the *Gobitis* opinion seemed to be especially nettled that its author was Justice Frankfurter, who had long been considered a champion a civil liberties. In private correspondence to Justice Stone, the lone justice to break with the Court's majority, several observers paired their praise for his eloquent dissent with sharp criticism of Frankfurter. A letter sent to Stone by the British Socialist Harold Laski, a friend of both of men, was typical on this score. "First and foremost, I want to tell you how right I think you are in that educational case from Pennsylvania and, to my deep regret, how wrong I think Felix [Frankfurter] is."[10]

A Congregational minister named Charles Hager made a similar point in a letter to Stone. "I dare believe that the time will come when your children, if you have them, will be as proud of your dissent in this case as on any other act of your progressive career. . . . Especially I am disappointed with Frankfurter."[11]

Several of those who commended Stone correctly predicted that his dissent would be long remembered as a landmark defense of civil liberties. Assistant Attorney General Thurman Arnold expressed the views of many when he complimented Stone:

> I think that your dissenting opinion in the salute-to-the-flag case is not only sensible but courageous. I congratulate you. It shows a sense of proportion which people are too apt to lose in these days. Ten years from now everyone who knows you will be proud that you dissented.[12]

MOB VIOLENCE

Tragically for the Jehovah's Witnesses, the public's reaction to the *Gobitis* opinion went beyond rhetorical salvos aimed at members of the Supreme Court. The flag salute case was unique in the annals of American legal history because of the extraordinarily violent response it precipitated among members of the general public, many of whom misinterpreted the Court's decision as an indictment of the Witnesses' loyalty. Historian Peter Irons neatly summarized the impact of the opinion: "Supreme Court decisions often are criticized, and some are disobeyed, but few have ever provoked as violent a public reaction as the *Gobitis* opinion. Frankfurter's words unleashed a wave of attacks on Witnesses across the country."[13]

Minersville, Pa.
Nov. 5, 1935

Our School Directors
Dear Sirs

I do not salute the flag because I have promised to do the will of God. That means that I must not worship anything out of harmony with God's law. In the twentieth chapter of Exodus it is stated, "Thou shalt not make unto thee any graven image, nor bow down to them nor serve them for I the Lord thy God am a jealous God visiting the iniquity of the fathers upon the children unto the third and fourth generation of them that hate me. I am a true follower of Christ. I do not salute the flag because I do not love my country but I love my country and I love God more and I must obey His commandments.

Your Pupil,
Billy Gobitas

Student William Gobitas wrote a letter dated November 5, 1935, to the directors of the Minersville, Pennsylvania, school district explaining that he refused to salute the flag because it conflicted with his religious beliefs as a Jehovah's Witness. William's father, Walter, sued the school district after his children were expelled for refusing to salute the flag. In *Minersville School Dist. v. Gobitis* (1940)—the family name was misspelled in the records—the Supreme Court upheld compulsory flag saluting, but a strong dissenting opinion by Justice Harlan Stone remains as a landmark defense of civil liberties. —William Gobitas Papers, reprinted with permission of Lillian Gobitas Klose

Among those who felt the public's wrath was Lillian Gobitas, one of the schoolchildren who had challenged the flag salute regulation. She later recounted her own response to the Court's decision and the storm of violence it helped touch off.

It never really occurred to us that the court's decision would be anything but favorable. After all, we had won the previous two cases [in the lower courts]. But on the morning of June 3, 1940, Mom and I were working in the kitchen with the radio playing in the background. Suddenly a newscast came on. The judges had decided against us— and not by a mere margin, but by 8 to 1! Mom and I just stood there, frozen in disbelief. . . .

This decision unleashed an almost unimaginable wave of terror. Across the country, it was open season on Jehovah's Witnesses. People thought they were doing their patriotic duty by attacking us.[14]

One of the worst anti-Witness incidents occurred in Kennebunk, Maine, where townspeople attacked a Kingdom Hall operated by the sect. The *Boston Globe* described how the mob destroyed the building.

The mob made two visits and set two fires. The first burned out part of the building's interior but was extinguished quickly. The second . . . completed the destruction. Before each of the fires the mob ransacked the building . . . and removed tracts, furnishings and members' personal belongings. These were burned in piles in a street of this ordinarily placid town. A man and woman were "roughed up" in the second sacking of the headquarters. Identified only as Biddeford [a small town nearby] members of the Witnesses, they were taken to the town line and released. . . . Neither was hurt, police said, but the man's shirt was "torn from his back." Hours after firemen doused the last ember, club-carrying townspeople milled around the building, and someone affixed a small American flag to the charred front of the hall.[15]

The *New York Herald Tribune* was among the many newspapers to draw a direct link between the outbreak of anti-Witness violence and the Supreme Court's opinion in *Gobitis*.

We have the "liberal" members of the Supreme Court to thank—at least in part—for the religious riots which have been breaking out in Maine. This conservative New England state has seen little lynching or other lawlessness; but the Supreme Court's recent decision that the Jehovah's Witnesses must salute the flag seems to have convinced several hundred Maine rustics that it is their personal responsibility to see this decree carried out.[16]

An incident in Texas demonstrates the clear connection between the Court's opinion in *Gobitis* and violence against Jehovah's Witnesses. As the local sheriff looked on, a mob forced a group of Witnesses to leave a small town. The sheriff later told reporter Beulah Amidon what had caused the disturbance. "Jehovah's Witnesses. They're running them out of here. They're traitors—the Supreme Court says so. Ain't you heard?" Amidon recognized that the sheriff's misinterpretation of the meaning of the *Gobitis* opinion was widespread and that it foretold horrific consequences for Witnesses throughout the country. "North and South, East and West, the Court decision has served to kindle mob violence against Jehovah's Witnesses."[17]

THE JUSTICES RESPOND

A steady drumbeat of such comments had an effect on three of the justices who had been part of the Supreme Court's majority in *Gobitis*. In an extraordinary move, Justices Douglas, Black, and Murphy explicitly backed away from the ruling. They did so in 1942 in another case involving Jehovah's Witnesses, *Jones v. Opelika*. Although the *Jones* opinion did not directly concern flag saluting (it covered several cases involving the application of municipal leafleting ordinances to religious proselytizing), the three justices used it to express their misgivings about the Court's handling of *Gobitis*.

> The opinion of the Court sanctions a device which in our opinion suppresses or tends to suppress the free exercise of a religion practiced by a minority group. This is but another step in the direction which *Minersville School District v. Gobitis* took against the same religious minority and is a logical extension of the principles upon which that decision rested. Since we joined in the opinion in the *Gobitis* case, we think this is an appropriate occasion to state that we now believe that it was also wrongly decided. Certainly our democratic form of government functioning under the historic Bill of Rights has a high responsibility to accommodate itself to the religious views of minorities however unpopular and unorthodox those views may be. The First Amendment does not put the right freely to exercise religion in a subordinate position. We fear, however, that the opinions in these [cases] and in the *Gobitis* case do exactly that.[18]

Just a year later, in *West Virginia Board of Education v. Barnette*, the Supreme Court took the extraordinary step of essentially reversing itself on the flag salute issue. Justice Jackson's eloquent majority opinion in *Barnette* (which focused more on free speech than religious liberty) sounded the death knell of *Gobitis* only three years after it had been handed down.

> The case is made difficult not because the principles of its decision are obscure but because the flag involved is our own. Nevertheless, we apply the limitations of the Constitution with no fear that freedom to be intellectually and spiritually diverse or even contrary will disintegrate the social organization. To believe that patriotism will not flourish if patriotic ceremonies are voluntary and spontaneous instead of a compulsory routine is to make an unflattering estimate of the appeal of our institutions to free minds. We can have intellectual individualism and the rich cultural diversities that we owe to exceptional minds only at the price of occasional eccentricity and abnormal attitudes. When they are so harmless to others or to the State as those we deal with here, the price is not too great. But freedom to differ is not limited to things that do not matter much. That would be a mere shadow of freedom. The test of its substance is the right to differ as to things that touch the heart of the existing order.
>
> If there is any fixed star in our constitutional constellation, it is that no official, high or petty, can prescribe what shall be orthodox in politics, nationalism, religion, or other matters of opinion or force citizens to confess by word or act their faith therein. If there are any circumstances which permit an exception, they do not now occur to us.
>
> We think the action of the local authorities in compelling the flag salute and pledge transcends constitutional limitations on their power and invades the sphere of intellect and spirit which it is the purpose of the First Amendment to our Constitution to reserve from all official control.[19]

The Court's repudiation of *Gobitis* was greeted favorably in most quarters. *Time* magazine, in a story headlined "Blot Removed," offered a typical response to the justices' decision in *Barnette*. "The U.S. Supreme Court this week reaffirmed its faith in the Bill of Rights—which, in 1940, it had come perilously close to outlawing."[20]

The Court's tumultuous journey from *Gobitis* to *Barnette* did not lay to rest controversies regarding the flag salute and the Pledge of Allegiance. In the 1988 presidential campaign, for example, Vice President

George H. W. Bush castigated his opponent, Michael Dukakis, for his veto, as governor of Massachusetts, of a measure that would have fined public school teachers in his state who failed to lead their classes in pledge exercises. And in 2000 a father in California filed a much-publicized lawsuit in which he asserted that a law mandating recitation of the Pledge of Allegiance in public schools violated the First Amendment's establishment clause because the oath forced pupils to use the phrase "under God." In 2004, in the case *Elk Grove School District v. Newdow,* the Supreme Court dismissed the father's claim, saying that he lacked legal standing to act on his daughter's behalf.

NOTES

1. "Rights and Privileges," *Washington Post,* June 4, 1940, 6.
2. "Problem in Freedom," *New York Times,* June 5, 1940, 24.
3. Quoted in John A. Garraty, ed. *Quarrels That Have Shaped the Constitution,* 2d ed. (New York: Harper and Row, 1987), 298.
4. "Oh, Well, We Were Just Wondering," *Des Moines Register,* June 7, 1940, 4.
5. "An Illiberal Court," *Chicago Tribune,* June 9, 1940, 17.
6. Press Release, American Civil Liberties Union, June 7, 1940.
7. John Haynes Holmes, "The Case of Jehovah's Witnesses, *Christian Century,* July 17, 1940, 896–898.
8. "The Flag Salute Case," *Christian Century,* June 19, 1940, 791–792.
9. "The Court Abdicates," *Christian Century,* July 3, 1940, 845–846.
10. Quoted in Shawn Francis Peters, *Judging Jehovah's Witnesses: Religious Persecution and the Dawn of the Rights Revolution* (Lawrence: University Press of Kansas, 2000), 69.
11. Quoted in ibid., 67.
12. Thurman Arnold to Harlan Fiske Stone, June 7, 1940, Stone Papers, Library of Congress.
13. Peter Irons, *The Courage of Their Convictions: Sixteen Americans Who Fought Their Way to the Supreme Court* (New York: Penguin, 1990,) 22.
14. Lillian Gobitas Klose, "The Courage to Put God First," *Awake!* July 22, 1993, 15.
15. Quoted in Peters, *Judging Jehovah's Witnesses,* 79.
16. Quoted in ibid., 82.
17. Beulah Amidon, "Can We Afford Martyrs?" *Survey Graphic,* September 1940, 457–460.
18. *Jones v. City of Opelika,* 316 U.S. 584, at 623–624 (1942).
19. *West Virginia State Board of Education v. Barnette,* 319 U.S. 624, at 641–642 (1943).
20. "Blot Removed," *Time,* June 21, 1943, 16.

Ex parte Quirin

Louis Fisher

Ex parte Quirin
317 U.S. 1 (1942)

DECIDED: July 31, 1942 (per curiam)
October 29, 1942 (full opinion)

VOTE

CONCURRING: 8 (Harlan F. Stone, Owen J. Roberts, Hugo L. Black, Stanley F. Reed, Felix
Frankfurter, William O. Douglas, James F. Byrnes, Robert H. Jackson)

DISSENTING: 0

OPINION OF THE COURT: Stone

DID NOT PARTICIPATE: Frank Murphy

In *Ex parte Quirin* the Supreme Court upheld the jurisdiction of a military tribunal established by President Franklin D. Roosevelt to try eight German saboteurs, one of whom was Richard Quirin. After the terrorist attacks of September 11, 2001, the White House called the Court's World War II decision an "apt precedent" for President George W. Bush to authorize the creation of military tribunals to try noncitizens accused of providing assistance to the terrorists. On June 28, 2004, when the Supreme Court in *Hamdi v. Rumsfeld* placed some constraints on the president's power to try enemy combatants, the plurality decision, written by Justice Sandra Day O'Connor, referred to *Quirin* as "the most apposite precedent" for detaining U.S. citizens. In his dissenting opinion, Justice Antonin Scalia said that the German saboteur case "was not this Court's finest hour." Military tribunals have been controversial because they are created by presidents or military commanders without specific statutory support. Courts-martial, used to try military personnel, follow procedural rules adopted by Congress. In addition, tribunals have been used to try civilians, including U.S. citizens.

The eight Germans in the *Quirin* case traveled by two submarines to the United States in June 1942 to commit sabotage on industrial and economic targets, focusing on aluminum plants, bridges, and railways. Because one of the saboteurs (George Dasch) turned himself in to the FBI, the other seven were apprehended within a matter of weeks. Part of the purpose of creating a military tribunal instead of prosecuting them in civil court, with the glare of full press coverage, was to avoid publicizing the fact that Dasch had surrendered and helped the government locate his colleagues. President Roosevelt wanted Nazi Germany and other Axis powers to believe that the United States had a remarkable capacity for policing its borders and catching enemy spies. Also, Roosevelt wanted the death penalty to send a signal to would-be saboteurs. Had the eight men been tried in civil court, the maximum penalty would have been prison terms ranging between two and thirty years.

Four of the Germans had come ashore near Jacksonville, Florida, and the others landed at Amagansett, Long Island. After their arrest, President Roosevelt issued a proclamation on July 2 to create a military tribunal, which began its proceedings on July 8 on the fifth floor of the Justice Department. On July 21 the defense counsel informed the tribunal that the prisoners planned to apply for a writ of *habeas corpus,* a review of the legality of a person's imprisonment by government authority, in U.S. district court to test the constitutionality of Roosevelt's proclamation. The district court turned down the petition for a writ on July 28, and oral argument began the following day before the Supreme Court. After two days and nine hours of oral argument, the Court on July 31 upheld the jurisdiction of the tribunal, and the trial concluded on August 1. A verdict two days later found all eight men guilty, and six were electrocuted on August 8.

The Court's decision on July 31 consisted of a short *per curiam* (by the court), an unsigned opinion, announcing that the tribunal had jurisdiction to proceed. The *per curiam* explained that the Court was acting "in advance of the preparation of a full opinion which necessarily will require a considerable period of time for its preparation and which, when prepared, will be filed with the Clerk." In other words, the Court was upholding the jurisdiction of the tribunal without providing a legal justification. The full opinion, containing the legal reasoning, was not released until October 29. Because six of the saboteurs had already been executed, the Court's full opinion could not possibly admit to any legal or constitutional deficiencies in the tribunal proceedings.

RESPONSES IN THE PRESS

Some press accounts were critical of the Court for even taking the case. An editorial in the *Los Angeles Times* of July 29, 1942, objected to the "totally uncalled-for summoning of the United States Supreme Court in extraordinary session to pass on the question of *habeas corpus*." For the most part, however, the Court received credit for meeting in special session in the middle of the summer to consider the legal rights of the Nazi saboteurs. To many in the media, American standards of justice had been proudly displayed. After the two days of oral argument, a *Washington Post* editorial remarked:

> Americans have faith in their institutions, confidence in their inherent strength. Even in as desperate a crisis as that which faces our Nation and other free nations today, we do not propose to imitate the enemy, but only to act in accordance with the precepts of law and right. For that reason there is an element of the sublime in the action of the Chief Justice in calling this extraordinary session of the court.[1]

On August 9 the *Post* said of the *per curiam*: "Americans can have the satisfaction of knowing that even in a time of great national peril we did not stoop to the practices of our enemies." The *New York Times* believed that the country "drew a long breath of relief" when the Court issued its *per curiam* and predicted that the full opinion, "which will be made public later on, will go into our constitutional history beside the [*Ex parte*] *Milligan* decision, delivered in 1866."[2] (See page 34.) The *Chicago Daily Tribune* reacted to the *per curiam* by saying:

> There is probably no other country in the world in which the jurisdiction of a military court to handle such a case would have been given so much as a moment's question. The fact that our government was required to prove its right to try the suspects under military law has had the effect, and quite probably the intended effect, of pointing the contrast between totalitarian justice and American justice. That is all to the good.[3]

For those who wondered why the men were tried instead of being placed against a wall and shot, the *New York Times* took the high ground: "We had to try them because a fair trial for any person accused of crime, however apparent his guilt, is one of the things we defend in this war."[4] The *New Republic* also expressed satisfaction with the judicial proceedings: "It is good to know that even in wartime and even toward the enemy we do not abandon our basic protection of individual rights. . . . And it is undoubtedly a good thing for Americans to know, and to tell the world, that they have invoked the rule of law even in the case of enemy saboteurs."[5]

The initial public reaction to the *per curiam* was almost wholly one of praise. A rare dissenting note about the judicial process came from Norman Cousins of the *Saturday Review of Literature*:

> You don't have to dangle your saboteurs before you and poke them with democracy to prove to them they are having a fair trial. There was no need for a summary execu-

tion, but there was similarly no need to make a farce out of justice, when everyone knew at the very start of the trial what the outcome would be. If the saboteurs *actually had a chance,* it would be different, but they didn't; we knew it, and they knew it.[6]

A similar evaluation came from constitutional scholar Edward S. Corwin, who viewed the Court's full opinion as "little more than a ceremonious detour to a predetermined end."[7] John P. Frank, who had clerked for Justice Black in 1942 and watched the internal proceedings, remarked that the Court "sent the defendants to their deaths some months before Chief Justice Stone was able to get out an opinion telling why."[8]

A CRITICAL LEGAL ANALYSIS

Justice Frankfurter was sufficiently troubled by the full decision to ask his former student, Frederick Bernays Wiener, an expert on military justice, to offer his views on how well the Court had acquitted itself. Wiener was unsparing in his criticism. He prepared three analyses for Frankfurter, sending them in letters on November 5, 1942, and January 13 and August 1, 1943. Each pointed out serious deficiencies in the Court's work.

The first letter credited the Court for taking "the narrowest—and soundest—ground" in holding that the eight saboteurs were "war criminals (or unlawful belligerents) as that term is understood in international law," and that "under established American precedents extending back through the Revolution, violators of the laws of war were not entitled, as a matter of constitutional right, to a jury trial." He complimented the Court for clarifying certain aspects of the Civil War case, *Ex parte Milligan,* and for "putting citizenship in its proper perspective in relationship to war offense." Still, he criticized the Court for creating a "good deal of confusion as to the proper scope of the Articles of War insofar as they relate to military commissions." Weaknesses in the decision flowed "in large measure" from the Roosevelt administration's disregard for "almost every precedent in the books" when it established the military tribunal.

Wiener complimented the Court for correcting some of the "extravagant dicta" in the majority's opinion in *Milligan* and for treating the U.S. citizenship of one of the Germans, Herbert Haupt, as irrelevant in deciding the tribunal's jurisdiction to try him for a violation of the law of war. Where Wiener "parted company" with the Court was in what he considered its careless or uninformed handling of the Articles of War enacted by Congress. The Court said that Article of War 15 preserved the concurrent jurisdiction of military commissions with courts-martial. In contrast, Wiener argued that the legislative history of Article 15 demonstrated that it was intended as a *restriction* on military commissions, which had extended their authority to offenses punishable by courts-martial. During the Civil War, military commissions had repeatedly and improperly assumed jurisdiction over offenses better handled by courts-martial.

To Wiener, Congress was authorized by the Constitution to limit the jurisdiction of military tribunals by statute, and it seemed to him "perfectly plain that the Articles of War are applicable to military commissions to the extent that they in terms purport to apply to such tribunals." The fact that President Roosevelt appointed the members of the tribunal did not give it a free charter. If the president appointed a general court-martial, it would still be subject to the provisions of the Articles of War. The power of the president to appoint did not make a tribunal "immune from judicial scrutiny." Passages from the *Digest of Judge Advocate General's Opinions* showed that military tribunals are subject to restrictions just like courts-martial: "the rules which apply in these particulars to general courts-martial have almost uniformly been applied to military commissions."

Wiener next analyzed the Court's treatment of Article of War 46 (AW 46), which required that the trial record of a general court-martial or military commission be referred for review to the staff judge advocate or the judge advocate general. It seemed "too plain for argument" that AW46 required "legal review of a record of trial by military commission before action thereon by the reviewing authority; that the President's power to prescribe rules of procedure did not permit him to waive or override this requirement; that he did in fact do so; and that he disabled his principal legal advisers by assigning to them the task of prosecution." It would be difficult to craft a more sweeping condemnation.

Wiener denied that Roosevelt could justify his actions with the tribunal by citing his powers as commander in chief or by invoking implied or inherent executive authority: "I do not think any form of language, or any talk about the President's inherent powers as Commander in Chief, is sufficient to justify that portion of the precept, which, in my considered judgment, was palpably illegal." Having identified these legal and constitutional violations, Wiener nevertheless concluded that "not even this flagrant disregard of AW 46 was sufficient to justify issuance of the writ" of *habeas corpus*. The issue before the Court was whether the saboteurs were in lawful custody, not whether they could be sentenced "without benefit of the advice of staff judge advocate." Defense counsel Kenneth Royall had conceded in oral argument that the Court was not asked to correct procedural errors. Wiener made the same point: "Errors in procedure, and the question of petitioner's guilt or innocence, are beyond the scope of inquiry on *habeas corpus* to a military tribunal."

Wiener turned to other problems. Military commissions were normally appointed by War Department Special Orders, not by presidential proclamation or military order. He found only one precedent of using the judge advocate general of the Army as prosecutor, and it was one "that no self-respecting military lawyer will look straight in the eye: the trial of the Lincoln conspirators." Even in that sorry precedent, he said, "the Attorney General did not assume to assist the prosecution."

Wiener thought the saboteurs could have been "perfectly well" tried either by commissions appointed by the commanding generals of New York and Florida or by a military commission operating under the limitations of a general court-martial. The trial record, he said, should have been reviewed first by the judge advocate general before being sent to the president. Under Roosevelt's proclamation and military order, that was impossible. When a second group of German saboteurs infiltrated in November 1944 and were apprehended in New York City, they were tried along the lines suggested by Wiener.[9]

Two months later, in his second letter to Frankfurter, Wiener reported that he had "been digging a little deeper into the AW 46 matter, and while in a sense it is tied up with AW 501/2, it is necessary to discriminate between the various portions of AW 501/2." As to Article of War 46, a commanding general "may disregard his staff JA's advice, but he is bound to have it before him before he acts." Under Article of War 501/2, the president may also disregard his staff judge advocate, but "there is this exception, that in presidential cases the President's approval is final—there is no one to review after him as there is in the case of subordinate commanders." Wiener regarded the conclusion as "inescapable that AW 46 and ¶2 of AW 501/2 read together require that the record of trial by a military commission appointed by the President must go to the B/R [board of review] and the JAG." There was no basis to contend that a presidential military commission is subject to procedures that vary from ordinary military commissions "except where statute makes it so." The Constitution vested authority in Congress, not the president, to "define and punish . . . Offences against the Law of Nations." Both AW 46 and paragraph 2 of AW 501/2 "imposed such limitations" on the president.

In his third letter, Wiener repeated his position that the eight Germans, coming into U.S. territory in civilian clothes as unlawful belligerents, had no constitutional right to a jury trial. He analyzed the administration's argument—accepted by the Court—that AW 15 provided an affirmative direction by Congress that offenses against the law of war should be tried by military commissions. Wiener disagreed. The legislative history of AW 15, which first appeared in 1916, made it "at least doubtful whether Congress had any affirmative legislation in mind." Brig. Gen. Enoch H. Crowder, judge advocate general of the Army from 1911 to 1923, explained to Congress in 1916 that AW 15 was included to clarify two points: that it was not the intent in legislating on courts-martial to exclude trials by military commissions, and that military commanders "in the field in time of war" had the option of using either one:

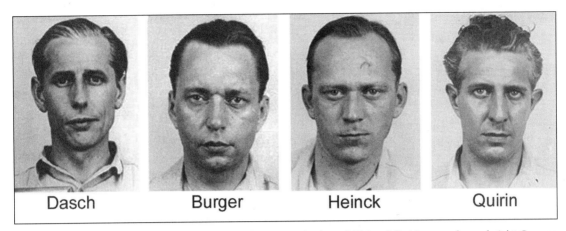

Dasch | Burger | Heinck | Quirin

George John Dasch, Ernest Peter Burger, Heinrich Harm Heinck, and Richard Quirin were four of eight German saboteurs arrested in 1942 after their submarines landed on Long Island, New York. President Franklin Roosevelt ordered them tried by a military tribunal, but the Germans' lawyers cited the precedent in the Civil War case *Ex parte Milligan* (1866) in seeking a civilian trial. In a unanimous Supreme Court decision upholding the power of the military commission, Justice Harlan Stone distinguished *Quirin* from *Milligan* on the grounds that the Germans were enemy agents rather than U.S. citizens. —AP Wide World Photos

A military commission is our common-law war court. It has no statutory existence, though it is recognized by statute law. As long as the articles embraced them [a number of persons included in AW 2 who are also subject to trial by military commission] in the designation "persons subject to military law" and provided that they might be tried by court-martial, I was afraid that, having made a special provision for their trial by court-martial, it might be held that the provision operated to exclude trials by military commission and other war courts; so this new article was introduced. . . .

It just saves to these war courts the jurisdiction they now have and makes it a concurrent jurisdiction with courts-martial, so that the military commander in the field in time of war will be at liberty to employ either form of court that happens to be convenient.[10]

Wiener omitted from the second paragraph Crowder's concluding sentence: "Both classes of courts have the same procedure." Congress did not intend military tribunals to manufacture their own rules and regulations. When Congress created the judge advocate general in 1862, it directed his office to receive, "for revision, the records and proceedings of all courts-martial and military commissions." The review procedure was identical for both. Roosevelt's proclamation, however, authorized the military tribunal to depart from those procedural safeguards whenever it decided it was appropriate or necessary.

These letters from Wiener must have had an impact on Frankfurter. In 1953, when the Court was considering whether to sit in summer session to hear the espionage case of Ethel and Julius Rosenberg (see page 184), someone recalled that the Court had sat in summer session in 1942 to hear the saboteur case. Frankfurter wrote: "We then discussed whether, as in *Ex parte Quirin,* 317 U.S. 1, we might not announce our judgment shortly after the argument, and file opinions later, in the fall. Jackson opposed this suggestion also, and I added that the *Quirin* experience was not a happy precedent."[11] In an interview on June 9, 1962, Justice Douglas made a similar comment: "The experience with *Ex parte Quirin* indicated, I think, to all of us that it is extremely undesirable to announce a decision on the merits without an opinion accompanying it. Because once the search for the grounds, the examination of the grounds that had been advanced is made, sometimes those grounds crumble."[12]

LAW REVIEW ARTICLES

In general, the articles that first appeared in law journals were brief descriptions of *Quirin*, offering little in the way of analysis, judgment, or evaluation.[13] Somewhat more perceptive were two articles by Robert E. Cushman in 1942, although he wrote quickly and without access to many of the facts that would become public within a few years.[14] A piece in the *Harvard Law Review* noted that, as a result of "certain powers vested exclusively in Congress by the Constitution, it would seem that Congress has the basic power to create military commissions."[15]

Several participants in the tribunal wrote law review articles of greater interest. Judge Advocate General Myron C. Cramer discussed his experience in handling the prosecution with Attorney General Francis Biddle, but he wrote before the full opinion was released and covered only the bare facts that had already been made public. Yet Cramer offered this compliment: "In the gravest times of war, our highest court convened quickly during midsummer in extraordinary session to hear and weigh the arguments of counsel for petitioners and Government, in a manner characteristic of its spirit and traditions."[16]

An article by Col. F. Granville Munson, who assisted Cramer during the trial, was also limited to matters of public record and written in advance of the full opinion. Munson made this distinction between courts-martial and military tribunals: "A court-martial has no authority to make rules for the conduct of its proceedings. Its procedure is rather rigidly prescribed in the *Manual for Courts-Martial* (1928) which, by Executive order of November 29, 1927, is prescribed for the government of all concerned."[17] He also pointed out that a general court-martial must have as one of its members a "law member" (an officer of the judge advocate general's department, if available), who would rule on the admissibility of evidence. The military tribunal for the saboteurs lacked a law member. In "several important particulars" (such as peremptory challenges) the rules followed by the tribunal "were at variance with the statutory provisions for general courts-martial."

A more extensive treatment, written after the full opinion was issued, appears in an article by attorney Cyrus Bernstein. He still promoted the misconception that the FBI found Dasch and not the other way around: "As he fell afoul of the F.B.I. special agents' net, one of the men made a full confession."[18] Bernstein did highlight an *ex post facto* issue in Roosevelt's proclamation, which increased the maximum penalty of sabotage from thirty years to death: "Congress could not have passed an *ex post facto* law of that tenor; Congress could not have authorized the President to issue such a proclamation." Bernstein also pointed to a conflict of interest for Biddle. The proclamation authorized the attorney general, with the approval of the secretary of war, to make exceptions to the prohibition against remedies or proceedings in the civil courts, and yet Biddle also served as prosecutor. Similarly, Bernstein noted that Cramer's participation with the prosecution eliminated the customary JAG review of a military commission's decision.

LATER VIEWS OF *QUIRIN*

By far the most shallow, error-ridden account appears in Francis Biddle's 1962 memoir. He wrote that the four Germans who landed at Amagansett threatened the Coast Guardsman "with revolvers."[19] Nothing in the record supports that claim. Biddle might have been relying on a memo he wrote to Roosevelt on June 19, 1942, claiming that one of the four Germans at Amagansett "covered the Patrolman with a gun."[20] Biddle was in error then and merely repeated it. He said that Dasch "forced $350" into the guardsman's hand.[21] The figure is either $300 (Dasch's intent) or $260 (what the guardsman actually received). Oddly, Biddle's June 19 memo had it right: $260. According to Biddle, the FBI "was on the job in a few minutes," although eight or so hours would be a better estimate. He heaped praise on FBI Director J. Edgar Hoover: "All of Edgar Hoover's imaginative and restless energy was stirred into prompt and effective action. His eyes were bright, his jaw set, excitement flickering around the edge of his nostrils when he reported the incident to me." Biddle speculated, with no evidence, that "a particularly brilliant FBI agent, probably attending the school in sabotage where the eight had been trained, had been able to get on the inside."[22]

These and other errors—incorrect names, dates, and facts—lead one to question how a major participant in the military tribunal, and one so close to the record, could stray so far from it.

Chief Justice Stone's biographer, Alpheus Thomas Mason, explained Stone's dilemma in trying to draft the full opinion that would do the least damage to the judiciary. The Court could do little other than uphold the jurisdiction of the military tribunal, being "somewhat in the position of a private on sentry duty accosting a commanding general without his pass." Stone was well aware that the judiciary was "in danger of becoming part of an executive juggernaut."[23]

Recent studies of *Quirin* have been quite critical of the Court. According to Michal Belknap, Stone went to "such lengths to justify Roosevelt's proclamation" that he preserved the "form" of judicial review while "gutt[ing] it of substance." So long as the justices marched to the beat of war drums, the Court "remained an unreliable guardian of the Bill of Rights."[24] In a separate article, Belknap described a memo that Frankfurter wrote while the full opinion was being written as evidence of a "judge openly hostile to the accused and manifestly unwilling to afford them procedural safeguards."[25] David J. Danelski regarded the full opinion in *Quirin* as "a rush to judgment, an agonizing effort to justify a *fait accompli*." The opinion marked a victory for the executive branch, but for the Court "an institutional defeat." The lesson for the Court, Danelski writes, is to "be wary of departing from its established rules and practices, even in times of national crisis, for at such times the Court is especially susceptible to co-optation by the executive."[26]

NOTES

1. *Washington Post,* July 31, 1942.
2. *New York Times,* August 1, 1942.
3. *Chicago Daily Tribune,* August 1, 1942.
4. *New York Times,* August 9, 1942.
5. *New Republic,* August 10, 1942.
6. Norman Cousins, *Saturday Review of Literature,* August 10, 1942.
7. Edwin S. Corwin, *Total War and the Constitution* (New York: Alfred A. Knopf, 1947), 118.
8. John P. Frank, *The Marble Palace* (New York: Alfred A. Knopf, 1972), 249.
9. Louis Fisher, *Nazi Saboteurs on Trial: A Military Trial and American Law* (Lawrence: University Press of Kansas, 2003), 138–144.
10. Ibid., 133.
11. "Memorandum Re: Rosenberg v. United States, Nos. 111 and 687, October Term 1942," June 4, 1954, Frankfurter Papers, Harvard Law School.
12. Conversation between Justice William O. Douglas and Prof. Walter F. Murphy, June 9, 1962, 204–205, Seeley G. Mudd Manuscript Library, Princeton University.
13. See, for example, "Notes: Jurisdiction of Military Tribunals," *Illinois Law Review* 37 (November-December 1942): 265; George T. Schilling, "Saboteurs and the Jurisdiction of Military Commissions," *Michigan Law Review* 41 (December 1942): 481.
14. Robert E. Cushman, "Ex parte Quirin et al.—The Nazi Saboteur Case," *Cornell Law Quarterly* 28 (November 1942): 54; Robert E. Cushman, "The Case of the Nazi Saboteurs," *American Political Science Review* 36 (December 1942): 1082.
15. Note: "Federal Military Commissions: Procedure and 'Wartime Base' of Jurisdiction," *Harvard Law Review* 56 (January 1943): 631, 639.
16. Myron C. Cramer, "Military Commissions: Trial of the Eight Saboteurs," *Washington and Lee Review and State Bar Journal* 17 (November 1942): 247, 253.
17. F. Granville Munson, "The Arguments in the Saboteur Trial," *University of Pennsylvania Law Review* 91 (November 1942): 239, 250.
18. Cyrus Bernstein, "The Saboteur Trial: A Case History," *George Washington Law Review* 11 (February 1943): 131, 136.
19. Francis Biddle, *In Brief Authority* (Garden City, N.Y.: Doubleday, 1962), 326.
20. Memo from Biddle to Roosevelt, June 19, 1942, PSF "Departmental File, Justice: Biddle, Francis, 1941–43," Box 56, Franklin D. Roosevelt Library.

21. Biddle, *In Brief Authority,* 326.

22. Ibid., 328.

23. Alpheus Thomas Mason, "*Inter Arma Silent Leges:* Chief Justice Stone's Views," *Harvard Law Review* 69 (1956): 806, 830, 831.

24. Michal Belknap, "The Supreme Court Goes to War: The Meaning and Implications of the Nazi Saboteur Case," *Military Law Review* 89 (1980): 59, 83, 95.

25. Michal Belknap, "Frankfurter and the Nazi Saboteurs," *Yearbook 1982* (Washington, D.C.: Supreme Court Historical Society, 1983), 66.

26. David J. Danelski, "The Saboteurs' Case," *Journal of Supreme Court History* 1 (1996): 61, 80.

Japanese Internment Cases

Melvin I. Urofsky

Hirabayashi v. United States
320 U.S. 81 (1943)

> DECIDED: June 21, 1943
> VOTE
> > CONCURRING: 9 (Harlan F. Stone, Owen J. Roberts, Hugo L. Black, Stanley F. Reed, Felix Frankfurter, William O. Douglas, Frank Murphy, Robert H. Jackson, Wiley B. Rutledge)
> > DISSENTING: 0
> OPINION OF THE COURT: Stone
> CONCURRING OPINION: Douglas
> CONCURRING OPINION: Murphy
> CONCURRING OPINION: Rutledge

Korematsu v. United States
323 U.S. 214 (1944)

> DECIDED: December 18, 1944
> VOTE
> > CONCURRING: 6 (Harlan F. Stone, Hugo L. Black, Stanley F. Reed, Felix Frankfurter, William O. Douglas, Wiley B. Rutledge)
> > DISSENTING: 3 (Owen Roberts, Frank Murphy, Robert H. Jackson)
> OPINION OF THE COURT: Black
> CONCURRING OPINION: Frankfurter
> DISSENTING OPINION: Roberts
> DISSENTING OPINION: Murphy
> DISSENTING OPINION: Jackson

Ex parte Endo
323 U.S. 283 (1944)

> DECIDED: December 18, 1944

In the worst violation of civil liberties in American history, the U.S. government forcibly transferred 110,000 persons of Japanese origin—70,000 of them American citizens—away from their homes, jobs, and property; locked them in detention centers; and kept some of them there up to four years.

Immediately after the attack on Pearl Harbor in December 1941, the general attitude toward the Japanese American population, nearly all of whom lived on the West Coast, remained fairly tolerant. "Let's not get rattled," urged the *Los Angeles Times;* most of the Japanese in this country were "good Americans, born and educated as such," and the paper urged its readers that "there be no precipitations, no riots, no mob law." Gen. John L. DeWitt, head of the West Defense Command, termed the idea of evacuating Japanese from the coastal areas "damned nonsense!"

But prejudice against the Japanese dated back decades before the war. After Congress passed the Chinese Exclusion Act in 1882, Californian nativists began a campaign to keep the Japanese out of the country too. Because of their low numbers, the Japanese at first attracted little attention, even though they had begun to buy up small farms in supposedly barren areas and, through hard work, make them enormously productive. Papers soon carried headlines and editorials on "the Yellow Peril," and in 1906 the San Francisco school board agreed to transfer all Japanese students to the segregated school already reserved for the Chinese. Anti-Japanese organizations sought to bar further land purchases, and in 1913 the California legislature passed the Alien Land Law prohibiting purchases or leasing of land by aliens ineligible for citizenship. When Congress passed the Immigration Restriction Act of 1924, which reduced the quotas on nearly all groups, it singled out the Japanese for total exclusion, despite the protests of the State Department.

Given this background, it was little wonder that within six weeks of the attack on Pearl Harbor, the initial tolerance gave way to a full-throated cry to get Japanese Americans, all of whom allegedly might be saboteurs or spies, away from the West Coast, which alarmists claimed would soon be invaded by Emperor Hirohito's forces. The government had no evidence of even a single instance of sabotage by a Japanese American, but public hysteria demanded that the military do something. General DeWitt, now eager to accommodate, began a campaign to secure approval for the mass removal of the Japanese. The respected columnist Walter Lippmann, after a talk with DeWitt, informed his readers that "nobody's constitutional rights include the right to reside and do business on a battlefield. There is plenty of room elsewhere for him to exercise his rights."[1] A few days later, the less-restrained columnist Westbrook Pegler called for every Japanese man and woman to be put under armed guard, "and to hell with habeas corpus until the danger is over."[2]

Military analysts at this time viewed the Pacific as a Japanese lake, and, in fact, until the Battle of Midway in June 1942, it appeared that nothing could stop the Imperial Fleet or prevent an invasion of the West Coast. Moreover, the treatment of Japanese Americans, unfair as it was, came nowhere close to the way the Japanese and Germans treated minority groups in the countries they occupied.

JAPANESE RELOCATION

On February 19, 1942, without discussing it with his cabinet, President Franklin D. Roosevelt signed Executive Order 9066. Some critics of the relocation say that the president bears little responsibility for the program, that he had no part in originating or developing it, and, with so many other war-related demands on his time and energy, he did not recognize the problem. Others point out that the president is, under the Constitution, the chief executive of the United States and therefore responsible for what executive agencies and officers do. Protests against 9066 and warnings from his own attorney general ought to have alerted the president to the political and constitutional dangers of relocation; furthermore, Roosevelt augmented and continued the program through other executive orders and personally prohibited its discontinuation until after the 1944 election.

Executive Order 9066 authorized the secretary of war and certain military officers to designate parts of the country as "military areas" from which any and all persons might be excluded and in which travel restrictions might be imposed. Roosevelt issued the order solely on his power as commander in chief, but army lawyers feared the actions that were necessary to implement 9066 might not withstand court scrutiny on such a narrow base. They wanted more authority, and they got it on March 21, 1942, when Congress enacted the major provisions of 9066 into law and added stringent penalties for those who resisted relocation.

Although relocated families could stay together, they had to leave their homes and jobs; property owners suffered enormously because they had to dispose of their holdings in a matter of days and accept whatever price they could get. Inside the camps, despite a variety of busywork activities, they had little to do. Amazingly, the 110,000 men, women, and children responded cooperatively for the most part. A number of Nisei men (Japanese Americans born in the United States) volunteered to serve in the army, and their unit, the 442d Regimental Combat Team, became one of the most highly decorated in the European theater of operations.

The relocation program, the government's most serious invasion of individual rights in the nation's history, proceeded on racist assumptions and brought forth astounding statements such as that of Rep.

Leland Ford, R-Calif., that "a patriotic native-born Japanese, if he wants to make his contribution, will submit himself to a concentration camp." Despite the absence of evidence of disloyalty, the entire Japanese American population—including native-born citizens—stood condemned, because, as General DeWitt put it, "A Jap is a Jap."

Contrasting with the treatment of Japanese on the West Coast was the favorable treatment of Italians on the East Coast. After Mussolini's declaration of war against the United States in December 1941, some 600,000 Italians—more than 10 percent of the entire Italian American community—were still Italian citizens and were automatically labeled as "enemy aliens." But the Roosevelt administration had been actively cultivating Italian voters, and the president instructed Attorney General Nicholas Biddle to cancel that designation. The announcement was made to a cheering 1942 Columbus Day crowd in New York's Carnegie Hall, just weeks before the congressional elections.

THE RELOCATION CASES

The constitutional basis for Roosevelt's executive orders and subsequent congressional legislation left much to be desired, but they received the imprimatur of the nation's highest tribunal. The first case resulting from the internment program to reach the Court was *Hirabayashi v. United States* (1943). Gordon Hirabayashi, a University of Washington senior and a native-born citizen, was arrested for failing to report to a control center and for violating the curfew. In protest to the evacuation order, Hirabayashi had walked into an FBI office and handed an agent a four-page letter outlining his reasons for resisting the orders. The Court sustained the legitimacy of the curfew but evaded any ruling on the wider implications of the relocation program. Chief Justice Stone, for a unanimous Court, held that the power to impose a curfew in wartime clearly lay within the presidential war powers as well as congressional authority. He noted the gravity of the situation (which no one questioned) and the possible disloyalty of some Japanese Americans (which no one could prove), and said that the Court ought not challenge the discretion of the military in interpreting the war powers broadly. Any discrimination based on race, while "odious to a free people," had clearly been relevant to the situation, and Congress had properly taken it into account.

That unanimity, however, was hard purchased, and Justice Frankfurter, acting with Stone's approval, brought a great deal of pressure on reluctant members of the Court. He wrote to Justice Murphy:

> Do you think it is conducive to the things you care about, including the great reputation of this court, to suggest that everybody is out of step except Johnny, and more particularly the Chief Justice and seven other Justices of this Court are behaving like the enemy and thereby playing into the hands of the enemy. Compassion is, I believe, a virtue enjoined by Christ. Well, tolerance is a long, long way from compassion—and can't you write your views with such expressed tolerance that you won't make people think that when eight others disagree with you, you think their view.[3]

Justices Murphy, Douglas, and Rutledge entered concurring opinions that practically amounted to dissents, especially Murphy's. He objected to any invasion of rights based on race, even in wartime. The curfew order, he noted, had "a melancholy resemblance" to the way Jews were being treated in Germany and Nazi-occupied Europe. But the three men reluctantly consented to what they considered an unconstitutional program because of the allegedly critical military situation.

The following year the Court heard another case testing the relocation program, and the majority again shied away from dealing with the central issue. Fred Korematsu, an American citizen, turned down because of ulcers when he volunteered for the army, had refused to leave the war zone. Justice Black's opinion for the majority in *Korematsu v. United States* (1944) separated the exclusion issue from that of detention and found the war power of Congress and the president sufficient to sustain the order. In wartime, civilians had to defer to military judgment and bear the resulting hardships that had always accompanied war. Somewhat disingenuously, Black denied that race had anything to do with Korematsu's arrest: he had been ordered to leave the war zone not because of his race, but because of military necessity.

Gordon Hirabayashi, center, who was imprisoned in Mount Lemmon, in Tucson, Arizona, during World War II, participates in a November 7, 1999, ceremony renaming the prison internment site after him. Hirabayashi and Fred Korematsu were appellants in the two Japanese internment cases (1943 and 1944) in which the Supreme Court upheld the war powers of Congress and the president to relocate Japanese Americans to prison camps. —AP Wide World Photos/Sergey Shayevich/Arizona Daily Star

This time, three justices, Murphy, Roberts, and Jackson, entered strenuous dissents. Justice Jackson wrote that Korematsu had been convicted of nothing more than "being present in the state whereof he is a citizen, near the place where he was born, and where he lived all his life." Jackson also attacked the cruel quandary that the military proclamations had created. On the one hand, they forbade Japanese Americans from leaving, and, on the other, forbade them from remaining, with the only option left open being "submission to custody, examination, and transportation out of the territory, to be followed by indeterminate confinement in detention camps."

Justice Roberts proved even blunter in his dissent, charging that Korematsu had been convicted "for not submitting to imprisonment in a concentration camp." Justice Murphy also dissented eloquently "from this legalization of racism" and exposed the central problem of the relocation program: it had been based solely on prejudice, on unproven fears that some members of one group, identifiable because of their ethnicity, might be disloyal. No similar action had been taken against German Americans or Italian Americans, despite the fact that some German Americans and German nationals were arrested for espionage and treason. Murphy wrote:

This exclusion of "all persons of Japanese ancestry, both alien and non-alien," from the Pacific Coast area on a plea of military necessity in the absence of martial law ought not to be approved. Such exclusion goes over "the very brink of constitutional power" and falls into the ugly abyss of racism.

In dealing with matters relating to the prosecution and progress of a war, we must accord great respect and consideration to the judgments of the military authorities who are on the scene and who have full knowledge of the military facts. The scope of their discretion must, as a matter of necessity and common sense, be wide. And their judgments ought not to be overruled lightly by those whose training and duties ill-equip them to deal intelligently with matters so vital to the physical security of the nation.

At the same time, however, it is essential that there be definite limits to military discretion, especially where martial law has not been declared. Individuals must not be left impoverished of their constitutional rights on a plea of military necessity that has neither substance nor support. Thus, like other claims conflicting with the asserted constitutional rights of the individual, the military claim must subject itself to the judicial process of having its reasonableness determined and its conflicts with other interests reconciled. . . .

Civilian Exclusion Order No. 34, banishing from a prescribed area of the Pacific Coast "all persons of Japanese ancestry, both alien and non-alien," clearly does not meet that test. Being an obvious racial discrimination, the order deprives all those within its scope of the equal protection of the laws as guaranteed by the Fifth Amendment. It further deprives these individuals of their constitutional rights to live and work where they will, to establish a home where they choose and to move about freely. In excommunicating them without benefit of hearings, this order also deprives them of all their constitutional rights to procedural due process. Yet no reasonable relation to an "immediate, imminent, and impending" public danger is evident to support this racial restriction which is one of the most sweeping and complete deprivations of constitutional rights in the history of this nation in the absence of martial law. . . .

I dissent, therefore, from this legalization of racism. Racial discrimination in any form and in any degree has no justifiable part whatever in our democratic way of life. It is unattractive in any setting but it is utterly revolting among a free people who have embraced the principles set forth in the Constitution of the United States. All residents of this nation are kin in some way by blood or culture to a foreign land. Yet they are primarily and necessarily a part of the new and distinct civilization of the United States. They must accordingly be treated at all times as the heirs of the American experiment and as entitled to all the rights and freedoms guaranteed.[4]

The internment program and the Supreme Court's condoning it have been generally condemned. Recent evidence indicates that Solicitor General Charles Fahy knew that no military necessity justified the relocation and deliberately misled the Court in this area. Perhaps it is too much to expect the justices to remain free of the passions that inevitably sweep a nation during wartime, but there is a bitter irony in comparing Stone's "famous footnote" in *Carolene Products Co. v. United States* (1944), in which he called for a "more exacting judicial scrutiny" of racially directed legislation, and his opinion in *Hirabayashi*, which condemned discrimination in general, but approved of it in this application. Nor can one find much evidence of the concern for rights that later marked the careers of Black and Douglas. Only Murphy's position in the Japanese cases seemed fully consistent with his earlier opinions, but even he bowed to what the Court, and much of the nation, took to be military necessity.

The only case in which the Court displayed any concern for due process involved Mitsuye Endo. Unlike Hirabayashi and Korematsu, she did not violate the relocation orders, but voluntarily went to the Tanforan assembly center and then filed a *habeas corpus* petition. Despite the lengthy process, her case eventually reached the Supreme Court and was decided December 18, 1944, the same day as *Korematsu*. Endo's situation—she was a citizen, had been proven to be loyal, and had been detained anyway—provided her with a strong argument, especially when at that point in the war everyone realized that the internment program had been an excessive reaction to a threat that had never materialized. Writing for a unanimous Court, Justice Douglas fudged the issue of rights and relied on a narrow reading of the statute to require that Endo be immediately released.

COMMENTS PRIOR TO THE DECISIONS

In 1943, before the Court had handed down any decision, law professor Harrop Freeman, a Quaker and peace activist, published an article in the *Cornell Law Quarterly* evaluating the evacuation and internment orders. He placed the policy in the context of prior government action in wartime and showed how unprecedented the evacuation was both in nature and in scale. As for the government's argument of military necessity, Freeman found it completely unconvincing and based almost entirely on racial prejudice. What is surprising is that Freeman came to this conclusion, which he documented well, with access only to the relatively few documents that the government had released, such as press announcements, administrative rulings, and the brief filed in the *Hirabayashi* case. Later, Peter Irons and others who examined materials not made public at the time were able to show convincingly how great a role racial stereotyping played in the decision and implementation of the evacuation program. But Freeman presciently wrote: "When the final history of the Japanese evacuation is written, it will almost certainly appear that the decisions were made on misinformation, assumptions, prejudices [and] half truths." He wrote:

> *The Government's Claim of Military Necessity:* The government's justification for the west coast evacuation is based upon the Japanese successes in the Pacific and the alleged nonassimilation of the west coast Japanese by reason of continuous anti-Japanese agitation, and the policy of exclusion of Japanese aliens from immigration, from the right to become naturalized, from intermarriage, from owning land. The government points to these, to the belief in Shintoism, the continuance of Japanese language schools in the United States, and the possible retention of dual citizenship, and concludes that "it is entirely possible that an unknown number of Japanese may lack to some extent a feeling of loyalty toward the United States as a result of their treatment." In the footnote [referring to the government's brief in *Hirabayashi*] it is admitted, however, that "most of the evacuees are loyal to this country."
>
> *Expectations of Sabotage or Fifth Column Activity:* On December 7, 1941, the Territory of Hawaii was attacked and immediately martial law was declared. Yet at no time, though the Japanese in Hawaii constitute 38 per cent of the total population, has it been deemed necessary to conduct any evacuation, and the evidence on record . . . was all to the effect that there was no sabotage or fifth column activity before, during, or after Pearl Harbor and that persons of Japanese ancestry behaved with remarkable loyalty.
>
> The evidence of loyalty in the United States is equally clear. Persons who should know are direct in their testimony as to the loyalty of American citizens of Japanese ancestry in the United States. Government counsel conceded, in the circuit court of appeals in the *Hirabayashi* case, that there had been no acts of sabotage or disloyalty by American citizens of Japanese ancestry.[5]

Some commentators have defended the internment program and the Court's approval of it. Even before Japanese Americans began to challenge the curfew and evacuation orders in court, Prof. Charles Fairman of Stanford Law School, an acolyte of Felix Frankfurter, published a lengthy law review article justifying a wide range of powers the government could exercise in wartime. Admitting that "no one will suppose that all the Nisei are disloyal to the United States," he nevertheless asserted that it "would be fanciful to suppose that the opposite is true." Fairman articulated in academic language the very prejudices that the government had adopted in Executive Order 9066 and that the Court would validate the following year.

> The Japanese, including most of the Japanese-Americans, have lived among us without becoming a part of us. This is not to be charged to them as a fault. Fundamental differences in mores have made them inscrutable to us. Because of the absence of that frank

interchange by which human personality is revealed, the Nisei have remained largely unknown to their fellow citizens. . . . As a rough generalization—and since the attack on Pearl Harbor there has been opportunity to go on the assumption that among the Japanese communities along the coast there is enough disloyalty, potential if not active, to make it expedient to evacuate the whole. . . . When one considers the irreparable consequences to which leniency might lead, the inconvenience, great though it may be, seems only one of the unavoidable hardships incident to the war.[6]

Fairman went on to note that to avoid having courts strike down the evacuation program, all Congress had to do was exercise its power to suspend the writ of *habeas corpus* for the duration of the hostilities. An even more avid supporter of unlimited wartime powers, law professor Maurice Alexandre, anticipated the Court's opinion, essentially saying that while not a nice thing, it was war, and some people had to suffer. "Without doubt, the restrictions imposed upon the American-born Japanese are not pleasant. It is no light matter to be uprooted from one's home, and sent to unfamiliar surroundings, faced with the necessity of adjustment to a new mode of living. Nevertheless, the problem presented by the presence of the Japanese in this country should not be met with less harsh methods at the expense of effectiveness."[7]

REACTIONS IN THE PRESS

The nation's leading newspapers reported the exclusion cases, but editorial writers came close to ignoring them. In spring 1943 race riots in Detroit dominated the headlines and the editorial pages. Many editorial writers found the Court's decision in *Schneiderman v. United States,* upholding a naturalized citizen's rights to hold Communist views, more important than *Hirabayashi.* The two cases were handed down the same day.

The *Los Angeles Times,* a vociferous advocate of the relocation, hailed the *Hirabayashi* opinion. The decision

> is heartening news for the Pacific Slope, where opinion has held with similar unanimity that the presence of any Japs here is dangerous in wartime.
>
> Chief Justice Stone put the matter in a nutshell when he said that exclusion by military authority of any specified groups of persons is precisely analogous to exclusion of citizens from a fire area by firelines, or a regulation requiring people to stay indoors during a blackout. . . .
>
> In this case, law once more coincides with good, sound common sense. The decision makes it plain to commanders of threatened areas that their hands are not tied and that they may take any steps reasonably necessary for the protection of the populations committed to their care. . . .
>
> Agitation for the return of Japs to the Pacific Coast—which has gained recruits in high circles in Washington—gets its devastating answer from the clear analysis of the situation by Justice Stone and the unanimous opinion of the Supreme Court.[8]

The *San Francisco Chronicle,* while avoiding the racist tones of the *Los Angeles Times,* found the Court's unanimity an important step in quieting criticism of the evacuations. The opinion, the paper wrote,

> should put an immediate end to legal attempts to fight these regulations on constitutional grounds. . . . [The Court reasoned that] if General De Witt had reason to believe there were possible saboteurs among the people of Japanese blood resident in the military area under his command he had a right to impose restrictions on them whether

they were citizens or non-citizens. He could not be expected to wait until after sabotage had happened. It was his duty to prevent it.

The *Chronicle* did, however, go on to point out that the decision was not a blank check for arbitrary actions:

> The Court emphasized the point that any restrictions on citizens infringing their normal liberties must have a reasonable basis. Military commanders are not free to follow whims, and the Court, said the opinion, will be on guard against purely arbitrary military orders directed against civilians.[9]

While editorials in favor of the decision concentrated on the alleged unanimity of the decision, the *Washington Post* noted that the three concurring opinions were evidence that at least some of the justices entertained "grave misgivings" about the constitutionality of the program. The *Post* editorial writer seemed to think that the Court had very reluctantly gone along with the administration:

> The Supreme Court has performed a duty for which it obviously had little relish. The decision was without precise precedent, as were the tragic circumstances on the West Coast after Pearl Harbor out of which the case arose. "Today is the first time, so far as I am aware," Justice Murphy noted in his separate concurring opinion, "that we have sustained a substantial restriction of the personal liberty of citizens of the United States based on the accident of race or ancestry." . . .
>
> The Court carefully sheered away from any judgment on the validity of the Government's action in evacuating persons of Japanese ancestry from the West Coast and detaining them indefinitely in relocation centers. But that some of the justices entertain grave misgivings about this procedure seems apparent from the three concurring opinions. . . .
>
> Perhaps the Court should, before too long, pass upon the constitutionality of our continuing discrimination against American citizens because of their racial heritage. The outright deprivation of civil right which we have visited upon these helpless and, for the most part, no doubt, innocent people may leave an ugly blot upon the pages of our history.[10]

In December 1944 the German counteroffensive in Belgium, which at times seemed likely to push the Allies back to the Channel, was foremost in the nation's consciousness. In addition, the *Korematsu* opinion, and its companion, *Ex parte Endo*, came on the heels of an announcement from Gen. Henry Pratt, head of the Western Defense Command on December 17, 1944, that "those persons of Japanese ancestry whose records have stood the test of Army scrutiny during the past two years" would be released from internment after January 2, 1945. They would then be "permitted the same freedom of movement throughout the United States as other loyal citizens and law-abiding aliens."

The *Los Angeles Times* headlined its news story of Pratt's announcement "Outbreak of Violence Seen by Nips' Return," and labeled its editorial on the reversal of policy and the Court's December 18 decisions "We Shan't Pretend to Like It." It found the two Court opinions puzzling, one for approving a policy that the army now inexplicably abandoned, and the other for requiring so much due process for someone who, in its opinion, had been duly arrested and taken away.[11]

The *Chronicle*, which had approved the decision in *Hirabayashi* with some reservations, now applauded the *Korematsu* and *Endo* opinions, although it seemed to make too much of what the Court had actually done.

The decisions also fit well the pattern of Civil War rulings by the Supreme Court in cases involving assumption of extraordinary powers over citizens by the Government and the military. These uniformly upheld the Constitution but as uniformly were so managed, by timing or otherwise, so as not to be a handicap in the exigencies of war.

So, the Korematsu decision of yesterday upheld the validity of the evacuation order as of its time and emergency but gave no general warrant for such exercises of extraordinary power. Any future like case . . . will have to stand or fall on its own circumstances. Nor did the validity of the evacuation at the time it was made give it any continuing authority. As soon as the supporting circumstances ceased so did its legality. . . .

In general, these decisions of the Court with their accompanying concurrences and dissents strike a blow at racism. Justice Douglas summed it all up in, "Loyalty is a thing of heart and mind, not of race, creed or color." This, a universal truth, is the American denial of Hitlerism.[12]

On the East Coast, a *Philadelphia Inquirer* editorial applauded the *Endo* opinion and the demise of the War Department program and hoped that the racist sentiments that had prevailed in California against the Japanese would abate.

Many of our soldiers of Japanese blood have rendered valiant service to the American cause in Europe and in the Pacific. Large numbers have been returned to this country suffering from wounds and serious disabilities. This is something to remember when the loyalty of this racial group, as a whole, is called into question.[13]

The *Washington Post,* which had condemned *Hirabayashi* in 1943, also denounced the *Korematsu* decision, calling it the "legalization of racism." While endorsing the outcome in *Endo,* it denounced Justice Black's opinion sustaining the evacuation program and asked whether the Court "will ever be able to assert the rights of citizens against a plea of military necessity."[14]

In one of the strangest editorials on the case, the *New York Times,* which had editorially ignored *Hirabayashi,* noted that the Court had upheld the evacuation program.

Whether it was right and necessary to do so is another story. Of about 100,000 men, women and children ordered out, about two-thirds were citizens. Many of the younger men displayed their patriotism in combat in Italy and elsewhere, as did Japanese-Americans enlisted in Hawaii. In Hawaii, which was for a long time an actual war zone, it was not considered necessary to deport law-abiding inhabitants of Japanese descent. . . . Still, no harm seems to have been done.[15]

Contrary to the assertion in the *New York Times,* the great extent of that harm would slowly but inexorably become apparent after the war.

THE ATTACK ON THE DECISIONS BEGINS

The war in the Pacific had not ended before the first, and one of the most powerful, critiques of the cases appeared. Yale law professor Eugene V. Rostow termed the Supreme Court's decisions a "disaster," and for the most part that is how scholars ever since have viewed them.

Our war-time treatment of Japanese aliens and citizens of Japanese descent on the West Coast has been hasty, unnecessary and mistaken. The course of action which we undertook was in no way required or justified by the circumstances of the war. It was calculated to produce individual injustice and deep-seated social maladjustments of a cumulative and sinister kind. . . .

If the Court had stepped forward in bold heart to vindicate the law and declare the entire program illegal, the episode would have been passed over as a national scandal, but a temporary one altogether capable of reparation. But the Court, after timid and evasive delays, has now upheld the main features of the program. That step converts a piece of war-time folly into political doctrine, and a permanent part of the law. . . . For the first time in American legal history, the Court has seriously weakened the protection of our basic civil right, the writ of habeas corpus. It has established a precedent which may well be used to encourage attacks on the civil rights of citizens and aliens, and may make it possible for some of those attacks to succeed. It will give aid to reactionary political programs which use social division and racial prejudice as tools for conquering powers. As Mr. Justice Jackson points out, the principle of these cases "lies about like a loaded weapon ready for the hand of any authority that can bring forward a plausible claim of an urgent need."[16]

In another critique written at war's end, law professor and rights activist Nanette Dembitz charged the government with basing its evacuation program on racial prejudice and stereotyping. She took the Supreme Court to task for its abandonment of the high standards it normally used and its acceptance of government assertions that had little or no basis in truth.

On this question the Court departed from the relatively high standard of review which it had previously enunciated. The premises supporting the conclusion as to the application of the curfew were, according to the Government's argument, the potential disloyalty of at least a minority of the citizens of Japanese ancestry and the difficulty of identifying and restricting the potentially disloyal as a separate group from the loyal. . . . Rather than proving in the trial court the existence of the "Constitutional facts," the Government asked the Court to judicially notice the bases for a belief in the existence of various circumstances encouraging an attachment to Japan on the part of at least some of the second and third generations of the population of Japanese ancestry. . . . A "reasonable" man could not and would not have come to a positive conclusion, on the basis of the available documentary data, that most of the supposed influences toward disloyalty did in fact exist; a belief in their existence could not be said to rest on "reasonable or substantial grounds" insofar as the phrase connotes that a fact is established by a preponderance of evidence after the weighing of an adequate amount of data on both sides. . . .

While the Court's stated general criterion for determining whether an act is within the war power was whether the belief in its necessity is supported by reasonable and substantial grounds, it departed from this standard in reviewing the racial facts, if the terms "reasonable" and "substantial" have any meaning.[17]

Milton Eisenhower (President Dwight Eisenhower's brother), who for a short time headed the War Relocation Authority that supervised the internment, and who would later be president of Johns Hopkins University, noted in his memoirs that he had "brooded about this whole episode" for more than thirty years, and wondered how "an entire society can somehow plunge off course."

It would be comforting to heap the blame for the evacuation on some individual or group of individuals. General DeWitt is a likely candidate, as is the unyielding Colonel [Karl] Bendetson. Perhaps General [Allen W.] Gullion, the Provost Marshal General, or Assistant Secretary [John J.] McCloy. Or even Secretary [Henry L.] Stimson. President Roosevelt signed the fateful order, and must be ultimately responsible; perhaps he should bear the blame. Certainly his approval of the evacuation was a glaring example of how a busy president often makes a decision on inadequate evidence, simply because he is preoccupied with seemingly more pressing matters.

All these men—and many more—played key roles in the tragedy and all must share the responsibility. But I am convinced that *no one* fully understood at the time, or even knew about, all of the events that transpired between December 7, 1941, and March 1942, which led ultimately to the evacuation.

Only after the events had taken place could historians work their magic and reconstruct chaos into neat, logical, linear chronology. But, at the time, many forces were at work—military, political, economic, emotional, and racial. The principal actors in the drama frequently acted independently of each other. Often they were unaware of what the others were doing or thinking or how their decisions or actions related to other decisions or actions. I doubt that anyone saw the overall pattern that was emerging or how his actions contributed to that pattern.[18]

GOVERNMENT REPARATIONS

Following the civil rights movement of the 1950s and 1960s, prejudice against Japanese Americans began to decrease. Legal restraints about Issei (Japanese immigrants) owning land either disappeared from the statute books or were struck down in court. Japanese immigrants and their children became eligible for U.S. citizenship, and the admission of Hawaii, where the population was overwhelmingly Asian, helped break down racial barriers even further. Starting in the 1970s, a drive began to secure government recognition of the wrong done to Japanese Americans in the war. On February 19, 1976, President Gerald R. Ford issued a formal apology on behalf of the U.S. government in regard to the internment policy. In 1980 the Commission on Wartime Relocation and Internment of Civilians was established to hear testimony, review wartime documents, and make a recommendation as to the validity of reparations for the surviving evacuees. In 1983 the commission issued its report, *Personal Justice Denied,* in which it concluded that Executive Order 9066

> was not justified by military necessity, and the decisions that followed from it— exclusion, detention, the ending of detention, and the ending of exclusion—were not founded upon military considerations. The broad historical causes that shaped these decisions were race prejudice, war hysteria, and a failure of political leadership. . . . A grave personal injustice was done to the American citizens and resident aliens of Japanese ancestry who, without any individual review or any probative evidence against them, were excluded, removed and detained by the United States during World War II.[19]

The commission made five recommendations. First, Congress should pass a joint resolution, signed by the president, acknowledging the injustice of the evacuation and apologizing for "acts of exclusion, removal, and detention." Second, presidential pardons should be given to those charged with violation of the program regulations, such as curfew. Third, those who lost their jobs should be allowed to apply for "the restitution of positions, status or entitlements lost in whole or in part because of acts or events between December 1941 and 1945. Fourth, the commission recommended that Congress establish a fund for "educational and humanitarian purposes" to ensure that such gross violations did not happen again, and fifth, Congress should establish a $1.5 billion fund to provide personal redress. In 1988 Congress passed a bill embodying these five recommendations, and Ronald Reagan signed it into law in his last weeks in office. The reparation program went into effect later in the year over the signature of George H. W. Bush.

Although most Americans approved of these gestures at restitution, not everyone applauded. In a study of the reaction in letters to the editors, historian Roger Daniels noted that many people believed the

Japanese should also pay reparations. "Japan had bombed Pearl Harbor [and] the now rich Japanese government should make any payments that were due." A more frequent complaint was that the United States could not afford such an expense, and the surviving Japanese Americans did not need the money.[20]

Even some Japanese Americans were ambivalent about the redress program. Although most agreed with Art Yorimoto that reparations were justified—"I think we had it coming to us. What we went through was quite a bit"—but others thought that such things happened in wartime. "It was a war," stated one intern of the Amache camp. "I felt everyone was going through a hard time. I don't think we should get anything. Because I didn't think that anybody owed us anything. It was war. Everybody loses in a war. This is my idea. So [my husband and I] never fought for any money."[21]

For some, the apology was far more important than money. George Hirano related the story about his mother, who before her death declared, "I don't want [the money]. I want that apology from the president of the United States." Hirano agreed that "in the long run the apology remains clear in our minds, but whatever people did with the money is gone." For Yoshi Tanita and others, the apology and the reparations came too late. For "most of the Issei, you know our parents, were gone by the time the money came around to us. They were the ones who really deserved it."[22]

Although the commission concluded that the Supreme Court decisions on relocation had been "overruled in the court of history," those decisions are still on the books, and the fear remains that in some future crisis the argument of military necessity might again be used to limit the rights of citizens. The argument is not that far-fetched. At the Relocation Commission hearings, Wall Street attorney John J. McCloy, still unrepentant over his role in shaping the internment program as assistant secretary of war, pointed out that a major threat to American security, Cuba, existed less than ninety miles from the Florida coast and urged the commission not to recommend any restrictions that might hamper the government from responding to the threat of fifth columnists.

At the same time the Relocation Commission began its hearings, lawyers for Gordon Hirabayashi, Fred Korematsu, and others began the lengthy process in federal district courts on the West Coast to have their convictions overturned. Using evidence uncovered by Irons in researching his book on the relocation cases, the lawyers asked for the ancient and little-used writ of *coram nobis,* a final avenue of relief for persons who have been convicted of a crime and served their sentence, but who seek reversal of the judgment on the grounds that the original conviction was tainted by government misconduct. Irons had found evidence that not only did General DeWitt know that the Japanese Americans posed no security threat, but so did the government lawyers, especially John Fahy, who argued the cases before the Supreme Court.

In 1984 the court vacated Korematsu's conviction, and the other trials also resulted in a resounding defeat for the government. The Justice Department appealed one of the reversals but ran into a stone wall in the Ninth Circuit, which upheld the lower court's decision. In response to the government's claim that so much time had passed as to make the issue moot, Judge Mary M. Schroeder declared, "A United States citizen who is convicted of a crime on account of race is lastingly aggrieved." At that point the government decided not to appeal to the Supreme Court.

NOTES

1. Quoted in Peter Irons, *Justice at War* (New York: Oxford University Press, 1983).

2. Ibid.

3. Frankfurter to Murphy, June 10, 1943, Frankfurter Papers, Harvard Law School.

4. *Korematsu v. United States,* 323 U.S. 214, at 234 (1944).

5. Harrop A. Freeman, "Genesis, Exodus, and Leviticus: Genealogy, Evacuation, and Law," *Cornell Law Quarterly* 28 (1943): 414, 441, 446–447.

6. Charles Fairman, "The Law of Martial Rule and the National Emergency," *Harvard Law Review* 55 (June 1942): 1253, 1301–2.

7. Maurice Alexandre, "Wartime Control of Japanese Americans: The Nisei—A Casualty of World War II," *Cornell Law Quarterly* 28 (June 1943): 385, 404.

8. "Supreme Court Speaks Plainly on Jap Exclusion," *Los Angeles Times,* June 22, 1943.

9. "De Witt Upheld," *San Francisco Chronicle,* June 22, 1943.

10. "Stigma by Ancestry," *Washington Post,* June 25, 1943.

11. *Los Angeles Times,* December 19, 1944.

12. "Exclusion Order," *San Francisco Chronicle,* December 19, 1944.

13. "An Unjust Ban is Lifted," *Philadelphia Inquirer,* December 19, 1944.

14. "The Legalization of Racism," *Washington Post,* December 21, 1944.

15. "Exiles' Return," *New York Times,* December 22, 1944.

16. Eugene V. Rostow, "The Japanese American Cases—A Disaster," *Yale Law Journal* 54 (1945): 489, 491.

17. Nanette Dembitz, "Racial Discrimination and the Military Judgment: The Supreme Court's Korematsu and Endo decisions," *Columbia Law Review* 45 (1945): 175, 184–185.

18. Milton S. Eisenhower, *The President Is Calling* (Garden City: Doubleday, 1974), 125–126.

19. Commission on Wartime Relocation and Internment of Civilians, *Personal Justice Denied, Part 2: Recommendations* (Washington, D.C.: Government Printing Office, 1983), 5.

20. Roger Daniels, "Redress Achieved, 1983–1990," in *Japanese Americans: From Relocation to Redress,* ed. Roger Daniels, Sandra C. Taylor, and Harry H. L. Kitano (Seattle: University of Washington Press, 1991), 220–221.

21. Quoted in Robert Harvey, *Amache: The Story of Japanese Internment in Colorado during World War II* (Dallas: Taylor Trade Publishing, 2004), 210.

22. Ibid.

Dennis v. United States
Arthur J. Sabin

Dennis v. United States
341 U.S. 494 (1951)

DECIDED: June 4, 1951
VOTE
  CONCURRING: 6 (Fred M. Vinson, Stanley F. Reed, Felix Frankfurter, Robert H. Jackson, Harold H. Burton, Sherman Minton)
    DISSENTING: 2 (Hugo L. Black, William O. Douglas)
OPINION OF THE COURT: Vinson
OPINION CONCURRING IN JUDGMENT: Frankfurter
CONCURRING OPINION: Jackson
DISSENTING OPINION: Black
DISSENTING OPINION: Douglas
DID NOT PARTICIPATE: Tom C. Clark

The cold war that followed on the heels of World War II was the result of the failure to keep alive the alliance that won the war. Postwar political, military, and economic problems developed rapidly, creating conflicts between the Soviet Union and the United States. The result was a military standoff, a long cold war between the two superpowers that dominated the world diplomatic scene from 1946 to 1989.

Events such as the victory of the Communists over the Nationalists in China in 1949 and the Soviet Union's successful testing of its first atomic bomb that same year left the American public battered with distressing news. Even before then, however, there developed a need to identify a domestic enemy as the major cause of problems plaguing the United States. Many factors can be cited as sharing in the creation of a national paranoia: the need to explain why the World War II alliance had dissolved so quickly; the behavior of Stalin, who violated his promises to his former allies; and the ease with which the West fell back into the anti-Soviet attitudes that had existed since the end of World War I. The result was the so-called Red Scare—a growing fear that the Soviet Union was not only an international threat, but also the internal enemy, operating through the Communist Party in the United States. Efforts to identify subversives were capped by the initiation of the greatest peacetime loyalty investigation in U.S. history.

The high point in the investigation came on July 20, 1948, with FBI director J. Edgar Hoover's indictment of the national leadership of the U.S. Communist Party, including party secretary Eugene Dennis, under the Smith Act of 1940. This law made it a federal crime to advocate and teach the duty and necessity of overthrowing the U.S. government by force and violence. What the eleven arrested men were *not* accused of was any act or activity to accomplish these alleged goals. They had no cache of arms; they did not kill government officials or attack public buildings or take any active steps to overthrow the government. They wrote a lot and talked even more, but they took no action in furtherance of their alleged beliefs.

Given the times and the hysteria surrounding the trial in federal district court in Foley Square in Manhattan, the conviction of all defendants seemed assured. The testimony of FBI agents and informers, as well as former party members who testified against the party and its leadership, doomed any chance any of them had for acquittal. Evidence that the defendants had used false names, swore falsely to gain passports and the like, rubbed up against middle-class mores reflected in the members of the jury.

Most citizens and media applauded the trial and return of guilty verdicts against all eleven defendants. The trial judge also handed down contempt citations against all defense attorneys, calling for jail time for each of them. Most important, the Supreme Court had put its important and prestigious seal of approval on these prosecutions before the Communists' case itself came before the Court. With the exception of one case, every decision upon appeal dealing with the cold war Red Scare contained an endorsement of the government's position.

The Communist Party defendants appealed to the Second Circuit Court of Appeals after the guilty verdicts rendered in the district court.[1] That particular appeals court was considered quite special throughout the American justice system because it decided so many crucial issues and because one of the giants of American law, Learned Hand, was a member. Known to be protective of civil liberties, Hand saw the Red Scare as originating with frantic witch hunters, who, if allowed, would set up an inquisition, using hearsay and illicit tactics wherever nonconformity appeared. Surely an enlightened voice on the constitutionality of the Smith Act and those prosecuted under it would be heard.

Oral arguments before the court of appeals in *Dennis* took an exceptionally long three days, ending June 23, 1950. The next day North Korea invaded South Korea, and by the time the court's decision was issued on August 1, 1950, the United States was at war in Korea.

Hand's opinion came as a shock to those who believed he stood solidly for the interests of civil liberties and constitutional rights. Writing for a unanimous three-judge panel, Hand affirmed the conviction of the Communist Party leaders. He wrote that the United States, acting to suppress a danger, could properly prosecute those who appeared to seek overthrow of the government by force. The Smith Act, as applied to such a conspiracy, he added, did not unconstitutionally abridge freedom of speech. "In each case [courts] must ask whether the gravity of the 'evil,' discounted by its improbability, justifies such invasion of free speech as is necessary to avoid the danger," he wrote.

THE SUPREME COURT'S DECISION

Although it heard oral arguments in early December 1950, the Supreme Court took until June 4, 1951, to issue its decision in *Dennis*. Chief Justice Vinson, appointed by President Harry Truman, wrote an opinion affirming the trial and appellate court decisions. The crux of the case before the Court was whether sections of the Smith Act, under which the defendants were tried, violated the First Amendment. The majority stated that government had the power to prevent an armed rebellion; given this power, the issue was whether the Smith Act would pass constitutional muster as a means of protecting the U.S. government. The Court held that it did. The majority agreed with Judge Hand that the societal value of free speech must, on occasion, be subordinated to other values and considerations such as national security.

The result was a "grave and probable danger" test used to determine when circumstances were of such a threatening nature that Congress had the right to act to preemptively prevent their occurrence. In response to the argument that no overt acts had taken place, the Vinson opinion stated:

> Obviously, [this standard] cannot mean that before the government may act, it must wait until the putsch is about to be executed, the plans have been laid and the signal is awaited. If Government is aware that a group aiming at its overthrow is attempting to indoctrinate its members and to commit them to a course whereby they will strike when the leaders feel the circumstances permit, [preemptive] action by the Government is required.[2]

Justice Frankfurter, apparently uncomfortable with the majority's statement and with the way Judge Harold R. Medina had conducted the trial, was nevertheless willing to join in affirming the conviction. He wrote his views in a concurring opinion that ran twice as long (including an appendix) as the majority's. Justice Jackson's argument followed a different path. He said that a clear and present danger need not be found where a conspiracy is proven. Conspiracy was, in itself, a crime; the defendants were found guilty of a conspiracy. That, for him, seemed to be sufficient.

Justice Black based his brief dissent on the First Amendment:

> At the outset I want to emphasize what the crime involved in this case is, and what it
> is not. These petitioners were not charged with an attempt to overthrow the Govern-
> ment. They were not charged with overt acts of any kind designed to overthrow the
> Government. They were not even charged with saying anything or writing anything
> designed to overthrow the Government. The charge was that they agreed to assemble
> and to talk and publish certain ideas at a later date: The indictment is that they con-
> spired to organize the Communist Party and to use speech or newspapers and other
> publications in the future to teach and advocate the forcible overthrow of the Govern-
> ment. No matter how it is worded, this is a virulent form of prior censorship of speech
> and press, which I believe the First Amendment forbids. I would hold §3 of the Smith
> Act authorizing this prior restraint unconstitutional on its face and as applied.[3]

From that point, he argued that no clear and present danger existed, that the First Amendment "is the key-
stone of our Government, [and] that the freedoms it guarantees provide the best insurance against the
destruction of all freedom."[4]

Black closed his dissent with a prediction:

> Public opinion being what it now is, few will protest the conviction of these Commu-
> nist petitioners. There is hope, however, that in calmer times, when present pressures,
> passions and fears subside, this or some later Court will restore the First Amendment
> liberties to the high preferred place where they belong in a free society.[5]

The opening words of Justice Douglas's dissent are particularly meaningful, in light of the terrorist
attacks of September 11, 2001:

> If this were a case where those who claimed protection under the First Amendment
> were teaching the techniques of sabotage, the assassination of the President, the filching
> of documents from public files, the planting of bombs, the art of street warfare, and the
> like, I would have no doubts. The freedom to speak is not absolute; the teaching of
> methods of terror and other seditious conduct should be beyond the pale [of constitu-
> tional protection] along with obscenity and immorality.[6]

In Douglas's view, free speech had already destroyed the effectiveness of the Communist Party. Looking
back to the Great Depression, he noted that Communists had enjoyed little success in a time of serious
economic trouble. With the conditions of the country so greatly changed, he argued, "The country is not in
despair; the people know Soviet Communism; the doctrine of Soviet revolution is exposed in all its ugli-
ness and the American people want none of it."[7]

PRESS RESPONSES

The finding that eleven top Communist Party members were all guilty was welcomed in headlines and
editorials throughout the nation. The war in Korea was not going well; American blood was being shed in
the battle against communism overseas, making these domestic legal victories against the enemy welcome.
In an editorial reviewing the majority decision (ignoring the dissents), the *Los Angeles Times* stated:

> A time may come again when a Communist will be a harmless member of a political
> splinter party, when he can holler from his soapbox that it would be a good thing to
> burn the Capitol, hang the Cabinet and start on the way to a true "people's government."
> But that time is not now or in the foreseeable future. We are fighting Communism with

blood and money on both sides of the world; now the Supreme Court permits us to fight it at home. The weapon is an awkward one, but it is better than none at all.[8]

Many responses anticipated and welcomed a roundup of more Communist Party leaders; some warned of "Red violence" in the wake of the decision. In the *Chicago Tribune* of June 6, 1951, Eugene Dennis said the Court's action could be "reversed by the people." Both assertions were absurd: the idea that there would be a violent uprising of the remnants of the Communist Party was as realistic as Dennis's belief that the "people" disagreed with the majority's verdict and would somehow "reverse" it.

James E. McInerney, an assistant attorney general, announced the impending prosecutions of an estimated 2,500 local Communist leaders.[9] This prediction was echoed by *Newsweek* on June 18, 1951, when it headlined: "Communists: Worse Days Coming" and speculated on a list of new targets for Smith Act prosecutions. Both *Dennis* dissenters, especially Justice Douglas, were vilified by some of the more extreme voices. Rep. Roy O. Woodruff, R-Mich., the accuser in an article entitled "Aid To Foe Charged To Justice Douglas," called for the justice to resign for giving "aid and comfort" to America's enemies.[10]

Douglas's dissent also raised the ire of syndicated newspaper commentators such as Fulton Lewis Jr., who stated: "Douglas peddles a lot of the same stuff mouthed by liberals, who come crying out of the woods every time a Communist gets into trouble." The article was clipped by a reader and sent to Douglas with a note that included the question, "How in the name of God did a nut, screwball and crackpot like you get on the bench of the Supreme Court?"[11]

The newspapers and magazines that criticized the *Dennis* majority were few in number. They included the *St. Louis Post-Dispatch,* the *New York Post,* and the *Louisville Courier-Journal.* As the weeks went by, however, some publications had second thoughts about the verdict. In an editorial on June 20, 1951, the *Christian Century* praised the result, but after its editors read the commentary in the *St. Louis Post-Dispatch* and the *Louisville Courier-Journal,* as well as an advertisement placed in the *New York Times* by some leading civil libertarians, the paper shifted position, noting that it felt uncomfortable with the deeper implications of the Court's majority opinions.

The *New Republic* editorial "What the Court Has Destroyed" opened with the line: "On June 4, 1951, the Supreme Court of the U.S. paid tyranny the tribute of imitation." Calling the majority decision "the most dramatic delinquency of the Court," it concluded that "the great damage lies in the deterioration of the American spirit of freedom."[12]

Overlooked by most commentators was another decision of the Supreme Court issued the same day as *Dennis.* Seventeen people who worked for the city of Los Angeles and who had been fired for refusing to execute non-Communist affidavits and take an oath relating to their political views lost their appeal to the Court, 6–3. The case was *Garner v. Board of Public Works of Los Angeles* (1951). Regarding the *Dennis* case, a *New Republic* editorial pointed out, "Whatever its ultimate impact may be on all citizens, through weakening the First Amendment, its immediate impact falls on only a small band of conspirators." In contrast, the *Garner* decision was important to about 3 million public servants. In validating the Los Angeles loyalty-test scheme and upholding the firing of civil servants without respect to prohibitions based on arguments of *ex post facto* or bill of attainder, "the Court has placed Constitutional force behind the efforts of states and municipalities to use oaths to drive political non-conformists from public office."[13] The editorial claimed the decision in *Garner* would sustain such oath programs in at least thirty-three states and several cities and maintained that "all of these expurgatory oath programs have now been judicially anointed and sanctified." Citing the slim majority upholding the legality of the oath, the editorial lamented the change in the composition of the Court brought on by the deaths of Justices Frank Murphy and Wiley B. Rutledge, who the writer presumed would have joined the dissenters and created a majority that would have overturned the oath as unconstitutional.[14]

Under the headline "Press Cites Red Case Ruling [*Dennis*] as Safeguarding [the] Future of the U.S.," the *St. Louis Post-Dispatch* quoted the *New York Times* assessment that the verdict "ensures liberty shall not be abused to its own destruction."[15] The *Post-Dispatch* then featured a survey of twelve newspapers. All were quoted as expecting the result and approving the majority's decision. In responding to the Court's action, each editorial writer emphasized what seemed most important about *Dennis*. For example, the *Minneapolis Star* said:

> The Star believes—despite deep misgivings about its consequences for the free speech principle—that Chief Justice Vinson made the only possible decision in the case of the 11 Communist leaders. The Communist party in America intends to come to power by murdering people who oppose it. The political color of Communist doctrine can scarcely excuse conspiracy to commit murder. The free speech principle cannot be stretched that far in law, however far it may be stretched in philosophy.

And the *New Orleans Times-Picayune* wrote:

> With the conviction's sustainment goes affirmation of the federal act upon which the prosecution was based. Thus yesterday's decision both establishes the right of the United States to protect itself against the "clear and present danger" created by a conspiracy to overthrow its government by force and violence, and validates the method prescribed by Congress to meet that danger.

The same day the *St. Louis Post-Dispatch* printed these quotes, it ran its own editorial on *Dennis*. The editor's reaction can be viewed as the paradigm for those questioning the wisdom of the Court. Under the title "Six Men Amend the Constitution," the editorial said:

> There is no greater right in all the world than the right to hold free opinions and to express them without fear of reprisal by those in authority.
>
> This right is the very heart of American democracy. Keep it secure and the free way of life will survive. Take it away and the free way of life will die within itself, whether or not attack ever comes [from] the outside.
>
> Jefferson, Madison, Mason, and the others who started the weak little republic 100 years ago were not afraid of the right to inquire and expound and advocate. By formal amendment these wise men and their fellow citizens, with great deliberation, wrote into the first article of the Bill of Rights the guarantee that "Congress shall make no law abridging the freedom of speech." . . .
>
> What a strange and distressing contrast a century and a half later present. By now the feeble little nation has grown to be the strongest power in all the world. Yet the successors of Jefferson and his compatriots in high office are not merely less bold. They even retreat in fear of the free exchange of ideas.
>
> This is the context in which the Supreme Court decision in the case of the Communist leaders must be set. Chief Justice Vinson, with the concurrence of Justices Reed, Frankfurter, Jackson, Burton, and Minton, leads the gravest departure from the guarantee of freedom of speech in our history.
>
> These six justices say that the Communists by organizing "to *teach* and *advocate* the overthrow of the Government of the United States by force and violence *created* a 'clear and present danger' of an attempt to overthrow the Government by force and violence."
>
> They cite no overt acts of force.
>
> They present no record of violence.
>
> They find danger both clear and present through teaching and advocacy alone.
>
> Never before has such a restriction been placed on the right to hold opinions and to express them in the United States of America. . . .

What is important in this case is what has now been done internally to our own historic liberty. The two Justices who have the courage to dissent against this self-inflicted wound do so with words that history will mark.

Justice Black says: "This is a virulent form of prior censorship of speech and press." Deploring this "watering down" of the First Amendment, the senior Justice holds the applied sections of the Smith Act "unconstitutional on their face."

Justice Douglas joins Justice Black with this memorable protest: Never until today has anyone seriously thought that the ancient law of conspiracy could constitutionally be used to turn speech into seditious conduct. Full and free discussion has been the first article of our faith. It has been the safeguard of every religious, political, philosophical, economic, and racial group amongst us. . . .

Six men have amended the United States Constitution without submitting their amendment to the states for ratification. That is the nub of this decision.[16]

Most mainstream newspapers' editorials covered the same issues in terms of the meaning of the *Dennis* case. The *Chicago Daily Sun-Times* was typical of those favoring the decision:

Containing Communism at Home

THE AMERICAN PEOPLE have a new weapon with which to fight the insidious Communist fifth column on the home front.

The U.S. Supreme Court has ruled that our democratic society can protect itself by making it a crime to conspire to advocate the overthrow of the government by force.

No longer will wily, double-talking, home-grown Reds be able to shield their conspiracy to overthrow the government by force by hiding behind the Bill of Rights. Freedom of speech, the Supreme Court has ruled, can be limited by the government when such speech is used to build a conspiracy to overthrow our society.

The court broke a new trail in law. It found that there was a "clear and present danger" to the United States by the very existence of the conspiracy. Many legal scholars, dissenting Justice Douglas included, believe that there can be no "clear and present danger" unless a speech is followed by some immediate injury to society. The court ruled that "it is the existence of the conspiracy which creates the danger." It said:

> Obviously the words [clear and present danger or grave and probable danger] cannot mean that before the government may act it must wait until the putsch is about to be executed, the plans have been laid and the signal is awaited.

The government can act—as it did in this case—when it is aware that a group aiming at its overthrow plans to strike as speedily as circumstances would permit.

These are key words. The court made plain that it is not concerned with soapbox orators who cry, Comrades, let us march on the city hall. Such persons usually do not present a clear and present danger, because they are generally ignored. But, in the case of the Communist leaders, Americans are endangered by a group of well-disciplined party members, ideologically attuned to Russia, who teach the duty and necessity of destroying our government by force *whenever the time is ripe to do so.*

This is something new in America, and Chief Justice Vinson acknowledged that the high court was confronted with a situation never before it in the past. . . .

The Supreme Court decision does not outlaw the Communist party as a political group. The decision does not legalize suppression of legitimate political opinion and criticism of our way of life. We can still meet that challenge by open and free discussion. But the U.S. is finally catching up to those who plot with a foreign government violently to change our way of life.[17]

The Thorn Tree

This cartoon from the *Christian Science Monitor* suggests that the U.S. uproot the "tree of communism" with enlightened policies rather than cutting away at free speech. The cartoon was published in 1948, the same year that twelve leaders of the Communist Party were indicted for advocating the overthrow of the government. Three years later, the Supreme Court in *Dennis v. United States* (1951), upheld the constitutionality of a federal law criminalizing such advocacy, even if the threat is not imminent.—Paul Carmack / © 1948 The Christian Science Monitor (www.csmonitor.com) All rights reserved.

Nationwide news magazines reported the verdict and highlighted the dissents by printing parts of the arguments of Justices Black and Douglas. The titles "Black Day for the Reds" and "Communists: Worse Days Coming" reveal the points of view.[18]

Two magazines of liberal commentary, the *New Republic* and the *Nation* were clearly on the side of Black and Douglas. Said the *New Republic*:

> With fewer words, the dissenting Justices Black and Douglas challenged the majority on the meaning of the First Amendment, on the interpretation of "clear and present danger," and on the constitutionality of the Smith Act. Both pointed out that the 11 top Communists were not convicted on charges of conspiracy to overthrow the government (which could have led to prosecution under the country's conspiracy laws) but rather that "they conspired to organize the Communist Party and to use speech or newspapers and other publications to teach and advocate . . . overthrow of the government."[19]

The press, with few exceptions, assured Americans that they could sleep better because of the Supreme Court's seemingly patriotic interpretation of the Smith Act. The Communist Party suffered a significant blow in having these eleven top party functionaries jailed. The *Dennis* decision was followed by the prosecution of state party leaders throughout the nation, using the Smith Act, now codified as a legitimate exercise of legislative power. Joining the few newspapers and magazines that opposed *Dennis,* the American Civil Liberties Union, fearing the impact on dissent and First Amendment rights, announced its disapproval.

CONGRESSIONAL RESPONSE

Another forum for reaction to *Dennis* was the *Congressional Record.*[20] Once again, most statements by members of Congress, or material reprinted at their behest, reflected approval of the outcome. But Sen. William Langer, R-N.D., and those disagreeing had articles, such as "Six Men Amend the Constitution," reprinted in full.

On June 6, 1951, Rep. Jacob K. Javits, R-N.Y., remarked:

> Mr. Speaker, the Supreme Court on Monday in upholding the Constitutionality of the Smith Act—making it a felony to teach or advocate the overthrow of the Government by force—and sustaining the convictions of the 11 Communist leaders has made one of the momentous judicial decisions of our time. It has established the bedrock of the law on internal security. No longer is it necessary for the Government to consider legislation involving civil liberties and civil rights in an atmosphere of self-preservation. The Supreme Court has given to the Government an effective safeguard for its own preservation.

Javits then submitted an editorial he felt was "pertinent" to the issue:

FREEDOM WITH SECURITY

> The Supreme Court's decision upholding the conviction of the 11 Communist leaders is the most important reconciliation of liberty and security in our time. The five opinions handed down in this case contain ample evidence of long and deep soul-searching. That process brought six of the eight Justices who took part in the deliberations to a firm conviction that the Smith Act is constitutional and that the Communist leaders were properly convicted under it. The Court has demonstrated once more that our system, with all its respect for individual freedom, is not (to borrow words from Chief Justice Hughes) "an imposing spectacle of impotency."[21]

One reaction to the Supreme Court's confirmation of guilt was that the decision drew the needed line between personal liberties and the threat to national security. Those supporting the *Dennis* outcome hailed the use of the "clear and present danger test," as modified by Judge Hand's language and used by the majority, as the answer to the perplexing question of the limits of political dissent.

Rep. Thomas J. Lane, D-Mass., had an article from the issue of the *Christian Science Monitor* reprinted in the *Congressional Record* as representative of those who took a more careful, more nuanced position on the meaning of the *Dennis* decision. It said in part:

> As to the effects of the decision: If a balance has needed restoring in favor of governmental powers to deal with subversive teachings, the Supreme Court has restored it. But the basic problem remains still poised on the knife edge between liberty and security. Having thus reinforced security, it behooves Americans to be all the more watchful of their individual liberty.
>
> The decision may allay many fears. It is to be hoped, therefore, that it will rather stabilize public thinking than . . . [set off a] witch hunt.[22]

In all, only about a dozen entries in the *Congressional Record* comment on *Dennis,* and most of them were reprints of newspaper articles. The paucity of notice can be explained in a number of ways, including the continuing Korean War and the emerging power of Sen. Joseph McCarthy, R.-Wis., who made his reputation by alleging that Communist sympathizers had infiltrated the federal government. Not that communism was left behind as a topic for discussion. On the contrary, new venues were found to discuss, warn about, and generally condemn any and all aspects of communism. In essence, instead of cooling down, the matter of Communists and the Communist Party actually heated up as McCarthy took center stage and Hoover went after lower-level party members. The Republican Party beat the anti-Communist drum as the 1952 national election came into view.

COMMUNISTS' RESPONSE

One newspaper, the *Worker* (daily) and the *Sunday Worker,* attacked the results in the *Dennis* case in the strongest terms made more dramatic by the use of political cartoons. This paper was the official organ of the Communist Party. In type that covered two-thirds of the front page, the paper announced on June 5, 1951

Supreme Court Upholds Foley Sq. Frameup, 6–2

Black Says 1st Amendment Scuttled; Communists to Demand Rehearing-

Under a further headline, "CP Will Continue Fight For Peace," the paper published Eugene Dennis's response. Part of what Dennis wrote follows:

> In an atmosphere of war hysteria, the Truman Court majority voted to substitute the Smith thought-control-Act for the Constitution's First Amendment, which clearly forbids Congress to make any law abridging the people's right of free speech, press, assembly or worship. Its refusal to consider the case of the lawyers for the 11 Communist leaders strikes a blow at the historic freedom of Americans to their own counsel as well as the right of attorneys zealously to defend their clients and uphold the Constitution. . . .
>
> The sole "guilt" of the Communist leaders is their advocacy of peace and social progress—their opposition to war and fascism. The Communist Party does not now advocate—and never has advocated—the forcible overthrow of the Government. It has worked—and will continue to work—for peace and democracy, for the unity of the people against atomaniacs [people who oppose individualism], against Labor's foes and against the lynchers of the Negro people.

The "strategy" was for the Communists to move for rehearing, which is rarely granted, before the Supreme Court as soon as possible. In support of this move, individual readers and organizations were asked to write to President Truman (an interesting idea considering that Communists and the *Worker* had and would continue to blame him for the cold war) asking that he reverse what the Supreme Court had done.

During the next weeks, the *Worker* attempted to put the best face possible on the situation. The paper cited individuals and organizations who had announced their opposition to the decision. Unsurprisingly, most were from Communist Party members or affiliates. Every newspaper item that questioned the wisdom of the majority or in any way criticized them was reprinted in the *Worker* to boost party morale. In addition, a variety of persons and organizations who were not Communists, or even liberals, raised serious civil rights issues by questioning whether the majority had invaded and substantially weakened the liberties set forth in the Constitution.

Dennis also made a strong argument:

> We warn the American people that reaction here, as in Nazi Germany, will not stop with the Communists. Reaction will try to exploit this decision not only to seek to sup-

press the Communist Party but to smash the trade unions, sharpen the terror against the Negro people and stifle the growing peace movement.[23]

What the Communist leadership did not understand was that most American workers did not feel threatened by the *Dennis* decision. Their national concerns were with the Korean War, inflation, the atom bomb, and internal subversion. The threats to the First Amendment rights that were recognizable in the *Dennis* majority, people felt, were more than compensated for by the belief that an internal enemy had been defeated. In 1951 most citizens regarded Hoover and McCarthy as heroes, not perverted prosecutors who threatened the United States and the Constitution. The victory of the government in *Dennis* meant that precedent had been established to prosecute Communists in federal courts throughout the nation. With one exception, the Supreme Court refused to review any of these decisions.

Justice Black was correct when he said that only in calmer times would the First Amendment be restored to its rightful place in protecting political dissent, but that process began sooner than Black anticipated. On June 17, 1957, the Court handed down its decision in four cases that substantially reduced the ability of the government to prosecute Communists using the *Dennis* precedent. In the lead case, *Yates v. United States,* the Court ruled that the government in pursuing Smith Act prosecutions had to show more than mere advocacy of revolt; rather, the government had to prove that acts or efforts to instigate action had taken place. Because the government could not meet that test, prosecutions of Communists for the most part stopped. Despite the controversy *Yates* engendered among conservative anti-Communists, calmer days had indeed returned.

NOTES

1. *United States v. Dennis,* 183 F.2d 201 (2d Cir. 1950).
2. *Dennis v. United States,* 341 U.S. 494, at 509 (1951).
3. Ibid., at 579.
4. Ibid.
5. Ibid., at 580.
6. Ibid., at 581.
7. Ibid., at 588.
8. "A Clear and Present Danger," *Los Angeles Times,* June 5, 1951.
9. "Reds Plan A Fight To Save Politburo," *New York Times,* June 15, 1951.
10. *New York Times,* June 3, 1951.
11. Douglas Papers, Box 205, Library of Congress.
12. *New Republic,* June 18, 1951.
13. Ibid., July 1956.
14. Ibid., June 18, 1951.
15. *St. Louis Post-Dispatch,* June 5, 1951.
16. Ibid.
17. *Chicago Daily Sun-Times,* June 6, 1951.
18. *Time,* "Black Day for the Reds," June 11, 1951; *Newsweek,* "Communists: Worse Days Coming," June 18, 1951.
19. *New Republic,* n.d.
20. *Congressional Record,* 82d Cong., 1st sess., January 3, 1951–October 20, 1951.
21. *Washington Post,* June 6, 1951.
22. *Christian Science Monitor,* June 6, 1951.
23. *Worker,* June 5, 1951.

Rosenberg v. United States

Harvey Rishikof

Rosenberg v. United States
346 U.S. 273 (1953)

DECIDED: June 19, 1953
VOTE
  CONCURRING: 6 (Fred M. Vinson, Robert H. Jackson, Stanley F. Reed, Harold H. Burton, Tom C. Clark, Sherman Minton)
  DISSENTING: 3 (Hugo L. Black, Felix Frankfurter, William O. Douglas)
OPINION: *Per curiam*
OPINION OF THE COURT: Vinson
CONCURRING OPINION: Jackson (Vinson, Reed, Burton, Clark, Minton)
CONCURRING OPINION: Clark (Vinson, Reed, Jackson, Burton, Minton)
DISSENTING OPINION: Black
DISSENTING OPINION: Frankfurter
DISSENTING OPINION: Douglas

Julius Rosenberg, a thirty-two-year-old electrical engineer, and his wife Ethel, thirty-five, were arrested in the summer of 1950 and executed on June 19, 1953, for conspiracy to commit espionage. Their fourteen-day trial, which also included Morton Sobell as a defendant and co-conspirator, began in late March 1951 and was followed by twenty-seven months of appeals that helped define the cold war struggle against communism. The case went before the United States Supreme Court seven times on different motions and requests for *habeas corpus, certiorari,* and rehearing, and the Second Circuit issued three opinions upholding the sentences. The case was a foil for the Korean War, and the executions have remained a *cause célèbre* for more than five decades, as the controversy continues to be debated in books, law reviews, and academia.

A 2001–2002 exhibit on the Rosenbergs at the New-York Historical Society was described in these terms:

> The Rosenbergs Reconsidered: The Death Penalty in the Cold War Era presents artifacts of the 1950s trial, juxtaposed with cultural objects that embody the spirit of the times and reactions to the case. A magazine cover exemplifies nuclear fear with a hypothetical illustration of a bomb striking Manhattan; the New York painter Ralph Fasanella depicts the trial and the surrounding Red Scare as a threat to democracy that resembled the all too recent book burnings in Nazi Germany; photographs of marchers clashing at the White House pit clemency advocates against anti-communist picketers carrying pro–capital punishment signs and shouting "Fry 'em!" while protest posters from Mexico and France demonstrate the international response to the double death sentence. The exhibit also features a selection of original documents from the Rosenberg trial now housed in the New York City branch of the National Archives, including mug shots, a Jell-O box used as a recognition signal for couriers, financial records and drawings of nuclear bomb parts sketched by David Greenglass after he became a witness for the prosecution.[1]

Note: The views expressed in this article are those of the author and do not reflect the official policy or position of the National Defense University, the National War College, the Department of Defense, or the U.S. government. Sincere thanks go to Rachel Cook for her research assistance.

The alleged spy ring was discovered in 1950 when a list of Russian Communist spies was found in Germany, revealing the name of Klaus Fuchs, a Manhattan Project nuclear physicist. Fuchs had been selected by the British government to work on the atomic bomb and "implosion theory" at Los Alamos, New Mexico. When arrested in England, Fuchs admitted to transmitting atomic secrets to the Soviet Union and implicated Harry Gold as one of his American couriers for intelligence material. Gold in turn named Greenglass, who had been a machinist at Los Alamos. Greenglass then confessed he had become involved in espionage on the urging of his older sister, Ethel Rosenberg, and her husband, Julius. In addition, Max Elichter and Morton Sobell, Young Communist League members and friends of Julius, were revealed to be part of the ring under the direction of Julius.

The issue at the center of the case was this conspiracy to steal the secrets of the atomic bomb. What sparked intensive debate that continues to this day, however, was the imposition of the death penalty for both Rosenbergs that orphaned their two sons, Michael, ten, and Robert, six. The *New York Daily News* reported on June 23, 1953, that the day after his parents' executions, Michael warned reporters, "The judges of the future will look back at this case with great shame." Sobell, the third defendant at the trial, was given a thirty-year prison sentence. Judge Irving R. Kaufman did not give him the death penalty "only because his complicity was not proved equal to that of the Rosenbergs." The previous December, Gold had received a thirty-year sentence. Ruth Greenglass, David's wife, was not indicted even though she had been mentioned as a co-conspirator. David Greenglass was sentenced to fifteen years.

REACTIONS TO THE TRIAL AND SENTENCES

Contemporary opinion on the left maintained the Rosenbergs were martyrs, innocent victims of a frame-up, who were being punished for their Jewish heritage. To the courts and mainstream opinion, however, the conspiracy was "worse than murder" and a betrayal equal to or greater than that of Benedict Arnold. For example, on June 22, the day after the executions, Ralph McGill, publisher of the *Atlanta Constitution*, wrote in an editorial that the Rosenbergs, the atom spies, through "traitorous chores cost the lives of thousands of American soldiers and placed in jeopardy the nation itself." The prosecutor, U.S. Attorney Irving H. Saypol, did not ask for the death penalty, nor was his recommendation solicited, nor was a jury involved in the decision. Saypol, however, pointed out that death was the maximum penalty for wartime espionage for a foreign nation. Judge Kaufman, who sent the Rosenbergs to their deaths, declared his reasons from the bench:

> I consider your crime worse than murder. Plain deliberate contemplated murder is dwarfed in magnitude by comparison with the crime you have committed. In committing the act of murder, the criminal kills only the victim. . . . But in your case, I believe your conduct in putting into the hands of the Russians the A-bomb has already caused, in my opinion, the Communist aggression in Korea, with the resultant casualties exceeding 50,000 and who knows but that millions more of innocent people may pay the price of your treason. Indeed, by your betrayal you undoubtedly have altered the course of history to the disadvantage of our country. No one can say that we do not live in a constant state of tension. We have evidence of your treachery all around us every day for the civilian defense activities throughout the nation are aimed at preparing us for an atom bomb attack.[2]

The *New York Times* on April 6, the day after the criminal trial, highlighted the fact that the Rosenbergs' death sentences were reported as the first under the Espionage Act of 1917, which imposed death as a maximum penalty for espionage in wartime. In peacetime the maximum penalty would have been twenty years in prison. Emanuel Bloch, the Rosenbergs' attorney, again made the argument that the defendants were victims of politics rather than law, and he argued, "I repeat that these defendants assert their innocence and will continue to assert it as long as they breathe. They believe that they are victims of political hysteria, and that their sentence was based upon extraneous political considerations having no legitimate or legal connection with the crime charged against them." Before the sentences were passed on the Rosenbergs, Bloch said the case might have international repercussions.

> Great efforts are being made to bring the United States and Russia into an orbit of understanding, the lawyer said. This case has reached such importance that your sentence will be radioed around the world in three minutes. We are not at war with the Soviet Union, although the Soviet Union is regarded as an enemy. Who knows but that tomorrow the Soviet Union and the United States may reach an accord?[3]

The *New York Times* story quoted liberally from the prosecutor, allowing him to assert that he was not moved by "any spirit of malice, hatred, or revenge" when he made his case for conviction.

> The law under which the defendants were tried specifically omits reference to espionage in favor of a nation with whom this country is at war. . . . It is clear that this omission was conscious. The framers of the law understood the lesson of history that the uneasy ally of convenience of one day can really be preparing to be tomorrow's enemy. The Nazi-Soviet Pact of August, 1939, which unloosed the flood gates of World War II, is still fresh in our memory. What sort of allies were the Nazis and the Russians at that time? When the Nazis attacked Russia, did Russia become an ally of ours by choice? . . . The greatest issue of our age is the struggle of our free society for survival against the vast forces of Communist totalitarianism. These defendants were the agents of antagonistic forces which might well be preparing to overwhelm us. A society which does not defend itself is not worthy of survival.[4]

The left-wing *National Guardian* began a series of articles to overturn on appeal the "terrible injustice" of the "calamitous precedent" and covered the story continually in midsummer. The *National Guardian* also contributed to the formation of the National Committee to Secure Justice in the Rosenberg Case, and from time to time Ethel Rosenberg sent letters to the paper from prison. Similar committees were founded in Britain, France, and Italy. Typical of the *National Guardian* was a story that compared the Rosenbergs to others wrongly accused or convicted:

> Is the Rosenberg case the Dreyfus case of the cold-war America? Is it the Sacco-Vanzetti case of this year when the nightmare Truman war program demands the destruction of militant labor opposition? Is it the Reichstag Fire Trial at a time when the protest from the political Left must at all costs be silenced?
> . . . The possibility of removing all Constitutional checks on the hounding of left-wing Americans depends on the government's ability to convince the public that all such persons are a "real and present danger" to national security.
> . . . Upholding the conviction of the Rosenbergs would go far toward enabling the government to make any member of any of the 200-odd organizations officially labeled "subversive " subject to arrest as a "spy."

To the mainstream, the *National Guardian* was a publication described in 1949 by the California Committee on Un-American Activities as notoriously Stalinist in its staff, writers, management, and content.[5]

THE APPEALS: JUDICIAL AND PUBLIC

The Rosenbergs' first appeal was to the U.S. Court of Appeals for the Second Circuit. In February 1952 Judge Jerome Frank wrote for a unanimous court that the Espionage Act had been applied properly, that the jury had made up its own mind about the government's co-conspirator witnesses, that the judge had conducted the trial fairly, and that the imposition of the death penalty was not "unconstitutional." The

Across from the White House in January 1953, demonstrators rally in support of clemency for condemned spies Ethel and Julius Rosenberg. The couple, sentenced to death in 1951, appealed to the Supreme Court. Justice William O. Douglas issued a stay of execution, but in *Rosenberg v. United States* (1953) the full Court vacated the stay, and the husband and wife were executed. —AP Wide World Photos

court noted, however, that no civil court had ever imposed death in an espionage case before, but that the sentence did not violate the Eighth Amendment by shocking "the conscience and sense of justice of the people of the United States."

Leading attorneys were surprised by the harshness of the sentences and corresponded privately to different jurists when the first *certiorari* application was denied by the Supreme Court. In November 1952 C. C. Burlingham, one of the elder statesmen of the New York bar, wrote to Justice Frankfurter requesting that the death sentences be viewed in a comparative law perspective, noting, "The British gave [Klaus] Fuchs only 14 years or less. Canada gave its traitors only a few short years. The R's [Rosenbergs] treason was when we were friends of Russia. We must not go back to the 16th century."[6]

With the denial of the first *certiorari* petition in October 1952 and the motion for rehearing in November, a series of collateral attacks followed in the lower courts resulting in two more circuit court opinions and subsequent denials of review by the Supreme Court. In the Supreme Court denials of *certiorari,* when stays were granted, Justices Black and Frankfurter expressed a desire to hear the case. On the second appeal before the Second Circuit, in December 1952, the defense team raised the issue that prejudicial newspaper publicity had created a "a communal prejudgment of guilt," particularly the indicting of a Mr. William Perl for perjury in denying knowing the Rosenbergs while Ruth Greenglass was testifying. The defense team had not raised this issue at trial and requested neither a mistrial nor a judicial corrective instruction to the jury, so the panel rejected the claim. The appellate court summarily dismissed claims of perjury on the part of Greenglass and other witnesses. In May the *certiorari* petition to the Supreme Court was denied, and, because the trial judge had set the execution date for the week of June 15, the defense team launched three collateral attacks in the lower courts.

During the appeal period, pamphleteers such as Howard Fast for *Masses and Mainstream* stirred emotions with fiery editorial commentary mixing anti-Semitism, anticapitalism, and Marxist analysis. The left, critical of American liberalism and its perceived anti-Semitism, equated the legal process as weighted against justice:

> In a special way, the Rosenberg case defines the epoch we live in. Through the Rosenberg case the Truman administration squarely and undisguisedly uses the death penalty for those who stand in opposition to it. More subtly, perhaps than Adolph Hitler proceeded, more cleverly, perhaps, but with the same tactic, the Truman administration seeks to inflame anti-Semitism.
>
> I do not say this is Germany in 1933. This is America in 1952, and for that very reason the masses of American people still have both the time and the strength to say, "Ethel and Julius Rosenberg must not and shall not die!"
>
> It is time we learned that we live in a period when the human race is indivisible. There are no more strangers to mankind. The Rosenbergs have been offered up by the men of war, the men of death, the lords of the atom, the lords of pain, of greed, of hunger, and of destruction. If the sacrifice is made, then our own flesh and blood will burn, and particularly will those of us who are Jews have committed the deepest sin, the sin of breaking faith with all of the holy dead who fought against and who died fighting against, the monster of fascism.[7]

Responding to the allegations of anti-Semitism and the intense campaign to frame the trial as anti-Jewish conspiracy, the Anti-Defamation League under the auspices of the National Community Relations Advisory Council in June 1952 issued the following statement:

> For some months the Anti-Defamation League has been alert to an intensive propaganda campaign being promoted by a Communist-inspired group which seeks to create the false impression that Ethel and Julius Rosenberg, convicted atom spies, have been the victims of an alleged anti-Semitic frame-up. This campaign has been slanted to agitate Jewish people throughout the US and the world in an effort to gain adherents and thereby give the entire project an appearance of being promoted by Jews as such. The following statement has just been released by all the Jewish agencies constituent to the National Community Relations Advisory Council, alerting American Jewry to this "fraudulent" effort.
>
> Any group of American citizens has a right to express its views as to the severity of the sentence in any criminal case. Attempts are being made, however, by a Communist-inspired group called the National Committee to Secure Justice in the Rosenberg Case, to inject the false issue of anti-Semitism into the Rosenberg case. We condemn these efforts to mislead the people of this country by unsupported charges that the religious ancestry of the defendants was a factor in the case. We denounce this fraudulent effort to confuse and manipulate public opinion for ulterior political purposes.[8]

WHITE HOUSE ROLE

The Rosenberg trial began during the administration of Harry S. Truman, but he left office without acting on the case. Significant public demonstrations took place in front of the White House, as supporters attempted to convince the president to grant clemency. Between December 27, 1952, and January 17, 1953, for twenty-one days and nights, demonstrators participated in the "White House Clemency Vigil." Numbers fluctuated between 500 and 750, according to the press and radio. On the last few days the *Washington Star* and the *National Guardian* estimated the number at close to 2,000. The vigil ended once it became clear Truman would not act and the issue of executive clemency would fall to the next president, Dwight D. Eisenhower. On February 11, 1953, Eisenhower denied the petition for executive clemency filed by the Rosenbergs. In denying the petition, he stated:

> These two individuals have been tried and convicted of a most serious crime against the people of the United States. They have been found guilty of conspiring with intent and reason to believe that it would be to the advantage of a foreign power, to deliver to the agents of that foreign power certain highly secret atomic information relating to the national defense of the United States. The nature of the crime for which they have been found guilty and sentenced far exceeds that of the taking of the life of another citizen; it involves the deliberate betrayal of the entire Nation and could very well result in the death of many, many thousands of innocent citizens. By their act these two individuals have, in fact, betrayed the cause of freedom for which free men are fighting and dying at this very hour.
>
> The courts have provided every opportunity for the submission of evidence bearing on this case. In this time-honored tradition of American justice, a freely selected jury of their fellow citizens considered the evidence in this case and rendered its judgment. All rights of appeal were exercised and the conviction of the trial court was upheld after full judicial review, including that of the highest court in the land. I have made a careful examination into this case, and I am satisfied that the two individuals have been accorded their full measure of justice. There has been neither new evidence nor have there been mitigating circumstances which would justify altering this decision and I have determined that it is my duty, in the interest of the people of the United States, not to set aside the verdict of their representatives.[9]

In response to President Eisenhower's denial, the National Committee to Secure Justice in the Rosenberg Case took out full-page advertisements in the *National Guardian* that proclaimed:

**Ethel and Julius Rosenberg
CAN BE SAVED!**

**The President Can Reconsider His Denial of Clemency!
Lend your voice NOW to the sentiments of Pope Pius XII, leader of 28 Protestant
denominations, and the world's leading rabbis**

Wire, Phone, Write
**President Eisenhower: Reconsider!
Commute Rosenberg Death Sentences**

Funds Desperately Needed!
**$25,000 needed within 5 days for legal steps and campaign for clemency
Checks may be out to Joseph Brainin, Chairman, or to
NATIONAL COMMITTEE TO SECURE JUSTICE TO THE ROSENBERG CASE**
1095 Sixth Avenue, New York 18, N.Y.   Telephone Brant 9-9694 [10]

The same day it ran the ad, the *National Guardian* highlighted the role of Pope Pius XII and contended that his plea for clemency had been suppressed. The story quoted Apostolic Delegate Amleto Cicognani from the Vatican's paper, *L'Osservatore Romano,* as saying:

> At the request of the Holy See, the Apostolic Delegation last December communicated to the Dept. of Justice the fact that the Holy Father had received numerous and urgent appeals in behalf of Julius and Ethel Rosenberg, which out of motives of charity proper to his Apostolic Office without being able to enter into the merits of the cases, His Holiness felt appropriate to bring to the attention of the U.S. civil authorities.[11]

Also on that day the paper reported that Attorney General Herbert Brownell Jr. and Daniel M. Lyons, the pardons attorney at the Department of Justice, had both recommended clemency to the president. The paper reported on another round-the-clock vigil that had begun on Valentine's Day. Scattered through the crowd were signs with a variety of messages, including:

> Professor Einstein says he has grave doubts
> "The sentence is excessive and cruel" The Churchmen
> Mr. President 3,000 ministers have appealed to you
> The *Jewish Examiner:* "The punishment of the Rosenbergs is extremely harsh"
> The Electric Chair can't kill the doubts in the Rosenberg Case
> The Court of Appeals says a new trial should have been granted
> Afro-American says there are grave doubts in the case
> Justice in the U.S. must not be more vindictive than in other countries—*Jewish Chronicle*

The demonstrations and protest persisted as the last round of collateral legal attacks wound their way to the Supreme Court. In the final act of what had been a judicial marathon, the Supreme Court denied any *habeas corpus* or hearing and, in the eleventh hour, vacated Justice Douglas's motion for a stay of execution. New appellate attorneys, under the name of Irwin Edelman, as a friend to the court, raised what Justices Douglas, Black, and Frankfurter believed deserved briefing and argument. The crux of the issue was whether the death penalty could be imposed without the recommendation of the jury for a crime involving the disclosure of atomic secrets when a part of the crime occurred after 1946, the effective date of the Atomic Energy Act. To the majority this issue did not apply because the Atomic Energy Act had not superseded the Espionage Act, which did not require a jury verdict, and they were not predisposed to more judicial review.

In the words of *Time* magazine, on June 29, 1953:

> It was Monday, the last day of judgment before the U.S. Supreme Court recessed for summer vacation. It was also, or so it seemed, the last hope before the bar of justice for Julius and Ethel Rosenberg. For the sixth time, the mousy little engineer and his wife, waiting in Sing Sing's death house, had petitioned the highest tribunal, this time for a stay of execution and review of their trial. For the sixth time, a majority of the nine Justices rejected a Rosenberg appeal.

In the view of the *Nation,* attorney Edelman had not made friends in his "friend of the court" brief:

> Expelled from the Communist Party in 1947, Edelman did not turn informer or renegade. . . .
> One of the justices referred to him as a "vagrant," citing a court decision from which it clearly appears that Edelman had raised and carried to the Supreme Court of California an important free-speech issue. . . .

In the last tragic chapter it was Edelman who came forward as the "friend" of the Rosenbergs to raise the point, over the objection of the Rosenbergs' accredited counsel, that won a stay and might, if it had been raised earlier, have won a review. . . .

On the night the Rosenbergs were executed, the intrepid Edelman was chased from Pershing Square by an angry crowd.[12]

During the cold war, character attacks were not restricted to those representing the Rosenbergs. The response to the Douglas dissenting opinion was quite sharp in some quarters, if somewhat slow to develop. On March 13, 1957, a resolution was submitted to the Georgia General Assembly. The resolution characterized Justice Douglas's participation in the Rosenberg case:

That in the case of the infamous Julius and Ethel Rosenberg, convicted and sentenced to death for war time espionage, because of the sale of atomic secrets to communist Russia, decided June 19, 1953, reported in 346 U.S. 273, Justice Douglas wilfully granted an order to stay the execution of said Russian spies. Said stay order was granted by Justice Douglas on the intervention of a stranger to said Rosenbergs, and to their case, which intervention was even opposed by the Rosenberg counsel of record. Said stranger who was thus accommodated by Justice Douglas was an irresponsible character whose conviction as a dissolute person by the State of California had been affirmed by the United States Supreme Court, with the same Associate Justice Douglas dissenting, less than six months previously (*Edelman v. State of California*, January 12, 1952, 344 U.S. 357).

That misdemeanor on the part of Douglas made it necessary for the Court to hold a special term to set aside said stay order, which, the Court states, promised many more months of litigation in a case which had otherwise run its full course and in which said Rosenbergs' plea for stay orders and other dilatory tactics had been denied for the sixth time over a period of more than two years after their conviction and sentence to death, and that the question raised by the said stay order had been considered by the full Court on its merits and denied.

That in said decision, Justices Frankfurter and Black supported the unlawful action of Justice Douglas, thereby using their judicial offices to give aid and comfort to the communist enemy, in violation of Section 3 of the Fourteenth Amendment of the United States Constitution.[13]

On the day of the execution, President Eisenhower again refused to grant executive clemency. In his statement he made clear that the courts had thoroughly reviewed the issues on several appeals and that the severity of the crime dictated the outcome:

Within the last two days, the Supreme Court, convened in a special session, has again reviewed a further point which one of the justices felt the Rosenbergs should have an opportunity to present. This morning the Supreme Court ruled that there was no substance to this point.

But what was that "point"? Was it information from Edelman's brief? Eisenhower continued:

I am convinced that the only conclusion to be drawn from a history of this case is that the Rosenbergs have received the benefit of every safeguard which American justice can provide. . . .

Throughout the innumerable complications and technicalities of this case, no judge has ever expressed any doubt that they committed most serious acts of espionage. Accordingly, only most extraordinary circumstances would warrant executive intervention in this case. . . . The execution of two human beings is a grave matter, but even graver is the thought of the millions of dead whose death may be directly attributable to what these spies have done. . . .

[W]hen in their most solemn judgment the tribunals of the United States have adjudged them guilty and the sentence just, I will not intervene in this matter.[14]

VENONA AND REACTIONS TO THE EXECUTIONS

The story of the public response to the Rosenberg case is not complete without a discussion of the revelations contained in the U.S. Army's Signal Intelligence Service *Venona Cables Project.* Venona was the code name for a counterintelligence project that read intercepted and encoded cables between Moscow and its intelligence officers in the West between 1943 and the mid-1950s and deeply influenced the government officials in the case. The cables helped identify the atomic spy ring and its participants—Klaus Fuchs, David Greenglass, and Julius Rosenberg—and their involvement in the process of extracting bomb-grade uranium.

Critical to the government's case against the Rosenbergs was what Greenglass had supplied to the Soviets through Julius's efforts: notes and a diagram for a high explosive lens to detonate an atomic bomb. While in New York, under Julius's encouragement, Greenglass was introduced to a Russian intelligence officer with scientific knowledge that was captured in a decoded 1944 Venona message to Moscow as follows:

> "Osa" [Ruth Greenglass] has returned from a trip to see "Kalibar" [David Greenglass]. "Kalibar" express his readiness to help in throwing light on the work being carried on at Camp 2 [Los Alamos] and stated that he had already given thought to this question earlier. "Kalibar" said that the authorities of the Camp were openly taking all precautionary measures to prevent information about "Enormous" [the atomic bomb project] falling into Russian hands. This is causing serious discontent among the progressive workers. . . . [In] the middle of January "Kalibar" will be in "Tyre" [New York City]. "Liberal" [Julius Rosenberg], referring to his ignorance of the problem, expresses the wish that our man should meet "Kalibar" and interrogate him personally. He asserts that "Kalibar" would be very glad of such a meeting. Do you consider such a meeting advisable? If not, I shall be obliged to draw up a questionnaire and pass it to "Liberal." Report whether you have any questions of priority interest to us.[15]

As for Ethel Rosenberg's direct involvement in espionage, the only Venona cable concerning her is a November 28, 1944, communiqué that mentions her knowledge of her husband's work:

> Information on LIBERAL's wife. . . . Surname that of her husband, first name ETHEL. 29 years old. Married five years. Finished secondary school. . . . Sufficiently well developed politically. Knows about her husband's work and the role of METR [probably Joel BARR or ALFRED SARANT]. . . . In view of delicate health does not work. Is characterized positively and as a devoted person.[16]

Subsequently, it has been revealed that perjury may have taken place during the trial testimony in that Ethel never typed up notes for Julius or participated in meetings concerning the conspiracy with David and Ruth Greenglass.

As the government files reflect, FBI Director J. Edgar Hoover urged the FBI to build a case against Ethel for leverage: "There is no question" but that "if Julius Rosenberg would furnish details of his extensive espionage activities, it would be possible to proceed against other individuals. [P]roceeding against his wife might serve as a lever in this matter."[17] The plan failed to force Julius Rosenberg to confess.

The day after the execution, the left-wing press castigated the government. Representative of the reaction was the front page story of the New York-Harlem edition of the *Worker* that began with the banner headline: "WE DIE INNOCENT" and proclaimed "Their Nobility Will Triumph." It continued with a harrowing description of Ethel Rosenberg's death.

> Ethel and Julius Rosenberg were murdered in the electric chair because they would not buy their lives from the FBI by agreeing to "finger" other innocent Americans to feed more fake "spy" hysteria.
>
> They died after they sent their final clemency message to their fellow Americans and the world. Julius, who in his final days spoke with contempt of "the rotten deals" the Eisenhower government was offering him through U.S. Attorney General Herbert Brownell, was placed in the electric chair at 8:04 p.m. daylight time and was pronounced dead three minutes later. He stood erect and then looked straight ahead as he was placed into the death machine.
>
> Ethel, mother of two children, Michael, 10, and Bobby, 6, was placed in the chair at 8:11 and was pronounced dead at 8:16. Just before she was strapped into the death instrument, Ethel turned and kissed on the cheek Mrs. Helen Evans, a prison matron who had attended her for more than two years as she lived alone in the empty, isolated woman's death-cell block.
>
> Mrs. Evans, who was almost in tears, mumbled something to the doomed mother, patted her on the shoulder, and then faltered from the death chamber.
>
> Just a half hour before Ethel was strapped in the chair, President Eisenhower read a letter from her pleading for her life and that of her husband. Her plea was flung aside by the President with the comment it was without merit.
>
> While an agonized and shocked humanity all over the earth hoped and pleaded with Eisenhower not to kill the couple against whom there was not an iota of evidence, the executioner threw the switch. The sun went down over the Hudson as they died.
>
> After the fourth shock, guards removed one of the two straps from Mrs. Rosenberg and the doctors applied their stethoscopes. But they were not sure she was dead. Executioner Francel came to them from his switchboard.
>
> "Want another?" he asked.
>
> The doctors nodded. The guards replaced the [leg strap.][18]

In England the Rosenbergs' supporters asked the prime minister to intervene. The *Manchester Guardian* reported:

> A deputation from a "Save the Rosenbergs" protest meeting held at Marble Arch, London last night, called at No.10 Downing Street where it was told the Prime Minister was at Chartwell. Members of the deputation, which was led by the Rev. Stanley Evans, then motored to Chartwell. When they arrived in the lane outside Sir Winston's home, Mr Evans and Professor Bernal found about twenty supporters of the National Rosenberg Defence Committee. They had scribbled a note addressed "Dear P.M.," and asking the Prime Minister to appeal direct "to President Eisenhower over the Transatlantic telephone immediately." In reply they received a typewritten note saying: "It is not within my duty or my power to intervene in this matter. (Signed) Winston Churchill."
>
> This reply was handed to the deputation at midnight, and the gates of Chartwell were closed for the night. In London, fifty demonstrators who had earlier stated they intended to keep an all-night vigil at No.10 Downing Street found police had cordoned off both entrances by the time they arrived at 12.50 a.m. At one o'clock this morning in

Manchester a crowd of two hundred stood quietly outside the offices of the "Manchester Guardian" waiting for news of the Rosenberg executions.

The crowd stood in silence until the executions were announced at 1.45 a.m. The news was received in silence, and members of the crowd, most of them men, maintained a two minutes' silence for the Rosenbergs. Afterwards they moved off to the steps of the Royal Exchange in Cross Street where the meeting pledged itself to continue the fight to clear the name of the Rosenbergs and "to pin the blame where it rightly belongs."

A telegram sent earlier to the Queen had asked her to use her influence towards securing a reprieve.[19]

As for the Rosenbergs, they saw their sentence as part of the intensification of the cold war. According to his attorney, Emanuel Bloch, Julius said, on September 22:

> This death sentence is not surprising. It had to be. There had to be a Rosenberg Case because there had to be an intensification of the hysteria in America to make the Korean War acceptable to the American people. There had to be a hysteria and a fear sent through America in order to get increased war budgets. And there had to be a dagger thrust in the heart of the left to tell them that you are no longer gonna give five years for a Smith Act prosecution or one year for Contempt of Court, but we're gonna kill ya![20]

Indeed, Sen. Joseph McCarthy, R-Wis., used the Rosenberg case as a platform to further investigate the army and Communist spy rings. Julius Rosenberg was believed to have stolen radar and proximity fuse information from the Fort Monmouth, New Jersey, army base during his work as an electrical engineer there between 1940 and 1945. In October 1953 McCarthy claimed that Rosenberg had set up a wartime spy ring at Fort Monmouth that might still be in operation. Fort Monmouth was then known as the "house of spies." The claims and counterclaims led to subcommittee hearings from October through December on "Army Signal Corps Subversion and Espionage" at Fort Monmouth. First held at the Foley Square Federal Building in New York City (the site of the Rosenberg trial), the proceedings were finally moved to the Capitol building in Washington. The "Red Scare" movement would continue to use the Rosenberg case to its advantage through the period. As Senator McCarthy warned at his infamous hearings in 1954, "Either the army will give the names of men coddling Communists or we will take it [the investigation] before the Senate."[21]

LINGERING QUESTIONS

Each of the issues raised or suggested by the case and appeals has continued to be controversial: the imposition of the death penalty, particularly for Ethel Rosenberg; the refusal of Julius and Ethel Rosenberg to come forward with their participation and their willingness to sacrifice for the cause; Judge Kaufman's conduct and his *ex parte* communications; the FBI's use of witnesses and the Venona tapes; the Supreme Court's unwillingness to hold a hearing on the interpretation of the statutes; the real significance of the information that was passed on to the Soviet Union; the quality of the legal defense and the lawyers' refusal to raise the statutory problems earlier; the more lenient sentences granted other participants and co-conspirators; the role of anti-Semitism, and finally, the effect of the cold war psychology on the trial and appeals.

Robert L. Stern, acting solicitor general, who argued the final case before the Supreme Court on June 18, 1953, had the following reflection when the Court vacated the stay and allowed the executions to take place:

> The imposition of death sentences on the Rosenbergs may well have been the result of bad luck. The most important factor was probably the assignment of the case to then

District Judge Kaufman, who was a tough judge for criminal defendants generally as well as for the Rosenbergs. If Klaus Fuchs had been captured and tried in the United States instead of England, Judge Kaufman might have known that he rather than the Rosenbergs and Greenglass was primarily responsible for the disclosure of atomic bomb secrets to the Soviet Union, and thus for the loss of American lives during the Korean War. And only between the fall of 1949 and 1954 was the Supreme Court . . . so composed as to have been likely to have overridden Justices Black, Frankfurter and Douglas. *(Note: In 1949 liberal Justices Frank Murphy and Wiley Rutledge died and were replaced by the more conservative Tom Clark and Sherman Minton. In 1953, within a few months of the Rosenberg decision, Chief Justice Vinson died and was replaced by Earl Warren, and in 1955 John Harlan replaced Robert Jackson.)*

What I knew at the time and what I have learned since leaves me with no doubt as to the Rosenbergs' guilt. I was not at all sure that a death sentence was warranted, particularly for Mrs. Rosenberg. Even though we were at war in 1944 and 1945, when the atomic secrets were transmitted to it, Russia was not then an enemy of the United States but an ally. The reason given by Judge Kaufman for imposing such a sentence was substantially undermined by the subsequent disclosure that Klaus Fuchs had almost certainly turned over much more damaging information to the Soviet Union at or about the same time. But the severity of a sentence within lawful limits is not within the province of appellate judges or lawyers to decide. . . . I am not persuaded that the capital punishment provision of the 1946 Atomic Energy Act governed a conspiracy which in large part was effectuated before 1946. I would not be so sure if all or most of the acts had occurred thereafter, even though the literal words of sec. 10(b) (6) still seem to me to be decisive.[22]

Yet, as Stern pointed out in 1990, the true contribution of the Rosenbergs to the bomb or, more important, to the communism cause of the time, still remains debatable:

Recently released information indicates that the secrets the Rosenbergs passed to the Soviet Union were more valuable than previously believed. In tapes recorded after his forced retirement, but withheld from his earlier memoirs, Nikita Khruschev stated expressly: "I was part of Stalin's circle when he mentioned the Rosenbergs with warmth. I cannot specifically say what kind of help they gave us, but I heard from both Stalin and Molotov, then Minister of Foreign Affairs, that the Rosenbergs provided very significant help in accelerating the production of our atom bomb. Let this be a worthy tribute to the memory of those people. Let my words serve as an expression of gratitude."[23]

NOTES

1. See http://www.nyhistory.org/rosenberg/evidence.html for a description of *The Rosenbergs Reconsidered: The Death Penalty In the Cold War Era*, at the New-York Historical Society, October 2, 2001–March 24, 2002.
2. See http://www.law.umkc.edu/faculty/projects/ftrials/rosenb/ROS_SENT.HTM.
3. William R. Conklin, "Atom Spy Couple Sentenced to Die; Aide Gets 30 Years," *New York Times*, April 6, 1953.
4. Ibid.
5. "Is This the Dreyfus Case of Cold War America?" *National Guardian*, August 15, 1951.
6. Burlingham to Frankfurter, November 17, 1952, Frankfurter Papers, Library of Congress.
7. Howard Fast, *Masses and Mainstream*, April 1952, 48–50.
8. Quoted in Herbert Romerstein and Eric Breindel, *The Venona Secrets* (Washington, D.C.: Regnery Publishing, 2000), 250.
9. See http://www.rosenbergtrial.org/docike.html.

10. *National Guardian,* Vol. 5, No. 18, February 19, 1953.

11. Ibid.

12. *Nation,* June 27, 1953.

13. "Impeachment of Certain U.S. Supreme Court Justices," No. 100, Georgia House Resolution No. 174-554d.

14. President's statement as reported in the *New York Times,* June 20, 1953.

15. Romerstein and Breindel, *Venona Secrets,* 235.

16. Robert Louis Benson and Michael Warner, eds., *Venona: Soviet Espionage and the American Response, 1939–1957* (Washington, D.C.: National Security Agency, Central Intelligence Agency, 1996), 381; see also Michael E. Parrish, "Essay on the Trials of the Century: Revisited: The Rosenberg 'Atom Spy' Case," *University of Missouri (KC) Law Review* 68 (2000): 601 n. 20.

17. Ronald Radosh and Joyce Milton, *The Rosenberg File: A Search for the Truth* (New York: Holt, Rinehart, and Winston, 1983), 99.

18. *The Worker,* June 21, 1953, 1.

19. "Execution of the Rosenbergs: 'Enemies of Democracy,' " *Manchester Guardian,* June 20, 1953.

20. See http://www.crimelibrary.com/terrorists_spies/spies/rosenberg/1.html.

21. See Army-McCarthy link at http://www.infoage.org/mccarthy.html; William B. Ewald Jr., *Who Killed Joe McCarthy?* (New York: Simon and Schuster, 1984), 20, 93, 156.

22. Robert L. Stern, "The Rosenberg Case in Perspective—Its Present Significance," *Supreme Court Historical Society Yearbook, 1990* (Washington, D.C.: Supreme Court Historical Society, 1991).

23. Ibid., note 10a.

Brown v. Board of Education of Topeka, Kansas

John W. Lemza

Brown v. Board of Education of Topeka, Kansas
347 U.S. 483 (1954)

DECIDED: May 17, 1954
VOTE
CONCURRING: 9 (Earl Warren, Hugo L. Black, Stanley F. Reed, Felix Frankfurter, William O. Douglas, Robert H. Jackson, Harold H. Burton, Tom C. Clark, Sherman Minton)
DISSENTING: 0
OPINION OF THE COURT: Warren

At 12:52 p.m. on May 17, 1954, before a quiet, packed gallery, Earl Warren. the recently appointed chief justice of the United States, read the Supreme Court's unanimous ruling in *Brown v. Board of Education*. The Court struck down the "separate but equal" doctrine established for U.S. public education in *Plessy v. Ferguson* (1896) (see page 75). The decision was underscored by Warren's simple pronouncement: "Separate educational facilities are inherently unequal." The ruling was the culmination of arguments before the Court that challenged school segregation laws in Delaware, Kansas, South Carolina, Virginia, and the District of Columbia.

The Court had requested that arguments on both sides of the school segregation question consider the history of the Fourteenth Amendment and its application to education. The results were found to be inconclusive, however, in part because public education in the South just after the Civil War was so primitive that no one had bothered to think about it, and because the original intent of the amendment's framers was not clear. Warren also briefly examined the *Plessy* doctrine and noted the extent of segregation in the North as well as the South. "In approaching this problem," he declared, "we cannot turn the clock back to 1868 when the Amendment was adopted, or even to 1896 when *Plessy v. Ferguson* was written." Warren went on to say, "We must consider public education in the light of its full development and its present place in American life throughout the Nation."

The Court noted that public education plays a crucial role in preparing individuals to become productive members of society. More important, education prepares them to be citizens and to participate in the pressing political choices facing the nation. When states undertook to provide education, they had to do so on equal terms for all. After reading through more than half the Court's opinion, Warren posed the central question: "Does segregation of children in public schools solely on the basis of race . . . deprive the children of the minority group of equal education opportunities?" After a brief pause he answered, "We believe it does." The chief justice then went on to declare that segregation of black schoolchildren

> from others of similar age and qualifications solely because of race generates a feeling of inferiority as to their status in the community that may affect their hearts and minds in a way unlikely ever to be undone. . . . Segregation with the sanction of law, therefore, has a tendency to retard the educational and mental development of Negro children.

The Court concluded that "in the field of public education the doctrine of 'separate but equal' has no place." Once the unanimous decision was announced, Warren later recalled, "A wave of emotion swept the room."

The significance of the decision was obvious. Members of the Court knew that the brief eleven-page opinion would be widely read and scrutinized. Warren realized that black Americans and many northern whites needed little convincing and that stubborn racists would never agree with the Court, regardless of the arguments. Instead, the hope was to reach those who could still be brought to understand the need to eliminate state-sanctioned segregation. Believing that "opinions should be short, readable by the lay public, non-rhetorical, unemotional and, above all, nonaccusatory," Warren saw this opinion as an opportunity to gain the understanding and support of as many southern whites as possible. So, with typical political astuteness, he attempted to ease acceptance of the decision by carefully couching its terms.

In the final paragraph of the *Brown* opinion, Warren noted the "wide applicability" of the Court's intention to order nationwide desegregation, but he recognized the emotional turmoil the decision could incite in the South. Therefore, intentional references to the complexity of the issue "because of the great variety of local conditions" and the delay in issuing implementing orders sent a signal to the South that the Court would allow time for the states to accustom themselves to the idea. Warren also hoped to win support and forestall the imposition of harsher solutions in the reluctant Jim Crow South by coaxing "the full assistance of the parties in formulating decrees." Finally, Warren carefully crafted the *Brown* opinion to apply to a single area, the legal segregation of children by race in primary and secondary schools. This was the group most likely to win public sympathy as victims of racism.

INTERNATIONAL REACTION

Until the *Brown* decision was rendered, international opinion of America's commitment to her own democratic ideals hung in the balance. The world seemed to watch and wait for a sign that racial equality in the West was much more than a social chimera. *Brown* provided that notice. Within an hour of Warren's announcement, the Court's opinion was broadcast in thirty-four languages via the Voice of America to Eastern Europe and the Far East. Although commentaries explained why school segregation existed in certain regions of the United States and not in others, they also emphasized that the issue was settled through a democratic process and not by dictatorial imposition or mob influence. The immediate reaction from the international community was overwhelmingly positive and had an important effect in elevating America's image abroad at a time when the nation was locked in a cold war geopolitical struggle with the Soviet Union. On May 21, 1954, the Municipal Council of Santos, São Paulo, issued a letter to the U.S. Embassy in Rio de Janeiro, applauding the *Brown* decision and noting that it established "the just equality of the races, essential to universal harmony and peace." The council also "desired that the Consul of that great and friendly nation [the United States] be officially notified of our desire to partake in the rejoicing with which the said decision was received in all corners of the civilized world."[1]

Newspapers in Africa followed suit and provided extensive coverage of the Court's decision. Although slightly skeptical over the pending implementation of the ruling, the newspapers reported the announcement with general enthusiasm. The *Afrique Nouvelle*, a weekly antidiscrimination watchdog, proclaimed, "At Last! Whites and Blacks in the United States on the same school benches," and concluded by saying "all the peoples of the world can salute with joy this measure of progress."[2] By August 1954 the U.S. Information Agency had reported to the National Security Council that "the decision [*Brown*] is regarded as the greatest event since the Emancipation Proclamation, and it removes from Communist hands the most effective anti-American weapon they had in Black Africa."[3]

These sentiments reflected the comments of Walter White, executive secretary of the National Association for the Advancement of Colored People (NAACP). In a May 28, 1954, interview with *U.S News & World Report*, White recalled conversations with diplomats from India who originally expressed concern that in their dealings with a racially arrogant America their skin color would cause them to "be treated as Negroes are treated in the United States."[4] The *Brown* ruling, White noted, acted as a salve to those worries:

> I think it is most important that we of the free world give both an inspiration and an
> example, as this Supreme Court decision does, to these people, so that they will see that

This billboard along a highway in Birmingham, Alabama, expresses the John Birch Society's opinion of Chief Justice Earl Warren. Many groups reacted negatively to Warren's support of civil rights, including his role in the landmark *Brown v. Board of Education* (1954), which banned racial segregation in public schools. —AP Wide World Photos

the Communist charge that democracy is decadent, is false, that dark-skinned people who constitute two thirds of the world population are not going to be denied, because of color, equal opportunity; and that is the most important step we can take to throw out Communism and raise American prestige.[5]

By 1956 the State Department was able to report that "Criticism of the United States because of color discrimination practices . . . has markedly declined in recent years, partly as a result of the Supreme Court decisions in the school segregation cases."[6] In the same spirit, an editorial in the liberal weekly *The Nation* carried the thoughts of a spokesman for Kenya's Luo tribe who applauded the decision: "America is right. . . . If we are not educated together, we will live in fear of one another. If we are to stay together forever, why should we have separate schools?" The editorial writer went on to reflect that the *Brown* decision was "especially welcome . . . since it enabled us and our friends abroad for the first time in some years to be equally and simultaneously enthusiastic about an important announcement from Washington." And he emphasized, "The decision was a fine antidote to the blight of McCarthyism and kindred fevers."[7]

RESPONSES FROM THE BLACK COMMUNITY

At home, the enthusiasm of the black community equaled that of the international community, but was tempered with a guarded optimism. The Associated Negro Press (ANP) national news service heralded the long-awaited ruling "as the most important court decision affecting Negroes since the Dred Scott decision in 1857," but it anticipated that the "opinion is expected to receive opposition from many white educators and local officials."[8] The news service assumed a wait-and-see position in light of the initial reactions by elements of the segregationist South:

> It remains to be seen whether or not some southern states will take drastic action to circumvent the high tribunal's ruling. Governors of Georgia and South Carolina earlier stated they would abolish public school systems in their states if segregation were outlawed. Now that that has occurred, it is up to the chief executives to act.[9]

On a different level, the weekly *Richmond Afro-American* reflected the immediate unbridled joy of its readership. Its May 22, 1954, headline shouted "Housing Is Next!" Page 1 columns predicted the "Inevitable end of segregation seen in this generation," declaring that "Divided buses, restaurants are next to go," and "Citizens hail court ruling as momentous." Some individual responses captured the effusive mood: "I felt darn good when I heard about the Supreme Court's decision. My first reaction was to think that my son will be able to go to a better school," and others reflected a wearied satisfaction: "I'm a citizen and I pay my taxes faithfully. Maybe now I and my family can begin to enjoy some of the benefits of our society like other people."[10]

The *Richmond Afro-American* also recorded the initial comments of black educators. Dr. Luther H. Foster, president of Tuskegee Institute, noted, "The Court's action is especially heartening to those citizens, who have often been denied full access to educational resources of their communities. The legal source of segregation is now removed." Dr. D. O. W. Holmes, president emeritus of Morgan State College, agreed: "From our viewpoint, it is very cheering to have the highest court make that decision for if the 14th Amendment forbids segregation in education, it forbids it in every other public function and will give a tremendous boost to all our other fights to end segregation." Yet his comments were realistic: "Of course, segregated schools won't end in some areas for a long time."[11]

Still, other concerns followed the banner scripts. Black teachers worried about their futures. Rufus Wells, editor of the *Richmond Afro-American*, asked the pressing question: "Now that the United States Supreme Court has declared school segregation unconstitutional, the big question is: What will happen to 112,000 colored teachers, principals, and supervisors?" But without a standing precedent he could offer only the obvious response, "A survey indicates there is no categorical answer. But it is generally agreed that the problem of teacher assimilation is the toughest one faced in the transition to a non-segregated school system in the South."[12]

Behind the joy, cautious optimism, and concerns, the NAACP girded itself for an expected fight and promised to push for full integration in the shortest possible time. Thurgood Marshall, the association's chief legal counsel (and future justice of the Supreme Court), warned that if any state attempted to delay or sidestep the Court's ruling, "NAACP lawyers will take the matter to court again. If they try it in the morning, we'll have them in court the next morning—or possibly that same afternoon."[13] The full text of a statement issued from the May 22-23, 1954, NAACP convention in Atlanta was subsequently dubbed the "Atlanta Declaration." It set forth, in no uncertain terms, the groundwork for a plan of action:

> We are instructing all of our branches in every affected area to petition their local school boards to abolish segregation without delay and to assist these agencies in working out ways and means of implementing the Court's ruling. The total resources of the NAACP will be made available to facilitate this great project of ending the artificial separation of America's children on the irrelevant basis of race and color.[14]

REACTIONS IN THE NORTH AND SOUTH

In comparison to the cautious, but determined, enthusiasm of the black community, the reaction of the majority of Americans to the *Brown* ruling seemed consistent with regional attitudes. The differences were evident in the several pages of editorial excerpts the *New York Times* ran the morning after Warren's announcement. The *New York Herald Tribune* piece proclaimed, "In the lives of nations there are moments when the ideal blazes forth with shattering intensity. Men see the truth they have known all along and yet have somewhat managed to deny. Such a moment comes with the clear, final decision of the court." Similarly, the *Des Moines Register* spoke of the Court's effort to begin "the erasure of one of American democracy's blackest marks," and the *Boston Herald* admitted, "We believe that Negroes have earned the right to be treated as first-rate citizens and earned it the hard way."[15]

In contrast to the northern press, southern editorials reflected a different set of moods. The *Atlanta Constitution* flatly claimed, "The court decision does not mean that Negro and white children will go to school together this fall. The court itself provides for a 'cooling off' period." The *Birmingham News* lamented, "This newspaper deeply regrets that the Supreme Court has come to a decision that a segregation of Negro and white students in the public schools is unconstitutional."[16] The Jackson, Mississippi, *Daily News* editor complained that the ruling was "the worst thing that has happened to the South since carpetbaggers and scalawags took charge of our civil government in Reconstruction days."[17]

These southern editorials were typical of that region's varied responses. As described by a reporter from Chattanooga, Tennessee, some southern leaders "spoke bitter words of defiance. Others ranged from sharp disagreement to predictions of peaceful and successful adjustment in accord with the ruling."[18] The most vociferous protests came from a chorus of known white supremacists; men such as Gov. Herman Talmadge, D-Ga., who "asserted that the Court's decision had reduced the Constitution to 'a mere scrap of paper.'" He added, "The Justices had blatantly ignored all law and precedent and usurped from the Congress and the people the power to amend the Constitution." Soon afterward Talmadge considered converting all state public schools to private institutions to escape the Court's ruling. A now-famous photograph showing the distressed governor, with his hand hiding a grimace upon hearing news of the Court's ruling, also graced a *Life* magazine article that proclaimed, "A Historic Decision for Equality."[19] Talmadge was joined in his outrage by Sen. Harry F. Byrd, D-Va., who called the decision "the most serious blow that has yet been struck against the rights of the states in a matter vitally affecting their authority and welfare," and Sen. James O. Eastland. D-Miss., who defiantly claimed that the South "will not abide by or obey this legislative decision by a political court."[20] Eastland also challenged the decision by claiming, "We will take whatever steps are necessary to retain segregation in education."[21] In even more provocative language, Eastland announced to a group of constituents that "the Constitution of the United States was destroyed because the Supreme Court disregarded the law and decided integration was right. . . . You are not required to obey any court which passes out such a ruling. In fact, you are obliged to defy it."[22] Despite this fiery rhetoric, certain strains of moderation came from other southerners who counseled a measured approach.

In the May 31, 1954, issue of the neo-liberal *New Republic,* Harold C. Fleming, a member of the Southern Regional Council in Atlanta, spoke of Talmadge's "rebel yells of defiance" as nothing more than "a jarring and isolated note," adding that "Other Southern Governors correctly sensed that their people were in no mood for secessionist rhetoric or obstructionist promises." Fleming went on to comment, "Certainly the decision was not popular with the great majority of white Southerners, but it had an authentic ring of justice and, in any case, was irrevocable."[23] Among those recommending a moderated approach was Sen. Spessard L. Holland, D-Fla., who offered hopeful predictions that the Court's far-reaching decision would not lead to "violent repercussions" and that "The vast majority will use moderation. They will examine very carefully just how this new law applies to them."[24]

Caution was the approach of men like Gov. Thomas Stanley, D-Va., who calmly noted that "it appears assured the decision of the Supreme Court will not affect the public schools next Fall," and "we shall have time to give full and careful consideration to means of arriving at an acceptable solution." Stanley's plan included meeting with the state board of education for "a preliminary discussion of the effect of the decision on Virginia" and appointing a special state commission to study the facts.[25] He also advocated the gathering of sixteen southern governors in Richmond with the hope that such a meeting "could serve a most useful purpose for the exchange of information and views." Some governors, such as Charley Johns, D-Fla., agreed, but others balked. Johnston Murray, D-Okla., said, "Each state has its own problems to consider in this. At a meeting about all we could do is tell what each State plans."[26] The wisdom of Stanley's course of action, however, was to make the most of the adjustment time implied by the Warren Court and avoid any rash action during the summer of 1954, unlike that of Gov. James F. Byrnes, D-S.C., who had also served briefly on the Supreme Court. Byrnes decided to cut off state money for new public school construction with the goal of forestalling integration. But Stanley had to feel confident with the editorial support of newspapers like the *Richmond News Leader,* which also advised:

> This is no time for rebellion. It is no time for surrender either. It is a time to sit tight, to think, to unite in a proposal that would win the Supreme Court's approval. . . . The profound implications of the court's opinion are well understood in the South, and now that the basic opinion has come . . . we can ponder those implications, and consider the best and wisest recommendation to offer to the court next Fall.[27]

THE SOUTH AND STATES RIGHTS

Regardless of whether southern editorial reactions to the *Brown* decision recommended conciliatory, balanced, or extreme measures, the Court's ruling did prick the one sensitivity common among the Jim Crow states that seemed to pass unnoticed in the North. That was the issue of states rights. Immediately after Warren's announcement a sampling of newspapers revealed a level of disquiet. The Charleston *News and Courier* declared that "[The ruling drives] another nail into the coffin of States' rights," and the Louisville *Courier-Journal* commented, "This decision amounts in effect not only to the judicial repeal of existing State laws but a judicially ordered alteration of the customs, habits and convictions of millions of Americans."[28] Virginia's attorney general, J. Lindsay Almond, declared that the *Brown* "decision is a drastic blow at the right of the sovereign State to maintain its own public school system without interference from the Federal government." Taking a political poke at President Dwight Eisenhower, he also charged that the "Republican party broke its 1952 campaign pledge when it prosecuted the segregation case . . . the party promised to restore States' rights."[29] But perhaps the strongest demonstration against the perceived violation of states rights could be found in the words of the Southern Manifesto.

Cobbled together by southern political leaders, the manifesto gave voice to their collective indignation over the apparent abrogation of states rights by the federal government through the Supreme Court. These politicians understood full well the meaning of the Court's intransigent declaration that it was the "supreme law of the land" and by implication every individual state executive and legislature was bound and sworn to uphold its decisions. Most disturbing, however, was their understanding that the "statement implies that all state officials, whether or not a party to a case, are obliged to immediately support, in word and deed, whatever the Court has said." It was painful for them to bear witness to an "aggressive judicial action [that] risked the Court's enforcement capabilities and, perhaps worse, abridged the rights of states and localities to manage their own schools."[30] This was the premise of the Southern Manifesto introduced on the floor of the Senate by Walter F. George, D-Ga., on March 12, 1956. It bore the endorsement of nineteen senators and seventy-seven House members collectively representing eleven southern states. Senator George's introduction presented the manifesto as the South's response to:

> the increasing gravity of the situation following the decision of the Supreme Court in the so-called segregation cases, and the peculiar stress in sections of the country where

this decision has created many difficulties, unknown and unappreciated, perhaps, by many people residing in other parts of the country.[31]

Under the heading "Declaration of Constitutional Principles," the manifesto charged: "The unwarranted decision of the Supreme Court in the public school cases is now bearing the fruit always produced when men substitute naked power for established law." It regarded this as part of a larger, more dangerous "trend in the Federal Judiciary undertaking to legislate, in derogation of the authority of Congress, and to encroach upon the reserved rights of the States and the people." Furthermore, the manifesto charged that the Court's actions were in a larger sense destroying the "amicable relations between the white and Negro races that have been created through 90 years of patient effort by the good people of both races." It also commended "the motives of those States which have declared the intention to resist forced integration by any lawful means," and with a dark foreboding resolved, "We pledge ourselves to use all means to bring about a reversal of this decision [Brown] which is contrary to the Constitution and to prevent the use of force in its implementation."[32]

For these advocates of states rights, the Brown decision triggered an argument centered on the violation of the sacred principle of "balance in State and Federal relations which keeps the whole watchworks moving," and they warned that unless the delicate balance was preserved, "the whole organism of American government will be subtly transformed, without the express consent of the people governed." It was an admonition that "the South's largest, most expensive, most important, most cherished institutions," the public schools, would be "thrown into potential jeopardy and chaos," and sounded a clarion call: "What is lost to the Southern States, in terms of political powers, is lost to all States; and the imposition of court-ordered prohibitions in one field makes the next imposition that much easier."[33]

Outside the states rights polemics, many southerners also saw the Brown decision and the pending desegregation of schools as an "affront to the natural order of things."[34] It transcended the conflict over respective powers and touched at history and tradition. For them, the "court's opinion read more like an expert paper on sociology than a Supreme Court opinion." It was a social experiment, "Relying more on the social scientists than on legal precedents."[35] Sen. Sam Ervin, D-N.C., attempted to address this point by describing how the issue tore at the social fabric of the South. He noted that segregationists "believe that 'man finds his greatest happiness when he is among people of similar cultural, historical, and social background.' " He further explained that "segregation did not prevent Southerners from 'forming warm and mutually helpful friendships with members of the other race. Interracial friendships of this character are, in fact, commonplace in the South.' " Segregation, it seemed, "fit well enough this ancient pattern," and disturbing it was unthinkable.[36] For those who supported it, segregation was more than a genteel balance between the races, it was logic based on hard ethnocentric reasoning.

In The Southern Case for School Segregation, which came several years after the Brown decision, James J. Kilpatrick, the conservative former editor of the Richmond Times-Dispatch, laid out the case for separation of the races based on aptitude and behavior. Citing studies and statistics that reinforced his position, Kilpatrick spoke for the white supremacists in his condemnation of Brown, resting his argument on "the hard core of truth in this whole controversy," the superiority of the white race. Pulling statistics from studies on crime, classroom performance, and social surveys generally constructed by like-minded intellectuals, Kilpatrick made his case for keeping the races segregated. His solution, widely accepted in the South at the time, was to press for separate-but-equal facilities. He also offered a challenge: "When the Negro race proves itself, in terms of Western values of maturity and achievement, it will be time enough to talk of complete social and economic integration."[37] Regardless of Kilpatrick's extreme personal philosophy in the face of federal judiciary pressures, his concluding prediction did come to pass: "I believe the South will maintain what I have termed essential separation of the races for years to come."[38]

CONCLUSION

The Supreme Court's ruling in *Brown v. Board of Education* had a galvanic effect throughout the nation and overseas. It was generally recognized as a long-overdue legal and moral victory in the North and among blacks nationwide. They saw the ruling as the natural consequence of a struggle for equality that began with Reconstruction. Leaders abroad saw it as a validation of the West's democratic principles and appreciated its effect in countering Communist rhetoric.

For the American South, the *Brown* decision signaled a subtle but dangerous shift in basic powers and a threat to a traditional social equilibrium. Southerners saw it as a usurpation of states rights by federal authority, a usurpation they believed would have a domino effect, beginning in the public schools and extending to all areas of state control. At another level it appeared as a threat to an established status quo that allowed the races to coexist in a society that was in reality separate, but hardly equal. Although the Court arrived at its decision in a manner that would call into question the limits of its judicial powers at the time, "It is important, after this passage of years, to place the opinion in perspective. It was humane, among the most humane moments in all our history." [39]

NOTES

1. Mary L. Dudziak, *Cold War Civil Rights: Race and the Image of American Democracy* (Princeton, N.J.: Princeton University Press, 2000), 107.

2. Ibid., 108.

3. Ibid., 109.

4. "What Negroes Want Now," *U.S. News & World Report,* May 28, 1954, 54, 56.

5. Ibid.

6. As cited in Dudziak, *Cold War Civil Rights,* 109.

7. Carey McWilliams, "The Climax of an Era," *Nation,* vol. 178, no. 22, May 29, 1954, 453.

8. Associated Negro Press, May 17, 1954.

9. Ibid.

10. *Richmond Afro-American,* May 22, 1954, 2.

11. Ibid., 8.

12. "End of segregation will not cost teachers' jobs," *Richmond Afro-American,* May 29, 1954, 1.

13. "NAACP promises to return to court if states delay action," *Richmond Afro-American,* May 22, 1954, 1.

14. "Atlanta Declaration," *Richmond Afro-American,* May 29, 1954, 1.

15. "Editorial Excerpts from the Nation's Press on Segregation Ruling," *New York Times,* May 18, 1954, 3.

16. Ibid.

17. "Editors View the Segregation Decision," *Richmond Times-Dispatch,* May 19, 1954, 22.

18. John N. Popham, "Reaction of South," *New York Times,* May 18, 1954, 1

19. *Life* magazine, vol. 36, no. 22, May 31, 1954, 11.

20. Richard Kluger, *Simple Justice: The History of Brown v. Board of Education and Black America's Struggle for Equality* (New York: Vintage Books, 1977), 710.

21. Robert C. Albright, "Southerners Assail Court Decision," *Washington Post,* May 18,1954, 1.

22. Quoted in J. Harvie Wilkinson, *From Brown to Bakke: The Supreme Court and School Integration: 1954–1978* (New York: Oxford University Press, 1979), 69.

23. Harold C. Fleming, "The South Will Go Along," *New Republic,* May 31, 1954.

24. Albright, "Southerners Assail Court Decision."

25. James Latimer, "Idea for State Stresses Equality of Facilities; Official Skirts Details," *Richmond Times-Dispatch,* May 19, 1954, 1.

26. "Stanley Invites South's Governors to Discuss School Problem Here," *Richmond Times-Dispatch,* May 20, 1954, 2.

27. "The Decision," *Richmond News Leader,* May 18, 1954, 10.

28. Excerpts from "Editors View the Segregation Decision," *Richmond Times-Dispatch,* May 19, 1954, 22.

29. As cited in "Governor to Call Meeting of State Leaders," *Richmond Times-Dispatch,* May 18, 1954, 2.

30. Wilkinson, *From Brown to Bakke,* 92, 94.

31. *Congressional Record,* March 12, 1956, 84th Cong., 2d sess., vol. 102, 4459–5560.

32. Ibid.

33. James J. Kilpatrick, *The Southern Case for School Segregation* (New York: Crowell-Collier Press, 1962), 106.

34. Robert J. Cottrol, Raymond T. Diamond, and Leland B. Ware, *Brown v. Board of Education: Caste, Culture, and the Constitution* (Lawrence: University Press of Kansas, 2003), 188.

35. James Reston, "A Sociological Decision," *New York Times,* May 18, 1954, 2.

36. Wilkinson, *From Brown to Bakke,* 36, 37.

37. Kilpatrick, *The Southern Case,* 26, 100.

38. Ibid., 192.

39. Wilkinson, *From Brown to Bakke,* 39.

Mapp v. Ohio

Carolyn Long

Mapp v. Ohio
367 U.S. 643 (1961)

DECIDED: June 19, 1961
VOTE
CONCURRING: 6 (Earl Warren, Hugo L. Black, William O. Douglas, Tom C. Clark, William J. Brennan, Potter Stewart)
DISSENTING: 3 (Felix Frankfurter, John Marshall Harlan (II), Charles E. Whittaker)
OPINION OF THE COURT: Clark
CONCURRING OPINION: Black
CONCURRING OPINION: Douglas
OPINION CONCURRING IN JUDGMENT: Stewart
MEMORANDUM OPINION: Stewart
DISSENTING OPINION: Harlan (Frankfurter, Whittaker)

In *Mapp v. Ohio* (1961) the United States Supreme Court extended the exclusionary rule to state criminal trials. The exclusionary rule bars prosecutors from using any evidence unlawfully seized in violation of the Fourth Amendment's prohibition against unreasonable searches and seizures. The decision in *Mapp* also ushered in the Warren Court's "criminal due process revolution." Under the leadership of Chief Justice Warren, the Court began using the process of "selective incorporation," to apply constitutional guarantees in the Bill of Rights to the states.

Dollree Mapp was convicted of possession of obscene materials in violation of Ohio state law and sentenced to seven years in jail. The material was discovered during an illegal search of her home by police officers who said they were looking for a man in connection with a recent bombing. The officers claimed they had a search warrant, but it was later learned that they did not. The legality of the search, however, was not an issue as the case moved through the state courts because, under Ohio law, evidence seized illegally was still admissible at trial. At that time, each state had the prerogative to choose whether to admit unlawfully seized evidence under the Supreme Court precedent *Wolf v. Colorado* (1949). In *Wolf* the Court declared that, although the "security of one's privacy against arbitrary intrusion by the police" was "implicit in 'the concept of ordered liberty' and as such enforceable against the states through the due process clause" of the Fourteenth Amendment, the exclusionary rule need not be extended to the states "as an essential ingredient of the right." Rather, it was up to each state to decide how to remedy a Fourth Amendment wrong. At the time *Wolf* was decided, sixteen states applied the exclusionary rule to Fourth Amendment violations, and thirty-one states, including Ohio, did not.

So *Mapp v. Ohio* was not appealed to the Supreme Court on Fourth Amendment grounds. Instead, Mapp's counsel relied on the First and Fourteenth Amendments, arguing that her conviction should be reversed because Ohio's anti-obscenity law was unconstitutionally vague. Reconsideration of *Wolf* was raised only as a minor point in an *amicus curiae* (friend of the court) brief by the American Civil Liberties Union, which at the end of the nineteen-page brief stated, almost as an afterthought:

> This case presents the issue of whether evidence obtained in an illegal search and seizure can constitutionally be used in a State criminal proceeding. We are aware of the view that this Court has taken on this issue in *Wolf v. Colorado*. It is our purpose by this paragraph to respectfully request that this Court re-examine this issue and conclude that the ordered liberty concept guaranteed to persons by the due process clause of the

Fourteenth Amendment necessarily requires that evidence illegally obtained in violation thereof, not be admissible in state criminal proceedings.

The Fourth and Fourteenth Amendment issue received only minute attention during oral arguments and during conference deliberations. And, at the end of the conference, a unanimous Court agreed that Mapp's conviction be reversed because the Ohio anti-obscenity law violated the First and Fourteenth Amendments. Several days later, however, Justice Clark, who was assigned to write the majority opinion, decided to write a decision reversing *Wolf* and imposing the exclusionary rule on the states.

The U.S. Constitution is silent on the exclusionary rule, as it is for remedies for any violation of constitutional rights. The Supreme Court had created the exclusionary rule in 1914 in *Weeks v. United States*. That case involved the illegal seizure of personal papers and material by federal officials, which the Court declared violated the Fourth Amendment. As a result, the Court reasoned, the evidence should have been excluded from trial. Justice William R. Day, writing for a unanimous Court, observed, "If letters and private documents can thus be seized and held and used in evidence against a citizen accused of an offense, the protection of the Fourth Amendment declaring his right to be secure against those searches and seizures is of no value, and, so far as those thus placed are concerned, might as well be stricken from the Constitution." *Weeks*, however, applied only to illegal searches and seizures by *federal* authorities in *federal* prosecutions. And the Court's decision a quarter of a century later in *Wolf* not to extend the rule to the states appeared to settle the issue until Dollree Mapp's case reached the Court.

Justice Clark began the majority decision in *Mapp v. Ohio* with the observation that since *Wolf*, "There has occurred a series of events which undercuts the continued vitality of the considerations which found expression in its basic reasoning" and that "the scales are weighted in favor of the *Weeks* doctrine." Among these considerations was that by then almost half of the states had adopted the exclusionary rule either by legislative or judicial decision, and that alternative remedies to Fourth Amendment violations were "worthless and futile" as evidenced by the thousands of unlawful searches and seizures that occurred each year.

Clark then offered three rationales to justify extending the exclusionary rule to the states. First, he explained, it was constitutionally required, because "the admission of the new constitutional right by *Wolf* could not consistently tolerate denial of its most important constitutional privilege, namely, the exclusion of the evidence which an accused had been forced to give by reason of the unlawful seizure. To hold otherwise is to grant the right but without its privilege and enjoyment." Exclusion, Clark reasoned, "compels respect for the constitutional guaranty in the only effectively available way—by removing the incentive to disregard it." Second, Clark argued that the exclusionary rule be applied to the states to preserve the imperative of judicial integrity—that judges not be a party to using illegally seized evidence: "Nothing can destroy a government more quickly than its failure to observe its own laws, or worse, its disregard of the charter of its own existence." And third, he suggested that the exclusionary rule be applied to the states in the same manner as the federal government in order to promote "federal-state cooperation in the solution of crime."

At the time *Mapp v. Ohio* was decided, twenty-four states still allowed unlawfully seized evidence in state criminal trials, and four states had partial exclusionary rules. The decision in *Mapp* meant that these states had to conform to the federal requirement and exclude such evidence from their criminal trials. In one fell swoop, the Supreme Court imposed the exclusionary rule on half the states in the Union. The breadth of the decision was extraordinary. By federalizing state criminal procedure, *Mapp v. Ohio* affected every local police precinct and courthouse in the country. Because most criminal cases are handled at the state and local level, the rule could potentially apply to hundreds of thousands of cases involving illegal police searches every year. *Mapp* significantly transformed police investigatory activities and the conduct of state criminal prosecutions. Later, the exclusionary rule was extended to police interrogations in *Miranda v. Arizona* (1966) (see page 245) and police line-ups in *United States v. Wade* (1967).

MAPP'S IMPACT

The significance of this decision was clear from the beginning and continued over the years. The *New York Times* called *Mapp* "historic" and "the most far-reaching constitutional step of the term."[1] Future justice Abe Fortas declared *Mapp* one of "the most radical decisions in recent times."[2] Justice Stewart, who did not join the majority opinion, but reversed Mapp's conviction on First Amendment grounds, characterized the decision as "perhaps the most important search-and-seizure case in history.[3] Political scientist Dennis D. Dorin observed:

> *Mapp* is more than a case that has been in the vortex of public controversy. . . . It is probably the Court's most important search and seizure ruling. As such, it is of substantial consequence to the discipline of criminal justice. No textbook purporting to deal with criminal procedure can be without it. It is a staple of just about every criminal law course in the curriculum.[4]

Mapp was also significant because it was the first in a series of decisions by which the Supreme Court nationalized guarantees in the Bill of Rights to regulate police conduct and protect the rights of the criminally accused. Using the "selective incorporation" approach, the Court declared rights guaranteed in the Fifth, Sixth, and Eighth Amendments to the Constitution fundamental and incorporated into the due process clause of the Fourteenth Amendment. *Mapp*'s influence as a catalyst for these later developments is unmistakable. Political scientist Lucas A. Powe noted, "*Mapp* opened the incorporation floodgates. Thereafter, any case raising an incorporation issue succeeded."[5] The Court's efforts have been described as the "criminal due process revolution" because the decisions drastically expanded the rights of criminal suspects and defendants in state courts.

Many legal scholars, as well as former Supreme Court justices, have stated that the Court's "due process revolution" was the Warren Court's most important legacy. As described by reporter Fred Graham, *Mapp v. Ohio* "signaled the beginning of a due process revolution that was to transform the rules of state law enforcement and criminal procedure and provoke the current protest that the Supreme Court is coddling criminals and handcuffing the police. . . . Never before had a country's judiciary undertaken to change the law as drastically as the United States Supreme Court did during this period."[6] As Erwin N. Griswold, then one of the Court's most effective defenders, wryly put it in 1965, "Some things have recently been found in the Federal Constitution that were not previously known to be there."[7]

Reaction to any Supreme Court decision varies according to the issue at stake, the population affected by the ruling, and its public policy implications. The decision in *Mapp* polarized the country. Many in the law enforcement community and members of conservative interest groups criticized the decision as a hindrance to police and a threat to public safety. As Prof. John Kaplan noted, "From a public relations point of view, it is the worst possible kind of rule because it only works at the behest of a person, usually someone who is clearly guilty, who is attempting to prevent the use against himself of evidence of his own crimes."[8] Those who favored the outcome, such as civil libertarians and liberal interest groups, did so on the basis that *Mapp* helped protect individuals from an overreaching state. Politicians and the public, who focused on the practical implications of the decision, split according to their political ideology, with significant majorities questioning the rule. Members of the legal academy were also divided in their response.

ACADEMIC AND LAW ENFORCEMENT RESPONSES

Much of the scholarly reaction to *Mapp v. Ohio* focused on the legitimacy of the Court's majority decision. Some provided a spirited defense of *Mapp* as necessary to achieve the promise of the Fourth Amendment. For example, law professor Sanford Jay Rosen explained:

Sometimes the Supreme Court employs a procedural device to guarantee a more general substantive right to all the members of our society. Thus, illegally seized evidence is excluded from state as well as from federal criminal trials in order to preserve the general right of privacy—the freedom of each inhabitant of this country from unreasonable intrusion by the government into his home or person, which has been best described as "the right to be let alone." [9]

Law professor Stanley Ingber went even further, suggesting that *Mapp* compels respect for the law. "For constitutionally guaranteed rights to represent something beyond simple platitudes, the remedy provided for their violation must have some measurable consequence that vindicates the right in a manner which 'invokes and magnifies the moral and educative force of the law. The exclusionary rule, of course, does provide this needed confirmation of the right of privacy of one's person and domain,' " Ingber wrote, quoting from a 1970 article on the exclusionary rule by Prof. Dallin Oaks.[10]

Others criticized the Court for unnecessarily overreaching. Harvard Law School professor Robert G. McCloskey echoed the sentiments of many when he observed that "an important change in constitutional law should be preceded by full-dress argument, insuring the most sober kind of judicial consideration, especially when the prevailing rule has been laid down comparatively recently and the issue is one of some intricacy."[11] The decision was also criticized for being a "judicial creation" not recognized in the Constitution or common law and a violation of the principle of federalism because of the Court's imposition of its view of "due process" on the states. Prof. Fred E. Inbau, in a 1961 address to the National District Attorneys' Association one month after *Mapp* was decided, called attention to what he called the "dangerous attitude" assumed by the Supreme Court. He observed that "the Court has taken it upon itself, without constitutional authorization, to police the police." It has also functioned at times as a super-legislative body.[12]

Members of the law enforcement community criticized the decision from a different point of view. Their focus was on the practical implications of the exclusionary rule. For example, Michael Murphy, former police commissioner of New York City, which has the largest police force in the country, described *Mapp*'s effect as "dramatic and traumatic." In 1965 he gave the University of Texas Law School's Annual Lecture on Law and the Free Society, in which he said, "The decisions arrived at in the peace and tranquility of chambers in Washington, or elsewhere, create tidal waves and earthquakes which require rebuilding of our institutions sometimes from their very foundations upward." Murphy lamented how implementation of the exclusionary rule consumed police resources. He explained:

> Retraining sessions had to be held from the very top administrators down to each of the thousands of foot patrolmen and detectives engaged in the daily basic enforcement function. Hundreds of thousands of man-hours had to be devoted to retraining 27,000 men. Every hour in the classroom was an hour lost from the basic function of the police department: the protection of life and property on the street.[13]

Some lamented the possible consequences of the exclusionary rule—the exclusion of reliable, often probative evidence from trial, which raised the possibility Benjamin Cardozo observed while serving on the New York Supreme Court: "The criminal is to go free because the constable has blundered."[14] Law professor Charles Alan Wright predicted, "Its cost to society is great and real. Hundreds or thousands of criminals go free each year because the police are found to have violated, in one way or another, the intricate body of law on when and how they may search."[15] Others suggested that the rule would alter the "truth seeking" function of the criminal justice system by taking the focus away from the guilt or innocence of the criminal defendant to "a search for police error." Such a development, they predicted, would lead to loss of confidence as the public learned of guilty criminals being freed on "technicalities."

Supporters of *Mapp* replied that such was the cost of the Fourth Amendment. Prof. Yale Kamisar, responding to police complaints about court-imposed restrictions on their investigative authority, noted:

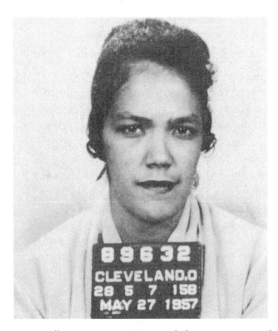

Dollree Mapp was arrested for possession of obscene materials seized during an illegal search. The American Civil Liberties Union, in an *amicus curiae* brief filed in *Mapp v. Ohio* (1961), raised the Fourth Amendment issue on which her case was decided. The Court said illegally obtained evidence could not be used against the accused at trial. — The Granger Collection, New York

Police and prosecutors strenuously resist what they like to call "tighter restrictions" on their powers. But more often than not, what they are really bristling about is tighter *enforcement* of long-standing restrictions. Thus, many in law enforcement reacted to the adoption of the exclusionary rule as if the guarantees against unreasonable search and seizure *had just been written!* They talked as if and acted as if the exclusionary rule *were* the guarantee against unreasonable search and seizure. What disturbed them so much was that the courts were now operating on the same premise.[16]

And, Stanley Ingber observed, the rule is actually directed at the integrity of the criminal justice system, rather than individual law enforcement officers:

The legitimate purpose of exclusion is not to place sanctions upon the specific officer, but to impose them upon the legal system in whose name he is functioning. Exclusion not only vindicates the right violated, but also eliminates the appearance of a system that encourages practically what it condemns rhetorically.[17]

Although some supporters of the exclusionary rule concede that it may result in suppression of evidence of a crime, they note that it was the unlawful police activity, not the rule, that led to the suppression. More often than not, the evidence would not have been discovered were it not for the illegal search.

POLITICAL RESPONSES

Another way to evaluate the public response to *Mapp v. Ohio* is to examine how the political branches reacted. Since the 1960s *Mapp* has had a noticeable effect on judicial nominations and led to legislative efforts to modify or abolish the exclusionary rule. At the same time, the Court under Warren E. Burger and William H. Rehnquist have effectively narrowed the thrust of the exclusionary rule by limiting its application and by cutting back on the substantive reach of the Fourth Amendment.

Mapp v. Ohio and the Supreme Court's criminal due process rulings resonated across the country. Unfortunately, as Fred Graham noted, these controversial decisions could not have come at a worse time. "History has played cruel jokes before, but few can compare with the coincidence in timing between the rise in crime, violence, and racial tensions in the United States and the Supreme Court's campaign to strengthen the rights of criminal suspects against the state."[18] The increase in crime was on the public's mind and was a major issue on the national political agenda. Although it is likely that for a number of reasons, including demographic changes, crime would have been on the rise regardless of the Warren Court's decisions, the fact that the two occurred simultaneously practically ensured the public would associate the increase in crime with the Court's decisions. Politicians who opposed *Mapp* were more than willing to exploit the apparent link between it and the increase in crime.

In 1964 Republican presidential candidate Barry Goldwater blamed the rising crime rate on the Democrats' "soft-on-crime" approach. Goldwater's bid for the White House was unsuccessful, but President Lyndon Johnson, realizing that the critique resonated with the country, focused on crime as a major domestic policy issue. On July 23, 1965, he signed Executive Order 11236, which created the President's Commission on Law Enforcement and the Administration of Justice in response to "the urgency of the Nation's crime problem and the depth of ignorance about it." The bipartisan commission investigated the causes of crime and delinquency over the next two years and in 1967 published "The Challenge of Crime in a Free Society." The report acknowledged that the Warren Court had handed down several criminal procedure decisions that affected the administration of justice, but it did not blame the Court for the rising crime rate. In regard to *Mapp v. Ohio* and the merits of the exclusionary rule, the report claimed:

> America's adherence to these principles not only demands complex and time consuming court procedures, but also in some cases forecloses the proof of facts altogether. Guilty criminals may be set free because the court's exclusionary rules prevent the introduction of a confession or of seized evidence.[19]

The report went on to state:

> Nevertheless, these limitations on prosecution are the product of two centuries of constitutional development in this country. They are integral parts of a system for balancing the interests of the individual and the state that has served the nation well.[20]

President Johnson later proposed the Omnibus Crime Control and Safe Streets Act, which requested additional federal funding for grants, research, and pilot projects to state and local governments to improve their police, courts, and correctional systems to address the crime problem. The Warren Court's criminal procedure decisions did not, however, survive unscathed. While deliberating Johnson's bill, conservative southern senators were able to amend the bill to include provisions that essentially reversed *Miranda v. Arizona* (1966) (see page 245) and provide new standards for the admission of confessions and eyewitness testimony in federal courts. Those provisions were never enforced, and the Court later declared them unconstitutional, but the fact that Congress had enacted them illustrated politicians' and the public's uncertainty about the legitimacy of the Warren Court criminal procedure decisions. Also, while the legislation was being considered, southern senators led an effort to oppose Johnson's nomination of Justice Abe Fortas to replace Chief Justice Warren, who was retiring. During Fortas's Senate confirmation hearings, the legitimacy of the Warren Court's criminal procedure decisions played a central role, and Fortas later asked the president to withdraw his name from consideration when it became obvious that he would not be confirmed.

In 1968 presidential candidate Richard Nixon took a page from Goldwater's campaign strategy and blamed Democrats for being soft on crime. Nixon's "law and order campaign" faulted the Warren Court for its "liberal excesses." The cumulative impact of the criminal procedure rulings, Nixon argued, "has been to set free patently guilty individuals on the basis of legal technicalities." In his acceptance speech at the 1968 Republican National Convention, Nixon spoke of how the courts "have gone too far in weakening the peace forces against the criminal forces of this country." President Nixon had four opportunities to fill openings on the Court. He selected candidates who reflected his conservative political and judicial philosophy and who he believed would reverse the Warren Court's controversial criminal procedure decisions. His successful appointments of Warren Burger as chief justice, and Harry A. Blackmun, Lewis F. Powell, and William Rehnquist as associate justices, illustrated, in part, that his criticism of the Warren Court resonated with a majority in the Senate.

It appeared as if *Mapp v. Ohio*'s days might be numbered. The new chief justice had a reputation as a champion of law and order and as an outspoken critic of the Warren Court's criminal procedure jurisprudence, in particular, the exclusionary rule. Burger alleged that the rule damaged the integrity of the criminal justice system. "A vast number of people are losing respect for the law and the administration of justice," he argued, "because they think that the Suppression Doctrine is *defeating* justice." The Burger Court was successful in limiting the *Mapp* exclusionary rule, but it did not reverse the decision outright.

Unable to secure a judicial reversal of *Mapp* and the exclusionary rule, the Nixon administration called upon Congress to address the issue. Although the legislative effort was directed at the federal exclusionary rule, rather than its application to the states, the popularity of the effort reflected the fact that many still opposed the idea that illegally seized evidence must be excluded from trial. In the first session of the 92d Congress in 1971, Sen. Lloyd Bentsen, D-Texas, introduced S 2657, which would modify the federal exclusionary rule to apply only to those illegal searches and seizures considered "substantial." Bentsen said his bill would "provide the courts with the opportunity to weigh the gravity of the crime charged to a defendant and then consider the seriousness and circumstances of the offense in seizing or searching for evidence." He argued that the bill was necessary to "restore some semblance of reason and balance to the rules by which we administer the fourth amendment to see that justice is done."[21] The bill was introduced in 1972, with an amendment allowing victims of an illegal search to sue the government for up to $25,000 in actual and punitive damages. The bill did not pass.

The effort to address the exclusionary rule gained new ground during President Ronald Reagan's two terms in office. In 1981 Reagan, citing crime as one of the major domestic policy issues facing the country, asked Attorney General William French Smith to look into the issue. The attorney general's Task Force on Violent Crime published a report that attacked the Warren Court's criminal procedure revolution as a major reason for the increase in crime since the 1960s, and *Mapp v. Ohio* was one of its main targets. The report faulted the exclusionary rule for "barring evidence of the truth, however important, if there is any investigative error, however unintended or trivial." It noted that in its "present application the exclusionary rule not only depresses police morale and allows criminals to go free when constables unwittingly blunder, but it diminishes public respect for the courts and our judicial process." The report concluded with a recommendation that Congress legislatively carve out a "good faith" exception to the exclusionary rule, that "evidence which is obtained as a result of a search or seizure which is otherwise admissible shall not be excluded in the criminal proceeding brought by the United States if the search or seizure was undertaken in a reasonable, good faith belief that it was in conformity with the Fourth Amendment to the Constitution."[22]

To President Reagan's frustration, repeated legislative efforts to moderate the effects of the exclusionary rule failed. He was also disappointed with the Burger Court's inability to launch the expected counterrevolution. Moreover, in this term he had only one opportunity to appoint a conservative justice, Sandra Day O'Connor, to the Court. In 1985, at the beginning of his second term, he asked his new attorney general, Edwin Meese III, to find a way to address the Warren Court's "liberal excesses." Meese subsequently ordered the Office of Legal Policy, the research arm of the Justice Department, to study the "current status of the truth seeking function of the criminal justice system." The project yielded eight reports, and the second in the series, "The Search and Seizure Exclusionary Rule," strongly condemned *Mapp v. Ohio*. The report concluded that the exclusionary rule was judicially created and not supported by "the original intent or meaning" of the Constitution and questioned its ability to effectively deter police misconduct. In addition, the report highlighted the "costs" of the exclusionary rule in terms of lost convictions. Although it conceded that the actual number was minimal, they were characterized as high in absolute terms. "Losing that many convictions certainly poses serious dangers to the community, and there is evidence that the number of lost convictions is concentrated particularly among certain crimes generally perceived as serious, e.g. weapons and drug offenses."[23]

The report also noted that these lost convictions had led to other costs as well, including "public anger and the heightened fear of crime that may result from the release or truncated prosecution of serious criminals even in a small number of cases." It urged the administration to pursue a litigation campaign to encourage the Supreme Court to reverse *Mapp v. Ohio*. "It is important to take advantage of the Court's increasing lack of confidence in the exclusionary rule as a deterrent to police misconduct, to highlight the costs of continued reliance on the rule, and to persuade the court that alternatives exist that effectively redress and deter violations."[24]

Despite passage of two major crime control bills during Reagan's second term, Congress was still unable to reverse *Mapp v. Ohio* or modify the federal exclusionary rule. One reason for the lack of impetus behind such an effort was that Congress believed Reagan's appointments to the Court would do the job for them. Rehnquist was elevated to chief justice, and the new justices, Antonin Scalia, Lewis Powell, and Anthony Kennedy, gave Reagan a solidly conservative Court. The Rehnquist Court limited the application of the exclusionary rule in much the same manner as the Burger Court; it also cut back on an accused person's substantive rights under the Fourth Amendment.

Mapp v. Ohio and the exclusionary rule have fallen from the national political agenda. Today, most of the activity on this issue is found in the states, which, thanks to "new judicial federalism," are doing more to strengthen the exclusionary rule rather than dismantle it. According to new judicial federalism, the U.S. Constitution provides only a minimal level of protection for constitutional rights and liberties, and a state court has the power to interpret its constitution more generously to provide greater protection for constitutional rights. A number of state supreme courts are pursuing this option; frequently these courts have declined to recognize the so-called "good-faith" exception to the exclusionary rule, resulting in a resurgence of support for the rule. It also appears that law enforcement officials, formerly the greatest critics of the rule, have now come to accept it.

In 1988 the American Bar Association, after conducting a two-year study on the impact of constitutional protections on crime control, published its findings, which acknowledged the advantages of the exclusionary rule. Based on testimony from hundreds of judges, prosecutors, defense attorneys, and police officers, the study concluded that "the exclusionary rule neither causes serious malfunctioning of the criminal justice system nor promotes crime." Moreover, it noted that law enforcement officials, "toward whom the deterrent force of the exclusionary rule is primarily directed," reported that the rule was not a "serious obstacle to their job." In fact, the study found that many "police officials also report that the demands of the exclusionary rule and resulting police training on Fourth Amendment requirements have promoted professionalism in police departments across the country." It concluded that the

> exclusionary rule appears to be providing a significant safeguard of Fourth Amendment protections for individuals at modest cost in terms of either crime control or effective prosecution. This "cost," for the most part, reflects the values expressed in the Fourth Amendment itself, for the Amendment manifests a preference for privacy and freedom over that level of law enforcement efficiency which could be achieved if police were permitted to arrest and search without probable cause or judicial authorization.[25]

The real problem facing the criminal justice system, the study summarized, was the inadequacy of resources available to detect and address crime.

NOTES

1. *New York Times*, June 25, 1961.
2. Bernard Schwartz, *Super Chief* (New York: New York University Press, 1983), 391.
3. Potter Stewart, "The Road to Mapp v. Ohio and Beyond: The Origins, Development, and Future of the Exclusionary Rule in Search-and-Seizure Cases," *Columbia Law Review* 83 (1983): 1367.

4. Dennis D. Dorin, " 'Seize the Time': Justice Tom Clark's Role in *Mapp v. Ohio*," in *Law and the Legal Process,* ed. Victoria L. Swigert (Beverly Hills: Sage, 1982), 22.

5. Lucas A. Powe, *The Warren Court and American Politics* (Cambridge: Harvard University Press, 2000), 195.

6. Fred Graham, *The Self-Inflicted Wound* (New York: Macmillan, 1970), 28.

7. Quoted in ibid., 28.

8. John Kaplan, "The Limits of the Exclusionary Rule," *Stanford Law Review* 26 (1974): 1038.

9. Sanford Jay Rosen, "Contemporary Winds and Currents in Criminal Law, With Special Reference to Constitutional Criminal Procedure: A Defense and Appreciation," *Maryland Law Review* 27 (1967): 103, 109.

10. Stanley Ingber, "Defending the Citadel: The Dangerous Attack of "Reasonable Good Faith,' " *Vanderbilt Law Review* 36 (1983): 1511, 1536.

11. Robert G. McCloskey, *The Modern Supreme Court* (Cambridge: Harvard University Press, 1972), 244.

12. Fred Inbau, speech, July 26, 1961, reprinted in Fred Inbau, "Public Safety v. Individual Civil Liberties: The Prosecutor's Stand," *Journal of Criminal Law, Criminology and Political Science* 53 (1962): 85, 329.

13. Michael Murphy, "Judicial Review of Police Methods in Law Enforcement," *Texas Law Review* 44 (1966): 939, 941.

14. *People v. DeFore* 242 NY 13, 21, 150 NE 585, 587 (1926).

15. Charles Alan Wright, "Must the Criminal Go Free If the Constable Blunders?" *Texas Law Review* 50 (1972): 741.

16. Yale Kamisar, "On the Tactics of Police-Prosecution Oriented Critics of the Courts," *Cornell Law Quarterly* 49 (1964): 436, 440.

17. Stanley Ingber, "Defending the Citadel," 1511, 1536.

18. Graham, *The Self-Inflicted Wound,* 4.

19. *The Challenge of Crime in a Free Society: A Report by the President's Commission on Law Enforcement and Administration of Justice* (Washington, D.C.: U.S. Government Printing Office, 1967), 126.

20. Ibid.

21. *Congressional Digest,* Senate floor debate, October 6, 1971.

22. *The Attorney General's Task Force on Violent Crimes, Final Report* (Washington, D.C.: U.S. Department of Justice, 1981), 17.

23. *Report to the Attorney General: The Search and Seizure Exclusionary Rule* (Washington, D.C.: U.S. Department of Justice, Office of Legal Policy, 1986), 23.

24. Ibid., vi–vii.

25. "Criminal Justice in Crisis: A Report to the American People and the American Bar on Criminal Justice in the United States: Some Myths, Some Realities, and Some Questions for the Future" (Washington, D.C.: American Bar Association, Criminal Justice Section, 1988).

Engel v. Vitale

Bruce J. Dierenfield

Engel v. Vitale
370 U.S. 421 (1962)

DECIDED: June 25, 1962
VOTE
    CONCURRING: 6 (Earl Warren, Hugo L. Black, William O. Douglas, Tom C. Clark, John Marshall Harlan (II), William J. Brennan Jr.)
    DISSENTING: 1 (Potter Stewart)
OPINION OF THE COURT: Black
CONCURRING OPINION: Douglas
DISSENTING OPINION: Stewart
DID NOT PARTICIPATE: Felix Frankfurter, Byron R. White

In the mid-twentieth century, about half of America's 35,000 public school districts permitted religious exercises of one kind or another, including reading from the King James Bible, baccalaureate services, and spoken prayer. Such devotions had aroused little controversy until 1958 when the Herricks public school district in New Hyde Park, Long Island, instituted a prayer prepared by the New York State Board of Regents. The twenty-two-word prayer, whose purpose was to fight communism abroad and juvenile delinquency at home, was: "Almighty God, we acknowledge our dependence upon Thee, and we beg Thy blessings upon us, our parents, our teachers and our Country." Participation was voluntary: students could remain silent or leave the classroom during the prayer, but this informal policy hardly made the prayer voluntary in the minds of Steven Engel, Monroe Lerner, Daniel Lichtenstein, Lenore Lyons, and Lawrence Roth, whose children attended public schools in the district. With the legal assistance of the New York Civil Liberties Union, these parents filed suit against the school board president, William Vitale Jr., to stop the prayer as a violation of the First Amendment, which forbids "an establishment of religion."

On June 25, 1962, in *Engel v. Vitale,* the U.S. Supreme Court dropped a bombshell when it invalidated the regents' prayer. Justice Black, a Franklin Roosevelt appointee, held that the prayer was clearly unconstitutional because a government body had placed its official "stamp of approval" on what was obviously a "religious activity." A state-mandated prayer, no matter how brief, "non-denominational," or voluntary, was contrary to the spirit and command of the First Amendment. An abridgment of the establishment clause, Black wrote, "does not depend upon any showing of direct governmental compulsion," only "the enactment of laws which establish an official religion." Before delivering a heart-felt history lesson about church-state relations, Black declared, "It is no part of the business of government to compose official prayers for any group of the American people to recite as a part of a religious program carried on by government." Black did not cite a single substantive case to support his argument, an omission that provided valuable ammunition to *Engel*'s critics.

Black foresaw that his decision would create a strong backlash, so he preemptively denied that the Court was hostile toward religion. He asserted that it was "neither sacrilegious nor antireligious to say that . . . government . . . should stay out of the business of writing or sanctioning official prayers and leave that purely religious function to the people themselves." In footnote 21, Black permitted short references to religion contained in government mottoes or ceremonies. School children were "officially encouraged to express love for our country by reciting historical documents," such as the Declaration of Independence and the National Anthem, which refer to a supreme being.

In a concurring opinion, Justice Douglas, another Roosevelt appointee, went much further and in so doing aroused the greatest fears of *Engel's* critics. In his view, any government-financed religious activity was illegal, including military/congressional chaplains, tax exemptions for churches, and the slogan "In God We Trust" on the nation's currency. "For me," he wrote, "the principle is the same no matter how briefly the prayer is said." Any audience for prayer—whether in a school, court, or legislature—is a "captive audience." Douglas dipped into psychology to protect the nonconformist student who might be "induced to participate for fear of being called an 'oddball.' " As Douglas summarized his thought, "[T]he atheist or agnostic—the nonbeliever—is entitled to go his own way. . . . [I]f government interferes in matters spiritual, it will be a divisive force."

The sole dissenter was Justice Stewart, Dwight Eisenhower's appointee, who interpreted the regents' prayer as a compromise between those who wanted to pray and those who did not. In the absence of clear coercion, he thought that the prayer was voluntary and therefore permissible. Faulting the other justices for misapplying the First Amendment and brushing aside "the religious traditions of our people," Stewart observed that divine supplications emanated from a number of institutions, including the Supreme Court. He reminded his colleagues that the president is sworn in under an oath to God, Congress opens its sessions with prayer, and the *Star-Spangled Banner,* which mentions God in the fourth verse, was designated as the nation's anthem by Congress. None of these examples established religion, Stewart maintained. They simply recognize the "deeply entrenched and highly cherished spiritual traditions of our Nation." School prayer was yet another example, in Stewart's mind. More fundamentally, Stewart could not comprehend how "an official religion" was established "by letting those who want to say a prayer say it," particularly one that was so brief and nonsectarian in nature. To clinch his argument, Stewart noted that Jefferson's wall-of-separation metaphor is "nowhere to be found in the Constitution."

INITIAL RESPONSES

At the time, legal scholars could not agree on what *Engel* meant. Erwin Griswold, the dean of Harvard Law School, thought it was "unfortunate" that the case ever reached the Supreme Court. Once there, Griswold could not understand how the Court could have misinterpreted the First Amendment phrase, "Congress shall make no law," because Congress had made no law in this instance. Further, he found it "difficult to see how what was done in New York, with respect to the school prayer there, can appropriately be regarded as an establishment of religion." On the contrary, he portrayed the regents' prayer as the simple "free exercise of religion." Paul Freund, a Harvard law professor who had taught one of Engel's attorneys, saw the developing controversy as yet another episode in which the Court was to serve as a kind of lightning rod for public discontent over a volatile issue. In this case, more than in others, "the lightning rod is blamed for the lightning." John Satterfield, the president of the American Bar Association, disagreed with *Engel* and would have dissented from the majority opinion had he been a member of the Court. Satterfield pulled a coin from his pocket and pointed to the inscription, "In God We Trust." He stated flatly that "If the use of that prayer is unconstitutional, then the words on this coin are also unconstitutional."

When the decision was announced, the *Engel* petitioners expressed considerable relief. Frances Roth, Lawrence's wife, confessed to a reporter, "We're so excited, we can't think straight." In the midst of the excitement, she sounded an appropriate note of caution: "We think there'll still be much misunderstanding." Almost immediately, the petitioners were ostracized and subjected to a torrent of abuse. Threatening phone calls arrived around the clock, with some anonymous callers vowing to kidnap the petitioners' children and blow up their cars. Hate letters accused them of destroying America. Clergymen branded the Roths as devils, and thugs from the American Nazi party arrived on their doorstep with signs reading, "GODLESS ATHEIST." The Roths discovered a bomb in their basement and gasoline-soaked rags lit in the shape of a cross on their lawn. Schoolyard fights broke out involving the petitioners' children, who were derided as "Jew bastards."[1] Given the high price of defending religious liberty, it is hardly surprising that none of the petitioners has written a memoir of the case.

Constitutional historians maintain that *Engel* was a "wildly unpopular" decision, one of the most excoriated and evaded decisions in American history.[2] The sweeping language of *Engel* alarmed, then angered, a clear majority of Americans because it appeared that the Supreme Court had not only "kicked God out of the schools" but also launched a full-scale attack on the nation's religious underpinnings. The Gallup poll found that fully 79 percent of Americans approved of prayers and Bible-reading in public schools, despite the Court's ruling. In large measure, the public perceived that the Court was well on its way to disestablishing Protestantism as America's unofficial religion, thereby eliminating second-class citizenship for minority religious groups such as Christian Scientists, Jehovah's Witnesses, Jews, and Mormons. Sociologist Will Herberg concluded that the vast majority of Americans "resented [*Engel*] as a violation of the American way of life" and predicted that they would nullify it to prevent a "completely secular culture."[3] One striking statement of the intense feelings over *Engel* came from Georgia's Methodist bishop, John Owen Smith, who compared the ruling to "taking a star or stripe off the flag."[4]

The Supreme Court itself contributed to public unrest over *Engel*. Leonard Levy, a leading First Amendment scholar, wrote at the time, "The Court has reaped the scorn of a confused and aroused public because it has been inconsistent; moreover, its past compromises failed to prepare the public for a principled decision."[5] Because the public had "little patience with legal distinctions," it simply could not understand how the Court could uphold subsidized bus rides for parochial school children and strike down prayers in public schools. And the Court repeatedly stirred the constitutional pot. Major decisions concerning obscenity, communism, and reapportionment preceded *Engel,* and others concerning Bible-reading (*Abington v. Schempp,* 1963) and the rights of the accused would soon follow. A cry arose from the right wing that Chief Justice Warren must be impeached. Candy manufacturer Robert Welch and his anti-Communist John Birch Society paid for hundreds of billboards across the country that demanded Warren's job. Protesters from an obscure organization known as the Committee to Restore God and Prayer in Our Schools picketed the White House, waving signs that read, "The Flag Is Next" and "Remove Warren, Restore God." The Liberty Lobby spread vicious rumors that Warren had murdered his father and covered it up. Court-bashing became a national pastime.

The conservative press fanned the flames of anger over *Engel,* especially by interviewing politicians facing an indignant electorate. Much of the heavily negative media response stemmed from incomplete or inaccurate reporting, producing confusion over the actual ruling. Of the forty-two largest metropolitan newspapers that commented on *Engel,* a majority opposed the decision as a sign of moral decay. The *Wall Street Journal* castigated the "violent wrecking of the Constitution's language," which it called "symptomatic of a broader move in the nation toward the rigid exclusion of all traces of religion in the public schools." A particularly strong rebuke came from the *Los Angeles Times,* which accused the Court of having fallen under the sway of "a small group of guardhouse sophists."[6] The result, the *Times* argued, was to make a "burlesque show of the world's first complete declaration of religion toleration." Likewise, the *New York Mirror* lambasted the Court and the opinion's author: "It is difficult to understand how any six men in the United States could agree on this decision, written by Justice Hugo Black, who started his political career in the Ku Klux Klan but who, on the bench, became the leader of the radical left. Here is a decision without a quoted precedent, with no roots in law, with no historic basis."[7] The *New York Daily News* called for open defiance: "If this device is eventually prohibited by an atheistic, agnostic or what-have-you Supreme Court majority, other dodges and end-runs can be figured out by active minds in religious circles. Sooner or later, such tactics should make a complete monkey and dead-letter out of Monday's Warren Court ruling."[8] Stinging editorials against *Engel* also appeared in the *Baltimore Sun, Birmingham News, Boston Globe, Chicago Tribune, Kansas City Star, New York News, San Francisco News-Call Bulletin,* and *Washington Star.* A cartoon in the Hearst newspaper chain depicted a judge chiseling off the word "God" from "In God We Trust." In counterpoint, the moderate *New York Herald Tribune* was amazed at "the sight of so many otherwise responsible newspapers getting completely swept off their feet by the tide of emotionalism."[9]

Angry editorials were soon followed by angry letters to the editor, which ran more than three to one against the ruling. Richard DiLoreto of Jamaica, Long Island, expressed the disgust of most letter-writers:

"WHAT DO THEY EXPECT US TO DO — LISTEN TO THE KIDS PRAY AT HOME?"

—from *Straight Herblock* (Simon & Schuster, 1964), courtesy of the Prints & Photographs Division, Library of Congress, LC-DIG-ppmsca-03478

Almighty God has been given his walking papers. He is persona non grata in America's public schools. He has become controversial. From this day forward, whomsoever shall dare utter His name in prayer in our public school shall incur the wrath of our highest tribunal and shall be summarily punished. His divine law has been superseded by the mortal law of the Supreme Court of the United States of America. The Supreme Judge has Himself been judged and found unconstitutional by six of His peers. Our Declaration of Independence says that man has been endowed by his Creator with certain unalienable rights. Is this now to be changed to read that man has been endowed by the Supreme Court with certain unalienable rights? Are we moving forward into a new era of enlight[en]ment which supplants infinite God with finite man?[10]

Hoping to ride out the storm, Jews sent very few letters to the press.

Other periodicals were more restrained in their reactions. *Newsday* wrote, "The ruling was a bad one, but the headlong rush to amend the Constitution is equally bad. . . . We must accept the decision while seeking other means to preserve the principle of a Supreme Being for our children." "Monday's decision," the *Atlanta Constitution*'s editorial said, "has not dealt a blow to religion. . . . On the contrary, it has fortified constitutional guarantees that our Government must leave each individual free to worship in his own way." David Lawrence, the editor of the *U.S. News & World Report*, determined that:

The Supreme Court . . . has barred "official" prayers in public schools. But it hasn't barred prayer. It hasn't barred the teaching of morality or the philosophy of human brotherhood, or the spread of knowledge concerning Christianity or Buddhism or any of the other religions of the world. To permit in public schools the study of codes of human behavior is not to create "an establishment of religion."[11]

Supportive editorials also appeared in the *Chicago Sun-Times, Cleveland Plain Dealer, Detroit News, Hartford Courant, Louisville Courier-Journal, Milwaukee Journal, New York Post, Pittsburgh Post-Gazette, New York Times, New York Herald Tribune, Rochester Democrat and Chronicle, St. Louis Post-Dispatch,* and *Washington Post.*

POLITICAL RESPONSES

Most politicians heaped scorn on *Engel.* Two former Republican presidents were stunned by the decision. Herbert Hoover, then in his late eighties, described the ruling as "a disintegration of one of the most sacred of American heritages" and urged Congress to approve a constitutional amendment guaranteeing "the right to religious devotion in all governmental agencies."[12] Dwight Eisenhower was also appalled by the ruling:

> I always thought that this nation was essentially a religious one. I realize, of course, that the Declaration of Independence antedates the Constitution, but the fact remains that this document was our certificate of national birth. It specifically asserts that we as individuals possess certain rights as an endorsement from our common creator—a religious concept.[13]

The governors, meeting at their annual conference, voted nearly unanimously to recommend a constitutional amendment that "will make clear and beyond challenge the acknowledgment of our nation and people of their faith in God and permit the free and voluntary participation in prayer in our public schools."[14] Although Gov. Nelson Rockefeller, R-N.Y., abstained from this resolution, he nevertheless hoped that "adjustments" could be made so that the regents' prayer could continue. Even a modified regents' prayer could help inculcate belief "in the brotherhood of man and the fatherhood of God" in young people.[15]

In Congress, everyone on record condemned the decision. The early leader of this contingent was Frank Becker, R-N.Y., a Roman Catholic who represented the Herricks school district. His oft-quoted remark that the *Engel* decision was "the most tragic in the history of the United States" typified the despair, if not outright hostility, expressed by most senators and representatives.[16] Sen. Prescott Bush, R-Conn., President George W. Bush's grandfather, characterized the decision as "unfortunate, divisive, and quite unnecessary."[17] Becker and Bush were joined by a phalanx of Southern Democrats, who fumed that *Engel* was a misbegotten and unacceptable victory for atheism. They firmly believed that history was on their side, arguing that the Fourteenth Amendment had not been adopted legally, which prevented the Court from applying the First Amendment and its establishment clause to the states. By charging ahead anyway, the Court had unconstitutionally usurped state power in the domain of religion. *Engel* provided conservatives with a heaven-sent opportunity to attack the Warren Court. The anti-Warren billboards that had sprouted after *Brown v. Board of Education* (1954) (see page 197) were modified to add the phrases "Save Prayer" and "Save America." One Florida representative even proposed buying a Bible "for the personal use" of each justice. With the fall elections approaching, most politicians had to bow to public demands to denounce *Engel.*

Among the congressional reactions were:

> *Sen. James Eastland, D-Miss.:* "In the minds of little children not versed in the intricacies of law, [*Engel*] can well create the fixed impression that the act of praying to God is in itself unconstitutional wherever the prayer might be uttered."

> *Sen. Sam Ervin Jr., D-N.C.:* "I should like to ask whether we would be far wrong in saying that in this decision the Supreme Court has held that God is unconstitutional and for that reason the public school must be segregated against Him?"

Sen. A. Willis Robertson, D-Va.: "The Supreme Court has decided several cases in the past few years in favor of atheists and agnostics; however, this is the most extreme ruling it has made. . . . We will not stand for this any longer."

Sen. Herman Talmadge, D-Ga.: "For some years now the members of the Supreme Court have persisted in reading alien meanings into the Constitution. . . . [T]hey have sought, in effect, to change our form of government. But never in the wildest of their excesses . . . have they gone as far as they did on yesterday. . . . It was an outrageous edict which has numbed the conscience and shocked the highest sensibilities of the Nation."

Rep. George Andrews, D-Ala.: "They put the Negroes in the schools and now they've driven God out."

Rep. Mendel Rivers, D-S.C.: "What is wrong with this prayer? Only a court composed of agnostics could find its defects. . . . I know of nothing in my lifetime that could give more aid and comfort to Moscow than this bold, malicious, atheistic and sacrilegious twist of this unpredictable group of uncontrolled despots." [18]

Newsweek columnist Kenneth Crawford accused Southern Democrats of being "not a little demagogic" in reviling the Court. He accused Senator Robertson of "acting like Savonarola in modern dress, surrounded by colleagues feeding his righteous wrath." The Bible-belt Democrats, Crawford wrote, had damned the Court for handing down "an atheistic anti-prayer, anti-church decision that will have the effect of turning American youth away from the nation's religious heritage." Such shrill accusations were dishonest representations of Black's opinion, which narrowly confined itself to public school prayers written and sponsored by government officials. For Crawford, most of the fault for the brouhaha over *Engel* fell at the feet of lawyers-turned-politicians who knew better. [19]

The Supreme Court received a record 5,000 letters—mostly negative—on *Engel* in the first month. More than 13,500 copies of the decision were sold by early 1964, the greatest demand for any opinion in memory. The public outcry was so great that some of the justices felt obliged to respond to their critics—a highly unusual occurrence. Warren anticipated the outcry and ignored it, but Black answered each critical letter he received. Clark felt enough heat to defend the ruling in a San Francisco speech to the American Bar Association, an almost unprecedented step. Criticizing press coverage as misinformed, he noted that the ruling had not outlawed religious observances in the public schools. Rather, the Court had upheld the Constitution, which, he said, provides "that both state and federal governments shall take no part respecting the establishment of religion or prohibiting the free exercise thereof. 'No' means 'No.' That was all the Court decided." [20] Some northern Democrats tried to calm the furor. Emanuel Celler, D-N.Y., the powerful House Judiciary Committee chairman, did not see that the Court had "any other choice" but to invalidate the prayer because "all parties agreed that the prayer was religious in nature. This being so, it ran contrary to the First Amendment—which is well grounded in history and has served to save the United States from religious strife." [21] Addressing the National Catholic Laymen's Retreat Conference in Portland, Oregon, Sen. Eugene McCarthy, D-Minn., criticized some of his colleagues who were "just 'demagoging' " because the Court had done "the only thing [it] could do." [22] Former president Harry Truman said simply, "the Supreme Court, of course, is the interpreter of the Constitution," implying that he backed the ruling. [23] In a press conference two days after the ruling, John F. Kennedy, the first Roman Catholic president, cautiously attempted to puncture the ballooning hostility to *Engel* by urging Americans to set aside their personal feelings about the explosive decision:

> The Supreme Court has made its judgment, and a good many people obviously will disagree with it. Others will agree with it. But I think that it is important for us if we are

going to maintain our constitutional principle that we support the Supreme Court decisions even when we may not agree with them. In addition, we have in this case a very easy remedy and that is to pray ourselves. And I would think that it would be a welcome reminder to every American family that we can pray a good deal more at home, we can attend our churches with a good deal more fidelity, and we can make the true meaning of prayer much more important in the lives of all of our children.[24]

Having been singed by bigotry in his quest for the presidency, Kennedy was not about to break his promise of religious neutrality and reawaken society's still-powerful undercurrent of anti-Catholicism.

RELIGIOUS LEADERS' RESPONSES

The faith community was sharply divided by the decision. The leading voices against *Engel* came from the Roman Catholic church, even though Justice Brennan, the Court's only Catholic, concurred in the decision. By now, the church preferred devotions in public schools, even devotions that were not strictly Catholic, to counter what it saw as disturbing trends toward secularism, materialism, and atheism. On this point, the American cardinals were of a single mind. Francis Spellman of New York professed to being "shocked and frightened" by the decision, which, he insisted, "strikes at the very heart of the Godly tradition in which America's children have for so long been raised."[25] Part of his concern, no doubt, was the implication that state aid for parochial schools was illegal. Richard Cushing of Boston warned that the Soviets would use *Engel* to fuel anti-American propaganda. "It is ridiculous," he commented, "to have a motto like 'In God We Trust' on our coins and to begin legislative sessions with a chaplain's prayer, and at the same time prevent children from opening classes with public school prayer."[26] In Los Angeles, James McIntyre called the decision "positively shocking and scandalizing to one of American blood and principles."[27] The bishop of the Dallas–Fort Worth diocese forecast that "American public schools will have to start bootlegging religion into the classrooms."[28]

Protestants were split on school prayer. Some prominent ministers and theologians, including Norman Vincent Peale and Reinhold Niebuhr, condemned *Engel,* but the National Council of Churches of Christ, which represented tens of millions of Protestants, supported it. Dean Kelley, a council executive, predicted, "Many Christians will welcome this decision" because it "protects the religious rights of minorities and guards against the development of 'public school religion,' which is neither Christianity nor Judaism, but something less than either [of these great faiths]."[29] The council nevertheless insisted that a way had to be found in the public schools to recognize the importance of religion in American life. The Lutheran Church of America thought the decision was hardly worth noticing because the regents' prayer was perfunctory. Franklin Clark Fry, president of the 3.2 million-member denomination, observed, "When the positive content of faith has been bleached out of prayer, I am not too concerned about retaining what is left."[30] Three influential religious magazines—the liberal *Christian Century,* the conservative *Christianity Today,* and *Presbyterian Life*—all backed the Court's ruling. Baptists had traditionally opposed any intermingling between religion and the government, and the Joint Baptist Committee on Public Affairs—a prominent lobbying organization for 17 million members—endorsed *Engel.* Its executive director, C. Emanuel Carlson, did not find the decision disturbing because he saw no real religious value for children in reciting such prayers. Herschel Hobbs, president of the Southern Baptist Convention, sent a warning to the Senate that any constitutional amendment for school prayer would invite "disaster."[31]

At the same time, *Engel* helped create a new faction that viewed the separation of church and state as a legal fiction aimed at openly confessing Christians. Most white Protestants in the South denounced the decision. The 1.5 million-member National Association of Evangelicals termed the ruling "regrettable."[32] Evangelist Billy Graham, the nation's most celebrated Southern Baptist minister, scorned *Engel* as "another step toward the secularization of the United States." He cautioned Americans:

Followed to its logical conclusion, we will have to take the chaplains out of the armed forces, prayers cannot be said in Congress, and the President cannot put his hand on the Bible when he takes the oath of office. The framers of our Constitution meant we were to have freedom of religion, not freedom from religion. . . . God pity our country when we can no longer appeal to God for help.[33]

Louie Newton, former president of the Southern Baptist Convention, remarked: "We just weren't ready for six men to tell us that our fathers and mothers were all wrong about this business of acknowledging God as the supreme ruler of the universe."[34] James Pike, the maverick Episcopal bishop of San Francisco, joined the chorus of critics. The Court, he claimed, had "deconsecrated the nation." The Rt. Rev. Percy Goddard, suffragen bishop of the Episcopal Diocese of Texas, compared the decision to the public prayer room in the United Nations: "They removed the cross so they wouldn't offend the Jews. They removed the Star of David so they wouldn't offend the Mohammedans. They wound up with a tree stump—a stump of nothing."[35]

SUPPORT FOR *ENGEL*

Many in the African American community supported the decision. Southern Baptist minister Martin Luther King Jr., then mired in a civil rights campaign in Albany, Georgia, praised *Engel* as "sound and good, reaffirming something that is basic in our Constitution."[36] Three leading black papers, including the *Amsterdam News, Chicago Defender,* and *Pittsburgh Courier,* also endorsed the decision. The NAACP, which had never previously commented on a church-state matter, passed a unanimous resolution at its national convention favoring the *Engel* decision.

The staunchest defenders of *Engel* included most humanists, Jews, and Unitarians. They generally believed that religion in public schools unconstitutionally coerced all schoolchildren and therefore represented an illegal establishment of religion. Gerald Wendt, editor of *The Humanist,* described the decision as "a godsend to Humanists—' a desirable thing which comes unexpectedly as if sent by God.' "[37] Except for some Orthodox Jews who feared that the Court would next outlaw federal aid to Hebrew schools, Jewish sentiment was overwhelmingly behind the decision. The American Jewish Committee, the American Jewish Congress, the Anti-Defamation League of B'nai B'rith, the Commission of Social Action of Reform Judaism, and the Synagogue Council of America hailed the decision as "a splendid reaffirmation of a basic American principle [that] adds another safeguard for freedom of religion in the United States."[38] Leo Pfeffer, American Jewish Congress's general counsel and a preeminent church-state scholar, praised *Engel* as in line with the American belief "that religion is a private matter." He asked pointedly, "Is God only in the public schools? Why can't children be taught to pray in the home? There are certain responsibilities of parenthood which should not be forwarded to the public schools." Pfeffer reminded audiences that "the Catholics and not the Jews" pushed for the secularization of the public schools beginning with the lawsuits of the late nineteenth century. The *American Jewish World* credited the First Amendment and decisions such as *Engel* for "the unfettered development of religion, on the one hand, and the enrichment of democracy, on the other."

While praising the *Engel* decision, Jews worried that it had revived anti-Semitism and was therefore a Pyrrhic victory. The Jesuit weekly *America*—ordinarily admired for its liberal and fair-minded views—published a tactless editorial, "To Our Jewish Friends," which mirrored Roman Catholic wrath everywhere. The editor called the decision "asinine," "unrealistic," "doctrinaire," and "stupid," which "spits in the face of our history, our tradition and our heritage as a religious people." He did not blame all Jews for ousting organized school prayer, just a "small but overly vocal segment" within Jewry. He also accused Jews of opposing parochial school funding and Sunday-closing laws. The "time has come," he said, "for these fellow citizens of ours to decide among themselves precisely what they conceive to be the final objective of the Jewish community in the United States—in a word, [they must decide] what bargain they are willing to strike as one of the minorities in a pluralistic society." The *America* editor did not mention that President Kennedy defended the Court and its decisions.[39]

Jews were appalled by the article. American Jewish Congress president Joachim Prinz said it was a sorry day for religious liberty in the United States when efforts to protect the guarantees of the First Amendment "should evoke thinly veiled threats of anti-Semitism from so respectable a journal of opinion as *America*." Leo Pfeffer charged that the magazine, "in the guise of predicting anti-Semitism, they are in fact encouraging it." Albert Vorspan and Rabbi Sidney Regner, speaking for the Union of American Hebrew Congregations, wondered aloud what Catholic reaction would be if a Jewish magazine published a similarly caustic editorial entitled, "To Our Catholic Friends," warning Catholics to stop campaigning for government money to parochial schools lest a wave of anti-Catholic bigotry arise. The Synagogue Council of America and the National Community Relations Advisory Council scored *America*'s editorial as "repugnant" for its suggestion that "any group must barter its right to free speech in exchange for its security."

To dampen the blazing controversy, *Commonweal,* a liberal lay Catholic publication, criticized its sister journal. *Commonweal* thought *America* had chosen a "very odd" method of combating any signs of rising anti-Semitism. It advised its readership:

> If there is . . . any real danger of anti-Semitism among Catholics, then it is Catholics who ought to be warned. . . . It does little good—as Catholics ought to know—to be told, much less warned, by others whether to press one's claims or not. . . . After centuries of Christian persecution of the Jews, it would be a monumental irony to accuse Jews of fostering anti-Semitism. If the result of the prayer decision is to break down community relations, the fault of this breakdown will lie with those Americans who single out particular groups to blame for the decision. [40]

DEFIANCE TO *ENGEL*

The reaction to *Engel* among educators was split. New York State officials accepted the ruling with "regret," but leaders in almost half of the other states breathed defiance to it. In places where community sentiment for religion in the classroom was strong, local school boards searched for ways to circumvent the Court's decision. In Alabama, for example, the fire-eating superintendent of education insisted that public schools should retain religious practices "regardless of what the Supreme Court says." The Oklahoma City school superintendent announced that Bible-reading would continue. State officials in Mississippi, North Carolina, and South Carolina passed off the responsibility for following *Engel* to the teachers, which meant that prayers would remain in most classrooms. Even beyond Dixie, resistance was evident. On Long Island, school officials replaced the regents' prayer with silent meditation or the fourth stanza of the national anthem, which declares, "And this be our motto: 'In God is our trust.'" In New Jersey, the state supreme court upheld the reading of five Old Testament verses each day and permitted the recital of the Lord's Prayer. In Pennsylvania, one school official declared: "What the hell! It's illegal, but they can't put us in jail. All they can do is get an injunction."[41]

In the decades since *Engel* was decided, Christian fundamentalists and evangelicals pressured Congress and other political bodies to protect their religious values and practices. They saw American society disintegrating rapidly as evidenced by poor test scores, juvenile delinquency, illicit drug use, sexual promiscuity, teenage pregnancy, and family dissolutions. These conservatives expected that "corporate verbal prayer" was the one sure way to stem the hemorrhaging of moral virtue. Virginia Baptist preacher Jerry Falwell explained that "the decay in our public school system suffered an enormous acceleration when prayer and Bible reading were taken out of the classroom. . . . Our public school system is now permeated with humanism. The human mind has been deceived, and the end result is that our schools are in serious trouble."[42] To restore school prayer, conservatives formed sophisticated lobbying organizations, including Falwell's Moral Majority, the Christian Coalition, and American Center for Law and Justice (founded by televangelist Pat Robertson, son of Senator Robertson), Religious Roundtable, Christian Voice, Project Prayer, the Rutherford Foundation, and First Priority of America, among others. These groups proposed several ways to restore religion in the public schools, including provision for moments of silence, posting the Ten Commandments, allowing students to pray at the flagpole before school begins and to meet in Bible meetings after school ends, inviting clergy to give graduation prayers, and arranging for students to give devotions on public address systems before Friday night football games. On Capitol Hill, politicians continued introducing constitutional amendments to overturn *Engel* and sought to strip the Supreme Court of jurisdiction over school prayer cases. Some "Christian amendments" sought to recognize the "Lordship of Jesus Christ" over the United States.

Most of these avenues have failed, and the appetite to keep fighting for school prayer has diminished noticeably in recent years. This waning enthusiasm owes much to the repeated failure of Congress to impeach a Supreme Court justice or approve a school prayer amendment and the Supreme Court's repeated unwillingness to sanction devotions in public schools. Moreover, once the Court had sanctioned abortion a decade after *Engel,* conservative Christians concentrated their energies on what they saw as an abomination and a national sin. "Secular schools" paled in comparison to "the murder of the unborn."

The defense of religious liberty is eminently sensible. Because the United States has the greatest religious diversity on earth, a one-size-fits-all generic prayer, like New York's regents' prayer, delivered by rote each morning, is as impractical as it is meaningless. Justice Black said as much in an extemporaneous remark while reading the *Engel* decision: "The prayer of each man from his soul must be his and his alone. That is the genius of the First Amendment."

NOTES

1. Fred Friendly and Martha Elliott, *The Constitution, That Delicate Balance: Landmark Cases That Shaped the Constitution* (New York: Random House, 1984), 119, 126.
2. Gregg Ivers, *To Build a Wall: American Jews and the Separation of Church and State* (Charlottesville: University Press of Virginia, 1995), 137.
3. Helen Dewar, "Theologian Sees Public Revolt over School Prayer Ban," *Washington Post,* July 4, 1962, A20.
4. "The Court Decision—and the School Prayer Furor," *Newsweek,* July 9, 1962, 43.
5. William Hachten, "Journalism and the School Prayer Decision," *Columbia Journalism Review* (Fall 1962): 7.
6. Ibid.
7. Ibid., 9.
8. Ibid.
9. Philip Kurland, "The Regents' Prayer Case: Full of Sound and Fury, Signifying . . ." *Supreme Court Review* (1962): 2.
10. *Long Island Press,* June 28, 1962, 12.
11. David Lawrence, "Is Prayer in Schools Really Barred?" *U.S. News & World Report,* July 9, 1962, 100.
12. Alexander Burnham, "Court's Decision Stirs Conflicts," *New York Times,* June 27, 1962, 20.
13. Ibid.
14. "Governors Seek Prayer Measure," *New York Times,* July 4, 1962, 8.
15. Fred Hechinger, "Challenges Are Predicted—30% of All Schools Use Some Rite," *New York Times,* June 26, 1962, 17.
16. *Congressional Record,* 87th Cong., 2d sess., June 26, 1962, 11719.
17. Robert Alley, *School Prayer: The Court, the Congress, and the First Amendment* (Buffalo: Prometheus Books, 1994), 109.
18. *Congressional Record,* 87th Cong., 2d sess., June 26, 29, 1962, 11675, 11708–9, 11719, 11732, 12235; *Congressional Quarterly Almanac 1962* (Washington, D.C.: Congressional Quarterly, 1963), 240.
19. Kenneth Crawford, "The Prayer Debate," *Newsweek,* July 16, 1962, 28.
20. Religious News Service, *Religious Herald,* August 23, 1962, 3.
21. Anthony Lewis, "Both Houses Get Bills to Lift Ban on School Prayer," *New York Times,* June 27, 1962.
22. Religious News Service, *Religious Herald,* August 16, 1962, 3.
23. Edward Folliard, "Pray More at Home and Church," *Washington Post,* June 28, 1962, A1.

24. *Public Papers of the Presidents of the United States: John F. Kennedy 1962* (Washington, D.C.: Government Printing Office), 259–260.

25. Alexander Burnham, "Edict Is Called a Setback by Christian Clerics—Rabbis Praise It," *New York Times,* June 26, 1962, 17.

26. Alexander Burnham, "Court's Decision Stirs Conflicts," *New York Times,* June 27, 1962, 20.

27. Fred Hechinger, "Many States Use Prayer in School," *New York Times,* June 26, 1962, 17.

28. "The Court Decision—and the School Prayer Furor."

29. Burnham, "Edict Is Called a Setback."

30. "The Court Decision—and the School Prayer Furor."

31. *New York Times,* July 1, 1962.

32. Burnham, "Edict Is Called a Setback."

33. Ibid.

34. "The Court Decision—and the School Prayer Furor."

35. Ibid.

36. Leo Pfeffer, *Church, State, and Freedom* (Boston: Beacon Press, 1967), 469.

37. Paul Blanshard, *Religion and the Schools: The Great Controversy* (Boston: Beacon Press, 1963).

38. Burnham, "Edict Is Called a Setback."

39. "To Our Jewish Friends," *America,* September 1, 1962, 665–666.

40. "On Warning Jews," *Commonweal,* September 7, 1962, 483–484.

41. Ben Franklin, "Pennsylvanians Lead School Prayer Revolt," *New York Times,* March 26, 1969, 20.

42. Jerry Falwell, *Listen, America!* (New York: Bantam Books, 1980), 178.

Reynolds v. Sims

Peter G. Renstrom

Reynolds v. Sims
377 U.S. 533 (1964)

DECIDED: June 15, 1964
VOTE

CONCURRING: 8 (Earl Warren, Hugo L Black, William O. Douglas, Tom C. Clark, William J. Brennan Jr., Potter Stewart, Byron R. White, Arthur J. Goldberg)
DISSENTING: 1 (John Marshall Harlan (II))
OPINION OF THE COURT: Warren
CONCURRING OPINION: Clark
CONCURRING OPINION: Stewart
DISSENTING OPINION: Harlan

The apportionment controversy began in Colonial America when political representation was based on locality, regardless of the size and importance of towns. After the Revolutionary War, representation began shifting to a population basis except for the Great Compromise at the Constitutional Convention, which gave each state equal representation in the U.S. Senate. State legislatures based on population began appearing in the nineteenth century as suffrage expanded. Many sections of the country, however, continued giving representation to political units such as counties. This deviation was a deliberate response to factors such as the closing of the Western frontier, rapidly increasing urban populations, and distrust of big city political bosses. Malapportionment of state legislatures was an attempt to preserve rural control of the political system, and by the 1960s extensive disparities could be found not only in virtually every state legislature but also the U.S. House of Representatives.

The Warren Court's involvement in the reapportionment question began with *Baker v. Carr* (1962). Sixteen years earlier, the Court had held in *Colegrove v. Green* (1946) that legislative malapportionment cases presented "peculiarly political" questions that ought to be resolved by the political branches rather than the judiciary. In *Baker* the Court abandoned this ruling and said that federal courts could indeed consider apportionment questions. A year later, in *Gray v. Sanders* (1963), the Court introduced the "one person, one vote" standard, which calls for legislatures to draw political districts to encompass equal numbers of voters. The Court then used *Gray* to strike down Georgia's congressional districting in *Wesberry v. Sanders* (1964). The malapportionment problem in *Wesberry* was similar to that of many states: legislative district boundaries had not changed for decades, and the largest districts had at least twice as many people than the smallest. Often the ratio of largest to smallest districts was thirty, forty, or more to one. Rural areas were advantaged by malapportionment, and rural-dominated state legislatures and congressional districts led the resistance to redistrict.

Wesberry did not involve the state's congressional districts—federal courts clearly could require state legislators to redraw congressional district boundaries. Ordering reapportionment of state legislative districts was a different matter. States regarded such federal judicial intervention as a frontal assault on their sovereignty. Significant alteration of state legislative districts would have at least two other consequences—legislative power would shift from rural to urban areas, and many rural incumbent legislators would lose their seats.

Four months after *Wesberry*, the Court announced its decision in *Reynolds v. Sims*. Alabama's 1901 constitution created a bicameral state legislature of 106 House members and 35 senators, based on equal population. Although redistricting was to follow each national census, the Alabama districts had not been redrawn since 1901 despite substantial population shifts. The state constitution had eventually been amended to represent each county in the legislature regardless of population. The most populous House district was sixteen times larger than the least populous, and the most populous Senate district was forty-one times greater than the smallest. Rural areas were disproportionately represented. Urban voters filed suit to have the Alabama districts declared unconstitutional on equal protection grounds.

Anticipating the litigation, the Alabama legislature devised two reapportionment plans in 1962. A three-judge U.S. district court declared the existing system unconstitutional and rejected the proposed alternatives. The court imposed a temporary, population-based plan, and Alabama appealed to the U.S. Supreme Court. In oral argument, U.S. Solicitor General Archibald Cox advanced the political equality rationale for redistricting—that if "it violates our fundamental precepts to give one class of voters more weight in an election for governor, it does the same in an election for representatives." Those defending the existing apportionment system relied on two arguments. First, they cited the so-called "federal analogy" to defend the apportionment of one house on the basis of area rather than population. They argued that the Framers of the Constitution favored the apportionment of state legislatures along federal lines, believing that houses not based on population in state legislatures would protect minorities and provide balanced representation. Second, they contended that it was both rational and justifiable to base apportionment systems on many factors, including but not requiring population. Representation of political subdivisions, a desire to reduce the size of constituencies, and protection of the interests of less-populous areas were among factors that might reasonably justify deviation from exact adherence to an equal population standard.

The Warren Court decided fifteen cases in 1964 dealing with state legislative reapportionment issues. Six of these, including *Reynolds,* were decided on June 15, 1964, with decisions in the other nine cases announced the following week. In all fifteen cases the Court struck down existing state districts and the proposed new districts with less than equal populations. *Reynolds,* decided over the single dissent of Justice Harlan, was the case chosen to articulate the Court's basic position on the state redistricting issue. Chief Justice Warren wrote the Court's opinion in *Reynolds* and the other cases decided on June 15.

After the decisions in *Baker, Wesberry* and *Gray,* the rulings in *Reynolds* and the other 1964 apportionment cases were expected, but Warren's uncompromising opinion identifying population as the only basis for apportionment surprised many on both sides of the controversy. The Court regarded the inequality of representation as a suffrage issue, citing various franchise cases that had invalidated the "dilution" or "debasement" of a citizen's fundamental right to vote. The *Gray* and *Wesberry* decisions had laid down guidelines, but *Baker* had offered no standards for the lower courts to determine whether a state legislature was unconstitutionally apportioned. *Reynolds* provided some answers. Most important was that the federal analogy cannot be used to sustain state apportionment plans on any basis other than population—in other words, seats in both houses of bicameral legislatures must be apportioned on a population basis. Furthermore, plans for non-population-based apportionment approved through statewide referendum or initiative process were invalid.

Chief Justice Warren indicated that the Court's primary task in post-*Baker* redistricting cases was to determine whether there is any justification for departing from an equal population basis for apportioning seats in state legislatures. The answer was an unequivocal no. Legislators, he suggested, "represent people, not trees or acres. Legislators are elected by voters, not farms or cities or economic interests." As long as ours is a "representative form of government," and legislatures are the "instruments of government elected directly by and directly representative of the people, the right to elect legislators in a free and unimpaired fashion is a bedrock of our political system." If a state allows that the votes of citizens in one part of the state should be given "two times, or five times, or ten times the weight of votes of citizens in another part of the state, it could hardly be contended that the right to vote of those residing in the disfavored area had not been effectively diluted." Weighting votes differently "merely because of where [voters] happen to reside hardly seems justifiable."

The concept of equal protection has been traditionally viewed, Warren continued, as "requiring the uniform treatment of persons standing in the same relation to the governmental action questioned or challenged." Any "suggested criteria for the differentiation of citizens are insufficient to justify any discrimination, as to the weight of their votes, unless relevant to the permissible purposes of legislative apportionment." Representation schemes "once fair and equitable become archaic and outdated." The basic principle of representative government, however, "must remain, unchanged—the weight of a citizen's vote cannot be made to depend on where he lives. Population is, of necessity, the starting point for consideration and the controlling criterion for judgment in legislative apportionment controversies."

Finally, the Court concluded that the federal analogy argument was "inapposite and irrelevant to state legislative districting schemes." The federal system of representation in the two houses of Congress is one "conceived out of compromise and concession indispensable to the establishment of our federal republic." We do not believe, Warren continued, "that the concept of bicameralism is rendered anachronistic and meaningless when the predominant basis of representation in the two state legislative bodies is required to be the same—population." Even if the controlling criterion for apportioning representation is required to be the same in both houses "does not mean that there will be no differences in the composition and complexion of the two bodies." Slight deviation from the population standard is permissible so long as divergence is grounded on "legitimate considerations incident to the effectuation of a rational state policy." History, economic, or other sorts of group interests, however, are "impermissible factors in attempting to justify disparities from population-based representation."

The *Reynolds* rationale governed the other five cases also decided on June 15, 1964. The Court struck down districting schemes from New York (*WMCA, Inc. v. Lomenzo*), Maryland (*Maryland Committee v. Tawes*), Virginia (*Davis v. Mann*), and Delaware (*Roman v. Sincock*). In each of these states, small minorities of the population could elect legislative majorities. The most extreme case involved the Delaware House, where a majority could be achieved by only 18.5 percent of the state's population.

The sixth case in the June 15 group, *Lucas v. Forty-fourth Colorado General Assembly*, presented an additional question for the Court. In 1962 the voters of Colorado had decisively rejected a system providing equal popular representation in both houses, adopting instead one that took into account other factors. This plan gave control of the state House to 45.1 percent of the population, while a Senate majority could come from only 33.2 percent of the population. Colorado contended that a majority of voters agreed to dilute their own voting power. Warren categorically dismissed the argument. "An individual's constitutionally protected right to cast an equally weighted vote cannot be denied even by a vote of [the] state's electorate." The contention that the plan was valid because it was the choice of the people, who could change it later, was also rejected. "Except as an interim remedial procedure justifying a court in staying its hand temporarily, we find no significance in the fact that a nonjudicial, political remedy may be available for the effectuation of asserted rights to equal representation in a state legislature."

At the time of the *Reynolds* decision, the Warren Court was already under fire from various quarters. Substantial resentment remained from the 1954 decision in *Brown v. Board of Education* (see page 197) and subsequent school desegregation cases. Opposition also stemmed from the Warren Court's criminal rights rulings and its decisions in the school prayer (see *Engel v. Vitale*, page 215) and Bible-reading cases. Furthermore, there was unhappiness, especially strong in rural communities, with *Gray* and *Wesberry*. Even before *Reynolds*, some members of Congress advocated reducing the Court's appellate jurisdiction or nullifying particular decisions by amending the Constitution. In late 1962 the General Assembly of the States, a group of state legislators affiliated with the Council of State Governments, proposed that state legislatures petition Congress to call a constitutional convention to consider several amendments to the federal Constitution. Among them was one that sought to create a Court of the Union composed of the chief justices of state supreme courts to review decisions of the U.S. Supreme Court that related to states rights. Another would have withdrawn state legislative apportionment issues from the appellate jurisdiction of federal courts, including the Supreme Court. The National Legislative Conference, also affiliated with the Council of State Governments and composed of state legislators, headed the campaign for these amendments, arguing they were essential to the preservation of the powers of the states.

Few Supreme Court decisions have had the political impact of *Reynolds v. Sims*. Within two years, the constituency maps of virtually all state legislatures had changed dramatically. Rural domination in a number of largely urban states disappeared. Politicians and political insiders thought *Reynolds* and the other 1964 reapportionment decisions were of "blockbuster" proportions. This view, however, was not fully shared or appreciated by the public. In late July 1964 the Gallup organization polled people on the *Reynolds* ruling. The ruling was described and respondents were told that the number of legislators from urban areas would likely increase with a commensurate loss in rural representatives. Forty-seven percent of the sample approved of the ruling, 30 percent disapproved, and 23 percent had no opinion. Party affiliation made little difference—49 percent of Democrats approved of *Reynolds*, as did 47 percent of Republicans, and 43 percent of independents. Fifty-six percent of those living in the East approved of *Reynolds*, higher than any other region, with the closest margin of approval in the South, 40 percent to 34 percent. Predictably, residents of large communities (more than 50,000) were more approving of *Reynolds* (56 percent) than residents of smaller communities; residents of communities of less than 50,000 disapproved of *Reynolds* 40 percent to 39 percent. Constant in these data was the large number of respondents—25 percent—who had no opinion. In many respects, the redistricting issue was more important to politicians and political activists than to the population at large.[1]

POLITICAL RESPONSES

The plaintiff's attorneys in the Alabama cases immediately petitioned the federal court to order immediate reapportionment of the state legislature, but the court delayed action to give the legislature additional time to act. When more than a year passed with the legislature giving no indication of compliance, the three-judge federal court prepared to order reapportionment. The U.S. Justice Department participated as *amicus curiae* and submitted, along with the other parties to the suit, proposals for a judicial remedy to Alabama's apportionment problem. Although the legislature was in session when the court order was issued, it adjourned without acting, and Democratic governor George Wallace was forced to call the legislature back into special session. In a statewide televised address to the legislators, Wallace took aim at the president, Congress, and the federal courts. The "very fabric of our American system is being torn to shreds," Wallace said. The Supreme Court, he continued, ruled that the "people do not have the power to determine how and in what manner their state governments shall be formed." Alabama was "compelled" to change its legislature "to meet the dictates" of a Supreme Court decision that was but "one example of steam roller tactics employed against the people." The Court, Wallace said, was the "most revolutionary force in the nation today," sanctioning the occupation of communities "by thousands of out-of-state riff-raff, Communists, and fellow travelers, kooks, beatniks, prostitutes and bums" and handcuffing "local law enforcement personnel who seek to prevent depredations against the peace and order." Following Wallace's address, the legislators struggled over reapportionment until September 23, 1965, when both houses finally adopted a redistricting plan.

Anthony Lewis of the *New York Times* suggested that few of the Court's decisions had "stunned this hardened capital city" as had these apportionment decisions. Spokesmen for both the Democratic and Republican parties reacted favorably to *Reynolds*, at least initially. John M. Bailey, chair of the Democratic National Committee, spoke of the "beginning of the end of archaic apportionment systems," adding that "this is something the Democratic Party had long advocated and fought for and certainly welcomes." His Republican counterpart, William E. Miller, praised *Reynolds* as "being in both the country's interest and the Republican party's interest." Support for *Reynolds* would soon diminish, especially among Republicans.[2]

Southern Republican and Democratic members of Congress introduced more than 100 measures to curb the role of the Court in suits affecting state patterns of apportionment. *Reynolds* provoked heated rhetoric, with Rep. Paul Findley, D-Ill., calling it the Court's most "unwise" action and suggesting Illinois would be "subject to Chicago machine politics from that day forward."[3] Rep. William Tuck, D-Va., a former governor, was even more outspoken than Findley in criticizing the Court. The day after *Reynolds*, he said the decision marked a "new and shocking interference by the federal judiciary with the right of the sovereign states to conduct their domestic affairs" and "strikes obstructively at the Federal Union." He introduced a bill both denying federal district courts' jurisdiction over state apportionment cases and withdrawing appellate jurisdiction from the Supreme Court in all state reapportionment cases. Tuck claimed his bill was necessary to "preserve the Constitution . . . already bleeding from assaults made on it by the Supreme Court."[4] He said his "double-barreled" approach was required to resolve one of the "most serious problems confronting the country today." He continued:

ANIMAL FARM

SOME ARE MORE EQUAL THAN OTHERS

1 RURAL AREA VOTE =100 CITY VOTES

—from *Herblock: A Cartoonist's Life* (Times Books, 1998), courtesy of the Prints & Photographs Division, Library of Congress, LC-DIG-LC-DIG-ppmsc-03534

> The Warren Supreme Court as at present constituted is creating a revolution that will destroy our Government as we have known it and as it has existed since established by the Founding Fathers of the Republic. . . . Unless the Warren Court is curbed and divested of some of the powers which they have unlawfully assumed and arrogated to themselves, the State and local governments will become nothing more than the hollow shells of a lost liberty.
>
> The reapportionment decision undertakes to reduce the legislative assemblies and officials of the various States to mere pawns in the hands of these inferior Federal courts who have, as they did in Virginia, nullified and negated laws duly enacted, terminated offices established under our State constitution, peremptorily ordered the Governor of a great commonwealth when to call the assembly into special session, and, in addition, have . . . ascribed to themselves the power to instruct the people of the State when to hold elections. Such unprecedented and unwarranted conduct rightfully subjects these courts to the reproach and firm reprimand on the part of many thoughtful Americans. [The legislation I have proposed is designed] to free the people of the United States from the unbridled clutches of our highest court.[5]

The House Judiciary Committee held hearings on the Tuck (and other) proposals, but it was generally assumed that the committee would not send any anti-Court proposal to the floor for a vote because committee chair Emanuel Celler, D-N.Y., vigorously opposed the Tuck measure as well as other "Court-curbing" initiatives. On August 19 Celler said:

> [I] deem this bill a rather vicious attack upon the Supreme Court, and I use the word "vicious" advisedly, because any time any one of those who will vote for this bill or who

advocates the passage of this bill finds his constitutional rights invaded or eroded or taken away from him, he will flee to Supreme Court as a haven to protect those very rights. And now those who support this bill would subvert that very haven. . . .

[Further,] there is a violation of the separation of powers. This bill denies all Federal courts jurisdiction in apportionment cases. . . . Today it is apportionment cases over which the Supreme Court and the Federal court shall have no jurisdiction. Tomorrow this Congress can say the Federal courts shall have no jurisdiction over antitrust cases. The next day it shall have no jurisdiction over criminal cases, that it shall have no jurisdiction over the Bill of Rights. Finally, what would happen to the Supreme Court? You would render the Supreme Court a nullity. . . . Then you would have a legislative dictatorship that violates the principle of separation of powers.[6]

The House Rules Committee bypassed the Judiciary Committee and voted to bring the Tuck proposal directly to the House floor. Rep. Howard Smith, D-Va., the Rules Committee chair, believed passage of the Tuck bill was necessary for "curbing a power-mad, rampaging" Supreme Court from "running roughshod" over Congress, the states, and the American people. Celler protested the Rules Committee action saying, "Tammany Hall in its wildest moments would never have tried anything like this." On the strength of a coalition of Southern Democrats and Republicans, the House approved the Tuck measure on August 19, 1964, by a vote of 218 to 175.[7]

Meanwhile, in a separate maneuver, Sen. Everett Dirksen, R-Ill., attached a rider to an appropriations bill calling for a two-year delay in implementing *Reynolds*. Dirksen thought that two years would be enough time to secure ratification of a constitutional amendment allowing one house of state legislatures to be apportioned on a nonpopulation basis. Dirksen spoke frequently in favor of his proposal, and in his inimitable way often featured the states rights theme. Soon after offering the appropriations rider, he said:

I believe somewhere in the Constitution I read a clause which states that the power that is not delegated to the Federal Government is reserved to the people. By "people" we mean the States. That clause is still there. Perhaps it is bemusing and even amusing to a great many people. I always thought that those old-timers who came to Philadelphia to fabricate that Constitution in 1787 knew what they were about when they said, "so much power belongs to the Federal Government, and no more; and the rest of it we keep in our tight fists."[8]

One of those leading the opposition to the Dirksen proposal was Sen. Paul Douglas, D-Ill. Douglas observed:

It is improper for Congress to try to overrule the Supreme Court in matters of constitutional law. That is precisely what the Dirksen amendment would do. Therefore, our objections to the Dirksen amendment are founded on these facts. First, long continued and accumulating abuses in reapportionment were for the first time being redressed by the decisions of the Supreme Court and inferior Federal courts to reapportion in some fairly close proportion to population; and the cities and the suburbs were for the first time being given hope they could escape from the legislative shackles with which they were bound.[9]

A filibuster was subsequently successful in preventing the Dirksen rider from coming to a vote. In the meantime, Sen. Strom Thurmond, R-S.C., blocked referral of the Tuck bill to the Senate Judiciary Committee, preferring instead to bring it directly to the Senate floor. Following the Democratic National Convention, the Senate did not invoke cloture against the antirider filibuster. As a result, Senate Majority Leader Mike Mansfield, D-Mont., introduced a nonbinding "sense of Congress" resolution directing courts to allow legislatures "reasonable time" to comply with the redistricting orders. Thurmond's attempt to substitute the Tuck proposal for this resolution was defeated, and an amended version, in the form of a foreign aid bill rider, passed in the Senate by a 44 to 38 vote on September 24, 1964. The compromise version directed courts to allow state legislatures one session plus a month to comply with court orders and allowed states to use existing district boundaries provided no court orders had been issued; the resolution did not affect court orders issued before the resolution was adopted. House opponents of *Reynolds* were so incensed by the mild Senate resolution that the conference committee purged it from the foreign aid measure. The net result of all this was that *Reynolds* remained intact.

Anti-Court sentiment in Congress took a different direction in July 1964 when the Senate sought to reduce a pay increase previously approved by the House for Supreme Court justices. The bill's sponsor, Sen. Gordon Allott, R-Colo., tried to argue that his proposal should not be taken "in the spirit of criticism of the decisions of the Supreme Court," but the motive was clear. The Allott amendment was denounced in the House as an "act of vengeance" communicating to the Court that "if you do not decide cases the way we believe, we will engage in reprisals against you." A conference committee eventually restored part of the reduction, but the justices did not receive the original amount provided in the House bill or a raise equal to the salary increases of the lower federal judges.[10]

Sen. Barry Goldwater, R-Ariz., eager to win southern support for his presidential candidacy, denounced *Reynolds* as a prime example of the Court's disrespect for limited government. Some Democrats praised *Reynolds* as taking the Court's other recent civil rights and voting rights decisions to their logical conclusion. Other Democrats, however, including President Lyndon Johnson, wondered if the justices had gone too far in *Reynolds*. No matter the point of view, there was widespread agreement that a "constitutional milestone had been reached." A *New York Times* editorial suggested the reapportionment decisions of 1964 easily surpassed the *Brown* desegregation ruling as the most significant ruling of the Warren Court era.[11]

Within a month of the *Reynolds* decision, the Republican National Convention adopted its platform, which included a call for a constitutional amendment partially reversing the ruling and allowing states to depart from population as the basis for representation in one house of their bicameral legislatures. The Democratic National Convention was more divided on reapportionment, but, deferring to the wishes of President Johnson, did not include any statement on the issue in its platform. It was apparent, however, that the Court's 1964 apportionment decisions would not receive the broad-based support of Democrats who responded favorably to *Baker v. Carr* two years earlier.

Apportionment became a central component of Goldwater's bid for the presidency—one of the "moral-constitutional issues" that formed the ideological core of Goldwater's presidential campaign. Indeed, the Goldwater campaign targeted the Court, attacking many of its important constitutional rulings dating back as far as the 1930s. In addition to the reapportionment decisions were the Warren Court decisions expanding procedural protections for criminal defendants in state trials, decisions restricting censorship of allegedly obscene literature, decisions relating to subversion and internal security, and the school prayer and Bible-reading decisions. Goldwater charged

> that the Supreme Court has abandoned the principle of judicial restraint, with respect to acts of Congress with which it disagreed but which are founded on legitimate exercise of legislative power. Today's Supreme Court is the least faithful to the constitutional tradition of limited government of the three branches of Government. . . . [The Court's decisions] are defended on the grounds that results are desirable; that it really isn't good for children to say prayers in school and that it is really desirable to have state legislatures, in their entirety, apportioned on a one-man, one-vote basis. This is raw and naked power. The question under our system of government is not simply what decision is right, but also who has the right to decide. Only when the latter question is answered should the former be considered.[12]

Not since the liberal attacks on the Court during the New Deal era had constitutional issues played such a prominent role in national electoral politics. Illustrative of the extent of anti-Court sentiment among 1964 Republican convention delegates was the response to hearing the chief justice's name. Warren had been a Republican governor of California and his party's vice presidential nominee in 1948, but the mere mention of his name produced a "chorus of boos" from the delegates. During his campaign Goldwater continued to label the Court the "least faithful branch," but the Democrats' restrained response to *Reynolds* limited the extent to which the Republicans could exploit the reapportionment issue nationally.

AFTER THE 1964 ELECTION

The voters ended the presidential hopes of Goldwater and the Republican Party in 1964, but the attacks on the Court's apportionment decisions persisted. A move to convene a national constitutional convention to address the reapportionment issue had begun even before the decision in *Reynolds.* By May 1965, twenty-five state legislatures had adopted resolutions calling for such a constitutional convention. These resolutions also urged Congress to remove the jurisdiction of the federal courts in apportionment cases. It was generally believed that many members of Congress had serious reservations about a constitutional convention, and that the real objective of those advocating a convention was to force Congress to propose its own apportionment amendment reversing *Reynolds v. Sims* as a way to avoid a constitutional convention.

On January 6, 1965, Senator Dirksen, the Republican minority leader, introduced S.J. Res. 2, a proposed amendment to the Constitution allowing the states to include factors other than population in the apportionment of either their senate or house chambers. The Dirksen proposal prompted a vigorous lobbying effort by a wide array of groups with support and opposition following largely predictable lines. The U.S. Chamber of Commerce, National Association of Manufacturers, American Farm Bureau Federation, National Farmers Union, National Grange, National Cattlemen's Association, and many other farm organizations formed the core of interest group support for the amendment. The opposition groups included the AFL-CIO and other member unions, the American Civil Liberties Union, the National Association for the Advancement of Colored People, Americans for Democratic Action, American Jewish Congress, Congress of Racial Equality, the U.S. Conference of Mayors, and the American League of Cities.

The number of states pressing for a constitutional convention on the reapportionment issue seemed to indicate the Dirksen proposal would be passed. Opponents of a convention realized that fewer petitions favoring a convention would come from legislatures with completed redistricting, and the strategy of opponents, therefore, was to delay a vote as long as possible. Failing to get his amendment reported favorably out of the Senate Judiciary Committee, Dirksen brought his proposal to a Senate vote as a substitute for a resolution designating a National American Legion Baseball Week. The proposal would allow one house of a bicameral state legislature to be apportioned on the basis of population, geography, or political subdivision. The proposal required that any apportionment scheme using a population alternative be approved in a statewide vote.

The Senate debate on the Dirksen substitute was highly charged. Sen. Paul Fannin, R-Ariz., argued that the measure would "restore to the people a right which the Supreme Court has wrongfully taken from them." Without the amendment, Sen. Milward Simpson, R-Wyo., said the "one person, one vote principle" would produce "roughshod dominance by urban bosses." Sen. Walter Mondale, D-Minn., saw the issue much differently. It was not an urban-rural controversy in his view, but a controversy between people "entitled to equal representation . . . and those who feel that certain citizens should be given greater influence in government than others." Mondale dismissed the federal analogy argument suggesting instead that state governments "do not consist of a federation of political subdivisions as does the federal government." As the vote on Dirksen neared, opponents addressed the issue from another angle, arguing that the amendment could be used to perpetuate racial discrimination by weighting white-controlled political subdivisions in one house of a state legislature.[13] The vote on the Dirksen amendment was 57 to 39 in favor, but seven votes short of the two-thirds vote needed to pass a constitutional amendment.

A year later the Senate rejected another Dirksen initiative, which again sought to reverse *Reynolds* and permit states to apportion one house of their legislatures on a nonpopulation basis. The Senate vote, taken on April 20, 1966, was 55 to 38 in favor, again falling short. The defeat effectively ended congressional efforts to set aside *Reynolds.* By the end of the year, the intensity of the opposition to the reapportionment issue had subsided. Rural interests continued in their efforts to prevent migration of legislative control to urban and suburban areas, but these efforts were uniformly unsuccessful. The shift from malapportioned state legislatures to those in compliance with *Reynolds* substantially ended by the 1966 election. The states that had not reapportioned by that time were redistricted by court mandate. In addition, the Supreme Court extended the "one person, one vote" principle to municipal and county governments, further cementing the principle into the evolving political culture. By mid-1967 a number of state petitions calling for a constitutional convention remained, but the drive for a convention had lost momentum. As important, the politics associated with President Johnson's domestic agenda and the continuing war in Vietnam diverted attention from both the reapportionment issue and the federal courts. Senator Dirksen's death in 1969 removed the leading congressional opponent to the "one person, one vote" principle from the national political stage.

That same year, Gallup ran another poll on reapportionment asking if the respondents would favor continuing the equal population districting plans or returning to plans in place before *Reynolds.* Fifty-two percent preferred the redrawn districts, 23 percent favored the pre-*Reynolds* plans, and 25 percent had no opinion. More than 55 percent of those living in communities of more than 50,000 preferred the new plans, and less than 20 percent preferred the earlier arrangements. The margins were closer among residents of small communities, but substantially in favor of the redrawn districts—48 percent to 26 percent among respondents in communities of 2,500-49,000, and 46 percent to 33 percent with residents of communities under 2,500. This small community (under 2,500 people) subset of the sample was the only group that had disapproved of *Reynolds* in 1964. Republicans, Democrats, and independents all preferred the new plans by margins of more than 2 to 1. Finally, the population-based plans were preferred 60 percent to 20 percent in the West, 51 percent to 25 percent in the Midwest, 50 percent to 23 percent in the South, and 49 percent to 23 percent in the East. In each region, the remaining respondents split about evenly between the earlier plan and no opinion categories. As these data suggest, the *Reynolds* decision and its "one person, one vote" principle for state legislative districts had gained acceptance throughout the country.

NOTES

1. These and all subsequent polling data are from George Gallup, *The Gallup Poll: Public Opinion 1935–1971,* Vol. 3, 1969–1971 (New York: Random House, 1971).

2. *New York Times,* June 17, 1964, 29.

3. *Congressional Quarterly Almanac 1964* (Washington, D.C.: Congressional Quarterly, 1965), 390.

4. Richard C. Cortner, *The Apportionment Cases* (Knoxville: University of Tennessee Press, 1970), 238.

5. *Congressional Record,* 89th Cong., 1st sess., January 5, 1965, 106–107.

6. *Congressional Record,* 88th Cong., 2d sess., August 19, 1964, 20236–7.

7. Cortner, *The Apportionment Cases,* 238.

8. *Congressional Record,* 88th Cong., 2d sess., August 13, 1964, 19446–7.

9. Ibid., September 23, 1964, 22561.

10. Cortner, *The Apportionment Cases,* 237.

11. *New York Times,* June 18, 1964.

12. Ibid., September 12, 1964.

13. *Congressional Quarterly Almanac 1965* (Washington, D.C.: Congressional Quarterly, 1966), 529.

Griswold v. Connecticut

John W. Johnson

Griswold v. Connecticut
381 U.S. 479 (1965)

DECIDED: June 7, 1965
VOTE

CONCURRING: 7 (Earl Warren, William O. Douglas, Tom C. Clark, John Marshall Harlan (II), William J. Brennan Jr., Byron R. White, Arthur J. Goldberg)
DISSENTING: 2 (Hugo L. Black, Potter Stewart)

OPINION OF THE COURT: Douglas
CONCURRING OPINION: Goldberg (Warren, Brennan)
OPINION CONCURRING IN JUDGMENT: Harlan
OPINION CONCURRING IN JUDGMENT: White
DISSENTING OPINION: Black (Stewart)
DISSENTING OPINION: Stewart (Black)

Americans value privacy as one of their most cherished rights. Yet the word "privacy" is not mentioned anywhere in the U.S. Constitution. Notwithstanding episodic appearances in the law of torts, a constitutional safeguard for privacy did not emerge until the middle of the twentieth century. What finally brought privacy under the aegis of the federal constitution was a 1965 U.S. Supreme Court decision known as *Griswold v. Connecticut.*

Griswold involved the Court's review of a nineteenth-century relic—an 1879 state law that made the use of artificial birth control illegal in Connecticut. Under this law, individuals residing in the state and using artificial contraceptives such as diaphragms or condoms could be fined, as could those who counseled or abetted others in the use of such devices. Practically speaking, the law had been widely ignored since its appearance on the statute books. Individuals or couples wishing to practice birth control routinely purchased over-the-counter contraceptives. In addition, middle- and upper-class Connecticut women sought and received birth control advice from private physicians. The most pronounced effect of the law was that it outlawed birth control clinics and, therefore, discouraged the practice of birth control by the state's poorest women. From World War I to the early 1960s, dozens of measures were introduced in the Connecticut state assembly to remove the injunction against birth control from the state's statute books. Because of the pervasive influence of Connecticut's Roman Catholic clergy and some conservative Protestants, however, all the proposed legislative attempts to dislodge the 1879 law proved unsuccessful. These failures ultimately led birth control advocates to resort to litigation.

Judicial attempts to overturn the prohibition on birth control failed in 1940, 1943, and 1961 because of procedural technicalities in the lawsuits. A successful legal challenge to the law commenced when Estelle Griswold, the executive director of the Planned Parenthood League of Connecticut (PPLC), and C. Lee Buxton, a Yale University physician, opened a birth control clinic in New Haven in November 1961. As the PPLC anticipated, the authorities closed the clinic after its first day of operation, and Griswold and Buxton were placed on trial for their "crimes." Losing at the state level, Griswold and Buxton appealed to the U.S. Supreme Court. Their attorneys made the argument that the 1879 law violated the privacy of the two defendants and unnamed married couples who sought contraceptive services from the clinic.

THE OPINION IN *GRISWOLD*

In a 7–2 decision, the Supreme Court agreed with Griswold and Buxton. In striking down "a silly law," the nation's highest court enunciated what many legal reformers and jurists had long campaigned for—a constitutional right of privacy. Writing for the Court's majority, Justice Douglas held that the "penumbra" or "emanations" of selected portions of five of the first ten amendments established "zones of privacy" sufficiently broad to afford married couples the constitutional right to engage in the intimate act of sexual intercourse with artificial contraceptives. Several of Douglas's concurring brethren suggested competing bases for a constitutional right of privacy. Justices Black and Stewart dissented vehemently.

The statute dispatched in *Griswold v. Connecticut* was of immediate practical importance only to the small number of Connecticut married couples who did not have access to birth control counseling at the time. The principal significance of *Griswold* has proven to be its resonance since the mid-1960s as a rationale for extending the constitutional right of privacy to all Americans. For example, *Griswold* was the major precedent for the right of a woman to choose an abortion and for the rights of same-sex couples to engage in intimate sexual acts. Furthermore, fealty to *Griswold* has served as perhaps the most important litmus test for members of Congress to pass upon the "constitutional correctness" of presidential nominees to the U.S. Supreme Court. Finally, since the enunciation of the decision in June 1965, *Griswold* has held a bellwether status in constitutional law: a few legal commentators have hailed Douglas's opinion as brilliantly creative; a majority of members of the legal community reacting to the decision, however, have agreed with the result reached by Douglas but found fault with his reasoning; and a vocal minority of legal experts have never accepted the constitutionality of a right of privacy and continue to regard Douglas's majority opinion in *Griswold* as a *bête noire* of legal reasoning.

Six justices wrote opinions in *Griswold*. Justice Douglas in the "opinion of the Court" found several amendments in the Bill of Rights that provided his basis for overturning the Connecticut statute. Douglas wrote in part:

> [S]pecific guarantees in the Bill of Rights have penumbras, formed by emanations from those guarantees that help give them life and substance. . . . Various guarantees create zones of privacy. The right of association contained in the penumbra of the First Amendment is one. . . . The Third Amendment in its prohibition against the quartering of soldiers "in any house" in time of peace without the consent of the owner is another facet of that privacy. The Fourth Amendment explicitly affirms the "right of the people to be secure in their persons, houses, papers, and effects, against unreasonable searches and seizures." The Fifth Amendment in its Self-Incrimination Clause enables the citizen to create a zone of privacy which government may not force him to surrender to his detriment. The Ninth Amendment provides: "The enumeration in the Constitution, of certain rights, shall not be construed to deny or disparage others retained by the people." . . .
>
> The present case . . . concerns a relationship lying within the zone of privacy created by several fundamental constitutional guarantees. And it concerns a law which, in forbidding the *use* of contraceptives rather than regulating their manufacture or sale, seeks to achieve its goals by means having a maximum destructive impact upon that relationship. . . . Would we allow the police to search the sacred precincts of marital bedrooms for telltale signs of the use of contraceptives? The very idea is repulsive to the notions of privacy surrounding the marriage relationship.
>
> We deal with a right of privacy older than the Bill of Rights—older than our political parties, older than our school system. Marriage is a coming together for better or for

worse, hopefully enduring, and intimate to the degree of being sacred. It is an association that promotes a way of life, not causes; a harmony in living, not political faiths; a bilateral loyalty, not commercial or social projects. Yet is an association for as noble a purpose as any involved in our prior decisions.[1]

In a concurring opinion, Justice Goldberg wrote:

The Ninth Amendment to the Constitution may be regarded by some as a recent discovery and may be forgotten by others, but since 1791 it has been a basic part of the Constitution which we are sworn to uphold. To hold that a right so basic and fundamental and so deep-rooted in our society as the right of privacy in marriage may be infringed because that right is not guaranteed in so many words by the first eight amendments to the Constitution is to ignore the Ninth Amendment and to give it no effect whatsoever.[2]

The dissenters found no basis in the Constitution for overturning what they agreed was a bad law. Justice Black wrote:

[T]he law is every bit as offensive to me as it is to my Brethren of the majority . . . who, reciting reasons why it is offensive to them hold it unconstitutional. There is no single one of the graphic and eloquent strictures and criticisms fired at the policy of this Connecticut law either by the Court's opinion or by those of my concurring Brethren to which I cannot subscribe—except their conclusion that the evil qualities they see in the law make it unconstitutional. . . .

I get nowhere in this case by talk about a constitutional "right of privacy" as an emanation from one or more constitutional provisions. I like my privacy as well as the next one, but I am nevertheless compelled to admit that government has a right to invade it unless prohibited by some specific constitutional provision.[3]

In a separate dissent, Justice Stewart agreed with Black.

Since 1879 Connecticut has had on its books a law which forbids the use of contraceptives. . . . I think this is an uncommonly silly law. . . . But we are not asked in this case to say whether we think this law is unwise, or even asinine. We are asked to hold that it violates the United States Constitution. And that I cannot do.[4]

INITIAL RESPONSES

Immediate reactions to the decision came from the litigants, their attorneys, and others close to the case. Contacted by the press on the day of the decision, Dr. Buxton stated, "It's a great advance for married couples in our state to be able to live a normal life without breaking the law."[5]

Fowler Harper, the attorney who helped frame the litigation in *Griswold,* did not live long enough to see the results of his efforts. His widow, Miriam Harper, sent a handwritten note to Justice Douglas:

Having lived with Fowler through almost every fact of the Birth Control Case for the past many years, I could not refrain from writing to tell you how pleased Fowler would have been with your opinion this week. It is one of the great sadnesses of [my] life that he could not see his work come to fruition. . . . Fowler's cause was always for the civil rights of people, and in this case to keep the sanctity of the home and the marital relationship. I feel the outcome of this case is a fitting memorial to Fowler and will have widespread effects.[6]

Thomas I. Emerson, a Yale law professor and constitutional scholar, took *Griswold* to the U.S. Supreme Court when Harper became too ill to proceed. Emerson was clearly gratified by the Court's decision in the birth control case. Shortly after learning of the outcome, he wrote:

> The precise source of the right of privacy is not as important as the fact that six Justices [White did not join the majority on a constitutional right of privacy] found such a right to exist, and thereby established it for the first time as an independent constitutional right. It was a bold innovation. . . . [T]he creation of a right to privacy is a step with enormous consequences. The concept of limited government has always included the idea that governmental powers stop short of certain intrusions into the personal life of the citizen. This is indeed one of the basic distinctions between absolute and limited government.[7]

The editorial response to the decision was for the most part favorable. The liberal-leaning *New York Times,* for example, wrote:

> The Supreme Court's 7-2 decision invalidating Connecticut's birth-control law is a milestone in the judiciary's march toward enlarged guardianship of the nation's freedoms. It establishes a new "right of privacy." . . . A reasonable and convincing argument can be made—and was made by the dissenters—that this infringement on personal freedom represented in the laws of Connecticut and many other states should have been corrected by the legislatures. But the fact is that it was not corrected. To what forum but the Supreme Court could the people then repair, after years of frustration, for relief from bigotry and enslavement? [8]

An editorial in a Midwest paper expressed a different view:

> "The specific guarantees in the Bill of Rights have penumbras" which create associated rights, Justice William O. Douglas . . . declared in overturning Connecticut's ban on birth control clinics because they violate a newly-created right of privacy. . . . Douglas's choice of the word [penumbra] may have been unfortunate, for the Constitution goes into full eclipse when the Supreme Court makes an addition to the Bill of Rights simply because the justices think it is needed. . . . The "right of privacy" which the majority of justices enunciated in this case was made up out of whole cloth. References to some items in the Bill of Rights were merely made to satisfy the legal niceties. The Supreme Court . . . has made itself a legislature beyond the reach of the people.[9]

In summing up the Supreme Court's term, the *New Republic* said of *Griswold:*

> The Supreme Court has had a relatively quiet term, which it ended rather spectacularly last week by declaring Connecticut's anti-birth control statute unconstitutional. . . . [In contrast to assertions in the dissent of Justice Black], the majority . . . was legislating no more than it had in *Brown v. Board of Education,* and a good deal less than it did in the reapportionment case. It held only that a statute directed at the *use* of contraceptives could not stand in a state that does not prohibit manufacture or effectively forbid sales; and a state that did not trouble to treat married couples at all differently from frolicking teen-agers.[10]

James D. Carroll, writing in the liberal periodical the *Nation,* endorsed the ruling:

> In *Griswold v. Connecticut,* the birth-control case handed down on June 7, the Supreme Court confounded most of the informed members of its public by giving

Estelle Griswold, executive director of the Connecticut Planned Parenthood League, and Cornelia Jahncke, president of the Planned Parenthood League of Connecticut, celebrate the Supreme Court's decision in *Griswold v. Connecticut* (1965), invalidating the state's anticontraception law.—The Granger Collection, New York.

everyone something and no one everything. June 7 was one of those days when it was impossible to tell the good guys on the Court from the bad. While Justices Harlan and Black in the background were decorously exchanging the mantles of judicial restraint and judicial activism, in the foreground Justices Douglas and Goldberg were excitedly announcing the discovery of a general constitutional right to marital privacy and the rediscovery of the Ninth Amendment to the Constitution. . . . The recognition by the Court of the Ninth Amendment is of fundamental importance as an affirmation of the Court's intention to protect the sovereignty and dignity of the individual. In a way, this recognition constitutes the declaration of a new Bill of Rights for the 20th century.[11]

RELIGIOUS COMMUNITY REACTS

A number of American religious leaders and journals of religious opinion offered their reactions to the decision. Archbishop Henry J. O'Brien of Hartford issued the following statement upon learning of the decision in *Griswold:* "Catholics, in common with our fellow citizens, recognize this decision of the court as a valid interpretation of constitutional law. However, I must emphasize that this is a juridical opinion, and in no way involves the morality of the question. Artificial contraception remains immoral by the law of God."[12]

The Reverend Robert Drinan, dean of the Boston College of Law, had this reaction: "I agree with the majority that the Connecticut law is in fact an invasion of the right to privacy, but I share dissenting Justice Black's misgivings about the scope and thrust of the majority opinion with respect to the alleged constitutional basis for the right to privacy." Martin Work, president of the National Council of Catholic Men, offered a positive comment in the wake of *Griswold*: "It was a wise decision in the pluralistic society of today. The [Connecticut birth control] laws were an unwarranted invasion of privacy."[13]

The liberal Catholic journal *Commonweal*—in an editorial and a feature article—deplored, not the decision, but the situation that had made it necessary to go to court:

> If there was anything clearly unfortunate about the Supreme Court decision, it was the fact that a constitutional decision was required in the first place. With no violation whatever even of the most hoary Catholic jurisprudential principles, the Connecticut hierarchy could have ceased long ago opposing the almost yearly attempts to have the law changed in the Connecticut legislature. . . . The entire round of court struggles was unnecessary, a dubious tribute to the power of a determined minority to impose their moral values on others. Will it happen again somewhere? Probably, for the Catholic community has learned its lessons slowly and in the hard way. The Supreme Court is an expensive tutor.[14]

William Ball, a noted constitutional attorney and writer on church-state issues, contributed an article to *Commonweal*, in which he took Justice Black to task for suggesting an extreme remedy:

> While it will be important to attempt to see what effects the Court's decision will have upon future policy developments and legislative psychology on the birth control front, it is equally important to put these considerations out of mind when examining the decision as a matter of constitutional law. The majority are now being arraigned for having fumbled for a constitutional basis on which to rest their proposition of privacy, but they might better be praised for the zealousness of their search. But Justice Black's suggestion that the slow processes of amendment would therefore need to be gone through in order to establish such a right smacks of a literalism little known in our constitutional jurisprudence since the days of John Marshall.[15]

The *Christian Century*, a liberal magazine aimed at mainline Protestants, applauded the Court's decision:

> When the United States Supreme Court held unconstitutional Connecticut laws banning the use and dissemination of birth control information and devices it did something more than reverse laws which for years have been farcically ineffective and the butt of numerous coarse jokes. It sustained—to use the court's words—"a right of privacy older than the Bill of Rights, older than our political parties, older than our school system." . . . The decision rescued marriage in Connecticut from desecrating implications and honored it in words comparable to those which in church manuals affirm the sacredness of the married state.[16]

LEGAL PROFESSIONALS' RESPONSE

Griswold was hailed by many students of American law as the most important decision of the Supreme Court's 1964-1965 term, and the academic legal community paid a great deal of attention to the several opinions in the case. Few of the more than thirty legal scholars and law students writing in the law reviews in the two years after the decision, however, felt that any of the six members of the Court who wrote opinions in the case "got it right." For example, the *Harvard Law Review* said:

As among those voting to strike down the law, a policy of judicial restraint might suggest that Mr. Justice Douglas's opinion is preferable since it adopts the narrowest ground necessary to reach that result. This ground may have been the only one commanding sufficient support among the Justices—and the public—to make reversal possible, and in any case the Court may have justifiably chosen to leave to the state legislatures as much as possible of the overhaul many think desirable in the area of birth control and similar laws. Nevertheless, since Mr. Justice Douglas's opinion emphasizing Connecticut's prohibition of use as the crux of the law's infirmity, a case involving a law prohibiting sale of contraceptives would confront the Court with a very difficult choice between upholding the law and abandoning the reasoning of Griswold. This dilemma might have been avoided by a broader holding in Griswold: that married couples have a right to use contraceptives.[17]

Two law professors commented on the *Griswold* opinions in the *Michigan Law Review*. Robert G. Dixon Jr. questioned the wisdom of finding a constitutional right.

When an "uncommonly silly law" produces the "most significant decision" of the Supreme Court term, and the seven-man majority has to be held together with four opinions, some inquiry is in order. . . . The actual result in *Griswold* may be applauded, but to reach this result was it necessary to play charades with the Constitution?[18]

Paul G. Kauper chided Justice Black for not applying the same standards of protection for individual rights in *Griswold* as he did in a case involving the associational rights of railroad workers.

In his dissenting opinion Mr. Justice Black reaffirmed and enlarged upon the basic view [he has long] expressed . . . that the Court has no business invalidating state legislation that does not violate the specifics of the Bill or Rights or other specifics found in the Constitution. The whole fundamental rights theory is anathema to him as an expression of judicial subjectivity and natural rights philosophy. . . . Yet it will be recalled that it was Mr. Justice Black who . . . [employed] a more extensive and more distinctly marginal use of the first amendment than the use of the specifics to protect the right of privacy in the *Griswold* case. To exclude the privacy of marital association from protection under the Bill of Rights, while using the first amendment as an umbrella for the kind of association in the . . . [railroad] case, appears to be a case of straining at gnats while swallowing a camel.[19]

THE EFFECT OF *GRISWOLD* ON SOCIETY AND THE COURT

In the immediate aftermath of *Griswold v. Connecticut,* a number of Court watchers predicted that the newly announced right of privacy would soon be enlisted to advance the rights of individuals confronted by overzealous law enforcement officers. In particular, constitutional experts argued that government use of wiretapping or electronic eavesdropping in criminal matters would be struck down as a violation of an accused person's right of privacy. That did not occur. What did take place in the realm of privacy in the forty years following *Griswold* was a controversial stream of court decisions touching the most intimate aspects of personal life.

In *Eisenstadt v. Baird* (1972) the Court enlisted the principle of the *Griswold*'s right of privacy to extend the constitutional coverage in the use of artificial contraceptives to unmarried individuals. In 1973 the Court majority cited *Griswold* with favor in *Roe v. Wade,* upholding a woman's right to an abortion in the first trimester of her pregnancy (see page 299). Most of the Court's subsequent abortion decisions have cited *Griswold* as a link in the chain of precedents covering a woman's right to an abortion. *Griswold* has also made an appearance in cases involving the issues of child custody and the right to withhold medical treatment for terminally ill patients.

In *Bowers v. Hardwick* (1986) the Supreme Court majority refused to extend the right of privacy to shield the intimate acts of homosexuals. In 2003, however, in *Lawrence v. Texas,* the Court explicitly overruled *Bowers,* citing *Griswold* as a precedent (see page 367). Later in 2003, building upon the reasoning of *Lawrence* and *Griswold,* the Supreme Judicial Court of Massachusetts held that the state's marriage law was unconstitutional as a violation of the principle of equal protection because it did not permit the marriage of same-sex couples.

> Marriage . . . bestows enormous private and social advantages on those who choose to marry. Civil marriage is at once a deeply personal commitment to another human being and a highly public celebration of the ideals of mutuality, companionship, intimacy, fidelity, and family. "It is an association that promotes a way of life, not causes; a harmony in living, not political faiths; a bilateral loyalty, not commercial or social projects." Griswold v. Connecticut. . . . Because it fulfils yearnings for security, safe haven, and connection that express our common humanity, civil marriage is an esteemed institution, and the decision whether and whom to marry is among life's momentous acts of self-definition. . . . We declare that barring an individual from the protections, benefits, and obligations of civil marriage solely because that person would marry a person of the same sex violates the Massachusetts Constitution.[20]

This decision set off a national firestorm over the legality of gay marriage and led to the proposal in Congress for a constitutional amendment to proscribe same-sex marriage. As long as the legality of same-sex marriages remains one of the hot button topics in American constitutional law, the *Griswold* precedent will be intoned with favor or derided as an example of judicial imperiousness.

Griswold has been an important focus of every Supreme Court confirmation hearing since the mid-1980s. Members of the Senate Judiciary Committee have grilled nominees regarding their views on the constitutionality of the right of privacy and the derivative right to an abortion. All of these nominees—save one—were willing to acknowledge the legitimacy of a constitutional right of privacy. The exception was Robert H. Bork, a federal appellate judge, nominated by President Ronald Reagan in 1987. The confirmation hearings were among the longest, and perhaps the most contentious, in the nation's history. Opposition to his nomination grew stronger as Bork was challenged to defend a statement on *Griswold* and privacy that he had advanced in a 1971 law review article:

> The *Griswold* decision has been acclaimed by legal scholars as a major advance in constitutional law, a salutary demonstration of the Court's ability to protect fundamental human values. I regret to have to disagree. . . . The Court's *Griswold* opinion, by Justice Douglas, and the array of concurring opinions . . . all failed to justify the derivation of any principle used to strike down the Connecticut anti-contraception statute or to define the scope of the principle. . . . The *Griswold* opinion fails every test of neutrality. The derivation of the principle was utterly specious, and so was its definition. In fact, we are left with no idea of what the principle really forbids. . . . We are left with no idea of the sweep of the right of privacy and hence no notion of the cases to which it may or may not be applied in the future. . . . Every clash between a minority claiming freedom and a majority claiming power to regulate involves a choice between the gratification of the two groups. When the Constitution has not spoken, the Court will be able to find no scale, other than its own value preferences, upon which to weigh the respective claims to pleasure.[21]

Testifying before the Judiciary Committee, Bork directed the following reply to Sen. Edward Kennedy, D-Mass.:

> Let me repeat about this created, generalized, and undefined right to privacy in *Griswold.* Aside from the fact that the right was not derived by Justice Douglas in any traditional mode of constitutional analysis, . . . we do not know what it is. We do not know what it covers. It can strike at random. For example, the Supreme Court has not applied the right of privacy consistently and I think it is safe to predict that the Supreme Court will not. . . . Privacy to do what, Senator? . . . Privacy to use cocaine in private? Privacy for businessmen to fix prices in a hotel room? We just do not know what it is.[22]

The Judiciary Committee voted against the nomination, 9-5. The committee report states:

> The committee believes that Judge Bork's position on the right to privacy exposes a fundamentally inappropriate conception of what the Constitution means. Judge Bork's failure to acknowledge the "right to be let alone" illuminates his entire judicial philosophy. If implemented on the Supreme Court, that philosophy would place at risk the salutory developments that have already occurred under the aegis of that right and would truncate its further elaboration.[23]

On June 7, 2005, several stories in the American press marked the fortieth anniversary of the Court's decision in *Griswold v. Connecticut.* As newspapers and legal experts noted on this occasion, *Griswold* has proven to be the primary legal precedent in the creation and expansion of the constitutional right to privacy, especially in the context of intimate personal matters such as contraception, abortion, the right to die, and the rights of same-sex couples.

NOTES

1. *Griswold v. Connecticut,* 381 U.S. 479, at 484, 485–486 (emphasis in original).
2. Ibid., at 491.
3. Ibid., at 507, 509–510.
4. Ibid., at 527.
5. Quoted in Peter Kihss, "Bill for Liberalizing New York Statute Goes to State Senate," *New York Times,* June 8, 1965, 35.
6. Miriam Harper to William O. Douglas, June 8, 1965, Box 1347, William O. Douglas Papers, Library of Congress, Washington, D.C.
7. Thomas I. Emerson, "Nine Justices in Search of a Doctrine," *Michigan Law Review* 64 (December 1965): 229.
8. "Right of Marital Privacy," *New York Times,* June 9, 1965, 46A.
9. "Abortion Laws Invalid Under Court Decision?" *Waterloo* [Iowa] *Daily Courier,* June 9, 1965, 4.
10. "End of Term Decisions," *New Republic,* June 19, 1965, 7–8 (emphasis in original).
11. James D. Carroll, "The Forgotten Amendment," *Nation,* September 6, 1965, 121–122.
12. Quoted in Kihss, "Bill for Liberalizing New York Statute."
13. Ibid.
14. Editorial, "The Connecticut Decision," *Commonweal,* June 25, 1965, 428.
15. William B. Ball, "The Court and Birth Control," *Commonweal,* July 9, 1965, 492.
16. Editorial, "Supreme Court Reverses Birth Control Law," *Christian Century,* June 23, 1965, 796.
17. "The Supreme Court, 1964 Term," *Harvard Law Review* 79 (1965): 164.
18. Robert G. Dixon Jr., "The *Griswold* Penumbra: Constitutional Charter for an Expanded Law of Privacy?" *Michigan Law Review* 65 (December 1965): 197, 218.
19. Paul G. Kauper, "Penumbras, Peripheries, Emanations, Things Fundamental and Things Forgotten: The *Griswold* Case," in ibid., 255–256.

20. *Goodridge v. Department of Public Health,* 440 Mass. 309, at 322, 344 (2003).

21. Robert H. Bork, "Neutral Principles and Some First Amendment Problems," *Indiana Law Journal* 47 (Fall 1971): 8–9.

22. U.S. Congress, Senate Committee on the Judiciary, *Hearings on the Nomination of Robert H. Bork To Be an Associate Justice of the United States Supreme Court,* 100th Cong., 1st sess., 1987, Committee Report, 150.

23. U.S. Congress, Senate Committee on the Judiciary, *Nomination of Robert H. Bork To Be an Associate Justice of the United States Supreme Court,* 100th Cong., 1st sess., 1987, Committee Report, 36.

Miranda v. Arizona

B. Keith Crew

Miranda v. Arizona
384 U.S. 436 (1966)

DECIDED: June 13, 1966
VOTE

> CONCURRING: 5 (Earl Warren, Hugo L. Black, William O. Douglas, William J. Brennan Jr., Abe
> Fortas)
> DISSENTING: 4 (Tom C. Clark, John Marshall Harlan (II), Potter Stewart, Byron R. White)

OPINION OF THE COURT: Warren
OPINION CONCURRING IN PART, DISSENTING IN PART: Clark
DISSENTING OPINION: Harlan (Stewart, White)
DISSENTING OPINION: White (Harlan, Stewart)

In *Miranda v. Arizona* and three companion cases, the Supreme Court established the now familiar requirement that persons detained by the police be informed of certain rights. Specifically, *Miranda* connects the Fifth Amendment right against self-incrimination with the Sixth Amendment right to counsel. That suspects had the right to remain silent and the right to be represented by legal counsel, and that they had to be informed of these rights, had already been established in *Gideon v. Wainwright* (1963) and *Escobedo v. Illinois* (1964). In *Miranda* the Court addressed the questions of who must inform suspects of their rights, when suspects must be informed, and how. The Court said the police must inform suspects of their rights before interrogating them, usually by reciting the words adapted from the Court's published opinion:

> You have the right to remain silent; if you give up the right to remain silent, anything
> that you say can and will be used against you in a court of law; you have the right to
> speak to an attorney and have one present during questioning; if you cannot afford an
> attorney, one will be appointed to represent you.

Furthermore, the police must obtain an intelligent waiver of these rights, typically done by asking: "Do you understand each of these rights as I have explained them? With these rights in mind, do you wish to talk to us now?"

Prior to *Miranda*, confessions were admissible provided they were held to be voluntary. The voluntariness standard was satisfied if the suspect was believed to be physically and mentally sound. In practice, this practice meant that the burden was on the defense to prove that a confession had been coerced or had been given by a defendant who was emotionally or mentally unstable at the time. After *Miranda*, the police had to prove that the suspect had been informed of the rights and had given an intelligent waiver.

The ruling also clarified when a person was considered to be in custody because it is the fact of being in custody that triggers the requirement. Basically, a person is defined as in custody when a reasonable person would conclude that he or she is not free to leave the scene. It does not matter if the police have officially pronounced the individual to be under arrest.

The most controversial part of the ruling was the application of the exclusionary rule (see *Mapp v. Ohio*, page 206). Self-incriminating statements including full confessions, no matter how voluntarily made, would henceforth be inadmissible as evidence if they were obtained without the defendant first being informed of his or her rights.

Along with the constitutional issues, the *Miranda* case addressed a fundamental division in the professional ideology of law enforcement regarding the use of confessions. Some people believed that voluntary confessions were the best type of evidence, while others believed that reliance on confessions encouraged sloppy police work and abuse of defendants. Although no abuse was alleged in Ernesto Miranda's case, it is evident that Chief Justice Warren was concerned with this issue. In writing the opinion of the Court, he addressed at length the temptation to coerce confessions, citing several documented examples of torture and intimidation used by police. In a strongly worded dissenting opinion, Justice Harlan stated that such concerns were exaggerated. He predicted dire consequences for society, asserting, "The social costs of crime are too great to call the new rules anything but a hazardous experimentation."

Miranda was a small-time criminal whose record included several sex crimes. In 1963 he was arrested in Phoenix, Arizona, and charged with the kidnapping and rape of one woman and armed robbery of another. When police told him that both victims had identified him in a lineup, Miranda confessed. He signed a written confession that included a typed paragraph stating the confession was made voluntarily and with full knowledge of his legal rights. At the trial, Miranda's court-appointed attorney based his defense almost entirely on trying to get the confession thrown out on the grounds that Miranda had not been informed of his rights and had waived those rights without the advice of a lawyer. The investigating officers admitted in testimony that they had not advised Miranda of his right to have an attorney present.

The American Civil Liberties Union (ACLU) took an interest in the case when it was appealed. With the ACLU assisting, the conviction in the rape case was appealed to the U.S. Supreme Court, which in 1965 agreed to hear it. Oral arguments for *Miranda* and three other appeals took place February 28 and March 1, 1966. On March 2 the *New York Times* reported that during the oral arguments the justices "disclosed their feelings to an unusual degree," and the paper speculated that a clash of opinions that had already been formed was imminent. On June 13 the Court released its decision, overturning Miranda's conviction, on the grounds that suspects must be informed of their rights before any self-incriminating statements they give may be used as evidence. Miranda, in the meantime, continued serving his sentence on the robbery charge. He was later retried and again convicted on the rape and kidnapping charge, this time without the contested confession.

In *Miranda* and the other three cases the Court reviewed together, the basis for the appeal was either the defendant had not been informed of his rights or the police had not documented that the defendant had waived his rights. In *Vignera v. New York,* the defendant had made self-incriminating statements to the police, and again later to an assistant district attorney. The defense attorney attempted to have these statements excluded at the trial on the grounds that the defendant had made them without being informed of his rights. In *California v. Stewart,* the defendant was held in custody for five days, during which he was interrogated nine times. After the ninth interrogation, he signed a confession. In *Westover v. United States,* the defendant was held and interrogated by Kansas City police for several hours, then turned over to the FBI, who continued the interrogation. The FBI agents persuaded the defendant to sign a statement confessing to two bank robberies. That signed confession contained statements that the defendant had been informed of his rights, but there was no documentation that he had been informed prior to being questioned. The lengthy interrogations in *Stewart* and *Westover* illustrate the use of pressure to elicit confessions, a practice some would consider abusive. No such abuse was alleged in *Miranda* or *Vignera;* rather, the Court ruled that inculpatory statements made without the defendant being informed of his rights (and the consequences of waiving those rights) were inadmissible, period. And, because Miranda's appeal was listed first, we speak today of "Miranda rights," not "Stewart" or "Vignera" rights.

Miranda was decided by a narrow 5–4 margin, which mirrored the public's divided opinion. The intensity of the controversy reflects the delicate balancing act confronting democracies, between protecting

```
PD 47
Rev 8/73   METROPOLITAN POLICE DEPARTMENT

              WARNING AS TO YOUR RIGHTS

You are under arrest. Before we ask you any questions, you must
understand what your rights are.

You have the right to remain silent.  You are not required to say
anything to us at any time or to answer any questions. Anything
you say can be used against you in court.

You have the right to talk to a lawyer for advice before we ques-
tion you and to have him with you during questioning.

If you cannot afford a lawyer and want one, a lawyer will be pro-
vided for you.

If you want to answer questions now without a lawyer present
you will still have the right to stop answering at any time. You
also have the right to stop answering at any time until you talk
to a lawyer.
```

```
                                    WAIVER

1.  Have you read or had read to you the warning as to your
    rights? _____

2.  Do you understand these rights?  _____

3.  Do you wish to answer any questions?  _____

4.  Are you willing to answer questions without having an
    attorney present? _____

5.  Signature of defendant on line below.

    _____

6.  Time _____        Date _____

7.  Signature of Officer _____

8.  Signature of Witness _____
```

The Miranda warning was mandated by the Supreme Court decision in *Miranda v. Arizona* (1966), which invalidated Ernesto Miranda's conviction on rape and kidnapping charges because police had not informed him of his rights against self-incrimination before he confessed to the crimes. The wording here is typical of what has become familiar from television dramas. Notably, the Court did not specify the exact language to be used when informing a suspect of his or her rights.

society and safeguarding individual rights. Public reactions to the Court's decision were inevitably framed by the often contradictory values of crime control and due process.

Not surprisingly, those most outraged by the *Miranda* ruling were prosecutors and the law enforcement communities, whose professional values emphasize crime control. The National District Attorneys Association (NDAA), an organization representing prosecuting attorneys in most of the nation's jurisdictions, along with the attorneys general of twenty-eight states, had filed *amicus curiae* (friend of the court) briefs. The NDAA brief urged the Court to maintain the status quo or, at least, not impose the exclusionary rule. The NDAA submitted statistical data collected from its members purporting to show that restrictions on the use of confessions would substantially reduce the number of convictions in criminal cases. The brief filed by the states' attorneys general argued that the states were not prepared to provide counsel at the pre-arraignment stage.

On the other side, the ACLU, which emphasizes the due process values, had filed an *amicus curiae* brief in support of restrictions on interrogation. The ACLU brief quoted police training manuals at length, concluding that generally accepted interrogation techniques were in fact intended to compromise, even violate, the subject's rights. Seeking to link the Fifth and Sixth Amendment rights, the ACLU argued that access to an attorney was necessary to protect defendants from the psychological pressure to confess inherent in the experience of being interrogated in isolation.

The ACLU and defense attorneys were generally pleased with the ruling. ACLU executive director John Pemberton, however, thought the Court did not go far enough in setting the new requirements. Pemberton said in the *New York Times* on June 14 that an attorney should be present before a defendant could intelligently waive his or her rights. Maricopa County's public defender Vernon Croaff referred to the distrust of police interrogation tactics when he expressed the hope that the ruling would force the police to be "investigators, instead of con men."[1]

REACTIONS FROM LAW ENFORCEMENT

Reactions to the *Miranda* decision were varied, although those who opposed the ruling tended to respond more intensely and emotionally than those who supported it. The decision was front-page news across the nation, and was clearly considered to be a change of major importance. Newspaper accounts tended to emphasize the generally negative reactions from prosecutors and law enforcement officials, perhaps creating the impression that a majority viewed the ruling as disastrous. The *Arizona Republic* of June 14 summed up this response with its headline, "Ruling Handcuffs Police." In Iowa the same day the *Waterloo Courier* quoted Democratic governor Harold Hughes as saying that the Court "just about took off the right arm of the detective." Public statements from law enforcement officials disappointed in the ruling followed three themes: that interrogation of suspects was essentially eliminated because defense attorneys would surely advise their clients to remain silent; that the Court was giving unfair advantage to criminals; and that the ruling would put society at risk by allowing criminals to go free. Duane Nedrud, speaking for the NDAA, asserted that *Miranda* "will effectively prevent any worthwhile interrogation. Fewer crimes will be solved; even fewer crimes will be prosecuted." Maricopa County Attorney Robert Corbin, whose office prosecuted Miranda's original trial, was quoted as saying, "God help us, God help the public."[2]

A sampling of statements by law enforcement officials illustrates the concern that interrogation had been vitiated if not eliminated. In an editorial in *Police Chief* magazine, Quinn Tamm, executive director of the International Association of Chiefs of Police, saw the police as "hamstrung" by an intrusive Court that put the rights of lawbreakers ahead of the rights of society.[3] A captain in the Des Moines Police Department called the ruling "ridiculous," stating: "Basically, we're trying to get at the truth, that's all. Now we can't, because we'll always have to have an attorney standing by who can just say 'keep your mouth shut.' "[4]

A county sheriff interviewed by a midwestern newspaper was clearly unhappy with the decision. He apparently misunderstood an important part of the ruling, however, because *Miranda* does not make a voluntary confession inadmissible:

> With decisions like that, they [the Court] doesn't want law enforcement. . . . If a man wants to tell you what he's done, it wouldn't be admissible . . . they are protecting the rights of the offender and completely disregarding the rights of the victim.[5]

A comment from another sheriff from the same state shows how central interrogation was to the professional values of the police:

> They went to extremes to deny peace officers something I consider their right. The criminal has all the advantages and the peace officer all the disadvantages. It makes our job much more difficult.[6]

The response from law enforcement was not entirely negative. Although the executive director of the International Association of Chiefs of Police blasted the decision a few months later, an official spokesperson for that group stated that the ruling in *Miranda,* "isn't so earthshaking; most professional police officers in this country have long felt that you should advise a suspect of his right to remain silent and to have counsel."[7]

In contrast to the horrified response of the Maricopa County prosecutors, other prosecutors were not upset by the ruling. For example, Samuel Olsen, the county prosecutor from Wayne County, Michigan, was quoted in the June 14 *New York Times* as saying, "So far as we are concerned there is absolutely nothing new in this decision."

Some, however grudgingly, acknowledged that police must become more professional in their approach to evidence. For example, in the *Des Moines Register* of June 14, a police captain stated that the decision "will call for better trained personnel, who will have to rely more on technical and physical evidence, and less on interrogation." This type of reform and professionalization of the police was precisely what Chief Justice Warren intended to encourage. Warren pointed out in the Court's opinion that in *Miranda* and each of the companion cases, there was enough other evidence to convict. Indeed, Ernesto Miranda was swiftly reconvicted without the confession.

PUBLIC RESPONSE

The general public's initial reaction to the *Miranda* decision was also mixed. A Gallup poll conducted shortly after the Court released its ruling asked, after a brief summary of the ruling, "Do you think the Supreme Court's ruling on confession was good or bad?" The pollsters put that question only to people who said they had followed the issue, about 40 percent of individuals polled. Of these, 24 percent thought it was a "good" decision, 46 percent thought it was a "bad" decision, and 30 percent had no opinion.[8] In a Roper Center poll conducted in December 1966, 56 percent felt that the "police should be allowed to be tougher," while 32 percent felt that the *Miranda* restrictions were correct and fair. The Roper poll may indicate a hardening of public attitudes had occurred, perhaps influenced by the hostile public statements of the decision's opponents. But, because the questions were worded differently in the two polls, it is not possible to compare them directly or to use them to establish a trend. It is reasonable, however, to conclude that the majority of American citizens did not support the Court's decision.

By the time of the *Miranda* decision, the Supreme Court under Chief Justice Warren had already established itself as an activist judiciary determined to enforce the rights of downtrodden and despised groups, including criminals. The Warren Court was cheered by liberals and derided by conservatives. *Miranda* was just one in a series of cases in which the Court extended the constitutional protections of suspects and defendants. Unfortunately, this "rights revolution" that strengthened the due process barriers that police and prosecutors face occurred at the same time that the United States was experiencing an unprecedented rise in crime. Conservative politicians blamed the increasing crime rates in part on liberal judges who were "soft" on crime. The bitterest denouncements of the *Miranda* ruling came from prosecutors and sheriffs. Whether elected or politically appointed, people who serve in these positions promise to be "tough on crime." The accusation that the Court protected the rights of criminals at the expense of the rights of victims resonated with a significant segment of the citizenry.

The conservative belief that *Miranda* and other decisions lead to dangerous criminals being released to commit more crimes was reinforced in the popular culture and mass media. Television shows and Hollywood movies began featuring the reading of rights as a dramatic element. The plot device of a dangerous criminal being set free on a "technicality," such as not being read the *Miranda* warnings, became standard fare. Popular entertainment has probably contributed to three common misperceptions about the role of the *Miranda* warnings. First, the warnings do not have to be given at the moment a suspect is placed under arrest, but before questioning begins. Second, some believe that failure to read the warnings automatically leads to the suspect's release. Television and movie crime dramas often present the reading of rights as if it were the "magic" words as in the children's game of "Simon Says." In reality, evidence gathered independently of the suspect's statements is not affected. Third, popular entertainment often exaggerates the impact of "technicalities" on the criminal justice process.

ATTEMPTS TO RESTRICT *MIRANDA*

Within two years of the *Miranda* decision, Congress passed Statute 3501, which made the giving of the *Miranda* warnings only one among several ways to render a confession admissible. Law enforcement agencies basically ignored Statute 3501 on the assumption that it would be ruled unconstitutional. Several challenges resulted in exceptions to the *Miranda* rules. *Harris v. New York* (1971) permits an illegally obtained confession to be admitted into evidence if the defendant takes the stand and the prosecution tries to impeach the defendant, that is, demonstrate that she or he committed perjury. The Court ruled in *Michigan v. Mosley* (1975) that a defendant does not have to be read the warnings again if an interrogation is interrupted and a different officer resumes the questioning. In *New York v. Quarles* (1984) the Court created a public safety exception, holding that police may ask suspects questions before advising them of their rights when the safety of an officer or citizen is immediately threatened, such as by the presence of a firearm. Undercover police may question a suspect without reading the *Miranda* warnings or revealing that they are the police; but once formal charges are made, the suspect must be given the warnings. This case was *Illinois v. Perkins* (1990). Although some liberals and civil libertarians see these decisions as eroding the constitutional protections of *Miranda,* most legal experts regard them as clarifications that pose no serious threat to its basic principles. Although conservatives continued to express anger over *Miranda,* it has gradually become an accepted fact of life in American justice.

For "law and order" conservatives, *Miranda* came to symbolize the perceived excesses of the Warren Court. President Richard Nixon drafted a message to Congress in 1969, asking Congress to consider amending the Constitution to "soften the effects of recent Supreme Court decisions." That memorandum focused on *Miranda.*[9] Although he made no serious effort to amend the Constitution, Nixon consistently nominated new Supreme Court justices who opposed the rights revolution of the Warren Court.

Conservatives' opposition to *Miranda* was exemplified by the efforts of Edwin Meese, attorney general during Ronald Reagan's administration. Meese signaled his intention to overturn or modify *Miranda* in a speech delivered at Vanderbilt University in 1987. His main objection to the *Miranda* rules was the application of the exclusionary rule. Therefore, Meese was also critical of *Mapp v. Ohio,* which extended the exclusionary rule to the states. Meese's position was that truth was more important than legal procedure:

> To most of us the point of a criminal trial is to determine whether the defendant did what he is accused of and to impose a just sentence if he is convicted on the basis of that determination. Getting the correct answer in this context is of the utmost importance. Mistakes in one direction will falsely brand innocent people as criminals and punish them unjustly. Mistakes in the other direction, freeing guilty defendants, also have dire consequences. Dangerous individuals may be set loose upon society, public respect for the legal system may be diminished, and, most importantly, justice will not be done. The objectives of protecting the public from the offender and deterring others from committing crimes cannot be achieved if guilt is not accurately established. These objectives are not casual concerns, but the basic reasons that a criminal justice system exists. If the truth cannot be discovered and acted on, the criminal justice system fails in its basic mission. Indeed, the state itself fails in its most fundamental responsibility.[10]

In addition to the Vanderbilt speech, a 128-page report prepared by Meese's staff at the Justice Department in 1986 confirmed that the department was seeking an appropriate case to challenge *Miranda.* The report stated: "The interesting question is not whether *Miranda* should go, but how we should facilitate its demise. . . . We regard a challenge to *Miranda* as essential."[11]

The Justice Department under Meese did not find a suitable case to challenge *Miranda.* The best chance for the Supreme Court to overturn *Miranda* came in 2000 with *Dickerson v. United States.* The position of the Clinton administration was, however, different from that of the Reagan administration. Presented by Janet Reno, President Bill Clinton's attorney general, the government's position was that the *Miranda* rules be retained.

Charles Dickerson was detained for questioning by the FBI regarding a bank robbery. He was interrogated twice. The first interview was conducted without the *Miranda* warnings, and some dispute existed over whether he was properly informed of his rights before the second interview. The information he gave resulted in a search of his apartment and the arrest of his codefendants. The confession was suppressed at his trial, but the prosecution successfully appealed to the Fourth Circuit of Appeals, citing Statute 3501.

The Supreme Court, with a more conservative membership than the Warren Court, surprised many with its 7–2 decision upholding *Miranda.* Only Justices Antonin Scalia and Clarence Thomas dissented. Chief Justice William H. Rehnquist, a long-time critic of *Miranda,* wrote the majority opinion, in which he cited precedent, noting that after more than thirty years, *Miranda* had become established as a principle of law. Furthermore, the *Miranda* warnings have proven to be "workable in practice."

Much of the debate over *Miranda* was empirical in nature. Opponents had predicted that the police would be less successful in solving cases, that fewer convictions would be obtained, and that more crimes would be committed. Paul Cassell, a law professor and critic of *Miranda*, submitted an *amicus curiae* brief in *Dickerson*. Among other things, the brief cited Cassell's own work on the impact of *Miranda*. Cassell estimated that *Miranda* had caused a 16 percent decrease in the rate of confessions, resulting in a net loss of 3.8 percent of convictions.[12] Some observers disagree that this is a significant impact. Moreover, Cassell's study has been criticized for methodological flaws. One critic estimates that the lost conviction rate attributable to *Miranda* is actually less than 1 percent.[13]

Compared to *Miranda*, negative reactions to *Dickerson* were fewer and more subdued. Opinion polls conducted following the *Dickerson* case showed that the vast majority of the public had come to accept and support the rule that police must give the *Miranda* warnings. A Roper poll conducted in 2000 showed that 86 percent of the public agreed with the central elements of the ruling, that police must inform suspects of their rights to remain silent and to have an attorney. A Gallup poll the same year puts the level of public support at 96 percent. People remain divided over the exclusionary rule, however. About half believe that confessions obtained without defendants being informed of their rights should be admissible.[14]

After nearly forty years, *Miranda* appears to be firmly established. The widespread public acceptance, and the fact that a mostly conservative Supreme Court upheld it, renders it less volatile as a political issue. Informing suspects of their rights is now simply how the police are expected to act. It has been said that "School children are more likely to recognize the *Miranda* warnings than the Gettysburg Address."[15] A new verb, "mirandize," has entered the language. As Chief Justice Rehnquist wrote in the *Dickerson* case, "*Miranda* has become embedded in routine police practice to the point where the warnings have become part of our national culture." Unless a serious alternative to the exclusionary rule emerges, police and prosecutors will have to accommodate the fact that they cannot use confessions, no matter how voluntary, without documenting that the suspect was properly "mirandized."

NOTES

1. Richard C. Cortner and Clifford M. Lytle, *Constitutional Law and Politics: Three Arizona Case Studies* (Tucson: University of Arizona Press, 1971), 53.

2. Ibid., 52–53.

3. Quinn Tamm, *Police Chief,* vol. 33, July 1966, 6.

4. *Des Moines Register,* June 14, 1966.

5. *Waterloo Courier,* June 14, 1966.

6. *Des Moines Register,* June 14, 1966.

7. *New York Times,* June 14, 1966.

8. *The Gallup Poll: Public Opinion 1935–1971,* Vol. 3 (New York: Random House, 1972), 2021.

9. *New York Times,* April 18, 1969, 34.

10. Edwin Meese, "Promoting Truth in the Courtroom," *Vanderbilt Law Review* 40 (1987): 271–274.

11. *New York Times,* January 21, 1987.

12. P. G. Cassell and B. S. Hayman, "Police Interrogation in the 1990s: An Empirical Study of the Effects of *Miranda,*" *UCLA Law Review* 43 (February 1996): 860.

13. Stephen J. Schulhofer, "*Miranda*'s Practical Effect: Substantial Benefits and Vanishingly Small Costs," in *The Miranda Debate: Law, Justice, and Policing,* ed. Richard A. Leo and George C. Thomas (Boston: Northeastern University Press, 1998), 205.

14. The Gallup Organization, June 27, 2000; www.gallup.com.

15. Leo and Thomas, *The Miranda Debate,* xv.

Loving v. Virginia

Peter Wallenstein and Erin K. Mooney

Loving v. Virginia
388 U.S. 1 (1967)

DECIDED: June 12, 1967

VOTE

CONCURRING: 9 (Earl Warren, Hugo L. Black, William O. Douglas, Tom C. Clark, John
Marshall Harlan (II), William J. Brennan Jr., Potter Stewart, Byron R. White,
Abe Fortas)

DISSENTING: 0

OPINION OF THE COURT: Warren

OPINION CONCURRING IN JUDGMENT: Stewart

Richard Loving, who was white, and Mildred Jeter, who was not, wanted to get married, but he was pretty sure they could not do so in their home state, Virginia. In June 1958 they drove the 100 miles north from their community in Caroline County to Washington, D.C., where no law against interracial marriage could keep them from having a wedding ceremony. Back in Virginia, they were rudely awakened one night a few weeks later and arrested. They learned that the same law that prevented their getting married in Virginia also made it a serious crime—one carrying a prison term of one to five years—for them to go out of state to get married and then return to Virginia and live together. Clearly guilty under Virginia law, in a plea bargain in January 1959 they accepted exile from the state for twenty-five years in lieu of a year in jail. They later challenged their convictions and the constitutionality of the law under which they had been arrested. In 1967 the U.S. Supreme Court, ruling for the first time directly on state laws restricting interracial marriage, struck down such laws as in conflict with the Fourteenth Amendment.

Although the decision in *Loving v. Virginia* was unanimous when it finally came, nothing of the sort could have been realistically predicted much before that time. A great deal of the rhetoric in the 1950s and 1960s against desegregated public schools had swirled around the hot-button issue of putting white girls in the same classrooms as black boys. So high were the feelings expressed among white southerners that the Court had twice in the 1950s declined to rule on cases concerning interracial marriage that had been appealed to it. By the time the Court acted in 1967, it was possible not only to decide the case the way it did, and to do so with unanimity, but also to escape a firestorm afterwards.

Laws against interracial marriage—especially, but far from only, between Caucasians and African Americans—had a firm footing in American law. Most states outside the South, as well as every state in the South, had such laws at one time or another, and between 1913 and 1948, thirty of the forty-eight states did. During Reconstruction, some courts in the Deep South had ruled that the Fourteenth Amendment invalidated miscegenation laws, but those decisions soon fell by the wayside. In *Pace v. Alabama* (1883), the Supreme Court ruled in favor of a miscegenation law, albeit one dealing with unmarried interracial couples, so not directly addressing the matter of marriage. And in *Maynard v. Hill* (1888), the Court held more generally that marriage "has always been subject to the control of the [state] Legislature." Through much of the twentieth century, therefore, there seemed little hope of obtaining a Court decision that miscegenation statutes were unconstitutional.

Yet, beginning in the 1920s, a series of Supreme Court decisions supported privacy, and by the 1940s other decisions proved favorable to African Americans' civil rights. Responsive to these two streams of decisions, and keenly aware of the nation's recent war with Nazi Germany, in 1948 a state supreme court acted against racial restrictions in marriage. In *Perez v. Sharp* the Supreme Court of California, in a 4–3 decision, ruled the state's miscegenation law unconstitutional. Combining the considerations of race and privacy, one member of the California court's majority observed: "If the right to marriage is a fundamental right, then it must be conceded that an infringement of that right by means of a racial restriction is an unlawful infringement of one's liberty." The antimiscegenation regime had, it seemed, moved past its high tide.

In 1954, moreover, the U.S. Supreme Court overturned the doctrine of *Plessy v. Ferguson* (see page 75) that segregation statutes could be constitutional, so far as public education was concerned. (See *Brown v. Board of Education,* page 197.) In the months that followed, challenges to miscegenation laws came to the Court from Alabama and Virginia. Unprepared to address interracial marriage, however, the Court deflected both cases. And into the 1960s, states across the South held firm in their retention of such laws. Outside the South, by 1965 the last of the states with miscegenation laws had repealed them.

In 1963, after more than four years in exile, Richard and Mildred Loving decided to challenge the law under which they had been convicted. In January 1965 Judge Leon M. Bazile wrote out a rationale for their conviction in his court six years earlier. Drawing on language and ideas that had been voiced in any number of court rulings across the previous century in support of miscegenation laws, Judge Bazile concluded:

> Almighty God created the races white, black, yellow, malay and red, and he placed them on separate continents. And but for the interference with his arrangement there would be no cause for such marriages. The fact that he separated the races shows that he did not intend for the races to mix.[1]

Meanwhile, in 1964, in *McLaughlin v. Florida,* the Supreme Court overruled *Pace v. Alabama.* Expressly limiting its ruling to a Florida law related to unmarried couples, the Court refused to invalidate the Florida law against interracial marriage *per se.* But relying on *Brown* and other cases, a unanimous Court said: "The central purpose of the Fourteenth Amendment was to eliminate racial discrimination emanating from official sources in the States." Two justices went further, insisting that they could not "conceive of a valid legislative purpose . . . which makes the criminality of an act depend upon the race of the actor."

In *Loving v. Virginia* the Court not only agreed to consider the constitutionality of a law banning interracial marriage, but it decided the case on broad, not narrow, grounds. A unanimous Court acknowledged *Maynard v. Hill* but imposed limits on its reach. For most purposes, state legislatures could continue to regulate the institution, but, in view of the Fourteenth Amendment, states could no longer restrict marriage to same-race couples. On equal protection grounds, and on due process grounds as well, Virginia's miscegenation law must fall, and so must similar laws in fifteen other states.

The most fervent comments on the decision came from the relieved couple. Never loquacious, Richard Loving summed up his feelings, "We're just really overjoyed." Mildred Loving, who shunned the limelight as well, was equally enthusiastic. "I feel free now," she said. Richard Loving, able at last to live in freedom with his wife and their three children in their home community, built a house for them. Years later, still living in that house, Mildred Loving said of the Supreme Court's ruling that it "changed our life a lot. We moved our family into our community in Caroline County without fear of going to prison."

COMMENTATORS IN LAW AND RELIGION

With the Supreme Court appearing on the cusp of scrutinizing laws against interracial marriage, Alfred Avins, a law professor at Memphis State University Law School, urged in 1966 that the laws be left alone.

The Supreme Court's 1964 decision in *McLaughlin v. Florida* seems to portend the demise in that Court of state laws forbidding interracial marriage. These laws ... have been upheld as constitutional by every appellate court which has considered the point, with the single exception of the [1948 California decision]. But the Court's decision in *McLaughlin* to overrule *Pace v. Alabama* evidently means that the justices intend to raze every constitutional landmark, however ancient and once-respectable, which permits the states to draw distinctions between the races. It requires no special perspicacity to see that anti-miscegenation laws are in jeopardy. . . .

I therefore am led to conclude that the fourteenth amendment does not forbid state laws preventing interracial marriage or extra-marital sexual relations. The matter remains subject to the state police power. Whatever the fate, therefore, of these laws in the present United States Supreme Court, the abiding Constitution of the United States, which I believe will ultimately prevail, makes these anti-miscegenation laws completely valid.[2]

Another legal scholar, Walter Wadlington, wrote a companion article in the same issue of the *Virginia Law Review*. Wadlington agreed with Avins that "an analysis of the intentions of the framers of the document is proper in explaining the historical setting from which the Constitution and its amendments are derived," but then they parted company.

To the extent that succeeding generations find a fuller meaning in the ideals which the language of their forefathers expresses, and rely upon that language in developing their own sense of value, the law must provide them with the freedom to apply the words of the Constitution in a manner consonant with their own understanding. . . .

. . . Although only a criminal provision is directly in issue in the *Loving* case, the constitutional arguments reach the very heart of the miscegenation law. The fundamental question is whether a man and his wife—and their children—should suffer at the hands of the law because they choose to marry across racial lines. *Loving v. Commonwealth* thus poses the constitutional issues clearly, and the Supreme Court should now make it clear that bans on interracial marriage have no place in a nation dedicated to the equality of men.[3]

Quite aside from what any statute or court might say or not say about interracial marriage, religious concerns about the matter were widely expressed in the 1960s. The *Christian Century* went to press with a faith-based perspective, "Interracial Marriage: A Christian View," in June 1967, just as the Supreme Court was preparing to hand down its ruling in *Loving*. Dr. James P. Carse, described as an instructor in the history and literature of religion at New York University, saw interracial unions as an answer to the race crisis. Shortly after Carse's piece was published—and shortly, too, after *Loving* was announced—the *Christian Century* printed an editorial response, "Pluralism Preferred," commenting on Carse's almagamationist prescription.

First, we are in complete agreement with Carse's presupposition that "in marriage, as in Christ, there is neither white nor Negro." . . .

Second, we agree with Carse that it is part of the duty of the church to help produce a climate in which interracial marriage is accepted as casually as—to use his illustration—a marriage between a Swede and an Italian. In striking down Virginia's ban against marriage between whites and nonwhites—and in effect all such prohibition in this country—the United States Supreme Court eliminated state-induced prejudice against interracial marriage. It is the duty of the church to show that such marriages are not only permissible but honorable. State laws declaring racial intermarriage illegal indoctrinated the people with the idea that such marriage is also immoral. The church has a principal role to play in removing that stigma.[4]

EDITORIAL RESPONSES IN VIRGINIA

Newspapers across Virginia not only reported the *Loving* decision but also commented on it. The African American voice of the Tidewater region, the *Norfolk Journal and Guide,* declared in "Freedom of Choice at the Altar":

> It is highly improbable that Monday's Supreme Court 9–0 decision outlawing Virginia's anti-miscegenation laws will change the prevailing marriage patterns in the Old Dominion. The unanimous decision, as a matter of fact, was anticipated.
>
> The ever broadening views of the Supreme Court justices with respect to purely personal relationships, and their increasing intolerance of restrictions on human conduct based on race, color or religion, had virtually assured the nation that the decision handed down Monday was on its way. . . .
>
> There should be no noticeable increase in the number of mixed marriages in Virginia as a result of the court ruling. Prospective grooms have always enjoyed the privileges of withholding their requests for the bride's hand, and brides since the memory of man runneth not to the contrary, have had the privilege and the authority to prevent mixed marriages simply by saying "no."
>
> What makes this Supreme Court decision so desirable is that it lifts an onerous and brutalizing stigma from Negro Virginians by knocking down that psychological barrier which, in effect, told them and the world that no Negro is good enough to be the husband or wife of a white Virginian.
>
> To Mr. and Mrs. Loving, whose married life has been lived virtually in a gold fish bowl for the last several years, our best wishes that they now may enjoy the privacy they always wanted, the happiness they expected to find in their mutual adventure, and the right to walk upright among their fellow Virginians and fellow Americans, their heads high, their dignity unabridged.
>
> They have done an incalculably great service for their community, their state, and their nation. Had they been less persevering, the legal battle to end Virginia's oppression on the marital front might have been forfeited long ago.[5]

In an editorial the *Norfolk Virginian-Pilot,* with a predominantly white readership, accepted the results as "inevitable":

> The Supreme Court's unanimous decision of yesterday striking down Virginia's anti-miscegenation law—and, by implication, similar statutes in 15 other states—was inevitable. "This Court has consistently repudiated distinctions between citizens solely because of their ancestry," wrote Mr. Chief Justice Warren. And so it has.
>
> . . . While the case at issue involved a Caroline County white man and Negro woman, who were convicted as criminals, the restriction they defied applied also to whites and members of brown and yellow races, including Chinese and Filipinos. But Virginia was inclined to arrest only whites and Negroes, although it withheld such marital civil rights as adoption, inheritance, and divorce from other racially mixed couples as well.
>
> In defending the Caroline County conviction (*Loving v. Virginia*) the State contended that only criminal provisions were concerned. Evidently, then, it sought to avoid any

Richard and Mildred Loving fought to overturn Virginia's law prohibiting interracial marriage. In *Loving v. Virginia* (1967), the Supreme Court unanimously ruled that state measures outlawing such marriages violate the Fourteenth Amendment. — AP Wide World Photos

holding in the case on the question of the validity of the anti-miscegenation law's civil sections. In contradiction to that, the Virginia Supreme Court of Appeals relied heavily on the prior decision (*Naim v. Naim*) involving an annulment action, rather than a criminal prosecution, when it ruled against the Caroline marriage and set the stage for yesterday's final ruling.[6]

From a small city in western Virginia, the *Roanoke Times* had this to say on its editorial page:

When the infamous Dred Scott case was decided by the Supreme Court in 1857, Chief Justice Taney observed that the country's attitude toward Negroes was indicated by its laws against interracial marriage. Those laws, he concluded, put "a stigma of the deepest degradation upon the whole race." In part, the court used that evidence of public attitudes to justify its decision that Negroes could not be American citizens.

Before the ink was barely dry on the Dred Scott decision, the nation was caught up in a tragic Civil War that ultimately would reverse the Supreme Court's non-citizenship sentence for Negro Americans. But for more than 100 years, there remained the "stigma of the deepest degradation."

This week that stigma finally was shattered. Appropriately enough, it was the Supreme Court that again was called upon to right a grevious wrong that still symbolized second-class citizenship for over 20 million Americans. Twelve years ago the court declined to take such action, desperately seeking to prevent a further outbreak of racial antagonism in Old Confederacy states still reeling from the previous year's historical school desegregation decision. . . .

To most Americans, marriage between whites and Negroes will continue to be viewed as wrong. If only because of social inhibitions, intermarriage will not occur except in a small percentage of cases. But the legal obstacle to such marriages has been erased . . . and so too the "stigma of the deepest degradation." The sensitive issue of race and sex will remain dominant in Negro-white relations for the foreseeable future, of course. But a state-administered caste system has been laid to final rest. . . .

"The law," Mrs. Loving once said, "should allow persons to marry anyone he wants." Because of *Loving v. Virginia*, the law so allows.[7]

THURGOOD MARSHALL, NOMINEE TO THE U.S. SUPREME COURT

By 1967 white Americans were living in a post-*Brown*, post–Civil Rights Act, and post–Voting Rights Act world; they had already acclimated themselves to a large measure of racial equality under the law. Terming "inevitable" the continued transformation in the status of African Americans, an editorial in Richmond's *News Leader* tied the *Loving* decision on Monday, June 12, to the nomination the next day of the first black nominee to the U.S. Supreme Court, Thurgood Marshall. The *Richmond News Leader* said:

> It is an arresting coincidence that news of the invalidation of miscegenation laws and appointment of the first Negro to the Supreme Court of the United States should be conveyed on the same front page. In a way, the two events testify to the swiftness with which the Negro's status is being altered.
>
> The large number of States that, at one time or the other, have had laws against mixed marriages was a consensus expression of apprehension and disapproval. The formal prohibition of mixed marriages now belongs to the past. Custom and personal inclination will now rule in this area. . . .
>
> The nullification of miscegenation laws and the appointment of Mr. Marshall were as inevitable as the morning's sunrise. That President Johnson appointed Mr. Marshall for political reasons and with the expectation that it will help him to another term in the White House is evident. But it is also evident that Mr. Marshall's formal qualifications to be a justice are generous and flawless by any test.[8]

And Marshall was eminently qualified: after a successful career with the NAACP Legal Defense Fund, which had brought many civil rights lawsuits to the Court, he served four years as a judge on the Second Circuit Court of Appeals and two years as U.S. solicitor general.

Regardless of whether the *Loving* decision might be regarded as "inevitable," it was by no means accepted without opposition. The meaning—even the validity—of the Fourteenth Amendment, the bedrock of the civil rights movement, came up for debate during Marshall's confirmation hearings in the Senate. Most members of the Senate Judiciary Committee supported the nomination, but several Southern Democrats expressed serious misgivings. They were worried about a constellation of recent Supreme Court rulings, among them *Loving*. That particular decision had been decided by a unanimous Court, so no single justice could have reversed the outcome, but it continued to rankle. On July 19 Sen. Strom Thurmond of South Carolina, who was still a Democrat in those days, challenged Marshall on the decision. The nominee deflected the question.

> *Senator Thurmond.* Do you know of any specific evidence relating to antimiscegenation laws which was presented to the Supreme Court in *Loving v. Virginia* which contradicted the historical evidence of the Commonwealth of Virginia that the 14th

amendment was not intended to affect antimiscegenation laws, and if you do not know of such evidence, how do you justify the Court saying that the historical evidence was not conclusive?

Judge Marshall. I am not familiar with the case. I am only familiar with the opinion. I did not read the record in that case.

Senator Thurmond. That's a recent case—

Judge Marshall. Yes, sir. . . . It was one of 150 this term, 150-odd, and I can't read the records of all of them.[9]

LOVING AND THE LAW AND CULTURE OF RACE AND MARRIAGE

Survey data from the time indicate that white Americans were growing less insistent that laws against interracial marriage should remain in place. When the National Opinion Research Center asked, "Do you think there should be laws against marriages between blacks and whites?" the proportion of white respondents who said yes was 62 percent in 1963, 60 percent in 1964 (the year of the ruling in *McLaughlin*), and 56 percent in 1968 (one year after the *Loving* decision). Then the support for such laws slipped more sharply, to 50 percent in 1970 and 40 in 1972, and by the end of the century it had reached 12 percent.

During the time the Lovings' case was back in the courts, national news magazines followed the story. In March 1966, for example, *Life* magazine published an illustrated article, "The Crime of Being Married." And immediately after the Supreme Court handed down its decision, *Time* and other magazines commented favorably on it. Characterizing antimiscegenation laws as "repugnant indeed," *Time* observed:

> In recent years, the court had several times passed up the chance to slap down interracial marriage bans. Presented squarely with the issue, however, the court was ringingly clear. . . . No state anti-miscegenation law will be able to stand in view of that unqualified, uncompromising finding.[10]

Some weeks later, in September 1967, the topic returned to the headlines when Margaret Elizabeth Rusk, whose father was Dean Rusk, the U.S. secretary of state, married an African American man, Guy Gibson Smith. *Ebony, Time,* and *Newsweek* all carried stories. *Time* put a photograph of the couple, shown arm in arm exiting the church, on its September 29 front cover, with the caption "Mr. and Mrs. Guy Smith: An Interracial Wedding." But the magazines did not all hit the same note in their coverage: *Ebony* was warmly accepting in its tone, and *Newsweek* more reserved.

In a number of cases already in state or federal court at the time of the ruling, the decision in *Loving* determined the outcome. One such case had been brought in federal court by an interracial Delaware couple that had been denied a marriage license in March 1967. On June 26, the court ruled in favor of the couple, basing the verdict on the *Loving* decision from two weeks earlier:

> The plaintiff [William Wesley] Davis is a "Negro" and the plaintiff [Sandra Jean] Drummond is a "white person" within the meaning of the Delaware statutes. . . . [They] requested that a marriage license be issued to them. Members of the staff of the Clerk of the Peace [of New Castle County] . . . refused to give the plaintiffs a marriage license, declaring that they were ineligible because under the law of Delaware intermarriage was prohibited between a Negro and a white person. [Mabel V. Roman] Gately [Clerk of the Peace] testified that a refusal to process an application for a marriage license was the invariable practice of her office when it appeared that a Negro and a white person desired a license to marry each other. . . .
> . . . A fundamental civil right, the right to marry, is here involved. . . .

... The thrust of the Virginia statutes at issue in *Loving* and that of the Delaware statutes ... is to prohibit marriage and its consummation on the grounds of race alone. The ruling of the Supreme Court clears the board of all racial barriers to marriage.[11]

In Oklahoma, the *Loving* decision was applied in an inheritance case. In *Dick v. Reaves,* a person's right to inherit property on the basis of a marriage was contested, on the grounds that the marriage had been interracial and therefore invalid. That is, the argument went, the marriage had been between a "person of African descent" and a Native American, someone "not of African descent" and thus "white" under Oklahoma law. The Oklahoma Supreme Court handed down its decision on July 11, 1967, a few weeks after *Loving.*

In view of ... *Loving v. Virginia,* .. holding that Virginia miscegenation statutes violate the United States Constitution, we feel compelled at this time to again review the long-standing view of this Court. ...

In accordance with this clear mandate of the Supreme Court of the United States, we ... expressly overrule all prior decisions of this Court to the contrary.

... the marriage of Martin Dick and Nicey Noel Dick was valid, regardless of the racial ancestry of either party to the marriage.[12]

The ability of two people to enter into a marriage, no matter their racial identities, was no longer a matter of doubt once the Supreme Court rendered its judgment as to the unconstitutionality of the traditional restraints. The federal ruling in the Delaware case exemplified the way that, although mop-up work might be required in a number of states, it was clear that interracial couples would soon be able to marry and live in any state. The state court's ruling in the Oklahoma case offered another reminder that ancillary issues had always been part of the legal controversy and social significance swirling about antimiscegenation laws and their enforcement. Just as that case dealt with inheritance, a later case, *Sidoti v. Palmore* (1984)—which, like *Loving,* went to the Supreme Court—addressed child custody. Early on, however, efforts emerged that would also apply the reasoning in *Loving* to same-sex marriage, and that effort appeared as controversial and challenging as the earlier campaign against miscegenation statutes had been.

LOVING AND SAME-SEX MARRIAGE

Beginning in 1970, cases began appearing in state courts contesting whether the logic of *Loving* might apply to same-sex marriages. The first of these to go to a state supreme court was argued in Minnesota. Richard John Baker and James Michael McConnell tried to get a marriage license, were refused, and appealed the decision to the Minnesota Supreme Court. Their attorney, Michael Wetherbee, drew on *Loving* to argue the case:

The refusal of respondent to issue the marriage license deprives appellants of liberty and property without due process of law contrary to the mandate of the Fourteenth Amendment to the United States Constitution. ...

In *Loving v. Commonwealth of Virginia* ... the issue was whether Virginia's anti-miscegenation statute prohibiting marriages between persons of the white race and any other race was constitutional. The Court struck down the statute. ...

The discrimination in this case is one of gender. ... Just as Virginia was attempting to maintain White Supremacy in *Loving,* Minnesota is attempting to maintain "heterosexual supremacy" here by denying to appellants one of the basic rights of Man. But even assuming that the interpersonal orientation of appellants is irrelevant to this case, there is no more rational reason for discriminating against appellants on account of their sex than there was in *Loving,* on account of their race.[13]

The state, in its brief, chose not to address *Loving,* but the Minnesota Supreme Court rejected the idea that *Loving* had any bearing on the case at hand:

> Virginia's antimiscegenation statute, prohibiting interracial marriages, was invalidated solely on the grounds of its patent racial discrimination. . . . *Loving* does indicate that not all state restrictions upon the right to marry are beyond reach of the Fourteenth Amendment. But in common sense and in a constitutional sense, there is a clear distinction between a marital restriction based merely upon race and one based upon the fundamental difference in sex.[14]

Baker and McConnell's attempt to convert *Loving* into a successful attack on restrictions against same-sex marriage did not succeed. Nor did the efforts of other same-sex couples in cases in the 1970s and 1980s. Beginning in the 1990s, however, state courts in Hawaii, Alaska, and Vermont proved receptive to the approach, renovated though it was to draw primarily on provisions in state constitutions.

In *Goodridge v. Department of Public Health* (2003), the Supreme Judicial Court of Massachusetts repeatedly drew upon the logic and the language in *Loving* to conclude that Massachusetts should permit same-sex marriage. Moreover, the Massachusetts court deployed both the California case from 1948, *Perez v. Sharp,* and the *Loving* decision to explain that although it was true that no consensus, in the nation or in any state, had yet formed to endorse gay marriage, the courts need not wait for such a consensus to emerge before declaring a right:

> For decades, indeed centuries, in much of this country (including Massachusetts) no lawful marriage was possible between white and black Americans. That long history availed not when the Supreme Court of California held in 1948 that a legislative prohibition against interracial marriage violated the due process and equality guarantees of the Fourteenth Amendment . . . or when, nineteen years later, the United States Supreme Court also held that a statutory bar to interracial marriage violated the Fourteenth Amendment. . . . As both *Perez* and *Loving* make clear, the right to marry means little if it does not include the right to marry the person of one's choice, subject to appropriate government restrictions in the interests of public health, safety, and welfare. . . . In this case, as in *Perez* and *Loving,* a statute deprives individuals of access to an institution of fundamental legal, personal, and social significance—the institution of marriage—because of a single trait: skin color in *Perez* and *Loving,* sexual orientation here. As it did in *Perez* and *Loving,* history must yield to a more fully developed understanding of the invidious quality of the discrimination.[15]

Indeed, the Massachusetts court observed, "Neither the *Perez* court nor the *Loving* Court was content to permit an unconstitutional situation to fester because the remedy might not reflect a broad social consensus."

In the 1990s, nearly three decades after *Loving* was decided, a collection of books came off the press, some of them by women who described themselves as the mothers of mixed-race children and others by children with multiracial identities. As the fortieth anniversary of the Court's ruling approached, most Americans had made their peace with the decision, as it applied to the law of race and marriage, and many seemed to be prepared to consider the merits of applying the decision to same-sex relationships. Debates continued over the definition of marriage—and over the orientation of the Constitution, the jurisdiction of federal and state authority, and the roles of the courts on the law of marriage. Much of that debate—what is the meaning of *Loving* for same-sex marriages?—takes place in law journals and in courtrooms. And much of it continues in political campaigns, on the floor of Congress, and in state legislatures, churches, and newspapers.

NOTES

1. Leon M. Bazile, January 1965 opinion, in case file of *Loving v. Commonwealth* (Record No. 6163), Virginia Law Library, Richmond, Va.

2. Alfred Avins, "Anti-Miscegenation Laws and the Fourteenth Amendment: The Original Intent," *Virginia Law Review* 7 (November 1966): 1224, 1255.

3. Walter Wadlington, "The *Loving* Case: Virginia's Anti-Miscegenation Statute in Historical Perspective," ibid., 1214, 1223.

4. "Pluralism Preferred," *Christian Century*, July 5, 1967, 859, 860.

5. "Freedom of Choice at the Altar," *Norfolk Journal and Guide*, June 17, 1967.

6. "A Unanimous Court," *Norfolk Virginian-Pilot*, June 13, 1967, 14.

7. "Wedlock: A 'Fundamental Freedom,' " *Roanoke Times*, June 14, 1967, 6.

8. "The Inevitable," *Richmond News Leader*, June 14, 1967, 6.

9. *Hearings on the Nomination of Thurgood Marshall, of New York, to Be an Associate Justice of the Supreme Court of the United States*, 90th Cong.,1st sess. (Washington, DC: Government Printing Office, 1967), 175.

10. "Anti-Miscegenation Statutes: Repugnant Indeed," *Time*, June 16, 1967, 45–46.

11. *Davis v. Gately*, 269 F.Supp. 996, 997, 998, 999 (1967).

12. *Dick v. Reaves*, 434 P.2d 295, 297, 298 (1967).

13. Brief for Richard John Baker and James Michael McConnell, case file of *Baker v. Nelson*, in the Minnesota State Law Library, Saint Paul, 62, 63, 73, 74.

14. *Baker v. Nelson*, 291 Minn. 310, at 314–315 (1970).

15. *Goodridge v. Department of Public Health*, 440 Mass. 309, at 325, 326, 327–328 (2003).

Tinker v. Des Moines Independent Community School District

John W. Johnson

Tinker v. Des Moines Independent Community School District
393 U.S. 503 (1969)

DECIDED: February 24, 1969
VOTE

CONCURRING: 7 (Earl Warren, William O. Douglas, William J. Brennan Jr., Potter Stewart, Byron R. White, Abe Fortas, Thurgood Marshall)
DISSENTING: 2 (Hugo L. Black, John Marshall Harlan (II))
OPINION OF THE COURT: Fortas
CONCURRING OPINION: Stewart
CONCURRING OPINION: White
DISSENTING OPINION: Black
DISSENTING OPINION: Harlan

The first big American protest against the war in Vietnam took place in Washington, D.C., in November 1965. Among the several thousand demonstrators marching and listening to speeches in the nation's capital over the Thanksgiving holiday was a contingent of about fifty Iowans, who, on the bus ride home, discussed how to best witness in their home communities the spirit of nonviolent objection to the American military presence in Southeast Asia. One course of action they settled upon was to encourage high school and college students who had strong feelings about the propriety of the conflict to express those concerns by wearing black armbands to their classes on predetermined dates the following month.

School administrators in Des Moines, Iowa's capital and its largest city, caught wind of this plan and hastily passed a resolution forbidding students from wearing black armbands to the city's schools to express their sentiments about the war. Defying the board's decree, a few dozen of the city's 18,000 public school students wore black armbands on the agreed upon dates—December 16 and 17, 1965. Among those sent home or suspended for defying the school board were sophomores Christopher Eckhardt and John Tinker, and John's eighth-grade sister, Mary Beth. The Tinkers and young Eckhardt maintained that they had put on the armbands not to protest the war *per se* but to express their sorrow for its casualties—Vietnamese as well as Americans—and in support of the idea of extending the anticipated Christmas truce to allow for the conduct of peace talks.

The suspensions sparked a public furor in Des Moines and other parts of Iowa. On the one hand, some Iowans were angry at the temerity of the students for defying a school rule; on the other, some were indignant at what they saw as the chilling impact on free expression resulting from the school district's ban. Two stormy school board meetings took place over the 1965-1966 Christmas holidays. At the second, a divided board upheld the suspensions but agreed to permit the students to return to school provided they did so without black armbands. Retaining the support of the Iowa Civil Liberties Union (ICLU) and a young lawyer named Dan Johnston, the students and their parents elected to challenge the legality of the suspensions in court. Pending a legal resolution, however, the students returned to classes without armbands on their sleeves.

Among the arguments raised in federal district court by Johnston and the ICLU was that the school board, acting in its capacity as an agent of state government, had denied the students their First Amendment right of free symbolic expression by prohibiting the armbands. The board's attorneys countered that school administrators were well within their rights to prohibit the armbands to preserve discipline and order in the classroom. The school board prevailed at the district court and appellate court levels, but the

Mary Beth Tinker and her brother, John, were suspended from their Des Moines, Iowa, high school for wearing black armbands to protest the Vietnam War. In *Tinker v. Des Moines* (1969), the Supreme Court ruled that the suspensions violated the students' First Amendment rights. — The Granger Collection, New York

Tinkers and Eckhardt succeeded in convincing the U.S. Supreme Court to accept review of the lower court decisions. While the case was working its way through the courts in the 1966-1968 period, escalation of the Vietnam War touched off hundreds of student protests—many of them quite violent—at colleges and universities around the country. The week before oral argument before the Court, the nation elected Richard Nixon to the presidency in one of the most divisive electoral contests in the twentieth century.

OPINIONS IN *TINKER*

The Supreme Court's decision in *Tinker v. Des Moines*, handed down February 24, 1969, found in favor of the students by a 7-2 margin. The opinion of the Court, written by Justice Fortas, held for the first time in American history that the protections of the Bill of Rights extended to students. Distinguishing the polite, silent wearing of armbands in the Des Moines public schools from the raucous protests at a number of American institutions of higher learning, Fortas ruled that students possess the right to free expression, symbolic or literal, provided that their actions are "not substantially disruptive" of the educational process:

> First Amendment rights, applied in light of the special characteristics of the school environment, are available to teachers and students. It can hardly be argued that either students or teachers shed their constitutional rights to freedom of speech or expression at the schoolhouse gate.[1]

Justice Fortas continued with a reminder that free speech often involves risk:

> The problem presented by the present case does not relate to regulation of the length of skirts or the type of clothing, to hair style or deportment. . . . It does not concern

aggressive, disruptive action or even group demonstrations. Our problem involves direct, primary First Amendment rights akin to "pure speech." The school officials banned and sought to punish petitioners for a silent, passive expression of opinion, unaccompanied by any disorder or disturbance on the part of petitioners. There is here no evidence whatever of petitioners' interference, actual or nascent, with the school's work or of collision with the rights of other students to be secure and to be let alone. Accordingly, this case does not concern speech or action that intrudes upon the work of the school or the rights of other students. . . .

The District Court concluded that the action of the school authorities was reasonable because it was based upon their fear of a disturbance from the wearing of the armbands. But, in our system, undifferentiated fear or apprehension of disturbance is not enough to overcome the right to freedom of expression. Any departure from absolute regimentation may cause trouble. Any variation from the majority's opinion may inspire fear. Any word spoken, in class, in the lunchroom or on the campus, that deviates from the views of another person, may start an argument or cause a disturbance. But our Constitution says we must take this risk . . . ; and our history says that it is this sort of hazardous freedom—this kind of openness—that is the basis of our national strength and of the independence and vigor of Americans who grow up and live in this relatively permissive, often disputatious, society.

In order for the State in the person of school officials to justify prohibition of a particular expression of opinion, it must be able to show that its action was caused by something more than a mere desire to avoid the discomfort and unpleasantness that always accompany an unpopular viewpoint. Certainly where there is no finding and no showing that the exercise of the forbidden right would "materially and substantially interfere with the requirements of appropriate discipline in the operation of the school," the prohibition cannot be sustained.[2]

Justice Black, the Court's most senior member, filed an angry dissent. Black declared that the act of wearing armbands in the Des Moines schools in 1965 was, in fact, unsettling to the educational process and that proper adolescent behavior in the schools should be governed by the admonition "children should be seen and not heard." Black wrote:

I think the record overwhelmingly shows that the armbands did exactly what the elected school officials and principals foresaw it would, that is, took the students' minds off their classwork and diverted them to thoughts about the highly emotional subject of the Vietnam war. And I repeat that if the time has come when pupils of state-supported schools . . . can defy and flaunt orders of school officials to keep their minds on their own school work, it is the beginning of a new revolutionary era of permissiveness in their country fostered by the judiciary.[3]

Justice Black then pointed out what children should be doing in school:

The original idea of schools, which I do not believe is yet abandoned as worthless or out of date, was that children had not yet reached the point of experience and wisdom which enabled them to teach all of their elders. It may be that the Nation has outworn the old-fashioned slogan that "children are to be seen not heard," but one may, I hope, be permitted to harbor the thought that taxpayers send children to school on the premise that at their age they need to learn, not teach.[4]

Black expressed his dismay at the Court's giving license to future misbehavior by students:

One does not need to be a prophet or the son of a prophet to know that after the Court's holding today that some students in Iowa schools and indeed in all schools will be ready, able, and willing to defy their teachers on practically all orders. This is the more unfortunate for the schools since groups of students all over the land are already running loose, conducting break-ins, sit-ins, lie-ins, and smash-ins. Many of these student groups . . . have already engaged in rioting, property seizures and destruction. . . . It is no answer to say that the particular students here have not yet reached such high points in their demands to attend classes in order to exercise their political pressures. Turned loose with law suits for damages and injunctions against their teachers like they are here, it is nothing but wishful thinking to imagine that young, immature students will not soon believe it is their right to control the schools rather than the right of the States that collect the taxes to hire the teachers for the benefit of the pupils. This case, therefore, wholly without constitutional reasons in my judgment, subjects all the public schools in the country to the whims and caprices of their loudest-mouthed, but maybe not their brightest, students. . . . I wish, therefore, wholly to disclaim any purpose on my part, to hold that the Federal Constitution compels the teachers, parents, and elected school officials to surrender control of the American public school system to public school students.[5]

THOSE CLOSEST TO THE CASE REACT

While Court watchers and constitutional experts divided along the judicial fault lines identified by Fortas and Black, the principals and their attorneys in *Tinker v. Des Moines,* also reacted to the Court's decision. Mary Beth Tinker, in a piece she wrote a few weeks after the decision, spoke for herself and her brother:

> We are often asked our reaction to the case and to the recent decision of the Supreme Court. . . . [O]ur reaction at this time is no more important than the reaction of any other person. We happen to have started the spark to get the case going, but now it is in the hands of the people. . . . [T]he "movement" in this country has progressed beyond black armbands. People are thinking that the Vietnam war is just one bad product of a basically corrupt society. People are not content to mourn silently for Vietnam's dead. They want to act in a way that will get to the basis of a government that would carry on such a war, a government that drafts boys to fight and die unwillingly in it, and that starves its poor to pay for it.[6]

John Tinker added:

> This decision has come at a time when many Americans are afraid of students. . . . It is ironic . . . that they should think that by claiming certain rights we were in some way destructive of the educational system. . . . If school systems cannot . . . provide students with the rights to which they are entitled, then they will be changed, and should be. . . . The Armband Case should provide a . . . springboard for further student rights. I believe that this is in the best interest of our country and of the democratic system as a whole.[7]

Justice Black had predicted near the end of his dissenting opinion in Tinker that the majority ruling in the case would usher in an "era of permissiveness" in the country. In response to that, Christopher Eckhardt's father, William Eckhardt, retorted: "Let's hope so! Without permissiveness, democracy is a word without meaning."[8]

Dan Johnston, the attorney for the Tinkers and Eckhardt, was working in his Des Moines law office when he learned of the Supreme Court's decision in his clients' favor. He later recalled his initial reaction as being "satisfaction but not surprise." He believed he "had an excellent chance to win the armband case from the very beginning." At the time of the oral argument he knew that he was not going to obtain Justice Black's vote, but the vehemence of Black's dissent was, nevertheless, distressing.[9]

In the late 1960s Edgar Bittle was a young attorney with the Des Moines law firm of Herrick, Langdon, Sandblom, and Belin. The senior partner, Alan Herrick, spearheaded the firm's handling of the *Tinker* case for the school board throughout the proceedings, and Bittle assisted him. He recalled Herrick being upset with the Supreme Court opinion for not recognizing the degree of disturbances that the armbands had set off in the Des Moines schools. Although Bittle was also disappointed with the majority ruling in the case, he acknowledged that it served to prod the Des Moines school district to move in the "right direction" by encouraging it to craft realistic disciplinary policies.[10]

PRESS REACTIONS TO *TINKER*

Tinker v. Des Moines attracted a substantial degree of attention from the press. The *New York Times* fully approved of the ruling, noting in an editorial:

> In a fascinating decision, Justice Fortas—speaking for the 7 to 2 majority—said in effect that the Court is not going to worry about or interfere with disciplinary rules and trivia such as hair length, clean ears, blue jeans or miniskirts. But the Court definitely intends to protect legitimate protest—by armband, button, or placard—as part of the general right of freedom of expression. . . . Justice Fortas cut through a forest of extraneous matter in placing these students within the First Amendment. . . . The majority of justices felt—we think, rightly—that a line could and should be drawn between free expression and disorderly excess. A close reading of the facts and decision shows that there is no license given here to riot, to interfere with classroom work, or to substitute the Court for the thousands of school boards. Freedom of expression—in an open manner by those holding minority or unpopular views—is part of the vigor and strength of our schools and society. So long as it does not obstruct the right of others in the class.[11]

A local newspaper, the *Des Moines Register,* also applauded and considered the school board's claims that it would no longer have disciplinary authority to be a gross exaggeration:

> Justice Black's prediction that the ruling will encourage students to defy their teachers "on practically all orders" probably will make school administrators nervous as they envision students politicking and demonstrating in school classrooms and corridors. But there is nothing in the ruling that gives sanction to disorderly or obstructive behavior. The ruling does not tie the hands of school authorities in the face of breaches of discipline or conduct likely to cause trouble in the schools. The Des Moines armband case would not have arisen if authorities hadn't panicked and over-reacted to plans by a handful of youngsters to show up in school with some black cloth on their arms. The Supreme Court ruling is an admonition to school officials that panic is no substitute for calm judgment and common sense when free speech is at stake. The ruling is important notice also to students that disruptive conduct in the schools has no claim to protection under the Constitution.[12]

Despite his paper's approval of the ruling, *New York Times* columnist Fred Graham, who often wrote critically of the Warren Court's activism, believed that "despite efforts by Justice Fortas to confine the ruling to narrow limits, . . . [the majority opinion] may make it more difficult for public schools to censor student publications or to purge school libraries or curriculums of 'objectionable' materials. Principals and deans may also encounter legal difficulty when they attempt to discipline student protesters."[13]

Ronald Ostrow, a columnist for the *Des Moines Register,* seemed to be trying to reassure readers that the Court had not given high school students a license to behave like the protesters at the nation's riot-torn universities:

> The recent Supreme Court decision upholding the right of a few Des Moines students to silently protest the Vietnam war sounded, at the same time, a clear warning for college demonstrators. In essence, the warning was that the court does not sanction interfering with classwork or engaging in substantial disorder or injuring the rights of others. The court seems to have clearly warned students guilty of any such practices that it will not upset actions by university officials suspending or expelling them—and perhaps will even agree to more stringent crackdowns by law enforcement officials. . . . Four times in the opinion by Justice Abe Fortas, the court went out of its way to point out, in effect, that a school in Des Moines was no Berkeley, no Columbia, no San Francisco State College. The stress clearly was on orderly, non-disruptive protest.[14]

A syndicated columnist for the paper was far less sanguine than Ostrow. Instead, he took his cue from Justice Black's dissent about the harmful effects that the majority opinion would have on the ability of school authorities to maintain the orderly environment necessary for learning:

> The high court has sent tremors running through the educational system by its dictum that symbolic free speech may emerge from the mouths of babes at school, the school board and Justice Hugo Black to the contrary notwithstanding. The Good Schoolkeeping stamp of approval was placed by the court on the wearing to class in Des Moines of black armbands four years ago by children . . . protesting the Vietnam war. . . . There is little question about the court majority's intent. It was to define the right of free expression by students of whatever age on the playground, the cafeteria, the campus and even the classroom, and then to set the bounds of that expression as a guide for the courts and school authorities in determining where the student protest movement can begin and where it must stop. Where it can begin is so broad and where it must stop is so vague that Justice Black, in outraged dissent, is probably right that the protest movement has been turned loose to try to run the schools and colleges—with the threat of lawsuits for damages and injunctions against teachers and school authorities.[15]

LETTERS TO THE COURT

The decision in *Tinker* prompted ordinary citizens to write letters to the Supreme Court. Found in the private papers of the justices, such letters constitute a repository of raw public reaction to a high profile decision. A few of the letters on *Tinker* were addressed to Justice Fortas. One letter read:

> Hon. Abe Fortas.
>
> Sir: I have completed the reading of your opinion in . . . *Tinker v. Des Moines.* . . . While no one can reasonably, under ordinary circumstances, be opposed to the wearing of black arm bands in the school setting, it seems to me that the breadth of your opinion raises some grave questions, indeed. . . . I must ask with utmost sincerity whether the schools are now, in the light of your decision and interpretation, to be used as propaganda organs for any and all organizations who are able to gain even one disciple among our student body who will distribute their sometimes corrosive literature.[16]

A letter from an individual possessing some professional expertise with children questioned the wisdom of the decision:

Dear Justice Fortas,

I read the newspaper accounts of the Supreme Court's decision to find [your approval of] permissible "silent, passive expressions of opinion" by school children in the classroom. I am amazed at the poor judgement of the court in entering this area. It would seem to me that if the court had any confidence at all in the mother-wisdom of a nation it would have remained silent on this point. . . . As executive director of a children's agency I however feel very strongly that the shades and nuances of a child's interaction with his teacher are far better left alone. . . . Heaven knows that I would not support a tyrannical teacher, but once the implication is there that the teacher does not have adequate authority, any red blooded child is tempted to take advantage of this. . . . The Supreme Court seems to forget that both the rights and the responsibilities of children are different from those of adults.[17]

By far the largest number of communications on *Tinker* were mailed to Justice Black, whose dissent clearly resonated with the public. Most of the letters were critical of the majority decision and endorsed Justice Black's dissent:

The Honorable Hugo L. Black.

My dear Mr. Justice,

Please allow me to express my appreciation for, and my complete concurrence with, your dissent concerning the recent ruling of the Court regarding the Iowa school case, as written by Mr. Justice Abe Fortas. Far too many youths today are, to quote an old popular song, "Runnin' Wild." Permissiveness seems to be the name of the game. . . . Speaking of permissiveness, . . . I am old-fashioned enough to believe that a large share of the blame should be laid at the doorstep of the parents. . . . One hears quite a bit about lack of communication between parent and child. I say Hogwash! When I was a youngster, my mother had a very good means of communication. It was called "Hairbrush." And I seldom failed to get the message.[18]

Black also heard from educators:

Dear Justice Black,

We wish to applaud you on your recent dissent delivered to your fellow justices for the decision they rendered in the Des Moines, Iowa school district case forbidding the wearing of black arm bands. Every day we witness this very obvious lack of respect for authority exercised by the young people we come in contact with in our school system and other systems nearby that we are involved with. . . . It makes no difference whether it is a Kindergarten student who refuses to write his name or a college student who says the administration is wrong—they are students and are supposed to be going to school because they do not know everything there is to know. So where do they get off saying they should set the rules, be consulted on what the rules are, or have the right to ignore them? . . . Again we thank you for taking a stand and want you to know there are other people who agree with you and support you.[19]

But not all of Black's correspondents agreed with him:

Dear Justice Black,

I want to express my great displeasure with your dissenting opinion in the case announced yesterday of the high school students who wore black armbands to their

Iowa school. How are we to prepare our young people to become full and responsible citizens if they are not allowed to experience the opportunity to exercise, peacefully, the rights of citizenship? Surely you have not found the button which, when pushed, will turn a person into a conscientious and knowledgeable citizen overnight upon reaching the age of 21. . . . You have, in this dissenting opinion, done a disservice to our country.[20]

One letter writer pointed to Black's reputation as a supporter of First Amendment rights:

Dear Mr. Justice Black,

This evening I had a chance to read your dissenting opinion on . . . *Tinker v. Des Moines*. . . . I was outraged. I had always assumed that a man of your background and reputation of insight and erudition would not be prone to such neanderthal political, social and educational opinions. . . . My thought is that the . . . symbolic protest on the part of the Iowa students is not coequal with those distinctly irrational and militant protests [on college campuses] to which you referred. . . . With your dissenting opinion in this case you are, curiously, opining counter to your own previous record as a civil libertarian.[21]

At least one letter writer promised to take matters into his own (untutored) hands:

To the Judge of the Supreme Court,

You don't have to worry about the laws breaking down. We are organizing a secret club to bring criminals to justise. We won't dress any different but will FIX all trouble makers in our school. Everyone says we are helpless but we know different. . . . P.S. There are 8 of us.[22]

THE LEGAL COMMUNITY RESPONDS

As the first Supreme Court decision extending Bill of Rights protections to students, *Tinker v. Des Moines* caught the eye of the American legal community. Approximately fifteen articles, case notes, and comments on *Tinker* appeared in legal periodicals in the two years following the decision. The writers split about evenly as to whether the Supreme Court had rendered the proper decision. Many of the articles noted that *Tinker* left it up to future courts to determine on a case-by-case basis what student expression meant and in what context it constituted "material and substantial interference" with a school's operation. Other articles emphasized that the opinions in *Tinker* dealt with the protection of political speech and did not concern themselves with student appearance or deportment. Finally, most of the legal commentators could not resist commenting upon Justice Black's diatribe against students choosing to confront authority.

The *Harvard Law Review* clearly approved of the decision:

The *Tinker* Court thought that the first amendment protects a learning process in state schools which is open, vigorous, disputatious, disturbing—a robust dialectic in which error is combatted with reason, not fiat. School authorities may never merely suppress "feelings with which they do not wish to contend," nor may they treat students as "closed-circuit recipients" of the dominant opinions of the community. The Court stressed that personal intercommunication among students outside the classroom is one of the activities to which the schools are dedicated. Noting that exercise of fundamental freedoms often entails risk, the Court said a school may not silence its students simply "to avoid the discomfort and unpleasantness that always accompany an unpopular viewpoint." In short, the Court adopted the view that the process of education in a democracy must be democratic.[23]

Political science professor Theodore Denno enthusiastically applauded the idea that children had rights deserving constitutional protection and that this would be good for society:

> *Tinker* is a pathfinder in that children themselves, claiming the common rights of citizenship within their institutional/legal school environment, have been recognized by our supreme constitutional tribunal as proper subjects for those rights. . . . A society which is too proud to listen to its children, too afraid that they may "disturb" it, is probably a society too afraid to look itself in the eye. During the course of history there was probably precious little difference between Mary Beth Tinker's message of the black armband and the twelve year old boy who spoke to the elders in the temple. This time the men in the black robes got wise. How will it be with the rest of us?[24]

Although a bit more cautious than Denno, attorney Jerry Benezra also thought that *Tinker* sent the right message, although he pointed out that such rights had to be exercised carefully within the context of the classroom. He went on, however, to distance himself from what he saw as Justice Black's myopic view of the schoolroom:

> The *Tinker* Court has "pointed the way" in making it clear to school authorities that they cannot act without due regard for the substantial constitutional rights of the students under their control. To do otherwise now clearly carries with it the possibility of litigation. Likewise the Court has "pointed the way" for students who desire to express their views within the school environment. To arm themselves with constitutional safeguards they must exercise these rights without materially or substantially interfering with the rights of their fellow students, or with the interests of the school authorities in maintaining classroom discipline and decorum. . . .
>
> Justice Black contended that petitioner's armbands would have a deleterious effect on the concentration of fellow students, thereby distracting from that *singleness of purpose* which a state has a right to preserve in its classrooms. By this reasoning, it would appear that every non-conformity may be deemed by its very nature, to be a distraction. . . . Therefore, the practical effect would be to totally deprive the student of his constitutional rights merely because he enters the door of the schoolhouse. However, the import of the *Tinker* decision is that it rejects such deprivation.[25]

On the other hand, both Carl Aspelund, then a law student, and Wake Forest law professor Hugh Divine thought the rationale of *Tinker* was wrong: a school was not a public forum, and by implication students did not enjoy the same rights as adults. Moreover, the *Tinker* majority clearly did not understand the obligations of school authorities. Aspelund wrote:

> It is submitted that the case does establish a bad precedent. School is not the place to wear a badge or emblem that would spark controversy. The state does have a reasonable interest in making sure that classroom order is maintained. A series of arguments about a highly inflammatory subject such as Viet Nam can very easily disrupt the operation of any class.[26]

Divine saw it from the educators' point of view:

> [A] court without professional training should hesitate to reverse an administrator's recommended method of operating his school unless the court is thoroughly convinced that the method is violating a student's constitutional rights. There is no reason for thinking the average judge inherently has the qualifications to take charge of the disciplinary problems of the schools. . . . The disturbing thing about the *Tinker* opinion is not

the result in the specific case, but the lack of indication by the Court of any idea of the problem as seen by the school administrators.[27]

Case Western Reserve law professor Paul Haskell noted that *Tinker* did not give students license to speak and behave improperly; rather, it spread the umbrella of the First Amendment only over traditionally protected speech—that involving political issues.

> The freedom afforded high school students by the *Tinker* decision should be as applicable to such discussion as it is to expression in the field of national social and political issues. Student advocacy of disregard of school rules and procedures and student ridicule of school administrators and teachers, however, are in a different category and are distinguishable from . . . [political speech].[28]

TINKER AS PRECEDENT

The broad language favoring student rights in Justice Fortas's opinion in *Tinker v. Des Moines* was substantially qualified—some would say "undercut"—by Supreme Court decisions rendered in the 1980s. The disjunction between *Tinker* and rulings in two important student rights cases that followed more than a decade later provides an object lesson in the difference between the Warren Court and the Burger and Rehnquist Courts. In the first of these cases, *Bethel School Dist. No. 403 v. Fraser* (1986), a majority upheld a school principal's suspension of a student for employing sexual innuendos in a speech before a school assembly. In the second, *Hazelwood School District v. Kuhlmeier* (1988), the Court sustained the right of a principal to excise from a student newspaper two articles on controversial topics. Strident dissents from holdover members of the Warren Court were filed in both cases.

Compare the majority views in *Fraser* by Chief Justice Burger and in *Hazelwood* by Justice White, with their limited view of student rights, and the respective dissents by Justices Marshall and Brennan, with the underlying philosophy of *Tinker*.

In *Fraser*, Chief Justice Burger wrote:

> This Court acknowledged in *Tinker v. Des Moines* . . . that students do not "shed their constitutional rights to freedom of speech or expression at the schoolhouse gate." . . . The marked distinction between the political "message" of the armbands in *Tinker* and the sexual content of respondent's speech in this case seems to have been given little weight by the Court of Appeals. In upholding the students' right to engage in a nondisruptive, passive expression of a political viewpoint in *Tinker,* this Court was careful to note that the case did "not concern speech or action that intrudes upon the work of the schools or the rights of other students." It is against this background that we turn to consider the level of First Amendment protection accorded to . . . utterances and actions before an official high school assembly attended by 600 students. . . . We hold that petitioner School District acted entirely within its permissible authority in imposing sanctions in response to his [Fraser's] offensively lewd and indecent speech. Unlike the sanctions . . . imposed on the students wearing armbands in *Tinker,* the penalties imposed in this case were unrelated to any political viewpoint. The First Amendment does not prevent the school officials from determining that to permit a vulgar and lewd speech such as respondent's would undermine the school's basic educational mission. . . . Justice Black, dissenting in *Tinker,* made a point that is especially relevant in this case: "I wish therefore, . . . to disclaim any purpose . . . to hold that the Federal Constitution compels the teachers, parents, and elected school officials to surrender control of the American public school system to public school students." [29]

Justice Marshall wrote:

> I dissent from the Court's decision . . . because in my view the School District failed to demonstrate that respondent's remarks were indeed disruptive. The District Court and Court of Appeals conscientiously applied *Tinker v. Des Moines* . . . and concluded that the School District had not demonstrated any disruption of the educational process. I recognize that the school administration must be given wide latitude to determine what forms of conduct are inconsistent with the school's educational mission; nevertheless, where speech is involved, we may not unquestioningly accept a teacher's or administrator's assertion that certain pure speech interfered with education. Here the School District, despite a clear opportunity to do so, failed to bring in evidence sufficient to convince either of the two lower courts that education at Bethel School was disrupted by respondent's speech. I therefore see no reason to disturb the Court of Appeals' judgment.[30]

Writing for the Court in *Hazelwood School District v. Kuhlmeier,* Justice White distinguished between this case and *Tinker:*

> The question whether the First Amendment requires a school to tolerate particular student speech—the question that we addressed in *Tinker*—is different from the question whether the First Amendment requires a school affirmatively to promote particular student speech. The former question addresses educators' ability to silence a student's personal expression that happens to occur on the school premises. The latter question concerns educators' authority over school-sponsored publications, theatrical productions, and other expressive activities that students, parents, and members of the public might reasonably perceive to bear the imprimatur of the school. . . . A school must be able to set high standards for the student speech that is disseminated under its auspices—standards that may be higher than those demanded by some newspaper publishers or theatrical producers in the "real" world—and may refuse to disseminate student speech that does not meet those standards. In addition, a school must be able to take into account the emotional maturity of the intended audience in determining whether to disseminate student speech on potentially sensitive topics. . . . Accordingly, we conclude that the standard articulated in *Tinker* for determining when a school may punish student expression need not also be the standard for determining when a school may refuse to lend its name and resources to the dissemination of student expression. Instead, we hold that educators do not offend the First Amendment by exercising editorial control over the style and content of student speech in school-sponsored expressive activities so long as their actions are reasonably related to legitimate pedagogical concerns.[31]

Justice Brennan, in dissent in *Kuhlmeier,* wrote:

> In *Tinker,* this Court struck the balance. We held that official censorship of student expression—there the suspension of several students until they removed their armbands protesting the Vietnam war—is unconstitutional unless the speech "materially disrupts classwork or involves substantial disorder or invasion of the rights of others . . . ." School officials may not suppress "silent, passive expression of opinion, unaccompanied by any disorder or disturbance on the part of" the speaker. . . . This Court applied the *Tinker* test just a Term ago . . . , upholding an official decision to discipline a student for delivering a lewd speech in support of a student-government candidate. The Court today

casts no doubt on *Tinker*'s vitality. Instead it erects a taxonomy of school censorship, concluding that *Tinker* applies to one category and not another. On the one hand is censorship "to silence a student's personal expression that happens to occur on the school premises." On the other hand is censorship of expression that arises in the context of "school-sponsored . . . expressive activities that students, parents, and members of the public might reasonably perceive to bear the imprimatur of the school." The Court does not, for it cannot, purport to discern from our precedents the distinction it creates. . . . Even if we were writing on a clean slate, I would reject the Court's rationale for abandoning *Tinker* in this case.[32]

CONCLUSION

In retrospect, *Tinker v. Des Moines* can be characterized as the last gasp of the liberal, activist Warren Court. Fortas resigned under an ethical cloud unrelated to this case a few months after delivering the opinion in *Tinker,* and Chief Justice Warren retired in the summer of 1969. In the years following, the Burger and Rehnquist Courts substantially modified the *Tinker* precedent. Nevertheless, *Tinker* remains the country's leading judicial decision on the constitutional rights of students.

The Court has not rendered a major student rights decisions since *Kuhlmeier.* Given, however, several distressing episodes of violence in American schools in the 1990s—climaxed by the student killings in Columbine, Colorado, in April 1999—civil liberties groups of late have reported little tolerance for student symbolic expression of any form. Black armbands in 1965 now appear quaint; black trench coats strike parents, school officials, and judges as ominous and threatening.

NOTES

1. *Tinker v. Des Moines,* 393 U.S. 503, at 506 (1969).
2. Ibid., at 508–509.
3. Ibid., at 518.
4. Ibid., at 522.
5. Ibid., at 525–526.
6. Mary Beth Tinker, "The Case of the Black Armbands," *Youth* 20, no. 8, April 20, 1969, 21–22.
7. Ibid., 21.
8. William Eckhardt, "The Black Arm Band Story," *Journal of Human Relations* 17 (1969): 510.
9. Dan Johnston, interview by author, May 17, 1994.
10. Edgar Bittle, interview by author, April 29, 1994.
11. "Armbands Yes, Miniskirts No," *New York Times,* February 27, 1969.
12. "The Armband Case," *Des Moines Register,* February 27, 1969.
13. Fred P. Graham, "High Court Upholds a Student Protest," *New York Times,* February 25, 1969.
14. Ronald J. Ostrow, "Campus Rioters Warned By Court in D.M. Ruling," *Des Moines Register,* February 26, 1969.
15. Richard Wilson, "Fears Armband Decision Opens Way for Students to Disrupt Education," *Des Moines Register,* March 4, 1969.
16. Edwin Schneider to Abe Fortas, March 25, 1969, Hugo Black Papers, Manuscript Division, Library of Congress, Washington, D.C.
17. G. Lewis Penner to Fortas, February 27, 1969, ibid.
18. Arthur V. Watkins to Hugo L. Black, February 28, 1969, ibid.
19. Jesse E. Walters and 24 other school staff to Black, February 27. 1969, ibid.
20. David M. Peterson to Black, February 26, 1969, ibid.
21. James Meyer to Black, February 4, 1970, ibid.
22. Anonymous to Black, n.d., ibid.
23. "The Supreme Court, 1968 Term," *Harvard Law Review* 83 (1969): 159.

24. Theodore F. Denno, "Mary Beth Tinker Takes the Constitution to School," *Fordham Law Review* 38 (October 1969): 35–36, 62.

25. Jerry E. Benezra, "Constitutional Law—Freedom of Expression—*Tinker v. Des Moines, . . .*" *Suffolk University Law Review* 4 (Fall 1969): 175, 173 (emphasis in original).

26. Carl L. Aspelund, "Constitutional Law—Free Speech Rights of School Children," *Loyola Law Review* 16 (1969–1970): 176.

27. Hugh W. Divine, "A Note on *Tinker,*" *Wake Forest Law Review* 7 (October 1971): 543–544.

28. Paul G. Haskell, "Student Expression in the Public Schools: *Tinker* Distinguished," *Georgetown Law Journal* 59 (October 1970): 52.

29. *Bethel School Dist. No. 403 v. Fraser,* 478 U.S. 675, at 680–681, 685–686 (1986).

30. Ibid., at 690.

31. *Hazelwood School District v. Kuhlmeier,* 484 U.S. 260, at 270–273 (1988).

32. Ibid., at 280–283.

Wisconsin v. Yoder

Shawn Francis Peters

Wisconsin v. Yoder
406 U.S. 205 (1972)

> DECIDED: May 22, 1972
> VOTE
> > CONCURRING: 6 (Warren Burger, William J. Brennan Jr., Potter Stewart, Byron R. White, Thurgood Marshall, Harry A. Blackmun)
> > DISSENTING: 1 (William O. Douglas)
>
> OPINION OF THE COURT: Burger
> CONCURRING OPINION: Stewart (Brennan)
> CONCURRING OPINION: White (Brennan, Stewart)
> DISSENTING OPINION: Douglas
> DID NOT PARTICIPATE: Lewis F. Powell Jr., William H. Rehnquist

In the fall of 1968, authorities in New Glarus, Wisconsin, charged three Amish fathers—Wallace Miller, Jonas Yoder, and Adin Yutzy—with violating Wisconsin's compulsory school attendance statute, which required all children to attend school until they reached the age of sixteen. The district attorney alleged that the three Amish farmers had broken the law because, in keeping with their faith's traditions, they had removed their children from school once they turned fourteen.

William Ball, the attorney who defended the Amish, argued that application of the school attendance statute to the Amish violated their right to the free exercise of religion. To comply with the law, he claimed, the Amish would have to forsake their religious beliefs, which included a proscription against school attendance beyond the age of fourteen. Ball asserted that the First Amendment clearly protected the Amish from being forced to sacrifice their religious freedom. An argument focusing on parental rights formed the second prong of Ball's defense strategy. He claimed that the state's action was unconstitutional because it violated the right of the Amish defendants to direct the upbringing of their children. Ball insisted that two U.S. Supreme Court opinions supported the claims of the Amish in the Wisconsin school attendance case. The Court's opinion in *Sherbert v. Verner* (1963) provided strong judicial safeguards for religious liberty, and its ruling in *Pierce v. Society of Sisters* (1925) furnished stout protections for the rights of parents.

But not all judicial precedent favored Ball and his clients. Throughout the New Glarus case, the state of Wisconsin pointed out that Amish parents living in other states had made similar challenges to the constitutionality of school attendance laws, and they had lost each time. The state also referred to language in several U.S. Supreme Court opinions that explicitly acknowledged its right to enforce education regulations, including statutes mandating school attendance. Some of these passages appeared in the same opinions that defense attorney Ball cited to bolster his arguments in favor of the Amish.

Ball attempted to refute the state's claims by mounting an exhaustive defense. He brought in expert witnesses from as far away as Philadelphia to testify on behalf of his clients. Their ranks included Temple University's John Hostetler, the nation's leading scholarly authority on the Amish, and an expert on public school regulation from the University of Chicago. Although the state's case was far less impressive (Hostetler's testimony alone lasted longer), a judge found the three Amish men guilty of a misdemeanor and ordered them to pay a token fine of five dollars. Ball and the New Glarus Amish had better luck when they appealed *Wisconsin v. Yoder* to the Wisconsin Supreme Court in 1971. With only one justice dissenting, it reversed the convictions of Miller, Yoder, and Yutzy.

The state of Wisconsin appealed this decision to the U.S. Supreme Court, which handed down its ruling in *Wisconsin v. Yoder* on May 15, 1972. Citing the protections of religious liberty conferred by the First and Fourteenth Amendments, the justices affirmed the lower court's ruling in favor of Miller, Yoder, and Yutzy. The application of the compulsory attendance law to the New Glarus Amish was unconstitutional, Chief Justice Warren Burger wrote in the Court's majority opinion, in part because the record of the case amply demonstrated that its impact on their religious liberty was "not only severe, but inescapable, for the Wisconsin law affirmatively compels them, under threat of criminal sanction, to perform acts undeniably at odds with fundamental tenets of their religious beliefs."

Many observers have lauded Chief Justice Burger's opinion in *Wisconsin v. Yoder* as a signal moment for religious liberty. But some critics have insisted that the Court botched the case. A legion of scholarly observers has argued that the justices plainly flouted the First Amendment's establishment clause by conferring special judicial protections on members of a single religious faith. Others have concluded that the Court, by focusing its attention on shielding the religious liberty of the Amish parents, neglected the interests of those most affected by the outcome of the case—Amish children. The majority's chief critic on this score was Justice Douglas, who wrote a customarily withering partial dissent in *Yoder.* (He agreed with the Court's holding only as it applied to Jonas Yoder, whose daughter Freida was the only child to testify at the fathers' trial.) Burger's majority opinion focused on the rights of parents, but Douglas emphasized that "children themselves have constitutionally protected interests." Burger had ignored these interests, Douglas groused, by focusing so much attention on protecting the parents' religious liberty.

It is perhaps a testament to *Yoder's* complexity that debates over its merits have continued long after the opinion lost much of its vitality as judicial precedent. After chipping away at it for several years, the Supreme Court essentially demolished *Yoder's* religious liberty holding in its controversial opinion in *Employment Division of Oregon v. Smith* (1990) (see page 341). Although the justices distinguished this ruling from *Yoder,* noting that the Amish case involved parental rights as well as religious liberty, *Smith* nevertheless sharply restricted protections for religious practice.

INITIAL REACTIONS

Perhaps the most intriguing responses to the outcome of *Wisconsin v. Yoder* came from the people whose liberties had been at stake in the case—the Amish themselves. Although the defendants expressed some satisfaction that their side had prevailed in the case, they also showed some ambivalence about their participation in it. Indeed, Jonas Yoder, the lead defendant, seemed almost anguished. "I feel that we had a miracle made for us, and I don't feel like making words. I'm really glad to have it over with. It was a long struggle. . . . I wish it had been anybody else. I don't feel [it] was worth it." For his part, Wallace Miller, another Amish defendant in *Yoder,* seemed relatively unconcerned about the case's outcome. "I'm glad it went our way. I thought it might—I hoped it would, that is. I wasn't worried about it. I figured we'd take what came."[1]

Others who had been involved in the winning side of the case, however, were more enthusiastic about the outcome. Thomas Eckerle, a Wisconsin attorney who had helped Amish defendants, seemed pleased that the justices had ruled in favor of his clients:

> I'm delighted. It seemed to me to boil down to some good, decent people who wanted to follow their conscience. It's just a matter of simple religious freedom. There are a lot of other overtones and ramifications to the case, but they all pale next to the religious freedom issue.[2]

Acting under the aegis of the National Committee for Amish Religious Freedom, a coalition of religious leaders, academics, and civil libertarians also had helped shepherd the case through the courts. The organization's leader, William Lindholm, gave the ruling high marks. "Needless to say, we are tremendously happy on behalf of these people who have been persecuted for these last two decades," he said. "Basically, it is a victory for religious freedom."[3]

Hostetler echoed the praise voiced by Eckerle and Lindholm:

> The decision of the Supreme Court, upholding the right of the Amish to train their own children on completing eight years of schooling, finally puts an end to the years of harassment the Amish have suffered in one state or another. No longer must they choose between criminal sanctions on the one hand and abandoning their religious practices and view of education which sustains their community on the other. This landmark decision will force many educators to take a fresh look at the education of minority groups. Something has been seriously wrong with our public policy and the education of our minority groups. At issue was not learning the basic skills, but basic values. When culturally different children attend a school that teaches an unattainable identity, an identity that would demand the rejection of the values of the home, of parents, the tribe, or the street, and even the color of their skin, what can be expected but alienation and rebellion? Public policy in this country has operated on the "melting pot" theory—molding immigrant peoples to be exactly like one another—thus obliterating cultural differences. With the Court's decision, there is now protection against the coercive powers of the state to obliterate cultural differences of no harm to anyone.[4]

Understandably, the losers in *Wisconsin v. Yoder* were not quite as enthusiastic about its outcome. William Kahl, Wisconsin's superintendent of public instruction, seemed unsure about the long-term significance of the decision, declaring, "We don't know what the wider implications of the decision are."

Although Russell Monroe, the superintendent of schools in New Glarus, appeared to share some of Kahl's uncertainty about the impact of the decision, he saw a silver lining in the triumph of the Amish. The decision, he maintained, "will have very little immediate impact on the school district. But the long-range effect on Wisconsin and the country may be great. At least our truancy officers will be able to quit making reports on them."[5]

In the days following the opinion's announcement, others with an interest in the case weighed in with their own appraisals. Many of these assessments were positive. E. Harold Hallows, chief justice of the Wisconsin Supreme Court, seemed elated that his lower court ruling had been upheld. "It's wonderful. This is a very important case in this area. You've got a clash between what the state thinks should be compulsory education and a parent's conscience."[6]

Marvin Karpatkin, general counsel for the American Civil Liberties Union (ACLU), also praised the ruling:

> The decision goes to a greater length than ever before in extending the constitutional umbrella over the heterogeneity of American religious impulses. Prior decisions of lower courts had held against the Amish in school cases, and against other sects and individuals involved in other legal confrontations, on the questionable distinction between "beliefs" and "actions." The distinction has its origins in a 92-year old Supreme Court decision that affirmed a polygamy conviction of a Utah Territory Mormon. Without any citation of precedent other than a statute of King James I—which made polygamy a capital offense—the Supreme Court dismissed the defense that polygamy was a basic tenet of the Mormon religion and opined that while laws cannot interfere with religious beliefs, they may interfere with religious practices. Now that the "belief"-"action" dichotomy has been swept away, many other religious practices may receive constitutional protection.[7]

A group of Amish children return from school near Intercourse, Pennsylvania, in 1999. In *Wisconsin v. Yoder* (1972), the Supreme Court found in favor of three Amish families who claimed that their rights were violated by Wisconsin's requirement that children be enrolled in school until the age of sixteen. The parents were convicted of violating the law when they removed their children from school after they had completed the eighth grade.—AP Wide World Photos/Rusty Kennedy

PRESS RESPONSES

Throughout 1972 and 1973, writers in a number of mainstream newspapers and periodicals commented on the Supreme Court's decision in *Yoder,* and the decision also served as the topic of several articles in law reviews. These critical assessments were mixed at best. Some observers, such as conservative columnist Russell Kirk, not only lauded the *Yoder* decision as a notable moment for religious liberty but also voiced hope that its protections could be extended to members of other minority groups who bristled at state regulation.

> Praise be, the Old Order Amish won't have to migrate to Brazil. For the Supreme Court of these United States, . . . has declared that a state government has no right to compel Amish children to attend public schools. . . .
>
> [The Court has] upheld the decision of Wisconsin's supreme court "that although education is a subject within the constitutional power of a state to regulate, there is no such a compelling interest in two years' high-school compulsory education as will justify the burden it places upon the [Amish] appellants' free exercise of their religion." So the Old Order Amish, after decades of tribulation, at least are emancipated from the tyranny of truant officers. But what of other parents who object strenuously to being compelled

to send their children to public schools? The Supreme Court's decision in Wisconsin v. Yoder applies only to the Amish and, by reasonable extension, to such other close-knit religious sects as protest on principle against having their children secularized and forcibly integrated into the schools of *technos* that would make the children so many tiny identical factors in an enormous producer-consumer equation. Must everybody else submit to educational dragooning?[8]

The Catholic journal *America* also hinted that members of other faiths might benefit from the Court's opinion in *Yoder.*

> The case is significant because it reassuringly demonstrates that American democratic society battered and ambiguous as it may be, can still mobilize within its constitutional framework the resources for checking powerful, unimaginative bureaucracies. Since the Amish, a tiny minority of self-reliant, unworldly farming people, refuse to litigate, a national coalition of lawyers, educators and clergymen took up their cause and won it. In the bleak spring of 1972, this is one piece of cheerful news. The decision itself is significant because the Court has judged that when the principle of religious freedom conflicts with another principle such as the state's right to regulate education, religious freedom should, as the greater value, be given primacy. This is a point, incidentally, that defenders of government aid for church-related schools have urged within the context of a clash between religious freedom and the no-establishment clause.[9]

Newspapers generally praised the decision. In Eau Claire, Wisconsin, for example, the *Leader-Telegram* endorsed Chief Justice Burger's majority opinion.

> In what is certain to be one of the landmark cases of the Burger Court, now steadfastly charting its own course, [a] majority [of] justices upheld a Wisconsin Supreme Court ruling that Amish parents need not obey Wisconsin law compelling education beyond eighth grade. Justices in both courts reasoned that to do so would seriously endanger if not destroy free exercise of religious beliefs by the Amish. There is reason to cheer high court recognition of freedom of worship at a point where it comes into conflict with the state's interest in universal education. . . .
>
> For religious freedom [the Court's decision] is solid endorsement of the right of parents to determine the educational pursuits of their children beyond the eighth grade at their own expense, where public school attendance can be shown to threaten long-established beliefs. For Amish children, it constitutes state recognition of the validity of their parents' religious views on limiting relations with the outside world. It promises for the Supreme Court, more cases to come on the adequacy of public education and whether or not other sects qualify for similar exemptions.[10]

Larger and better-known newspapers, such as the *Chicago Tribune,* offered similar praise.

> Jonas Yoder and other members of the Old Order Amish religion were convicted in a Wisconsin court of violating the compulsory attendance law and fined $5 each. They won on appeal in the Wisconsin Supreme Court, but then the state appealed. Now they have won in the federal Supreme Court. For a lawsuit over a $5 fine to go so far is evidence that it was one of extraordinary interest. . . .
>
> The question before the courts was whether or not the state's interest in enforcing the compulsory (to age 16) school attendance law outweighed the contention that for the Amish to comply with this law would violate their constitutionally protected religious

freedom. No conflict between generations was involved; there was no showing that the Amish children involved wanted to go to high school. Most of us non-Amish people can join the satisfaction that the Amish must feel in the Supreme Court's opinion.

As Chief Justice Burger said, "A way of life that is odd or even erratic but interferes with no rights or interests of others is not to be condemned because it is different." That the Amish are unoffending people no one disputes. For generations they have, different or not, survived and even prospered. They are hard working, self-reliant, effective in teaching their children a way of life that is productive and fulfilling in its way. The Old Order Amish now have the Supreme Court's explicit blessing in resisting extinction by involuntary assimilation into general patterns. Most of us would rather see than be Old Order Amish, but the United States is a bit more free for us all because the Amish won their case.[11]

In its editorial lauding the Court's *Yoder* ruling, the *New York Times* credited the Court for fashioning a narrow opinion that would be applicable only to the Amish:

The Supreme Court decision upholding the right of Amish parents in Wisconsin not to send their children to school beyond the eight elementary grades fits logically into an evolving pattern of constitutional interpretations designed to protect religious principles against inroads by secular power. The opinion by Chief Justice Burger amounts to a concession that, in view of the sect's rejection of virtually all the trappings of modern life, compulsory high school instruction would constitute an assault on the Amish dogma: "Be not conformed to this world."

The . . . ruling follows the landmark decision of *Pierce v. Society of Sisters* which, in 1925, upheld the right of parents to send their children to religious rather than public schools. But Justice Burger deliberately narrowed the impact by stressing that Amish opposition to high school instruction is based on long-established life style and religious doctrine rather than on some new theories about education and child rearing. This reservation should prevent the ruling from being used as a battering ram against compulsory education by those who, for political rather than religious reasons, consider the schools a coercive tool of the state. Although this aspect of the opinion will be characterized as illiberal by contemporary education's more radical critics, the Court is wise not to allow momentary dissatisfaction with the public schools to overshadow their past achievements and their continuing key role in a free and open society.[12]

CRITICISM OF THE DECISION

But other comments about the *Yoder* decision were less positive. Although no one seemed to have an unkind word to say about the Amish themselves, critics writing for both academic and popular audiences pointed out myriad apparent shortcomings in the ruling that shielded their religious liberty. In Green Bay, Wisconsin, for instance, the *Press-Gazette* paired its praise for the court with criticism:

The United States Supreme Court decision regarding Amish people and Wisconsin's compulsory education law appears to continue stronger than ever the absolute interpretation of freedom of religion of the First Amendment to the Constitution. . . .

[One] concern is the language of the decision written by Chief Justice Burger defining what sort of a religion may qualify in this decision. The Amish have "convincingly demonstrated the sincerity of their religious beliefs [for 300 years]. It cannot be overemphasized that we are not dealing with a way of life and mode of education by a group claiming to have recently discovered some progressive or more enlightened process for rearing children in modern life. . . . The very concept of ordered liberty precludes allowing every person to make his own standards on matters of conduct in which society as a whole has important interests," Justice Burger said.

But this implies that the age of a religious movement determines its validity and that there is order only in large numbers. This is dangerously close to a point of view in earlier times which the First Amendment was specifically written to guard against. The Supreme Court in recent decisions concerning objectors to military service has ruled that membership in an organized religious organization is not essential, and this appears inconsistent with some of the wording in the Amish case.[13]

The journal *Church and State* sounded another cautious note about the Court's opinion in *Yoder.*

On May 15 the United States Supreme Court ruled Amish parents may be exempted from full compliance with state compulsory school attendance laws, [but] the whole problem and the Court's response to it are not quite as simple as newspaper headlines may have suggested. . . .

Some of the praise for the ruling stemmed from the view that secondary education, public or private, is necessarily hostile to Amish views. Educators know, however, that a school can be respectfully neutral toward all religious traditions represented in a school and hostile toward none. Another problem raised by the ruling is the Court's attempt to limit its applicability to the Amish. Is the Court saying that the Amish have rights that might not be accorded to other sects or individuals? In Wisconsin v. Yoder the Supreme Court may well have raised more questions than it answered. Time alone will reveal the full implications of this complex decision.[14]

More strident criticism came from the likes of scholar Walter Berns, a professor of political science at the University of Toronto. Berns and others critics maintained that the Supreme Court's approach to the Amish school attendance case was deeply flawed.

The Court has never before held that one's religious convictions entitle him to an exemption from the requirements of a *valid* criminal statute. This is new law, and of a dangerous sort. It is dangerous because if one is entitled to disobey a law that is contrary to his religious beliefs, and entitled as well to define his own religious beliefs, the proliferation of sects and of forms of worship will be wonderful to behold: drug cultists, snake worshippers, income-tax haters—why, in Shelley's words, the sense faints picturing them all. But there will be no stopping this religious revival (or what, for legal purposes, will be labeled a religious revival), short of permitting public officials, and ultimately the judges, to do precisely what the Supreme Court has insisted they may not do, namely, get in the business of distinguishing the honest profession of faith from the dishonest, the genuine from the spurious. . . .

[I]n Yoder's case the Court took the first step in this heretofore prohibited direction by drawing a line between the religious and the secular; it did this by emphasizing that the exemption being carved out for this religious group could not be claimed by other kinds of groups, "however virtuous and admirable" may be their "way of life."[15]

For his part, Robert H. Bork, the noted conservative jurist, believed that the Supreme Court had erred in *Yoder* by reading the First Amendment's two religion clauses too broadly.

The Court has . . . read the religion clauses so expansively as to bring the prohibition of the establishment of religion into direct conflict with the guarantee of free exercise.

The classic example is *Wisconsin v. Yoder*. Amish parents objected to the state's school attendance laws, stating that their religion prohibited them from allowing their children to attend public school after the eighth grade. The Wisconsin statute required attendance to the age of sixteen and was in no way aimed at religion. The Supreme Court found the law a violation of religious freedom and held that the Amish children need not comply with it as other children must. Quite aside from the question of whether the decision was right or wrong, it makes plain that the religion clauses have been brought into conflict with each other. Had Wisconsin legislated an exception for the Amish, that favoritism clearly would have held a forbidden establishment of religion. Thus, in the name of the free exercise of religion, the Supreme Court, according to its own criteria, established a religion.[16]

Such criticisms held little weight with Prof. James D. Gordon III of Brigham Young University Law School. Writing in 1996, Gordon cited the *Yoder* opinion as a landmark in the Supreme Court's history:

> *Wisconsin v. Yoder* was the high water mark of religious liberty under the Free Exercise Clause of the First Amendment. . . .
>
> Despite its minor flaws, Yoder is a shining symbol of religious tolerance. It is a thoughtful and careful effort to accommodate religious differences and protect free exercise of religion. It reasonably defends that which reason cannot fully explain, powerfully protects the powerless, shelters a community from the community that shelters it, and subordinates positive law to a sincere interpretation of divine law. Yoder transcends a plurality of paradoxes as it contemplates the paradoxes of pluralism.[17]

NOTES

1. Quoted in "New Glarus Group Takes News Calmly," *Wisconsin State Journal* (Madison), May 16, 1972, 1.
2. Quoted in " 'It's a Miracle,' Yoder Declares," *Capital Times* (Madison), May 15, 1972, 1.
3. Quoted in ibid.
4. Quoted in "Amish Authority Gives Comments on Decision," *Monroe* (Wisconsin) *Evening Times,* May 17, 1972, 1.
5. Quoted in "New Glarus Group Takes News Calmly."
6. Quoted in " 'Wonderful', Says Justice," *Monroe Evening Times,* May 16, 1972, 1.
7. "Support for the Religious Dissenter," *New York Times,* June 4, 1972.
8. Russell Kirk, "The Amish Case," *National Review,* July 7, 1972, 747.
9. "The Court Finds for the Amish," *America,* May 27, 1972, 554.
10. "Court Upholds Amish," *Eau Claire Leader-Telegram,* May 18, 1972, A4.
11. "A Victory for the Amish," *Chicago Tribune,* May 29, 1972, 8.
12. " 'Simple Life' Upheld," *New York Times,* May 20, 1972, 32.
13. "Freedom of Religion First," *Green Bay Press-Gazette,* May 21, 1972, 10.
14. "The Amish Ruling and Religious Liberty," *Church and State,* July-August 1972, 6–7.
15. Walter Berns, "Ratiocinations," *Harper's,* March 1973, 36–42.
16. Robert H. Bork, *The Tempting of America: The Political Seduction of the Law* (New York: Free Press, 1990), 247–248.
17. "*Wisconsin v. Yoder* and Religious Liberty," *Texas Law Review* 74 (1996): 1237–40.

Flood v. Kuhn

Gregg Ivers

Flood v. Kuhn
407 U.S. 258 (1972)

DECIDED: June 19, 1972
VOTE

CONCURRING: 5 (Warren E. Burger, Potter Stewart, Byron R. White, Harry A. Blackmun, William H. Rehnquist)
DISSENTING: 3 (William O. Douglas, William J. Brennan Jr., Thurgood Marshall)
OPINION OF THE COURT: Blackmun
CONCURRING OPINION: Burger
DISSENTING OPINION: Douglas, Marshall (Brennan)
DID NOT PARTICIPATE: Lewis F. Powell

On June 18, 1972, the U.S. Supreme Court turned back Curt Flood's challenge to major league baseball's (MLB) "reserve clause." The decision ended a battle that had begun on Christmas Eve, 1969, when Flood informed baseball commissioner Bowie Kuhn that he would not accept a trade from his team of eleven seasons, the St. Louis Cardinals, to the Philadelphia Phillies.

The reserve clause essentially stated that the teams had the right to renew a player's contract following each season. This meant that all rights to a player's contract belonged to the team, and a player could never escape from that club or seek competing bids from other teams. Players were not even able to invalidate a contract by sitting out for a year and then returning to the game. In essence, the club could buy, sell, or trade a player via his contract as if the player were livestock.

In his letter to Kuhn, Flood wrote that he was not a "piece of property to be bought and sold irrespective of [his] wishes" and likened the reserve clause, the system created by the owners, to slavery. Flood argued that the Court's previous decisions involving labor practices in major league baseball, *Federal Baseball Club v. The National League* (1922) and *Toolson v. New York Yankees* (1953), were wrong because they permitted club owners to restrain trade in violation of the Sherman Antitrust Act of 1890. Since 1880 club owners had inserted the reserve clause into the standard uniform contracts issued to all players, regardless of team. The few players who had tested this system prior to Flood's challenge were banished for life.[1]

In the *Federal Baseball* decision, Justice Oliver Wendell Holmes Jr., writing for a unanimous Court, accepted the owners' position that professional baseball should be exempt from federal antitrust law because it did not qualify as interstate commerce. Holmes concluded that professional baseball games were merely intrastate "exhibitions" played for the public's enjoyment.[2] The Court upheld MLB's exemption from the Sherman Act in *Toolson,* ruling that minor league players had no right to offer their services to other organizations owned by MLB once their contracts had expired. The Court concluded that Congress had had thirty years to repeal baseball's antitrust exemption and chosen not to do so. Moreover, the majority did not budge from Holmes's earlier characterization of major league baseball as "intrastate commerce."[3] Two justices, Harold Burton and Stanley Reed, dissented from the *Toolson* majority's position on the interstate commerce question. After reviewing the extensive and complex nature of professional baseball's business operations, which included minor league teams in Cuba, Mexico, and Canada, Burton wrote that it was a "contradiction in terms to say that the defendants in the cases before us are not now engaged in interstate trade or commerce as those terms are used in the Constitution of the United States or the Sherman Act."[4]

Burton's view did not carry the day, but it demonstrated a minor crack in the façade of the Court's position on the reserve clause, and it was a factor in the decision of the Major League Baseball Players Association (MLBPA) to support Curt Flood's request to challenge the reserve clause in court.

THE COURT'S HOLDING

Writing for a 5–3 majority, Justice Blackmun, although agreeing with Justice Burton's *Toolson* dissent that major league baseball was clearly interstate commerce within the power of Congress to regulate, relied on *stare decisis* (respect given to prior court decisions) and ruled that Congress, not "this Court," should take appropriate corrective action. Blackmun acknowledged that no special reason existed for MLB's exemption—he referred to it as an aberration—from the federal antitrust laws that applied to professional hockey, golf, football, and boxing. He simply cited the Court's previous rulings in *Federal Baseball* and *Toolson* and said that, however misguided those decisions had been, there was no compelling reason for the Court to disturb them when Congress was better and more appropriately positioned to remedy the problem. Of MLB's exemption, Blackmun wrote: "It is an aberration that has been with us now for a half a century, one heretofore deemed fully entitled to the benefit of *stare decisis,* and one that has survived the Court's expanding concept of interstate commerce. It rests on a recognition and an acceptance of baseball's unique characteristics and needs."[5]

Justice Blackmun, by all accounts, loved the game. He had grown up in the Twin Cities of Minneapolis-St. Paul and was a devoted Minnesota Twins fan. He was also clearly smitten with baseball's romantic imagery in the American consciousness. The first section of his opinion was sub-headed THE GAME and included this soliloquy on baseball's professional origins and ode to many of the game's greats:

> It is a century and a quarter since the New York Nine defeated the Knickerbockers 23 to 1 on Hoboken's Elysian Fields June 19, 1846, with Alexander Jay Cartwright as the instigator and the umpire. The teams were amateur, but the contest marked a significant date in baseball's beginnings. That early game led ultimately to the development of professional baseball and its tightly organized structure.
>
> The Cincinnati Red Stockings came into existence in 1869 upon an outpouring of local pride. With only one Cincinnatian on the payroll, this professional team traveled over 11,000 miles that summer, winning 56 games and tying one. Shortly thereafter, on St. Patrick's Day in 1871, the National Association of Professional Baseball Players was founded and the professional league was born.
>
> The ensuing colorful days are well known. The ardent follower and the student of baseball know of General Abner Doubleday; the formation of the National League in 1876; Chicago's supremacy in the first year's competition under the leadership of Al Spalding and with Cap Anson at third base; the formation of the American Association and then of the Union Association in the 1880's; the introduction of Sunday baseball; inter-league warfare with cut-rate admission prices and player raiding; the development of the reserve "clause"; the emergence in 1885 of the Brotherhood of Professional Ball Players, and in 1890 of the Players League; the appearance of the American League, or "junior circuit," in 1901, rising from the minor Western Association; the first World Series in 1903, disruption in 1904, and the Series' resumption in 1905; the short-lived Federal League on the majors' scene during World War I years; the troublesome and discouraging episode of the 1919 Series; the home run ball; the shifting of franchises; the expansion of the leagues; the installation in 1965 of the major league draft of potential new players; and the formation of the Major League Baseball Players Association in 1966.

Then there are the many names, celebrated for one reason or another, that have sparked the diamond and its environs and that have provided tinder for recaptured thrills, for reminiscence and comparisons, and for conversation and anticipation in-season and off-season: Ty Cobb, Babe Ruth, Tris Speaker, Walter Johnson, Henry Chadwick, Eddie Collins, Lou Gehrig, Grover Cleveland Alexander, Rogers Hornsby, Harry Hooper, Goose Goslin, Jackie Robinson, Honus Wagner, Joe McCarthy, John McGraw, Deacon Phillippe, Rube Marquard, Christy Mathewson, Tommy Leach, Big Ed Delahanty, Davy Jones, Germany Schaefer, King Kelly, Big Dan Brouthers, Wahoo Sam Crawford, Wee Willie Keeler, Big Ed Walsh, Jimmy Austin, Fred Snodgrass, Satchel Paige, Hugh Jennings, Fred Merkle, Iron Man McGinnity, Three-Finger Brown, Harry and Stan Coveleski, Connie Mack, Al Bridwell, Red Ruffing, Amos Rusie, Cy Young, Smokey Joe Wood, Chief Meyers, Chief Bender, Bill Klem, Hans Lobert, Johnny Evers, Joe Tinker, Roy Campanella, Miller Huggins, Rube Bressler, Dazzy Vance, Edd Roush, Bill Wambsganss, Clark Griffith, Branch Rickey, Frank Chance, Cap Anson, Nap Lajoie, Sad Sam Jones, Bob O'Farrell, Lefty O'Doul, Bobby Veach, Willie Kamm, Heinie Groh, Lloyd and Paul Waner, Stuffy McInnis, Charles Comiskey, Roger Bresnahan, Bill Dickey, Zack Wheat, George Sisler, Charlie Gehringer, Eppa Rixey, Harry Heilmann, Fred Clarke, Dizzy Dean, Hank Greenberg, Pie Traynor, Rube Waddell, Bill Terry, Carl Hubbell, Old Hoss Radbourne, Moe Berg, Rabbit Maranville, Jimmie Foxx, Lefty Grove. The list seems endless.[6]

Myth, legend, and romance aside, Blackmun then fired the equivalent of a called strike three: "[W]hat the Court said in *Federal Baseball* in 1922 and what it said in *Toolson* in 1953, we say again here in 1972: the remedy, if any is indicated, is for congressional, and not judicial, action."[7] Chief Justice Burger, who grew up with Blackmun in the Twin Cities, commented that baseball's exemption from federal antitrust law was a "mistake," but feared that any radical change to baseball's labor practices would have a negative impact on too many people. Burger added that it was time for Congress to act.

Dissenting, Justice Douglas took a different view. He was the only justice hearing the *Flood* case who was on the Court when *Toolson* was decided. A blunt man with an equally blunt writing style, Douglas wrote that "while I joined the Court's opinion in *Toolson* . . . I would now correct what I believe to be its fundamental error. . . . This Court's decision in *Federal Baseball* . . . made in 1922, is a derelict in the stream of law that we, its creator, should remove." Almost to a man, the justices were annoyed with Blackmun's opening paean to baseball, finding it silly and beneath the Court's dignity. But Douglas dared to capture that sentiment in print: "Only a romantic view of a rather dismal business account over the last 50 years would keep that derelict in midstream."[8]

Douglas also reminded his colleagues that the Court's modern commerce clause jurisprudence effectively began with the constitutional revolution of 1937, when the justices began to approve New Deal legislation. "The power of Congress was recognized as broad enough to reach all phases of the vast operations of our industrial system," Douglas wrote.[9] He concluded, "An industry so dependent on radio and television as is baseball and gleaning vast interstate revenues would be hard put today to say with the Court in the Federal Baseball case that baseball was only a local exhibition, not trade or commerce. There can be no doubt 'that were we considering the question of baseball for the first time upon a clean slate' we would hold it to be subject to federal antitrust regulation. The unbroken silence of Congress should not prevent us from correcting our own mistakes."[10] Justice Thurgood Marshall agreed with Douglas on this last point, writing separately that "this Court should correct its own errors."[11]

FLOOD'S REACTION

The Court's sympathies to Flood's position were of little consolation to the former three-time All Star and seven-time Gold Glove winner, who was an integral part of two World Series championship teams. Flood sat out the 1970 season and returned briefly in 1971 when he was "traded" by the Phillies, which owned his rights, despite his refusal to report to them, to the Washington Senators. Flood's time away from baseball did not serve his skills well. After signing a $110,000 per year contract, which was $20,000 more than the Cardinals had paid him in 1969, his last season with the team, Flood played just thirteen games. He batted only .200 and showed little of the grace and panache that had led *Sports Illustrated* to label him, in his prime, the greatest defensive centerfielder since Willie Mays.

Flood sacrificed his career to take a stand on principle, lost, left baseball, and moved to Europe, the only place, it seemed, where he could escape the labels of "ingrate," "traitor," and even "Communist" that had been heaped upon him by professional baseball's owners and their allies in the sporting press. Twenty-five years later, however, the baseball establishment would have a very different view of Curt Flood's legacy to the game, as events simmering below the surface of *Flood v. Kuhn* received a jump start from the Court's decision. While the owners may have popped champagne corks and lit expensive cigars to celebrate their victory over the players, the MLBPA saw something very different in *Flood's* outcome.

St. Louis Cardinals center fielder Curt Flood, pictured here in 1965, fought being traded to the Philadelphia Phillies, informing Major League Baseball commissioner Bowie Kuhn that he was not "a piece of property to be bought and sold irrespective of my wishes." Flood lost his battle when in *Flood v. Kuhn* (1972) the Supreme Court upheld the league's exemption to antitrust laws. — AP Wide World Photos

OWNERS, PLAYERS, AND THE PRESS REACT

The MLB team owners' lead counsel, John Gaherin, cautioned the owners about interpreting Flood's defeat as an end to the players' efforts to seek mobility and better compensation. "Read the decision more closely. The justices said you're not covered by the Sherman Antitrust Act. But if you were, you'd get your pants taken off. And they invited Congress to do something about it." Several owners bristled at Gaherin's suggestion, but he refused to say what they wanted to hear: "Fellas, this is the twentieth century. You can't get anybody, drunk or sober, to agree that once a fella goes to work for the A&P, he has to work for the A&P the rest of his life." Gaherin told the owners to pay particular attention to Marvin Miller, the executive director of the MLBPA. Miller, who had enjoyed a successful career as a labor negotiator on behalf of the United Steelworkers and other major labor organizations before going to work for the MLBPA, considered baseball players among the "most exploited" workers in America. If they thought Miller was going to roll over and encourage the players to play dead because the Supreme Court had ruled against Curt Flood, Gaherin said, they were mistaken. "Marvin's going to be pouring gas all over the floor and lighting matches"[12] The owners did not believe him, but Gaherin was right.

The owners, perhaps distracted by the *Flood* case, were not paying close attention to the rumblings among the rank-and-file of the MLBPA. Angered by the refusal of the owners to negotiate with them in good faith over health insurance, pensions, and other benefits after the 1971 season, the player representatives from each team voted 47-0 (with one abstention) to authorize a players' strike upon expiration of the yearly agreement between the MLBPA and the owners. Accordingly, Miller called Gaherin shortly after midnight on March 31, 1972, to inform him that the players would not play in any more spring training games or start the season until they had reached satisfactory terms for a new agreement. The owners were flabbergasted and refused to believe that the game's star players, some of whom were now making the unheard figure of $150,000 per year, would refuse to play. But the players stood their ground, and the owners could not have possibly taken any comfort when Willie Mays stood by Miller's side and told the players that if they "didn't hang together, everything we've worked for will be lost."[13]

Predictably, the players found few allies for their cause either in public opinion or in the baseball press, which was still overwhelmingly a public relations tool for the owners. Too many people had played baseball growing up and simply could not fathom how anyone could be unhappy being paid—sometimes very well—to play a child's game. Reporters referred to the players as "privileged" and "pampered" at a time when the average salary was less than $40,000 per year and unflatteringly referred to Miller as a "labor boss." The *Sporting News*, then America's premier baseball publication, called the players' strike "the darkest moment in sports history." (The *Sporting News* was headquartered in St. Louis, and Cardinals owner Augustus Busch, the beer magnate, was among the hardest of the hard-liners in defense of baseball's historic position on the reserve clause and other labor issues.) But several other owners, knowing full well they would lose money by the millions if they did not soon reach an agreement with the players, told Gaherin to negotiate with Miller behind the scenes. On April 13 the players and owners settled the benefits issue, and play began on April 15. For the first time ever, a professional sport started its season late due to a strike by its players.[14]

FURTHER LABOR DEVELOPMENTS

The strike was not the last headache the owners would face during the 1972 season. Another disgruntled Cardinal, a switch-hitting catcher named Ted Simmons, with two years in the major leagues, refused to sign the contract he was offered for the 1972 season. Simmons viewed baseball's uniform players contract the same way that Miller did—that at the end of one year a player's obligation to his team was complete and he was free to offer his services around the league. Miller had told the players this in one meeting after another leading up to the 1972 season. Few players had the nerve to test it because they knew the consequences. Because no owner would negotiate with a player under contract to another team, a player's refusal to sign meant banishment from the game. Simmons wanted a $30,000 contract to play the 1972 season, and Cardinal management was willing to go only as high as the low twenties. Simmons refused to give in, recalling, "When someone representing the [baseball] establishment said, 'This is what you'll do,' I was just bulletproof enough, naïve enough, and political enough to say, 'I'm not going to.' "[15]

Simmons played his hand correctly. Cardinal management continued to field Simmons, who played the first half of the season without a contract. Cardinal general manager Bing Devine told Simmons that his salary would be cut back to the minimum, $12,000, if he did not sign. With Miller advising him along the way, Simmons, who was having his best season yet and earned a spot on the National League's All-Star Team, held firm at $30,000. And it was during the All-Star break that the Cardinals finally gave in to Simmons. Sitting in his hotel room, Simmons received a call from Devine, who offered new terms. For the first time in baseball history, a team was prepared to offer a player a *multiyear* contract. The Cardinals would agree to pay Simmons $30,000 for the 1972 season and $45,000 for the 1973 season. Simmons was elated. Miller was happy for him but had secretly hoped that he could use this standoff to test the reserve clause with an arbitrator. The owners had bought themselves more time, but change was in the offing, and there was nothing they could do about it.

Miller achieved another major victory in 1974, when an arbitrator ruled in favor of Jim "Catfish" Hunter in a contract dispute with Oakland Athletics owner Charlie Finley. Hunter's contract called for Finley to purchase a $50,000 insurance annuity *during the season* to be paid directly to a company designated by Hunter. After realizing that he could not deduct the cost of the annuity from his tax return until after Hunter received his first payment, Finley refused to pay the company directly. He offered to pay Hunter, but that violated the terms of his contract. At first, the arbitrator ordered Finley to make the payment to Hunter's insurance company and voided the star pitcher's contract. But he said nothing about Hunter's status following his decision. Miller wanted a clear ruling on Hunter's status: the breach of contract by Finley made Hunter a free agent. The arbitrator, Peter Seitz, agreed. After the 1974 season, "Catfish" Hunter became professional baseball's first free agent.[16] A bidding war for Hunter's services resulted in a $3.8 million dollar contract over five years. His last contract with Oakland had been for two years at $100,000 per year.

Hunter's case did not establish free agency, a common misperception attributed to his victory over Finley. The arbitrator did not void the reserve clause or deal with the other questions raised by the Flood case. In 1975 two pitchers succeeded in persuading Seitz to declare Section 10A of the Uniform Player's Contract a violation of federal law.[17] Andy Messersmith, who played for the Los Angeles Dodgers in 1974 without a contract and was at the height of his powers, and Dave McNally, who left the Montreal Expos at the beginning of the 1974 season to retire, argued they were now free agents because they were never under contract. Free agency was born, and the game was never the same.

Since 1975 the MLBPA has gone on strike three times. The 1981 mid-season players' strike yielded more benefits for them, but, with average salaries now around $196,000 per year, public opinion was firmly on the side of the owners. In 1985 the players went on strike in August after playing the season without a new basic agreement. After twenty-four hours, the players and owners reached an agreement, with neither side eager to walk off a cliff this late in the season. The 1985 strike added a new twist to public perception of the players as ungrateful and greedy. For the first time, the owners turned over their books to an independent economist, who revealed the owners' personal earnings from baseball. The public learned that the owners made a lot of money, and that the value of their franchises continued to increase regardless of what they paid themselves.

Whether one's sympathies lay with the owners or the players, almost everyone agreed that baseball's next major "work stoppage," as the phrase now went, in 1994 was an unmitigated disaster for the game. Play stopped in August, and, after a series of self-imposed deadlines, negotiations between the MLBPA and the owners ended. For the first time ever, the World Series was canceled. Attendance dropped off precipitously for years, until Mark McGuire and Sammy Sosa's 1998 battle to eclipse Roger Maris's single season homerun record of sixty-one drew fans back to the game, with McGuire ultimately hitting seventy homers. Their graciousness to each other and to the Maris family was a public relations bonanza for a game that was just starting to recover from the black eye it had sustained four years before. In September Cal Ripken Jr., a star shortstop for the Baltimore Orioles, ended his consecutive games streak at 2,632, having surpassed Yankee legend Lou Gehrig during the 1995 season. Ripken's modesty also helped restore the image of individual players as capable of more than outrageous contract demands.

CURT FLOOD'S PERSONAL LEGACY

In January 1997, between Ripken's pursuit of Gehrig's streak and the McGuire-Sosa homerun chase, Curt Flood, no longer considered a pariah of the game, died of throat cancer. Two weeks later, Rep. John

Conyers, D-Mich., introduced the Curt Flood Act, designated H.R. 21 in honor of Flood's uniform number, which extended coverage to baseball players under federal antitrust law and finally put to rest the Court's decisions in *Federal Baseball, Toolson,* and *Flood.* (President Bill Clinton signed the Curt Flood Act into law on October 27, 1998.) Conyers noted that Flood's experience in the game included confrontation with racial injustice. Flood was the only African American player on his minor league team, the High Point, North Carolina, Hi-Toms, during the 1950s and was thus subject to the Jim Crow laws of the South. He was not permitted to use gas station restrooms when the team bus stopped for food and bathroom breaks; he could not eat in restaurants with his teammates or dress in the same locker-rooms. Flood spoke of his experience to documentary filmmaker Ken Burns, who interviewed him for his series on the history of baseball. Said Flood:

> After the end of the first game you take off your uniform and you throw it into a big pile. . . . [But the clubhouse manager] sent my uniform to the colored cleaners which was probably 20 minutes away and there I sat while the other guys were on the field. [The crowd has] really been giving me hell all day long, and now I'm sitting there stark naked waiting for my uniform to come back from the cleaners and the other guys were out on the field. So finally they get my uniform back and I walk out on the field . . . boy you'd think that I had just burned the American flag [18]

When Flood died, President Clinton wrote a condolence letter to Flood's widow:

> Dear Mrs. Flood:
>
> Hillary and I were saddened to learn of your husband's death, and we extend our deepest sympathy. Curt Flood was a man of extraordinary ability, courage and conviction. His achievements on the field were matched only by the strength of his character. While there are no words to ease the pain of your loss, I hope you can take comfort in the knowledge that Curt will be remembered by so many Americans as one of baseball's finest players and a lasting influence on the sport he loved so much.
>
> We hope that the loving concern and support of your family and friends will sustain you during this difficult time. You are in our thoughts and prayers.
>
> Sincerely,
>
> Bill Clinton [19]

Donald Fehr, who succeeded Marvin Miller as executive director of the MLBPA in 1983, commented: "Baseball players have lost a true champion. A man of quiet dignity, Curt Flood conducted his life in a way that set an example for all who had the privilege to know him. When it came time to take a stand at great personal risk and sacrifice, he stood firm for what he believed was right." Hank Aaron, baseball's all-time home run leader and one of its greatest all-around players, was more direct: "Flood was crucified for taking his stand." [20]

Learning of Flood's illness, the Baseball Assistance Team (B.A.T.), a group formed to help former major league players who were unable to cope with medical bills or other difficulties, came to Flood's aid. Ironically, the president of B.A.T, Joe Garagiola, had testified against Flood during the trial phase of his lawsuit. After Flood's death, Garagiola said, "I thought if the reserve clause went, baseball was going. I was so wrong I can't begin to tell you. It took a lot of guts for him to do what he did." [21]

But it was Flood who captured his legacy best:

> I lost money, coaching jobs, a shot at the Hall of Fame. But when you weigh that against all the things that are really and truly important, things that are deep inside you, then I think I've succeeded. People try to make a Greek tragedy of my life, and they can't

do it. I'm too happy. Remember . . . the American dream? That if you worked hard enough and tried hard enough and kicked yourself in the butt, you'd succeed? Well, I think I did, I think I did.[22]

NOTES

1. Gregg Ivers and Kevin T. McGuire, eds., *Creating Constitutional Change: Clashes over Power and Liberty in the Supreme Court* (Charlottesville: University of Virginia Press, 2004), 21–22.

2. *Federal Baseball Club v. The National League,* 259 U.S. 200, at 208–209 (1922).

3. *Toolson v. New York Yankees,* 346 U.S. 356, at 357 (1953).

4. Ibid.

5. *Flood v. Kuhn,* 407 U.S. 258, at 282 (1972).

6. Ibid., at 260–264.

7. Ibid., at 288.

8. Ibid., at 286.

9. Ibid.

10. Ibid.

11. Ibid., at 292.

12. John Helyar, *Lords of the Realm: The Real History of Baseball* (New York: Villard Books, 1994), 127.

13. Ibid., 119.

14. Ibid., 119–120.

15. Ibid., 120.

16. Marvin Miller, *A Whole Different Ball Game: The Sport and Business of Baseball* (New York: Simon & Schuster, 1991), 226–229.

17. *National and American League Professional Baseball Clubs v. Major League Baseball Players Ass'n,* 66 Lab. Arb. Rep., Bureau of National Affairs 101 (1976).

18. See http://thomas.loc.gov/cgi-bin/query/F?r105:1:./temp/~r105lIS0F:e0:.

19. Ibid.

20. Quoted by Thomas Boswell, *Washington Post,* January 22, 1997.

21. Quoted by Murray Chass, *New York Times,* January 21, 1997.

22. See http://xroads.virginia.edu/~CLASS/am483_97/projects/brady/legacies.html.

Furman v. Georgia

B. Keith Crew

Furman v. Georgia
408 U.S. 232 (1972)

DECIDED:: June 29, 1972

VOTE

CONCURRING: 5 (William O. Douglas, William J. Brennan, Potter Stewart, Byron R. White, Thurgood Marshall)

DISSENTING: 4 (Warren Burger, Harry A. Blackmun, Lewis F. Powell Jr., William H. Rehnquist)

OPINION: *Per curiam*

OPINION CONCURRING IN JUDGMENT: Douglas

OPINION CONCURRING IN JUDGMENT: Brennan

OPINION CONCURRING IN JUDGMENT: Stewart

OPINION CONCURRING IN JUDGMENT: White

OPINION CONCURRING IN JUDGMENT: Marshall

DISSENTING OPINION: Burger (Blackmun, Powell, Rehnquist)

DISSENTING OPINION: Blackmun

DISSENTING OPINION: Powell (Burger, Blackmun, Rehnquist)

DISSENTING OPINION: Rehnquist (Burger, Blackmun, Powell)

In a series of cases in the 1970s, the U.S. Supreme Court considered whether the death penalty should be abolished as violating the Eighth Amendment prohibition against "cruel and unusual punishment." Doing so would entail no easy bit of jurisprudence because capital punishment is clearly mentioned in the Constitution and was obviously taken for granted by its Framers. The Fifth and Fourteenth Amendments forbid the federal and state governments from depriving anyone of life without due process of law; therefore, they imply that the government may take life as long as it follows due process. Nevertheless, a *de facto* moratorium on executions had begun in 1967, and, as a number of appeals in capital cases moved through the courts, many expected the Supreme Court to abolish the death penalty.

The pivotal case in the series was *Furman v. Georgia* (1972). William Furman was an African American who lived in Savannah, Georgia, where he was born. He was mentally deficient, possibly from a childhood brain injury, and had a penchant for burglarizing houses when he was under the influence of alcohol. During one such episode, he entered the residence of a white family. The owner surprised Furman, who tripped and fell, inadvertently discharging the pistol he was carrying. The bullet struck and killed the homeowner. The NAACP took an interest in the case, and its lawyers took the lead in filing the appeals. The possibility that racial discrimination was a factor in Furman's death penalty, along with the interest taken in the case by the nation's foremost civil rights organization, no doubt played a part in the Supreme Court agreeing to hear the case, even though it had less than a year before upheld capital punishment in *McGautha v. California* (1971).

In *Furman* the Supreme Court struck down existing state and federal capital punishment statutes, effectively abolishing capital punishment. The abolition was not permanent, however, because the justices stopped short of declaring capital punishment *per se* unconstitutional. Instead, the Court directed its ruling at the procedures used in imposing the death penalty and the unfair distribution of justice permitted by those procedures. In other words, the Court did not rule that the death penalty was unconstitutionally cruel and unusual; rather, it ruled that the "wanton" and "freakish" application of capital punishment permitted under existing law was cruel and unusual. States that wished to retain or reinstate capital punishment had to craft new legislation that satisfied the principles established in the *Furman* decision. Although new capital punishment statutes were upheld in *Gregg v. Georgia* in 1976, and executions resumed in 1977, the Court can fairly be said to have applied *Furman* rather than overturned it.

One of the main issues in these cases was the amount of discretion allowed juries in imposing the death penalty. In *McGautha v. California,* the Court had upheld the "untrammeled discretion of the jury in the power to pronounce life or death in capital cases." Because untrammeled discretion was linked to arbitrary, capricious, and discriminatory imposition of the death penalty, the Court ruled in *Furman* that guidelines were necessary. Justice White suggested that statutes mandating capital punishment for certain categories of crime would be acceptable.

It is unusual for the Court to overturn a previous decision as quickly as it did with *Furman* overturning *McGautha.* Justices Stewart and White were the swing votes, joining Justices Douglas, Brennan, and Marshall, the three-judge minority in *McGautha,* to form the five-judge majority in *Furman.*

Several other features of the *Furman* decision are noteworthy. Most outstanding is that all nine justices wrote separate opinions. The opinion of the Court was a brief paragraph written *per curiam* ("by the court"). Usually, one justice is assigned by the chief justice (or the most senior justice in the majority, if the chief justice is in the minority) to write the opinion of the Court. The majority agreed that capital punishment was cruel and unusual, but each member offered different reasons for reaching that conclusion. Brennan and Marshall were the only justices to assert that capital punishment *per se* was cruel and unusual. Each relied heavily on the doctrine of "evolving standards of decency" formulated by the former chief justice, Earl Warren, in *Trop v. Dulles* (1958). Douglas, Stewart, and White based their opinions on the procedures by which the death penalty was imposed. Although each stressed different aspects, their main arguments followed the same path: (1) juries and judges had a wide range of discretion regarding whether to sentence a convicted person to death; (2) such discretion resulted in the arbitrary and capricious imposition of the ultimate punishment, so that there was no consistent logic associated with who lived and who died; and (3), therefore, the procedures and statutes that produced these results were unconstitutional. As Justice Douglas said in his opinion:

> It would seem incontestable that the death penalty inflicted on one defendant is "unusual" if it discriminates against him by reason of his race, religion, wealth, social position, or class, or if it is imposed under a procedure that gives room for the play of such prejudices.[1]

In addition to the arbitrariness of the application of death sentences was the issue of proportionality. The two companion cases to *Furman* involved men sentenced to death for rape. In neither case was the victim killed. Rape was a capital crime only in southern states, where death sentences and executions were applied almost exclusively to black men convicted of raping white women. In 1970 the U.S. Court of Appeals for the Fourth Circuit had ruled that capital punishment for rape was "unconstitutionally disproportionate."[2] Although circuit court opinions do not set precedent for the nation, *Furman* was understood by many to have upheld the Fourth Circuit ruling.

Another notable feature of this case was the political division underlying the various opinions. President Richard Nixon's four appointees to the Court cast the four dissenting votes. Nixon had openly stated his intentions to appoint "strict constructionists" to counteract the "activist" legacy of the Warren Court. In addition, the Warren Court, fairly or unfairly, had been labeled by many as "soft" on crime, and Nixon selected nominees in part for their reputations for being "tough" on crime.

REACTIONS TO THE DECISION

Public reactions to the Court's ruling in *Furman v. Georgia* reflected the preexisting philosophical and political divisions about the death penalty. Abolitionists and civil rights advocates celebrated, although some felt that the Court had not gone far enough. Proponents of the death penalty reacted with concern, sometimes outrage, and called for new capital punishment legislation. Others reacted with confusion, which was understandable given the various opinions of the Supreme Court justices. Lawyers and legislators predicted that further challenges would be made and that a second Supreme Court ruling would be necessary to decide the fate of people on death row.[3] *Congressional Digest* devoted its January 1973 issue to the topic, stating, "Confusion resulting from the Supreme Court's ruling has resulted in a variety of responses among the States to different—and frequently conflicting—interpretations of how the decision affects their capital punishment laws."

In Georgia, where the *Furman* case and the case associated with the restoration of capital punishment, *Gregg v. Georgia,* both originated, the coverage of the Supreme Court ruling was extensive. The conflicting reasons and emotions associated with the complex issue of capital punishment were exemplified by the reaction of Georgia's governor (and future Democratic president), Jimmy Carter. Reacting to the news of the Court's decision with self-described "mixed emotions," Carter stated that while he was "relieved" by the decision, he was unsure if the death penalty should be abolished. He said, "In a way, I am relieved that this ruling has come, but at the same time, I do feel the additional responsibility to re-examine the laws."[4]

Two themes dominated the public statements of those who were opposed to the Court's decision in *Furman.* The first was the belief that the liberals on the Court had overstepped their authority. The second was that the liberal justices were dangerously lax on criminals and had removed a necessary deterrent to crime. Sen. Herman Talmadge, D-Ga., clearly felt the Court had exceeded its authority. "Five of the nine members of the Supreme Court have once again amended by usurpation the Constitution," he said. "We have had too much of that already."[5] Sen. James Eastland, D-Miss., chairman of the Senate Judiciary Committee, announced that his committee would "take up" the issue, adding, "This is a matter solely within the prerogatives of the states. The Supreme Court is again legislating and destroying our system of government."[6]

Sam Nunn, at the time a state representative and candidate for the U.S. Senate, referred to the case as illustrating the need for a constitutional amendment requiring Supreme Court justices to face the voters every six years to retain their seats: "We have got to end this dictatorship created by judges appointed for a lifetime."[7]

In contrast to the view that the ruling violated states' rights and legislative authority, the *New Republic* editorialized that the legislators were unlikely to "take the risk of unpopular, though principled, decisions." This publication was more concerned with the fact that the four Nixon appointees voted as a bloc, concluding that the "image of the Court as an independent institution" was threatened.[8]

The second theme, that capital punishment was an effective deterrent and essential to protecting society from crime, was assumed by many pro–capital punishment figures, such as Rep. Louis Wyman, R-N.H., who asserted that the decision was "harmful to the nation, faced as it is with rising crime."[9] Wyman, a former president of the National Association of Attorneys General, was voicing an opinion common among prosecuting attorneys. The U.S. district attorney for the Savannah area stated, "I've always agreed with capital punishment. I think it's a great deterrent force from a practical standpoint."[10] Lewis Slaton, the district attorney for Fulton County (Atlanta), offered the following commentary in response to the ruling:

> The decision is a setback to adequate enforcement of criminal laws. In certain instances, we have needed capital punishment. . . . I have always disliked capital punishment, but I considered it an unpleasant necessity in some cases.[11]

John Inman, the chief of police in Atlanta, was slightly more emphatic in stating a similar view:

> I think it's terrible . . . the ruling removes a definite deterrent to major crimes. It shows we're still placing too much emphasis on the rights of criminals, to the detriment of law abiding citizens.[12]

Some took this stance to the extreme, suggesting that the Court's decision was an endorsement of rape and murder and a threat to civilization itself. Lt. Gov. (and former governor) Lester Maddox, known for his

After he was sentenced to die in the electric chair, William Furman, a twenty-six-year-old black man convicted of murdering a white woman, challenged the constitutionality of the death penalty. In *Furman v. Georgia* (1972), the Supreme Court focused on the imposition and carrying out of capital punishment, determining it cruel and unusual punishment. — Reuters

segregationist politics, pronounced it a "bleak and sad day," and called the decision a "license for anarchy, for rape and for murder." Maddox predicted that the ruling would lead to vigilante justice.[13] Echoing these sentiments was James Floyd, an influential member of the Georgia House of Representatives: "This is one of the saddest days in American history. We're going back to the days of the jungle." The image of the jungle was also invoked by a federal prosecutor, U.S. District Attorney John Stokes Jr., who said the *Furman* ruling was "a giant leap back into the law of the jungle."[14] One of the most bitter reactions came from an Atlanta homicide detective who told a reporter:

> All these criminals out here are going to have a field day. I hope the judges who voted against capital punishment are the first to get hit.[15]

SUPPORT FOR THE OPINION

Contrary opinion saw capital punishment as a barbarous relic of the past rather than a necessity for preserving order. Ruste Kitfield, executive director of the American Civil Liberties Union of Georgia, concluded her interview with the press by saying, "The death penalty just didn't belong with a civilized society."[16] The *Washington Post* editorial took a position supporting the Court, stating, "We trust that the death chambers will now be dismantled."[17]

Opponents of the death penalty often emphasized the belief that it had been misused. Kitfield, for example, believed that the fear of the death penalty was unfairly used to intimidate defendants into pleading guilty. She asserted that some of these individuals were innocent, but pleaded guilty rather than risk getting the electric chair.[18] Like many death penalty opponents, Kitfield also felt that the death penalty was unfairly imposed, targeting "the poor, the black, and the forgotten."[19]

Some of the more supportive reactions came from somewhat surprising sources. Although the majority of police officers interviewed for a sidebar story in the *Atlanta Constitution* were decidedly pro–death penalty, one officer stated

I've never believed in capital punishment. . . . There are some people in prison who should never get out. But I don't think we should kill them either.[20]

Ellis MacDougall, Georgia's corrections director, believed that trials would be fairer without the death penalty for juries to "all of a sudden get squeamish about." He went on to say:

We're going to see more people go to prison who should go to prison. In the end we're going to see society more protected in some respects. The way we've used capital punishment it's not really a deterrent.[21]

One of the unexpected celebrators of the *Furman* decision was the man in charge of carrying out the death sentence in Georgia. E. B. Caldwell was the warden of Reidsville State Penitentiary, the site of Georgia's electric chair. A long-time opponent of capital punishment, Warden Caldwell delivered the news to the death row inmates personally, "smiling broadly" as he announced that the Supreme Court had overturned capital punishment.[22]

Given the importance of racial disparities in the imposition of capital punishment to the *Furman* decision, the race issue was given surprisingly little attention in the major Atlanta newspapers. The *Journal* noted that the fact that the three cases involved black defendants from southern states "raised the side issue of racial discrimination." Notably absent from both papers' coverage were statements from black public figures or representatives of civil rights groups such as the NAACP. The *Constitution* ran an article focused on death row inmates, including pictures and references to race. An attorney for one black inmate convicted and sentenced by an all-white jury was quoted as saying:

This will take a lot of pressure off black people . . . the majority of the people in prison are black and a lot of them are on death row. This is a step in the right direction.[23]

LEGISLATIVE ACTION

Furman v. Georgia was the catalyst for what in effect became a state-by-state national referendum on the death penalty. In Georgia, Governor Carter called for a reexamination of the laws. One concern was whether life sentences would provide an adequate alternative deterrent. Like most states at that time, Georgia had indeterminate sentencing. Under this system, an inmate serving a life sentence was eligible for parole after serving seven years. "Seven years is not adequate for a convicted murderer or rapist," said Carter. The vast majority of state officials agreed that changes would be necessary in the sentencing and parole laws.[24]

Adjusting to the absence of a death penalty was not the primary issue for many others, who immediately took action toward reinstating it. Representative Wyman proposed a constitutional amendment that would permit state legislatures and the U.S. Congress to enact laws authorizing the death penalty for murder.[25] The amendment never went forward, but it proved unnecessary. Three of the majority and all of the dissenting opinions stated or implied that death penalty legislation designed to prevent the arbitrary and discriminatory use of capital punishment could meet with the Court's approval. *Furman,* therefore, was a virtual invitation to the legislative branch to restore capital punishment by writing new laws. The point was not lost on legislators who supported capital punishment. The day after the *Furman* decision was announced, the chairs of the Georgia Senate and House judiciary committees scheduled joint hearings to draft new death penalty legislation. The House committee chair stated, "We certainly want to conform to the Supreme Court ruling and have the legislation ready to do so."[26] And James "Sloppy" Floyd, an influential Democratic state representative, asserted, "We've got to have a death penalty," and he went on to indicate that he would propose his own legislation and consider any other proposed new laws.[27]

Furthermore, state legislators were already aware that new laws would have to be written so that imposition of the death penalty would be proportional and consistent. Rep. Wayne Snow, a Democrat, acknowledged the point in his comments to the press:

> I agree that the death penalty for rape is too severe unless there is heinous activity connected which might warrant execution. The punishment should be according to the crime committed. Every crime has a degree of severity. . . . [Murder] has to be classified a little better than it is now.[28]

The most effective advocates for restoration of the death penalty were state attorneys general. In October 1972 a committee of eleven state attorneys general met in Oklahoma City to investigate ways of reinstating capital punishment. In December of that year, at its annual meeting, the National Association of Attorneys General endorsed model legislation drafted by the eleven-member committee. Thus, state legislators who wished to bring back capital punishment had essentially ready-made bills to consider.[29]

Although the Georgia legislature acted very quickly, Florida was the first state to pass new capital punishment legislation, which it enacted just five months after the decision in *Furman* was announced. Georgia quickly followed suit, putting its new law on the books in 1973, along with thirteen other states. Within three years of the *Furman* decision, twenty-nine states had rewritten their death penalty laws.

The states took two approaches to modify the previously "untrammeled discretion" of juries in capital cases and ensure that similar cases resulted in similar and proportionate punishments. One approach was to make the death penalty mandatory for certain categories of murder, thereby eliminating the jurors' discretion. This approach was rejected by the Supreme Court in *Woodson v. North Carolina* (1976). The Court seemed to be saying that in capital cases too much or too little discretion was unacceptable. The question was if a "just right" middle ground could be found.

Several states, including Georgia, were successful enough in legislating procedures that fell into the middle ground to ultimately restore capital punishment. The new laws required a bifurcated trial, with the jury determining guilt or innocence in the first phase and recommending a sentence in the second phase. Imposition of the death penalty required the jury to determine that one or more aggravating circumstance was present. Finally, the death sentence generated an automatic appeal, giving an appeals court the opportunity to compare the case to others to determine if the ultimate penalty was being applied consistently.

These newly rationalized procedures were mostly upheld by the Court in 1976 in *Gregg v. Georgia*. Troy Gregg received three death sentences, one for murder and two for robbery. Gregg had been convicted of killing and robbing two men who had given him and a hitchhiking companion a ride. The Court upheld the death penalty for the murder, but not for robbery. With the apparent new restriction to crimes involving deliberate taking of life, capital punishment was back. Executions resumed the following year.

Much of the controversy in the death penalty cases stemmed from the evolving standards principle. In his dissenting opinion in *Furman*, Chief Justice Warren Burger insisted that it was the duty and right of the legislative branch of government to enact laws reflective of changing standards. The events subsequent to *Furman* illustrate the power of a well-crafted dissenting opinion in influencing legal change. But were those legislators in touch with the will of the people? Prior to the moratorium on executions that preceded *Furman*, public support for the death penalty had plummeted. Public opinion polls conducted by Harris and Gallup found that the percentage of the public in favor of the death penalty had reached its low point in 1965 or 1966. According to a 1965 Harris poll, only 38 percent supported the death penalty; 47 percent opposed it.[30] Then public support began increasing again. By 1972, the year *Furman* was decided, a slim majority favored capital punishment.

PUBLIC OPINION ON THE DEATH PENALTY

Between the *Furman* and *Gregg* cases, public support for the death penalty continued to rise. By 1976 about two-thirds of the public were in favor capital punishment, a level that has remained steady since then. The table below shows the percentage favoring capital punishment from selected years of the General Social Survey.

Clearly, public attitudes shifted in favor of capital punishment after *Furman*. It seems reasonable to attribute some of that shift to the public reconsideration of the death penalty that accompanied the cases. The upward trend in public support also coincided with rising crime rates. Calls to reinstate the death penalty often followed news stories of heinous crimes. For example, the pilot of a commercial airliner that was hijacked called for capital punishment for air piracy. The pilot suggested a nationwide strike by pilots to force lawmakers to "get off their duffs and do something."[31]

TABLE 31-1

PERCENT FAVORING CAPITAL PUNISHMENT			
YEAR	TOTAL	WHITE	BLACK
1972	52.8	57.6	28.7
1976	65.4	67.5	41.1
2002	65.6	69.8	42.1

Source: National Opinion Research Center, 1972, 1976, 2002.

Although lawmakers do not universally or slavishly follow the opinion polls when crafting legislation, there can be little doubt that the opinion polls provided motivation and justification for the effort to restore the death penalty. The surveys certainly posed a difficulty for the "evolving standards" argument. But the troublesome subject of race is evident in public attitudes toward capital punishment, as shown by the table. Compared to whites, African Americans are significantly less likely to approve of the death penalty.

In *Furman v. Georgia,* the Supreme Court, far from settling the issue of whether the death penalty should be abolished, generated an intense reconsideration. Ultimately, the *Furman* decision can be credited with requiring some rationalization of capital punishment, so that current laws and procedures are guided by principles of fairness, proportionality, and consistency. Some empirical research suggests, however, that racial inequality in the imposition of the death penalty continues.[32] Criminologists and legal scholars also generally agree that the death penalty has no deterrent effect on violent crime.[33] Although a majority of the states permit capital punishment, and a majority of the public favors capital punishment for some crimes, the issue remains divisive. As the debate continues, perhaps the true legacy of *Furman* is the attention given to fairness by both sides.

NOTES

1. *Furman v. Georgia,* 408 U.S. 232, at 242 (1972).
2. *Ralph v. Warden,* 438 F.2d 786 (1970).
3. *U.S. News & World Report,* July 10, 1972, 25–27.
4. *Atlanta Constitution,* June 30, 1972.
5. *Atlanta Journal,* June 29, 1972.
6. *U.S. News & World Report,* July 10, 1972, 26.
7. *Atlanta Constitution,* June 30, 1972.
8. *New Republic,* July 15, 1972, 7–8.
9. *Waterloo Courier,* June 30, 1972.
10. *Atlanta Constitution,* June 30, 1972.
11. Ibid.
12. Ibid.
13. *Atlanta Journal,* June 29, 1972.
14. *Atlanta Constitution,* June 30, 1972.
15. Ibid.

16. Ibid.

17. *Washington Post,* June 30, 1972.

18. *Atlanta Constitution,* June 30, 1972.

19. *Atlanta Journal,* June 29, 1972.

20. *Atlanta Constitution,* June 30, 1972.

21. Ibid.

22. Ibid.

23. Ibid.

24. Ibid.

25. *Waterloo Courier,* June 30, 1972.

26. *Atlanta Constitution,* June 30, 1972.

27. Ibid.

28. Ibid.

29. *Congressional Digest,* January 1973.

30. Kathleen Maguire and Anne l. Pastore, eds., *Sourcebook of Criminal Justice Statistics 2000* (Washington, D.C.: U.S. Government Printing Office, 2001), 142.

31. *Washington Post,* July 6, 1972.

32. R. K. Bailey, "A Contemporary Review of Discriminatory Practices in the Implementation of Capital Punishment," *Forensic Examiner* (May-June 2003): 36–43.

33. See, for example, Robert Bohm, *Deathquest: An Introduction to the Theory and Practice of Capital Punishment in the United States* (Cincinnati: Anderson Publishing, 1999).

Roe v. Wade

James Z. Schwartz

Roe v. Wade
410 U.S. 113 (1973)

DECIDED: January 22, 1973
VOTE

CONCURRING: 7 (Warren Burger, William O. Douglas, William J. Brennan Jr., Potter Stewart, Thurgood Marshall, Harry A. Blackmun, Lewis F. Powell Jr.)

DISSENTING: 2 (Byron R. White, William H. Rehnquist)

OPINION OF THE COURT: Blackmun
CONCURRING OPINION: Burger
CONCURRING OPINION: Douglas
CONCURRING OPINION: Stewart
DISSENTING OPINION: White (Rehnquist)
DISSENTING OPINION: Rehnquist

In 1970 a young Texas woman challenged the constitutionality of a state law that prohibited abortion unless a mother's life was at risk. Norma McCorvey, known in her lawsuit as Jane Roe, sued the Dallas County prosecutor, Henry Wade, to prevent him from enforcing the law. Three years later, the U.S. Supreme Court issued a historic and controversial ruling in favor of Jane Roe. The ruling legalized abortion, transformed the nation's political landscape, and sparked bitter debates over reproductive rights, the power of the judiciary, and the role of religion in public life.

Roe v. Wade and its companion case, *Doe v. Bolton,* overturned all state antiabortion laws. Jane Roe had been denied an abortion in Texas, even though she claimed that her pregnancy resulted from a rape. She argued that the Texas statute violated her right to control her own body. Texas insisted that the state had a duty to protect the fetus. By the time the case reached the Supreme Court, Roe had long since given birth to her child and put it up for adoption. The Court rejected claims that the case was then moot— because pregnancy can occur more than once—and proceeded with its decision.

Writing for a 7–2 majority, Justice Blackmun based his ruling on the right to privacy, which the Court established in *Griswold v. Connecticut* (1965) (see page 235). In its *Griswold* ruling, the Court overturned a state law banning the sale and use of birth control devices. Blackmun expanded this right in *Roe,* asserting that the Fourteenth Amendment permitted women to end pregnancies. Additionally, Blackmun observed that efforts to prevent abortions were relatively recent. Common law had imposed far fewer restrictions on abortion than nineteenth-century American statutes did. The change had occurred mostly because of concerns about the safety of the procedure.

Blackmun, however, set limits on a woman's right to choose. In the first three months of pregnancy, a woman alone could decide whether to have an abortion. In the second trimester, the state could regulate the procedure to ensure a woman's health. During the final stage of pregnancy, when the fetus became "viable," and was able to survive outside the womb, the state could outlaw abortions.

Justice White dissented, observing that the majority had transformed a woman's "whim or caprice" into a right. He saw nothing in the Constitution to back this interpretation, and he criticized the Court for preventing states from determining whether the "continued existence and development of the fetus" took precedence over "a spectrum of possible impacts on the mother."

The case ended a long campaign to decriminalize abortion. Women's rights groups spearheaded the effort and by 1973 had convinced nineteen states to revise their abortion laws. The most impressive triumphs came in New York, Hawaii, Alaska, and Washington, where legislatures dropped most restrictions on abortion. Some observers hoped that Blackmun's ruling would end the battle over abortion.

Roe v. Wade had just the opposite effect. Rather than ending conflict, it ignited a firestorm of protest and created differences that continue to divide the nation. Many social conservatives condemn the decision on moral and religious grounds, and constitutional literalists condemn it on legal grounds, asserting that no right to privacy exists in the Constitution, that the justices ignored the rights of the fetus, and that the Court overstepped its authority in making a decision that should have been left to the states. Some conservative libertarians, however, praise the decision for reducing state power.

Liberals have been far more divided on *Roe* than have conservatives. Many applaud the ruling for guaranteeing a woman's right to choose and making a safe legal abortion generally available. Although most middle-class women could manage to circumvent antiabortion laws, the statutes forced poor women to risk their lives by going to unqualified practitioners. Others support abortion, but criticize the reasoning the Court used to establish reproductive rights. Such analysts criticize the ruling primarily on two grounds. First, like conservatives, they believe that the Court should have left the decision to the states. Second, liberals sometimes contend that Blackmun should have based his ruling on the equal protection clause in the Fourteenth Amendment, rather than on the right to privacy.

Roe has had profound political consequences. Outrage at the decision helped fuel the rise of the religious Right, which has sought to overturn *Roe* by passing a constitutional amendment to ban abortion, by electing presidents who will appoint more conservative judges to the federal judiciary, and by convincing state lawmakers to impose new restrictions on abortions. Seeking to satisfy one of its core constituencies, many Republicans have pledged to overturn *Roe* through appointments to the Supreme Court. Most Democrats have promised to defend the decision.

A gradually weakening majority in support of *Roe* on the Court has permitted states to restrict access to abortion. In *Webster v. Reproductive Health Services* (1989), the Court affirmed the constitutionality of a Missouri law that asserted the existence of life at conception and granted the fetus protectable interests, but, thanks to Justice Sandra Day O'Connor, did not reverse *Roe*. Three years later, in *Planned Parenthood v. Casey* (1992), the Court confronted a Pennsylvania law that also imposed restrictions on women seeking abortions. Although a 5–4 majority refused to overturn *Roe*, it eliminated *Roe*'s trimester scheme and permitted regulations that did not impose an "undue burden on women."

FAVORABLE REACTION TO *ROE*

Much of the mainstream press responded favorably to *Roe* when the ruling came down. The *New York Times* on January 24, 1973, applauded the decision, calling it a "major contribution to the preservation of individual liberties." The paper also hoped the ruling would end the bitter debate that had engulfed New York and other states that had recently legalized abortion.

> The Supreme Court has made a major contribution to the preservation of individual liberties and of free decision making by its invalidation of state laws inhibiting a woman's right to obtain an abortion in the first three months of pregnancy.
>
> The Court's 7-to-2 ruling could bring to an end the emotional and divisive public argument over what always should have been an intensely private and personal matter. It will end the argument if those who are now inveighing against the decision as a threat to civilization's survival will pause long enough to recognize the limits of what the court has done.
>
> It has not ordered any mother to have an abortion. It has left the decision where it belongs—to the woman and her physician—with the power of the state to interfere at later stages of pregnancy, governed essentially by considerations of maternal health. The court has performed a useful historical function by recalling that the initial spur for the

Anti-abortion rights demonstrators rally at the Minnesota Capitol in 1973 to protest the Supreme Court's decision in *Roe v. Wade* (1973) prohibiting state laws that criminalize abortion. — AP Wide World Photos

adoption of state laws banning abortion nearly a century ago was the great risk of maternal death involved in the surgical procedures then used. Now the risk arises out of perpetuating such archaic statutory prohibitions. The effect of these laws has been to force women, especially the young and the poor, to resort to abortion mills instead of expert hospital care when they are determined not to have an unwanted child.[1]

Two days after the *New York Times* editorial appeared, the more conservative *Wall Street Journal* also praised *Roe,* while expressing some doubts and worrying that Blackmun's trimester scheme was overly specific and might tread on the toes of state lawmakers.

We harbor certain reservations about Monday's Supreme Court decision allowing women to have pregnancies aborted, in their early stages, but on the whole, we think the court struck a reasonable balance on an exceedingly difficult question.

Our reservations have to do with whether the court stepped too far into the legislative arena and whether some of the technical aspects of its ruling might be misconstrued by those 46 states which now must set about to rewrite their abortion laws. But we haven't much quarrel with the core of the decision, which holds that the morality of abortion early in a pregnancy is a matter best left to the individual, her conscience and, perhaps, her church.

The high court decision rested on legal precedent and recent advances in medical science, not on the court's concept of morality. It could hardly have done otherwise, given the emotional content and imprecision of the moral, social and theological arguments for and against abortion.

Justice Blackmun, who wrote the majority opinion, relied heavily on court precedents that affirm a right of privacy to Americans. In what would appear to be a broadened interpretation of that right, he applied it, with certain reservations, to a woman's decision whether or not to terminate her pregnancy. He did not dismiss the rights of the unborn but his decision rested heavily on the finding that the "unborn have never been recognized in the law as persons in the whole sense. . . ."

[Blackmun's trimester approach] sounds a bit like law-giving, something that we would not wish to encourage from courts, since it is the responsibility of the Legislative Branch. We hope that as the decision is further interpreted it leaves legislatures some leeway in writing more specific rules.[2]

The *Nation,* a liberal journal of opinion, could hardly believe the decision had occurred. It saw *Roe* as a sign that the country was making progress on women's rights, noting that a decade earlier, no one could imagine this result. The magazine praised the women's rights activists who made the ruling possible and pointed out the disproportionate toll that abortion laws took on poor women. The editors, however, also raised questions about the motives of some groups supporting abortion that sought to limit the population growth among the poor to reduce the cost of welfare.

As recently as ten years ago, it was inconceivable that such a decision could have been handed down. What are the prerequisites for such a reversal of attitude at the highest judicial level? For one thing, there must be a special constituency, imbued with zeal, packing the force of reason, and pushing hard for a change in the law. Without an activist vanguard, the ancient concepts will not be questioned, much less critically examined. In the matter of abortion, Planned Parenthood, Women's Lib, liberal gynecologists and other groups provided the motive power.

Then the special constituency must have able and dedicated counsel who will painstakingly marshal not merely the law, but the facts of the situation to show the weaknesses in the accepted way of doing things, or not doing them. This branch of law is far more exacting—and unrewarding in terms of money—than, for instance, bankruptcy law. . . .

In the abortion controversy, it became clear, also, that gross discrimination was involved: the rich had no problem, the poor did, and more particularly the black poor on welfare. Even more than health care generally, the right to abortion depended on the economic status of those who desired it. Often, also, a progressive cause benefits for dubious reasons as well as ethically acceptable ones—might not the increasing tax burden of the "bums on welfare" be kept in check if their reproduction could be checked? This may have been a factor in the passage by the New York State legislature of a liberal abortion law, which has been generally successful.[3]

SOCIAL CONSERVATIVES AND CATHOLICS ON *ROE*

Catholics and other social conservatives were outraged by *Roe.* On March 2, 1973, the *National Review,* a conservative journal of opinion, condemned abortion as infanticide and called for a constitutional amendment to reverse the decision.

Senator James Buckley [C-N.Y.] will soon introduce a constitutional amendment to roll back the Supreme Court's pro-abortion ruling. (Rep. Lawrence J. Hogan [R-Md.]

has already introduced one in the House.) "The Supreme Court," says Senator Buckley, "has overturned not only a long line of legal precedent in this country, but more than two thousand years of human wisdom." He notes that the decision is based on a "right" that can be exercised only by destroying another's life. "If we find taking human life acceptable for purposes of social convenience under some circumstances, are we not going to pave the ground for taking of human life under other circumstances in order to meet other objectives of social convenience? . . . [This issue] goes to the heart of understanding what is known as the sanctity of life. I think that this is that what had distinguished Western civilization and that which must continue to distinguish it." (*Time*, ironically, underscored his point by noting approvingly that Soviet-bloc countries have had "permissive" and "liberal" abortion "for social as well as medical reasons.")

The National Conference of Catholic Bishops has now denounced the Court's decision, urged Catholics to disobey any "civil law that may require abortion," and pronounced excommunication on any Catholics who "undergo or perform an abortion." It furthermore urged Catholics to try to dissuade women from having abortions, and to work to find legal mean of overriding the decision, warning that all this would require "unified and persistent efforts."[4]

In one of the most critical analyses of the opinion, law professor John Noonan of the University of California-Berkeley (later a federal appellate judge) attacked *Roe*'s version of history and asserted that Blackmun had created rights that did not exist in the Fourteenth Amendment. Surprisingly, Noonan, whose article appeared in the same issue of the *National Review* as the editorial, echoed the *Nation* in arguing that abortion amounted to a subtle form of social engineering that aimed to limit the growth of the black population. Noonan wrote:

How did the Supreme Court reach this extraordinary result? In part through an inept use of history, in part through a schizophrenic style of judicial interpretation, in part through a conscious response to the needs of the technocracy.

Let us look at history. Justice Blackmun's opinion in [*Roe v.*] Wade contains a copious gob of it (Wade pp. 14–36). By and large it is a conscientious if pedestrian review of the relevant literature. But it is a history that is undigested—better said it is history that has been untasted. It has afforded no nourishment to the mind of the judge who set it out. He has not let it engage his spirit. He has not felt the pressure of loyalty to the persons of the past who have shaped our culture. He has not responded as a person to their perceptions.

Justice Blackmun describes with clarity the reason the American Medical Association led the fight in the nineteenth century for statutory protection of the embryo—"the popular ignorance of the true character of the crime—a belief even among mothers themselves that the fetus is not alive till after the period of quickening"; the consequent "unwarrantable destruction of human life" before the fifth month. He concludes, "The attitude of the profession may have played a significant role in the enactment of stringent abortion legislation during that period" (Wade, pp. 26–27). But the unimpeachable facts are apparently forgotten when Justice Blackmun discusses the claim that the purpose of American statutory law was not to protect the fetus, but to protect the mother from sepsis or other risks attendant on abdominal surgery in the unsanitary hospitals of the day. The Justice does not ask why the statutes then bar abortion by drug, or why this kind of surgery alone should have been made subject to the criminal law and customarily classed among "Crimes against the person."

If Justice Blackmun can read the history, cite the American Medical Association jeremiads, and trace the development of the law, and yet be uncertain as to the law's intent, it must be that he has failed to grasp, failed to integrate, the purposes which animated our ancestors in laying down a thick wall of protection about the baby in the womb. History for him has not been the evocation of persons in fidelity to their fundamental purposes. It has been a charade which is shuffled off the stage when the display of learning is completed.

What of the schizoid style of judicial interpretation favored by the Justice? On the one hand, he declares the Fourteenth Amendment, enacted in 1868, refers to a personal liberty which had escaped attention for over a century—a liberty which as Justice Rehnquist observes in dissent, would, if noticed, have invalidated the state statutes on abortion in force in 1868. Needless to say not a single word of history is adduced to show that the framers of the Fourteenth Amendment, the Congress which proposed it and the states which passed it, intended to legitimize abortion. In this branch of his opinion, Justice Blackmun is an evolutionist. Constitutions must be re-interpreted or remade to speak to the times. If liberty means one thing in 1868 and something entirely different in 1973, it is what one must expect of a basic document exposed to a variety of times and conditions. As Justice Blackmun says in an oblique reference to the process which he has followed, his holding is consistent "with the demands of the profound problems of the present day" (Wade, p. 50).

On the other hand, in determining the meaning of "person" in the Fourteenth Amendment's guarantee, the Justice is curiously wooden. He looks at what person meant literally at the time of the adoption of the Constitution. He notes what person must have meant in other clauses of the document. He observes that fetuses are not enumerated in the census. But he does not ask if the new biological data on the fetus compels the Court to be evolutionary in its definition of person as it is in its definition of liberty. He refrains from looking squarely at the facts of fetal existence. He takes the term person as if its meaning has been frozen forever. Contrary to the radical substance of the rest of his opinion, he is here, uniquely a strict constructionist. . . .

"Population growth, poverty and racial overtones" are mentioned by name only on page one of Wade as matters "tending to complicate the problem." They then disappear from view only to be embraced in the vague but comprehensive self-justification of the Court's holding: It is "consistent with . . . the demands of the profound problems of the present day" (Wade p. 50). Studiously ignored is the recommendation of the Rockefeller Commission that abortion be used as a secondary form of population control. Studiously ignored is the comment of black leaders like Jesse Jackson that what is being prepared by the welfare bureaucrats is a program of genocide in the womb. And yet the Court, looking back as it were on its handiwork, says its holding responds to profound problems of the present. What problems fall within the Court's solution but the problems of controlling population growth, the problems of welfare bureaucracy curtailing welfare rolls?[5]

Patrick T. Conley, an associate professor at Providence College who specialized in constitutional history, and Robert J. McKenna, an associate professor of politics at Salve Regina College, compared *Roe v. Wade* to the infamous *Dred Scott v. Sandford* decision of 1857 (see page 24) and condemned Blackmun for upholding a mother's right to privacy and casting aside the unborn child's right to life.

In the decade of the 1850s, one of the most vexing constitutional questions concerned the status of slavery in the federal territories. For reasons which historians have not yet fully fathomed, this issue became a vent for the economic, emotional, psychological, and moral disputes generated by the institution of slavery itself. . . . Then, in 1857, a Southern-dominated Supreme Court attempted to resolve this morally-charged dispute in what it considered to be a rational and impartial manner. The result was the Dred Scott decision in which the Court novelly employed the procedural Due Process Clause of the 5th Amendment to vindicate the pro-slave position. But it did so in disregard of historical precedents which made that view untenable. To compound its error, the Court contended that Negroes could not attain citizenship because such status contravened the intent of the Founding Fathers. . . .

On January 22, 1973, the United States Supreme Court, in magisterial fashion, undertook to resolve another moral controversy in the case of Roe v. Wade, and a companion case, Doe v. Bolton. These decisions concerned abortion, and here a right more fundamental than citizenship was at stake—at issue was the right to life. The Dred Scott analogy to Roe v. Wade is not an exercise in hyperbole; not only was a more basic right involved, but a much larger class was affected. In 1857, approximately 4,200,000 blacks and their descendants were judicially attainted, while in the year 1973 alone about 5 million living human fetuses will be shorn of their natural right to life for at least the first six months of their existence.

The right to privacy asserted by the Court is not only absent from the express provisions of the original Constitution, the Bill of Rights, and later Amendments, it is not generally recognized by law, custom, or by majority opinion. How could such an alleged right, therefore, be "so rooted in the traditional conscience of our people to be ranked as fundamental." It "simply fashions" says dissenting Justice White, "a new constitutional right for pregnant mothers and, with scarcely any reason or authority for its action, invests that right with sufficient substance to override most state abortion statutes."

The Court with equal effort could have "discovered" the unborn's right to life, invested it with "fundamental" status, and clothed it with judicial protection. This right is not explicit in any part of the Constitution, but unlike the right to abort, it is recognized by law, by custom, and by majority opinion.[6]

LIBERAL CRITICISM

Conservatives were not alone in castigating the decision. Some liberals also criticized it. The *New Republic* condemned the Court for trying to resolve a conflict better left to state lawmakers.

> Most states have abortion statutes. They are not uniform in their provisions. Some are old and some are new. All are currently in controversy and in flux. In their place, the Supreme Court has now prescribed a virtually uniform statute of its own, allowing very little variation. . . .
>
> There is a body of medical evidence now in existence, the Court tells us, showing that abortions during the first three months of pregnancy present no great risk. Well and good. . . . But the fetus is a potential life, and the Court acknowledges that society has a legitimate interest in it as such. And so does the individual—the woman and perhaps also the father—and the individual interest may be characterized as a claim to personal privacy, which in some contexts, all of them markedly different, the Constitution has been found to protect. The individual interest, the Court holds, completely overrides the interest of society in the first three months of pregnancy, and subject only to health regulations, also in the second. In the third trimester, society is in charge again.

Why? The Court never says. It simply asserts the result it has reached. That is all the Court can do because there is no answer that moral philosophy, logic, reason, or other materials of law can give to this question. If medical considerations were the only ones involved, perhaps a satisfactory rational answer could be arrived at. But as the court acknowledges, they are not. That is why the question is not for the courts, but should have been left to the political process, which in state after state can achieve not one but many accommodations and adjust them from time to time as attitudes change.[7]

A noted constitutional scholar, John Hart Ely, who had clerked for Chief Justice Earl Warren, is often cited as one of the most devastating critics of *Roe*. Ely contended that providing superprotection for a woman's right to choose was not "inferable from the language of the Constitution."

A woman's freedom to choose an abortion is part of the "liberty" the Fourteenth Amendment says shall not be denied without due process of law, as indeed is anyone's freedom to do what he wants. But "due process" generally guarantees only that the inhibition be procedurally fair and that it have some "rational" connection—though plausible is probably a better word—with a permissible governmental goal. What is unusual about Roe is that the liberty involved is accorded a far more stringent protection, so stringent that a desire to preserve the fetus's existence is unable to overcome it—a protection more stringent, I think it fair to say, than that the present Court accords the freedom of the press explicitly guaranteed by the First Amendment. What is frightening about Roe is that this super-protected right is not inferable from the language of the Constitution, the framers' thinking respecting the specific problem in issue, any general value derivable from the provisions they included, or the nation's governmental structure. Nor is it explainable in terms of the unusual political impotence of the group judicially protected vis-à-vis the interest that legislatively prevailed over it. . . . At times the inferences the Court has drawn from the values the Constitution marks for special protection have been controversial, even shaky, but never before has its sense of an obligation to draw been so obviously lacking.[8]

Catherine McKinnon, well-known as a radical feminist, asserted that reproductive rights should be based not on privacy as the Court held in *Roe,* but on equal protection, because antiabortion laws criminalize behavior that "only women need."

Because the social organization of reproduction is a major bulwark of women's social inequality, any constitutional interpretation of a sex equality principle must prohibit laws, state policies, or official practices and acts that deprive women of reproductive control or punish women for their reproductive role or capacity. . . . Women's right to reproductive control is a sex equality right because it is inconsistent with an equality mandate for the state, by law to collaborate with or mandate social inequality on the basis of sex, as such legal incursions do. This is not so much an argument for an extension of the meaning of constitutional sex equality as a recognition that if it does not mean this, it does not mean anything at all.

Under this sex equality analysis, criminal abortion statutes of the sort invalidated by Roe v. Wade violate equal protection laws. They make women criminals for a medical procedure only women need, or make others criminal for performing the procedure on women that only women need, when much of the need for this procedure as well as barriers to access to it have been created by social conditions of sex inequality. Forced motherhood is sex inequality. Because pregnancy can be experienced only by women, and because of the unequal social predicates and consequences pregnancy has for women, any forced pregnancy will always deprive and hurt one sex only as a member of her gender. Just as no man will ever become pregnant, no man will ever need an abortion, hence be in a position to be denied one by law. On this level, only women can be disadvantaged.[9]

Justice Ruth Bader Ginsburg, a former law professor, has argued that the Court should have issued a narrower ruling, overturning the Texas statute but leaving other antiabortion laws standing. Such a ruling would not have aroused the tremendous backlash that *Roe* produced and would have left the question in the hands of state legislatures. In 1985 she wrote:

> Roe ventured too far in the change it ordered. The sweep and detail of the opinion stimulated the mobilization of a right-to-life movement and an attendant reaction in Congress and state legislatures. In place of the trend "toward liberalization of abortion statutes" noted in Roe, legislatures adopted measures aimed at minimizing the impact of the 1973 rulings, including notification and consent requirements, prescriptions for the protection of fetal life, and bans on public expenditures for poor women's abortions.
>
> Professor Paul Freund explained where he thought the Court went astray in Roe, and I agree with his statement. The Court properly invalidated the Texas proscription, he indicated, because "[a] law that absolutely made criminal all kinds and forms of abortion could not stand up; it is not a reasonable accommodation of interests." If Roe had left off at this point and not adopted what Professor Freund called a "medical approach," physicians might have been less pleased with the decision, but the legislative trend might have continued in the direction in which it was headed in the early 1970s. "[S]ome of the bitter debate on the issue might have been averted," Professor Freund believed; "[t]he animus against the court might at least have been diverted to the legislative halls." . . .
>
> Roe, I believe, would have been more acceptable as a judicial decision if it had not gone beyond a ruling on the extreme statute before the court. The political process was moving in the early 1970s, not swiftly enough for advocates of quick, complete change, but majoritarian institutions were listening and acting. Heavy-handed judicial intervention was difficult to justify and appears to have provoked, not resolved conflict.[10]

The conflict over *Roe v. Wade* gained new life in 2005, when President George W. Bush nominated John G. Roberts Jr., a conservative federal appellate judge on the District of Columbia Circuit, to replace Chief Justice William H. Rehnquist. Right-to-life groups applauded the president's choice, while many supporting reproductive rights condemned it. Nor does the controversy over *Roe* seem likely to end anytime soon. That is because, in the words of Harvard law professor Laurence Tribe, the debate has become a "clash of absolutes" in which the opponents—liberal defenders of a woman's right to choose and social conservatives who believe that human life begins at conception—see little or no room for compromise.[11]

NOTES

1. *New York Times,* January 24, 1973.

2. *Wall Street Journal,* January 26, 1973.

3. *Nation,* February 5, 1973.

4. Editorial, *National Review,* March 2, 1973.

5. *National Review,* March 2, 1973.

6. Patrick T. Conley and Robert J. McKenna, "The Supreme Court on Abortion—A Dissenting Opinion," *Catholic Lawyer* (Winter 1973): 19, 25.

7. "Abortion," *New Republic,* February 10, 1973, 9.

8. John Hart Ely, "The Wages of Crying Wolf: A Comment," *Yale Law Journal* 82 (April 1973): 920, 935–937.

9. Catherine A. McKinnon, "Reflections on Sex Equality Under Law," *Yale Law Journal* 100 (March 1991): 1281, 1319–1320.

10. Ruth Bader Ginsburg, "Some Thoughts on Autonomy and Equality in Relation to *Roe v. Wade,*" *North Carolina Law Review* 63 (January 1985): 375, 381–382, 385.

11. Laurence Tribe, *Abortion: The Clash of Absolutes* (New York: W. W. Norton, 1992).

Regents of the University of California v. Bakke

Howard Ball

Regents of the University of California v. Bakke
438 U.S. 265 (1978)

> DECIDED: June 28, 1978
> VOTE: Multiple
> JUDGMENT OF THE COURT: Lewis F. Powell Jr.
> OPINION CONCURRING IN PART AND DISSENTING IN PART: William J. Brennan Jr., Byron R. White, Thurgood Marshall, Harry A. Blackmun
> OPINION CONCURRING IN PART AND DISSENTING IN PART: John Paul Stevens (Warren Burger, Potter Stewart, William H. Rehnquist)
> OPINION CONCURRING IN PART AND DISSENTING IN PART: White
> OPINION CONCURRING IN PART AND DISSENTING IN PART: Marshall
> OPINION CONCURRING IN PART AND DISSENTING IN PART: Blackmun

In the 1950s the United States experienced a general awakening regarding the brutal treatment of African Americans in the century after the Civil War. Powerful civil rights leaders and organizations emerged, including Martin Luther King Jr. of the Southern Christian Leadership Conference and Thurgood Marshall of the NAACP Legal Defense Fund. These and other civil rights groups attacked—through peaceful mass marches and through litigation—the very core of formalized racism in the South, including voting discrimination and the Jim Crow laws that governed all social relationships.

These actions led to the passage of major federal legislation, the 1964 Civil Rights Act and the 1965 Voting Rights Act. The bills addressed the reality of racial discrimination in public accommodations and employment as well as voting disfranchisement. They contained sections that, if properly implemented by federal and state officials, would remedy the wrongs that had been committed by whites against black citizens for more than 100 years. For example, Title VI of the 1964 Civil Rights Act prohibited discrimination based on race, color, national origin, and, later, sex in all institutions receiving federal funding. This section of the act was to become one of the two bases for arguing both in support of and opposition to the implementation of "affirmative action" admissions programs by college and university admissions officials.

Within a few years of the passage of the 1964 Civil Rights Act, university admissions committees, looking at the low numbers of minority students admitted to their undergraduate and graduate schools, began to develop and implement *preferential* minority affirmative action programs to "diversify" their student populations. For example, in 1968 the University of Washington School of Law, in an effort to remedy the "gross under-representation of certain minorities," created two pools of applicants: regular applications and those from adversely affected "social or ethnic backgrounds." Different criteria were used to evaluate applicants in the two groups; minority students were admitted with lower numerical scores than regular applicants, and within a few years the university's law school showed an increase in the number of minorities in attendance.

In 1970 the brand new University of California-Davis medical school implemented another type of affirmative action program: set-aside seats for minority applicants. Initially, eight of the fifty seats in the UC-Davis medical school were "set aside" for minority students. By 1973, when the enrollment doubled, so did the set aside for minority students. In that year, about 800 minority students were attending medical school in the United States, most at two predominantly black schools: Meharry Medical School in

Tennessee and Howard University's medical school in Washington, D.C. By the mid-1970s the *minority-preferential* affirmative action admission program had become the norm across the United States, and black student admissions had risen to about 1,200 students in 1978. The great majority of undergraduate and professional schools—especially at "elite" schools such as Harvard and Yale—used various kinds of affirmative action programs, separately or combined. By 1978, when *Bakke* was decided, many of these affirmative action programs had been in practice for almost a decade.

Allan Bakke, a white male, was employed as an engineer at the National Aeronautics and Space Agency (NASA) during this formative period of affirmative action development in higher education. He had graduated from the University of Minnesota in 1962 with a degree in mechanical engineering. In 1967, after serving two tours as a U.S. Marine captain in Vietnam, he became a research engineer at NASA's Ames Research Center in northern California. He married and had a family. Due in part to his experiences in Vietnam, however, Bakke began to plan for a career change to medicine. In 1972, at age thirty-two and far older than the typical medical school applicant, Bakke applied to about one dozen medical schools, including UC-Davis, which he preferred because of his family location.

His scores on the Medical College Admission Test (MCAT) and his other education statistics indicated that he was in the top tier of applicants. But UC-Davis, using its set-aside admissions process, rejected Bakke. In May 1973 he was turned down by UC-Davis and all the other schools. A few rejections noted that Bakke's age was a major factor in the admissions committee decision. In September Bakke was rejected for early admission into UC-Davis. In April 1974, after a terse interview with UC-Davis admissions committee staff, Bakke was again turned down.

Undaunted, Bakke filed suit in May 1974 in the Yolo County, California, Superior Court. This legal action came one month after the U.S. Supreme Court dismissed *DeFunis v. Odegaard* for "mootness." Marco DeFunis, a white man, had been denied admission by the University of Washington School of Law, which employed a preferential affirmative action admissions protocol. He appealed to the Washington courts and was allowed to attend the law school while the litigation continued. He was in his final semester when, in February 1974, the U.S. Supreme Court heard oral argument. By a 5–4 decision, the Court dismissed the suit as moot because DeFunis was about to graduate, and therefore his case no longer constituted the type of controversy necessary for a court to decide an issue.

Bakke's legal arguments were based on statutory and constitutional grounds. First, because UC-Davis was receiving federal funds, Title VI of the 1964 Civil Rights Act prohibited the university from discriminating on the basis of race in their admissions processes. Second, the Fourteenth Amendment's equal protection clause prohibited *any* state official—including the Board of Regents of the public University of California system—from discriminating on the basis of race or any other neutral factor.

THE COURT'S COMPLICATED DECISION

In November 1974 the Superior Court ruled that UC-Davis's preferential set-aside admissions program was unconstitutional, but, unlike DeFunis, Bakke was not permitted to attend school until the final outcome of his suit. In May 1975 the regents appealed the decision of the lower court judge to the California Supreme Court. In September 1976, by a vote of 6–1, the California Supreme Court validated the lower court judgment and ordered Allan Bakke admitted to the UC-Davis medical school.

In December the regents appealed the state supreme court decision to the U.S. Supreme Court, and the order admitting Bakke to medical school was stayed pending the result of the appeal. In February 1977 the Court granted *certiorari* (a decision to hear an appeal from a lower court), and oral arguments were scheduled for October, when Bakke would be almost thirty-eight years old.

In the months leading up to oral argument, nearly 60 *amicus curiae* (friend of the court) briefs, representing the views of more than 100 interest groups, were filed with the Court. In addition, the Court asked the new president, Democrat Jimmy Carter, elected in November 1976, to file an *amicus* brief expressing the views of the United States on the controversial question of preferential affirmative action in higher education programs.

Oral argument took place on October 11, 1977. Six days later the justices requested supplemental briefs on the Title VI question. Throughout the debates within the Court, the justices were split on the constitutionality of affirmative action admission programs.

Four—Chief Justice Burger and Justices Rehnquist, Stevens, and Stewart—believed that both types of affirmative action programs, the set-aside and those that used the race or ethnicity of an applicant in a positive manner, were inadmissible because they ran afoul of the Fourteenth Amendment's equal protection clause and/or Title VI. Stevens, who wrote for the quartet, was adamant that the case *not* be decided on constitutional grounds but rest on the Title VI argument.

Three others, Justices Brennan, Marshall, and White, maintained that *all* affirmative action programs were constitutional. They believed, from beginning to end, that both the Fourteenth Amendment and Title VI allowed institutions receiving federal funds to provide for temporary and transitional and *benign* affirmative action admissions programs in order to redress a century of discrimination against black and other minority applicants.

Two justices, Powell and Blackmun, did not circulate memos until December 1977 (Powell) and May 1978 (Blackmun). Powell's circulation in December, which was to be the judgment for the Court, argued that race could be used as a positive factor in admission decisions and cited Harvard College's admissions protocol. Diversity, he maintained, was a compelling reason for creating affirmative action programs for college admissions. Powell concluded, however, that the UC-Davis and other affirmative action admission protocols that set aside a certain number of seats for black and other minority students was an unconstitutional quota.

The 4–3–1 stalemate stood until late spring 1978. Blackmun had been away from the Court because of a medical problem, and his colleagues awaited his views. If he came down on the side of his friend, Chief Justice Burger, there would be five votes to affirm the California courts and end all affirmative action in higher education policies and practices; and Burger expected Blackmun to vote that way. When Blackmun circulated his opinion on May 1, however, it came down squarely on the side of the three justices who argued that affirmative action programs were constitutional and that the California courts were wrong when they invalidated the UC-Davis medical school admissions program.

Thus, by mid-May the voting alignment was quite complicated. Burger, Stevens, Stewart, and Rehnquist *joined* Powell's opinion striking down quotas or set-aside affirmative action admissions programs. But they *dissented* from Powell's observation that race could be taken into consideration in the college admissions process. Brennan, Marshall, Blackmun, and White *joined* Powell's opinion regarding the use of race as a factor in admissions decisions, but they *dissented* from Powell's assertion that set-asides or quotas used in an admission process were unconstitutional. On June 28, 1978, the Court announced its unusual decision. The day before, Powell sent a note to his colleagues: "It is difficult to refer—with brevity—to the various authors and joiners of the several [six] opinions. . . . As I am a 'chief' with no 'Indians,' I should be in the rear rank, not up front."

How the Solomon-like *Bakke* decision was reported on June 29 depended on the newspaper's point of view. Conservative papers screamed: "White Student Wins Reverse Bias Case" (*Chicago Sun-Times*). Liberal papers announced: "Affirmative Action Upheld" (*Washington Post*). The *Los Angeles Times* ran two stories about the case on its front page: "Historic Ruling Strikes Down Davis Quotas" and "School Ruling Seen as a Victory for Civil Rights." Who won? The *Wall Street Journal* story was probably the most valid of these media assessments. Its banner: "The Decision Everyone Won." Bakke began medical school at UC-Davis in September 1978, six years after he applied. He graduated four years later at age forty-two and took a residency at the Mayo Clinic in Minnesota. He continued to practice medicine in Minnesota, his home state.

Allan Bakke is followed by reporters after his first day at the medical school of the University of California at Davis in 1978. Originally denied admission, Bakke sued the university over its affirmative action program, which he claimed disadvantaged white applicants. In *Regents of the University of California v. Bakke* (1978), a divided Supreme Court rejected racial quotas but allowed race to be considered as one of many factors in admissions. Bakke was subsequently admitted. —AP Wide World Photos/Walt Zeboski

BAKKE'S IMPACT, 1978–2003

The *Bakke* case was a watershed affirmative action decision that had a major impact on institutions of higher education and graduate professional programs. It was the first substantive opinion by the U.S. Supreme Court regarding the constitutionality of college and university admissions programs that took the race of applicants into positive account when deciding who was to be admitted.

Bakke was also part of the continuing political and philosophical debate, often hostile, within the Court as well as in the halls of academia and society at large. The controversy over affirmative action policy centered on the notions of equality and "getting ahead" in a democratic society that has emphasized the notion of merit as the criterion for success in America. As supporters of affirmative action argued from the beginning of the struggle in the 1960s, however, for minorities and women, the meritocracy was a fiction. Equality between the races did not exist with regard to joining a union, getting a good job, buying or renting a house, or going to college. Instead, inequality, Jim Crow laws, discrimination, and segregation made a mockery of the idea of merit.

In the 1960s the situation began to change with the emergence of the public policy of affirmative action. As a way of overcoming past inequity, the preferential use of race and ethnicity and gender was incorporated into legislation and federal regulations, and the U.S. Supreme Court validated these political actions. Because of the often-violent history of racial discrimination and segregation, supporters of affirmative action maintained that the state had to move "beyond simple, race neutral non-discrimination." President Lyndon B. Johnson gave voice to the new notion in a June 1965 commencement speech at Howard University:

You do not wipe away the scars of centuries by saying [to the African American]: Now you are free to go where you want, and do as you desire. . . . You do not take a person who for years has been hobbled by chains and liberate him, bring him up to the starting line of a race and then say "You are free to compete with all the others," and still justly believe you have been completely fair. Thus it is not enough just to open the gates of opportunity. All our citizens must have the ability to walk through the gates. *This is the next and more profound stage of the battle for civil rights.* We seek not just freedom but opportunity. We seek not just legal equity but human ability, not just equality as a right and a theory but equality as a fact and equality as a result.[1]

Minorities and women trying to pull themselves out of "gateless poverty *just cannot do it alone* because of the endless years of hatred and hopelessness," said the president. Minorities need additional help from government programs that make the playing field level for the first time in American social and economic history. A few months later, Johnson's chairman of the newly created Equal Employment Opportunity Commission (EEOC), Franklin D. Roosevelt Jr., said:

We assume that merit employment is morally right and that most companies are living up to the civil rights law, but there's room for them *to go beyond the law* and it will be good for them and for the community. [Affirmative action programs call for] more *aggressive leadership and recruitment* and participation by private business in promoting equal employment opportunity . . . *more than is required by law:* We must go out looking for potential [minority] employees . . . let them know they are welcome in places where doors were once closed . . . and give them special training so that they may qualify.[2]

Countering these arguments were groups that insisted on racial, ethnic, and gender *neutrality* and claimed that the preferential use of race and ethnicity and gender violated the Constitution and went against the essential values of American society. For the critics, on and off the federal courts, the U.S. Constitution was a "color-blind" fundamental law, one that brooked no unjust discrimination based on an individual's race, ethnicity, or sex. Curiously, in the 1972 presidential campaign against Democratic candidate George McGovern, President Richard Nixon, whose administration cautiously supported affirmative action programs in his first term, voiced the anger of the anti–affirmative action, pro-meritocracy community:

Every man, woman, and child should be free to rise as far as his talents, and energy, and ambitions will take him. This is the American dream. But into that dream has entered a specter, the specter of a quota democracy—where men and women are advanced not on the basis of merit or ability, but solely on the basis of race, or sex, or color, or creed. . . . You do not correct an ancient injustice by committing a new one.[3]

At the same time as *Bakke* extended affirmative action to college admissions practices, the EEOC extended its reach into higher education by requiring institutions of higher learning to establish "goals" and "timetables" for recruiting faculty and staff who were underrepresented in college academic and administrative departments. Irving Kristol, a fiery opponent of affirmative action, said that the EEOC guidelines were

a discriminatory quota system—based on race, color, religion, sex, and national origin—imposed on college faculties. [The federal bureaucrats were the culprits because they claim] that a "goal" plus a "timetable" does not add up to a quota. Of all the lies to emanate from Washington in recent years, this is the most dispiriting—it is such a blatant lie, perceived by everyone involved to be a lie, in elementary logic a lie, on the record a lie.[4]

J. Stanley Pottinger, one of the federal bureaucrats in the Department of Health, Education, and Welfare, had a brief response to Kristol's broadside: "Balderdash. That is the biggest crock I have ever heard." The "goals" and "timetables," he said, "[are] not rigid and inflexible quotas that must be met."[5]

And the argument continued. "To treat our black students equally, we have to treat them differently," said Vanderbilt University's chancellor, Alexander Heard, a supporter. His view mirrored that of Justice Blackmun, who wrote in his *Bakke* opinion, "We must first take account of race. . . . *And in order to treat some persons equally we must treat them differently.* We cannot—we dare not—let the Equal Protection Clause perpetuate racial superiority."

Opponents of *Bakke,* such as conservative Republicans Terry Eastland and William Bennett, argued that the case was

> Supremely a conflict between two ideas of equality, one the idea of numerical equality, as represented by the academic institution, the University of California, and the other the ideal of moral equality, as represented by the individual, Allan Bakke.[6]

Other conservatives were not as charitable in their criticism of *Bakke.* For example, Robert H. Bork, a highly regarded conservative law professor at the time, said, simply: "Those who supported the UCD affirmative action plan challenged in *Bakke,* especially those on the U.S. Supreme Court, were *the hard-core racists of reverse discrimination.*"[7]

For twenty-five years *Bakke* was the only precedent on point regarding the validity of affirmative action in higher education. It reflected the clash of views between those who argued for race neutrality and those who argued for true equality. In two cases, *Grutter v. Bollinger* and *Gratz v. Bollinger,* which began in 1999 and were decided in June 2003, the U.S. Supreme Court again took up the argument that had been taking place out of court regarding merit versus equality. In *Grutter,* the Court, 5–4, reaffirmed the validity of the *Bakke* decision.

Bakke had invalidated set-aside affirmative action programs, but validated the use of race and ethnicity as positive factors that would enable a university's admissions process to diversify its student population. *Bakke*'s "implementing population"—college and university admissions officers, faculty, and administrators—very quickly reoriented their affirmative action programs to align with the judgment of the Court. Doing so meant ending all set-aside programs and developing an affirmative action program, modeled along the lines of Harvard's, as Justice Powell suggested in his opinion. By 1990 almost 12 percent of students attending institutions of higher learning in America were African Americans.

The presidential elections in the 1980s focused, in part, on the emergent issue of affirmative action in business, industry, and education. Republican politicians condemned *Bakke* and other Supreme Court decisions that validated affirmative action programs in both the public and private sectors. Democrats defended affirmative action as an appropriate remedial policy for more than a century of discrimination. The Republicans won the elections of 1980, 1984, and 1988, and supporters of affirmative action steeled themselves for the expected legislative, executive, and judicial actions that would end the concept.

With six vacancies during the Republican administrations of Ronald Reagan and George H. W. Bush, a newly constituted Supreme Court emerged between 1981 and 1992. By 1993 only three justices who supported affirmative action in higher education—White, Blackmun, and Stevens—remained. The sextet of new jurists were all perceived as conservatives: Sandra Day O'Connor, Antonin Scalia, Anthony Kennedy, David Souter, and Clarence Thomas and, elevated to the center seat by Reagan, William Rehnquist. This new majority was able to narrow and finally overturn earlier Supreme Court decisions regarding the validity of affirmative action programs in government contracting and business in cases such as *City of Richmond, Virginia v. Croson* (1989), and *Adarand Constructors v. Peña* (1995).

During the presidential elections of 1992 and 1996, the Republican presidential candidates, George Bush and Bob Dole (who, until he was nominated, was a long-time supporter of affirmative action programs), ran on platforms that condemned affirmative action in higher education programs and promised to appoint justices who would, joining the conservatives already on the Court, overturn *Bakke*. Democrat Bill Clinton won both elections, however, and, through executive actions and his appointments to the U.S. Supreme Court—Ruth Bader Ginsburg replaced White in 1993, and Steven Breyer replaced Blackmun in 1994—temporarily ended the assault on *Bakke*. Clinton's view of affirmative action was a positive one, and his instructions to his administrators was simple: "Mend it, don't end it."

In the mid-1990s, however, *Bakke* came under attack by conservative politicians, such as Gov. Pete Wilson, R-Calif., and conservative legal pressure groups such as the Center for Individual Rights in a number of states including California, Florida, Massachusetts, Texas, and Washington, among others. The views of Ward Connerly, a member of the Board of Regents of the University of California, reflect perfectly those of the anti–affirmative action movement. He believes that "there is a deeply rooted culture of equality in America that transcends political correctness, partisanship, and ideology."

> We can trace this culture back to the Declaration of Independence: "We hold these truths to be self-evident, that all men are created equal." . . . When Martin Luther King Jr. led the nation through the tumultuous civil rights era, beginning with the public bus boycott in Montgomery in 1955, he invoked that culture of equality in calling on America to "live out the true meaning of your creed." The principle of equality has been embraced by liberal Democrats and conservative Republicans alike, from Lyndon Johnson to Ronald Reagan.
>
> The debate about affirmative action preferences is fundamentally about the rights and responsibilities of American citizenship. *It is about whether we will have a system of government and a social system in which we see each other as equals.* Although often lost in the rhetorical clamor about its benefits, race-based affirmative action as a concept is, at its core, a challenge to the relationship between individuals and their government. It is a direct threat to the culture of equality that defines the character of the nation.
>
> Those who support affirmative action programs contend that such programs are necessary to provide equal opportunity for women and minorities. . . . But when you strip away all the rhetoric about "leveling the playing field" and "building diversity," preferential policies reduce themselves to two essential questions. First, are white males entitled to the same assertion of civil rights and equal treatment under the law as women and minorities? Second, how much longer is the nation going to maintain policies that presume that American-born black people are mentally inferior and incapable of competing head-to-head with other people, except in athletics and entertainment? We cannot resolve the issue of race in America without coming to terms with these two questions. And we certainly cannot reconcile the conflicts about affirmative action preferences without answering these questions.[8]

If the conservatives were stalled at the national level in their effort to end affirmative action, they could, through elections, initiatives, referenda, propositions, constitutional amendments, and legal actions, end affirmative action programs at the state level. Indeed, Connerly's efforts in California and Washington influenced voters in both states to pass propositions banning affirmative action programs in their jurisdictions.

In 1996, 54 percent of Californians approved Proposition 209, euphemistically called the "California Civil Rights Initiative: A Prohibition Against Discrimination of Preferential Treatment by State and Other Public Entities." It became Article I, Section 31, of the California Constitution: "The state shall not discriminate against, or grant preferential treatment to, any individual or group on the basis of race, sex, color, ethnicity, or national origin in the operation of public employment, education, or public contracting." Civil rights groups challenged the constitutionality of the proposition, but the California courts validated the proposition, and in 1997 the U.S. Supreme Court denied *certiorari*.

By 1999 minority law school admissions in California had dropped 71 percent. This drop in enrollment was so precipitous that the university regents quickly developed a new general admission policy for all institutions in the UC system: the top 4 percent of graduates in every high school in the state were guaranteed admission to any one of the UC schools.

In November 1998 almost 70 percent of voters in Washington State approved Initiative 200, patterned after California's Proposition 209. For more than a year, Connerly and his anti–affirmative action political action groups, aggressively—and successfully—campaigned for the initiative. The ballot asked voters: "Shall government be prohibited from discriminating or granting preferential treatment based on race, sex, color, ethnicity, or national origin in public employment, education, and contracting."

Connerly's rhetoric continuously emphasized that *equality* is the critical principle in America, not "race."

> America should embrace the notion that we don't want race, whatever "race" is; I always put that in quotes because I'm not sure anymore. What I think is that we need to get comfortable with this notion of equality. We need to get comfortable that regardless of your sexual orientation, your religion, your age, your color or where your ancestors came from, if you are an American citizen, you have a package of rights, civil rights. We are going to disburse those rights and when you interact with your government we are going to treat you without regard to those considerations. We are not going to take into account all of those factors and how we deal with you as a government.
>
> We will practice, practice, practice living with that creed. We won't fudge it to make up for the past. We won't fudge it because we think that somehow we are better off if we have more of these and more of those. We are going to live by that rule.[9]

Connerly and his group, the American Civil Rights Coalition, also campaigned in Florida toward the end of the 1990s. After *Bakke,* Florida higher education officials created a statewide affirmative action program that significantly diversified its higher education student population. By 1999 at the University of Florida, formerly the all-white flagship institution, African American and Hispanic American students made up more than 16 percent of the school's enrollment. Throughout the state, in 1999, 64 percent of university students were Caucasian, 14 percent were black, and another 14 percent were Hispanic.

Connerly was effective in influencing the views of Floridians. By 1999 a whopping 84 percent of voters polled supported a ban on preferential treatment of certain minorities. Before the issue was placed on the ballot, however, in mid-November 1999 Republican governor Jeb Bush issued two executive orders ending the use of race and ethnicity as factors in the university admissions process and barring the use of set-asides in state contracting actions. The orders, called the "One Florida Initiative," were similar to the California regents' actions; they guaranteed the top 20 percent of high school graduates a university education in one of the state's universities. That same year, the Board of Trustees of the University of Massachusetts system unilaterally ended the state's higher education affirmative action admissions program. Connerly has continued to campaign across the country, moving from Michigan to New York to Massachusetts and other states in his effort to provide support for anti–affirmative action group activities.

In Texas another approach was used to minimize or eradicate the impact of the *Bakke* decision. In 1996 the U.S. Court of Appeals for the Fifth Circuit heard a case that challenged the constitutionality of the University of Texas Law School's affirmative action program. The law school's admission practices were based on certain annual recruitment "goals," not quotas: 10 percent Hispanic American and 5 percent African American admissions. Cheryl Hopwood and four other Caucasians not admitted to the law school challenged the policy. They claimed, as DeFunis and Bakke had argued two decades earlier, that such an admission policy violated the Fourteenth Amendment's equal protection clause. They lost in the district court.

The three-judge circuit court panel, all conservatives appointed by Reagan and Bush, unanimously over-turned the district judge's conclusions upholding the Texas program. They also appeared to have *invalidated* Justice Powell's judgment in *Bakke,* quite a unique action of a lower federal appeals court! The panel referred to the Powell's as a "lonely opinion." Powell's view in *Bakke,* two of the judges wrote, "is not binding prece-dent because [much of the opinion] was joined by no other justice." The third judge in the panel disagreed with his colleagues: if *Bakke* were to be declared dead, he claimed, the U.S. Supreme Court should do it.

The trio concluded that the affirmative action program was unconstitutional because it "carries the danger of stigmatic harm." Ironically, the judges used the very argument Thurgood Marshall employed when he, for the NAACP, had asked the U.S. Supreme Court in 1952 to strike down the 1896 "separate but equal" *Plessy v Ferguson* precedent (see page 75). In 1952 the "stigmatic harm" allegedly befell black young-sters attending segregated schools; in 1996 it allegedly harmed young white adults who were denied admis-sion to the University of Texas Law School. In June 1996 the Court declined to grant *certiorari* in *Hopwood.* As a result, the decision, apparently overturning *Bakke,* was the law of the land in the Fifth Circuit—Mis-sissippi, Louisiana, and Texas. Its impact was immediate. Only twenty-three black and Hispanic students began law school at the University of Texas in 1997, and in 1998 only seven minority students were admit-ted to the law school.

Texas legislators responded to *Hopwood* by creating the "Texas Top Ten Plan." Similar to actions in California and Florida, Texas guaranteed that the top 10 percent of high school graduates could attend any of the state's public colleges or universities. This plan affected undergraduate admissions only. A year after the U.S. Supreme Court declined to review *Hopwood,* Hispanic American enrollments in graduate educa-tion in Texas dropped by 64 percent, and that of African Americans tumbled 88 percent.

This was how matters stood at the end of the twentieth century. *Bakke* was still precedent across the United States, except for the states covered by the Fifth Circuit and for states whose voters had acted to end all public affirmative action programs. *Bakke* had been the *imprimatur,* the legitimization, by the nation's highest court, of the practice of preferential and temporary affirmative action higher education admissions processes. From 1978 to 1999 African American enrollments had increased by more than 30 percent, and by more than 40 percent in graduate and professional schools. Overall Hispanic American enrollments were even higher: more than a 50 percent increase in this time period. Similar increases were seen in this same period for medical school admissions of black and Hispanic applicants. The increase in minority stu-dents attending and graduating from U.S. medical schools was more than 40 percent.

With the rise of ideologically conservative legal action groups, new legal challenges to *Bakke* were to be expected. In 1999 lawyers for the Center for Individual Rights (CIR), the same organization that had repre-sented Cheryl Hopwood and others in 1996, began arguing on behalf of white students, both undergradu-ate and professional school applicants to the University of Michigan who had been denied admission. Curt Levey, legal and public affairs director of the CIR, expressed the group's basic argument against affirmative action in higher education. After oral arguments in the Court in 2003, Levey was asked whether "it is your view that race should never be used in admissions decisions?" He answered:

> Yes, it is. If the last 25 years since the *Bakke* decision have taught us anything it's that schools can't be trusted to use race as just a small factor in seeking intellectual diversity. Instead this nation's elite schools have almost universally used it as a superfactor to achieve racial balancing. Since if you give them an inch the schools will take a mile, it's important now for the court to draw a bright line and say that applicants must be con-sidered as individuals without regard to race. Their position is that racial preferences are the only way to achieve racial diversity. But they have to argue that because if they were to admit that there is a race-neutral way of doing it their racial preferences would be per se unconstitutional under current Supreme Court precedent. . . . While the Center for Individual Rights does not endorse any specific race-neutral alternatives, *we do believe*

that the general approach of race-neutral alternatives based on actual disadvantage is a powerful step in the right direction. More importantly, race-neutral methods are presumed constitutional absent evidence to the contrary. Whereas Michigan's racially discriminatory admissions system is presumed unconstitutional unless the university meets its burden of showing that diversity is not just important but so compelling that it can overcome the bedrock principle of the civil rights movement, namely, that people should not be judged on the basis of their race.[10]

The U.S. Court of Appeals for the Sixth Circuit validated Michigan's undergraduate and graduate preferential admissions programs. The Supreme Court granted *certiorari* because, as Justice O'Connor said, "[There is] a question of national importance [that must be addressed]: Whether diversity is a compelling interest that can justify the narrowly tailored use of race in selecting applicants for admission to public universities." The Court handed down its decisions in *Grutter,* the law school admissions case, and *Gratz,* the undergraduate admissions case, in June 2003, reaffirming the *precedential* value of *Bakke.*

The undergraduate admissions process, ruled the Court in a 6–3 opinion, with Chief Justice Rehnquist writing for the majority in *Gratz,* was too similar to the quota process prohibited in *Bakke* and was "not narrowly tailored to achieve a compelling interest in diversity." In *Grutter,* however, the Court concluded, 5–4, that the affirmative action admission process was narrowly tailored to achieve the compelling educational goal of diversity. In her decision for the Court, perhaps addressing the *Hopwood* judges, O'Connor strongly reaffirmed the potency of Powell's opinion *for the Court* in *Bakke.* His opinion, she wrote, was the *"touchstone for constitutional analysis of race-conscious admission policies"* for *all* universities and colleges, both public and private.

> Today we hold that the Law School has a compelling interest in attaining a diverse student body. It has been 25 years since Justice Powell first approved the use of race to further an interest in student body diversity. . . . Since that time, the number of minority applicants with high grades and test scores has indeed increased. We expect that 25 years from now, the use of racial preferences will no longer be necessary to further the interest approved today.

Unmistakenly, *Grutter* overturned the *Hopwood* opinion and enabled colleges and universities in Texas, Louisiana, and Mississippi to once again implement narrowly tailored preferential admissions policies to further diversity their student bodies. What the full impact of the University of Michigan cases may be another story for scholars to investigate.

NOTES

1. Quoted in Howard Ball, *The Bakke Case* (Lawrence: University Press of Kansas, 2000), 11–12.
2. Quoted in Terry Anderson, *The Pursuit of Fairness: A History of Affirmative Action* (New York: Oxford University Press, 2004), 90.
3. Quoted in ibid., 139.
4. Quoted in ibid., 144.
5. Ibid.
6. Quoted in Ball, *Bakke Case,* 15.
7. Quoted in ibid. 142.
8. Ward Connerly, "On the Defensive: Quota Defenders Are Having a Tough Time," *National Review On-Line,* April 15, 2005, www.nationalreview.com/document/connerly200504150756.asp.
9. Ward Connerly, "The Cancer of Race," *National Review On-Line,* January 2, 2003, www.nationalreview.com.
10. Curt Levey, "Affirmative Action: Affirmed," *Court TV On-Line,* June 24, 2003, www.courttv.com/talk/chat _transcripts/2003/0624affirmact-levey.html, emphasis added.

Wallace v. Jaffree

Jason E. Whitehead

Wallace v. Jaffree
472 U.S. 38 (1985)

DECIDED: JUNE 4, 1985

VOTE

CONCURRING: 6 (William J. Brennan Jr., Thurgood Marshall, Harry A. Blackmun, Lewis F. Powell Jr., John Paul Stevens, Sandra Day O'Connor)

DISSENTING: 3 (Warren Burger, Byron R. White, William H. Rehnquist)

OPINION OF THE COURT: Stevens

CONCURRING OPINION: Powell

OPINION CONCURRING IN JUDGMENT: O'Connor

DISSENTING OPINION: Burger

DISSENTING OPINION: White

DISSENTING OPINION: Rehnquist

In *Wallace v. Jaffree* the Supreme Court struck down a 1982 Alabama law that authorized a one-minute period of silence in public schools for "meditation or voluntary prayer." Ishmael Jaffree, an attorney and the father of three elementary school children in Mobile, claimed the law violated the First Amendment's prohibition on the establishment of religion, and he filed suit against the governor of the state, George C. Wallace.

Writing for a 6–3 majority, Justice Stevens held that Alabama's law constituted an establishment of religion in violation of the First Amendment of the U.S. Constitution. It was clear from the record, Justice Stevens concluded, that Alabama's purpose in authorizing the moment of silence was not secular, but designed to promote religious activity. The law violated the first prong of the establishment clause test laid out in *Lemon v. Kurtzman* (1971), as well as the "established principle that the government must pursue a course of complete neutrality toward religion." Despite this holding, however, the Court also indicated a willingness to uphold other moment-of-silence laws that do not mention or clearly encourage prayer. In one dissenting opinion, Chief Justice Burger accused the majority of showing "not neutrality, but hostility toward religion." In a separate dissent, Justice Rehnquist reviewed the historical evidence for the metaphor of a "wall of separation" between church and state, arguing that it is based on "bad history" and had "proved useless as a guide to judging." Accordingly, Rehnquist concluded, the metaphor should be "frankly and explicitly abandoned."

The case is significant because it reinforced a long line of decisions outlawing state-sponsored prayer in public schools—beginning in 1962 with *Engel v. Vitale* (see page 215). It also marked a change from what had been the Court's view of the establishment clause—that it allowed some accommodation of religion by government. The division between Justice O'Connor, who voted with the majority, and Justice Rehnquist, who voted with the minority, presaged a continuing disagreement on the Court over whether the Court should continue the "strict neutrality" approach or should switch to a more accommodating approach to church-state relations.

Wallace v. Jaffree immediately re-ignited a virulent and acrimonious debate over the place of religion in American life and over the place of the Supreme Court in the American political system. On the one side, many conservatives—including those on the burgeoning religious Right—saw the decision as one more attempt by liberals and secular humanists to eradicate religion from the public sphere. They also saw the decision as the latest example of illegitimate activism by a Supreme Court out of touch with the values of ordinary Americans. They argued that the Court should strictly interpret the words of the Constitution in light of the original intent of the Framers, rather than imposing its own liberal political preferences. On the other side, many liberals saw *Wallace v. Jaffree* as further vindication of their long-established belief that government and religion should mix only rarely and minimally, if at all. They saw Alabama's moment-of-silence law as an attempt by religious conservatives and others to impose their narrow religious preferences on children who had no choice but to cooperate. In their eyes, the Court had acted heroically by ensuring that public schools welcomed children from all religious backgrounds.

SURPRISE, RELIEF, AND OUTRAGE

The decision came as somewhat of a surprise to many scholars and Court watchers. For example, Dean Jesse H. Choper of the University of California-Berkeley School of Law, an expert on church-state issues, exclaimed: "I bet . . . I've given 20 speeches around the country predicting it would come down the other way."[1] Noted *New York Times* reporter Linda Greenhouse put this surprise in the context of the Court's previous establishment clause decisions: "In declaring unconstitutional Alabama's 'moment of silence' statute, the Court signaled an unexpected about-face in its approach to the relationship between church and state."[2] Immediately after the decision was announced, she wrote:

> The Court has given abundant signals in the last few years that it was ready to relax its
> long emphasis on the strict separation of church and state. . . . But that tone was absent
> from the [*Jaffree*] opinion . . . which in its emphasis on government neutrality toward
> religion instead provided a strong reaffirmation of the traditional approach.[3]

But no one was more surprised than the people actually involved in the lawsuit. Plaintiff Ishmael Jaffree exclaimed: "I'm excited. Excited is an improper word, I'm ecstatic, surprised."[4] On the other side, the defendant, Gov. George C. Wallace, D-Ala., said he was "disturbed and disappointed" by the ruling.[5] The former president of the local school board, Dan Alexander, was defiant: "We think the majority of the folks in this country want voluntary vocal prayer in the classroom. That's what we're going to continue fighting for."[6]

Others closely involved in the case were equally determined. Alabama state senator Donald Holmes, who wrote Alabama's moment-of-silence law, vowed to continue the fight: "I'll never give up and I think this is an issue that most Americans . . . will not give up on."[7] Douglas T. Smith, an eighth-grade science teacher in Alabama, who had filed his own lawsuit against Jaffree, was dumbfounded: "I stand in shock . . . . It's like they're saying I have freedom of speech as long as I say what the state wants me to say. . . . When you remove any mention of God from the school system . . . that tells the students our country doesn't think God is important."[8]

President Ronald Reagan's Justice Department had sided with Alabama and participated as an *amicus curiae* (friend of the court). A department spokesperson chose to look on the bright side: "We regret that the court did not agree with our position. . . . We are pleased, however, that the court did not hold that the moment-of-silence laws now existing in some two dozen states offend the Constitution."[9]

Rex Lee, the U.S. solicitor general when *Jaffree* was argued, expressed the same mixture of surprise and relief. On the one hand, he said, "I really thought we would win it." On the other hand, he rejoiced in the limited nature of the Court's holding and speculated on how much room it left open for voluntary prayer:

> I think it's of greater symbolic importance than anything. It is true that the court held
> that . . . this particular statute enacted by the state of Alabama is unconstitutional. But,
> as I read the court's decision, it also quite clearly holds that, properly enacted, moment-
> of-silence statutes will not run afoul of the Constitution. . . . And I would also go further
> . . . and argue rather forcefully that it would be indeed an anomaly under the aegis of a
> free exercise clause or a freedom of religion clause to then say that if a moment of silence

statute in general is permissible, that . . . it is permissible to use [it] for every purpose except one, and that is for silent expression by the individual.[10]

Those closest to President Reagan, however, seemed more upset. At a speech before the American Bar Association (ABA), Attorney General Edwin Meese III seized on *Jaffree* as an example of the Court's liberal waywardness. He accused the Court of wandering "at large in a veritable constitutional forest" by issuing opinions, such as *Jaffree*, which are "more policy choices than articulations of constitutional principle." The original intent of the establishment clause, he asserted, "was to prohibit religious tyranny, not to undermine religion generally."[11] Requiring "strict neutrality between religion and nonreligion," as *Jaffree* did, "would have struck the founding generation as somewhat bizarre."[12]

President Reagan's responses were initially muted, but grew more critical over time. When asked about the decision when it was announced, White House spokesman Larry Speakes declined comment: "We haven't had the opportunity to review it. . . . We don't generally comment on Supreme Court decisions unless they're outrageous."[13] It did not take long for the administration to decide the case was sufficiently outrageous. Speaking to Alabama's congressional delegation, Reagan said *Jaffree* showed "we still have an uphill battle before us" in protecting religious freedom.[14] The next fall, when asked about Meese's comments before the ABA, the president largely agreed with them:

> Over recent years, we have had courts that tended to legislate rather than interpret the Constitution. Their ruling against prayer in schools is kind of strange in a body that opens with prayer and that has over its doorway "In God We Trust." I am opposed to the idea of a formal prayer in school and a dictated prayer by officialdom or school authorities or anyone else. What I am in favor of is eliminating a court decision that tells a generation of young people coming up through our schools that prayer is unacceptable in certain public areas. The Congress of the United States opens with prayer. I think the Supreme Court went beyond its province there.[15]

RIGHTEOUS INDIGNATION

The most vocal and consistent criticisms of *Jaffree* came from groups on the burgeoning religious Right. Rev. Jerry Falwell, founder of the Moral Majority, was quick to attack the case as one more example of liberal judges attempting to remove God from the public arena and impose a kind of thought control on America's youth:

> The ruling in my opinion is atrocious. It places religious children in second class citizenship. If the court . . . had simply said a moment of silence is [un]constitutional, period, without the additional comment that forbid[s] school teachers to suggest . . . that prayer is one option among many, . . . they would not have established this country as an atheistic state. But because they did add that, they were saying really . . . that one may think immoral thoughts or atheistic thoughts or whatever, but no thought about God—that is forbidden in the USA. And that sounds more like the Soviet Union than this country.[16]

Political columnist Cal Thomas, a Moral Majority spokesman, called the decision "ludicrous." He said the case reinforced "the philosophy in our public schools and many other institutions today . . . that a dose of God is more hazardous to your health than a dose of herpes or drugs."[17] He predicted, however, that the ruling would actually be counterproductive by increasing support for a constitutional amendment allowing school prayer—an issue that would have "just gone away" if not for *Jaffree*.[18]

Roy C. Jones, legislative director of the Moral Majority, agreed with this analysis. He called the ruling a "gross misinterpretation of the Constitution," which provided further evidence of the Court's "open

This cartoon by Bill "Whitey" Sanders appeared during the fallout over the school prayer decision in *Wallace v. Jaffree* (1985), in which the Supreme Court struck down an Alabama law that authorized a one-minute period of silence in public schools for "meditation or voluntary prayer." Despite its ruling, the Court expressed a willingness to uphold other moment-of-silence laws that do not expressly promote prayer. —Bill Sanders, *The Milwaukee Journal*, with permission by Kentucky Library and Museum, Western Kentucky University

hostility" to religion: "Students cannot be expected to shed their religious beliefs and practices each time they enter their classrooms." He predicted that *Jaffree* would be "the spark which will start our momentum moving again for a congressional solution to this problem, either through a constitutional amendment or by limiting the court's jurisdiction on this matter."[19] Summing up the Moral Majority's spin on the decision Jones claimed, "We don't view this decision as a defeat, but we view it as a victory."[20]

Other conservative religious figures and groups also saw the case as a watershed moment in church-state relations. Robert Grant, from the Christian Voice, called the ruling "stupid, sad and shameful."[21] Tim LaHaye, of the American Coalition for Traditional Values, called it a "tragic day in American history," because the case represents a "breakdown in values."[22] James McClellan, director of the Center for Judicial Studies, agreed that the ruling was actually a victory for advocates of school prayer: "That cat is out of the bag and the pro-prayer groups now have a rallying point they did not have before."[23]

Other noted conservative leaders took up the call against the *Jaffree* decision and in favor of amending the Constitution. Gov. John Ashcroft, R-Mo., a future senator and U.S. attorney general, attacked the Court's "phobic response to the six-letter word 'prayer.' " Conservative activist Paul Weyrich expanded on this idea, claiming that "it means the f-word is protected, but you still can't think [about] God." Legendary fund-raiser Richard Viguerie agreed with calls by the religious Right for legislative action: "We're going to turn the heat up on Congress." [24]

Columnist George Will further summed up the conservative reaction to the perceived silliness and inconsistency of the *Jaffree* decision:

> What injury does a moment of silence do, even if the legislature hopes children will use it for prayer? The only "injury" is to a few litigious adults—self-appointed thought police—whose injury is the annoyance they feel about what might be in a child's mind, or a legislature's hopes. . . . The court has [previously] said legislatures may pay chaplains, but now a suit is coming that seeks to prevent the use of public funds to print chaplains' prayers, presumably because exposure of non-legislators to the chaplains' works would "establish" religion. I hope such cases inundate the court until the justices fall on their knees (not on government property, of course, lest "excessive entanglement" occur) and pray for relief from the consequences of their anti-constitutional cleverness. [25]

SUPPORT FOR NEUTRALITY

At the other end of the spectrum, liberal religious groups praised the ruling, sometimes in lavish terms. James M. Dunn, from the Baptist Joint Committee, called the decision "proper" and asserted that it was well-founded. Echoing this sentiment, Dean Kelly, president of the National Council of Churches, said the decision was exactly "what the court should have decided." But, unlike his more conservative counterparts, Kelly did not think the decision was really a repudiation of school prayer at all: "The court has held that it is not the business of the government to sponsor prayer . . . in public schools. That's not to say children can't pray in the way Jesus said in the Sermon on the Mount—which is in their hearts." [26]

Civil liberties groups were also pleased with the decision. Activists at Americans United for the Separation of Church and State (AU) saw it as a welcome reinforcement of their core philosophy. Rev. Robert Maddox asserted that "the Supreme Court has again affirmed that government should not meddle in religion." [27] Likewise, AU spokesperson Joe Conn called it a "strong reaffirmation of separation of church and state." [28]

The American Civil Liberties Union (ACLU) also welcomed the decision. Legal director Burt Neuborne, was initially "delighted" that the Court was "courageous" enough to "not back away" from its previous rulings on the separation of church and state. Later, Neuborne speculated on the societal benefits of the Court's neutral approach:

> The [*Jaffree*] decision reaffirms the Supreme Court's traditional insistence that there be a serious wall between church and state. . . . I think [this] has been one of the most important protections that we have in our society, [so] that we never suffer the kinds of agony that you see around the world, in Northern Ireland or Lebanon. It is a protection that guarantees that religion and politics don't mix. And well-meaning people who try to find ways to mix them by trying an end-run around the Supreme Court were blocked today because the Supreme Court closed that door very firmly. [29]

Disagreeing with those who saw *Jaffree* as a repudiation of student prayer, ACLU legislative counsel Barry Lynn asserted that the ruling did "nothing to restrain genuine religious expression" by students but simply "makes clear that organized religious activities have no place in the schools, even if they are silent." [30]

This feeling was shared by the editorial boards at major national newspapers, who generally favored the ruling. The *New York Times* praised the theory of neutrality championed by the Court:

The decision's importance lies in its adherence to the principle of government neutrality with respect to religion. Neutrality need not be arid or hostile, said Justice John Paul Stevens in an opinion for six members of the Court. Indeed, "religious beliefs worthy of respect are the product of free and voluntary choice by the faithful," not of Government-sponsored worship.... The Court's reasonable approach will not still the clamor from those who don't like the Constitution the way it is. But it will encourage the majority of Americans who support it, and its protection against state interference in matters of faith.[31]

The *Washington Post*'s editorial board was equally pleased:

As an indication of the justices' strong commitment to retaining the separation of church and state in the public schools . . . it is heartening. Prayer is personal, private and protected. Nothing prevents an individual child from praying silently in any place at any time, including a period during the school day set aside for silence. It would be impossible to enforce such a prohibition even if the state wanted to. But neither can the government force or encourage religious practice in a diverse and free society, especially in schoolrooms where attendance is compulsory and children are under pressure to conform. The court is clear in announcing that any state's attempt to subvert these basic and cherished principles will not be allowed.[32]

Finally, the editorial page of the *Christian Science Monitor*, while favoring prayer, nevertheless hailed the case as a check against the repression of nonreligious viewpoints:

The start of such repression can come under the most innocuous of guises, in which those seeking to protect both religious and state independence are claimed to oppose an obviously useful practice—such as prayer during the school day.... Nothing can keep the individual from praying fervently, constantly, in gratitude or in need, or simply to stay in touch with the spiritual presence of intelligent good in his experience. The state can neither say when to pray nor in what manner or moment the Maker should reveal himself. The state is no party to revelation.... Only confusion, especially for children, can come from using public law and facilities to compel the individual's attention toward a practice that is essentially a private matter between him and his Maker. We applaud the court's decision.[33]

THE FIGHT MOVES TO CONGRESS

Responding to the calls of religious conservatives for legislative action, Congress's initial reaction to the *Jaffree* decision revolved around the possibility of a constitutional amendment. Sen. Strom Thurmond, R-S.C., chairman of the Senate Judiciary Committee, believed that was the correct course. He said of *Jaffree*, it "underscores the need for Congress to rectify this situation by quickly approving a constitutional amendment restoring the right of voluntary prayer or silent meditation in our public schools."[34] Likewise, Sen. Jesse Helms, R-N.C., attacked the ruling as an "unwise and unjust decision, delivering a slap in the face to the vast majority of Americans who favor school prayer." He later added that "it's time for Congress to stand up to the Supreme Court and to withdraw federal jurisdiction over school prayer."[35]

Sen. Orrin Hatch, R-Utah, was particularly outspoken about the misguided nature of the decision and what should be done about it:

The most recent [*Jaffree*] case was particularly objectionable because it outlawed silent prayer and mediation due to the perception of a majority of the Justices that the State of Alabama had evinced an intent to endorse religion.... The Supreme Court's

erroneous interpretations have created a regime in which the State has become antago-
nistic, even hostile, toward religious views. . . . The student is educated in political theory and sex education, music and art, baseball and football, hygiene and home
economics; indeed, he is instructed in virtually everything conducive to a constructive
character, yet even a moment of silent prayer may not be part of a balanced school
day. . . . In the name of honoring the intent of the authors of the Constitution and preserving the religious prerogatives of school students and all Americans, the Congress
should act to correct the Supreme Court's misconceived rulings.[36]

Republican members of the House of Representatives picked up on the theme, saying the Court's
decision was inconsistent with the religious heritage of the nation. Rep. Joe Linus Barton, R-Texas, noted
with irony that

the Supreme Court itself begins its sessions with the invocation, "God save the United
States and this Honorable Court." And we ourselves begin each session with a specific
prayer to a very specific God. . . . Therefore, I would like to suggest that the Supreme
Court's so-called neutrality is nothing more than an attempt to remove any connection
whatsoever between Government and religion.[37]

Rep. William Wilfred Cobey Jr., R-N.C., agreed with many on the religious Right when he accused the
Court of actually favoring the religion of "secular humanism" in the guise of religious neutrality:

Perhaps [*Jaffree*'s] line of reasoning could have some validity were it not for the fact
that "secularism" is today a vast and growing religion—a nontheistic religion, but a religion, nonetheless. . . . In the Court's attempt to take a neutral position toward theistic
beliefs in cases such as *Wallace v. Jaffree,* it has swung the pendulum wholly to the side of
the secular humanists. . . . The Court has turned its back on the God who has blessed
our country and our Nation so richly and it has done this under the false pretense of
neutrality. . . . The prayer issue is only one manifestation of this, but it is an issue that we
must take out of the Court's hands. We can do this by passing a constitutional amendment providing for voluntary prayer in schools.[38]

Although congressional supporters of the *Jaffree* decision were not as vocal as its opponents, at least
one liberal Republican lawmaker and several Democrats praised the Court and rejected the need for any
legislative action. Sen. Lowell Weicker, R-Conn., thought the decision was "great." He said, "I think that the
First Amendment remains intact, undiluted, and I might add that I don't think it needs any watering down
whether from Alabama or subsequently from the Congress of the United States."[39]

Rep. Gary Ackerman, D-N.Y., harkened back to earlier congressional rejections of a school prayer
amendment and characterized proponents of school prayer as intolerant:

Although I feel our position has been constitutionally vindicated by today's ruling,
those who would like to tear down the wall that the framers of our nation so carefully
constructed will no doubt not be deterred by today's Supreme Court action. . . . However, the constitutional safeguards that were placed in the paths of those who seek to
impose their religious doctrines upon others will be stymied—at least for the time
being. . . . I commend the U.S. Supreme Court for once again safeguarding this nation's
religious liberties and our citizens' firmly entrenched right to believe and worship as
they desire.[40]

Finally, others, like Rep. William D. Edwards, D-Calif., downplayed the significance of the Court's
opinion, noting that

the Court did not rule that all moment of silence plans are unconstitutional. The Court noted that silent voluntary prayer was not prohibited by the law. Only those laws or policies which encourage prayer or which have no secular purpose were affected by [*Jaffree*]. . . . The Court did not break new ground . . . but merely set forth the fundamental proposition: that government sponsorship or encouragement of prayer cannot pass constitutional muster. . . . The Court's decision in *Jaffree* merely upheld the law as we have known it for over 20 years. It was a wise, just, and courageous decision.[41]

This major ideological disagreement continued later that summer, when Congress debated whether to bring an existing school prayer amendment to the full House. The amendment's sponsor, Rep. Thomas N. Kindness, R-Ohio, saw *Jaffree* as perhaps the beginning of a larger effort by the Court to restrict basic constitutional rights:

If the courts are willing to limit . . . the right to free exercise of religion, if the words of prayer are involved, if that is the manner of speech, and if the setting where peaceable assembly takes place is a public school setting, then what is next? . . . What is next in terms of freedom of the press? It is a little hard to imagine that the Court would rule that a newspaper did not have the right to print a prayer, perhaps daily, in its newspaper; on its masthead perhaps. . . . However, if we allow the deterioration of our constitutional rights, court decision by court decision, then perhaps we will face that prospect in the future. . . . I would ask my friends in the fourth estate to look closely at the language of the first amendment and to consider how their freedom of the press will look 20 years from now if the present trend goes unchecked. I submit that it would be well worth their time.[42]

Rep. Patrick L. Swindall, R-Ga., echoed these sentiments, and those of many religious Right activists, by comparing the logic of *Jaffree* to the condition of religious believers in Communist countries.

[Some] will say that all this controversy is much ado about nothing, since no power on earth, including this Court and Congress, can stop any teacher from opening the day of school with moment of silence for pupils to meditate, to plan their day, or to pray if they voluntarily elect to do so. The point I would like to make is . . . that that argument is equally applicable today in the Soviet Union, behind the Iron Curtain, where in fact you may pray wherever and whenever you want to, provided you do not let anybody know about it.[43]

In the fall, this disagreement spilled over into a separate debate over a proposal to remove school prayer cases from the Supreme Court's jurisdiction. The bill's sponsor, Senator Helms, agreed with President Reagan and Attorney General Meese that the *Jaffree* decision was an example of a renegade liberal court:

The problem in the prayer matter, as in so many areas of constitutional law, is runaway Federal judges bent on imposing their own personal views of good public policy on the American public irrespective of the Constitution. More often than not in recent years, these views have been hostile to both the Constitution and long-standing American traditions. It is no understatement to say that American society has been radically altered in the recent past because of activist Federal judges. . . . We in Congress have tolerated this judicial usurpation long enough in many areas of the law, and particularly in the area of school prayer. It is time to put a stop to this usurpation and school prayer is a good place to start.[44]

Sen. Don Nickles, R-Okla., agreed with this assessment, placing his vote on the Court-stripping amendment in the context of a protest over *Jaffree:*

> *Wallace v. Jaffree* presented the Justices with the opportunity to return religious free-dom to schools.... Unfortunately, instead of moving back to the direction established by our Founding Fathers, the Supreme Court restricted our intended religious freedoms even further by ruling in opposition to a moment of silence in the classroom.... I sup-port [the amendment] ... as a signal of my strong disagreement ... with the U.S. Supreme Court's rulings which are moving us toward an increasingly secular society.[45]

A year later, long after these proposed amendments had been rejected or abandoned, the controversy over *Jaffree* surfaced again, this time during the debate over President Reagan's nomination of Justice Rehnquist for the position of chief justice. Many Democratic senators used Rehnquist's *Jaffree* dissent, which called for the abandonment of the metaphor describing a "wall of separation" between church and state, to paint Rehnquist as a conservative extremist.

Sen. Tom Harkin, D-Iowa, a future presidential hopeful, placed in the record an editorial from Daven-port, Iowa's *Quad City Times,* which criticized Rehnquist's dissent: "Should the Rehnquist interpretation of the establishment clause ever command a court majority ... the ramification would be enormous and harmful to the tranquil church-state relations enjoyed in our country."[46]

On the other side of the aisle, Republican senators turned these arguments around, claiming that opponents of school prayer were the real extremists. Senator Hatch responded to Rehnquist's critics by asserting that

> if this vote [in *Jaffree*] makes an individual too "extreme" to serve on the Supreme Court, then Chief Justice Burger and Justice White, a Kennedy appointment, would also be disqualified. They also voted to sustain Alabama's authority to permit silent prayer.... It just may be the case that those who are out of the mainstream on these church-State issues are those Senators who found themselves without a prayer after los-ing the vote in the Judiciary Committee.[47]

In the end, the lasting significance of *Wallace v. Jaffree* may not lie in its impact on the Supreme Court's establishment clause jurisprudence, nor in the ability of its opponents to generate immediate changes in the constitutional landscape. Rather, the true and lasting significance of the case may be the way it served as a training exercise for both sides in the culture war that broke out in earnest toward the end of the twentieth century. Social conservatives certainly used the decision to raise money and support for their national and grass-roots efforts to "take back" the country from the "liberal elite." Just as certainly, progres-sives and leftists used *Jaffree* to try to marginalize right-wing attempts to "turn back the clock" to a more "narrow, closed-minded" society. Perhaps only a victory or an armistice in this culture war—within which *Jaffree* was only one small battle—will provide the perspective to assess the case's long-term impact.

NOTES

1. David Lauter, "Moment-of-Silence Ruling Comes as a Surprise; Administration Expected Victory," *National Law Journal,* June 17, 1985, 5.
2. Linda Greenhouse, "The Court's New Line on Religion Isn't So New," *New York Times,* June 9, 1985, D5.
3. Linda Greenhouse, "High Court Upsets Moment's Silence for Pupil Prayer," *New York Times,* June 5, 1985, A1.
4. ABC News Transcripts, *World News Tonight,* June 4, 1985.
5. Al Kamen, "Prayer Ban in Schools Reaffirmed; Supreme Court Strikes Down Alabama Law," *Washington Post,* June 5, 1985, A1.
6. ABC News Transcripts, *World News Tonight,* June 4, 1985.
7. Ibid.

8. "Plaintiff in Prayer Suit Says the Case Hurt His Children," *New York Times,* June 5, 1985, B5.

9. Elder Witt, "Court Ruling Spurs New School Prayer Drive," *CQ Weekly Report,* June 8, 1985, 1111.

10. Educational Broadcasting and GWETA Transcripts, *MacNeil/Lehrer NewsHour,* June 4, 1985, Transcript #2527.

11. Faye A. Silas, "Meese Rips Court: Charges Unclear Direction," *ABA Journal* (September 1985): 17.

12. Stuart Taylor Jr., "Meese, In Bar Group Speech, Criticizes High Court," *New York Times,* July 10, 1985, A13.

13. Kathy Sawyer, "Conservatives Renew Bid for School Prayer Laws; Supreme Court Ruling Widely Denounced," *Washington Post,* June 6, 1985, A7.

14. Gerald M. Boyd, "Reagan Affirms Basis for Hanoi Ties," *New York Times,* June 7,1985, A3.

15. "Heading for Geneva; 'We Have a Strength We Haven't Had Before,' " interview with Ronald Reagan, *U.S. News & World Report,* November 18, 1985, 30.

16. ABC News Transcripts, *World News Tonight,* June 4, 1985.

17. "School Prayer's Bad Day in Court," *U.S. News & World Report,* June 17, 1985, 9.

18. Sawyer, "Conservatives Renew Bid for School Prayer Laws."

19. Witt, "Court Ruling Spurs New School Prayer Drive."

20. ABC News Transcripts, *World News Tonight,* June 4, 1985.

21. "School Prayer's Bad Day in Court."

22. Kamen, "Prayer Ban in Schools Reaffirmed."

23. Sawyer, "Conservatives Renew Bid for School Prayer Laws."

24. Michael S. Serrill, "Uproar over Silence: The Court Again Stirs the School-Prayer Debate," *Time,* June 17, 1985, 52.

25. George F. Will, "The Court's Moral Microscope," *Washington Post,* June 9, 1985, D7.

26. Kamen, "Prayer Ban in Schools Reaffirmed."

27. "School Prayer's Bad Day in Court."

28. Witt, "Court Ruling Spurs New School Prayer Drive."

29. Educational Broadcasting and GWETA Transcripts, Transcript #2527.

30. Witt, "Court Ruling Spurs New School Prayer Drive."

31. "Neutral, Not Hostile, to Religion," *New York Times,* June 6, 1985, A26.

32. "A Moment of Clarity," *Washington Post,* June 6, 1985, A26.

33. "Protecting Religion," *Christian Science Monitor,* June 6, 1985, 21.

34. Witt, "Court Ruling Spurs New School Prayer Drive."

35. Sawyer, "Conservatives Renew Bid for School Prayer Laws."

36. Orrin Hatch, "School Prayer," *Congressional Record,* September 10, 1985, 131 Cong Rec S 11148.

37. Joe Barton, "Supreme Court Attempts to Sever Government and Religion," *Congressional Record,* August 1, 1985, 131 Cong Rec H 7060.

38. William Cobey, "Sign Discharge Petition; No. 1," *Congressional Record,* October 29, 1985, 131 Cong Rec H 9272.

39. ABC News Transcripts, *World News Tonight,* June 4, 1985.

40. Gary Ackerman, "High Court Flunks School Prayer," *Congressional Record,* June 4, 1985, 131 Cong Rec E 2533.

41. William Edwards, "Supreme Court Decision Is Wise, Just, and Courageous," *Congressional Record,* June 5, 1985, 131 Cong Rec H 3814.

42. Thomas Kindness, "School Prayer Amendment," *Congressional Record,* July 30, 1985, 131 Cong Rec H 6882.

43. Patrick Swindall, "School Prayer Amendment," *Congressional Record,* July 30, 1985, 131 Cong Rec H 6875.

44. Jesse Helms, "School Prayer," *Congressional Record,* September 10, 1985, 131 Cong Rec S 11148.

45. Don Nickles, "School Prayer," *Congressional Record,* September 10, 1985, 131 Cong Rec S 11148.

46. Tom Harkin, "Nomination of William H. Rehnquist to be Chief Justice of the United States," *Congressional Record,* September 17, 1986, 132 Cong Rec S 12781.

47. Orrin Hatch, "Nomination of William H. Rehnquist to be Chief Justice of the United States," *Congressional Record,* September 12, 1986, 132 Cong Rec S 12467.

Texas v. Johnson

Robert Justin Goldstein

Texas v. Johnson
491 U.S. 397 (1989)

DECIDED: June 21, 1989
VOTE

CONCURRING: 5 William J. Brennan Jr., Thurgood Marshall, Harry A. Blackmun, Antonin
Scalia, Anthony M. Kennedy

DISSENTING 4 William H. Rehnquist, Byron R. White, John Paul Stevens, Sandra Day
O'Connor

OPINION OF THE COURT: Brennan
CONCURRING OPINION: Kennedy
DISSENTING OPINION: Rehnquist (White, O'Connor)
DISSENTING OPINION: Stevens

What might be termed the "cult of the American flag" developed during and after the Civil War. Before then, the flag played little role in daily life; it flew only over federal buildings, never from private homes or businesses. The Civil War–era glorification of the flag led, perhaps inevitably, to its subsequent expropriation for a wide range of mundane nonofficial uses, as politicians and commercial interests figuratively and literally began wrapping themselves in flags. Debate then erupted over what became known as "flag desecration," a term that, by definition, implies profaning a sacred object. By the late nineteenth century, veterans and patriotic groups had begun campaigns to outlaw the alleged commercial and political misuse of the flag. As a result, between 1897 and 1932 all of the (then) forty-eight states passed laws banning flag desecration, generally defined to include placing any marks on the flag (partly in response to politicians who placed their pictures and slogans across flags), using it for advertising purposes or "publicly" mutilating, tramping, defacing, defiling, "defying," or casting "contempt" upon it, either "by words or act."

A flurry of flag desecration prosecutions occurred during World Wars I and II—many for verbally abusing flags—but otherwise little attention was paid to the issue until Vietnam War protesters began burning flags. In 1967 Congress passed the first federal flag desecration law, making it a crime to "knowingly" cast contempt upon the flag by "publicly mutilating, defacing, defiling, burning or trampling upon it." Advertising and mainstream "political" use of the flag were not mentioned. During the war, probably more than 1,000 flag desecration prosecutions were initiated and invariably aimed at instances of political protest, while flag usage to express pro-war sentiment went unhindered. The most severe penalty, a four-year jail term, was meted out to a Texas teenager convicted for burning a piece of flag-like bunting in a Dallas park.

Court rulings concerning the constitutionality of flag desecration laws were in a state of advanced confusion until 1989. The Supreme Court had upheld a state law used to prosecute selling beer bottles with flag illustrations on the labels in a 1907 case, *Halter v. Nebraska,* which had been challenged as infringing property, rather than free speech, rights, but by the 1960s most people regarded advertising and mainstream political use of the flag as patriotic. Challenges to Vietnam War prosecutions based on free speech claims yielded hopelessly divided state court rulings, and the Supreme Court repeatedly evaded the central First Amendment issue—symbolic speech—raised by physical flag desecration. For example, in *Street v. New York* (1969), the Court struck down a flag-burning conviction on the strained grounds that Sidney Street might have been found guilty solely for his incidental verbal abuse of the flag, thus violating the principle that "the public expression of ideas may not be prohibited merely because the ideas are themselves offensive to some of their hearers."

Controversy over respect for the flag resurfaced during the 1988 presidential campaign, when successful Republican candidate George H. W. Bush repeatedly criticized Democratic contender Michael Dukakis for vetoing, when he was governor of Massachusetts (in clear compliance with a 1943 Supreme Court ruling), a legislative proposal to require daily public school recitation of the Pledge of Allegiance. Bush repeatedly asked, "What is it about the American flag which upsets this man so much?" Shortly after Bush's election, a huge national controversy erupted in early 1989 over a Chicago art display in which an American flag was placed on the floor; the U.S. Senate quickly voted, 97–0, to amend the 1967 federal law to ban such conduct.

The June 21, 1989, Supreme Court ruling in *Texas v. Johnson,* which upheld on free speech grounds the right to burn or otherwise "desecrate" flags for protest purposes, therefore, was issued when political, public, and media interest in the issue was already high. In a 5–4 ruling, with the majority opinion written by Justice Brennan, the Court held that a Texas law had been unconstitutionally applied in connection with a 1984 Dallas flag burning in protest of the imminent renomination of President Ronald Reagan by the Republican National Convention there. The Court first held that the "expressive, overtly political nature" of Gregory Lee Johnson's conduct was "both intentional and overwhelmingly apparent" and therefore presumptively protected free speech, absent a compelling overriding state interest. The Court then rejected the two allegedly compelling interests advanced by Texas: (1) the need to protect the peace, held "not implicated," because "no disturbance of the peace actually occurred or threatened to occur because of Johnson's burning of the flag"; and (2) the need to protect the flag's symbolic value, rejected on the grounds that Texas was ultimately seeking to prevent citizens from conveying "harmful" messages. The Court said that such an interest violated the "bedrock principle underlying the First Amendment," namely "that the Government may not prohibit expression of an idea simply because society finds the idea itself offensive or disagreeable." The Court concluded that the "principles of freedom and inclusiveness that the flag best reflects" would be reaffirmed by its decision: "We do not consecrate the flag by punishing its desecration, for in doing so we dilute the freedom that this cherished emblem represents."

Justice Kennedy joined the majority opinion, but also wrote an extraordinary concurring opinion that expressed his "distaste for the result," which he said had taken a "painful" and "personal toll" on him. He said he felt compelled to support it because "it is poignant but fundamental that the flag protects those who hold it in contempt" and flag burning was "speech, in both the technical and fundamental meaning of the Constitution."

Justice Stevens and Chief Justice Rehnquist (joined by Justices White and O'Connor) wrote separate dissents, filled with patriotic oratory, which essentially argued that ordinary legal principles did not apply to the flag. Stevens wrote that the flag was "unique" and not subject to legal doctrines that might apply "to a host of other symbols" because "this case has an intangible dimension that makes those rules inapplicable." In a bitter dissent, Rehnquist also termed the flag "unique" and rejected what he termed the majority's suggestion that it could not be exempted from the "marketplace of ideas" because it was "not simply another 'idea' or 'point of view' competing for recognition," as "millions of Americans regard it with an almost mystical reverence" and a "uniquely deep awe and respect." According to Rehnquist, it was a "high purpose" of a democratic society for majorities to ban what they regarded as "inherently evil and profoundly offensive" conduct, whether "murder, embezzlement, pollution or flag burning."

EARLY OPPOSITION TO *JOHNSON*

The *Johnson* ruling touched off what one newspaper termed a "firestorm of indignation" and what *Newsweek* termed "stunned outrage" across the United States. In the House of Representatives various members rose to attack the ruling and defend the flag. Dan Burton, R-Ind., introduced his remarks with a musical selection:

Mr. Speaker, George M. Cohan wrote:
You're a grand old flag,
You're a high flying flag,
And forever in peace may you wave,
You're the emblem of the land I love,
The home of the free and the brave,
Every heart beats true,
Under red, white and blue,
Where there's never a boast or a brag,
But should old acquaintance be forgot,
Keep your eyes on the grand old flag.
Mr. Speaker, Mr. Cohan must be turning in his grave.

Americans have fought and died for that flag all over the world. Many have given their lives just because they did not want it to touch the ground, if you can believe that, during combat.

Yesterday the Supreme Court ruled on a case that involved a Communist, Gregory "Joey" Johnson a member of the Revolutionary Communist Youth Brigade. . . .

What are we coming to in this country? . . .

Mr. Speaker, the Judiciary in this country has gone too far. Shame . . . on these judges [who voted for the majority], Justice William Brennan, Justice Harry Blackmun, Justice Anthony Kennedy, Justice Thurgood Marshall, and Justice Antonin Scalia; shame on you, shame on you.[1]

Rep. Douglas Applegate, D-Ohio, was incensed:

Mr. Speaker, I am mad as heck. We have witnessed the greatest travesty in the annals of jurisprudence when the U.S. Supreme Court allowed the destruction of our greatest of American symbols. What in God's name is going on?

One and a quarter million of our American veterans fought and died throughout our history to defend this flag and what it stands for.

The flag right here in this Chamber that we pledge to, we can take it down, throw it on the floor, step on it, defecate on it, do anything we want, burn it, as long as we have a message, and the Court is going to say it is all right. . . .

Are there any limitations? Are they going to allow fornication in Times Square at high noon? . . .

What we need is a constitutional amendment.[2]

The White House received hundreds of letters, from the famous and the unknown, denouncing the opinion. One, on Frank Sinatra's letterhead, dated June 29, 1989, read:

Dear Mr. President:

I applaud you long and loud for your reaction to the Supreme Court ruling which permits the burning of the banner which you so proudly hail to the world.

Be assured, Sir, I march in your parade, with millions of our fellow countrymen and women who are outraged at the behavior of those to whom our flag in flames receive the benediction of the First Amendment behind which too many have hidden for too long.

And I must add that if torching the ultimate symbol of decency and freedom in the world is our generation's expression of freedom of speech then surely the matter now rejected by the Court must enter the legislative arena where this monumental wrong must be righted.

Respectfully,

s/ Francis Albert

Assistant District Attorney Kathi Drew of Dallas County, Texas, speaks to reporters outside the Supreme Court in 1989. Drew had earlier argued that flag burners such as Gregory Lee Johnson, left, should be criminally punished. The Court disagreed and in *Texas v. Johnson* (1989) declared that flag-burning deserves First Amendment protection.—AP Wide World Photos/Bob Daugherty

Two letters, handwritten in block letters, were dated June 29 and June 24, 1989, respectively. The first went to President Bush, and the second to the Supreme Court with a copy sent to the president:

Dear Mr. President Bush:

I am 6½ years old. My name is Bobby. Get rid of the bad people in the Supreme Court that hurt my flag. No one should hurt my flag. You don't burn my flag. You don't spit or cuss the flag. They go to jail if they do. I LOVE America and my flag. Please don't hurt my flag, my beautiful flag of freedom.

Sincerely,

Robert B.

To the Supreme Court Justices:

My name is Bobby. I am 6½ years old. You broke the law. My American flag is a religious, patriotic symbol. You made treason. You must go to jail for breaking the law. I LOVE America—LAND of the FREE!!! So should you!!!

Sincerely,

Robert B.[3]

RESOLUTIONS AND A PROPOSED AMENDMENT TO OVERTURN *JOHNSON*

According to Sen. Strom Thurmond, R-S.C., the *Johnson* ruling had "opened an emotional hydrant across our country demanding immediate action to overturn it." Within a week of the ruling, 172 members of the House and 43 senators sponsored 39 separate resolutions calling for a constitutional amendment. The Senate voted 97–3 to express "profound disappointment" with the Court's ruling and approved an attempt to overturn *Johnson* legislatively. The Senate's resolution read:

Whereas the first amendment to the United States Constitution lies at the core of our Nation's concept of ordered liberty;

Whereas the flag of the United States is the most profound symbol of our ideals, aspirations, and indeed our identity as a nation;

Whereas the flag stands for our very being, including our commitments to freedom, justice, equal opportunity, and peace;

Whereas Americans have always displayed the flag as a living symbol of our Nation and the values for which it stands;

Whereas the burning of the American flag is an affront to our American heritage and an affront to the American people;

Whereas millions of Americans have fought valiantly, and many thousands have died, to protect this sacred symbol of nationhood, from the beginning of the Republic through the two World Wars, the Korean conflict, the Vietnam conflict, to the present, and that those who risked and gave their lives for our country are profoundly offended by the desecration of this sacred emblem;

Whereas the Congress and forty eight States have enacted laws to protect against desecration of the flag;

Whereas the Senate expressed its respect for the flag as recently as March 16, 1989, when on a vote of 97–0, it passed S. 607, prohibiting the displaying of the flag on the floor or ground;

Whereas throughout the history of our Nation, the Supreme Court has properly defended and protected the first amendment rights of our Nation's citizens;

Whereas the United States Supreme Court yesterday rendered a decision in the case of *Texas v. Johnson*, No. 88-155, finding unconstitutional a Texas statute prohibiting the desecration of the flag, determining that this conduct is an act of "symbolic speech" protected by the first amendment;

Whereas the Congress has believed that the act of desecrating the flag is clearly not "speech" as protected by the first amendment; and that analogous acts, such as desecrating a public monument such as the Lincoln Memorial, would never be tolerated as speech;

Whereas it appears that yesterday's decision may invalidate the Federal and State laws prohibiting desecration of the flag:

Therefore, be it Resolved,

That the Senate hereby

(1) expresses its profound disappointment that the Texas statute prohibiting the desecration of the flag was found to be unconstitutional;

(2) expresses its continued commitment to preserving the honor and integrity of the flag as a living symbol of our Nation and its aspirations and ideals;

(3) intends to make an immediate study of the impact of yesterday's Supreme Court decision on Federal and state laws prohibiting the desecration of the flag, and to seek ways to restore sanctions against such reprehensible conduct; and

(4) urges the American people to continue to display proudly the American flag as a symbol of our Nation and the values for which it stands.[4]

The House of Representatives voted 411–15 to express "profound concern" with the decision:

Whereas for more than 2 centuries the flag of the United States has stood as the paramount symbol of unity for the Nation by transcending political and geographical divisions;

Whereas millions of men and women have served under the flag of the United States in the Armed Forces since the beginning of the Republic, through 2 world wars and in Korea and Vietnam, and many thousands sacrificed their lives in defense of freedom;

Whereas the Congress has commemorated the unique status of the flag through the enactment of detailed legislation prescribing its proper display and treatment;

Whereas desecration of the flag is an act so offensive to individuals in the United States that it may be considered an incitement to violence; . . .

Whereas the decision of the Court calls into question the validity of [the 1967 federal law] prescribing criminal penalties for desecration of the flag, as well as statutes enacted by 48 of the 50 States prohibiting the burning of the flag:

Now, therefore, be it Resolved,

That the House of Representatives hereby

(1) expresses its profound concern over the Supreme Court's decision in *Texas v. Johnson;*

(2) expresses its continued commitment to preserving the honor and integrity of the flag as a living symbol of our Nation and its aspirations and ideas;

(3) condemns all actions intended to desecrate the American flag; and

(4) urges the American people to continue to display proudly the flag of the United States as a symbol of our Nation and the values for which it stands.[5]

President Bush, who in the 1988 campaign had made much of his support of the flag, spoke at the Iwo Jima Memorial near Arlington National Cemetery on June 30, 1989, formally introducing a proposed constitutional amendment to overturn the *Johnson* decision:

All across America—above farmhouses and statehouses, schools and courts and capitols—our flag is borne on the breeze of freedom. And it reminds Americans how much they've been given and how much they have to give. Our flag represents freedom and the unity of our nation. And our flag flies in peace, thanks to the sacrifices of so many Americans. . . .

Patriotism is not a partisan issue; it's not a political issue: Our purpose today transcends politics and partisanship.

And we feel in our hearts, and we know from our experience, that the surest way to preserve liberty is to protect the spirit that sustains it. And this flag sustains that spirit. And it's one of our most powerful ideas. And like all powerful ideas, if it is not defended, it is defamed. To the touch, this flag is merely fabric. But to the heart, the flag represents and reflects the fabric of our nation—our dreams, our destiny—our very fiber as a people. . . .

Free speech is a right that is dear and close to all. It is in defense of that right, and the others enshrined in our Constitution, that so many have sacrificed. But before we accept dishonor to our flag, we must ask ourselves how many have died following the order to "Save the Colors!" We must ask how many have fought for the ideals it represents. And we must honor those who have been handed the folded flag from the casket at Arlington.

If the debate here is about liberty, then we cannot turn our backs on those who fought to win it for us. We can't forget the importance of the flag to the ideals of liberty and honor and freedom. To burn the flag, to dishonor it, is simply wrong. . . .

And what that flag embodies is too sacred to be abused. . . .

This amendment preserves the widest conceivable range of options for free expression. It applies only to the flag, the unique symbol of our nation. . . .

For the sake of the fallen, for the men behind the guns, for every American, we will defend the flag of the United States of America.

Thank you. God bless this flag. And God bless the United States of America.[6]

The language of the proposed amendment was introduced in a joint resolution of Congress:

Proposing an amendment to the Constitution of the United States authorizing the Congress and the States to prohibit the physical desecration of the flag of the United States.

Whereas the flag of the United States of America is a national symbol of such stature that it must be kept inviolate;

Whereas the physical desecration of the flag should not be considered constitutionally protected speech; and

Whereas physical desecration may include, but is not limited to, such acts as burning, mutilating, defacing, defiling or trampling on the flag, or displaying the flag in a contemptuous manner: Now, therefore, be it

Resolved by the Senate and the House of Representative of the United States of America in Congress assembled (two-thirds of each House concurring therein), That the following article is proposed as an amendment to the Constitution of the United States, which shall be valid to all intents and purposes as part of the Constitution when ratified by the legislatures of three-fourths of the several States within seven years after the date of its submission for ratification:

ARTICLE

"The Congress and the States shall have power to prohibit the physical desecration of the flag of the United States."[7]

STATE AND LOCAL REACTIONS CRITICAL OF *JOHNSON*

Within two weeks of the Court's decisions, one or both legislative chambers in sixteen states adopted resolutions attacking the ruling and/or demanding a constitutional amendment to overturn it. Typical is that of the Texas legislature, whose law the Court had overturned in *Johnson*. House Concurrent Resolution No. 18 said:

Whereas the United States flag belongs to all Americans and ought not be desecrated by any one individual, even under principles of free expression, any more than we would allow desecration of the Declaration of Independence, Statue of Liberty, Lincoln Memorial, Yellowstone National Park, or any other common inheritance that the people of the land hold dear;

Whereas the United States Supreme Court, in contravention of this postulate, has by a narrow decision held to be a First Amendment freedom the license to destroy in protest this cherished symbol of our national heritage;

Whereas whatever legal arguments may be offered to support this contention, the incineration or other mutilation of the flag . . . is repugnant to all those who have saluted it, paraded beneath it on the Fourth of July, been saluted by its half-mast configuration, or raised it inspirationally in remote corners of the globe where they have defended the ideals of which it is representative; and. . .

Whereas the members of the Legislature of the State of Texas, while respectful of dissenting political views, themselves dissent forcefully from the court decision echoing the

beliefs of all patriotic Americans that this flag is our flag, and not a private property subject to a private prerogative to maim or despoil in the passion of individual protest;
and. . . .

Whereas this legislature concurs with the court minority that the Stars and Stripes is
deserving of a unique sanctity, free to wave in perpetuity over the spacious skies where
our bald eagles fly, the fruited plain above which our mountain majesties soar, and the
venerable heights to which our melting pot of peoples and their posterity aspire; now,
therefore, be it

Resolved, That the 71st Legislature of the State of Texas . . . hereby petition the Congress . . . to propose to the states an amendment to the United States Constitution, protecting the American flag and 50 state flags from willful desecration and exempting such
desecration from constitutional construction as a First Amendment right.[8]

Hundreds of local government officials across the country also joined in the clamor. The Board of
Supervisors of Los Angeles County, California, wrote to President Bush:

Dear Mr. President:

We are outraged at the recent Supreme Court decision to allow desecration of the
United States Flag, this Nation's most sacred symbol of freedom and liberty for all.

Therefore we strongly urge Congress to promptly enact legislation that would make it
illegal to destroy or desecrate the United States flag.[9]

Donald F. Munch, the borough manager of Schuylkill Haven, Pennsylvania, also wrote to the president:

Dear President Bush:

Our little town is nestled among the rolling hills of Central Pennsylvania. While we
are rural, we are not deaf to affairs outside our little haven. The recent Supreme Court
decision concerning "free expression" has invaded our world like a swarm of locusts.

We're appalled to think that anyone can relegate our Flag to a position of a "symbol."
It simply is not a symbol to us. It's a living reminder of what is so great about this Country. The many men and women who have defended our Living Flag, the many men and
women who have died for an idea that all men have a right to determine their own destinies, would not rest easily if they believed our Flag was merely a symbol.

If we may be so bold as to speak for our six thousand citizens, hear us loud and clear
WE DO NOT WANT TO SEE OUR FLAG DESECRATED. We support any action the
Congress or the President would take to forever make that a criminal offense.

From the best little damned town in Central Pennsylvania, where the Flag of the
United States of America is alive and well; we are

Sincerely yours,

[Signed.][10]

Although judges rarely speak out on such matters, Judge Francis C. Jackson of the Golden, Colorado,
county court, wanted President Bush to know that he sided with him against the Supreme Court:

Dear Mr. President:

I am writing this letter in response to your action in speaking out against the
Supreme Court decision allowing people to burn the American Flag. I have been a Judge

for 14 years and for the first time in my career I found it difficult to put on my robe and take the bench.

Please Mr. President, lead the fight to get the flag protected by Constitutional amendment!

Yours truly,

[Signed.][11]

In contrast to the overwhelming thrust of early political and public opinion, most newspapers strongly supported the *Johnson* ruling on First Amendment grounds. The *New York Times* declared on June 23 that by placing "such a high value on free expression," the decision had delivered a "message for patriotic Americans to be proud of," one that would allow the flag to "wave more proudly than ever." Similarly, the June 26 *Christian Science Monitor,* noting that conservative justices Scalia and Kennedy had joined the Court majority, said the ruling "shows that the grand idea of free speech is not the property of the left or the right, but is the bedrock value of the American vision."

A small minority of newspapers, however, criticized the *Johnson* ruling, sometimes in extremely vehement terms. The June 23 *Washington Times* termed Brennan's majority opinion "tedious pedantry" which would "weaken the psychic and emotional substratum on which American freedom rests" and facilitate the "further subversion of our nation's characteristic ideas through calculated insults to their symbols." The same day's *New York Daily News,* in an editorial headed, "Okay, go on, burn their robes!" termed the ruling "dumb" and held the Court in "naked contempt" of the American people by displaying "pompous insensitivity to the most beloved symbol of the most benevolent form of government ever to appear on this Earth."

A July 3, 1989, *Newsweek* poll indicated that 71 percent of the public favored a constitutional amendment to overturn *Johnson.* By October, 1.5 million people had signed petitions to that effect.

The legal and popular arguments critical of the *Johnson* ruling ultimately boiled down to the argument that the flag, as the best-known symbol of "freedom" and the nation, was "unique" and "special," and that, although dissent was a legitimate and critical part of the democratic process, desecrating the flag went "too far." Typical of political figures' reactions was that of Bob Dole, R-Kan., minority leader of the Senate, who declared that "freedom of speech is a constitutional guarantee that America holds dear, but we draw the line when it comes to our flag." President Bush proclaimed that the flag was a "unique national symbol" and that he felt "viscerally about burning the American flag."

SUPPORT FOR THE *JOHNSON* RULING

The clear minority who backed the *Johnson* decision vigorously maintained that, at a time when Americans were applauding East Europeans for tearing out hated Communist symbols from their national flags and condemning the Communist Chinese for their brutal suppression of mass demonstrations in Beijing, "the land of the free" would be true to its basic democratic principles only if even the most offensive peaceful expressions of political dissent were protected. In House committee hearings on proposals to overturn *Johnson* by way of a constitutional amendment or a new law, Charles Fried, Harvard law professor and former solicitor general in the Reagan administration, urged that no action be taken to seek to override *Texas v. Johnson:*

> Gregory Lee Johnson's burning of the American flag was a vile and distressing act. I do not like coming here to urge you to leave alone the laws and Constitution that say he may not be punished for that act. . . .
>
> I came here from Czechoslovakia, a country with a deep and humane tradition of democratic values, crushed first by the Nazis and then by the Soviets and their disgusting

little puppets. To the Czechs, at least from the days when Woodrow Wilson befriended the nation's first President Thomas Masaryk, America was a model and ideal. So America, its traditions and values and its flag are important to me. Foremost among those values is the principle that no one shall be punished for his political expressions—no matter how offensive or bizarre. That commitment to liberty is our first and greatest contribution to the history of mankind. . . .

I beg you not to tamper with our tradition. [Others] have testified that a statute might be drawn that would pass constitutional muster. . . . I very much hope that no such statute will be passed. I agree with the judgment that whatever the technicalities, the evident purpose of such a statute would still be to punish acts of expression, acts that do no harm except as they express political convictions—mistaken and sordid as those convictions are. . . .

I hope and pray that we will not act—that no statute be passed and of course that the Constitution not be amended. In short, I believe the *Johnson* case is right not just as a matter of present constitutional law. It is right in principle. . . . As for the likes of Gregory Lee Johnson, let us simply turn our backs on him.[12]

Sen. Bob Kerrey, D-Neb., also spoke out against an amendment:

At first, I, like most Americans, was outraged by the decision [in *Texas v. Johnson*]. It seemed ridiculous to me that flag burning could be a protected act. . . .

I joined with 96 other Senators expressing our disagreement with the decision.

As I prepared to head home for the fourth of July recess, I declared my disbelief at our apparent impotence in protecting this symbol of American freedom.

Then, during the recess, I read the decision [and] was surprised to discover that I agreed with the majority [and] found the majority argument to be reasonable, understandable, and consistent with those values which I believe make America so wonderful. . . .

Today, I declare that I do not support any of the constitutional amendments which are being offered. . . .

Today, I am even skeptical about the need to pass anti–flag burning laws at the state or the federal level. . . . Today, I am disappointed that the strength of leadership shown by President Bush in his travels to Poland and Hungary was not shown here at home. President Bush did not stand before the angry and distressed mob to stop us in our tracks before we had done something we would regret. He did not offer words that calmed us and gave us assurance that the Nation was not endangered. Instead of leading us, President Bush joined us.

The polls showed support for a constitutional amendment and so the President yielded to his political advisers. . . . The President chose the path of least resistance and greatest political gain. . . .

There is simply no line of Americans outside this building or in this Nation queuing up to burn our flag. On the face of the evidence at hand it seems to me that there is no need for us to do anything. . . .

America is the beacon of hope for the people of the world who yearn for freedom from the despotism of repressive governments. This hope is diluted when we advise others that we are frightened of flag burning. . . .

Chief Justice Rehnquist, in his disappointing dissent, asserts that men and women fought for our flag in Vietnam. In my case I do not remember feeling this way. . . . I do not remember giving the safety of our flag anywhere near the thought that I gave the safety of my men. . . .

America—the home of the free and the brave . . . does not need our Government to protect us from those who burn a flag.[13]

Another voice speaking out against a constitutional amendment came from James H. Warner, a former prisoner of war in Vietnam:

As I stepped out of the aircraft [after being released from captivity in Vietnam], I looked up and saw the flag. I caught my breath, then, as tears filled my eyes, I saluted it. I never loved my country more than at that moment. . . . I cannot compromise on freedom. It hurts to see the flag burned, but I part company with those who want to punish the flag burners. . . .

I remember one interrogation [by the North Vietnamese] where I was shown a photograph of some Americans protesting the war by burning a flag. "There," the officer said. "People in your country protest against your cause. That proves that you are wrong."

"No," I said. "That proves I am right. In my country we are not afraid of freedom, even if it means that people disagree with us." The officer was on his feet in an instant, his face purple with rage. He smashed his fist on the table and screamed at me to shut up. While he was ranting I was astonished to see pain, compounded by fear, in his eyes. I have never forgotten that look, nor have I forgotten the satisfaction I felt at using his tool, the picture of the burning flag against him. . . .

We don't need to amend the Constitution in order to punish those who burn our flag. They burn the flag because they hate America and they are afraid of freedom. What better way to hurt them than with the subversive idea of freedom? Spread freedom. . . . Don't be afraid of freedom, it is the best weapon we have.[14]

FLAG PROTECTION ACT

Opponents of the constitutional amendment managed to postpone a vote on it until fall 1989, when it failed in the Senate. One reason for the defeat was that a legislative alternative, the Flag Protection Act (FPA), had overwhelmingly passed both houses of Congress in October. The FPA declared itself "content neutral," but provided punishment for anyone who "knowingly mutilates, physically defiles, burns, maintains on the floor or ground, or tramples" upon the flag.

A few days after passage of the FPA, a group of protesters challenged the validity of the new law by burning an American flag on the steps of the Capitol. They issued a statement:

At midnight this past Friday, October 27, the new national flag statute went into effect, outlawing desecration of the U.S. flag. . . . These dangerous moves to shut people up and shut people down in the name of the red, white and blue are not in the interest of the majority. Today, they try to suppress political expression in the name of the flag, tomorrow what next will become forbidden? We need only look at Nazi Germany to see an answer to that. . . .

Especially in a political climate marked by increasing racism, assaults on women's rights, calls for an enforced oppressive moral code, censorship, intervention in other countries and overall escalating attacks on the people, all [flag burners] deeply felt the need to defy a law that would make the flag a religious icon and its worship mandatory. . . .

To the government that has made flag desecration illegal, we defy your law. And we challenge you. Arrest us. Test your statute. Take it back to your Supreme Court and try once again to claim it is consistent with your constitutional standards of free speech. . . .

This flag means one thing to the powers that be and something else to all of us. Everything bad this system has done and continues to do to people all over the world has been done under this flag. No law, no amendment will change it, cover it up, or stifle that truth. So to you we say, Express yourself! Burn this flag. It's quick, it's easy, it may not be the law, but it's the right thing to do.

FIGHT THE FASCIST FLAG LAW NO FLAG AMENDMENT

NO MANDATORY PATRIOTISM[15]

In *United States v. Eichman* (1990), the Supreme Court struck down the FPA, essentially declaring, by the same 5–4 majority as in *Johnson,* that it really meant what *Johnson* had said. President Bush quickly renewed his endorsement of a constitutional amendment, but by then public passion over the issue had died down. The revived amendment, which President Bill Clinton opposed, but not passionately, and President George W. Bush supported, but not passionately, received the necessary two-thirds majority in the House six times between 1995 and 2005. It fell a few votes short in the Senate in 1995 and 2000.

NOTES

1. *Congressional Record,* June 22, 1989, H3002.
2. Ibid., H3005.
3. George H. W. Bush Presidential Library, White House Office Records Management, Support File, Judicial-Legal Matters.
4. S. Res. 151, adopted by the U.S. Senate, *Congressional Record,* June 22, 1989, S7189.
5. Resolution adopted by the U.S. House of Representatives, *Congressional Record,* June 27, 1989, H3228.
6. *Weekly Compilation of Presidential Documents,* vol. 25, no. 26, July 3, 1989, 1006–8.
7. Senate Joint Resolution 180, 1989.
8. *Congressional Record,* September 7, 1989, S10825.
9. George H. W. Bush Presidential Library, White House Office Records Management, Support File, Judicial-Legal Matters.
10. Ibid., Heraldry-Flags-Presidential Seal File.
11. Ibid., Box 6.
12. *Statutory and Constitutional Responses to the Supreme Court Decision in* Texas v. Johnson, *Hearings Before the Subcommittee on Civil and Constitutional Rights of the House Committee on the Judiciary,* 101st Cong., 1st sess., 1989, serial no. 24, 222–260.
13. *Congressional Record,* July 18, 1989, S18102-03.
14. James H. Warner, op ed in *Washington Post,* July 11, 1989.
15. Statement by four flag burners arrested at the Capitol steps, October 30, 1989, in Joint Appendix, *United States v. Eichman* and *United States v. Haggerty,* Nos. 89-1433 and 89-1444, in the Supreme Court of the United States, October term, 1989, 55–57.

Employment Division, Department of Human Resources of Oregon v. Smith

Carolyn Long

Employment Division, Department of Human Resources of Oregon v. Smith
494 U.S. 872 (1990)

> DECIDED: April 17, 1990
> VOTE
>   CONCURRING: 6 (William H. Rehnquist, Byron R. White, John Paul Stevens, Sandra Day
>   O'Connor (in part), Antonin Scalia, Anthony M. Kennedy)
>   DISSENTING: 3 (William J. Brennan Jr., Thurgood Marshall, Harry A. Blackmun)
> OPINION OF THE COURT: Scalia
> OPINION CONCURRING IN JUDGMENT: O'Connor
> DISSENTING OPINION: Blackmun (Brennan, Marshall)

In *Employment Division of Oregon v. Smith* the U.S. Supreme Court ruled that the state of Oregon had rightfully denied unemployment benefits to two members of the Native American Church. The two employees were fired for ingesting peyote, a substance proscribed by state law, in a religious ceremony. The significance of this case went far beyond the two individual claimants, however. In *Smith,* a slim majority of the Court also ruled that the free exercise clause of the First Amendment protects religious activity only when the state has acted in a manner that was "specifically directed" at religiously inspired behavior. It does not safeguard individuals from "compliance with an otherwise valid law prohibiting conduct that the state is free to regulate." The decision came as a surprise to many because in the previous three decades the Court had evaluated religious claims using the same standard of scrutiny, regardless of whether or not the government action was specifically directed at religious behavior.

Al Smith and Galen Black were dismissed from their jobs as drug and alcohol treatment counselors at the Douglas County Council on Alcohol and Drug Abuse Prevention and Treatment (ADAPT) facility, a private, nonprofit treatment center, after their employer learned they had ingested peyote as part of a Native American Church ceremony. Several western states exempted peyote from their list of controlled substances, but Oregon did not. Smith and Black subsequently applied for and were denied unemployment benefits because the state determined that they were discharged "for misconduct connected with work." State law allowed that benefits could be denied under such circumstances. Smith and Black argued that the denial of benefits constituted a burden on their religious activity, protected under the free exercise clause of the First Amendment. As their separate cases moved through the Oregon courts, both claimants won their constitutional challenge, and their unemployment compensation was reinstated. In its *Employment Division v. Smith* decision, the Oregon Supreme Court described how it evaluated Smith's free exercise challenge: once an individual has shown that an application of a law places a significant burden on his or her free exercise of religion, the state must then demonstrate that the constraint on the religious activity is the "least restrictive means" of achieving a "compelling" state interest. If it is unable to do so, the religious adherents should be granted an exemption to the law.

The U.S. Supreme Court established this "strict scrutiny" or "compelling state interest" test in *Sherbert v. Verner,* a 1963 decision involving a state's denial of unemployment compensation to a Seventh-Day Adventist who was fired from her job because she refused to work on Saturdays, her faith's Sabbath. In this decision the Court declared that the free exercise of religion was a preferred freedom, subject to the highest level of judicial scrutiny, regardless of whether the violation was the result of a direct or indirect government action. Subsequent to this decision, the Court applied this standard to free exercise challenges where the claimant was able to prove a "substantial burden" on his religion. Many claimants were unsuccessful because the state was able to show that its interests were sufficiently compelling. Moreover, in *Goldman v. Weinberger* (1985) the Supreme Court refused to apply this high level of scrutiny to free exercise challenges to military regulations or, in *O'Lone v. Estate of Shabazz* (1987), to prison regulations. Until 1990 state and federal courts had consistently used strict scrutiny analysis to evaluate free exercise challenges.

In *Employment Division of Oregon v. Smith,* Justice Scalia, speaking for the majority, declared that, according to his reading of the Court's free exercise jurisprudence, neutral, generally applicable laws had never been limited by the free exercise clause of the First Amendment. The cases where the Court had applied this high level of scrutiny, he explained, were exceptions to this general rule. He explained that "it is a permissible reading . . . that if prohibiting the exercise of religion is not the object of the [law] but is merely the incidental effect of a generally applicable and otherwise valid provision, the First Amendment has not been offended." To evaluate challenges to this type of government action, he noted, the courts should employ the "reasonableness" or "rational basis test." Under this standard, the lowest level of scrutiny employed by courts, if the law in question is reasonable and rationally related to the state's goals, then it is constitutional. The Court suggested that religious proponents resort to the democratic political process for the protection of their religious practices. Although appeals to the legislature would admittedly place minority religions at "a relative disadvantage," the decision concluded "that unavoidable consequence of democratic government must be preferred to a system in which each conscience is a law unto itself or which judges weigh the social importance of all laws against the centrality of all religious beliefs."

INITIAL REACTIONS

The Court's decision in *Smith* took many by surprise, a reaction typified by the sentiments of David Frohnmayer, Oregon's attorney general, who argued the case on behalf of the Employment Division:

> We had no clue that the Court would reconsider free exercise doctrine. We thought we had won on the *Sherbert v. Verner* test. . . . Did I think that *Sherbert* would be discarded? It had just been reaffirmed. And that came as a total shock. We hadn't briefed it, we hadn't argued it, we hadn't been questioned about it, and we hadn't suggested it.[1]

An overwhelming majority of people in the religious and civil liberties communities unhappily agreed with Frohnmayer. Many had expected, at worst, a decision denying the respondents' request for unemployment compensation based upon the state's "compelling interest" in controlling drug use. Instead, the Court removed an entire category of laws from the protection of the free exercise clause, and, in their view, impacted religious liberty for all Americans.

The case, which had not received much media attention up to this point, was widely denounced in the popular press. Writing in the *Washington Post,* civil libertarian Nat Hentoff lamented the fact that the Court had relegated protection of the free exercise of religion to the political branches of government. "Almost in time for the celebrations of the bicentennial of the Bill of Rights, Justice Scalia has interpreted this quintessential part of the First Amendment to be a majoritarian rule rather than a protection of individual conscience. Maybe it's just as well James Madison isn't around for the champagne."[2] The Indian community was also incensed. In particular, Native people were shocked at the Court's ethnocentric perspective regarding the use of peyote in religious ceremonies. Rueben Snake, a member of the Nebraska Winnebago tribe and a lifelong Native American Church member, criticized the Court for equating the sacramental use of peyote with "the tragedy of drug abuse." The Court's unwillingness to protect an unfamiliar religion when it was previously willing to protect popular religions was even noted in the overseas press. In its review of the case, the *Economist* noted, "During Prohibition, the large Catholic minority won congressional support for communion wine. Now, apparently, a smaller minority simply takes its lumps."[3]

Al Smith, the central figure in the case, was surprised by the media firestorm and simply stated, "I was only going to Church."[4]

The harshest criticism was found in the reaction of legal scholars. William Bentley Ball, a well-known constitutional law scholar stated, "What first appeared to be a trivial free exercise challenge to an unemployment compensation ruling has resulted in a constitutional fault of San Andreas proportions."[5] University of Chicago law professor Michael McConnell called the decision "undoubtedly the most important development in the law of religious freedom in decades," and University of Texas law professor Douglas Laycock, well known for his scholarship in this area, found it difficult to comprehend the Court's sudden departure from its earlier free exercise decisions. "The opinion appears to be inconsistent with the original intent, inconsistent with the constitutional text, inconsistent with doctrine under other constitutional clauses, and inconsistent with precedent. It strips the free exercise clause of independent meaning."[6] Within a short period, several dozen scholarly articles harshly criticized Scalia's reasoning and result. Few could hide their surprise at the Court's change in jurisprudence. A handful of scholars supported the decision, but they were in the distinct minority. Criticism of the decision was directed at what many believed was the Court's effort to purposely misread and misinterpret Supreme Court precedent to justify its reasoning. One scholar called it "troubling, bordering on the shocking." Others described it as "strained," "untrustworthy," "internally inconsistent," "fiction," and even "bizarre."

The Court was also criticized for engaging in judicial activism. Rather than limit the decision to the immediate case at hand, and rule only on the question of unemployment compensation, the Court reached beyond the issue posed at bar and established a new standard to govern free exercise challenges. Ironically, in the same term as *Smith,* the Court had applied strict scrutiny analysis in *Swaggart Ministries v. Cal. Bd. of Equalization* (1990) and in two cases the previous term, *Texas Monthly, Inc. v. Bullock* and *Hernandez v. Commissioner of IRS.* In each of these cases the state prevailed against the free exercise challenge because the claimants were unable to fulfill the requirement that they prove the government action placed a burden on their religious exercise. But the Court had not signaled that it was considering a reevaluation of its free exercise jurisprudence. The critics argued that the broader question of the applicability of the free exercise clause to neutral, generally applicable laws should have been fully briefed by attorneys. Critics also claimed that the solution posed by the Court—that religious adherents appeal to the legislative process to request religious exemptions from neutral, generally applicable laws that burdened religious beliefs—was inappropriate because it would disproportionately disadvantage smaller, less politically powerful religious groups. They concluded that the unwillingness of the Court majority to shield religious liberty beyond what was already offered by the political process was inconsistent with the Court's previous free exercise jurisprudence and antithetical to the very purpose of the Bill of Rights.

The day after the Court's ruling, legal experts with the American Jewish Congress joined Smith's attorneys on a petition for rehearing. By the time the brief was filed several weeks later, dozens of religious and civil liberties group belonging to the Coalition for the Free Exercise of Religion (CFER) had signed it. CFER, which formed after the decision was handed down, was an extraordinarily eclectic alliance representing both sides of the ideological spectrum, from organizations on the left, such as the American Civil Liberties Union (ACLU), the American Jewish Congress, Americans United for Separation of Church and State, and the Baptist Joint Committee on Public Affairs, and organizations from the right, such as the Christian Legal Society, Home School Legal Defense Association, the National Association of Evangelicals, and People for the American Way. Fifty-five constitutional law scholars also signed the brief. Attached to it was a recently published *Harvard Law Review* article, "The Origins and Historical Understanding of Free Exercise of Religion" by Professor McConnell. [7] The article was a significant scholarly effort that traced the origins of the free exercise clause. It illustrated the historical roots of accommodation of religious activity under the Constitution, and coalition members believed it might persuade the Court to at least reconsider its revision of free exercise jurisprudence. This effort ended in mid-June 1990 when the Court denied the request for a rehearing.

CONGRESSIONAL RESPONSE

While the petition for rehearing was being drafted, the Coalition decided to pursue a legislative response to *Smith*. Morton Halperin, director of the Washington office of the ACLU and chair of CFER; Dean Kelley, general counsel for the National Council of Churches; and Oliver Thomas and J. Brent Walker, general and associate counsel of the Baptist Joint Committee, worked on the strategy. Halperin took the lead and contacted Rep. Steven Solarz, D-N.Y., known for his work in enacting Public Law 100-180 in response to *Goldman v. Weinberger*. In *Goldman* the Court denied an Orthodox Jew an exemption to an Air Force regulation that prevented individuals from wearing a yarmulke (skullcap), which was a requirement of his faith. The legislative decision spearheaded by Solarz reversed this decision in part by allowing military personnel to wear "unobtrusive religious headgear."

Nat Lewin, a prominent Washington attorney known for his work on religious liberty issues, joined Halperin and Solarz on the legislative response to *Smith*. The three came up with the Religious Freedom Restoration Act (RFRA). The proposed legislation, modeled after the 1965 Voting Rights Act, relied on Section 5 of the Fourteenth Amendment, which, they argued, empowered Congress to draft legislation to protect religious liberty. The legislation, if enacted, would not explicitly overturn or reverse the Supreme Court's decision in *Smith*; rather, it would circumvent the ruling by providing petitioners with federal statutory protection for free exercise challenges. RFRA required the federal government and state governments to use strict scrutiny analysis—discarded under *Smith*—to evaluate all free exercise claims, regardless of whether the government action was directed at an individual's religious activity or was an "incidental effect" of a neutral, generally applicable law. CFER, pleased that RFRA would restore the pre-*Smith* standard, embraced the legislative response. At these early meetings, coalition members agreed that the best response to *Smith* was to write a general law to protect religious liberty for all Americans. They would avoid focusing on legislation to protect the sacramental use of peyote, which proved controversial for some CFER members. That issue could be addressed separately. Another issue arose that would prove to be a major stumbling block to RFRA, however. Several pro-life groups expressed concern that the measure might create a statutory right to abortion by allowing women to argue that they had a free exercise right to terminate a pregnancy.

The Religious Freedom Restoration Act was introduced to the public at a news conference on June 26, 1990. Oliver Thomas, who spoke for CFER, said

> Coalitions come and go but mostly—in the volatile field of church-state relations—they go. That's why this motley gathering of unlikely cohorts is historic. Although perennial adversaries, these groups are joining voices to say to the United States Supreme Court that religious liberty is not a luxury to be gratuitously bestowed by a beneficent majority.[8]

As hearings on RFRA got under way in the House in September, support for the legislation was both bipartisan and broad based. Solarz, opening the hearings, described *Smith* as a "devastating blow to religious freedom in the U.S." and characterized RFRA as a "narrowly crafted, legislative response to the radical work of an activist Supreme Court majority." Witnesses urged Congress to act aggressively to ensure protection for religion. As Douglas Laycock explained:

> By creating judicially enforceable statutory rights, Congress can call on the powers of the judiciary that the Court feared to invoke on its own. Because the rights created would be statutory, Congress can retain a voice that it could not have retained if the Court had acted on its own. By legislating generally, for all religion, instead of case-by-

case for particular religions, Congress can reduce the danger that it will not respond to the needs of small faiths.[9]

In addition to support from academia, representatives from national religious groups, including Rev. Robert P. Dugan, public affairs director of the National Association of Evangelicals, an association of more than fifty thousand churches from seventy-eight denominations, and Rev. John H. Buchanan Jr., chair of the People for the American Way Action Fund, a nonpartisan constitutional liberties union, testified on behalf of the legislation. A companion bill, S 3254, was introduced in the Senate the following month, but the session ended before hearings could be held.

Opposition to RFRA grew in 1991 during the 102d Congress. The abortion issue, which was raised early on, gained strength as a major impediment to successful passage of the legislation. Representatives from the United States Catholic Conference and the National Right to Life Committee strongly denounced the proposed legislation, and, although several legal scholars once again testified on behalf of the bill, others expressed reservations about its constitutionality. Despite this opposition, the bill was favorably reported out of committee and approved by a voice vote in the House. A companion bill, sponsored by Sen. Orrin Hatch, R-Utah, and Sen. Edward Kennedy, D-Mass., and twenty-one cosponsors, was introduced in the Senate. The Judiciary Committee tackled similar issues about RFRA's impact on abortion and its constitutionality, but the bill died in committee as the congressional session came to a close.

The following year, Bill Clinton was elected president. He had endorsed RFRA as a presidential candidate. His support and the Supreme Court decision in *Planned Parenthood v. Casey* (1992), which affirmed *Roe v. Wade*'s (see page 299) central holding that abortion rights were protected under a general right to privacy in the due process clause of the Fourteenth Amendment, paved the way for successful passage of RFRA. Clinton signed it into law on November 16, 1993. At the signing ceremony the president noted:

> The power to reverse the Court by legislation . . . is a power that is rightly, hesitantly and infrequently exercised by the United State Congress. But this is an issue in which that extraordinary measure was clearly called for. . . . This act reverses the Supreme Court's decision in Employment Division against Smith and reestablishes a standard that better protects all Americans of all faiths in the exercise of their religion in a way that I am convinced is far more consistent with the intent of the Founders of the Nation than the U.S. Supreme Court decision.[10]

RFRA provided federal statutory protection for the exercise of religion, ensuring that any local, state, or federal law that places a substantial burden on an individuals' religion is subject to the high level of protection found in strict scrutiny analysis, or the "compelling government interest test." If government is unable to meet its burden, the religious challenger will be granted an exception to the law.

NATIVE AMERICANS' RELIGIOUS FREEDOM

While RFRA was moving through Congress, a separate legislative effort on behalf of Native Americans' religious freedom was also moving forward. In 1991 the American Indian Religious Freedom Coalition launched a national campaign for federal legislation to protect Indian religious freedom. Rueben Snake led the effort. He contacted Sen. Daniel Inouye, D-Hawaii, chair of the Senate Committee on Indian Affairs, to discuss the coalition's legislative strategy.

In May 1993 Inouye and seven cosponsors introduced S 1021, the Native American Free Exercise of Religion Act. As with RFRA, much of the conversation focused on whether Congress had the authority to enact this type of legislation, but the academics who testified argued that it did. Resistance to the legislation came primarily from individuals representing forestry and mining industries, who were concerned that federal legislation protecting sacred land might affect their industries. They also said the legislation would show preference for Native American religion, a violation of the establishment clause. The Clinton administration pledged support for an amended bill.

Because it was clear the support for legislative protection for the religious use of peyote transcended party lines, with no formal opposition, coalition members decided to introduce this as a separate measure. That year President Clinton also signed an executive memorandum that protected eagle feathers and parts and instructed heads of executive departments and agencies to simplify the process of collection and transfer of eagle parts for religious purposes. Clinton's action on this issue, the coalition believed, made federal legislation unnecessary. Protection for the religious rights of incarcerated Indians, which had not received a great deal of attention, also was abandoned because many in Congress believed RFRA would provide an adequate forum for prisoners' challenges. In addition, coalition members decided to pursue the effort to protect sacred sites separately. That proposal was losing support because representatives from forestry and extraction industries continued to lobby against it, and in 1994 the bill died in committee.

The House passed legislation to protect the religious use of peyote by a unanimous voice vote, and the Senate passed it by an overwhelming majority; on October 6, 1994, President Clinton signed it into law. The law added a new section to the American Indian Religious Freedom Act of 1978, which exempts Indian religious use of peyote in *bona fide* traditional ceremonies from state and federal controlled substance laws and prohibits discrimination for the use of peyote, including denial of benefits from public assistance programs. The law provides that the Drug Enforcement Agency and the state of Texas continue to regulate the distribution of peyote, which is found in a small geographic area in Texas. It also allows federal and state authorities to place "reasonable" limitations on peyote use by individuals employed in "safety sensitive jobs."

More than four years after the Supreme Court used Al Smith's challenge to Oregon's prohibition against possession of peyote as its opportunity to address the status of the free exercise clause of the Constitution, Congress successfully enacted comprehensive legislation that protected this ancient religious ritual in all fifty states of the Union. John Echohawk, the executive director of the Native American Rights Fund, reflecting on the long battle, said:

> We got a bad Supreme Court case and this decision that ostensibly denies constitutional rights to practice the religion of the Native American Church, and it took a super effort on the church's part and our effort here to salvage a federal statutory right for the church to use peyote in their ceremonies. It was something we weren't at all sure we were able to get. But we were forced to do that, so at least we salvaged something. That is the most important thing in the end. But it was very tough.[11]

But this would not be the final word on *Employment Division of Oregon v. Smith* and religious freedom under the Constitution. In the four years following passage of RFRA, several hundred RFRA-related cases were decided in the lower courts. The cases ranged from frivolous challenges to prison regulations prohibiting the use of illicit drugs to legitimate requests for protection such as Indian prisoners seeking access to use of sweat lodges and Orthodox Jewish prisoners' requests for religious materials to practice their faith. Although the results were mixed—many claimants were unable to meet the requirement that the government action placed a substantial burden on their religious exercise—those that did found the courts more likely to grant them an exemption to the law under RFRA. CFER carefully tracked these cases because the members knew the constitutionality of the law would eventually be challenged in court. In cases where this occurred, CFER would file a generic legal brief drafted by Mark Stern of the American Jewish Congress and Prof. Laycock defending the constitutionality of the bill.

It was only a matter of time, however, before the Supreme Court weighed in to assess the constitutionality of a law that circumvented one of its decisions. In late October 1987 the Court granted certiorari to *City of Boerne v. Flores,* a case concerning a zoning dispute that began several weeks after Congress enacted RFRA. St. Peter the Apostle Catholic Church, which had outgrown its building, wanted to demolish it and build a new 700-seat church. A city landmark commission had denied the request for a building permit because the church was located in a historic preservation district. The church argued the denial placed a substantial burden on its parishioners' ability to freely practice their religion and that, because the city did not have a compelling interest in historic preservation, it should be granted an exemption to the ordinance and be allowed to build a new church. The city argued that RFRA was unconstitutional, based on an argument presented by Cardozo Law School professor Marci Hamilton. [12] The Supreme Court agreed, ruling that Congress exceeded its authority when it enacted RFRA because it attempted to substantively define the free exercise clause inappropriately under its Fourteenth Amendment, Section 5, power, which is limited to remedial legislation to enforce the amendment's guarantee of civil rights. Interpretation of constitutional rights, which RFRA was characterized as doing, is a power reserved for the judiciary. The Court also ruled that the legislation intruded upon states' rights by imposing the "compelling state interest" balancing test on challenges to state and local government action that infringed on religious liberty.

The decision in *Boerne* was a blow to members of CFER and to those in Congress who had led the effort to enact RFRA. They immediately began new discussions on how to address *Smith* under another part of the Constitution that would withstand scrutiny by the Supreme Court. A two-prong attack followed. The first was a federal effort to rewrite RFRA to avoid constitutional problems, and the second was a multistate effort to enact "mini-Religious Freedom Acts" all over the country. These laws would require state courts to use "strict scrutiny" analysis or the "compelling government interest" test to evaluate all religious challenges, including challenges to neutral, generally applicable laws that the Supreme Court decided in *Smith* were not subject to protection under the First Amendment.

The federal effort culminated in the proposed "Religious Liberty Protection Act" based upon Congress's Article I power under the spending and commerce clauses; the bill was introduced in Congress in 1998 and 1999. Although it received initial support in the House, the legislative effort has since lost steam, especially in light of a number of Supreme Court decisions that cast doubt on congressional legislative efforts that potentially intrude on states' rights. Efforts at the state level have been only slightly more successful. In 1998 Religious Freedom Acts were introduced in nineteen states, and passed in Connecticut, Florida, and Rhode Island; Alabama used the initiative process to protect religious liberty under its state constitution. Progress was made in other states as well, but concerns raised by prison officials and requests for exemptions to antidiscrimination laws are often sufficient to kill the legislation. The battle for state legislative solutions continues, however. In addition, renewed support for "new judicial federalism" is apparent in many states. The state courts can interpret their own constitutions to provide greater protection for constitutional rights than under the federal Constitution, and this has led to situations where religious liberty claims to neutral, generally applicable laws are evaluated using "strict scrutiny" analysis.

NOTES

1. Interview with John Frohnmayer, Eugene, Oregon, May 26, 1997.

2. As quoted in Garrett Epps, *To an Unknown God: Religious Freedom on Trial* (New York: St. Martin's Press, 2001), 228.

3. As cited in ibid., 229.

4. Interview with Al Smith, Breckenheim, Germany, July 16, 1998.

5. As quoted in Carolyn N. Long, *Religious Freedom and Indian Rights: The Case of Oregon v. Smith* (Lawrence: University Press of Kansas, 2000), 197.

6. Michael McConnell, "Accommodation of Religion: An Update and a Response to the Critics," *George Washington Law Review* 60 (March 1992): 685–742; Douglas Laycock, "The Supreme Court's Assault on Free Exercise and the Amicus Brief That Was Never Filed," *Journal of Law and Religion* 8 (1993): 99–114.

7. Michael McConnell, "The Origins and Historical Understanding of Free Exercise of Religion," *Harvard Law Review* 103 (1990): 1409–1476.

8. Statement of Oliver Thomas, general counsel, Baptist Joint Committee, Washington, D.C., June 26, 1990.

9. "The Religious Freedom Restoration Act of 1990," *Hearings Before the Subcommittee on Civil and Constitutional Rights and the Subcommittee on Criminal Justice of the Committee on the Judiciary,* 101st Cong., 2d sess., September 27, 1990.

10. Statement of President William Jefferson Clinton, Washington, D.C., November 16, 1993.

11. Interview with John Echohawk, May 18, 2000.

12. Marci Hamilton, "The Religious Freedom Restoration Act: Letting the Fox into the Henhouse Under Cover of Section 5 of the Fourteenth Amendment," *Cardozo Law Review* 16 (December 1994): 357–398.

Church of the Lukumi Babalu Aye v. City of Hialeah

David M. O'Brien

Church of the Lukumi Babalu Aye v. City of Hialeah
508 U.S. 520 (1993)

DECIDED:: June 11, 1993

VOTE

CONCURRING: 9 (William H. Rehnquist, Byron R. White, Harry A. Blackmun, John Paul Stevens, Sandra Day O'Connor, Antonin Scalia, Anthony M. Kennedy, David H. Souter, Clarence Thomas)

DISSENTING: 0

OPINION OF THE COURT: Kennedy

CONCURRING OPINION: Scalia (Rehnquist)

OPINION CONCURRING IN JUDGMENT: Blackmun (O'Connor)

OPINION CONCURRING IN JUDGMENT: Souter

In 1987 the city council of Hialeah, Florida, passed ordinances that made it a crime to possess and slaughter animals for ritual sacrifices. The council adopted the ordinances when Ernesto Pichardo announced the opening of a Santeria church, the Church of the Lukumi Babalu Aye. Santeria is rooted in the religious practices of the Lukumi people of what is now western Nigeria. Slaves brought to Cuba from the sixteenth to nineteenth centuries preserved their religious rituals but were forced to transform them. Because Cuba was dominated by the Roman Catholic church, the African religion became shrouded in secrecy. Conducted under the guise of worshipping Catholic saints or carried on in private homes, over time it became known as Santeria—"the way of the saints." In opening the church, Pichardo aimed to institutionalize the original religion and to perform its rites publicly, including ritual animal sacrifices.

The Lukumi church challenged the city's ordinances in federal district court as unconstitutional violations of the First Amendment's guarantee of the free exercise of religion. The district court upheld the ordinances upon concluding that they advanced three compelling government interests: the promotion of public health and safety, the prevention of cruelty to animals, and the prevention of the adverse psychological effect on children exposed to such sacrifices. That decision was affirmed by the Court of Appeals for the Eleventh Circuit.

Writing for the Court, Justice Kennedy reversed the appellate court's decision and struck down the ordinances. Kennedy's opinion commanded the support of only a plurality, but it nevertheless reaffirmed the cardinal principle of the free exercise clause that "government may not enact laws that suppress religious belief or practice." He did so by applying the analysis in *Employment Division, Department of Human Resources of Oregon v. Smith* (1990) (see page 341), in which the Court had declined to make exceptions for religious minorities from neutral and generally applicable laws. The ordinances failed *Smith*'s twin requirements of neutrality and general applicability. On the one hand, the combined language and legislative history of the ordinances established that Hialeah had targeted a religion and therefore failed the test of neutrality. The ban on "ritual animal sacrifice" swept too broadly. If Hialeah's interest was the proper disposal of animal carcasses, then the city could enact a general regulation on garbage disposal. Similarly, the city could prevent animal cruelty by narrower restrictions.

The ordinances also ran afoul of the requirement of general applicability. The city was "underinclusive" in preventing animal cruelty and promoting public health. Hialeah's interest in preventing animal cruelty fell short because the city allowed the killing of animals by virtually all other means except for ritual sacrifice. Fishing and hunting remained legal, along with the extermination of mice and rats and the use of animals in scientific experiments.

Although the Court's decision was unanimous, two justices wrote separate concurring opinions disagreeing with Kennedy's reasoning. Joined by Chief Justice Rehnquist Justice Scalia disagreed with the analysis of *Oregon v. Smith*'s requirements of neutral and generally applicable laws as "interrelated, rather than as substantially overlapping." In his view, nonneutral laws respecting the religious freedom could be generally applicable, precisely because they target particular religions. In addition, he disagreed with the focus on the motivations of Hialeah's city council when enacting the ordinances. Instead, he would have rested solely on the "plain meaning" of the ordinances, because legislative intent is frequently elusive, if not impossible to determine; here, the city council had specifically targeted the *ritual* killing of animals.

In another concurring opinion Justice Souter sharply disagreed with *Oregon v. Smith* and Justice Kennedy's reliance on it. He did not deem *Smith* germane to deciding the case and further argued that *Smith* should be overruled. It was well settled that the free exercise clause bars the government from discriminating against religious beliefs and practices. For him, Hialeah's ordinances were not neutral under any definition. He strenuously objected to the reliance on *Smith* because it introduced a narrow conception of government neutrality, namely, that a law must be neutral with respect to religion in its purpose and on its face. That did not go far enough in protecting religious freedom. A neutral and generally applicable law may still burden religious freedom by forbidding something that a religion requires or requiring something that a religion forbids.

In a third concurring opinion, which also reads more like a dissent, Justice Blackmun, joined by Justice O'Connor, maintained that the protection of the First Amendment extends beyond situations where the government targets religion with discriminatory legislation. Quoting from his dissent in *Oregon v. Smith*, he underscored that burdens on religious freedom "may stand only if the law in general, and the State's refusal to allow a religious exemption in particular, are justified by a compelling interest that cannot be served by less restrictive means." Unlike the plurality's opinion, he would have expressly applied the strict scrutiny test, under which there would be no question that regulations targeting religion are unconstitutional.

The Court's ruling was important in underscoring the free exercise clause's protection for religious freedom, especially for religious minorities. The decision was particularly crucial for Jews and Muslims who follow religious law in slaughtering animals. But it was a major setback for advocates of animal rights. Although the Court did not overturn *Oregon v. Smith*, it reaffirmed that government may neither discriminate against particular religious faiths nor target unpopular religions. Just months after the decision was issued, Congress passed the Religious Freedom Restoration Act of 1993 (RFRA), which would have overridden *Oregon v. Smith*, but in *City of Boerne v. Flores* (1997) RFRA was declared an unconstitutional exercise of congressional power. Therefore, although the government need not make exceptions for religious minorities from neutral and generally applicable laws—traffic and zoning laws, for example, and laws criminalizing the use of drugs, as in *Oregon v. Smith*—the holding in *Church of the Lukumi* made it clear that the government may not single out particular religions for discriminatory treatment.

The case generated controversy not just locally, but nationally. In Hialeah, a working class Hispanic community, Catholics and Protestant congregations denounced animal sacrifice as uncivilized. Some Cuban Catholics objected that publicly performing ritual animal sacrifices was demeaning to them. Some practitioners of Santeria opposed the public aspect of the sacrifice, which broke with the tradition of secrecy and invited harassment from animal rights activists.

Nationally, a wide coalition of religious organizations sided with the Church of the Lukumi Babalu Aye. They did so, not because they endorsed animal sacrifice, but because, after *Oregon v. Smith*, they worried that the Court might continue to further limit constitutional protection for religious freedom. By contrast, animal rights groups supported Hialeah and viewed the case as a potentially important step in the development of animal rights law.

One measure of the national controversy is the number of *amicus curiae* (friend of the court) briefs filed before the Supreme Court. The four *amici* briefs supporting the church were joined by nineteen groups, including the Americans United for the Separation of Church and State, the American Jewish Congress, the Baptist Joint Committee on Public Affairs, the Church of Jesus Christ of Latter-Day Saints, the National Association of Evangelicals, and the People for the American Way. Five briefs supported Hialeah and were joined by eighteen animal rights organizations, including the Humane Society of the United States, the Institute for Animal Rights Law, the International Society for Animal Rights, and People for the Ethical Treatment of Animals (PETA). The United States Catholic Conference filed a brief that supported neither side but asked the Court to overrule *Oregon v. Smith* and to broaden protection for religious freedom.

REACTIONS TO THE COURT'S RULING

The immediate reactions to the Court's decision were mixed and split between defenders of religious freedom and animal rights advocates. Following the announcement of the Court's decision, ABC aired an exchange with Pichardo, Barry W. Lynn, executive director of Americans United, and Marc Paulhus of the Humane Society, each offering sharply divergent reactions:

> *Ernesto Pichardo:* We must use the animals, offer the animals, and then consume the animals. They become part of our communion. . . .
>
> *Barry Lynn:* It's absolutely absurd for a city to permit the killing of animals for sport, for pest control, and for food, but to make it illegal to kill animals for religious purposes. . . .
>
> *Marc Paulhus:* We're totally stunned and, indeed, we are angry about this ruling. What it means is that tens of thousands of animals can now be legally sacrificed on the altar of religious freedom.[1]

At a news conference, Pichardo further elaborated on his reaction to the Court's decision. "We are amazed by the decision. As an immigrant, as a Cuban, I feel a great honor. This is why we came to the United States, because we have freedom of speech and freedom of religion."[2] Pichardo also said, "The decision is of profound significance. Animal sacrifice is an integral part of our faith. It is like our holy meal. The decision means that our people will no longer feel they are outlaws because of the way they worship God."[3]

Hialeah's mayor, Julio Martinez, was resigned to the ruling, but said, "I don't think anyone likes to see animal carcasses in front of your house or in front of your car when you're driving down the street. But the Supreme Court says that's what we have to put up with."[4] But he also told reporters that the city would enact no further legislation on the matter, in part because of the legal cost of defending the ordinances, which he estimated to be about $375,000. In his words, "That's a huge chunk of change that could have repaired a lot of streets and served a lot of hot breakfasts to children. I don't think the city of Hialeah can stand another bill this big."[5]

Ironically, several months before the Court handed down its ruling, Pichardo and other founders of the Church of the Lukumi Babalu Aye had voted to not perform ritual animal sacrifices in public. Yet, not all followers of Santeria agreed with their decision. Two weeks after the Court ruling, Rigoberto Zamora invited television crews and reporters to his apartment in Miami Beach, Florida, to witness the ritual sacrifice of nineteen animals, explaining, "What before we had to hide, now we can do in the open. We feel different now—but we have always done this, legal or not."[6]

Zamora's performing the rite in public angered not only animal rights activists, who protested outside his apartment, but also Pichardo, who now claimed, "Public offering of animals is offensive to our traditions and violates the privacy of the ritual. And it's our belief that it offends the sensibilities of the community at large."[7]

Zamora and Pichardo became embroiled in bitter public dispute, as reported in the Fort Lauderdale *Sun-Sentinel,* with Pichardo saying, "Zamora is a charlatan," and Zamora responding, "Pichardo thinks he is the pope of Santeria. The Supreme Court ruling has gone to his head."[8] Pichardo told reporters, "Zamora was informed two days prior to his conduct that his intent would be viewed as offensive to our religious traditions, as well as the general community."[9] Pichardo also said, "The First Amendment does allow individuals to do almost as they wish. But as a religious community, the leadership does have sanctioning power. He could end up totally isolated from that religious community."[10]

In the end, Zamora apologized, observing:

> I just wanted to demonstrate that we kill animals quickly. But others saw it from another point of view. They just saw an animal being killed and they're used to buying their meats in a supermarket. . . . It was an error on my part. It had a different effect than the one I was anticipating.[11]

PRAISE FOR THE DECISION

Despite the public quarrel, defenders of the Church of the Lukumi Babalu Aye and religious freedom praised the decision. Robyn Blummer of the Florida ACLU (American Civil Liberties Union) said, "This is a stunning victory for freedom of religion."[12] And, as Hillel Kuttler reported in the *Jerusalem Post:*

> Jewish community leaders on Friday welcomed a U.S. Supreme Court decision striking down local ordinances that prohibit animal sacrifice. . . .
>
> In issuing the ruling, the Court "reached the right decision on the substance of it," said Rabbi David Saperstein, director of the Reform movement's Religious Action Center.
>
> "It was encouraging to proponents of religious freedom that the Court maintains its strong belief that the government cannot ban religious practices solely on the grounds that they are exotic, unusual or distasteful to others," he said.[13]

The American Jewish Committee's legal director, Samuel Rabinove, observed: "Can the government ever forbid for religious purposes an activity it freely permits for all kinds of non-religious purposes? Happily, the U.S. Supreme Court said no—and said it resoundingly."[14]

In the *St. Petersburg Times* Thomas J. Billitteri reported support for the decision from across the religious spectrum:

> It's not every day that Baptists, Mormons and the National Association of Evangelicals are bound in common cause with Presbyterians, Lutherans and liberal groups such as Norman Lear's People for the American Way. . . .
>
> But when the U.S. Supreme Court announced its decision . . . religious-rights advocates, including many mainline churches, breathed a collective sigh of relief.
>
> Why? They feared that if the court had ruled against the Church of Lukumi Babalu Aye, government officials everywhere could restrict all sorts of religious practices—including mainstream ones.
>
> "We consider [it] an important win for religious liberty," said Forest Montgomery, counsel for the National Association of Evangelicals, which represents about 15-million Christians and 44 denominations. "It is a clear message to government officials that they can't single out a church for discriminatory legislation."

"In effect it was permissible to kill an animal for any reason in the city of Hialeah except a religious reason," said Oliver Thomas, general counsel of the Baptist Joint Committee, which represents 10 Baptist bodies and is separate from the fundamentalist-controlled national Southern Baptist Convention. "That sort of religious gerrymandering has no place in a society committed to freedom of conscience." . . .

"Many of the groups (that joined the case) think animal sacrifice is abhorrent," [Montgomery] said. "Certainly none of us take the position that it is proper theologically. But that is not the business of government to decide—whether a particular practice is proper theologically." . . .

"The law is made in cases involving very small or unpopular religious minorities," Thomas said. "Therein lies the danger. Frequently the public wants to find a way to hold against these unpopular groups without realizing that the law created for Rev. Moon, Jimmy Swaggart and the Santeria Church is the law that applies to the Presbyterian Church, the Baptist Church" and others.[15]

Douglas Laycock, a University of Texas law professor, who argued the church's case before the U.S. Supreme Court, was more cautious in celebrating the ruling:

> This case proves that *Smith* did not totally repeal the Free Exercise Clause. There is some Free Exercise Clause left, but I don't think there is much. . . . By itself, this case doesn't mean much, except that we're still protected against the worst types of religious persecution. From a historical perspective and from the perspective of religious liberty worldwide, that's important.[16]

Artist Xavier Cortada painted this representation of the Supreme Court decision in *Church of the Lukumi Babalu Aye v. City of Hialeah* (1993) as part of an exhibit for the Florida Supreme Court. In the ruling, the U.S. Supreme Court invalidated a city ordinance that banned ritual animal sacrifice. —Xavier Cortada, "Church of the Lukumi Babalu Aye v. City of Hialeah," 48" x 36" acrylic on canvas, 2004, www.cortada.com.

RESPONSES CONCERNING ANIMAL RIGHTS

Animal rights activists and organizations unanimously lamented the Court's decision. Roger Caras, president of the American Society for the Prevention of Cruelty to Animals, called the ruling "an obscene, bizarre and disastrous mistake."[17] Amy Bertsch of PETA denounced the ruling and told reporters that ritual animal sacrifice "is pretty vicious."[18]

Following the Court's ruling, the justices received numerous letters from animal rights supporters denouncing the decision. Chris DeRose, the president of Last Chance for Animals, in Tarzana, California, wrote to Justice Blackmun:

Dear Justice Blackmun:

On behalf of the LCA Board of Directors, staff, volunteers, and 60,000 members and supporters nationwide, please know that we are shocked at the Court's recent ruling defending the terrorizing, dismembering, and killing of animals in the name of "religion." The decision further illustrates our society's increasing desensitization toward violence, suffering, and death. We take a giant step backward.

In the words of Harvard University's medical professor Dr. Henry J. Bigelow, "Some day this nation will look back at animal sacrifice in the name of religion the way we now look back at burning at the stake in name of religion."

With this ruling the Court has condoned the willful violation of the humane statutes that we already have on the books. . . . The majority of religions use symbolic substitutes in their worship ceremonies, but the "santero" slits the throats of 15 animals.

I feel confident that this ruling has done much to undermine the public's confidence in the judgment of the Court.[19]

Nanci Alexander, the president of Animal Rights Foundation of Florida, also wrote to Blackmun:

As President and Speaker for over 4,000 members of the Animal Rights Foundation of Florida (ARFF), I can speak for all in expressing concern over the misinterpretation of the Court's ruling allowing animal sacrifices for the sake of "religious freedom."

The general public is concerned as well. Enclosed are several articles and editorials from individuals stunned over the recent ruling and the confusion by law-enforcement officials to enforce existing anti-cruelty laws. Also enclosed are letters from average Americans who do not understand how such a great system of justice could so miserably fail.[20]

Barbara A. Love, of the Humane Society of Lake County in Eustis, Florida, wrote:

TO THE MEMBERS OF THE SUPREME COURT

We are all appalled at the recent Supreme Court ruling allowing the sacrifice of animals for the sake of "religious freedom." We understand this decision has been erroneously interpreted to prohibit local and state authorities from enforcing anti-cruelty and humane slaughter ordinances when clear violations of the law are committed.

It is deplorable that we would allow any kind of animal sacrifice to continue in our country. We are under the impression that we are civilized!?![21]

Most newspaper editorials endorsed the Court's ruling for protecting religious pluralism. The *Baltimore Jewish Times,* for example, said in an editorial:

At first glance, the United States Supreme Court's decision last week to strike down a set of laws in Hialeah, Fla., that outlawed animal sacrifices would seem to have little relationship to the world as most of us know it. But look deeper. It's really an example of religious pluralism in action. . . .

It may be difficult for the rational Western mind to accept the belief that God smiles favorably on the ritual sacrifice of animals. Yet there are sincere religious people today in addition to Santerians who still engage in ritual sacrifice, and there are also some Jews who look forward to the restoration of such rites should the Temple be rebuilt in Jerusalem.

Moreover, there are those who argue that ritual circumcision and the process by which animals are slaughtered to render them kosher are both cruel and archaic practices that should be outlawed. If the courts were to uphold bans on these essential rites, observant Jews would virtually be prohibited from practicing Judaism.

This nation is filled with unpopular and unusual minorities that are difficult for the mainstream to comprehend. But as Jewish groups who supported the Santerians in this case understood, passing laws against practices that the majority disagrees with is a slippery slope.

Given recent widespread immigration from the Third World, it appears that this nation's future will be one of even greater diversity than we have known in the past. There will be many more instances of having to accept the beliefs of others that we may personally reject, lest our own beliefs someday be rejected.[22]

Newspapers and magazines published numerous letters to the editor. Most were critical, and some also attempted to explain, or interpret for the public, the Court's ruling. The *New York Times,* for example, published a letter from Gary L. Francione, the director of the Rutgers Law School Animal Rights Law Clinic:

To the Editor:

There has been confusion about the meaning of the Supreme Court's decision in Church of the Lukumi Babalu Aye. Contrary to what some may think, the Court did not hold animal sacrifices to be protected. Rather, the Court held that these practices could not be prohibited by legislation that was specifically intended to target religious practices alone.

A municipality may still ban animal sacrifices as long as the subject of regulation is the method of sacrifice, "not a religious classification that is said to bear some relationship to it." That is, regulation under a neutral anticruelty statute is still permissible. Moreover, a municipality may still ban all slaughter outside of licensed packinghouses or prohibit completely the keeping of certain types of animals in dwellings.

There is legitimate concern about the cruelty of Santeria sacrifices. . . .

Animals used in Santeria ceremonies are often kept in filthy and inhumane conditions, and deprived of food or water, for days before the ceremony. Decomposing animal bodies are disposed of in public places as part of the religious mandate.

Although every use of animals in our society is regulated by some body of law, Santeria practitioners insist on the absolute secrecy of their sacrificial practices. Neither the First Amendment nor common sense requires that.[23]

In the Dade County, Florida, *Jewish Journal,* Caren Lesser objected to the support for the Court's decision from the journal's editors and Jewish organizations, explaining:

I am Jewish. My younger brother and sister were bar/bat mitzvahed. . . . I am fascinated with my lineage and the heritage of the Jewish people. They have overcome so much adversity and risen above potential destruction. How can I not feel proud of my religion? I'll tell you how—and why I am so ashamed.

I stand on the "front lines," hold signs for television and newspaper cameras to see, write, letters, attend hearings—all to do my part for the world I live in. To protect animals. . . . Yet at the same time, I endure the burden of knowing that the so-called "leaders" of organizations representing the Jewish faith condone the torture, mutilation and mass murder of thousands of animals in the name of a cult called Santeria. . . .

Keep in mind that most every mass murderer from Ted Bundy to Jeffrey Dahmer started his "career" torturing, mutilating and killing animals first. What message are we sending to our children? What kind of religion supports these heinous acts. Not mine.[24]

The reactions of interest groups diverged in predictable ways that had originally led to the controversy. Those defending religious freedoms, like Americans United and the ACLU, as well as religiously affiliated organizations, praised the Court's ruling. Barry Lynn, in a special report, "The Supreme Court and Religious Liberty," in his group's journal, *Church & State,* observed:

Religious freedom took another small step forward when the Supreme Court, again unanimously, ruled that officials in Hialeah, Fla., may not ban the practice of animal sacrifice just because some people find it distasteful. While the ruling was a clear victory for religious freedom, the decision did little more than restate the obvious: Government may not pass laws designed solely to stamp out religious practices. Left in place were offensive legal principles devised by the court three years ago that allow government to regulate religion through laws deemed "neutral" and "generally applicable."[25]

But not even all *Church & State* readers agreed. Jonathan Spitz took issue with the idea that the Court's ruling was a victory for religious freedom:

By including animal sacrifice as a right of free religious exercise, the U.S. Supreme Court did not produce a "solid victory for religious freedom" as *Church & State* reports. In fact, by continuing to rely on the "generally applicable laws" standard for denying religious freedom established in the 1990 *Employment Division v. Smith* case, the justices effectively reaffirmed the principle of majoritarian control over religious exercise. . . .

Kennedy's statement, "[R]eligious beliefs need not be acceptable, logical, consistent, or comprehensible to others in order to merit First Amendment protection" is laughable in the wake of *Employment Division v. Smith.*

What the Court really means: Your religious beliefs are protected by the First Amendment if you're a drug-free carnivore.[26]

Animal rights activists and organizations continue their opposition. PETA's Web site, for example, maintains a page entitled "Animal Sacrifices: Cruel Rituals," which summarizes the sacrifice of animals by Santeria and other cults, and offers suggestions for action:

What You Can Do

If you discover evidence or have knowledge of any case of animal sacrifice or mutilation, contact the police. In addition, find out who in your town, county, or state investigates and enforces the anticruelty code (such as an officer from a humane society or SPCA) and provide him or her with a concise, written, factual statement.

One way to determine whether religious cults that practice animal sacrifice (such as Santeria) exist in your community is to consult your telephone yellow pages under religious suppliers or "botanicas." Botanicas are stores that sell beads and other supplies used in ritual sacrifice and other cult practices. . . .

Determine whether the zoning ordinance in your area prohibits the possession, breeding, and sale of any fowl or grazing animals in any residential and commercial area of your community; if not, organize a letter-writing campaign to city officials urging them to revise the ordinance. (This would create an obstacle for individuals who sell animals for sacrifice.)

Unfortunately, ordinances that specifically prohibit the killing or maiming of animals for ritualistic purposes can be problematic. However, . . [a]nimal sacrifices may still be banned as long as the subject of regulation is the method of sacrifice, "not a religious classification that is said to bear some relationship to it." In other words, regulation under a neutral anticruelty statute is still permissible. For example, a municipality can still, in effect, ban animal sacrifice by banning all slaughter outside licensed packing-houses or by prohibiting the keeping of certain animals in residential areas.

If all else fails, you can always visit or call your local newspapers or television stations and try to interest reporters in the story. A news story may force officials to act or scare the person causing the abuse into stopping.[27]

NOTES

1. ABC News, *World News Tonight with Peter Jennings*, June 11, 1993, available on Lexis/Nexis.

2. Quoted in Laurie Asseo, "Court Upholds Harsher Terms for Hate Crime," *Los Angeles Times*, June 13, 1993, A1.

3. Quoted in wire reports, "Court Throws Out Animal-Sacrifice Ban, Justices Say Florida Law Targeted Santeria," *Dallas Morning News*, June 12, 1993, A18.

4. Quoted in ibid.

5. Quoted in Larry Rohter, "Santeria Faithful Hail Court Ruling," *New York Times*, June 13, 1993, A34.

6. Quoted by Deborah Sharp, " 'We're a Religion, Just Like Any Other'; Santeria Priest Holds Sacrifices in Public," *USA Today*, June 28, 1993, A4.

7. Quoted by Associated Press, "Cult Marks Victory with Sacrifices," *Chicago Tribune*, June 27, 1993, C7.

8. Quoted by Luisa Yanez, "Santeria Priests Locked in Struggle for Power," *Sun-Sentinel*, July 31, 1993, A1.

9. Quoted in United Press International, "Santeria Priest Apologies for Sacrifices," July 2, 1993.

10. Quoted in AP-Special, "Animals Butchered as U.S. 'High Priest' Marks Court Victory," *Toronto Star*, June 27, 1993, A14.

11. Quoted in United Press International, "Santeria Priest Apologies for Sacrifices."

12. Quoted by Laurie Asseo, "Longer Prison Terms OK for 'Hate Crimes'; Unanimous Court Upholds Wis. Law," *Chicago Sun-Times*, June 11, 1993, A1.

13. Hillel Kuttler, "Jews 'Pleased' at U.S. Court Allowing Animal Sacrifices," *Jerusalem Post*, June 13, 1993, A1.

14. Quoted by Heidi B. Perlman, "Future of Hate Crime, Church-State Status Debated: Reactions to Supreme Court Rulings," *Jewish Advocate* (Boston), June 24, 1993, 1.

15. Thomas J. Billitteri, "Santeria Ruling Hailed as a Victory," *St. Petersburg Times*, June 19, 1993, Religion 1.

16. Quoted in Rob Boston, "Protecting the Unpopular," *Church & State* 46 (1993): 7–8.

17. Quoted by Asseo, "Longer Prison Terms OK."

18. Quoted by Cox News Service, "Animal Killings in Church Rites Gets Court Ok," *Cleveland Plain Dealer*, June 12, 1993, A8.

19. Chris DeRose to Harry A. Blackmun, July 12, 1993, in Papers of Justice Harry A. Blackmun, Box 611, Library of Congress.

20. Nanci Alexander to Blackmun, July 21, 1993, in ibid.

21. Barbara A. Love to members of the Supreme Court, n.d., in ibid.

22. Editorial, *Baltimore Jewish Times*, June 18, 1993, 8.

23. Gary L. Francione, letter to editor, "Court Isn't Protecting Animal Sacrifices," *New York Times*, July 1, 1993, A23.

24. Caren Lesser, letter to editor, "Religious Freedom Should Not Cost Animals' Lives," *Dade County Jewish Journal*, July 8, 1993, 12.

25. Barry W. Lynn, "A Special Report," *Church & State* 46 (1993): 3.

26. Jonathan Spitz, letters, "No Victory for Religious Freedom," *Church & State* 46 (1993): 22.

27. PETA Web site, www.peta.org/factsheet/files/FactsheetDisplay.asp?ID=77 (viewed July 27, 2004).

Bush v. Gore

Stephen J. Wermiel

Bush v. Gore
531 U.S. 98 (2000)

DECIDED:: December 12, 2000
VOTE
CONCURRING: 5 (William H. Rehnquist, Sandra Day O'Connor, Antonin Scalia, Anthony M. Kennedy, Clarence Thomas)
DISSENTING: 4 (John Paul Stevens, David H. Souter, Ruth Bader Ginsburg, Stephen G. Breyer)
OPINION: *Per Curiam*
CONCURRING OPINION: Rehnquist (Scalia, Thomas)
DISSENTING OPINION: Stevens (Ginsburg, Breyer)
DISSENTING OPINION: Souter (Stevens, Ginsburg, Breyer)
DISSENTING OPINION: Ginsburg (Stevens, Souter, Breyer)
DISSENTING OPINION: Breyer (Stevens, Souter, Ginsburg)

In an unsigned opinion for the Court, the justices ruled that counting damaged or otherwise uncounted ballots in Florida in the 2000 presidential election without uniform standards would violate the equal protection clause of the Fourteenth Amendment. The Court also ruled that it was too late to allow the Florida recount to continue because the legal deadline had arrived for the state to pick its representatives to the Electoral College.

In an unusual role for the Supreme Court, it effectively decided the outcome of the 2000 presidential contest between the Republican candidate, former Texas governor George W. Bush, and the Democrat, Vice President Al Gore, when it awarded Bush Florida's electoral votes. In the end only 537 votes separated the two candidates in Florida, with Bush coming out on top 2,912,790 to 2,912,253. Florida counted for 25 votes in the Electoral College where Bush was selected, 271 to 266, despite the fact that Gore won the total popular vote nationwide, 50,999,897 to 50,456,002.

Given its momentous impact, the Court's ruling is relatively short. The body of the decision runs eleven pages in the United States Reports, and the separate concurring opinion of Chief Justice Rehnquist is the same length. The four dissenting opinions of Justices Stevens, Souter, Ginsburg, and Breyer together total thirty-five pages.

The factual setting for the case was a complex and quickly moving election dispute that reflected the closeness of the race and the partisan differences between the candidates and their supporters. The dispute in Florida riveted much of the nation beginning late on election night, November 7, 2000, and lasting until December 13, 2000, the day after the Supreme Court ruling, when Gore said he would no longer try to fight the outcome.

With the outcome in Florida uncertain after the ballots were tallied, Gore had demanded that ballots in some counties be manually recounted. Those manual recounts would have occurred in only four counties, but would have taken longer than the deadline set by Florida's secretary of state, a Republican leader and Bush supporter. After the deadline passed, and after much legal maneuvering in several different state and federal courts simultaneously, the Florida Supreme Court waived the deadline and ruled that the manual recounts should proceed for an extended period. The U.S. Supreme Court heard arguments on December 1 on whether the state court decision conflicted with federal law or the U.S. Constitution. On December 4, 2000, the justices vacated the state court's extension of the recount deadline. In a unanimous, unsigned decision, the U.S. Supreme Court said there was too much uncertainty about the legal basis for the extension and ordered the Florida Supreme Court to reconsider its ruling. This move gave the appearance of the U.S. Supreme Court avoiding a decision on the merits of the case, but it had the effect of casting strong doubt on whether the recount could continue.

The Florida Supreme Court ruled four days later that some recounted ballots should be added to the totals and that other recounts should continue, a legal victory for Gore by a narrow 4–3 margin. Bush once more appealed to the U.S. Supreme Court. On December 9, the justices issued a stay that stopped the recount, and the case was argued again on December 11.

As with the first argument in the U.S. Supreme Court, interest and awareness were heightened nationally because the justices, who do not generally allow televising or radio broadcasting of their arguments, released audiotapes for broadcast as soon as the arguments ended. The national drama reached even greater heights on December 12, when the Court released its decision at about 10 p.m. The timing thrust television networks into hasty prime-time news bulletins, punctuated by the spectacle of usually unflappable correspondents standing on the front plaza of the Supreme Court, frantically flipping pages of the opinion live on camera, while trying desperately to figure out what the Court had done.

THE COURT'S DECISION

What the Court had done was declare that the Florida recounts posed a number of constitutional problems. The Court started with the premise that the Constitution does not guarantee a right to choose presidential electors, noting that the means of selecting electors is determined by state law. But once a state gives voters the right to choose electors, the Court said, the state must follow procedures—including those for recounts—that do not treat some voters differently from others. The Court said the Florida courts had not adopted "specific standards to ensure" that recounted ballots would be analyzed the same way from county to county or even "within a single county from one recount team to another." The Court also faulted the state court's proposed inclusion of the totals from a partially completed recount in one county.

These problems amounted to violations of the equal protection clause of the Fourteenth Amendment, the Court said. "When a Court orders a statewide remedy, there must be at least some assurance that the rudimentary requirements of equal treatment and fundamental fairness are satisfied," the Court stated. Finally, the Court said it was too late for Florida to adopt fair procedures and then resume the recount.

Oddly, the majority maintained that the equal protection principle announced in the case applied only in this instance and not in the future. "Our consideration is limited to the present circumstances, for the problem of equal protection in election processes generally presents many complexities," the majority declared.

In a concurring opinion joined by Justices Scalia and Thomas, Chief Justice Rehnquist added that the Florida Supreme Court had exceeded its authority and violated the intent of the Florida legislature to have the results certified by December 12. He said that the Florida legislature had chosen to have ballot counts completed by December 12 because that was the deadline by which, under federal law, a state's method of choosing electors for the Electoral College would be presumed valid and not subject to challenge.

In four separate opinions the dissenters split into two camps. All four thought that there was no basis for the U.S. Supreme Court second-guessing the judgment of the Florida Supreme Court or for terminating the recount in a way that would leave significant numbers of voters disenfranchised. In their opinions Justices Stevens and Ginsburg doubted whether continuing the recount was a significant violation of the equal protection clause. Justice Souter's dissent said the recount procedures might raise a valid equal protection concern, but that the state should have been given time to try to finish the recount under fair standards. Justice Breyer also thought the Bush side raised an important fairness and equality argument, but he said stopping the recount caused more unfairness than allowing it to continue.

It is obviously not a common occurrence for the Court to decide the outcome of a presidential election, and so the controversy that followed was not unexpected. Justice Breyer's dissent may have presaged the bitter, divisive fallout from the ruling. He warned at the end of his dissent:

> And, above all, in this highly politicized matter, the appearance of a split decision runs the risk of undermining the public's confidence in the Court itself. That confidence is a public treasure. It has been built slowly over many years, some of which were marked by a Civil War and the tragedy of segregation. It is a vitally necessary ingredient of any successful effort to protect basic liberty and, indeed, the rule of law itself. We run no risk of returning to the days when a President . . . might have said, "John Marshall has made his decision; now let him enforce it." But we do risk a self-inflicted wound—a wound that may harm not just the Court, but the Nation.

Justice Stevens was equally gloomy when he warned, "Although we may never know with complete certainty the identity of the winner of this year's Presidential election, the identity of the loser is perfectly clear. It is the Nation's confidence in the judge as an impartial guardian of the rule of law."

REACTIONS PRO AND CON

Because of the late-night release of the Supreme Court decision and its complexity, much of the reaction waited until December 13. Some of the first comments came from angry black leaders. At a rally in Tallahassee, Florida, Rev. Jesse Jackson said, "The election was essentially taken and stolen. . . . Today the emperor has no clothes and no shame."[1]

Republicans were quick to embrace the Court's decision. Rep. Tom DeLay, R-Texas, the majority whip, issued a statement: "The U.S. Supreme Court's decision reflects a proper and prudent enforcement of the Constitution. The Florida Supreme Court's ruling violated the vital limits on judicial authority and threatened to treat voters in an arbitrary and unfair manner."[2]

Initial reactions showed little sign of the passions cooling off. Anticipating a concession speech by Gore, the *NewsHour with Jim Lehrer* had the following heated exchange on December 13 between liberal commentator Mark Shields and conservative commentator Paul Gigot:

> *Mark Shields:* . . . probably more people will see and remember what he [Gore] says tonight than any event of the entire campaign because of the drama and the history surrounding it. . . .
>
> *Paul Gigot:* Well, I don't think this can be a garden variety concession speech because we haven't had a garden variety recount here. He has taken the country through an awful lot in the last five weeks by challenging the way he has. I don't think there is any question that there has been damage done, some damage to Bush. . . .
>
> *Mark Shields:* . . . I could not disagree more strenuously with Paul that Al Gore has to apologize for putting George Bush or the nation through anything. We do not know who won Florida. The decision has been made; the Supreme Court has ruled; and George Bush will be the president, but I mean to say that Al Gore put the country through something when he stood at 267 electoral votes with the popular lead, I don't—I really see no need at all for him to apologize for anything. I mean, what he did was totally legal. . . . I don't think you can say that responsibility for the past five weeks rests on Al Gore. . . .
>
> *Paul Gigot:* I don't think I ever used the word "apologize" and I wouldn't expect him to say I apologize but I do expect him to say, look, to begin to repair some of the damage

to the institutions and to the presidency of Bush. I mean, the courts haven't emerged out of this in terrific shape. They've been dragged into the electoral process, and I think by basically saying this is legitimate. Bush won it fair and square despite all of this—he could go a long way to help.[3]

That evening, Gore made a nationally televised speech in which he said:

> Now the U.S. Supreme Court has spoken. Let there be no doubt, while I strongly disagree with the Court's decision, I accept it. I accept the finality of this outcome which will be ratified next Monday in the Electoral College. And tonight, for the sake of our unity of the people and the strength of our democracy, I offer my concession. . . .
>
> Some have expressed concern that the unusual nature of this election might hamper the next president in the conduct of his office. I do not believe it need be so.[4]

Bush followed with a victory speech in which he sought to unify the nation:

> I believe things happen for a reason, and I hope the long wait of the last five weeks will heighten a desire to move beyond the bitterness and partisanship of the recent past.
>
> Our nation must rise above a house divided. Americans share hopes and goals and values far more important than any political disagreements.
>
> Republicans want the best for our nation, and so do Democrats. Our votes may differ, but not our hopes.
>
> I know America wants reconciliation and unity. I know Americans want progress. And we must seize this moment and deliver.
>
> Together, guided by a spirit of common sense, common courtesy and common goals, we can unite and inspire the American citizens.[5]

—copyright 2000 by Herblock in the *Washington Post*.

The speeches by Bush and Gore had the effect of shifting the focus among Washington political leaders to the transition and the new Congress. The bitter feeling among Democrats and elation among Republicans seemed to quickly give way in Washington to a back-to-work pragmatism. By the second day after the ruling, Bush was designating members of his cabinet and making plans to come to Washington to visit Capitol Hill, meet with House and Senate Democratic leaders, and try to establish a bipartisan spirit.

Sen. Tom Daschle, D-S.D., the minority leader, said, "What we need now is acceptance. We have a new president-elect. . . . Those who are in government have an urgent responsibility to prove to the American people that our government can still work for them." [6]

REACTIONS IN THE PRESS

But strident newspaper commentary did not subside so quickly. Op-ed columnists, split roughly along liberal and conservative lines, exchanged strongly worded ideas about the role of the Supreme Court and whether the credibility of the justices was permanently tarnished.

Columnist William Safire defended the Court on December 14, 2000, on the *New York Times* op-ed page:

> For the next few days . . . we can expect much learned hand-wringing about "the wound" the Supreme Court inflicted on itself by daring to hear, and to rule on, the hottest political case imaginable. . . . Though the Rehnquist court can expect much law-school derision for its activism in enforcing judicial restraint, it can lick its "wound" by considering how much tension it saved the Republic. [7]

Anthony Lewis, another *Times* columnist, expressed his concerns on December 16, 2000:

> The majority's rush to judgment has no credible explanation in the *per curiam* opin-ion. So the country is left with the impression that five justices acted as they did because they cared more about the result—ending the recount—than they did about the reason-ing that would compel it. . . .
>
> Deciding a case of this magnitude with such disregard for reason invites people to treat the court's aura of reason as an illusion.
>
> That would be a terrible price to pay. The Supreme Court must have the last word in our system because its role is essential to our structure of freedom.
>
> Preservation of the public respect on which the institution depends is far more important than who becomes president. [8]

Safire was right. There was plenty of law school derision. Perhaps nowhere was the depth of frustra-tion greater than among law professors who felt the U.S. Supreme Court had rendered itself an illegitimate institution.

In a news analysis on December 14, the *New York Times* quoted Prof. Suzanna Sherry of Vanderbilt Law School, who said, "There is really very little way to reconcile this opinion other than that they wanted Bush to win." The same article, by Supreme Court correspondent Linda Greenhouse, suggested that the *Bush v. Gore* episode "left behind an institution that many students of the court said appeared diminished, if not actually tarnished, by its extraordinary foray into presidential politics." [9]

Neal Katyal, a law professor at Georgetown University, wrote in an op-ed in the *Washington Post* on December 14:

> The price of George W. Bush's victory has been the immolation of America's last great standing institution: the Supreme Court. By elevating politics over principle, the court revealed itself to be no better than any other institution or actor that touched this election. Its decision will prompt an attack on the court from Congress, lower court judges and scholars. And the court has only itself to blame.
>
> The unsigned majority opinion can be summed up simply: It is lawless and unprece-dented. The Supreme Court has never, in its 200-year history, decided that if ballots can-not be counted with absolute perfection, they cannot be counted at all. . . . This break with the court's tradition is even more chilling when we consider that the Rehnquist

court has been built on the rock of respecting states' rights, not interfering with them.[10]

And writing in the *Los Angeles Times* on December 17, Yale Law School professor Akhil Amar wondered:

> Judged by ordinary standards of legal analysis, Bush v. Gore gets low marks. The core idea is that because the Florida recount was proceeding under somewhat uneven standards, it violated constitutional principles of equal protection. In some counties, dimpled chads might be counted; in other counties not. And so on.
>
> At first, this argument sounds plausible. But let's test it by traditional legal tools. As a matter of logic: If the Florida recount was constitutionally flawed, why wasn't the initial Florida count equally, if not more, flawed? It, too, featured uneven standards from county to county. . . .
>
> When my students ask about the case, I will tell them that we should and must accept it. But we need not, and should not, respect it.[11]

Conservatives were not reticent about answering the charges coming from academia. Washington lawyer Bruce Fein, a longtime conservative court-watcher, wrote on December 19 in the *Washington Times*:

> Except for result-oriented extremists, the precedent has left public confidence in the impartiality and integrity of the U.S. Supreme Court undisturbed. Neither Mr. Gore nor his surrogates nor Democrats in Congress have endorsed the partisanship charge. No clamors for impeachment or curtailing the jurisdiction or powers of the high court have been heard, in contrast to times past. . . .
>
> In sum, the world-riveting case proved one of the court's finest hours markedly superior to other participants in the drama and confirmed that our independent federal judiciary is a precious jewel in our constitutional crown.[12]

And in an analytical story, the *Los Angeles Times* on December 21 quoted John Yoo, a law professor at the University of California-Berkeley who later joined the Justice Department during Bush's first term:

> I think we should balance the short-term hit to the court's legitimacy with whether in the long run we can agree that it was in the best interest of the country to end the electoral crisis at an early date. People, like law professors, who spend their lives fixated on the court would rather have the court not do this than have the government up and running. I would rather have the divisive crisis over and the government put together than [preserve] the court's legitimacy for some unforeseen future need. The court has regularly intervened in cases [such as abortion and gay rights] . . . and my liberal colleagues never were troubled. I don't understand the great concern here where the court was intervening in a much deeper, more important, issue. . . . The costs to the court and the legal system were small and the benefit to the nation was high. The presidency is more important to the country than the Supreme Court's legitimacy.[13]

For much of the country, the rift over the election moved to a backburner. It would flare up occasionally in the middle of partisan squabbling and political strife. E. J. Dionne Jr. noted in a *Washington Post* story on January 28, 2001, that Republicans had adopted a new slogan to shout at complaining Democrats: "Get over it." He reported that during the inauguration, some protesters encountered celebrants of the president who declared, "Go meditate and get over it."[14]

But perhaps more than any other constituency in the country, some liberal law professors just could not get over it. There followed a wave of venting on Web sites, in magazines and law reviews, all at considerably greater length than the initial rounds of op-ed commentaries. And conservative legal scholars could not abide the continued focus on the 2000 election by their liberal counterparts.

THE CONTROVERSY CONTINUES

Jamin Raskin, a law professor at American University's Washington College of Law, wrote an essay entitled "Bandits in Black Robes" in March 2001:

> Quite demonstrably the worst Supreme Court decision in history, *Bush v. Gore* changes everything in American law and politics. The Rehnquist Court has destroyed any moral prestige still lingering from the Warren Court's brief but passionate commitment to civil rights. . . . *Bush v. Gore* was no momentary lapse of judgment by five conservative justices, but the logical culmination of their long drive to define an extra-constitutional natural law enshrining the rights of white electoral majorities, like the one that brought George W. Bush the White House.

> People do not want to believe that *Bush v. Gore* is actually the worst Supreme Court decision in our history because we want that title to belong for all time to the infamous *Dred Scott* decision (1857) . . . by comparison, a brilliantly reasoned and logically coherent decision. . . .

> By contrast, *Bush v. Gore*'s Emancipation Proclamation for pregnant chads mocks legal reasoning and represents an affront to the rule of law. It has no grounding in originalism or textualism, the watchwords of the conservatives. It constitutes an assault on federalism and the separation of powers, both of which conservatives pretend to love. And it makes a mockery of the phrase "judicial restraint." In a slapdash job of constitutional interpretation, the conservatives upended and ravaged four foundational relationships in our constitutional system. It usurped the role of the Florida Supreme Court in interpreting state law. It usurped the role of the American people by halting the counting of ballots in a presidential election and effectively choosing the president for them. It usurped Congress' powers to accept or reject the states' electoral college votes. And it reversed the proper distribution of powers in federal government by having Supreme Court justices appoint the president rather than vice versa.[15]

Yale Law School professor Jack Balkin wrote a fifty-one-page essay in the *Yale Law Journal* in 2001, in which he said:

> Legal academics rationalize bad judicial decisions all the time; that is part of their job description. Moreover, the fact that a few judges occasionally make mistakes in legal reasoning, even very egregious mistakes, should come as no surprise, nor should it cause one to lose faith in the rule of law, the U.S. Supreme Court, or in the system of judicial review. Likewise, the fact that a few judges occasionally decide cases because they secretly favor one party over another should also come as no surprise; nor should isolated examples of judicial corruption cause one to lose faith in a larger process of legal decision making. The problem with Bush v. Gore, I suspect, was the case was too salient an example of judicial misbehavior for many legal academics to swallow. It was no isolated fender bender in which a local judge helped out the son of a former law partner. Rather, the case decided the outcome of a presidential election and may well have determined who would sit on the Supreme Court and the lower federal courts for decades to come. . . . That the conservative Justices acted as they did suggested that

their partisanship was so thorough and pervasive that it blinded them to their own biases.[16]

Former judge and former law professor Robert H. Bork, writing in the *New Criterion* in March 2001, had a dramatically different view of the liberal criticism of the Supreme Court's ruling. Bork wrote:

> Cruder commentators, with which the print and electronic media and law school faculties are amply supplied, put the decision down to raw political partisanship. But the idea that each of the seven justices who found a constitutional violation and the five who voted to end the recounts immediately were voting for a Bush presidency is a bit too crass to be credited, particularly if you know the people involved.
>
> The more likely explanation is that the justices saw an election being stolen in Florida and that the Supreme Court of Florida was not only complicit but also willing to defy the U.S. Supreme Court.[17]

The halls of academia were not the only source of discussion about the lingering effects of the *Bush v. Gore* decision. The already unusual episode in the Court's history was marked by another unusual chapter. Justices Kennedy and Thomas discussed the need for the Court to decide the case during a congressional hearing on Court funding on March 29, 2001. "Sometimes it is easy to enhance your prestige by not exercising your responsibility, but that has not been the tradition of our court," Kennedy said, according to the *Washington Post* account. "The issues we decide are very difficult ones," he said. "Ultimately, the power and the prestige and the respect of the court depends on trust." Thomas, at the same hearing, commented: "It is on difficult issues that the court is required to be the court. If there was a way . . . to have avoided getting involved in that difficult decision . . . I would have done it."[18]

Justice O'Connor made similar comments in an appearance on NBC's *Dateline* news magazine show. "There was a great deal of criticism. It was a difficult case. It's too bad that it came up," the *Houston Chronicle* quoted her as saying. "We don't enjoy being thrust into the middle of political controversy. We don't always have a choice in what comes here," she said.[19]

The next phase in reaction was the publication of large numbers of books devoted to the episode. Among these were collections of essays: *Bush v. Gore: The Question of Legitimacy,* edited by Yale Law professor Bruce Ackerman, a vehement critic of the decision; *Bush v. Gore: The Court Cases and the Commentary,* edited by Dionne and *Weekly Standard* editor William Kristol; and *The Vote: Bush, Gore and the Supreme Court,* edited by University of Chicago Law professors Cass R. Sunstein and Richard A. Epstein. The latter two books attempted to achieve a balanced treatment with essays from various points of view.

Among the other individual works was one defending the Court's decision by Judge Richard Posner of the U.S. Court of Appeals for the Seventh Circuit, who wrote *Breaking the Deadlock: The 2000 Election, the Constitution, and the Courts.* There were also a number of books highly critical of the Court. Harvard Law School professor Alan Dershowitz weighed in with *Supreme Injustice: How the High Court Hijacked Election 2000.* Vincent Bugliosi, a former California prosecutor, released *The Betrayal of America: How the Supreme Court Undermined the Constitution and Chose Our President.* Douglas Kellner, a professor at the UCLA School of Education, wrote *Grand Theft 2000: Media Spectacle and a Stolen Election.* Professor Raskin wrote *Overruling Democracy: The Supreme Court vs. The American People.* And there were still others.

EFFECT ON 2004 ELECTION

As the 2004 presidential election season began, the anger of Democrats over the 2000 outcome began to resurface. First it showed up in slogans. "Re-elect Al Gore in 2004" signs, bumper stickers, and T-shirts appeared; and, when it was clear that Gore was not in the race, a variation proclaimed "Re-defeat Bush."

In the heat of the 2004 election, with Sen. John Kerry, D-Mass., locked in a tight race with President Bush, the concern over *Bush v. Gore* became more pronounced. Stuart Taylor Jr. wrote in the *National*

Journal a month before the election that legions of lawyers had been hired by both candidates to be prepared for election day battles. He warned:

> It seems all too possible that if the presidential election is close, the courts will once again put us through weeks of uncertainty and once again determine the outcome. The resulting explosion of bitterness could dwarf the one after Bush v. Gore, further depleting the legitimacy of our political and legal processes alike.[20]

Although some legal maneuvering was apparent immediately before election day 2004, the outcome was decided by the voters this time, and the courts played a minimal role. This result and the absence of postelection uncertainty was noted around the world, leading the *Courier-Mail* newspaper in Australia to observe on November 4, 2004, "The victory . . . gives Mr. Bush a legitimacy that he did not have after 2000, when the election was effectively decided by the US Supreme Court in Bush v. Gore."[21]

There is no way to know if the passage of time will mute the debate over the Court's ruling in *Bush v. Gore* and the decision will one day be seen as an aberration. Another possibility is that the voters face the same question every four years: Will the Supreme Court decide this election?

NOTES

1. "Black Democrats Angered by Supreme Court ruling," December 13, 2000, http://archives.cnn.com/2000/ALLPOLITICS/stories/12/13/african.americans/index.html (accessed February 20, 2005).
2. 2000 PR Newswire Association, Inc., December 13, 2000 (accessed at LexisNexis, October 24, 2004).
3. *NewsHour with Jim Lehrer,* http://www.pbs.org/newshour/shields&gigot/december00/sg_12-13.html (accessed February 20, 2005).
4. OnPolitics: Text: Vice President Gore Concedes Election, December 13, 2000, http://www.washingtonpost.com/wp-srv/onpolitics/elections/goretext121300.htm (accessed February 20, 2005).
5. ELECTION 2000: Governor George W. Bush Delivers Remarks, December 13, 2000, http://www.cnn.com/ELECTION/2000/transcripts/121300/bush.html (accessed February 20, 2005).
6. Deborah Barfield, "Democrats Vow To End partisan Bickering," *Newsday,* December 15, 2000, A04.
7. William Safire, "The Coming Together," *New York Times,* December 14, 2000, A39.
8. Anthony Lewis, "Abroad at Home: A Failure of Reason," *New York Times,* December 16, 2000, A19.
9. Linda Greenhouse, "The 43rd President: Another Kind of Bitter Split," *New York Times,* December 14, 2000, A1.
10. Neal Kumar Katyal, "Politics over Principle," *Washington Post,* December 14, 2000, A35.
11. Akhil Reed Amar, "Supreme Court: Should We Trust Judges?" *Los Angeles Times,* December 17, 2000, M1.
12. Bruce Fein, "Misguided Detractors," *Washington Times,* December 19, 2000, A1.
13. David G. Savage, Henry Weinstein, "Supreme Court Ruling: Right or Wrong?" *Los Angeles Times,* December 21, 2000, A24.
14. E. J. Dionne Jr., "We'll Get Over It If You Get Off Your High Horse," *Washington Post,* January 28, 2001, B01.
15. Jamin Raskin, "Bandits in Black Robes," *Washington Monthly,* March 2001.
16. Jack M. Balkin, "*Bush v. Gore* and the Boundary Between Law and Politics," *Yale Law Journal* 110 (June 2001): 1407, 1408.
17. Robert H. Bork, "Sanctimony Serving Politics: The Florida Fiasco," *New Criterion,* March 2001.
18. Charles Lane, "Two Justices Defend Court's Intervention in Fla. Dispute," *Washington Post,* March 30, 2001, A13.
19. Reuters, "O'Connor: Bush v. Gore Difficult Decision to Make," *Houston Chronicle,* January 27, 2002, A8.
20. Stuart Taylor Jr., "Inside Washington: Opening Argument, Imperial Judges Could Pick the President," *National Journal,* October 9, 2004.
21. "Bush Set for a Legitimate Second Term" (Queensland, Australia) *Courier-Mail,* November 4, 2004.

Lawrence v. Texas

Peter G. Renstrom

Lawrence v. Texas
539 U.S. 558 (2003)

DECIDED: June 26, 2003
VOTE

CONCURRING: 6 (John Paul Stevens, Sandra Day O'Connor, Anthony M. Kennedy, David H. Souter, Ruth Bader Ginsburg, Stephen G. Breyer)

DISSENTING: 3 (William H. Rehnquist, Antonin Scalia, Clarence Thomas)

OPINION OF THE COURT: Kennedy
CONCURRING OPINION: O'Connor
DISSENTING OPINION: Scalia (Rehnquist)
DISSENTING OPINION: Thomas

Lawrence v. Texas involved homosexuality, a hot-button issue for many Americans. Specifically, in this case the Court examined the Texas criminal sodomy law, which is designed to restrict certain sexual practices. In 1960 such laws existed in all fifty states. These laws did not define sodomy uniformly, but typically criminalized forms of nonprocreative sex such as anal or oral sex—practices regarded as "unnatural." Over the next two decades, half the states abandoned such regulations.

As late as 1986, however, in *Bowers v. Hardwick,* the Supreme Court upheld a Georgia man's conviction under that state's sodomy law. Justice Byron R. White, speaking for the majority in *Bowers,* categorically rejected the contention that "any kind of private sexual conduct between consenting adults is constitutionally insulated from state proscription." The right to engage in homosexual conduct is neither a fundamental right "deeply rooted" in the nation's "history and tradition nor implicit in the concept of ordered liberty." White characterized contentions to the contrary as "facetious." Despite the Court's ruling, only thirteen states retained sodomy laws into the twenty-first century; only four proscribed homosexual conduct. Texas was one of the four.

In 1860 Texas criminalized "abominable and detestable crimes against nature," a phrase understood to prohibit anal sex both for opposite- and same-sex couples. A revised statute was adopted in 1943 that made the prohibition specific for heterosexual and homosexual couples. Texas's Homosexual Conduct Law of 1973, under which John Lawrence and his partner, Tyron Garner, were prosecuted, banned oral and anal sex, but only by same-sex couples. Harris County officers responded to a reported weapons disturbance and entered Lawrence's apartment on September 17, 1998. They saw Garner and Lawrence engaged in a private, consensual sexual act and arrested them for deviant sexual intercourse under the Texas statute. A county court denied motions to quash the complaints, found Lawrence and Garner guilty, and fined them each $200 plus court costs of $141.25. Relying on *Bowers v. Hardwick,* the Texas appellate courts upheld the convictions.

Justice Kennedy's majority opinion indicated that the Supreme Court reviewed the case to consider whether Lawrence and Garner's convictions for adult consensual sexual intimacy in their home violated their liberty and privacy protected by the Fourteenth Amendment's due process and equal protection clauses. In a 6–3 decision, with Chief Justice Rehnquist and Justices Scalia and Thomas dissenting, the Court ruled for Lawrence and Garner. By a 5–4 vote, with Justice O'Connor joining the other dissenters, the Court formally overruled *Bowers.* In deciding *Lawrence,* the Court expanded the protective reaches of the right to privacy and the equal protection clause and created immunity from government regulation on a number of "moral values" issues, which could include same-sex marriage.

Kennedy spoke of constitutional protections preventing "unwarranted government intrusions" into private places. The state, he said, is "not omnipresent in the home." But these protections are more far-reaching, extending to "other spheres of our lives and existence, outside the home, where the State should not be a dominant presence"; these are freedoms that extend "beyond spatial bounds." In Kennedy's view, the *Lawrence* case involved personal liberty "in its spatial and more transcendent dimensions."

The laws at issue in *Bowers* and *Lawrence* purportedly did no more than prohibit particular sexual conduct. The Court, however, saw more "far-reaching consequences," touching upon the "most private human conduct, sexual behavior, and in the most private of places, the home." The Texas law sought to regulate a relationship that is "within the liberty of persons to choose without being punished as criminals." When sexuality finds "overt expression in intimate conduct with another person," Kennedy said, the conduct is "but one element in a personal bond that is more enduring." The Constitution "allows homosexual persons the right to make this choice."

Kennedy disputed the conclusion from *Bowers* that there is a long-standing history in the United States prohibiting homosexual conduct. Early American sodomy laws sought to prohibit all nonprocreative sexual activity and did not distinguish homosexual from heterosexual conduct. Far from having "ancient roots," American laws targeting same-sex couples is a relatively recent phenomenon. As a result, the historical grounds relied upon in *Bowers* are, said Kennedy, "overstated at the very least." The "deficiencies" in *Bowers* were also apparent by the number of states repealing their criminal sodomy laws after the ruling. Kennedy suggested that the Court's decisions in *Planned Parenthood v. Casey* (1992), which retained the privacy-based right to an abortion, and *Romer v. Evans* (1996), striking down a Colorado constitutional amendment prohibiting state action designed to protect the civil rights of homosexuals and bisexuals, further undermined *Bowers*. When a precedent is so weakened, Kennedy suggested, it must be reexamined. *Bowers* was "not correct when it was decided, . . . not correct today, [and] ought not to remain binding precedent."

The Texas law also had equal protection defects. Criminalizing homosexual conduct, Kennedy said, "is an invitation to subject homosexual persons to discrimination both in the public and in the private spheres." The stigma imposed "is not trivial." While the offense is "minor" in the Texas scheme, it "remains an offense with all that imports for the dignity of the persons charged." O'Connor's concurring opinion effectively focused this point. She said *Lawrence* raised a issue different from *Bowers*: whether "moral disapproval is a legitimate state interest to justify by itself a statute than bans homosexual sodomy, but not heterosexual sodomy." Moral disapproval of homosexuals is an "insufficient interest" for satisfying rational basis review under the equal protection clause, which requires that "all persons similarly situated should be treated alike." The Texas law, however, makes sodomy a crime only if a person "engages in deviate sexual intercourse with another individual of the same sex; it treats the same conduct differently based solely on the regulated group."

Kennedy emphasized the *Lawrence* case did not involve minors, persons who might be injured or coerced, persons in relationships where consent might not easily be refused, or public conduct. Equally important, the case did not require legal recognition of homosexual relationships as such. Rather, the case involved "two adults who, with full and mutual consent, engaged in sexual practices common to a homosexual lifestyle." They were entitled, in the Court's view, to "respect for their private lives," and the state cannot "demean their existence or control their destiny by making their private sexual conduct a crime." Quoting *Casey*, Kennedy concluded, "It is a promise of the Constitution that there is a realm of personal liberty which the government may not enter." The Texas statute furthers no legitimate state interest that can justify its "intrusion into the personal and private life of the individual."

Finally, Kennedy suggested the Court take an adaptive approach when interpreting the due process clauses of the Fifth and Fourteenth Amendments. He concluded that those who drew and ratified those amendments did not intend to foreclose expanding the reach of those clauses; they did not presume to know all the "components of liberty in its manifest possibilities." On the contrary, they knew "times can blind us to certain truths and later generations can see that laws once thought necessary and proper in fact serve only to oppress. As the Constitution endures, persons in every generation can invoke its principles in their own search for greater freedom."

Two justices wrote dissenting opinions in *Lawrence*. Justice Scalia, joined by Chief Justice Rehnquist and Justice Thomas, criticized the Court's reasoning in overruling *Bowers,* and he accused the majority of being "manipulative" with the doctrine of *stare decisis*. By using the same reasoning as *Lawrence,* he argued, *Roe v. Wade* (see page 299) should be overruled as well. Scalia contended that "societal reliance" on the principles underlying *Bowers* had been "overwhelming." Countless judicial decisions and legislative enactments have relied on the long-standing proposition that a governing majority's belief that "certain sexual behavior is immoral and unacceptable constitutes a rational basis for regulation." He saw overruling *Bowers* as a "massive disruption of the current social order." The Court has repeatedly held that "*only* fundamental rights qualify for this so-called 'heightened scrutiny' protection—that is, rights which are 'deeply rooted' in this Nation's history and tradition." The majority does not describe homosexual sodomy as a "fundamental right" or a "fundamental liberty interest." He said the Court's conclusion that the Texas statute furthers no "legitimate state interest" that can justify intrusion into the personal and private life of individuals is "so out of accord with our jurisprudence—indeed, with the jurisprudence of *any* society we know—that it requires little discussion." The Texas statute acts on the belief of its citizens that certain forms of sexual behavior are "immoral and unacceptable." This same interest, he argued, is furthered by criminal laws against fornication, bigamy, adultery, adult incest, bestiality, and obscenity. If the promotion of majoritarian sexual morality is not even a "*legitimate* state interest, none of the above-mentioned laws can survive rational-basis review."

In Scalia's view, the *Lawrence* opinion was overly influenced by a "law-profession culture that has largely signed on to the so-called homosexual agenda." The Court has "taken sides in the culture war, departing from its role of assuring, as neutral observer, that the democratic rules of engagement are observed." Debating and perhaps persuading one's fellow citizens is one thing, but "imposing one's views in absence of democratic majority will is something else." What Texas has chosen to do, Scalia concluded, is "well within the range of traditional democratic action, and its hand should not be stayed through the invention of a brand-new constitutional right by a Court that is impatient of democratic change."

Justice Thomas dissented separately and urged judicial restraint. Quoting Justice Potter Stewart's dissent in *Griswold v. Connecticut* (see page 235), he said he saw the Texas law as "uncommonly silly." Thomas indicated he would vote to repeal it were he in the Texas legislature. As a justice, however, he did not believe he was "empowered to help petitioners and others similarly situated. I can find nowhere in the Constitution a "general right of privacy," or as Kennedy termed it, the "liberty of the person both in its spatial and more transcendent dimensions."

LAWRENCE'S POTENTIAL IMPACT

Invalidating the Texas criminal sodomy law was among the less-significant consequences of the *Lawrence* ruling. Of the thirteen states with antisodomy statutes still on their books, only four targeted homosexual conduct exclusively, and none of the four regularly enforced these laws. The more significant consequences of *Lawrence* stemmed from the Court's reasoning and from a number of other issues grounded in homosexuality, especially same-sex marriage.

The Court's reasoning in *Lawrence* clearly supported the possibility for increased judicial scrutiny of state laws on due process and equal protection grounds. The Court's conclusion that the Texas sodomy law furthered no "legitimate state interest" could have a substantial impact on personal liberties jurisprudence generally and sexual liberty specifically. The Court's support of Lawrence and Garner's equal protection claim may also require further consideration of the asserted "morality justification."

In Houston, Tyrone Garner, left, and John Lawrence, right, celebrate the Supreme Court's decision in *Lawrence v. Texas* (2003), which struck down a Texas sodomy law and reversed *Bowers v. Hardwick* (1986). Gay rights advocates applauded the ruling.— Reuters/Richard Carson

The Court's ruling in *Lawrence* triggered a substantial backlash against homosexuals and gay rights as evidenced by the defense-of-marriage acts adopted in a number of states, state constitutional amendments banning same-sex marriage, the prospect of a federal constitutional amendment prohibiting same-sex-marriage, and the contraction (if not elimination) of some domestic partner benefits. Texas argued *Lawrence* largely on state sovereignty grounds and the need for judicial restraint in defining constitutional rights. In addition to their displeasure with the Court's unwarranted activism, social conservatives also saw a more fundamental issue—holding the line against advances in gay equality to preserve traditional sexual morality and family values. In their view, invalidation of sodomy laws represented another step toward allowing same-sex marriage. Both sides in the "culture war" over the place of homosexuals in American society considered the maintenance or defeat of sodomy laws as central, if only symbolically, to their respective causes.

Supporters and critics of *Lawrence* weighed in with superheated rhetoric. As a result, both sides rallied their supporters by magnifying the importance of the decision. The existence of sodomy laws, suggested Harvard law professor Laurence Tribe "was an excuse for harassment and discrimination, and a labeling of a whole group of people for whom this is the primary form of physical sexual intimacy as deviant and criminal. A lot of people feel the yoke has been lifted."[1] Joan Biskupic of *USA Today* called rejection of state antisodomy laws a "decisive endorsement of gay rights that is likely to become a milestone in U.S. law and culture."[2] Emory University law professor David Garrow said the decision was the "most libertarian majority opinion ever issued by the Supreme Court."[3] Stephen Wermiel, associate professor at American University's law school, saw *Lawrence* in more limited terms. The ruling was "narrowly written to give gay men and lesbians the right to private, consensual sex. That doesn't get me to a constitutional right to get married."[4] Harvard law professor Richard Fallon concurred. "It's one thing to say there's a fundamental right to sexual intimacy and another to say there's a fundamental right to marriage." "When people say the decision means a lot," suggested Mary Coombs of the University of Miami's law school, "what they're doing is not so much saying what it means but what they are going to argue it means. Part of what this will do is energize both the gay-rights movement and the Christian Fundamentalist right."[5]

SUPPORTING RESPONSES

Among the groups supporting the *Lawrence* ruling were the American Bar Association, American Civil Liberties Union (ACLU), American Psychological Association, Freedom to Marry, Gay and Lesbian Advocates and Defenders, Gay & Lesbian Alliance Against Discrimination, Human Rights Campaign, Institute for Justice, Lambda Legal Defense and Education Fund, Log Cabin Republicans, National Lesbian and Gay Law Association, and National Organization for Women.

Baltimore gay rights activist Jon Kaplan thought *Lawrence* might be the "start of big things for Maryland's gay and lesbian population."[6] David Smith, spokesman for the Human Rights Campaign, the nation's largest gay lobby, called it the "most significant case" to be decided by the Court related to equal rights for gays. To establish a "fundamental right to privacy for gay and lesbian Americans is a giant leap forward, and contained in there are links to marriage, child rearing . . . it's just not too far a leap." Charles Francis, founder and co-chairman of the Republican Unity Coalition, a group trying to improve acceptance of gays within the GOP, said the Court's rejection of *Bowers* has "practical significance, by putting gays on equal footing in substantive legal matters of employment, adoption, child custody and other matters."[7]

Kevin Cathcart, executive director of Lambda Legal, a leading gay civil rights organization, said *Lawrence* "closed the door on an era of intolerance and ushered in a new era of respect and equal treatment for gay Americans." The ruling "promises real equality to gay people in our relationships, our families, and everyday lives; it starts an entirely new chapter in our fight for equality for lesbian, gay, bisexual and transgendered people."[8] Elaine McNeely, founder of the New Hope Gay and Lesbian Task Force echoed that sentiment:

> This is a large step, but only the first step and it does open the door for other things. But we are not protected under the Declaration of Independence because "all men are created equal." If it would be written again they would say all people, black, white, male, female, gay or straight would be created equal. We just want the same rights and freedoms to love who we choose. Judges like Scalia are worried that we are a threat to traditional marriages. They only look at the sexual end. Heterosexuals don't have a monopoly on love.[9]

Some gay rights lawyers pointed to the many legal obstacles to establishing rights to gay marriage, but most observers acknowledged that the decision had profound legal and political implications. Ruth Harlow, legal director of the Lambda Legal Defense and Education Fund and the lead counsel for Lawrence and Garner, called the decision "historic and transformative." Suzanne Goldberg, a professor at Rutgers Law School, who represented Lawrence and Garner in the Texas courts, said the decision would affect "every kind of case" involving gay people, including employment, child custody and visitation, and adoption. It removes the "reflexive assumption of gay people's inferiority," Goldberg said. "*Bowers* took away the humanity of gay people, and this decision gives it back."[10] Elizabeth Birch, executive director of the Human Rights Campaign, offered similar sentiments:

> This is an historic day for fair-minded Americans everywhere. We are elated and gratified that the Supreme Court, in its wisdom, has seen discriminatory state sodomy laws

for what they are—divisive, mean-spirited laws that were designed to single out and marginalize an entire group of Americans for unequal treatment. Gay Americans are parents, children, brothers, sisters, friends, co-workers and churchgoers. This ruling opens the door for new advances toward full equality and should be viewed as a challenge to legislators to help pass important legal protections for GLBT [gay, lesbian, bisexual, transgendered] Americans—like employment nondiscrimination laws and comprehensive hate crimes legislation. The GLBT community owes a debt of gratitude to John Lawrence and Tyron Garner for letting their story be heard.[11]

Calling *Lawrence* a "historic decision with wide-ranging implications," the ACLU issued a press release. James Esseks, litigation director of the ACLU's Lesbian and Gay Rights Project, said:

> This decision will affect virtually every important legal and social question involving lesbians and gay men. For years, whenever we have sought equality, we've been answered both in courts of law and in the court of public opinion with the claim that we are not entitled to equality because our love makes us criminals. That argument—which has been a serious block to progress—is now a dead letter. From now on, cases and political debates about employment, custody and the treatment of same-sex couples should be about merit, not about who you love. With this decision, the Court has finally recognized that we are part of the American family. Now it's time for the rest of society to do the same. Our civil rights laws need to make the workplace fair, our schools safe, and to give basic respect to the relationships at the core of our lives—with partners and our children. By acknowledging that we are not criminals, this decision will make it far easier for us to get society to change.[12]

RESPONSES OPPOSING *LAWRENCE*

Among the groups criticizing the Court's decision in *Lawrence* were American Center for Law and Justice, American Family Association, American Values, Center for Law and Justice International, Center for Marriage Law, Concerned Women for America (CWA), Eagle Forum, Family Research Council, First Principles, Inc., Focus on the Family, Liberty Counsel, Liberty Legal Institute, Massachusetts Family Institute, National Clergy Council, Pro-Family Network, Pro-Family Law Center, and Traditional Values Coalition.

Tom Minnery, vice president for public policy at Focus on the Family, said the Court "continues pillaging its way through the moral norms of our country." If the people have no right to regulate sexuality, the "institution of marriage is in peril, and with it, the welfare of the coming generations of children." The ruling prohibits the states from preventing "sexual chaos in our culture." By "unlocking one of society's last social seatbelts," the Court has guaranteed "more fatal collisions lie just down the road."[13] Kelly Shackelford, chief counsel of Liberty Legal Institute, a Texas-based foundation, thinks gays can now claim that gay relationships are afforded liberty interests under the Constitution, "something which our Founders would never ha[ve] said." At the same time, the "atomic bomb would have been to create a fundamental right for homosexuality, similar to the so-called 'right' to abortion." In Shackelford's view, *Lawrence* stopped short of that.[14]

Jan LaRue, chief counsel for the CWA, said the *Lawrence* ruling came from:

> Supreme Court justices who believe in a "living" and "evolving" theory of the Constitution—it's as if the Founders wrote it on a blackboard and gave them an eraser and chalk. If there's no rational basis for prohibiting same-sex sodomy by consenting adults, then state laws prohibiting prostitution, adultery, bigamy, and incest are at risk. No doubt, homosexual activists will try to bootstrap this decision into a mandate for same-

sex marriage. Any attempt to equate sexual perversion with the institution that is the very foundation of society is as baseless as this ruling. Six lawyers robed in black have magically discovered a right of privacy that includes sexual perversion. More vaporous law emanating from "penumbras" that do not exist in the text of the Constitution. The Court has denied the people of Texas their constitutional right to decide what is immoral sexual behavior and replaced it with the Court's version. The majority didn't like the Texas sodomy statutes, so they struck them down.[15]

Rev. Lou Sheldon, president of the Traditional Values Coalition, promised that "people of faith are not going to lie down and allow their faith to be trampled because a politically correct Court has run amok." CWA president Sandy Rios predicted "moral Armageddon." Although states might be able to ban sexual practices that are obviously hurtful or exploitive of women or minors, she predicted that the "fear of legalized wantonness" would become a central issue in the 2004 presidential campaign. Scott Lively of the Pro-Family Law Center in Sacramento called the *Lawrence* decision "an error of biblical proportions." He predicted the result of *Lawrence* would be that the already "enormously powerful gay political lobby in our state [California] will consolidate its power" and secure adoption of "every item on its agenda." Bishop Wilton D. Gregory, president of the United States Conference of Catholic Bishops, said the Court mistakenly "chose to view homosexual behavior between consenting adults as a matter of privacy." In Gregory's view, sexual activity has "profound social consequences which are not limited to those immediately engaged in sexual acts." Sexual activity, Gregory continued, "belongs to the marital relationship between one man and one woman in fidelity to each other." Respect for the "purpose of human sexuality and the family" needs to be reaffirmed and "anything which reduces respect for them—such as [the *Lawrence*] decision—is to be deplored."[16]

The *Baltimore Sun* interviewed local clergymen on June 28. Bill Thomas, a Carroll County pastor, contended that the Bible teaches when a country "openly walks away from God's design for marriage and family, usually that culture suffers decline and sometimes devastation." Maryland legislator Emmett C. Burns Jr., who is also pastor of Rising Sun Baptist Church in Woodlawn, argued that *Lawrence* "opens the door for same sex marriage, and goes against the laws of nature. Men were not meant to be in love, in a romantic way, with men." Rev. Steven Hooker, pastor of New Beginnings Church of God in Bel Air, said the ruling underscores a perennial struggle between moral and humanistic concerns in America, but "we know the Bible completely condemns sodomy." He added that sexual acts should promote creation of life and that homosexuality represents the "imbalance of man's lust."

The American Society for the Defense of Tradition, Family, and Property (TFP) saw the moral and social consequences of *Lawrence* as far worse than those of *Roe v. Wade*. In granting constitutional protection to sodomy, the Court "renounced the duty imposed by Natural Law on every government to uphold morality in striving for the common good." The TFP called the decision a "major blow" to the "institution of the family and the very foundations of morality and society." *Lawrence* is "America's moral 9/11." With one decision, the Court "laid low the legal constructs of every state safeguarding public morality" and paved the way for destroying the country's many defense of marriage laws erected to "protect the sacred institutions of marriage and the family." *Lawrence* is a "blatant rejection of Natural Law and the moral code that has governed Western Civilization for 2,000 years." The decision "essentially affirms there is no morality." Further, the ruling allows for an interpretation so broad that "all state laws proscribing prostitution, adultery, bigamy, incest, sadomasochism, pedophilia, and bestiality are now at risk."[17]

Virginia C. Armstrong, national chairman of the Eagle Forum's Court Watch, was among the most outspoken critics. She said the horror of *Roe v. Wade* and *Lawrence* "lies in their results as well as their reasoning." These cases, more than any other two cases in American history, "call into question the ability of America's culture and constitutional system to survive." *Lawrence* "tramples state power, virtually ignoring the states' constitutionally-protected interest in protecting public health, safety, welfare and morality from the dangers of homosexual conduct." The decision "reeks with the message that homosexual conduct is, at the least, acceptable." Even legislation that is "largely symbolic and infrequently enforced has significant pedagogical value." Laws teach people "what they should and should not do." The judicial "destruction of a massive protective wall around public health, safety, morality and welfare leaves America wide open for a further plunge backward into Sodom and Gomorrah." In Armstrong's view, state laws prohibiting bestiality, incest, sibling intermarriage, polygamy, prostitution, spousal abuse, and drug use are likely to be "buried in the Supremes' hurry to legitimize [homo]sexual behavior." [18]

Armstrong saw *Lawrence* as the latest attack on marriage by the justices she referred to as the "Sodomy Six." She contended that *Lawrence* opened the door to "homosexual marriage and the legal status for similar homosexual arrangements." As a result, *Lawrence* "poses the gravest judicial threat to marriage in American history and is a stigmatic insult to the countless numbers of Americans who oppose homosexual conduct, not because they hate homosexuals, but because of their sincere, deeply held moral and/or religion values." She called on Congress to remove federal court jurisdiction from issues stemming from the 1996 federal Defense of Marriage Act. Longer term, Armstrong urged adoption of a constitutional amendment to protect more thoroughly marriage and the family.[19]

Ken Connor, president of the Family Research Council, said judicial activists have used once again "their fertile imagination to create rights that simply don't exist in the Constitution." In doing so, they have "imposed their own moral judgments in place of state legislatures and have thereby undermined the democratic process." [20] Connor went further on the *USA Today* opinion page:

> [*Lawrence*] is a direct attack on marriage. As Justice Scalia noted in his dissent, state laws against bigamy, same-sex marriage, adult incest, prostitution, masturbation, adultery, fornication, bestiality and obscenity are likewise sustainable only in light of *Bowers'* validation of laws based on moral choices. Indeed, the Court opened the door to all of this under an implicit "right to privacy" that appears nowhere in the Constitution. The court invented it in a 1965 case called *Griswold v. Connecticut*, when it "divined" a generalized right to privacy not from the actual test of the Constitution, but from vague and invisible legal oozings that were called "emanations" issuing from "penumbras" surrounding the words. Now the majority has extended the "right of privacy" to embrace homosexual sodomy. This decision is deeply flawed. . . . Will we rule ourselves, or be ruled by unelected black-robed oligarchs who disregard the Constitution to impose their own political agenda on the country?[21]

Jay Sekulow, legal director of the American Center for Law and Justice, a conservative legal advocacy group founded by Pat Robertson, said *Lawrence* reflects a "political approach to the law that we deplore." Rev. Jerry Falwell, an evangelical leader, said "this is probably as bad a day as the court has had on social issues since *Roe v. Wade*." The Court "put the right of privacy ahead of respect for community standards of morality which have prevailed for many years." Falwell said *Lawrence* would put the nation on a "slippery slope in which courts might approve bestiality, prostitution and the use of narcotics." He called *Lawrence* a "capitulation to the gay and lesbian agenda whose ultimate goal is the legalization of same-sex marriages." William Devlin, founder of Philadelphia-based Urban Family Council, a faith-based family advocacy organization, called the ruling a "case of the inmates running the asylum." He said *Lawrence* was a "bad decision for America, a bad decision for children, and a bad decision for families." [22]

SAME-SEX MARRIAGE

A few months after the *Lawrence* ruling, the focal point had shifted. The criminal sodomy issue examined in *Lawrence* moved to the back-burner; no state attempted to reenact a sodomy law. Rather, *Lawrence* became a proxy for higher stakes issues associated with homosexuality, especially the institution of marriage. On October 3, 2003, President George W. Bush proclaimed October 12–18, 2003, as Marriage Protection Week. In his press release, he referred to marriage as a "sacred institution" and indicated its protection is "essential to the continued strength of our society." Marriage Protection Week provided an "opportunity to focus our efforts on preserving the sanctity of marriage and on building strong and healthy marriages in America." Bush went on to say that marriage is a "union between a man and a woman, and my Administration is working to support the institution of marriage by helping couples build successful marriages and be good parents."[23]

Marriage Protection Week was grounded on the language of the Defense of Marriage Act of 1996 (DOMA), which declared that in everything pertaining to federal law, the word marriage "means only a legal union, between one man and one woman as husband and wife." In addition, it provided that no state shall be required to "give effect to a law of any other state with respect to same-sex marriage." Thirty-eight states enacted similar laws. The primary concern following *Lawrence* was that DOMA would be declared unconstitutional by so-called "activist judges," and the supporters of the law urged amending it to withdraw jurisdiction from all federal courts to hear any challenge.

On November 18, 2003, the Massachusetts Supreme Judicial Court provided impetus to the defense of marriage movement when it ruled the state had "failed to identify any constitutionally adequate reason" to deny gay and lesbian couples the right to marry. Three months later, the Massachusetts court held that full marriage rights were required and that any civil union measure would establish an "unconstitutional, inferior, and discriminatory status for same sex couples."[24] President Bush called the ruling "deeply troubling" and said that if "activist judges insist on redefining marriage by court order, the only alternative will be the constitutional process."[25]

Soon after the Massachusetts court's second pronouncement, and the beginning of San Francisco's issuance of same-sex marriage licenses in February 2004, rhetoric from both sides of the issue turned to politics. Opponents of same-sex marriage called for a federal marriage amendment. Rep. Marilyn Musgrave, R-Colo., had introduced a two-part amendment in the U.S. House in May 2002. The first section legally defined marriage as "only the union of a man and a woman." The second section provided that "neither federal or state constitutions or statutes shall be construed to require that marital status or the legal incidents thereof be conferred upon unmarried couples or groups." The measure was subsequently introduced in the U.S. Senate. On July 14, 2004, the Senate failed to cut off debate on the proposal, ending the possibility of an actual vote on its substance in 2004. A vote of sixty senators was needed to stop debate, but only forty-eight votes were recorded in favor, well short of the required two-thirds. In spite of the defeat, Senate Majority Leader Bill Frist, R-Tenn., promised the "issue is not going away."[26] President Bush expressed disappointment at the Senate vote and called upon "defenders of traditional marriage" not to relent in their efforts to keep activist judges from "redefin[ing] marriage for the rest of America." Many Republicans and their allies among Christian groups promised to use this issue to mobilize conservative voters in the November 2004 elections. "This is just the beginning of the process," said Gary Cass of the Center for Reclaiming America, an advocacy group founded by Rev. D. James Kennedy, a Florida evangelist.[27] A vote on another federal marriage amendment almost certainly will occur before the 2006 election. Gay rights activists anticipated the backlash from *Lawrence* and vowed to build on the "victory" by working for equality in "every town, city, school and place of employment in this country."[28]

The anti-*Lawrence* forces were able to gain momentum in the 2004 elections. President Bush was reelected, and with him the promise to pursue a federal marriage amendment. In addition, eleven states adopted constitutional amendments banning same-sex marriage. The objective of these amendments was to keep state courts from making decisions like those from Massachusetts. The country "overwhelmingly rejects same-sex marriage," said conservative activist Gary Bauer. "Our hope is that both politicians and activist judges will read these results and take them to heart."[29] The political response to *Lawrence v. Texas* has gone beyond criminal sodomy laws, and same-same marriage has become the new "moral values" battleground. Andrew Koppelman, a law professor at Northwestern University, suggested the upshot of the 2004 election is that the forum for the debate over marriage has shifted. "The gay marriage issue is being fought primarily in the culture, not in the courts."[30]

NOTES

1. Nancy Gibbs, "A Yea for Gays," *Time,* July 7, 2003, 39.
2. Joan Biskupic, "Decision Represents an Enormous Turn in the Law," *USA Today,* June 27, 2003, 5A.
3. Evan Thomas, "The War over Gay Marriage," *Newsweek,* August 7, 2003, 40.
4. Scott Calvert, "Ruling on Gays Stirs Up Emotions," *Baltimore Sun,* June 28, 2003.
5. Gibbs, "A Yea for Gays."
6. Calvert, "Ruling on Gays Stirs Up Emotions."
7. Carolyn Lochhead, "High Court Ruling Likely to Usher in New Era for Gays: Decision's Logic to Have Impact on Other Rights," *San Francisco Chronicle,* June 29, 2003.
8. Scott Frost, "Gay Rights Leaders Applaud Court Decision," *Trentonian,* June 28, 2003.
9. Ibid.
10. Linda Greenhouse, "Justices, 6–3, Legalize Gay Sexual Conduct in Sweeping Reversal," *New York Times,* June 26, 2003.
11. Human Rights Commission press release, June 26, 2003, www.hrc.org.
12. ACLU news release, http://www.aclu.org, June 26, 2003.
13. Karen Peterson, "Sodomy Rulings Gives Hope to Many," *New York Times,* June 26, 2003, 5A.
14. Pete Winn, "Court Strikes Down Texas Sodomy Law," June 26, 2003, *CitizenLink,* http://www.family.org.
15. "Supreme Court Wrong to Declare a Right to Sexual Perversion," June 26, 2003, http://cwfa.org.
16. "Conference President Criticizes Supreme Court Decision," June 27, 2003, http://www.sodomylaws.org.
17. "TFP Decries Supreme Court's Decision as America's 'Moral 9/11,' " June 26, 2003, http://www.sodomylaws.org.
18. Virginia C. Armstrong, *Eagle Forum,* July 18, 2003.
19. Ibid., October 15, 2003.
20. Family Research Council press release, http://www.frc.org, June 26, 2003.
21. Ken Connor, "Right to Privacy Goes Too Far," *USA Today,* June 27, 2003, 12A.
22. Kristin Smith, "Mixed Reviews on Court Ruling," *Delaware County Daily Times,* June 29, 2003.
23. White House press release, October 3, 2003.
24. Jennifer Peter, "Mass. High Court Rules for Gay Marriage," February 4, 2004, http://www.yahoo.com.
25. Rose Arce, "Massachusetts Court Upholds Same-Sex Marriage," February 6, 2004, http://www.cnn.com.
26. Helen Dewar and Alan Cooperman, "Senate Scuttles Amendment Banning Same-Sex Marriage," July 14, 2004, http://washingtonpost.com.
27. Ibid.
28. ACLU press release, June 26, 2003, http://www.aclu.org.
29. Eric Johnson, "Voters in 11 States Ban Same-Sex Marriage," November 3, 2004, http://www.PlanetOut.com.
30. Adam Liptak, "Caution in Court for Gay Rights Groups," *New York Times,* November 12, 2004.

McConnell v. Federal Election Commission

Melvin I. Urofsky

McConnell v. Federal Election Commission
540 U.S. 93 (2003)

DECIDED: December 10, 2003

VOTE

    CONCURRING: 5 (John Paul Stevens, Sandra Day O'Connor, David H. Souter, Ruth Bader Ginsburg, Stephen G. Breyer)

    DISSENTING: 4 (William H. Rehnquist, Antonin Scalia, Anthony M. Kennedy, Clarence Thomas)

OPINION OF THE COURT: Stevens, O'Connor

DISSENTING OPINION: Rehnquist

DISSENTING OPINION: Scalia

DISSENTING OPINION: Kennedy

DISSENTING OPINION: Thomas

Reformers attempting to change the way political campaigns are financed have been hard at work at this task since the middle of the twentieth century, and their efforts have yielded two major pieces of legislation. Congress passed the Federal Election Campaign Act (FECA) in 1971, and, following the revelations of the Watergate scandals, amended the measure not only to tighten reporting requirements but also to impose limits on how much contributors could give to campaigns and how much candidates and the political parties could spend. In *Buckley v. Valeo* (1976) the Supreme Court upheld most of the law, including limits on contributions, but struck down the caps on expenditures. In reasoning that has drawn criticism ever since, the majority drew a distinction between giving money to candidates, which the justices said did not constitute speech protected by the First Amendment, and expenditures by parties and candidates, which the Court said came under the umbrella of the speech clause's protection.

Ever since the *Buckley* decision, most academic commentators as well as some members of the Court found the distinction between contributions and expenditures artificial and indefensible as sound jurisprudential logic. More important, parties and candidates managed to find all sorts of ways to skirt the limits imposed by the FECA. The law regulated only so-called "hard money," the funds given directly to a candidate or party committee. It imposed no limits on groups, such as political action committees (PACs) or individuals, who could raise vast sums of "soft money" that fell outside many of the law's requirements. By the 1990s soft money funded nearly half the expenditures in federal campaigns. Moreover, running for office had become fabulously expensive, so that candidates spent an inordinate amount of time raising money. A person elected to the United States Senate, for example, had to raise an average of $15,000 a week every week throughout a six-year term to have sufficient funds to run for reelection. In the 2000 election cycle the cost of campaigning in federal elections for the first time exceeded $1 billion.

The high cost of campaigns, the growing reliance on special interests for large donations, and the bad odor attached to some of the fund-raising techniques of the Clinton administration finally gave reformers the popular support they needed to push a new campaign finance measure through Congress. Led by John McCain, R-Ariz., and Russell Feingold, D-Wis., in the Senate and Christopher Hays, R-Conn., and Martin Meehan, D-Mass., in the House, reformers secured passage of the Bipartisan Campaign Reform Act of 2002 (BCRA), and President George W. Bush reluctantly signed it into law. Among BCRA's provisions, the most important were an effort to do away with soft money, a redefinition of what constitutes campaign advertising, strict limits on contribution amounts and sources, and tougher disclosure and reporting requirements. It also prohibited minors from making contributions, because some contributors evaded the giving limits of FECA by channeling sums through other family members, including children and grandchildren. If faced by a wealthy, self-financing candidate, "poorer" candidates, according to the law, could exceed limits imposed on their expenditures.

BCRA and the case it generated, *McConnell v. Federal Election Commission,* represented a conflict between two theories of what government can do to regulate the campaign process. One argument held that the integrity of the political process, and the need to protect it from apparent as well as real corruption, constituted such an important interest for a democratic society that it justified some limits on the free speech guaranteed by the First Amendment. The opposing argument was that the protections of the First Amendment were inviolable. Political speech was the core value the amendment had been designed to protect, and if, at times, it became shrill or apparently chaotic, then the answer was not to regulate it but to allow more speech. As Justice William J. Brennan Jr. once noted, "Debate on public issues should be uninhibited, robust, and wide-open." Any limitations on speech, even in the name of trying to protect the integrity of the political system, would lead to a diminution of the most important of all rights, free speech.

Within hours after President Bush signed the measure into law, Sen. Mitch McConnell, R-Ky., who had fought against it, announced that he would challenge its constitutionality and welcomed other groups and individuals to join him. McConnell soon had more than eighty co-plaintiffs, including such unlikely bed-fellows as the National Rifle Association and the American Civil Liberties Union (ACLU), the AFL-CIO and the U.S. Chamber of Commerce, and state and national committees of the Republican and Democratic parties.

Normally, the Justice Department and the Federal Election Commission (FEC) would defend the constitutionality of such a law, but BCRA allowed any member of Congress standing to join in the suit. The bill's prime sponsors—Senators McCain and Feingold and Representatives Shays and Meehan—joined as defendants, and an influential Washington law firm represented them. Both sides, in fact, enjoyed the *pro bono* services of some of the nation's leading lawyers. In addition, the defense team received major help from the Pew Charitable Trusts, which funded a number of studies to provide the factual basis for the claim that the large amounts of money pouring into the political system generated not only the appearance of corruption but actual corruption as well.

The law provided for a "fast track" option: a special three-judge federal court would hear the constitutional challenges, which would then go on direct appeal to the U.S. Supreme Court. Congress and both political parties wanted a speedy resolution of the issue well before they began serious fundraising for the 2004 federal election cycle. The district court opinion proved so unwieldy, with the three judges split on almost every issue, that neither side could claim victory, and the plaintiffs and defendants immediately appealed to the Supreme Court. Recognizing the importance of the case, the justices ordered four hours of argument (instead of the usual one) on September 8, 2003, a full month before the Court's customary opening day. In a relatively speedy process, the Court announced its decision just three months later.

The Supreme Court split almost as badly as the court below, with eight different opinions handed down. The opinions reflected the basic dualism that had marked the entire debate over the bill—the need to protect the political system from the corruption of large amounts of money (expounded in the joint majority opinion of Justices Stevens and O'Connor) and the First Amendment rationale that political speech deserved the highest protection under the First Amendment and should not be restricted (articulated most forcefully in the dissenting opinions of Justices Scalia and Thomas).

The slim 5–4 majority that upheld the main provisions of the law relied heavily on the factual findings of Congress, reinforced in the Pew studies that the defense had cited—that large amounts of money in the political system could lead to corruption or its appearance. Time and again Stevens and O'Connor's joint opinion deferred to congressional fact-finding, and, although most people believe that in terms of policy-making, courts should defer to the legislative branch, in this case, as several commentators noted, the majority's deference led it to abandon independent First Amendment inquiry. In essence, the majority said that Congress had found a danger existed (although neither Congress nor the defense had been able to show any actual corruption), and the need to avert such danger constituted the compelling governmental interest necessary to impose some limits on the First Amendment. The majority opinion, however, failed to articulate any clear doctrinal consistency.

The various dissents have a firmer base in doctrine than the majority opinion because they enunciate what had been—until this case—accepted First Amendment jurisprudence for more than three decades. Government may not restrict speech without some compelling interest, and if government can meet the heavy burden of this proof, it must allow a narrowly tailored solution involving the least restrictive means. Moreover, of all types of speech, political speech is that most to be cherished and protected. The dissents by Scalia and Kennedy shredded the majority opinion and hit especially hard on the fact that the majority was allowing restrictions on speech without any proof of actual corruption. Congress's fear that at some point corruption *might* appear did not provide adequate justification.

SUPPORTERS' RESPONSES

Supporters of the law rejoiced. On the day of the decision, the four sponsors issued a simple two-sentence statement: "This opinion represents a landmark victory for the American people in the effort to reform their political system. Now that the Court has spoken, we must make sure that the law is properly interpreted and enforced." The next day, the *Washington Post* ran a story with the headline "McCain, Feingold & Co. Laugh Last." It began, "For nearly a decade, they were the Don Quixotes of Capitol Hill, whose crusades against the influence of big money in politics caused colleagues to snicker at their relentless optimism and zeal in the face of repeated defeats." But now that small band of reformers—McCain, Feingold, Shays, and Meehan—had the last laugh. McCain, who had made campaign finance reform the centerpiece of his bid for the Republican presidential nomination in 2000, was visiting the U.S. Naval Base at Guantánamo Bay, Cuba, when an aide called to inform him about the ruling. A reporter asked McCain if he had ever lost hope after years of congressional obstruction, delays, presidential vetoes, and court challenges. He laughed and said, "Did Don Quixote ever despair?"[1]

In his official statements, McCain reiterated that the bill reflected longtime citizen revulsion at the abuses in the system. "For years, poll after poll revealed the public's strong support for genuine campaign finance reform. These polls clearly marked the progress of public sentiment on this question." The polls, according to McCain, indicated that voters had lost faith in the basic integrity of the system. "That faith was shaken and it was imperative that Congress act."[2] In an interview on NBC's *Today* show, McCain said that he could "assure all Americans that no longer can a member of Congress or a senator pick up the phone, call a trial lawyer, a corporate head or a union leader and say, 'Write me a six- or seven-figure check. And, by the way, your legislation is coming up soon.'"[3]

His cosponsors echoed this theme. According to Shays, "We believed the cause was noble, it was worth fighting for, and we trusted each other." Feingold claimed that "the system had careened so far out of control that even members of Congress didn't want to be part of the system." Scandals involving corporate giants such as Enron gave them an added impetus. "We knew the bill would ultimately pass," Shays said, "because the system was going to get worse. . . . There would always be some new abuse."[4]

The Pew Charitable Trusts applauded the Court's decision. Rebecca W. Rimel, president and CEO of the foundation, declared:

> Polling shows that Americans continue to be frustrated with the state of campaigns and elections, and many are disconnecting from the process altogether. Cynicism has become widespread, and voter participation has been sliding downward for decades.

These cornerstones of democracy have drifted further away from their essential role as mechanisms by which citizens engage in political and public life.

One of the most troubling trends has been the growing and unaccountable influence of money in the campaign process. The average cost to win a House seat rose from $73,000 in 1976 to $918,000 in 2000. For a Senate seat, the cost increased from $595,000 to $7.3 million during the same time. Simply put, money—rather than citizens—has become the fuel that powers the current campaign system. That is why we have sponsored research to inject new ideas—and new public confidence—into the present campaign finance system.

Begun in 1996 and continuing today, these efforts have aimed to support regulatory reform and improvements in the federal campaign finance system, including:

- limits on the use of soft money;
- stronger issue advocacy provisions; and,
- better enforcement of existing and new laws.

The sweeping reform legislation passed by Congress and subsequent affirmation by the Supreme Court are important first steps to mending the broken campaign finance system. We expect to continue supporting efforts to shine light on the campaign finance activities of groups participating in elections, aid in the interpretation and enforcement of the campaign finance laws in the courts and Federal Election Commission, and identify new areas in which the system is in need of repair.[5]

Public Citizen, another group that was active in sponsoring BCRA and in defending it before the courts, also expressed its satisfaction. Public Citizen president Joan Claybrook and Alan B. Morrison, founder of the organization's litigation group, issued a joint statement:

Today's Supreme Court decision upholding every one of the key provisions of the McCain-Feingold campaign finance reform measure is a magnificent vindication of a decade of work by reform groups and key members of Congress who fought for its passage.

The decision helps ensure the removal of the corrupting influence of "soft money" from federal elections so that corporations and labor unions, as well as wealthy donors, will no longer be able to buy influence and access through our national political parties. The decision also will require that all broadcast ads run shortly before elections that are attempting to influence the election or defeat of candidates—referred to as "sham issue ads"—are funded by individual contributions, not from the treasuries of corporations and unions. Further, the sources of those funds will be made public.

Today's decision represents a home run when it comes to limiting the influence of special interests in our elections. The raising of soft money and the broadcasting of sham issue ads was accelerating exponentially. Had the Court failed to uphold this law, politicians and parties would have been further indebted to interest groups, and the airwaves would have remained saturated with ads benefiting candidates. Today, there is now hope that the erosion of our democracy is somewhat halted.

The majority of the Court clearly understood the two major challenges that Congress faced in regulating soft money and sham issue ads, and correctly concluded that Congress had addressed them in a careful manner that did not infringe on First Amendment rights. The new law does this while assuring that this massive circumvention of our campaign finance laws does not continue.

Republican senator John McCain of Arizona, left, and Democratic senator Russell Feingold of Wisconsin, center, discuss their campaign finance bill in March 2001. The bill became the Bipartisan Campaign Reform Act (BCRA) of 2002, whose provisions were challenged on free speech grounds by their Republican colleague Mitch McConnell of Kentucky in *McConnell v. Federal Elections Commission* (2003). The Supreme Court upheld BCRA's restriction on political parties' use of soft money and on some kinds of issue advertising, but struck down its prohibition on campaign contributions by minors. — Congressional Quarterly/Scott Ferrell

The majority of justices stated in their opinion that "money, like water, will always find an outlet." But as money seeks new outlets, Public Citizen will be on guard to be sure that its most corrosive influences on the political process are brought to the public's attention and that Congress remains ever-vigilant in safeguarding our democracy and the electoral process.[6]

Common Cause, which had been instrumental in a number of court cases to force the FEC to act and was a strong supporter of BCRA, called the decision "A major victory for democracy and all Americans." According to Common Cause president Chellie Pingree:

The American people wanted this law, Congress enacted it and now the Supreme Court has ruled it constitutional. The toxic link between donors who write six-figure checks and people in power at the highest levels of government has been severed for good.

Upholding the ban on soft money and the ban on corporations and labor unions directly funding some broadcast advertisements about federal candidates means that additional, meaningful campaign finance reforms can now follow. . . .

This struggle took more than a decade, but it proves that citizens can trump the power of special interests.[7]

MEDIA RESPONSE

Newspapers around the country in general praised the ruling. In California the *Alameda Times-Star* said it had just about given up hope that there would be meaningful reform, but Congress had acted, and now the Court had validated McCain-Feingold. The ruling "counters that pessimism and raises hope for such other proposed reforms as increased public financing of elections. . . . It also opens the door to further refinements as politics finds other streams through which its mother's milk—money—may flow." In an editorial, the *Times-Star* said that campaign finance reform, "the Rodney Dangerfield of American political policy—finally got some respect, and it came from the U.S. Supreme Court of Chief Justice William Rehnquist and Justices Antonin Scalia and Clarence Thomas, even though none of the conservative justices approve" of the law.[8]

On the East Coast, an op-ed piece in the *Boston Globe* by law professor Spencer Overton praised the decision, but warned that if Americans truly wanted to reform the system, other steps remained, especially empowering the average citizen by increasing the influence of the smaller contributor. Overton suggested a two-step solution. First, reward contributions of $100 or less by providing a four-to-one match from public funds. In the proposed revision to the presidential campaign funding law, candidates who emphasized small gifts would reap significant rewards and could therefore avoid the fat cats looking for favors or access. Second, Overton wanted this system extended to *all* federal elections, the House and Senate as well as the presidency.[9]

The Knight-Ridder papers carried similar editorials praising the *McConnell* decision, but they also warned that enacting McCain-Feingold and securing the Court's blessing did not automatically reform the system. "The nation will have to keep a close watch to see if the campaign finance reform law restores people's faith in democracy and actually limits the undue influence money has on politics, without making it too hard for political groups to make themselves heard."[10]

OPPONENTS' RESPONSE

On the other side, opponents of the law condemned the ruling. Senator McConnell's office released a terse comment:

> In a 5–4 decision today, a narrowly divided Supreme Court has unfortunately allowed Congress to diminish the ability of political parties and citizens groups to speak in the days before an election. Justice Kennedy correctly observed this decision replaces "respected First Amendment principles with . . . rules which dismantle basic protections for speech."
>
> This law will not remove one dime from politics. As the Majority opinion correctly observed, "money, like water, will always find an outlet." In fact, it already has. Wealthy donors like George Soros are writing multi-million dollar checks to fund massive special interest groups to run political ads. Outside special interest groups have become the modern day political parties. Soft money is not gone—it has just changed its address.[11]

The American Civil Liberties Union blasted the opinion as an unprecedented restriction on core political speech that is inconsistent with basic First Amendment values:

> The ACLU is a non-partisan organization that has never endorsed a candidate in its 83-year history. After today's decision, however, the ACLU runs the risk of criminal prosecution if it broadcasts an advertisement in the period preceding an election that urges voters to contact their Senator or Representative about important civil liberties legislation, if those officials also happen to be running for office.

Today's decision also means that the ACLU will face new hurdles if it seeks to broadcast advertisements during the ongoing presidential campaign discussing the position of the various candidates on the civil liberties consequences of the war on terrorism.

"The notion that the government can tell an organization like the ACLU when and how it should address important civil liberties issues is a form of censorship masquerading as campaign finance reform," said ACLU Executive Director Anthony D. Romero. "The fact that those restrictions have now been upheld by the Supreme Court is extremely disappointing."

As even today's decision recognizes, Romero noted, there is little likelihood that the new campaign finance restrictions will in fact reduce the flow of money into electoral politics. For that reason, he said, "the ACLU has repeatedly urged Congress to adopt a serious program of public financing for federal campaigns. We repeat that call today."

"Today's decision will do far more to restrict political speech than to curtail the influence of money on politics," Romero concluded. "More speech should not be seen as a threat to our democracy, but sadly, that is the message of the Court's decision."[12]

An angry Wayne LaPierre, head of the National Rifle Association (NRA), called the ruling

> the most significant change in the First Amendment since the Alien and Sedition Acts of 1798, which tried to make it a crime to criticize a member of Congress. This whole thing from the start has been an inside deal among politicians to stop criticism, whether it comes from us or from the Sierra Club. Well, we're going to be heard, and they're going to be surprised how loud we're going to be heard.[13]

The decision was "incomprehensible" to one of the nation's most respected First Amendment lawyers, Floyd Abrams, who had argued against the law on behalf of Senator McConnell. The Court's decision, running almost 300 pages, missed the fundamental importance of free speech, he said. "It almost reads like a tax case rather than a First Amendment case. In style, tone, and nature, it reads like an opinion about regulation by government of some sort of improper activity."[14]

In an on-line discussion just a few hours after the Court announced the decision, an "obviously disappointed" Kenneth W. Starr, the former solicitor general of the United States and the lead attorney for McConnell, predicted that the opinion would only encourage people to find other ways to get money into the process. He too quoted Justice O'Connor's comment that "money, like water, will always find an outlet." Starr noted, "People are already finding ways to influence political campaigns without running afoul of BCRA. I think we can expect to see further cycles of alleged 'abuses' followed by legislation. Only time will tell if the effort to take money out of politics altogether proves to be futile."

In response to a question of how much room the Court's decision leaves for future regulation, Starr was pessimistic.

> From my point of view, and the point of view of my clients, the Court's opinions contain some quite broad language, including language suggesting that restrictions are valid as long as they are necessary to prevent circumvention of other previously upheld restrictions (a rationale that, as the Chief Justice points out, is potentially limitless). Ultimately, I think that Congress, and not the Supreme Court, may be the body that brings a halt to the cycle of campaign regulation. I suspect that at least some of BCRA's supporters, having seen its draconian practical consequences, would vote differently today than they did two years ago. One thing is certain. It will be interesting to watch the law in this area unfold over the next few years.[15]

The academic and legal reaction to the decision proved almost unanimously negative. Lillian BeVier of the University of Virginia, a longtime advocate of political speech as the core of the First Amendment, found herself "largely dismayed" by the majority opinion, and she admitted, "One has, after all, been quite thoroughly vanquished."[16] Robert F. Bauer, a lawyer specializing in election law, lamented the decision as a signal of how little the Court valued another First Amendment right. The decision, he declared, "signals the effective demise of the right of association in campaign finance jurisprudence."[17] James Bopp Jr. and Richard E. Coleson, who represented several socially conservative groups in the case, angrily charged that the Court had abandoned "its role as guardian of free speech where and when it counts the most, while giving the unenumerated abortion right a highly protected status." The Court, they claimed, had shown Congress far too much deference, not in protecting the rights of the unborn, but in "protecting incumbent politicians from the people."[18] Two lawyers who represented the NRA, Charles J. Cooper and Derek L. Shaffer, charged that Title II of BCRA had been cut from the same cloth as the infamous Sedition Act of 1798, aimed specifically at stifling criticism of government and its elected members.[19]

Such criticisms from lawyers on the losing side were not surprising, but the analysis by the distinguished law professor Richard A. Epstein proved equally critical. He denounced the decision as "yet another backward step in the march of constitutional law." Even if one conceded that Congress had the power to enact laws aimed at preventing corruption or its appearance in electoral campaigns, it had done so in a heavy-handed manner that deserved not the acquiescence of the Court but "an instant and merciless repudiation." Although Epstein believed that judges should normally show deference to legislative policy judgments, he argued that courts also had an independent role to play, a role the Supreme Court had completely abandoned in the *McConnell* case. The "dense network of regulations" under BCRA promised full employment for a generation of lawyers, but the bottom line "is less political speech." For that the Court would have to bear much of the blame.[20]

ANTICIPATED RESULTS

Would BCRA work now that it had the blessing of the highest court in the land? Elizabeth Garrett, director of the University of Southern California Center for the Study of Law and Politics, thought that the disclosure aspects of the law would probably be fairly effective, but they were the act's least controversial aspects. Moreover, by confirming BCRA's requirements, the Court had put its stamp of approval on other forms of campaign financial disclosure, and these rules "are the most widespread regulation of the campaign finance system, and they are the sole regulation in several electoral arenas," such as state and local elections.[21] Beyond that, Prof. Samuel Issacharoff of Columbia University expected few positive results in straightening out the morass that campaign finance had become. If history were any guide, all BCRA would do is "prompt new forms by which money seeks to influence, cajole, inform, capture, and even corrupt." Although the law banned soft money and attempted to limit hard money, it, in fact, opened the gates to all sorts of hard money contributions, and in his view hard money could be just as corrosive an influence on the political process as soft.[22]

Prof. Robert C. Post of the Yale Law School suggested, however, that one ought to look at the opinion as part of the on-going dialogue between Congress and the Court over the extent of congressional powers. This Court had decided several high-profile cases in which the justices told Congress that it had no power to intrude on functions traditionally within the ambit of the states. "Things were getting pretty explosive," he noted, and he had little doubt that Justice O'Connor had been moved, at least in part, by "her political antennae. . . . The tension was too high, and she understood that the rhythm of the court's relationship with Congress had to be attended to, the pace of the conversation had to be lowered." In effect, "the Court gave Congress space to breathe."[23]

FEC chairman Bradley A. Smith could be expected to express delight with the ruling. But Smith, who in his academic years had been sharply critical of efforts to regulate campaign finance, attacked the ruling with as much vigor as did the NRA and the ACLU. The Supreme Court's decision, he wrote,

> was eminently predictable, but nonetheless stunning in the sweep of its language and the shallowness of its analysis. The majority simply had no response, and so did not try to respond, to the most simple and devastating critique made by the various dissents: that political speech now clearly has less constitutional protection than virtual child pornography, tobacco advertising, sexually explicit cable programs, dissemination of illegally received communications, nude dancing, defamation, cross burning, and flag burning. We need not analyze all of these cases here to grasp, intuitively, that something has gone seriously wrong in the Court's First Amendment jurisprudence.
>
> Historically, decisions that sharply curtail civil liberties, as does *McConnell*, have not stood well the test of time, and are looked upon as black moments in the Court's history. . . . Time will tell if *McConnell* suffers the same fate. . . .
>
> BCRA provides a new cudgel to attempt to silence or hinder opponents, while the Court's lax standard of review is sure to encourage more such efforts. When all is said and done, I suspect it will be the *McConnell* plaintiffs and the dissenting justices who will be remembered, not only for their principles, but for their pragmatism.[24]

Just as *Buckley* caused more problems than it resolved in terms of regulating campaign finance, *McConnell* is likely to have the same effect. The decision left far too many questions unanswered about what the First Amendment protects, and the Court may have a difficult time squaring this opinion with a situation in which it is far clearer that true political speech is being restricted. As the 2004 elections showed, people who have money and want to spend it in support of political candidates will find a way to do so.

NOTES

1. Helen Dewar, "McCain, Feingold & Co. Laugh Last," *Washington Post,* December 11, 2003.
2. John McCain, form letter, April 29, 2004.
3. Transcript, *Today,* December 11, 2003.
4. *Washington Post,* December 11, 2003.
5. Pew, press release, December 10, 2003, http://www.pewtrusts.com/ideas/ideas_item.cfm?content_id=2045&content_type_i.
6. Public Citizen, press release, December 10, 2003, http://www.citizen.org/pressroom/release.cfm?ID=1064 (viewed May 8, 2004).
7. Common Cause, press release, December 10, 2003, http://www.commoncause.org.news/default.cfm?ArtID−258.
8. "Court's Ruling Validates Campaign Finance Reform," editorial, *Alameda Times-Star,* December 14, 2003.
9. *Boston Globe,* December 12, 2003.
10. *St. Louis Post-Dispatch,* December 11, 2003.
11. Sen. Mitch McConnell, press release, December 10, 2003.
12. American Civil Liberties Union, press release, December 10, 2003, http://www.aclu.org/news/NewsPrint.cfm?ID=14560&c=261.
13. *Washington Post,* December 11, 2003.
14. Ibid.
15. *Washington Post* on-line discussion, December 10, 2003, http://www.washingtonpost.com/ac2/wp-dyn/A52956-2003Dec10?language=printer.
16. Lillian BeVier, "*McConnell v. FEC*: Not Senator Buckley's First Amendment," *Election Law Journal* 3 (2004): 127.
17. Robert F. Bauer, "*McConnell*, Parties, and the Decline of the Right of Association," ibid., 199.
18. James Bopp Jr. and Richard E. Coleson, "Electioneering Communication Versus Abortion," ibid., 205, 209.

19. Charles J. Cooper and Derek L. Shaffer, "What Congress Shall Make . . . ," ibid., 223.

20. Richard A. Epstein, "*McConnell v. FEC:* A Deadly Dose of Double Deference," ibid., 231.

21. Elizabeth Garrett, "*McConnell v. FEC* and Disclosure," ibid., 237.

22. Samuel Issacharoff, "Throwing in the Towel. . . ," ibid., 259.

23. *New York Times,* December 12, 2003.

24. Bradley A. Smith, "*McConnell v. FEC:* Ideology Trumps Reality, Pragmatism," *Election Law Journal* 3 (2004): 345, 346.

APPENDIXES

CONSTITUTION OF THE UNITED STATES

We the People of the United States, in Order to form a more perfect Union, establish Justice, insure domestic Tranquility, provide for the common defence, promote the general Welfare, and secure the Blessings of Liberty to ourselves and our Posterity, do ordain and establish this Constitution for the United States of America.

ARTICLE I

Section 1. All legislative Powers herein granted shall be vested in a Congress of the United States, which shall consist of a Senate and House of Representatives.

Section 2. The House of Representatives shall be composed of Members chosen every second Year by the People of the several States, and the Electors in each State shall have the Qualifications requisite for Electors of the most numerous Branch of the State Legislature.

No Person shall be a Representative who shall not have attained to the age of twenty five Years, and been seven Years a Citizen of the United States, and who shall not, when elected, be an Inhabitant of that State in which he shall be chosen.

[Representatives and direct Taxes shall be apportioned among the several States which may be included within this Union, according to their respective Numbers, which shall be determined by adding to the whole Number of free Persons, including those bound to Service for a Term of Years, and excluding Indians not taxed, three fifths of all other Persons.][1] The actual Enumeration shall be made within three Years after the first Meeting of the Congress of the United States, and within every subsequent Term of ten Years, in such Manner as they shall by Law direct. The Number of Representatives shall not exceed one for every thirty Thousand, but each State shall have at Least one Representative; and until such enumeration shall be made, the State of New Hampshire shall be entitled to chuse three, Massachusetts eight, Rhode-Island and Providence Plantations one, Connecticut five, New-York six, New Jersey four, Pennsylvania eight, Delaware one, Maryland six, Virginia ten, North Carolina five, South Carolina five, and Georgia three.

When vacancies happen in the Representation from any State, the Executive Authority thereof shall issue Writs of Election to fill such Vacancies.

The House of Representatives shall chuse their Speaker and other Officers; and shall have the sole Power of Impeachment.

Section 3. The Senate of the United States shall be composed of two Senators from each State, [chosen by the Legislature thereof,][2] for six Years; and each Senator shall have one Vote.

Immediately after they shall be assembled in Consequence of the first Election, they shall be divided as equally as may be into three Classes. The Seats of the Senators of the first Class shall be vacated at the Expiration of the second Year, of the second Class at the Expiration of the fourth Year, and of the third Class at the Expiration of the sixth Year, so that one third may be chosen every second Year; [and if Vacancies happen by Resignation, or otherwise, during the Recess of the Legislature of any State, the Executive thereof may make temporary Appointments until the next Meeting of the Legislature, which shall then fill such Vacancies.][3]

No Person shall be a Senator who shall not have attained to the Age of thirty Years, and been nine Years a Citizen of the United States, and who shall not, when elected, be an Inhabitant of that State for which he shall be chosen.

The Vice President of the United States shall be President of the Senate, but shall have no Vote, unless they be equally divided.

The Senate shall chuse their other Officers, and also a President pro tempore, in the Absence of the Vice President, or when he shall exercise the Office of President of the United States.

The Senate shall have the sole Power to try all Impeachments. When sitting for that Purpose, they shall be on Oath or Affirmation. When the President of the United States is tried, the Chief Justice shall preside: And no Person shall be convicted without the Concurrence of two thirds of the Members present.

Judgment in Cases of Impeachment shall not extend further than to removal from Office, and disqualification to hold and enjoy any Office of honor, Trust or Profit under the United States: but the Party convicted shall nevertheless be liable and subject to Indictment, Trial, Judgment and Punishment, according to Law.

Section 4. The Times, Places and Manner of holding Elections for Senators and Representatives, shall be prescribed in each State by the Legislature thereof; but the Congress may at any time by Law make or alter such Regulations, except as to thc Placcs of chusing Senators.

The Congress shall assemble at least once in every Year, and such Meeting shall [be on the first Monday in December],[4] unless they shall by Law appoint a different Day.

Section 5. Each House shall be the Judge of the Elections, Returns and Qualifications of its own Members, and a Majority of each shall constitute a Quorum to do Business; but a smaller Number may adjourn from day to day, and may be authorized to compel the Attendance of absent Members, in such Manner, and under such Penalties as each House may provide.

Each House may determine the Rules of its Proceedings, punish its Members for disorderly Behaviour, and, with the Concurrence of two thirds, expel a Member.

Each House shall keep a Journal of its Proceedings, and from time to time publish the same, excepting such Parts as may in their Judgment require Secrecy; and the Yeas and Nays of the Members of either House on any question shall, at the Desire of one fifth of those Present, be entered on the Journal.

Neither House, during the Session of Congress, shall, without the Consent of the other, adjourn for more than three days, nor to any other Place than that in which the two Houses shall be sitting.

Section 6. The Senators and Representatives shall receive a Compensation for their Services, to be ascertained by Law, and paid out of the Treasury of the United States. They shall in all Cases, except Treason, Felony and Breach of the Peace, be privileged from Arrest during their Attendance at the Session of their respective Houses, and in going to and returning from the same; and for any Speech or Debate in either House, they shall not be questioned in any other Place.

No Senator or Representative shall, during the Time for which he was elected, be appointed to any civil Office under the Authority of the United States, which shall have been created, or the Emoluments whereof shall have been encreased during such time; and no Person holding any Office under the United States, shall be a Member of either House during his Continuance in Office.

Section 7. All Bills for raising Revenue shall originate in the House of Representatives; but the Senate may propose or concur with Amendments as on other Bills.

Every Bill which shall have passed the House of Representatives and the Senate, shall, before it become a Law, be presented to the President of the United States; If he approve he shall sign it, but if not he shall return it, with his Objections to that House in which it shall have originated, who shall enter the Objections at large on their Journal, and proceed to reconsider it. If after such Reconsideration two thirds of that House shall agree to pass the Bill, it shall be sent, together with the Objections, to the other House, by which it shall likewise be reconsidered, and if approved by two thirds of that House, it shall become a Law. But in all such Cases the Votes of both Houses shall be determined by yeas and Nays, and the Names of the Persons voting for and against the Bill shall be entered on the Journal of each House respectively. If any Bill shall not be returned by the President within ten Days (Sundays excepted) after it shall have been presented to him, the Same shall be a Law, in like Manner as if he had signed it, unless the Congress by their Adjournment prevent its Return, in which Case it shall not be a Law.

Every Order, Resolution, or Vote to which the Concurrence of the Senate and House of Representatives may be necessary (except on a question of Adjournment) shall be presented to the President of the United

States; and before the Same shall take Effect, shall be approved by him, or being disapproved by him, shall be repassed by two thirds of the Senate and House of Representatives, according to the Rules and Limitations prescribed in the Case of a Bill.

Section 8. The Congress shall have Power To lay and collect Taxes, Duties, Imposts and Excises, to pay the Debts and provide for the common Defence and general Welfare of the United States; but all Duties, Imposts and Excises shall be uniform throughout the United States;

To borrow Money on the credit of the United States;

To regulate Commerce with foreign Nations, and among the several States, and with the Indian Tribes;

To establish an uniform Rule of Naturalization, and uniform Laws on the subject of Bankruptcies throughout the United States;

To coin Money, regulate the Value thereof, and of foreign Coin, and fix the Standard of Weights and Measures;

To provide for the Punishment of counterfeiting the Securities and current Coin of the United States;

To establish Post Offices and post Roads;

To promote the Progress of Science and useful Arts, by securing for limited Times to Authors and Inventors the exclusive Right to their respective Writings and Discoveries;

To constitute Tribunals inferior to the supreme Court;

To define and punish Piracies and Felonies committed on the high Seas, and Offences against the Law of Nations;

To declare War, grant Letters of Marque and Reprisal, and make Rules concerning Captures on Land and Water;

To raise and support Armies, but no Appropriation of Money to that Use shall be for a longer Term than two Years;

To provide and maintain a Navy;

To make Rules for the Government and Regulation of the land and naval Forces;

To provide for calling forth the Militia to execute the Laws of the Union, suppress Insurrections and repel Invasions;

To provide for organizing, arming, and disciplining, the Militia, and for governing such Part of them as may be employed in the Service of the United States, reserving to the States respectively, the Appointment of the Officers, and the Authority of training the Militia according to the discipline prescribed by Congress;

To exercise exclusive Legislation in all Cases whatsoever, over such District (not exceeding ten Miles square) as may, by Cession of particular States, and the Acceptance of Congress, become the Seat of the Government of the United States, and to exercise like Authority over all Places purchased by the Consent of the Legislature of the State in which the Same shall be, for the Erection of Forts, Magazines, Arsenals, dock-Yards, and other needful Buildings;—And

To make all Laws which shall be necessary and proper for carrying into Execution the foregoing Powers, and all other Powers vested by this Constitution in the Government of the United States, or in any Department or Officer thereof.

Section 9. The Migration or Importation of such Persons as any of the States now existing shall think proper to admit, shall not be prohibited by the Congress prior to the Year one thousand eight hundred and eight, but a Tax or duty may be imposed on such Importation, not exceeding ten dollars for each Person.

The Privilege of the Writ of Habeas Corpus shall not be suspended, unless when in Cases of Rebellion or Invasion the public Safety may require it.

No Bill of Attainder or ex post facto Law shall be passed.

No Capitation, or other direct, Tax shall be laid, unless in Proportion to the Census or Enumeration herein before directed to be taken.[5]

No Tax or Duty shall be laid on Articles exported from any State.

No Preference shall be given by any Regulation of Commerce or Revenue to the Ports of one State over those of another; nor shall Vessels bound to, or from, one State, be obliged to enter, clear, or pay Duties in another.

No Money shall be drawn from the Treasury, but in Consequence of Appropriations made by Law; and a regular Statement and Account of the Receipts and Expenditures of all public Money shall be published from time to time.

No Title of Nobility shall be granted by the United States: And no Person holding any Office of Profit or Trust under them, shall, without the Consent of the Congress, accept of any present, Emolument, Office, or Title, of any kind whatever, from any King, Prince, or foreign State.

Section 10. No State shall enter into any Treaty, Alliance, or Confederation; grant Letters of Marque and Reprisal; coin Money; emit Bills of Credit; make any Thing but gold and silver Coin a Tender in Payment of Debts; pass any Bill of Attainder, ex post facto Law, or Law impairing the Obligation of Contracts, or grant any Title of Nobility.

No State shall, without the Consent of the Congress, lay any Imposts or Duties on Imports or Exports, except what may be absolutely necessary for executing it's inspection Laws: and the net Produce of all Duties and Imposts, laid by any State on Imports or Exports, shall be for the Use of the Treasury of the United States; and all such Laws shall be subject to the Revision and Controul of the Congress.

No State shall, without the Consent of Congress, lay any Duty of Tonnage, keep Troops, or Ships of War in time of Peace, enter into any Agreement or Compact with another State, or with a foreign Power, or engage in War, unless actually invaded, or in such imminent Danger as will not admit of delay.

ARTICLE II

Section 1. The executive Power shall be vested in a President of the United States of America. He shall hold his Office during the Term of four Years, and, together with the Vice President, chosen for the same Term, be elected, as follows:

Each State shall appoint, in such Manner as the Legislature thereof may direct, a Number of Electors, equal to the whole Number of Senators and Representatives to which the State may be entitled in the Congress: but no Senator or Representative, or Person holding an Office of Trust or Profit under the United States, shall be appointed an Elector.

[The Electors shall meet in their respective States, and vote by Ballot for two Persons, of whom one at least shall not be an Inhabitant of the same State with themselves. And they shall make a List of all the Persons voted for, and of the Number of Votes for each; which List they shall sign and certify, and transmit sealed to the Seat of the Government of the United States, directed to the President of the Senate. The President of the Senate shall, in the Presence of the Senate and House of Representatives, open all the Certificates, and the Votes shall then be counted. The Person having the greatest Number of Votes shall be the President, if such Number be a Majority of the whole Number of Electors appointed; and if there be more than one who have such Majority, and have an equal Number of Votes, then the House of Representatives shall immediately chuse by Ballot one of them for President; and if no Person have a Majority, then from the five highest on the list the said House shall in like Manner chuse the President. But in chusing the President, the Votes shall be taken by States, the Representation from each State having one Vote; A quorum for this Purpose shall consist of a Member or Members from two thirds of the States, and a Majority of all the States shall be necessary to a Choice. In every Case, after the Choice of the President, the Person having the greatest Number of Votes of the Electors shall be the Vice President. But if there should remain two or more who have equal Votes, the Senate shall chuse from them by Ballot the Vice President.][6]

The Congress may determine the Time of chusing the Electors, and the Day on which they shall give their Votes; which Day shall be the same throughout the United States.

No Person except a natural born Citizen, or a Citizen of the United States, at the time of the Adoption of this Constitution, shall be eligible to the Office of President; neither shall any Person be eligible to that Office who shall not have attained to the Age of thirty five Years, and been fourteen Years a Resident within the United States.

In Case of the Removal of the President from Office, or of his Death, Resignation, or Inability to discharge the Powers and Duties of the said Office,[7] the Same shall devolve on the Vice President, and the Congress may by Law provide for the Case of Removal, Death, Resignation or Inability, both of the President and Vice President, declaring what Officer shall then act as President, and such Officer shall act accordingly, until the Disability be removed, or a President shall be elected.

The President shall, at stated Times, receive for his Services, a Compensation, which shall neither be encreased nor diminished during the Period for which he shall have been elected, and he shall not receive within that Period any other Emolument from the United States, or any of them.

Before he enter on the Execution of his Office, he shall take the following Oath or Affirmation:—"I do solemnly swear (or affirm) that I will faithfully execute the Office of President of the United States, and will to the best of my Ability, preserve, protect and defend the Constitution of the United States."

Section 2. The President shall be Commander in Chief of the Army and Navy of the United States, and of the Militia of the several States, when called into the actual Service of the United States; he may require the Opinion, in writing, of the principal Officer in each of the executive Departments, upon any Subject relating to the Duties of their respective Offices, and he shall have Power to grant Reprieves and Pardons for Offences against the United States, except in Cases of Impeachment.

He shall have Power, by and with the Advice and Consent of the Senate, to make Treaties, provided two thirds of the Senators present concur; and he shall nominate, and by and with the Advice and Consent of the Senate, shall appoint Ambassadors, other public Ministers and Consuls, Judges of the supreme Court, and all other Officers of the United States, whose Appointments are not herein otherwise provided for, and which shall be established by Law: but the Congress may by Law vest the Appointment of such inferior Officers, as they think proper, in the President alone, in the Courts of Law, or in the Heads of Departments.

The President shall have Power to fill up all Vacancies that may happen during the Recess of the Senate, by granting Commissions which shall expire at the End of their next Session.

Section 3. He shall from time to time give to the Congress Information of the State of the Union, and recommend to their Consideration such Measures as he shall judge necessary and expedient; he may, on extraordinary Occasions, convene both Houses, or either of them, and in Case of Disagreement between them, with Respect to the Time of Adjournment, he may adjourn them to such Time as he shall think proper; he shall receive Ambassadors and other public Ministers; he shall take Care that the Laws be faithfully executed, and shall Commission all the Officers of the United States.

Section 4. The President, Vice President and all civil Officers of the United States, shall be removed from Office on Impeachment for, and Conviction of, Treason, Bribery, or other high Crimes and Misdemeanors.

ARTICLE III

Section 1. The judicial Power of the United States, shall be vested in one supreme Court, and in such inferior Courts as the Congress may from time to time ordain and establish. The Judges, both of the supreme and inferior Courts, shall hold their Offices during good Behaviour, and shall, at stated Times, receive for their Services, a Compensation, which shall not be diminished during their Continuance in Office.

Section 2. The judicial Power shall extend to all Cases, in Law and Equity, arising under this Constitution, the Laws of the United States, and Treaties made, or which shall be made, under their Authority—to all Cases affecting Ambassadors, other public Ministers and Consuls;—to all Cases of admiralty and maritime Jurisdiction—to Controversies to which the United States shall be a Party;—to Controversies between two or more States;—between a State and Citizens of another State;—between Citizens of different States;—between Citizens of the same State claiming Lands under Grants of different States, and between a State, or the Citizens thereof, and foreign States, Citizens or Subjects.[8]

In all Cases affecting Ambassadors, other public Ministers and Consuls, and those in which a State shall be Party, the supreme Court shall have original Jurisdiction. In all the other Cases before mentioned, the supreme Court shall have appellate Jurisdiction, both as to Law and Fact, with such Exceptions, and under such Regulations as the Congress shall make.

The Trial of all Crimes, except in Cases of Impeachment, shall be by Jury; and such Trial shall be held in the State where the said Crimes shall have been committed; but when not committed within any State, the Trial shall be at such Place or Places as the Congress may by Law have directed.

Section 3. Treason against the United States, shall consist only in levying War against them, or in adhering to their Enemies, giving them Aid and Comfort. No Person shall be convicted of Treason unless on the Testimony of two Witnesses to the same overt Act, or on Confession in open Court.

The Congress shall have Power to declare the Punishment of Treason, but no Attainder of Treason shall work Corruption of Blood, or Forfeiture except during the Life of the Person attainted.

ARTICLE IV

Section 1. Full Faith and Credit shall be given in each State to the public Acts, Records, and judicial Proceedings of every other State. And the Congress may by general Laws prescribe the Manner in which such Acts, Records and Proceedings shall be proved, and the Effect thereof.

Section 2. The Citizens of each State shall be entitled to all Privileges and Immunities of Citizens in the several States.

A Person charged in any State with Treason, Felony, or other Crime, who shall flee from Justice, and be found in another State, shall on Demand of the executive Authority of the State from which he fled, be delivered up, to be removed to the State having Jurisdiction of the Crime.

[No Person held to Service or Labour in one State, under the Laws thereof, escaping into another, shall, in Consequence of any Law or Regulation therein, be discharged from such Service or Labour, but shall be delivered up on Claim of the Party to whom such Service or Labour may be due.][9]

Section 3. New States may be admitted by the Congress into this Union; but no new State shall be formed or erected within the Jurisdiction of any other State; nor any State be formed by the Junction of two or more States, or Parts of States, without the Consent of the Legislatures of the States concerned as well as of the Congress.

The Congress shall have Power to dispose of and make all needful Rules and Regulations respecting the Territory or other Property belonging to the United States; and nothing in this Constitution shall be so construed as to Prejudice any Claims of the United States, or of any particular State.

Section 4. The United States shall guarantee to every State in this Union a Republican Form of Government, and shall protect each of them against Invasion; and on Application of the Legislature, or of the Executive (when the Legislature cannot be convened) against domestic Violence.

ARTICLE V

The Congress, whenever two thirds of both Houses shall deem it necessary, shall propose Amendments to this Constitution, or, on the Application of the Legislatures of two thirds of the several States, shall call a Convention for proposing Amendments, which, in either Case, shall be valid to all Intents and Purposes, as Part of this Constitution, when ratified by the Legislatures of three fourths of the several States, or by Conventions in three fourths thereof, as the one or the other Mode of Ratification may be proposed by the Congress; Provided [that no Amendment which may be made prior to the Year One thousand eight hundred and eight shall in any Manner affect the first and fourth Clauses in the Ninth

Section of the first Article; and]¹⁰ that no State, without its Consent, shall be deprived of its equal Suffrage in the Senate.

ARTICLE VI

All Debts contracted and Engagements entered into, before the Adoption of this Constitution, shall be as valid against the United States under this Constitution, as under the Confederation.

This Constitution, and the Laws of the United States which shall be made in Pursuance thereof; and all Treaties made, or which shall be made, under the Authority of the United States, shall be the supreme Law of the Land; and the Judges in every State shall be bound thereby, any Thing in the Constitution or Laws of any State to the Contrary notwithstanding.

The Senators and Representatives before mentioned, and the Members of the several State Legislatures, and all executive and judicial Officers, both of the United States and of the several States, shall be bound by Oath or Affirmation, to support this Constitution; but no religious Test shall ever be required as a Qualification to any Office or public Trust under the United States.

ARTICLE VII

The Ratification of the Conventions of nine States, shall be sufficient for the Establishment of this Constitution between the States so ratifying the Same.

Done in Convention by the Unanimous Consent of the States present the Seventeenth Day of September in the Year of our Lord one thousand seven hundred and Eighty seven and of the Independence of the United States of America the Twelfth. IN WITNESS whereof We have hereunto subscribed our Names,

George Washington,
President and deputy from Virginia.

[The language of the original Constitution, not including the Amendments, was adopted by a convention of the states on September 17, 1787, and was subsequently ratified by the states on the following dates: Delaware, December 7, 1787; Pennsylvania, December 12, 1787; New Jersey, December 18, 1787; Georgia, January 2, 1788; Connecticut, January 9, 1788; Massachusetts, February 6, 1788; Maryland, April 28, 1788; South Carolina, May 23, 1788; New Hampshire, June 21, 1788.

Ratification was completed on June 21, 1788.

The Constitution subsequently was ratified by Virginia, June 25, 1788; New York, July 26, 1788; North Carolina, November 21, 1789; Rhode Island, May 29, 1790; and Vermont, January 10, 1791.]

AMENDMENTS

Amendment I (First ten amendments ratified December 15, 1791)

Congress shall make no law respecting an establishment of religion, or prohibiting the free exercise thereof; or abridging the freedom of speech, or of the press; or the right of the people peaceably to assemble, and to petition the Government for a redress of grievances.

Amendment II

A well regulated Militia, being necessary to the security of a free State, the right of the people to keep and bear Arms, shall not be infringed.

Amendment III

No Soldier shall, in time of peace be quartered in any house, without the consent of the Owner, nor in time of war, but in a manner to be prescribed by law.

Amendment IV

The right of the people to be secure in their persons, houses, papers, and effects, against unreasonable searches and seizures, shall not be violated, and no Warrants shall issue, but upon probable cause, supported by Oath or affirmation, and particularly describing the place to be searched, and the persons or things to be seized.

Amendment V

No person shall be held to answer for a capital, or otherwise infamous crime, unless on a presentment or indictment of a Grand Jury, except in cases arising in the land or naval forces, or in the Militia, when in actual service in time of War or public danger; nor shall any person be subject for the same offence to be twice put in jeopardy of life or limb; nor shall be compelled in any criminal case to be a witness against himself, nor be deprived of life, liberty, or property, without due process of law; nor shall private property be taken for public use, without just compensation.

Amendment VI

In all criminal prosecutions, the accused shall enjoy the right to a speedy and public trial, by an impartial jury of the State and district wherein the crime shall have been committed, which district shall have been previously ascertained by law, and to be informed of the nature and cause of the accusation; to be confronted with the witnesses against him; to have compulsory process for obtaining witnesses in his favor, and to have the Assistance of Counsel for his defence.

Amendment VII

In Suits at common law, where the value in controversy shall exceed twenty dollars, the right of trial by jury shall be preserved, and no fact tried by a jury, shall be otherwise re-examined in any Court of the United States, than according to the rules of the common law.

Amendment VIII

Excessive bail shall not be required, nor excessive fines imposed, nor cruel and unusual punishments inflicted.

Amendment IX

The enumeration in the Constitution, of certain rights, shall not be construed to deny or disparage others retained by the people.

Amendment X

The powers not delegated to the United States by the Constitution, nor prohibited by it to the States, are reserved to the States respectively, or to the people.

Amendment XI (Ratified February 7, 1795)

The Judicial power of the United States shall not be construed to extend to any suit in law or equity, commenced or prosecuted against one of the United States by Citizens of another State, or by Citizens or Subjects of any Foreign State.

Amendment XII (Ratified June 15, 1804)

The Electors shall meet in their respective states and vote by ballot for President and Vice-President, one of whom, at least, shall not be an inhabitant of the same state with themselves; they shall name in their ballots the person voted for as President, and in distinct ballots the person voted for as Vice-President, and they shall make distinct lists of all persons voted for as President, and of all persons voted for as Vice-President, and of the number of votes for each, which lists they shall sign and certify, and transmit sealed to the seat of the government of the United States, directed to the President of the Senate;—The President of the Senate shall, in the presence of the Senate and House of Representatives, open all the certificates and the votes shall then be counted;—The person having the greatest number of votes for President, shall be the President, if such number be a majority of the whole number of Electors appointed; and if no person have such majority, then from the persons having the highest numbers not exceeding three on the list of those voted for as President, the House of Representatives shall choose immediately, by ballot, the President. But in choosing the President, the votes shall be taken by states, the representation from each state having one vote; a quorum for this purpose shall consist of a member or members from two-thirds of the states, and a majority of all the states shall be necessary to a choice. [And if the House of Representatives shall not choose a President whenever the right of choice shall devolve upon them, before the fourth day of March next following, then the Vice-President shall act as President, as in the case of the death or other constitutional disability of the President.—][11] The person having the greatest number of votes as Vice-President, shall be the Vice-President, if such number be a majority of the whole number of Electors appointed, and if no person have a majority, then from the two highest numbers on the list, the Senate shall choose the Vice-President; a quorum for the purpose shall consist of two-thirds of the whole number of Senators, and a majority of the whole number shall be necessary to a choice. But no person constitutionally ineligible to the office of President shall be eligible to that of Vice-President of the United States.

Amendment XIII (Ratified December 6, 1865)

Section 1. Neither slavery nor involuntary servitude, except as a punishment for crime whereof the party shall have been duly convicted, shall exist within the United States, or any place subject to their jurisdiction.

Section 2. Congress shall have power to enforce this article by appropriate legislation.

Amendment XIV (Ratified July 9, 1868)

Section 1. All persons born or naturalized in the United States, and subject to the jurisdiction thereof, are citizens of the United States and of the State wherein they reside. No State shall make or enforce any law which shall abridge the privileges or immunities of citizens of the United States; nor shall any State deprive any person of life, liberty, or property, without due process of law; nor deny to any person within its jurisdiction the equal protection of the laws.

Section 2. Representatives shall be apportioned among the several States according to their respective numbers, counting the whole number of persons in each State, excluding Indians not taxed. But when the right to vote at any election for the choice of electors for President and Vice President of the United States, Representatives in Congress, the Executive and Judicial officers of a State, or the members of the Legislature thereof, is denied to any of the male inhabitants of such State, being twenty-one years of age,[12] and citizens of the United States, or in any way abridged, except for participation in rebellion, or other crime, the basis of representation therein shall be reduced in the proportion which the number of such male citizens shall bear to the whole number of male citizens twenty-one years of age in such State.

Section 3. No person shall be a Senator or Representative in Congress, or elector of President and Vice President, or hold any office, civil or military, under the United States, or under any State, who, having previously taken an oath, as a member of Congress, or as an officer of the United States, or as a member of any State legislature, or as an executive or judicial officer of any State, to support the Constitution of the United States, shall have engaged in insurrection or rebellion against the same, or given aid or comfort to the enemies thereof. But Congress may by a vote of two-thirds of each House, remove such disability.

Section 4. The validity of the public debt of the United States, authorized by law, including debts incurred for payment of pensions and bounties for services in suppressing insurrection or rebellion, shall not be questioned. But neither the United States nor any State shall assume or pay any debt or obligation incurred in aid of insurrection or rebellion against the United States, or any claim for the loss or emancipation of any slave; but all such debts, obligations and claims shall be held illegal and void.

Section 5. The Congress shall have power to enforce, by appropriate legislation, the provisions of this article.

Amendment XV (Ratified February 3, 1870)

Section 1. The right of citizens of the United States to vote shall not be denied or abridged by the United States or by any State on account of race, color, or previous condition of servitude.

Section 2. The Congress shall have power to enforce this article by appropriate legislation.

Amendment XVI (Ratified February 3, 1913)

The Congress shall have power to lay and collect taxes on incomes, from whatever source derived, without apportionment among the several States, and without regard to any census or enumeration.

Amendment XVII (Ratified April 8, 1913)

The Senate of the United States shall be composed of two Senators from each State, elected by the people thereof, for six years; and each Senator shall have one vote. The electors in each State shall have the qualifications requisite for electors of the most numerous branch of the State legislatures.

When vacancies happen in the representation of any State in the Senate, the executive authority of such State shall issue writs of election to fill such vacancies: *Provided,* That the legislature of any State may empower the executive thereof to make temporary appointments until the people fill the vacancies by election as the legislature may direct.

This amendment shall not be so construed as to affect the election or term of any Senator chosen before it becomes valid as part of the Constitution.

Amendment XVIII (Ratified January 16, 1919)

Section 1. After one year from the ratification of this article the manufacture, sale, or transportation of intoxicating liquors within, the importation thereof into, or the exportation thereof from the United States and all territory subject to the jurisdiction thereof for beverage purposes is hereby prohibited.

Section 2. The Congress and the several States shall have concurrent power to enforce this article by appropriate legislation.

Section 3. This article shall be inoperative unless it shall have been ratified as an amendment to the Constitution by the legislatures of the several States, as provided in the Constitution, within seven years from the date of the submission hereof to the States by the Congress.][13]

Amendment XIX (Ratified August 18, 1920)

The right of citizens of the United States to vote shall not be denied or abridged by the United States or by any State on account of sex.

Congress shall have power to enforce this article by appropriate legislation.

Amendment XX (Ratified January 23, 1933)

Section 1. The terms of the President and Vice President shall end at noon on the 20th day of January, and the terms of Senators and Representatives at noon on the 3d day of January, of the years in which such terms would have ended if this article had not been ratified; and the terms of their successors shall then begin.

Section 2. The Congress shall assemble at least once in every year, and such meeting shall begin at noon on the 3d day of January, unless they shall by law appoint a different day.

Section 3.[14] If, at the time fixed for the beginning of the term of the President, the President elect shall have died, the Vice President elect shall become President. If a President shall not have been chosen before the time fixed for the beginning of his term, or if the President elect shall have failed to qualify, then the Vice President elect shall act as President until a President shall have qualified; and the Congress may by law provide for the case wherein neither a President elect nor a Vice President elect shall have qualified, declaring who shall then act as President, or the manner in which one who is to act shall be selected, and such person shall act accordingly until a President or Vice President shall have qualified.

Section 4. The Congress may by law provide for the case of the death of any of the persons from whom the House of Representatives may choose a President whenever the right of choice shall have devolved upon them, and for the case of the death of any of the persons from whom the Senate may choose a Vice President whenever the right of choice shall have devolved upon them.

Section 5. Sections 1 and 2 shall take effect on the 15th day of October following the ratification of this article.

Section 6. This article shall be inoperative unless it shall have been ratified as an amendment to the Constitution by the legislatures of three-fourths of the several States within seven years from the date of its submission.

Amendment XXI (Ratified December 5, 1933)

Section 1. The eighteenth article of amendment to the Constitution of the United States is hereby repealed.

Section 2. The transportation or importation into any State, Territory, or possession of the United States for delivery or use therein of intoxicating liquors, in violation of the laws thereof, is hereby prohibited.

Section 3. This article shall be inoperative unless it shall have been ratified as an amendment to the Constitution by conventions in the several States, as provided in the Constitution, within seven years from the date of the submission hereof to the States by the Congress.

Amendment XXII (Ratified February 27, 1951)

Section 1. No person shall be elected to the office of the President more than twice, and no person who has held the office of President, or acted as President, for more than two years of a term to which some other person was elected President shall be elected to the office of the President more than once. But this Article shall not apply to any person holding the office of President when this Article was proposed by the Congress, and shall not prevent any person who may be holding the office of President, or acting as President, during the term within which this Article becomes operative from holding the office of President or acting as President during the remainder of such term.

Section 2. This article shall be inoperative unless it shall have been ratified as an amendment to the Constitution by the legislatures of three-fourths of the several States within seven years from the date of its submission to the States by the Congress.

Amendment XXIII (Ratified March 29, 1961)

Section 1. The District constituting the seat of Government of the United States shall appoint in such manner as the Congress may direct:

A number of electors of President and Vice President equal to the whole number of Senators and Representatives in Congress to which the District would be entitled if it were a State, but in no event more than the least populous State; they shall be in addition to those appointed by the States, but they shall be considered, for the purposes of the election of President and Vice President, to be electors appointed by a State; and they shall meet in the District and perform such duties as provided by the twelfth article of amendment.

Section 2. The Congress shall have power to enforce this article by appropriate legislation.

Amendment XXIV (Ratified January 23, 1964)

Section 1. The right of citizens of the United States to vote in any primary or other election for President or Vice President, for electors for President or Vice President, or for Senator or Representative in Congress, shall not be denied or abridged by the United States or any State by reason of failure to pay any poll tax or other tax.

Section 2. The Congress shall have power to enforce this article by appropriate legislation.

Amendment XXV (Ratified February 10, 1967)

Section 1. In case of the removal of the President from office or of his death or resignation, the Vice President shall become President.

Section 2. Whenever there is a vacancy in the office of the Vice President, the President shall nominate a Vice President who shall take office upon confirmation by a majority vote of both Houses of Congress.

Section 3. Whenever the President transmits to the President pro tempore of the Senate and the Speaker of the House of Representatives his written declaration that he is unable to discharge the powers and duties of his office, and until he transmits to them a written declaration to the contrary, such powers and duties shall be discharged by the Vice President as Acting President.

Section 4. Whenever the Vice President and a majority of either the principal officers of the executive departments or of such other body as Congress may by law provide, transmit to the President pro tempore of the Senate and the Speaker of the House of Representatives their written declaration that the President is unable to discharge the powers and duties of his office, the Vice President shall immediately assume the powers and duties of the office as Acting President.

Thereafter, when the President transmits to the President pro tempore of the Senate and the Speaker of the House of Representatives his written declaration that no inability exists, he shall resume the powers and duties of his office unless the Vice President and a majority of either the principal officers of the executive departments or of such other body as Congress may by law provide, transmit within four days to the President pro tempore of the Senate and the Speaker of the House of Representatives their written declaration that the President is unable to discharge the powers and duties of his office. Thereupon Congress shall decide the issue, assembling within forty-eight hours for that purpose if not in session. If the Congress, within twenty-one days after receipt of the latter written declaration, or, if Congress is not in session, within twenty-one days after Congress is required to assemble, determines by two-thirds vote of both Houses that the President is unable to discharge the powers and duties of his office, the Vice President shall continue to discharge the same as Acting President; otherwise, the President shall resume the powers and duties of his office.

Amendment XXVI (Ratified July 1, 1971)

Section 1. The right of citizens of the United States, who are eighteen years of age or older, to vote shall not be denied or abridged by the United States or by any State on account of age.

Section 2. The Congress shall have power to enforce this article by appropriate legislation.

Amendment XXVII (Ratified May 7, 1992)

No law varying the compensation for the services of the Senators and Representatives shall take effect, until an election of Representatives shall have intervened.

SOURCE: U.S. Congress, House, Committee on the Judiciary, *The Constitution of the United States of America, as Amended,* 100th Cong., 1st sess., 1987, H Doc 10094.

NOTES:
1. The part in brackets was changed by Section 2 of the Fourteenth Amendment.
2. The part in brackets was changed by the first paragraph of the Seventeenth Amendment.
3. The part in brackets was changed by the second paragraph of the Seventeenth Amendment.
4. The part in brackets was changed by the second paragraph of the Seventeenth Amendment.
5. The Sixteenth Amendment gave Congress the power to tax incomes.
6. The material in brackets was superseded by the Twelfth Amendment.
7. This provision was affected by the Twenty-fifth Amendment.
8. These clauses were affected by the Eleventh Amendment.
9. This paragraph was superseded by the Thirteenth Amendment.
10. Obsolete.
11. The part in brackets was superseded by Section 3 of the Twentieth Amendment.
12. See the Nineteenth and Twenty-sixth Amendments.
13. This amendment was repealed by Section 1 of the Twenty-first Amendment.
14. See the Twenty-fifth Amendment.

Baldwin, Henry

Birth: January 14, 1780, New Haven, Connecticut.

Education: Hopkins Grammar School, 1793; Yale College, 1797, LL.D., 1830; attended the law lectures of Judge Tapping Reeve; clerked for Alexander James Dallas.

Official Positions: U.S. representative; chairman, Committee on Domestic Manufactures.

Supreme Court Service: nominated associate justice by President Andrew Jackson January 4, 1830, to replace Bushrod Washington, who had died; confirmed by the Senate January 6, 1830, by a 41–2 vote; took judicial oath January 18, 1830; served until April 21, 1844; replaced by Robert C. Grier, nominated by President James K. Polk.

Family: married Marianna Norton, 1802; died 1803; one son; married Sally Ellicott, 1805.

Death: April 21, 1844, Philadelphia, Pennsylvania.

Barbour, Philip P.

Birth: May 25, 1783, Orange County, Virginia.

Education: read law on his own; attended one session at College of William and Mary, 1801.

Official Positions: member, Virginia House of Delegates from Orange County, 1812–1814; U.S. representative, 1814–1825, 1827–1830; Speaker of the House, 1821–1823; state judge, General Court for the Eastern District of Virginia, 1825–1827; president, Virginia Constitutional Convention, 1829–1830; U.S. district judge, Court of Eastern Virginia, 1830–1836.

Supreme Court Service: nominated associate justice by President Andrew Jackson February 28, 1835, to replace Gabriel Duvall, who had resigned; confirmed by the Senate March 15, 1836, by a 30–11 vote; took judicial oath May 12, 1836; served until February 25, 1841; replaced by Peter V. Daniel, nominated by President Martin Van Buren.

Family: married Frances Todd Johnson, 1804; seven children.

Death: February 25, 1841, Washington, D.C.

Black, Hugo L.

Birth: February 27, 1886, Harlan, Alabama.

Education: Birmingham Medical School, 1903–1904; University of Alabama Law School, LL.B., 1906.

Official Positions: police court judge, Birmingham, 1910–1911; county solicitor, Jefferson County, Alabama, 1914–1917; U.S. senator, 1927–1937.

Supreme Court Service: nominated associate justice by President Franklin D. Roosevelt August 12, 1937, to replace Willis Van Devanter, who had retired; confirmed by the Senate August 17, 1937, by a 63–16 vote; took judicial oath August 19, 1937; retired September 17, 1971; replaced by Lewis F. Powell Jr., nominated by President Richard Nixon.

Family: married Josephine Foster, February 1921; died 1951; two sons, one daughter; married Elizabeth Seay DeMerritte, September 11, 1957.

Death: September 25, 1971, Washington, D.C.

Blackmun, Harry A.

Birth: November 12, 1908, Nashville, Illinois.

Education: Harvard College, B.A., summa cum laude, 1929; Harvard Law School, LL.B., 1932.

Official Positions: clerk, Eighth Circuit Court of Appeals, 1932–1933; judge, Eighth Circuit Court of Appeals, 1959–1970.

Supreme Court Service: nominated associate justice by President Richard Nixon April 14, 1970, to replace Abe Fortas, who had resigned; confirmed by the Senate May 12, 1970, by a 94–0 vote; took judicial oath June 9, 1970; retired August 3, 1994; replaced by Stephen G. Breyer, nominated by President Bill Clinton.

Family: married Dorothy E. Clark, June 21, 1941; three daughters.

Death: March 4, 1999, Arlington, Virginia.

Blair, John, Jr.

Birth: 1732, Williamsburg, Virginia.

Education: graduated with honors from College of William and Mary, 1754; studied law at Middle Temple, London, 1755–1756.

Official Positions: member, Virginia House of Burgesses, 1766–1770; clerk, Virginia Governor's Council, 1770–1775; delegate, Virginia Constitutional Convention, 1776; member, Virginia Governor's Council, 1776; judge, Virginia General Court, 1777–1778; chief justice, 1779; judge, first Virginia Court of Appeals, 1780–1789; delegate, U.S. Constitutional Convention, 1787; judge, Virginia Supreme Court of Appeals, 1789.

Supreme Court Service: nominated associate justice by President George Washington September 24, 1789; confirmed by the Senate September 26, 1789, by a voice vote; took judicial oath February 2, 1790; resigned January 27, 1796; replaced by Samuel Chase, nominated by President Washington.

Family: married Jean Blair, December 26, 1756; died 1792.

Death: August 31, 1800, Williamsburg, Virginia.

Blatchford, Samuel

Birth: March 9, 1820, New York City.

Education: Columbia College, A.B., 1837.

Official Positions: judge, Southern District of New York, 1867–1872; judge, Second Circuit of New York, 1872 1882.

Supreme Court Service: nominated associate justice by President Chester Arthur March 13, 1882, to replace Ward Hunt, who had retired; confirmed by the Senate March 27, 1882, by a voice vote; took judicial oath April 3, 1882; served until July 7, 1893; replaced by Edward D. White, nominated by President Grover Cleveland.

Family: married Caroline Appleton, December 17, 1844.

Death: July 7, 1893, Newport, Rhode Island.

Bradley, Joseph P.

Birth: March 14, 1813, Berne, New York.

Education: Rutgers University, graduated 1836.

Official Positions: none.

Supreme Court Service: nominated associate justice by President Ulysses S. Grant February 7, 1870, succeeding James Wayne, who died in 1867 and whose seat remained vacant by act of Congress until 1870; confirmed by the Senate March 21, 1870, by a 46–9 vote; took judicial oath March 23, 1870; served until January 22, 1892; replaced by George Shiras Jr., nominated by President Benjamin Harrison.

Family: married Mary Hornblower in 1844; seven children.

Death: January 22, 1892, Washington, D.C.

Brandeis, Louis D.

Birth: November 13, 1856, Louisville, Kentucky.

Education: Harvard Law School, LL.B., 1877.

Official Positions: "people's attorney," Public Franchise League and Massachusetts State Board of Trade, 1897–1911; counsel, New England Policyholders' Protective Committee, 1905; special counsel, wage and hour cases in California, Illinois, Ohio, and Oregon, 1907–1914; counsel, Ballinger-Pinchot investigation, 1910; chairman, arbitration board, New York garment workers' labor disputes, 1910–1916.

Supreme Court Service: nominated associate justice by President Woodrow Wilson January 28, 1916, to replace Joseph R. Lamar, who had died; confirmed by the Senate June 1, 1916, by a 47–22 vote; took judicial oath June 15, 1916; retired February 13, 1939; replaced by William O. Douglas, nominated by President Franklin D. Roosevelt.

Family: married Alice Goldmark, March 23, 1891; two daughters.

Death: October 5, 1941, Washington, D.C.

Brennan, William J., Jr.

Birth: April 25, 1906, Newark, New Jersey.

Education: University of Pennsylvania, B.S., 1928; Harvard Law School, LL.B., 1931.

Official Positions: judge, New Jersey Superior Court, 1949–1950; judge, appellate division, New Jersey Superior Court, 1950–1952; associate judge, New Jersey Supreme Court, 1952–1956.

Supreme Court Service: recess appointment as associate justice by President Dwight D. Eisenhower October 16, 1956, to replace Sherman Minton, who had resigned; nominated as associate justice by President Eisenhower January 14, 1957; confirmed by the Senate March 19, 1957 by a voice vote; took judicial oath October 16, 1956; retired July 20, 1990; replaced by David H. Souter, nominated by President George Bush.

Family: married Marjorie Leonard, May 5, 1928, died 1982; two sons, one daughter; married Mary Fowler, March 9, 1983.

Death: July 24, 1997, Arlington, Virginia.

Brewer, David J.

Birth: June 20, 1837, Smyrna, Asia Minor.

Education: Wesleyan University, 1852–1853; Yale University, A.B., 1856; Albany Law School, LL.B., 1858.

Official Positions: commissioner, U.S. Circuit Court, Leavenworth, Kansas, 1861–1862; judge of probate and criminal courts, Leavenworth County, 1863–1864; judge, First District of Kansas, 1865–1869; Leavenworth city attorney, 1869–1870; justice, Kansas Supreme Court, 1870–1884; judge, Eighth Federal Circuit, 1884–1889; president, Venezuela-British Guiana Border Commission, 1895.

Supreme Court Service: nominated associate justice by President Benjamin Harrison December 4, 1889, to replace Stanley Matthews, who had died; confirmed by the Senate, December 18, 1889, by a 53–11 vote; took judicial oath January 6, 1890; served until March 28, 1910; replaced by Charles Evans Hughes, nominated by President William Howard Taft.

Family: married Louise R. Landon, October 3, 1861; died 1898; married Emma Miner Mott, June 5, 1901.

Death: March 28, 1910, Washington, D.C.

Breyer, Stephen G.

Birth: August 15, 1938, San Francisco, California.

Education: Stanford University, A.B., 1959; Oxford University, B.A., 1961; Harvard Law School, LL.B., 1964.

Official Positions: Law clerk to Justice Arthur J. Goldberg, 1964–1965; assistant to assistant attorney general, Antitrust Division, U.S. Justice Department, 1965–1967; assistant special prosecutor, Watergate Special Prosecution Force, 1973; special counsel, Senate Judiciary Committee, 1974–1975; chief counsel, Senate Judiciary Committee, 1979–1980; judge, U.S. Court of Appeals for the First Circuit, 1980–1994.

Supreme Court Service: nominated associate justice by President Bill Clinton May 13, 1994, to replace Harry A. Blackmun, who had retired; confirmed by the Senate July 29 1994, by an 87–9 vote; took judicial oath August 3, 1994.

Family: married Joanna Hare, 1967; two daughters, one son.

Brown, Henry B.

Birth: March 2, 1836, South Lee, Massachusetts.

Education: Yale University, A.B., 1856; studied briefly at Yale Law School and Harvard Law School.

Official Positions: U.S. deputy marshal for Detroit, 1861; assistant U.S. attorney, 1863–1868; circuit judge, Wayne County, Michigan, 1868; federal judge, Eastern District of Michigan, 1875–1890.

Supreme Court Service: nominated associate justice by President Benjamin Harrison December 23, 1890, to replace Samuel Miller, who had died; confirmed by the Senate December 29, 1890, by a voice vote; took judicial oath January 5, 1891; retired May 28, 1906; replaced by William H. Moody, nominated by President Theodore Roosevelt.

Family: married Caroline Pitts, July 1864; died 1901; married Josephine E. Tyler, June 25, 1904.

Death: September 4, 1913, Bronxville, New York.

Burger, Warren E.

Birth: September 17, 1907, St. Paul, Minnesota.

Education: attended the University of Minnesota, 1925–1927; St. Paul College of Law (now William Mitchell College of Law), LL.B., magna cum laude, 1931.

Official Positions: assistant U.S. attorney general, Civil Division, Justice Department, 1953–1956; judge, U.S. Court of Appeals for the District of Columbia, 1956–1969.

Supreme Court Service: nominated chief justice by President Richard Nixon May 21, 1969, to replace Chief Justice Earl Warren, who had retired; confirmed by the Senate June 9, 1969, by a 74–3 vote; took judicial oath June 23, 1969; retired September 26, 1986; replaced as chief justice by William H. Rehnquist, named by President Ronald Reagan.

Family: married Elvera Stromberg, November 8, 1933; one son, one daughter.

Death: June 25, 1995, Washington, D.C.

Burton, Harold H.

Birth: June 22, 1888, Jamaica Plain, Massachusetts.

Education: Bowdoin College, A.B., 1909; Harvard University, LL.B., 1912.

Official Positions: member, Ohio House of Representatives, 1929; director of law, Cleveland, 1929–1932; acting mayor of Cleveland, November 9, 1931–February 20, 1932; mayor of Cleveland, 1935–1940; U.S. senator, 1941–1945.

Supreme Court Service: nominated associate justice by President Harry S. Truman September 19, 1945, to replace Owen J. Roberts, who had resigned; confirmed by the Senate September 19, 1945, by a voice vote; took judicial oath October 1, 1945; retired October 13, 1958; replaced by Potter Stewart, appointed by President Dwight D. Eisenhower.

Family: married Selma Florence Smith, June 15, 1912; two daughters, two sons.

Death: October 28, 1964, Washington, D.C.

Butler, Pierce

Birth: March 17, 1866, Pine Bend, Minnesota.

Education: Carleton College, A.B., B.S., 1887.

Official Positions: assistant county attorney, Ramsey County, Minnesota, 1891–1893; county attorney, 1893–1897.

Supreme Court Service: nominated associate justice by President Warren G. Harding November 23, 1922, to replace William R. Day, who had retired; confirmed by the Senate December 21, 1922, by a 61–8 vote; took judicial oath January 2, 1923; served until November 16, 1939; replaced by Frank Murphy, nominated by President Franklin D. Roosevelt.

Family: married Annie M. Cronin, August 25, 1891; eight children.

Death: November 16, 1939, Washington, D.C.

Byrnes, James F.

Birth: May 2, 1879, Charleston, South Carolina.

Education: St. Patrick's Parochial School (never graduated); studied law privately; admitted to the bar in 1903.

Official Positions: court reporter, Second Circuit of South Carolina, 1900–1908; solicitor, Second Circuit of South Carolina, 1908–1910; U.S. representative, 1911–1925; U.S. senator, 1931–1941; director, Office of Economic Stabilization, 1942–1943; director, Office of War Mobilization, 1943–1945; secretary of state, 1945–1947; governor of South Carolina, 1951–1955.

Supreme Court Service: nominated associate justice by President Franklin D. Roosevelt June 12, 1941, to replace James McReynolds, who had retired; confirmed by the Senate June 12, 1941, by a voice vote; took judicial oath July 8, 1942; resigned October 3, 1942; replaced by Wiley B. Rutledge, appointed by President Roosevelt.

Family: Married Maude Perkins Busch, May 2, 1906.

Death: April 9, 1972, Columbia, South Carolina.

Campbell, John A.

Birth: June 24, 1811, Washington, Georgia.

Education: Franklin College (now the University of Georgia), graduated with first honors, 1825; attended U.S. Military Academy at West Point, 1825–1828.

Official Positions: Alabama state representative, sessions of 1837 and 1843; assistant secretary of war, Confederate States of America, 1862–1865.

Supreme Court Service: nominated associate justice by President Franklin Pierce March 21, 1853, to replace Justice John McKinley, who had died; confirmed by the Senate March 25, 1853, by a voice vote; took judicial oath April 11, 1853; resigned April 30, 1861; replaced by David Davis, nominated by President Abraham Lincoln.

Family: married Anna Esther Goldthwaite in the early 1830s; four daughters, one son.

Death: March 12, 1889, Baltimore, Maryland.

Cardozo, Benjamin N.

Birth: May 24, 1870, New York City.

Education: Columbia University, A.B., 1889; A.M., 1891; Columbia Law School, 1891, no degree.

Official Positions: justice, New York Supreme Court, 1913; judge, New York State Court of Appeals, 1913–1932; chief judge, 1926–1932.

Supreme Court Service: nominated associate justice by President Herbert Hoover February 15, 1932, to replace Oliver Wendell Holmes Jr., who had retired; confirmed by the Senate February 24, 1932, by a voice vote; took judicial oath March 14, 1932; served until July 9, 1938; replaced by Felix Frankfurter, nominated by President Franklin D. Roosevelt.

Family: unmarried.

Death: July 9, 1938, Port Chester, New York.

Catron, John

Birth: ca. 1786, Pennsylvania or Virginia.

Education: self-educated.

Official Positions: judge, Tennessee Supreme Court of Errors and Appeals, 1824–1831; first chief justice of Tennessee, 1831–1834.

Supreme Court Service: nominated associate justice by President Andrew Jackson March 3, 1837, to fill a newly created seat; confirmed by the Senate March 8, 1837, by a 28–15 vote; took judicial oath May 1, 1837; served until May 30, 1865; seat abolished by Congress.

Family: married Matilda Childress.

Death: May 30, 1865, Nashville, Tennessee.

Chase, Salmon P.

Birth: January 13, 1808, Cornish, New Hampshire.

Education: Dartmouth College, 1826.

Official Positions: U.S. senator, 1849–1855, 1861; governor of Ohio, 1856–1860; secretary of the Treasury, 1861–1864.

Supreme Court Service: nominated chief justice by President Abraham Lincoln December 6, 1864, to replace Chief Justice Roger B. Taney, who had died; confirmed by the Senate December 6, 1864, by a voice vote; took judicial oath December 15, 1864; served until May 7, 1873; replaced by Morrison R. Waite, appointed by President Ulysses S. Grant.

Family: married Katherine Jane Garniss, March 4, 1834; died December 1, 1835; married Eliza Ann Smith, September 26, 1839; died September 29, 1845; one daughter; married Sara Belle Dunlop Ludlow, November 6, 1846; died January 13, 1852; one daughter.

Death: May 7, 1873, New York City.

Chase, Samuel

Birth: April 17, 1741, Somerset County, Maryland.

Education: tutored by father; studied law in Annapolis law office; admitted to bar in 1761.

Official Positions: member, Maryland General Assembly, 1764–1784; delegate, Continental Congress, 1774–1778, 1784–1785; member, Maryland Committee of Correspondence, 1774; member, Maryland Convention and Council of Safety, 1775; judge, Baltimore Criminal Court, 1788–1796; chief judge, General Court of Maryland, 1791–1796.

Supreme Court Service: nominated associate justice by President George Washington January 26, 1796, to replace John Blair, who had resigned; confirmed by the Senate January 27, 1796, by a voice vote; took judicial oath February 4, 1796; served until June 19, 1811; replaced by Gabriel Duvall, nominated by President James Madison.

Family: married Anne Baldwin May 21, 1762; seven children, three of whom died in infancy; married Hannah Kitty Giles, March 3, 1784; two daughters.

Death: June 19, 1811, Baltimore, Maryland.

Clark, Tom C.

Birth: September 23, 1899, Dallas, Texas.

Education: Virginia Military Institute, 1917–1918; University of Texas, A.B., 1921; LL.B., 1922.

Official Positions: assistant district attorney, Dallas County, 1927–1932; special assistant, Justice Department, 1937–1943; assistant U.S. attorney general, 1943–1945; U.S. attorney general, 1945–1949; director, Federal Judicial Center, 1968–1970; judge, U.S. Court of Appeals, various circuits, by special arrangement, 1967–1977.

Supreme Court Service: nominated associate justice by President Harry S. Truman August 2, 1949, to replace Frank Murphy, who had died; confirmed by the Senate August 18, 1949, by a 73–8 vote; took judicial oath August 24, 1949; retired June 12, 1967; replaced by Thurgood Marshall, nominated by President Lyndon B. Johnson.

Family: Married Mary Jane Ramsey, November 8, 1924; one daughter, two sons.

Death: June 13, 1977, New York City.

Clarke, John H.

Birth: September 18, 1857, Lisbon, Ohio.

Education: Western Reserve University, A.B., 1877, A.M., 1880.

Official Positions: federal judge, U.S. District Court for Northern District of Ohio, 1914–1916.

Supreme Court Service: nominated associate justice by President Woodrow Wilson July 14, 1916, to replace Charles Evans Hughes, who had resigned; confirmed by the Senate July 24, 1916, by a voice vote; took judicial oath October 9, 1916; resigned September 18, 1922; replaced by George Sutherland, nominated by President Warren G. Harding.

Family: unmarried.

Death: March 22, 1945, San Diego, California.

Clifford, Nathan

Birth: August 18, 1803, Rumney, New Hampshire.

Education: Haverhill Academy; studied law in office of Josiah Quincy in Rumney; admitted to New Hampshire bar, 1827.

Official Positions: Maine state representative, 1830–1834; attorney general of Maine, 1834–1838; U.S. representative, 1839–1843; U.S. attorney general, 1846–1848; minister to Mexico, 1848–1849.

Supreme Court Service: nominated associate justice by President James Buchanan December 9, 1857, to replace Benjamin R. Curtis, who had resigned; confirmed by the Senate January 12, 1858, by a 26–23 vote; took judicial oath January 21, 1858; served until July 25, 1881; replaced by Horace Gray, nominated by President Chester A. Arthur.

Family: married Hannah Ayer, ca. 1828; six children.

Death: July 25, 1881, Cornish, Maine.

Curtis, Benjamin R.

Birth: November 4, 1809, Watertown, Massachusetts.

Education: Harvard University, graduated 1829 with highest honors; Harvard Law School, graduated 1832.

Official Positions: Massachusetts state representative, 1849–1851.

Supreme Court Service: nominated associate justice by President Millard Fillmore December 11, 1851, to replace Justice Levi Woodbury, who had died; confirmed by the Senate December 20, 1851, by a voice vote; took judicial oath October 10, 1851; resigned September 30, 1857; replaced by Nathan Clifford, nominated by President James Buchanan.

Family: married Eliza Maria Woodward, 1833; died 1844; five children; married Anna Wroe Curtis, 1846; died 1860; three children; married Maria Malleville Allen, 1861; four children.

Death: September 15, 1874, Newport, Rhode Island.

Cushing, William

Birth: March 1, 1732, Scituate, Massachusetts.

Education: graduated Harvard, 1751, honorary LL.D., 1785; honorary A.M., Yale, 1753; studied law under Jeremiah Gridley; admitted to the bar in 1755.

Official Positions: judge, probate court for Lincoln County, Massachusetts (now Maine), 1760–1761; judge, Superior Court of Massachusetts Bay province, 1772–1777; chief justice, Superior Court of the Commonwealth of Massachusetts, 1777–1780, Supreme Judicial Court, 1780–1789; member, Massachusetts Constitutional Convention, 1779; vice president, Massachusetts Convention, which ratified U.S. Constitution, 1788; delegate to electoral college, 1788.

Supreme Court Service: nominated associate justice by President George Washington September 24, 1789; confirmed by the Senate September 26, 1789, by a voice vote; took judicial oath February 2, 1790; served until September 13, 1810; replaced by Joseph Story, nominated by President James Madison.

Family: married Hannah Phillips, 1774.

Death: September 13, 1810, Scituate, Massachusetts.

Daniel, Peter V.

Birth: April 24, 1784, Stafford County, Virginia.

Education: privately tutored; attended Princeton University, 1802–1803.

Official Positions: member, Virginia House of Delegates, 1809–1812; Virginia Privy Council, 1812–1835; lieutenant governor of Virginia, 1818–1835; U.S. district judge, Eastern District of Virginia, 1836–1841.

Supreme Court Service: nominated associate justice by President Martin Van Buren February 26, 1841, to replace Justice Philip Barbour, who had died; confirmed by the Senate March 2, 1841, by a 22–5 vote; took judicial oath January 10, 1842; served until May 31, 1860; replaced by Samuel F. Miller, nominated by President Abraham Lincoln.

Family: married Lucy Randolph, 1809; died 1847; married Elizabeth Harris, 1853; two children.

Death: May 31, 1860, Richmond, Virginia.

Davis, David

Birth: March 9, 1815, Cecil County, Maryland.

Education: graduated Kenyon College, 1832; Yale Law School, 1835.

Official Positions: Illinois state representative, 1845–1847; member, Illinois Constitutional Convention, 1847; Illinois state circuit judge, 1848–1862; U.S. senator, 1877–1883.

Supreme Court Service: nominated associate justice by President Abraham Lincoln December 1, 1862, to replace John A. Campbell, who had resigned; confirmed by the Senate December 8, 1862, by a voice vote; took judicial oath December 10, 1862; resigned March 4, 1877; replaced by John Marshall Harlan, nominated by President Rutherford B. Hayes.

Family: married Sarah Walker, October 30, 1838; died 1879; one son (two children died in infancy); married Adeline Burr, March 14, 1883; two daughters.

Death: June 26, 1886, Bloomington, Illinois.

Day, William R.

Birth: April 17, 1849, Ravenna, Ohio.

Education: University of Michigan, A.B., 1870; University of Michigan Law School, 1871–1872.

Official Positions: judge, Court of Common Pleas, Canton, Ohio, 1886; first assistant U.S. secretary of state, 1897–1898; U.S. secretary of state, 1898; member, United States delegation, Paris Peace Conference, 1898–1899; judge, U.S. Court of Appeals for the Sixth Circuit, 1899–1903; umpire, Mixed Claims Commission, 1922–1923.

Supreme Court Service: nominated associate justice by President Theodore Roosevelt February 19, 1903, to replace George Shiras Jr., who had resigned; confirmed by the Senate February 23, 1903, by a voice vote; took judicial oath March 2, 1903; resigned November 13, 1922; replaced by Pierce Butler, nominated by President Warren G. Harding.

Family: married Mary Elizabeth Schaefer, 1875; four sons.

Death: July 9, 1923, Mackinac Island, Michigan.

Douglas, William O.

Birth: October 16, 1898, Maine, Minnesota.

Education: Whitman College, B.A., 1920; Columbia Law School, LL.B., 1925.

Official Positions: member, Securities and Exchange Commission, 1936–1939; chairman, 1937–1939.

Supreme Court Service: nominated associate justice by President Franklin D. Roosevelt March 20, 1939, to replace Louis D. Brandeis, who had retired; confirmed by the Senate April 4, 1939, by a 62–4 vote; took judicial oath April 17, 1939; retired November 12, 1975; replaced by John Paul Stevens, nominated by President Gerald R. Ford.

Family: married Mildred Riddle, August 16, 1923; divorced 1953; one son, one daughter; married Mercedes Hester Davison, December 14, 1954; divorced 1963; married Joan Martin, August 1963; divorced 1966; married Cathleen Ann Heffernan, July 1966.

Death: January 19, 1980, Washington D.C.

Duvall, Gabriel

Birth: December 6, 1752, Prince George's County, Maryland.

Education: classical preparatory schooling; studied law.

Official Positions: clerk, Maryland Convention, 1775–1777; clerk, Maryland House of Delegates, 1777–1787; member, Maryland State Council, 1782–1785; member, Maryland House of Delegates, 1787–1794; U.S. representative, 1794–1796; chief justice, General Court of Maryland, 1796–1802; presidential elector, 1796, 1800; first comptroller of the Treasury, 1802–1811.

Supreme Court Service: nominated associate justice by President James Madison November 15, 1811, to replace Samuel Chase, who had died; confirmed by the Senate November 18, 1811, by a voice vote; took judicial oath November 23, 1811; resigned January 14, 1835; replaced by Philip Barbour, nominated by President Andrew Jackson.

Family: married Mary Brice, July 24, 1787; died March 24, 1790; one son; married Jane Gibbon, May 5, 1795; died April 1834.

Death: March 6, 1844, Prince George's County, Maryland.

Ellsworth, Oliver

Birth: April 29, 1745, Windsor, Connecticut.

Education: A.B., Princeton, 1766; honorary LL.D., Yale (1790), Princeton (1790), Dartmouth (1797).

Official Positions: member, Connecticut General Assembly, 1773–1776; state's attorney, Hartford County, 1777–1785; delegate to Continental Congress, 1777–1784; member, Connecticut Council of Safety, 1779; member, Governor's Council, 1780–1785, 1801–1807; judge, Connecticut Superior Court, 1785–1789; delegate, Constitutional Convention, 1787; U.S. senator, 1789–1796; commissioner to France, 1799–1800.

Supreme Court Service: nominated chief justice by President George Washington March 3, 1796, to replace John Jay, who had resigned; confirmed by the Senate March 4, 1796, by a 21–1 vote; took judicial oath March 8, 1796; resigned September 30, 1800; replaced by John Marshall, nominated by President John Adams.

Family: married Abigail Wolcott, 1771; four sons, three daughters survived infancy.

Death: November 26, 1807, Windsor, Connecticut.

Field, Stephen J.

Birth: November 4, 1816, Haddam, Connecticut.

Education: graduated Williams College, 1837, class valedictorian; studied law in private firms; admitted to the bar in 1841.

Official Positions: Alcalde of Marysville, 1850; California state representative, 1850–1851; justice, California Supreme Court, 1857–1863.

Supreme Court Service: nominated associate justice by President Abraham Lincoln March 6, 1863, for a newly created seat; confirmed by the Senate March 10, 1863, by a voice vote; took judicial oath May 20, 1863; retired December 1, 1897; replaced by Joseph McKenna, nominated by President William McKinley.

Family: married Sue Virginia Swearingen, June 2, 1859.
Death: April 9, 1899, in Washington, D.C.

Fortas, Abe

Birth: June 19, 1910, Memphis, Tennessee.
Education: Southwestern College, A.B., 1930; Yale Law School, LL.B., 1933.
Official Positions: assistant director, corporate reorganization study, Securities and Exchange Commission, 1934–1937; assistant director, Public Utilities Division, Securities and Exchange Commission, 1938–1939; general counsel, Public Works Administration, 1939–1940, and counsel to the Bituminous Coal Division, 1939–1941; director, Division of Power, Department of the Interior, 1941–1942; undersecretary of the interior, 1942–1946.
Supreme Court Service: nominated associate justice by President Lyndon B. Johnson July 28, 1965, to replace Arthur J. Goldberg, who had resigned; confirmed by the Senate August 11, 1965, by a voice vote; took judicial oath October 4, 1965; resigned May 14, 1969; replaced by Harry A. Blackmun, nominated by President Richard Nixon.
Family: married Carolyn Eugenia Agger, July 9, 1935.
Death: April 5, 1982, in Washington, D.C.

Frankfurter, Felix

Birth: November 15, 1882, Vienna, Austria.
Education: College of the City of New York, A.B., 1902; Harvard Law School, LL.B., 1906.
Official Positions: assistant U.S. attorney, Southern District of New York, 1906–1909; law officer, Bureau of Insular Affairs, War Department, 1910–1914; assistant to the secretary of war, 1917; secretary and counsel, President's Mediation Commission, 1917; assistant to the secretary of labor, 1917–1918; chairman, War Labor Policies Board, 1918.
Supreme Court Service: nominated associate justice by President Franklin D. Roosevelt January 5, 1939, to replace Benjamin Cardozo, who had died; confirmed by the Senate January 17, 1939, by a voice vote; took judicial oath January 30, 1939; retired August 28, 1962; replaced by Arthur Goldberg, nominated by President John F. Kennedy.
Family: married Marion A. Denman, December 20, 1919.
Death: February 22, 1965, Washington, D.C.

Fuller, Melville W.

Birth: February 11, 1833, Augusta, Maine.
Education: Bowdoin College, A.B., 1853; studied at Harvard Law School and read law, 1853–1855.
Official Positions: member, Illinois House of Representatives, 1863–1864; member, Venezuela-British Guiana Border Commission, 1899; member, Permanent Court of Arbitration at the Hague, 1900–1910.
Supreme Court Service: nominated chief justice by President Grover Cleveland April 30, 1888, to replace Morrison R. Waite, who had died; confirmed by the Senate July 20, 1888, by a 41–20 vote; took judicial oath October 8, 1888; served until July 4, 1910; replaced as chief justice by Edward D. White, nominated by President William Howard Taft.
Family: married Calista Ophelia Reynolds, June 28, 1858; died 1864; two daughters; married Mary Ellen Coolbaugh, May 30, 1866; eight children, seven of whom survived childhood.
Death: July 4, 1910, Sorrento, Maine.

Ginsburg, Ruth Bader

Birth: March 15, 1933, Brooklyn, New York.
Education: Cornell University, B.A., 1954; attended Harvard University Law School, 1956–1958; graduated
Columbia Law School, J.D., 1959.
Official Positions: judge, U.S. Court of Appeals for the District of Columbia, 1980–1993.
Supreme Court Service: nominated associate justice by President Bill Clinton June 22, 1993, to replace
Byron R. White, who had retired; confirmed by the Senate August 3, 1993, by a 96–3 vote; took
judicial oath August 10, 1993.
Family: married Martin D. Ginsburg, 1954; one daughter, one son.

Goldberg, Arthur J.

Birth: August 8, 1908, Chicago, Illinois.
Education: Northwestern University, B.S.L., 1929; J.D., summa cum laude, 1930.
Official Positions: secretary of labor, 1961–1962; U.S. ambassador to the United Nations, 1965–1968.
Supreme Court Service: nominated associate justice by President John F. Kennedy August 29, 1962, to
replace Felix Frankfurter, who had retired; confirmed by the Senate September 25, 1962, by a
voice vote; took judicial oath October 1, 1962; resigned July 25, 1965; replaced by Abe Fortas,
nominated by President Lyndon B. Johnson.
Family: married Dorothy Kurgans, July 18, 1931; one daughter, one son.
Death: January 19, 1990, Washington, D.C.

Gray, Horace

Birth: March 24, 1828, Boston, Massachusetts.
Education: Harvard College, A.B., 1845; Harvard Law School, 1849.
Official Positions: reporter, Massachusetts Supreme Court, 1854–1864; associate justice, 1864–1873; chief
justice, 1873–1881.
Supreme Court Service: nominated associate justice by President Chester A. Arthur December 19, 1881, to
replace Nathan Clifford, who had died; confirmed by the Senate December 20, 1881, by a 51–5
vote; took judicial oath January 9, 1882; served until September 15, 1902; replaced by Oliver Wen-
dell Holmes Jr., nominated by President Theodore Roosevelt.
Family: married Jane Matthews, June 4, 1889.
Death: September 15, 1902, Nahant, Massachusetts.

Grier, Robert C.

Birth: March 5, 1794, Cumberland County, Pennsylvania.
Education: Dickinson College, graduated 1812.
Official Positions: president judge, District Court of Allegheny County, Pennsylvania, 1833–1846.
Supreme Court Service: nominated associate justice by President James K. Polk August 3, 1846, to replace
Justice Henry Baldwin, who had died; confirmed by the Senate August 4, 1846, by a voice vote;
took judicial oath August 10, 1846; retired January 31, 1870; replaced by William Strong, nomi-
nated by President Ulysses S. Grant.
Family: married Isabella Rose, 1829.
Death: September 25, 1870, Philadelphia, Pennsylvania.

Harlan, John Marshall

Birth: June 1, 1833, Boyle County, Kentucky.

Education: Centre College, A.B., 1850; studied law at Transylvania University, 1851–1853.

Official Positions: adjutant general of Kentucky, 1851; judge, Franklin County, 1858; state attorney general, 1863–1867; member, Louisiana Reconstruction Commission, 1877; member, Bering Sea Tribunal of Arbitration, 1893.

Supreme Court Service: nominated associate justice by President Rutherford B. Hayes October 17, 1877, to replace David Davis, who had resigned; confirmed by the Senate November 29, 1877, by a voice vote; took judicial oath December 10, 1877; served until October 14, 1911; replaced by Mahlon Pitney, nominated by President William Howard Taft.

Family: married Malvina F. Shanklin, December 23, 1856; six children.

Death: October 14, 1911, Washington, D.C.

Harlan, John M.

Birth: May 20, 1899, Chicago, Illinois.

Education: Princeton University, B.A., 1920; Rhodes scholar, Oxford University, Balliol College, B.A. in jurisprudence, 1923; New York Law School, LL.B., 1924.

Official Positions: assistant U.S. attorney, Southern District of New York, 1925–1927; special assistant attorney general, New York, 1928–1930; chief counsel, New York State Crime Commission, 1951–1953; judge, U.S. Court of Appeals for the Second Circuit, 1954–1955.

Supreme Court Service: nominated associate justice by President Dwight D. Eisenhower November 8, 1954, to replace Robert Jackson, who had died; confirmed by the Senate March 16, 1955, by a 71–11 vote; took judicial oath March 28, 1955; retired September 23, 1971; replaced by William H. Rehnquist, nominated by President Richard Nixon.

Family: married Ethel Andrews, November 10, 1928; one daughter.

Death: December 29, 1971, Washington D.C.

Holmes, Oliver Wendell, Jr.

Birth: March 8, 1841, Boston, Massachusetts.

Education: Harvard College, A.B., 1861; LL.B., 1866.

Official Positions: associate justice, Massachusetts Supreme Court, 1882–1899; chief justice, 1899–1902.

Supreme Court Service: nominated associate justice by President Theodore Roosevelt December 2, 1902, to replace Horace Gray, who had died; confirmed by the Senate December 4, 1902, by a voice vote; took judicial oath December 8, 1902; retired January 12, 1932; replaced by Benjamin N. Cardozo, nominated by President Herbert Hoover.

Family: married Fanny Bowdich Dixwell, June 17, 1872.

Death: March 6, 1935; Washington, D.C.

Hughes, Charles Evans

Birth: April 11, 1862, Glens Falls, New York.

Education: Madison College (now Colgate University), 1876–1878; Brown University, A.B., 1881, A.M., 1884; Columbia Law School, LL.B., 1884.

Official Positions: special counsel, New York state investigating commissions, 1905–1906; governor of New York, 1907–1910; U.S. secretary of state, 1921–1925; U.S. delegate, Washington Armament Conference, 1921; U.S. member, Permanent Court of Arbitration, 1926–1930; judge, Permanent Court of International Justice, 1928–1930.

Supreme Court Service: nominated associate justice by President William Howard Taft April 25, 1910, to replace David J. Brewer, who had died; confirmed by Senate May 2, 1910, by a voice vote; took judicial oath October 10, 1910; resigned June 10, 1916, to become Republican presidential candidate; replaced by John H. Clarke, nominated by President Woodrow Wilson; nominated chief justice February 3, 1930, by President Herbert Hoover, to replace Chief Justice Taft, who had retired; confirmed by the Senate February 13, 1930, by a 52–26 vote; took judicial oath February 24, 1930; retired July 1, 1941; replaced by Harlan F. Stone, nominated by President Franklin D. Roosevelt.

Family: married Antoinette Carter, December 5, 1888; one son, three daughters.

Death: August 27, 1948, Osterville, Massachusetts.

Hunt, Ward

Birth: June 14, 1810, Utica, New York.

Education: graduated with honors from Union College, 1828; attended Tapping Reeve law school.

Official Positions: member, New York Assembly, 1839; mayor of Utica, 1844; member, New York Court of Appeals, 1866–1869; New York State commissioner of appeals, 1869–1873.

Supreme Court Service: nominated associate justice by President Ulysses S. Grant December 3, 1872, to replace Samuel Nelson, who had retired; confirmed by the Senate December 11, 1872, by a voice vote; took judicial oath January 9, 1873; retired January 27, 1882; replaced by Samuel Blatchford, nominated by President Chester A. Arthur.

Family: married Mary Ann Savage, 1837; died 1845; three children; married Marie Taylor, 1853.

Death: March 24, 1886, Washington, D.C.

Iredell, James

Birth: October 5, 1751, Lewes, England.

Education: educated in England; read law under Samuel Johnston of North Carolina; licensed to practice, 1770–1771.

Official Positions: comptroller of customs, Edenton, North Carolina, 1768–1774; collector of customs, Port of North Carolina, 1774–1776; judge, Superior Court of North Carolina, 1778; attorney general, North Carolina, 1779–1781; member, North Carolina Council of State, 1787; delegate, North Carolina convention for ratification of federal Constitution, 1788.

Supreme Court Service: nominated associate justice by President George Washington February 8, 1790; confirmed by the Senate February 10, 1790, by a voice vote; took judicial oath May 12, 1790; served until October 20, 1799; replaced by Alfred Moore, nominated by President John Adams.

Family: married Hannah Johnston, July 18, 1773; two daughters, one son.

Death: October 20, 1799, Edenton, North Carolina.

Jackson, Howell E.

Birth: April 8, 1832, Paris, Tennessee.

Education: West Tennessee College, A.B., 1850; University of Virginia, 1851–1852; Cumberland University, 1856.

Official Positions: custodian of sequestered property for Confederate states, 1861–1865; judge, Court of Arbitration for Western Tennessee, 1875–1879; state legislature, 1880; U.S. senator, 1881–1886; judge, Sixth Federal Circuit Court, 1886–1891, U.S. Circuit Court of Appeals, 1891–1893.

Supreme Court Service: nominated associate justice by President Benjamin Harrison February 2, 1893, to replace Lucius Q. C. Lamar, who had died; confirmed by the Senate February 18, 1893, by a voice vote; took judicial oath March 4, 1893; served until August 8, 1895; replaced by Rufus W. Peckham, nominated by President Grover Cleveland.

Family: married Sophia Malloy in 1859; died 1873; six children, two died in infancy; married Mary E. Harding in April 1874; three children.

Death: August 8, 1895, Nashville, Tennessee.

Jackson, Robert H.

Birth: February 13, 1892, Spring Creek, Pennsylvania.

Education: Local schools in Frewsburg, New York; Albany Law School, 1912.

Official Positions: general counsel, Bureau of Internal Revenue, 1934–1936; assistant U.S. attorney general, 1936–1938; U.S. solicitor general, 1938–1939; U.S. attorney general, 1940–1941; chief U.S. prosecutor, Nuremberg war crimes trial, 1945–1946.

Supreme Court Service: nominated associated justice by President Franklin D. Roosevelt June 12, 1941, to replace Harlan F. Stone, who was promoted to chief justice; confirmed by the Senate July 7, 1941, by a voice vote; took judicial oath July 11, 1941; served until October 9, 1954; replaced by John M. Harlan, nominated by President Dwight D. Eisenhower.

Family: married Irene Alice Gerhardt, April 24, 1916; one daughter, one son.

Death: October 9, 1954, Washington, D.C.

Jay, John

Birth: December 12, 1745, New York City.

Education: privately tutored; attended boarding school; graduated from King's College (later Columbia University), 1764; clerked in law office of Benjamin Kissam; admitted to the bar in 1768.

Official Positions: secretary, Royal Boundary Commission, 1773; member, New York Committee of 51, 1774; delegate, Continental Congress, 1774, 1775, 1777, president, 1778–1779; delegate, New York provincial congress, 1776–1777; chief justice, New York State, 1777–1778; minister to Spain, 1779; secretary of foreign affairs, 1784–1789; envoy to Great Britain, 1794–1795; governor, New York, 1795–1801.

Supreme Court Service: nominated chief justice by President George Washington September 24, 1789; confirmed by the Senate September 26, 1789, by a voice vote; took judicial oath October 9, 1789; resigned June 29, 1795; replaced by Oliver Ellsworth, nominated by President Washington.

Family: married Sarah Van Brugh Livingston, April 28, 1774; died 1802; five daughters, two sons.

Death: May 17, 1829, Bedford, New York.

Johnson, Thomas

Birth: November 4, 1732, Calvert County, Maryland.

Education: educated at home; studied law under Stephen Bordley; admitted to the bar, 1760.

Official Positions: delegate, Maryland Provincial Assembly, 1762; delegate, Annapolis Convention of 1774; member, Continental Congress, 1774–1777; delegate, first constitutional convention of Maryland, 1776; first governor of Maryland, 1777–1779; member, Maryland House of Delegates, 1780, 1786, 1787; member, Maryland convention for ratification of the federal Constitution, 1788; chief judge, general court of Maryland, 1790–1791; member, board of commissioners of the Federal City, 1791–1794.

Supreme Court Service: nominated associate justice by President George Washington November 1, 1791, to replace John Rutledge, who had resigned; confirmed by the Senate November 7, 1791, by a voice vote; took judicial oath August 6, 1792; resigned February 1, 1793; replaced by William Paterson, nominated by President Washington.

Family: married Ann Jennings, February 16, 1766; died 1794; three sons, five daughters, one of whom died in infancy.

Death: October 26, 1819, Frederick, Maryland.

Johnson, William

Birth: December 27, 1771, Charleston, South Carolina.

Education: graduated Princeton, 1790; studied law under Charles Cotesworth Pinckney; admitted to bar in 1793.

Official Positions: member, South Carolina House of Representatives, 1794–1798; Speaker, 1798; judge, Court of Common Pleas, 1799–1804.

Supreme Court Service: nominated associate justice by President Thomas Jefferson March 22, 1804, to replace Alfred Moore, who had resigned; confirmed by the Senate March 24, 1804, by a voice vote; took judicial oath May 7, 1804; served until August 4, 1834; replaced by James M. Wayne, nominated by President Andrew Jackson.

Family: married Sarah Bennett, March 20, 1794; eight children, six of whom died in childhood; two adopted children.

Death: August 4, 1834, Brooklyn, New York.

Kennedy, Anthony M.

Birth: July 23, 1936, Sacramento, California.

Education: Stanford University, A.B., 1958; London School of Economics, 1957–1958; Harvard Law School, J.D., 1961.

Official Positions: judge, U.S. Court of Appeals for the Ninth Circuit, 1976–1988.

Supreme Court Service: nominated associate justice by President Ronald Reagan November 30, 1987, to replace Lewis F. Powell Jr., who had retired; confirmed by the Senate February 3, 1988, by a 97–0 vote; took judicial oath February 18, 1988.

Family: married Mary Davis, 1963; three children.

Lamar, Joseph R.

Birth: October 14, 1857, Elbert County, Georgia.

Education: University of Georgia, 1874–1875; Bethany College, A.B., 1877; Washington and Lee University, 1877.

Official Positions: member, Georgia legislature, 1886–1889; commissioner to codify Georgia laws, 1893; associate justice, Georgia Supreme Court, 1903–1905; member, mediation conference, Niagara Falls, Canada, 1914.

Supreme Court Service: nominated associate justice by President William Howard Taft December 12, 1910, to replace William Henry Moody, who had retired; confirmed by the Senate December 15, 1910, by a voice vote; took judicial oath January 3, 1911; served until January 2, 1916; replaced by Louis D. Brandeis, nominated by President Woodrow Wilson.

Family: married Clarinda Huntington Pendleton, January 30, 1879; two sons, one daughter.

Death: January 2, 1916, Washington, D.C.

Lamar, Lucius Q. C.

Birth: September 17, 1825, Eatonton, Georgia.

Education: Emory College, A.B., 1845.

Official Positions: member, Georgia House of Representatives, 1853; U.S. representative, 1857–1860, 1873–1877; U.S. senator, 1877–1885; secretary of interior, 1885–1888.

Supreme Court Service: nominated associate justice by President Grover Cleveland December 6, 1887, to replace William Woods, who had died; confirmed by the Senate January 16, 1888, by a 32–28 vote; took judicial oath January 18, 1888; served until January 23, 1893; replaced by Howell E. Jackson, nominated by President Benjamin Harrison.

Family: married Virginia Longstreet, July 15, 1847; died 1884; one son, three daughters; married Henrietta Dean Holt, January 5, 1887.

Death: January 23, 1893, Macon, Georgia.

Livingston, Henry Brockholst

Birth: November 25, 1757, New York City.

Education: graduated from College of New Jersey (Princeton), 1774; honorary LL.D., Harvard (1810), Princeton; studied law under Peter Yates; admitted to bar in 1783.

Official Positions: member, New York Assembly, Twelfth, Twenty-fourth, and Twenty-fifth sessions; judge, New York State Supreme Court, 1802–1807.

Supreme Court Service: nominated associate justice by President Thomas Jefferson December 13, 1806, to replace William Paterson, who had died; confirmed by the Senate December 17, 1806, by a voice vote; took judicial oath January 20, 1807; served until March 18, 1823; replaced by Smith Thompson, nominated by President James Monroe.

Family: married Catharine Keteltas, five children; married Ann Ludlow, three children; married Catharine Kortright, three children.

Death: March 18, 1823, Washington, D.C.

Lurton, Horace H.

Birth: February 26, 1844, Newport, Kentucky.

Education: Douglas University (University of Chicago), 1860; Cumberland Law School, L.B., 1867.

Official Positions: chancellor in equity, 1875–1878; judge, Tennessee Supreme Court, 1886–1893; judge, U.S. Court of Appeals for the Sixth Circuit, 1893–1909.

Supreme Court Service: nominated associate justice by President William Howard Taft December 13, 1909, to replace Rufus W. Peckham, who had died; confirmed by the Senate December 20, 1909, by a voice vote; took judicial oath January 3, 1910; served until July 12, 1914; replaced by James C. McReynolds, nominated by President Woodrow Wilson.

Family: married Mary Francis Owen, September 1867; three sons, two daughters.

Death: July 12, 1914, Atlantic City, New Jersey.

McKenna, Joseph

Birth: August 10, 1843, Philadelphia, Pennsylvania.

Education: Benicia Collegiate Institute, graduated in 1864; admitted to the bar in 1865.

Official Positions: district attorney, Solano County, California, 1866–1870; member, California Assembly, 1875–1876; U.S. representative, 1885–1892; judge, U.S. Ninth Judicial Circuit, 1892–1897; U.S. attorney general, 1897.

Supreme Court Service: nominated associate justice by President William McKinley December 16, 1897, to replace Stephen J. Field, who had retired; confirmed by the Senate January 21, 1898, by a voice vote; took judicial oath January 26, 1898; retired January 5, 1925; replaced by Harlan F. Stone, nominated by President Calvin Coolidge.

Family: married Amanda Frances Bornemann, June 10, 1869; three daughters, one son.

Death: November 21, 1926, Washington, D.C.

McKinley, John

Birth: May 1, 1780, Culpeper County, Virginia.

Education: read law on his own; admitted to the bar in 1800.

Official Positions: Alabama state representative, sessions of 1820, 1831, and 1836; U.S. senator, 1826–1831 and 1837; U.S. representative, 1833–1835.

Supreme Court Service: nominated associate justice by President Martin Van Buren September 18, 1837, for a newly created Supreme Court seat; confirmed by the Senate September 25, 1837, by a voice vote; took judicial oath January 9, 1838; served until July 19, 1852; replaced by John A. Campbell, nominated by President Franklin Pierce.

Family: married Juliana Bryan; married Elizabeth Armistead.

Death: July 19, 1852, Louisville, Kentucky.

McLean, John

Birth: March 11, 1785, Morris County, New Jersey.

Education: attended local school; privately tutored; read law with John S. Gano and Arthur St. Clair Jr.

Official Positions: examiner, U.S. Land Office, 1811–1812; U.S. representative, 1813–1816, chairman, Committee on Accounts; judge, Ohio Supreme Court, 1816–1822; commissioner, General Land Office, 1822–1823; U.S. postmaster general, 1823–1829.

Supreme Court Service: nominated associate justice by President Andrew Jackson March 7, 1829, to replace Robert Trimble, who had died; confirmed by the Senate March 7, 1829, by a voice vote; took judicial oath January 11, 1830; served until April 3, 1861; replaced by Noah H. Swayne, nominated by President Abraham Lincoln.

Family: married Rebecca Edwards, 1807; died 1840; four daughters, three sons; married Sarah Bella Ludlow Garrard, 1843; one son, died at birth.

Death: April 3, 1861, Cincinnati, Ohio.

McReynolds, James C.

Birth: February 3, 1862, Elkton, Kentucky.

Education: Vanderbilt University, B.S., 1882; University of Virginia, LL.B., 1884.

Official Positions: assistant U.S. attorney, 1903–1907; U.S. attorney general, 1913–1914.

Supreme Court Service: nominated associate justice by President Woodrow Wilson August 19, 1914, to replace Horace H. Lurton, who had died; confirmed by the Senate August 29, 1914, by a 44–6 vote; took judicial oath October 12, 1914; retired January 31, 1941; replaced by James F. Byrnes, nominated by President Franklin D. Roosevelt.

Family: unmarried.

Death: August 24, 1946, in Washington, D.C.

Marshall, John

Birth: September 24, 1755, Germantown, Virginia.

Education: tutored at home; self-taught in law; attended one course of law lectures at College of William and Mary, 1780.

Official Positions: member, Virginia House of Delegates, 1782–1785, 1787–1790, 1795–1796; member, Executive Council of State, 1782–1784; recorder, Richmond City Hustings Court, 1785–1788; delegate, state convention for ratification of federal Constitution, 1788; minister to France, 1797–1798; U.S. representative, 1799–1800; U.S. secretary of state, 1800–1801; member, Virginia Constitutional Convention, 1829.

Supreme Court Service: nominated chief justice by President John Adams January 20, 1801, to replace Oliver Ellsworth, who had resigned; confirmed by the Senate January 27, 1801, by a voice vote; took judicial oath February 4, 1801; served until July 6, 1835; replaced by Roger B. Taney, nominated by President Andrew Jackson.

Family: Married Mary Willis Ambler, January 3, 1783; died December 25, 1831; ten children.

Death: July 6, 1835, Philadelphia, Pennsylvania.

Marshall, Thurgood

Birth: July 2, 1908, Baltimore, Maryland.

Education: Lincoln University, A.B., cum laude, 1930; Howard University Law School, LL.B., 1933.

Official Positions: judge, Second Circuit Court of Appeals, 1961–1965; U.S. solicitor general, 1965–1967.

Supreme Court Service: nominated associate justice by President Lyndon B. Johnson June 13, 1967, to replace Tom C. Clark, who had retired; confirmed by the Senate August 30, 1967, by a 69–11 vote; took judicial oath October 2, 1967; retired October 1, 1991; replaced by Clarence Thomas, nominated by President George Bush.

Family: married Vivian Burey, September 4, 1929, died February 1955; married Cecilia Suyat, December 17, 1955; two sons.

Death: January 24, 1993, Bethesda, Maryland.

Matthews, Stanley

Birth: July 21, 1824, Cincinnati, Ohio.

Education: Kenyon College, graduated with honors, 1840.

Official Positions: assistant prosecuting attorney, Hamilton County, 1845; clerk, Ohio House of Representatives, 1848–1849; judge, Hamilton County Court of Common Pleas, 1851–1853; member, Ohio Senate, 1855–1858; U.S. attorney for southern Ohio, 1858–1861; judge, Superior Court of Cincinnati, 1863–1865; counsel, Hayes-Tilden electoral commission, 1877; U.S. senator, 1877–1879.

Supreme Court Service: nominated associate justice by President Rutherford B. Hayes January 26, 1881, to replace Noah Swayne, who had retired; no action by Senate; renominated by President James A. Garfield March 14, 1881; confirmed by the Senate May 12, 1881, by a 24–23 vote; took judicial oath May 17, 1881; served until March 22, 1889; replaced by David J. Brewer, nominated by President Benjamin Harrison.

Family: married Mary Ann Black, February 1843; died 1885; eight children; married Mary Theaker, 1887.

Death: March 22, 1889, Washington, D.C.

Miller, Samuel F.

Birth: April 5, 1816, Richmond, Kentucky.

Education: Transylvania University, M.D., 1838; studied law privately; admitted to the bar in 1847.

Official Positions: justice of the peace and member of the Knox County, Kentucky, court, an administrative body, in the 1840s.

Supreme Court Service: nominated associate justice by President Abraham Lincoln July 16, 1862, to replace Peter V. Daniel, who had died; confirmed July 16, 1862, by a voice vote; took judicial oath July 21, 1862; served until October 13, 1890; replaced by Henry B. Brown, nominated by President Benjamin Harrison.

Family: married Lucy Ballinger, November 8, 1842; died 1854; three children; married Elizabeth Winter Reeves, widow of his law partner, 1857; two children.

Death: October 13, 1890, Washington, D.C.

Minton, Sherman

Birth: October 20, 1890, Georgetown, Indiana.

Education: Indiana University, LL.B., 1915; Yale University, LL.M., 1917.

Official Positions: public counselor, Public Service Commission, 1933–1934; U.S. senator, 1935–1941; assistant to president, 1941; judge, Seventh Circuit Court of Appeals, 1941–1949.

Supreme Court Service: nominated associate justice by President Harry S. Truman September 15, 1949, to replace Wiley B. Rutledge, who had died; confirmed by the Senate October 4, 1949, by a 48–16 vote; took judicial oath October 12, 1949; retired October 15, 1956; replaced by William J. Brennan Jr., nominated by President Dwight D. Eisenhower.

Family: married Gertrude Gurtz, August 11, 1917; two sons, one daughter.

Death: April 9, 1965 in New Albany, Indiana.

Moody, William H.

Birth: December 23, 1853, Newbury, Massachusetts.

Education: Harvard College, A.B., cum laude, 1876; Harvard Law School, 1876–1877; read law with Richard Henry Dana.

Official Positions: city solicitor, Haverhill, 1888–1890; district attorney, Eastern District of Massachusetts, 1890–1895; U.S. representative, 1895–1902; secretary of the Navy, 1902–1904; U.S. attorney general, 1904–1906.

Supreme Court Service: nominated associate justice by President Theodore Roosevelt December 3, 1906, to replace Henry B. Brown, who had retired; confirmed by the Senate December 12, 1906, by a voice vote; took judicial oath December 17, 1906; retired November 20, 1910; replaced by Joseph R. Lamar, nominated by President William Howard Taft.

Family: unmarried.
Death: July 2, 1917, Haverhill, Massachusetts.

Moore, Alfred

Birth: May 21, 1755, New Hanover County, North Carolina.
Education: educated in Boston; studied law under his father; received law license, 1775.
Official Positions: member, North Carolina legislature, 1782, 1792; North Carolina attorney general, 1782–1791; trustee, University of North Carolina, 1789–1807; judge, North Carolina Superior Court, 1799.
Supreme Court Service: nominated associate justice by President John Adams December 6, 1799, to replace James Iredell, who had died; confirmed by the Senate December 10, 1799, by a voice vote; took judicial oath April 21, 1800; resigned January 26, 1804; replaced by William Johnson, nominated by President Thomas Jefferson.
Family: married Susanna Eagles.
Death: October 15, 1810, Bladen County, North Carolina.

Murphy, Francis W.

Birth: April 13, 1890, Sand (now Harbor) Beach, Michigan.
Education: University of Michigan, A.B., 1912, LL.B., 1914; graduate study, Lincoln's Inn, London, and Trinity College, Dublin.
Official Positions: chief assistant U.S. attorney, Eastern District of Michigan, 1919–1920; judge, Recorder's Court, Detroit, 1924–1930; mayor of Detroit, 1930–1933; governor general of the Philippines, 1933–1935; U.S. high commissioner to the Philippines, 1935–1936; governor of Michigan, 1937–1939; U.S. attorney general, 1939–1940.
Supreme Court Service: nominated associate justice by President Franklin D. Roosevelt January 4, 1940, to replace Pierce Butler, who had died; confirmed by the Senate January 16, 1940, by a voice vote; took judicial oath February 5, 1940; served until July 19, 1949; replaced by Tom C. Clark, nominated by President Harry S. Truman.
Family: unmarried.
Death: July 19, 1949, Detroit, Michigan.

Nelson, Samuel

Birth: November 11, 1792, Hebron, New York.
Education: graduated, Middlebury College, 1813.
Official Positions: postmaster, Cortland, New York, 1820–1823; presidential elector, 1820; judge, Sixth Circuit of New York, 1823–1831; associate justice, New York Supreme Court, 1831–1837; chief justice, New York Supreme Court, 1837–1845; member, Alabama Claims Commission, 1871.
Supreme Court Service: nominated associate justice by President John Tyler February 4, 1845, to replace Justice Smith Thompson, who had died; confirmed by the Senate February 14, 1845, by a voice vote; took judicial oath February 27, 1845; retired November 28, 1872; replaced by Ward Hunt, nominated by President Ulysses S. Grant.
Family: married Pamela Woods, 1819; died 1822; one son; married Catherine Ann Russell, ca. 1825; two daughters, one son.
Death: December 13, 1873, Cooperstown, New York.

O'Connor, Sandra Day

Birth: March 26, 1930, El Paso, Texas.

Education: Stanford University, B.A., 1950, Stanford University Law School, LL.B., 1952.

Official Positions: deputy county attorney, San Mateo, California, 1952–1953; assistant attorney general, Arizona, 1965–1969; Arizona state senator, 1969–1975, majority leader, state Senate, 1973–1974; judge, Maricopa County Superior Court, 1975–1979; judge, Arizona Court of Appeals, 1979–1981.

Supreme Court Service: nominated associate justice by President Ronald Reagan August 19, 1981 to replace Potter Stewart, who had retired; confirmed by the Senate September 21, 1981 by a 99–0 vote; took judicial oath September 26, 1981; announced retirement July 1, 2005.

Family: married John O'Connor, 1952; three sons.

Paterson, William

Birth: December 24, 1745, County Antrim, Ireland.

Education: graduated from College of New Jersey (Princeton), 1763; M.A., 1766; studied law under Richard Stockton; admitted to the bar, 1769.

Official Positions: member, New Jersey Provincial Congress, 1775–1776; delegate, New Jersey State Constitutional Convention, 1776; New Jersey attorney general, 1776–1783; delegate, U.S. Constitutional Convention, 1787; U.S. senator, 1789–1790; governor, New Jersey, 1790–1793.

Supreme Court Service: nominated associate justice by President George Washington March 4, 1793, to replace Thomas Johnson, who had resigned; confirmed by the Senate March 4, 1793, by a voice vote; took judicial oath March 11, 1793; served until September 9, 1806; replaced by Henry B. Livingston, nominated by President Thomas Jefferson.

Family: married Cornelia Bell, February 9, 1779; died 1783; three children; married Euphemia White, 1785.

Death: September 9, 1806, Albany, New York.

Peckham, Rufus W.

Birth: November 8, 1838, Albany, New York.

Education: Albany Boys' Academy; studied privately in Philadelphia.

Official Positions: district attorney, Albany County, 1869–1872; corporation counsel, City of Albany, 1881–1883; judge, New York Supreme Court, 1883–1886; judge, New York Court of Appeals, 1886–1895.

Supreme Court Service: nominated associate justice by President Grover Cleveland December 3, 1895, to replace Howell E. Jackson, who had died; confirmed by Senate December 8, 1895, by a voice vote; took judicial oath January 6, 1896; served until October 24, 1909; replaced by Horace H. Lurton, nominated by President William Howard Taft.

Family: married Harriette M. Arnold, November 14, 1866; two sons.

Death: October 24, 1909, Altamont, New York.

Pitney, Mahlon

Birth: February 5, 1858, Morristown, New Jersey.

Education: College of New Jersey (Princeton), A.B., 1879; A.M., 1882.

Official Positions: U.S. representative, 1895–1899; New Jersey State senator, 1899–1901; president, New Jersey Senate, 1901; associate justice, New Jersey Supreme Court, 1901–1908; chancellor of New Jersey, 1908–1912.

Supreme Court Service: nominated associate justice by President William Howard Taft February 19, 1912, to replace John Marshall Harlan, who had died; confirmed by the Senate March 13, 1912, by a 50–26 vote; took judicial oath March 18, 1912; retired December 31, 1922; replaced by Edward T. Sanford, nominated by President Warren G. Harding.

Family: married Florence T. Shelton, November 14, 1891; two sons, one daughter.

Death: December 9, 1924, Washington, D.C.

Powell, Lewis F., Jr.

Birth: September 19, 1907, Suffolk, Virginia.

Education: Washington and Lee University, B.S., 1929; Washington and Lee University Law School, LL.B., 1931; Harvard Law School, LL.M., 1932.

Official Positions: president of the Richmond School Board, 1952–1961; member, 1961–1969, and president, 1968–1969, Virginia State Board of Education; president of the American Bar Association, 1964–1965; president, American College of Trial Lawyers, 1968–1969.

Supreme Court Service: nominated associate justice by President Richard Nixon October 22, 1971, to replace Hugo L. Black, who had retired; confirmed by the Senate December 6, 1971, by an 89–1 vote; took judicial oath January 6, 1972; retired June 26, 1987; replaced by Anthony Kennedy, nominated by President Ronald Reagan.

Family: married Josephine M. Rucker, May 2, 1936; three daughters, one son.

Death: August 25, 1998, Richmond, Virginia.

Reed, Stanley F.

Birth: December 31, 1884, Minerva, Kentucky.

Education: Kentucky Wesleyan University, A.B., 1902; Yale University, A.B., 1906; legal studies, University of Virginia and Columbia University (no degree); graduate studies, University of Paris, 1909–1910.

Official Positions: representative, Kentucky General Assembly, 1912–1916; general counsel, Federal Farm Board, 1929–1932; general counsel, Reconstruction Finance Corporation, 1932–1935; special assistant to attorney general, 1935; solicitor general, 1935–1938.

Supreme Court Service: nominated associate justice by President Franklin D. Roosevelt January 15, 1938, to replace George Sutherland, who had retired; confirmed by Senate January 25, 1938, by a voice vote; took judicial oath January 31, 1938; retired February 25, 1957; replaced by Charles E. Whittaker, appointed by President Dwight D. Eisenhower.

Family: married Winifred Elgin, May 11, 1908; two sons.

Death: April 2, 1980, New York City.

Rehnquist, William H.

Birth: October 1, 1924, Milwaukee, Wisconsin.

Education: Stanford University, B.A., 1948, M.A., 1948; Harvard University, M.A., 1950; Stanford University Law School, LL.B., 1952.

Official Positions: law clerk to Supreme Court Justice Robert H. Jackson, 1952–1953; assistant U.S. attorney general, Office of Legal Counsel, 1969–1971.

Supreme Court Service: nominated associate justice by President Richard Nixon October 21, 1971, to replace John M. Harlan, who had retired; confirmed by the Senate December 10, 1971, by a 68–26 vote; took judicial oath January 7, 1972; nominated chief justice by President Ronald Reagan June 20, 1986; confirmed by the Senate, 65–33, September 17, 1986; took judicial oath September 26, 1986; replaced as associate justice by Antonin Scalia, nominated by President Reagan; served until September 3, 2005; replaced by John G. Roberts Jr., nominated by President George W. Bush.
Family: married Natalie Cornell, August 29, 1953; died October 17, 1991; one son, two daughters.
Death: September 3, 2005, Arlington, Virginia.

Roberts, John G., Jr.

Birth: January 27, 1955, Buffalo, New York.
Education: Harvard University, B.A., 1976; Harvard Law School, LL.B., 1979.
Official Positions: law clerk to Justice William Rehnquist, 1980–1981; special assistant to Attorney General, William French Smith, U.S. Justice Department, 1981–1982; associate counsel to President Ronald Reagan, 1982–1986; judge, U.S. Court of Appeals for the District of Columbia Circuit, 2003–2005.
Supreme Court Service: nominated associate justice by President George W. Bush July 19, 2005, to replace Sandra Day O'Connor, who announced her retirement on July 1, 2005; elevated to chief justice nominee upon death of Chief Justice William H. Rehnquist September 3, 2005; confirmed as chief justice by the Senate, September 29, 2005, by a 78–22 vote; took judicial oath September 29, 2005.
Family: married Jane Marie Sullivan in 1996; one daughter, one son.

Roberts, Owen J.

Birth: May 2, 1875, Germantown, Pennsylvania.
Education: University of Pennsylvania, A.B. with honors, 1895; LL.B. cum laude, 1898.
Official Positions: assistant district attorney, 1903–1906; special deputy attorney general, Eastern District of Pennsylvania, 1918; special U.S. attorney, 1924–1930; umpire, Mixed Claims Commission, 1932; chairman, Pearl Harbor Inquiry Board, 1941–1942.
Supreme Court Service: nominated associate justice by President Herbert Hoover May 9, 1930, to replace Edward T. Sanford, who had died; confirmed by the Senate May 20, 1930, by a voice vote; took judicial oath June 2, 1930; resigned July 31, 1945; replaced by Harold H. Burton, nominated by President Harry S. Truman.
Family: married Elizabeth Caldwell Rogers, 1904; one daughter.
Death: May 17, 1955, West Vincent Township, Pennsylvania.

Rutledge, John

Birth: September 1739, Charleston, South Carolina.
Education: privately tutored; studied law at the Middle Temple in England; called to the English bar February 9, 1760.
Official Positions: member, South Carolina Commons House of Assembly, 1761–1776; South Carolina attorney general pro item, 1764–1765; delegate, Stamp Act Congress, 1765; member, Continental Congress, 1774–1776, 1782–1783; president, South Carolina General Assembly, 1776–1778; governor, South Carolina, 1779–1782; judge of the Court of Chancery of South Carolina, 1784–1791; chief, South Carolina delegation to the Constitutional Convention, 1787; member, South Carolina convention to ratify U.S. Constitution, 1788; chief justice, South Carolina Supreme Court, 1791–1795; member, South Carolina Assembly, 1798–1799.

Supreme Court Service: nominated associate justice by President George Washington September 24, 1789; confirmed by the Senate September 26, 1789, by a voice vote; took judicial oath February 15, 1790; resigned March 5, 1791; replaced by Thomas Johnson, nominated by President Washington. Later sworn in by virtue of recess appointment as chief justice August 12, 1795; appointment not confirmed, and service terminated December 15, 1795.
Family: married Elizabeth Grimke, May 1, 1763; died 1792; ten children.
Death: July 18, 1800, Charleston, South Carolina.

Rutledge, Wiley B.

Birth: July 20, 1894, Cloverport, Kentucky.
Education: University of Wisconsin, A.B., 1914; University of Colorado, LL.B., 1922.
Official Positions: judge, U.S. Court of Appeals for the District of Columbia, 1939–1943.
Supreme Court Service: nominated associate justice by President Franklin D. Roosevelt January 11, 1943, to replace James F. Byrnes, who had resigned; confirmed by the Senate February 8, 1943, by a voice vote; took judicial oath February 15, 1943; served until September 10, 1949; replaced by Sherman Minton, nominated by President Harry S. Truman.
Family: married Annabel Person, August 28, 1917; two daughters, one son.
Death: September 10, 1949, York, Maine.

Sanford, Edward T.

Birth: July 23, 1865, Knoxville, Tennessee.
Education: University of Tennessee, B.A. and Ph.B., 1883; Harvard, B.A., 1884, M.A., 1889; Harvard Law School, LL.B., 1889.
Official Positions: special assistant to the U.S. attorney general, 1906–1907; assistant U.S. attorney general, 1907–1908; federal judge, U.S. District Court for the Middle and Eastern Districts of Tennessee, 1908–1923.
Supreme Court Service: nominated associate justice by President Warren G. Harding January 24, 1923, to replace Mahlon Pitney, who had retired; confirmed by the Senate January 29, 1923, by a voice vote; took judicial oath February 19, 1923; served until March 8, 1930; replaced by Owen J. Roberts, nominated by President Herbert Hoover.
Family: married Lutie Mallory Woodruff, January 6, 1891; two daughters.
Death: March 8, 1930, Washington, D.C.

Scalia, Antonin

Birth: March 11, 1936, Trenton, New Jersey.
Education: Georgetown University, A.B., summa cum laude, 1957; Harvard Law School, LL.B., magna cum laude, 1960.
Official Positions: general counsel, White House Office of Telecommunications Policy, 1971–1972; chairman, Administrative Conference of the United States, 1972–1974; assistant attorney general, Office of Legal Counsel, 1974–1977; judge, U.S. Court of Appeals for the District of Columbia Circuit, 1982–1986.
Supreme Court Service: nominated associate justice by President Ronald Reagan June 24, 1986, to replace William H. Rehnquist, who had been promoted to chief justice; confirmed by the Senate September 17, 1986, by a 98–0 vote; took judicial oath September 26, 1986.
Family: married Maureen McCarthy, 1960; nine children.

Shiras, George, Jr.

Birth: January 26, 1832, Pittsburgh, Pennsylvania.
Education: Ohio University, 1849–1851; Yale University, B.A., 1853, honorary LL.D., 1883; studied law at Yale and privately; admitted to the bar in 1855.
Official Positions: none.
Supreme Court Service: nominated associate justice by President Benjamin Harrison July 19, 1892, to replace Joseph P. Bradley, who had died; confirmed by the Senate July 26, 1892, by a voice vote; took judicial oath October 10, 1892; retired February 23, 1903; replaced by William R. Day, nominated by President Theodore Roosevelt.
Family: married Lillie E. Kennedy, December 31, 1857; two sons.
Death: August 2, 1924, Pittsburgh, Pennsylvania.

Souter, David H.

Birth: September 17, 1939, Melrose, Massachusetts.
Education: Harvard College, B.A., 1961; Oxford University (Rhodes Scholar), 1961–1963; Harvard University Law School, LL.B., 1966.
Official Positions: assistant attorney general, New Hampshire, 1968–1971; deputy attorney general, New Hampshire, 1971–1976; attorney general, New Hampshire, 1976–1978; associate justice, New Hampshire Superior Court, 1978–1983; associate justice, New Hampshire Supreme Court, 1983–1990; judge, U.S. Court of Appeals for the First Circuit, 1990.
Supreme Court Service: nominated associate justice by President George Bush July 23, 1990, to replace William J. Brennan Jr., who had retired; confirmed by the Senate October 2, 1990, by a 90–9 vote; took judicial oath October 9, 1990.
Family: Unmarried.

Stevens, John Paul

Birth: April 20, 1920, Chicago, Illinois.
Education: University of Chicago, B.A., 1941; Northwestern University School of Law, J.D., magna cum laude, 1947.
Official Positions: law clerk to Justice Wiley B. Rutledge, 1947–1948; associate counsel, Subcommittee on the Study of Monopoly Power, House Judiciary Committee, 1951; member, U.S. Attorney General's National Committee to Study the Antitrust Laws, 1953–1955; judge, Seventh Circuit Court of Appeals, 1970–1975.
Supreme Court Service: nominated associate justice by President Gerald R. Ford November 28, 1975, to replace William O. Douglas, who had retired; confirmed by the Senate December 17, 1975, by a 98–0 vote; took judicial oath December 19, 1975.
Family: married Elizabeth Jane Sheeren, 1942, divorced 1979; one son, three daughters; married Maryan Mulholland Simon, 1980.

Stewart, Potter

Birth: January 23, 1915, Jackson, Michigan.
Education: Yale College, B.A., cum laude, 1937; Yale Law School, LL.B., cum laude, 1941; fellow, Cambridge University, Cambridge, England, 1937–1938.

Official Positions: member, Cincinnati, Ohio, city council, 1950–1953; vice mayor of Cincinnati, 1952–1953; judge, Sixth Circuit Court of Appeals, 1954–1958.

Supreme Court Service: received recess appointment as associate justice by President Dwight D. Eisenhower October 14, 1958, to replace Harold H. Burton, who had retired; nominated associate justice by President Eisenhower January 17, 1959; confirmed by the Senate May 5, 1959, by a 70–17 vote; took judicial oath October 14, 1958; retired July 3, 1981; replaced by Sandra Day O'Connor, nominated by President Ronald Reagan.

Family: married Mary Ann Bertles, April 24, 1943; two sons, one daughter.

Death: December 7, 1985, Hanover, New Hampshire.

Stone, Harlan Fiske

Birth: October 11, 1872, Chesterfield, New Hampshire.

Education: Amherst College, A.B., 1894, M.A., 1897, LL.D., 1913; Columbia University, LL.B., 1898.

Official Positions: U.S. attorney general, 1924–1925.

Supreme Court Service: nominated associate justice by President Calvin Coolidge January 5, 1925, to replace Joseph McKenna, who had retired; confirmed by the Senate February 5, 1925, by a 71–6 vote; took judicial oath March 2, 1925; nominated chief justice by President Franklin D. Roosevelt June 12, 1941, to replace Chief Justice Charles Evans Hughes, who had retired; confirmed by the Senate June 27, 1941, by a voice vote; took judicial oath July 3, 1941; served until April 22, 1946; replaced by Fred M. Vinson, nominated by President Harry S. Truman.

Family: married Agnes Harvey, September 7, 1899; two sons.

Death: April 22, 1946, Washington, D.C.

Story, Joseph

Birth: September 18, 1779, Marblehead, Massachusetts.

Education: attended Marblehead Academy; graduated from Harvard, 1798; LL.D., 1821; read law under Samuel Sewall and Samuel Putnam; admitted to bar, 1801.

Official Positions: member, Massachusetts legislature, 1805–1808; Speaker of the House, 1811; U.S. representative, 1808–1809; delegate, Massachusetts Constitutional Convention, 1820.

Supreme Court Service: nominated associate justice by President James Madison November 15, 1811, to replace William Cushing, who had died; confirmed by the Senate November 18, 1811, by a voice vote; took judicial oath February 3, 1812; served until September 10, 1845; replaced by Levi Woodbury, nominated by President James K. Polk.

Family: married Mary Lynde Oliver, December 9, 1804; died June 1805; married Sarah Waldo Wetmore, August 27, 1808; seven children.

Death: September 10, 1845, Cambridge, Massachusetts.

Strong, William

Birth: May 6, 1808, Somers, Connecticut.

Education: Yale College, A.B., 1828; M.A., 1831.

Official Positions: U.S. representative, 1847–1851; Pennsylvania Supreme Court justice, 1857–1868.

Supreme Court Service: nominated associate justice by President Ulysses S. Grant February 7, 1870, to replace Robert C. Grier, who had retired; confirmed by the Senate February 18, 1870, by a voice vote; took judicial oath March 14, 1870; retired December 14, 1880; replaced by William B. Woods, nominated by President Rutherford B. Hayes.

Family: married Priscilla Lee Mallery, November 28, 1836; died 1844; two daughters, one son; married Rachel Davis Bull, a widow, November 22, 1849; two daughters, two sons.

Death: August 19, 1895, Lake Minnewaska, New York.

Sutherland, George

Birth: March 25, 1862, Buckinghamshire, England.

Education: Brigham Young (University) Academy, 1879–1881; University of Michigan Law School, 1882.

Official Positions: Utah state senator, 1896–1900; U.S. representative, 1901–1903; U.S. senator, 1905–1917; chairman, advisory committee to the Washington Conference for the Limitation of Naval Armaments, 1921; U.S. counsel, Norway–United States arbitration, The Hague, 1921–1922.

Supreme Court Service: nominated associate justice by President Warren G. Harding September 5, 1922, to replace Justice John H. Clarke, who had resigned; took judicial oath October 2, 1922; confirmed by the Senate September 5, 1922, by a voice vote; retired January 17, 1938; replaced by Stanley F. Reed, nominated by President Franklin D. Roosevelt.

Family: married Rosamund Lee, June 18, 1883; two daughters, one son.

Death: July 18, 1942, Stockbridge, Massachusetts.

Swayne, Noah Haynes

Birth: December 7, 1804, Frederick County, Virginia.

Education: studied law privately; admitted to the bar in Warrenton, Virginia, in 1823.

Official Positions: Coshocton County (Ohio) prosecuting attorney, 1826–1829; Ohio state representative, 1830 and 1836; U.S. attorney for Ohio, 1830–1841; Columbus city councilman, 1834.

Supreme Court Service: nominated associate justice by President Abraham Lincoln January 21, 1862, to replace John McLean, who had died; confirmed by the Senate January 24, 1862, by a 38–1 vote; took judicial oath January 27, 1862; retired January 24, 1881; replaced by Stanley Matthews, nominated by President Rutherford B. Hayes and renominated by President James A. Garfield.

Family: married Sarah Ann Wager, 1832; four sons, one daughter.

Death: June 8, 1884, New York City.

Taft, William Howard

Birth: September 15, 1857, Cincinnati, Ohio.

Education: Yale University, A.B., class salutatorian, 1878; Cincinnati Law School, LL.B., 1880.

Official Positions: assistant prosecuting attorney, Hamilton County, Ohio, 1881–1883; assistant county solicitor, Hamilton County, 1885–1887; judge, Ohio Superior Court, 1887–1890; U.S. solicitor general, 1890–1891; judge, U.S. District Court for the Sixth Circuit, 1892–1900; chairman, Philippine Commission, 1900–1901; governor general of the Philippines, 1901–1904; secretary of war, 1904–1908; president of the United States, 1909–1913; joint chairman, National War Labor Board, 1918–1919.

Supreme Court Service: nominated chief justice by President Warren G. Harding June 30, 1921, to replace Chief Justice Edward D. White, who had died; confirmed by the Senate June 30, 1921, by a voice vote; took judicial oath July 11, 1921; retired February 3, 1930; replaced by Chief Justice Charles Evans Hughes, nominated by President Herbert Hoover.

Family: married Helen Herron, June 19, 1886; two sons, one daughter.

Death: March 8, 1930, in Washington, D.C.

Taney, Roger Brooke

Birth: March 17, 1777, Calvert County, Maryland.

Education: graduated from Dickinson College in Pennsylvania, 1795, honorary LL.D.; read law in office of Judge Jeremiah Chase in Annapolis.

Official Positions: member, Maryland House of Delegates, 1799–1800; Maryland state senator, 1816–1821; Maryland attorney general, 1827–1831; chairman, Jackson Central Committee for Maryland, 1827–1828; U.S. attorney general, 1831–1833; acting secretary of war, 1831; U.S. secretary of the Treasury, 1833–1834 (appointment rejected by Senate).

Supreme Court Service: nominated chief justice by President Andrew Jackson December 28, 1835, to replace John Marshall, who had died; confirmed by the Senate on March 15, 1836, by a 29–15 vote; took judicial oath March 28, 1836; served until October 12, 1864; replaced by Salmon P. Chase, nominated by President Abraham Lincoln.

Family: married Anne Phoebe Carlton Key, January 7, 1806; died 1855; six daughters; one son died in infancy.

Death: October 12, 1864, Washington, D.C.

Thomas, Clarence

Birth: June 23, 1948, Pin Point, Georgia.

Education: Immaculate Conception Seminary, 1967–1968; Holy Cross College, B.A., 1971; Yale University Law School, J.D., 1974.

Official Positions: assistant attorney general, Missouri, 1974–1977; assistant secretary of education for civil rights, 1981–1982; chairman, Equal Employment Opportunity Commission, 1982–1990; judge, U.S. Court of Appeals for the District of Columbia, 1990–1991.

Supreme Court Service: nominated associate justice by President George Bush July 1, 1991, to replace Thurgood Marshall, who had retired; confirmed by the Senate October 15, 1991, by a 52–48 vote; took judicial oath October 23, 1991.

Family: married Kathy Grace Ambush, 1971; one son; divorced 1984; married Virginia Lamp, 1987.

Thompson, Smith

Birth: January 17, 1768, Dutchess County, New York.

Education: graduated Princeton, 1788; read law under James Kent; admitted to the bar, 1792; honorary law doctorates from Yale, 1824; Princeton, 1824; and Harvard, 1835.

Official Positions: member, New York state legislature, 1800; member, New York Constitutional Convention, 1801; associate justice, New York Supreme Court, 1802–1814; appointed to New York State Board of Regents, 1813; chief justice, New York Supreme Court, 1814–1818; secretary of the Navy, 1819–1823.

Supreme Court Service: nominated associate justice by President James Monroe December 8, 1823, to replace Brockholst Livingston, who had died; confirmed by the Senate December 19, 1823, by a voice vote; took judicial oath February 10, 1823; served until December 18, 1843; replaced by Samuel Nelson, nominated by President John Tyler.

Family: married Sarah Livingston, 1794; died September 22, 1833; two sons, two daughters; married Eliza Livingston; two daughters, one son.

Death: December 18, 1843, Poughkeepsie, New York.

Todd, Thomas

Birth: January 23, 1765, King and Queen County, Virginia.

Education: graduated from Liberty Hall (now Washington and Lee University), Lexington, Virginia, 1783; read law under Harry Innes; admitted to bar in 1788.

Official Positions: clerk, federal district for Kentucky, 1792–1801; clerk, Kentucky House of Representatives, 1792–1801; clerk, Kentucky Court of Appeals (Supreme Court), 1799–1801; judge, Kentucky Court of Appeals, 1801–1806; chief justice, 1806–1807.

Supreme Court Service: nominated associate justice by President Thomas Jefferson February 28, 1807, to fill a newly created seat; confirmed by the Senate March 3, 1807, by a voice vote; took judicial oath May 4, 1807; served until February 7, 1826; replaced by Robert Trimble, nominated by President John Quincy Adams.

Family: married Elizabeth Harris, 1788; died 1811; five children; married Lucy Payne, 1812; three children.

Death: February 7, 1826, Frankfort, Kentucky.

Trimble, Robert

Birth: November 17, 1776, Berkeley County, Virginia.

Education: Bourbon Academy; Kentucky Academy; read law under George Nicholas and James Brown; admitted to the bar in 1803.

Official Positions: Kentucky state representative, 1802; judge, Kentucky Court of Appeals, 1807–1809; U.S. district attorney for Kentucky, 1813–1817; U.S. district judge, 1817–1826.

Supreme Court Service: nominated associate justice by President John Quincy Adams April 11, 1826, to replace Thomas Todd, who had died; confirmed by the Senate May 9, 1826, by a 27–5 vote; took judicial oath June 16, 1826; served until August 25, 1828; replaced by John McLean, nominated by President Andrew Jackson.

Family: married Nancy Timberlake, August 18, 1803; at least ten children.

Death: August 25, 1828, Paris, Kentucky.

Van Devanter, Willis

Birth: April 17, 1859, Marion, Indiana.

Education: Indiana Asbury University, A.B., 1878; University of Cincinnati Law School, LL.B., 1881.

Official Positions: city attorney, Cheyenne, 1887–1888; member, Wyoming territorial legislature, 1888; chief justice, Wyoming Territory Supreme Court, 1889–1890; assistant attorney general, Department of the Interior, 1897–1903; judge, U.S. Court of Appeals for the Eighth Circuit, 1903–1910.

Supreme Court Service: nominated associate justice by President William Howard Taft December 12, 1910, to replace Edward D. White, who became chief justice; confirmed by the Senate December 15, 1910, by a voice vote; took judicial oath January 3, 1911; retired June 2, 1937; replaced by Hugo L. Black, nominated by President Franklin D. Roosevelt.

Family: married Dellice Burhans, October 10, 1883; two sons.

Death: February 8, 1941, Washington, D.C.

Vinson, Frederick Moore

Birth: January 22, 1890, Louisa, Kentucky.

Education: Kentucky Normal College, 1908; Centre College, A.B., 1909; LL.B., 1911.

Official Positions: commonwealth attorney, Thirty-second Judicial District of Kentucky, 1921–1924; U.S. representative, 1924–1929, 1931–1938; judge, U.S. Court of Appeals for the District of Columbia, 1938–1943; director, Office of Economic Stabilization, 1943–1945; administrator, Federal Loan Agency, 1945; director, Office of War Mobilization and Reconversion, 1945; secretary of the Treasury, 1945–1946.

Supreme Court Service: nominated chief justice by President Harry S. Truman June 6, 1946, to replace Chief Justice Harlan F. Stone, who had died; confirmed by the Senate June 20, 1946, by a voice vote; took judicial oath June 24, 1946; served until September 8, 1953; replaced by Earl Warren, nominated by President Dwight D. Eisenhower.

Family: married Roberta Dixson, January 24, 1923; two sons.

Death: September 8, 1953, Washington, D.C.

Waite, Morrison R.

Birth: November 27, 1816, Lyme, Connecticut.

Education: graduated from Yale College, 1837.

Official Positions: Ohio state representative, 1850–1852; representative to the Geneva Arbitration, 1871; president of the Ohio Constitutional Convention, 1873–1874.

Supreme Court Service: nominated chief justice by President Ulysses S. Grant January 19, 1874, to replace Salmon P. Chase, who had died; confirmed by the Senate January 21, 1874, by a 63–0 vote; took judicial oath March 4, 1874; served until March 23, 1888; replaced by Melville W. Fuller, nominated by President Grover Cleveland.

Family: married his second cousin, Amelia C. Warner, September 21, 1840; five children.

Death: March 23, 1888, Washington, D.C.

Warren, Earl

Birth: March 19, 1891, Los Angeles, California.

Education: University of California, B.L., 1912; J.D., 1914.

Official Positions: deputy city attorney, Oakland, California, 1919–1920; deputy district attorney, Alameda County, 1920–1925; district attorney, Alameda County, 1925–1939; California attorney general, 1939–1943; governor, 1943–1953.

Supreme Court Service: nominated chief justice by President Dwight D. Eisenhower September 30, 1953, to replace Chief Justice Fred M. Vinson, who had died; confirmed by the Senate March 1, 1954, by a voice vote; took judicial oath October 5, 1953; retired June 23, 1969; replaced by Warren E. Burger, nominated by President Richard Nixon.

Family: married Nina P. Meyers, October 14, 1925; three sons, three daughters.

Death: July 9, 1974, Washington, D.C.

Washington, Bushrod

Birth: June 5, 1762, Westmoreland County, Virginia.

Education: privately tutored; graduated College of William and Mary, 1778; read law under James Wilson; member, Virginia bar; honorary LL.D. degrees from Harvard, Princeton, and University of Pennsylvania.

Official Positions: member, Virginia House of Delegates, 1787; member, Virginia convention to ratify U.S. Constitution, 1788.

Supreme Court Service: nominated associate justice by President John Adams December 19, 1798, to replace James Wilson, who had died; confirmed by the Senate December 20, 1798, by a voice vote; took judicial oath February 4, 1799; served until November 26, 1829; replaced by Henry Baldwin, nominated by President Andrew Jackson.

Family: married Julia Ann Blackburn, 1785.

Death: November 26, 1829, in Philadelphia, Pennsylvania.

Wayne, James M.

Birth: 1790, Savannah, Georgia.

Education: College of New Jersey (Princeton University), 1808, honorary LL.B., 1849; read law under three lawyers including Judge Charles Chauncey of New Haven; admitted to the bar January 1811.

Official Positions: member, Georgia House of Representatives, 1815–1816; mayor, Savannah, 1817–1819; judge, Savannah Court of Common Pleas, 1820–1822; Georgia Superior Court, 1822–1828; U.S. representative, 1829–1835; chairman, Committee on Foreign Relations.

Supreme Court Service: nominated associate justice by President Andrew Jackson January 7, 1835, to replace William Johnson, who had died; confirmed by the Senate January 9, 1835 by a voice vote; took judicial oath January 14, 1835; served until July 5, 1867; replaced by Joseph Bradley, nominated by President Ulysses S. Grant.

Family: married Mary Johnson Campbell, 1813; three children.

Death: July 5, 1867, Washington, D.C.

White, Byron R.

Birth: June 8, 1917, Fort Collins, Colorado.

Education: University of Colorado, B.A., 1938; Rhodes Scholar, Oxford University, 1939; Yale Law School, LL.B., magna cum laude, 1946.

Official Positions: law clerk to Chief Justice Fred M. Vinson, 1946–1947; deputy U.S. attorney general, 1961–1962.

Supreme Court Service: nominated associate justice by President John F. Kennedy March 30, 1962, to replace Charles E. Whittaker, who had retired; confirmed by the Senate April 11, 1962, by a voice vote; took judicial oath April 16, 1962; retired June 28, 1993; replaced by Ruth Bader Ginsburg, nominated by President Bill Clinton.

Family: married Marion Stearns, 1946; one son, one daughter.

Death: April 15, 2002, Denver, Colorado.

White, Edward D.

Birth: November 3, 1845, Lafourche Parish, Louisiana.

Education: Mount St. Mary's College, Emmitsburg, Maryland, 1856; Georgetown College (University), Washington, D.C., 1857–1861; studied law at University of Louisiana (Tulane) and with Edward Bermudez; admitted to the bar in 1868.

Official Positions: Louisiana state senator, 1874; associate justice, Louisiana Supreme Court, 1878–1880; U.S. senator, 1891–1894.

Supreme Court Service: nominated associate justice by President Grover Cleveland February 19, 1894, to replace Samuel Blatchford, who had died; confirmed by the Senate February 19, 1894, by a voice vote; took judicial oath March 12, 1894. Nominated chief justice by President William Howard Taft December 12, 1910, to replace Melville Fuller, who had died; confirmed by the Senate December 12, 1910, by a voice vote; took judicial oath December 19, 1910; served until May 19, 1921; replaced as chief justice by former president Taft, appointed by President Warren G. Harding.

Family: married Virginia Montgomery Kent, November 1894.

Death: May 19, 1921, in Washington, D.C.

Whittaker, Charles E.

Birth: February 22, 1901, Troy, Kansas.

Education: University of Kansas City Law School, LL.B., 1924.

Official Positions: judge, U.S. District Court for Western District of Missouri, 1954–1956; judge, Eighth Circuit Court of Appeals, 1956–1957.

Supreme Court Service: nominated associate justice by President Dwight D. Eisenhower March 2, 1957, to replace Stanley Reed, who had retired; confirmed by the Senate March 19, 1957, by a voice vote; took judicial oath March 25, 1957; retired March 31, 1962; replaced by Byron R. White, nominated by President John F. Kennedy.

Family: married Winifred R. Pugh, July 7, 1928; three sons.

Death: November 26, 1973, Kansas City, Missouri.

Wilson, James

Birth: September 14, 1742, Caskardy, Scotland.

Education: attended University of St. Andrews (Scotland); read law in office of John Dickinson; admitted to the bar in 1767; honorary M.A., College of Philadelphia, 1776; honorary LL.D., 1790.

Official Positions: delegate, first Provincial Convention at Philadelphia, 1774; delegate, Continental Congress, 1775–1777, 1783, 1785–1787; delegate, U.S. Constitutional Convention, 1787; delegate, Pennsylvania convention to ratify U.S. Constitution, 1787.

Supreme Court Service: nominated associate justice by President George Washington September 24, 1789; confirmed by the Senate September 26, 1789, by a voice vote; took judicial oath October 5, 1789; served until August 21, 1798; replaced by Bushrod Washington, nominated by President John Adams.

Family: married Rachel Bird, November 5, 1771; died 1786; six children; married Hannah Gray, September 19, 1793; one son died in infancy.

Death: August 21, 1798, Edenton, North Carolina.

Woodbury, Levi

Birth: December 22, 1789, Francestown, New Hampshire.

Education: Dartmouth College, graduated with honors, 1809; Tapping Reeve Law School, ca. 1810.

Official Positions: clerk, New Hampshire Senate, 1816; associate justice, New Hampshire Superior Court, 1817–1823; governor, New Hampshire, 1823–1824; Speaker, New Hampshire House, 1825; U.S. senator, 1825–1831, 1841–1845; secretary of the Navy, 1831–1834; secretary of the Treasury, 1834–1841.

Supreme Court Service: nominated associate justice by President James K. Polk December 23, 1845, to replace Justice Joseph Story, who had died; confirmed by the Senate January 3, 1846, by voice vote; took judicial oath September 23, 1845; served until September 4, 1851; replaced by Benjamin R. Curtis, nominated by President Millard Fillmore.

Family: married Elizabeth Williams Clapp, June 1819; four daughters, one son.

Death: September 4, 1851, Portsmouth, New Hampshire.

Woods, William B.

Birth: August 3, 1824, Newark, Ohio.

Education: attended Western Reserve College for three years; graduated from Yale University, 1845.

Official Positions: mayor of Newark, Ohio, 1856; Ohio state representative, 1858–1862, Speaker in 1858–1860 and minority leader in 1860–1862; chancellor, middle chancery district of Alabama, 1868–1869; U.S. circuit judge for the Fifth Circuit, 1869–1880.

Supreme Court Service: nominated associate justice by President Rutherford B. Hayes December 15, 1880, to replace William Strong, who had retired; confirmed by the Senate December 21, 1880, by a 39–8 vote; took judicial oath January 5, 1881; served until May 14, 1887; replaced by Lucius Q. C. Lamar, nominated by President Grover Cleveland.

Family: married Anne E. Warner, June 21, 1855; one son, one daughter.

Death: May 14, 1887, Washington, D.C.

SOURCE: Adapted from Joan Biskupic and Elder Witt, *Congressional Quarterly's Guide to the U.S. Supreme Court,* 3d ed. (Washington, D.C.: Congressional Quarterly, 1997), 855–962. Updated by the author.

Succession Chart of . . .

YEAR	CHIEF JUSTICE	SEAT 2	SEAT 3	SEAT 4
1789	Jay	Rutledge, J.	Cushing	Wilson
1790–1791				
1791–1793		Johnson, T.		
1793–1795		Paterson		
1795	Rutledge, J.			
1796–1798	Ellsworth			
1799				Washington
1800				
1801–1803	Marshall, J.			
1804–1806				
1807–1810		Livingston		
1811			(vacant)	
1811–1823			Story	
1824–1826		Thompson		
1826–1828				
1829				
1830–1834				Baldwin
1835				
1836	Taney			
1837–1841				
1841–1843				
1844		(vacant)		
1845		Nelson		(vacant)
1846–1851			Woodbury	Grier
1852			Curtis	
1853–1857				
1858–1860			Clifford	
1861				
1862				
1863–1864				
1865	Chase, S.P.			
1866–1867				
1868–1869				
1870–1872				Strong
1873		Hunt		
1874–1877	Waite			
1877–1880				

. . . Supreme Court Seats

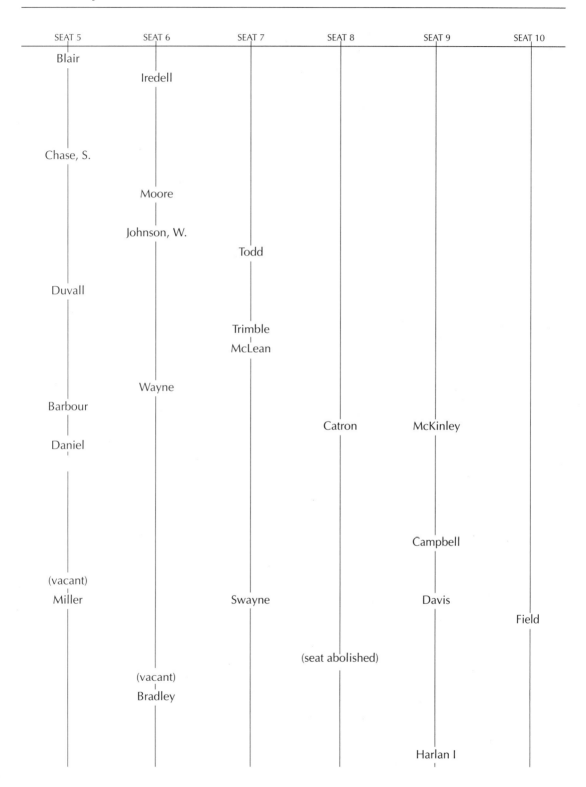

SEAT 5	SEAT 6	SEAT 7	SEAT 8	SEAT 9	SEAT 10
Blair					
	Iredell				
Chase, S.					
	Moore				
	Johnson, W.				
		Todd			
Duvall					
		Trimble			
		McLean			
	Wayne				
Barbour			Catron	McKinley	
Daniel					
				Campbell	
(vacant)					
Miller		Swayne		Davis	
					Field
			(seat abolished)		
	(vacant)				
	Bradley				
				Harlan I	

YEAR	CHIEF JUSTICE	SEAT 2	SEAT 3	SEAT 4
1881				Woods
1882–1887		Blatchford	Gray	
1888				Lamar, L.
1888–1889	Fuller			
1889–1890				
1891				
1892				
1893				Jackson, H.
1894–1895		White, E.		
1896–1897				Peckham
1898–1902				
1903–1906			Holmes	
1907–1909				
1910				Lurton
1910–1911	White, E.	Van Devanter		
1912–1914				
1914–1916				McReynolds
1916–1921				
1921–1922	Taft			
1922				
1923–1924				
1925–1930				
1930–1931	Hughes			
1932–1937			Cardozo	
1937		Black		
1938				
1939			Frankfurter	
1940–1941				
1941–1942	Stone			Byrnes
1943–1945				Rutledge, W.
1945–1946				
1946–1949	Vinson			
1949–1953				Minton
1953–1954	Warren			
1955–1956				
1957–1958				Brennan
1959–1962				
1962–1965			Goldberg	
1965–1967			Fortas	

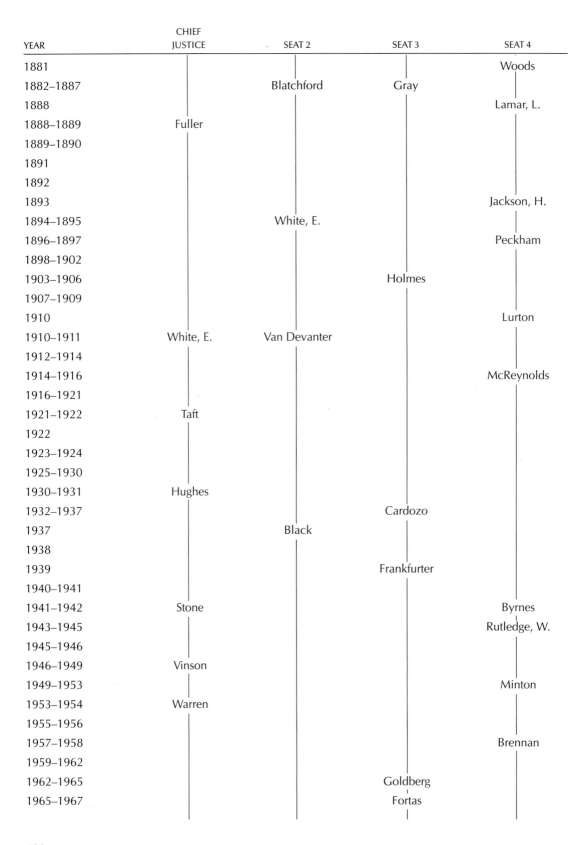

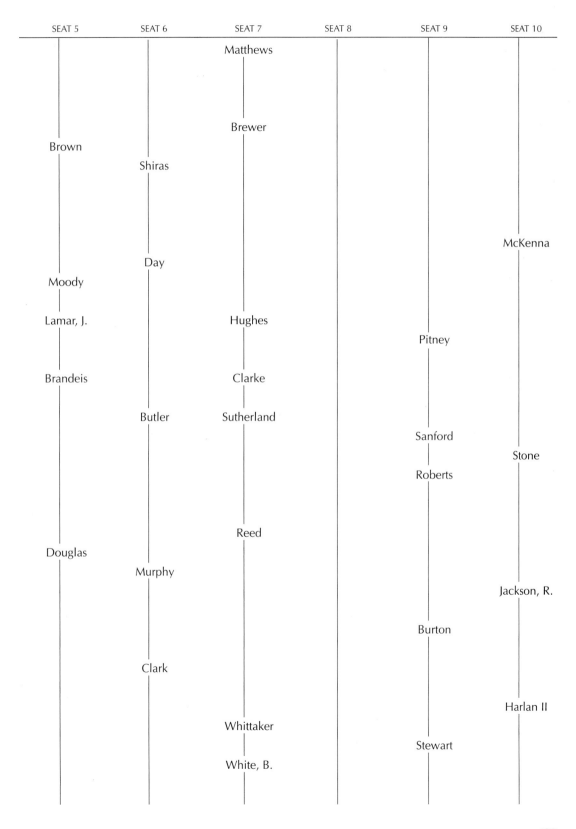

SEAT 5	SEAT 6	SEAT 7	SEAT 8	SEAT 9	SEAT 10
		Matthews			
		Brewer			
Brown	Shiras				
					McKenna
	Day				
Moody					
Lamar, J.		Hughes		Pitney	
Brandeis		Clarke			
	Butler	Sutherland		Sanford	
					Stone
				Roberts	
		Reed			
Douglas	Murphy				Jackson, R.
				Burton	
	Clark				Harlan II
		Whittaker		Stewart	
		White, B.			

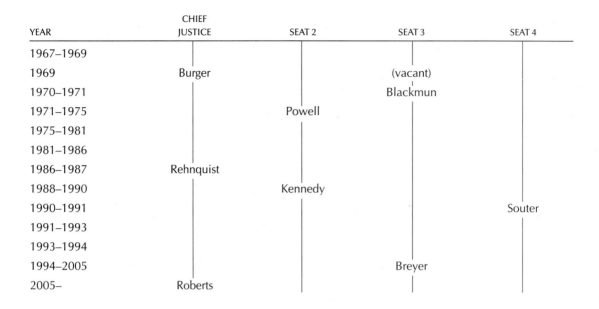

YEAR	CHIEF JUSTICE	SEAT 2	SEAT 3	SEAT 4
1967–1969				
1969	Burger		(vacant)	
1970–1971			Blackmun	
1971–1975		Powell		
1975–1981				
1981–1986				
1986–1987	Rehnquist			
1988–1990		Kennedy		
1990–1991				Souter
1991–1993				
1993–1994				
1994–2005			Breyer	
2005–	Roberts			

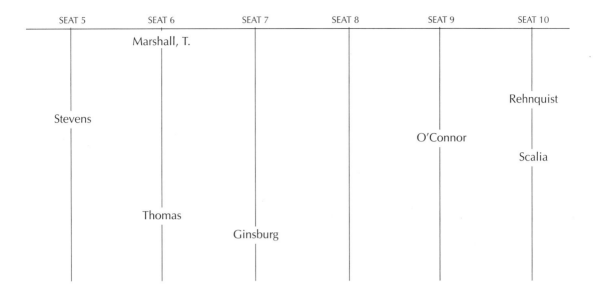

SEAT 5	SEAT 6	SEAT 7	SEAT 8	SEAT 9	SEAT 10
	Marshall, T.				
					Rehnquist
Stevens				O'Connor	
					Scalia
	Thomas				
		Ginsburg			

SOURCE: Kenneth Jost, ed. The Supreme Court A to Z, 3d. ed. (Washington, D.C.: CQ Press, 2003), 520–522.

THUMBNAIL SKETCH OF THE SUPREME COURT'S HISTORY

Court Era	Chief Justices	Defining Characteristics	Major Court Cases
Developmental Period (1789–1800)	John Jay (1789–1795) John Rutledge (1795) Oliver Ellsworth (1796–1800)	Low prestige: spotty attendance by justices, resignations for more "prestigious positions," hears about fifty cases Business of the Court: largely admiralty and maritime disputes Use of seriatim opinion practice	*Bingham v. Cabbot* (1795) *Bingham v. Cabot* (1798)
The Marshall Court (1801–1835)	John Marshall (1801–1835)	Establishment of Court's role in governmental process Strong Court support for national powers (especially commerce) over states' rights Use of "Opinions of the Court," rather than seriatim practice Beginning of systematic reporting of Court opinions Despite the importance of Court opinions interpreting the Constitution, the business of the Court continues to involve private law issues (maritime, property, contracts)	*Marbury v. Madison* (1803) *Fairfax's Devisee v. Hunter's Lessee* (1813) *Martin v. Hunter's Lessee* (1816) *McCulloch v. Maryland* (1819) *Gibbons v. Ogden* (1824) *Cherokee Nation v. Georgia* (1831) *Worcester v. Georgia* (1832) *Wheaton v. Peters* (1834) *Proprietors of Charles River Bridge v. Proprietors of Warren Bridge* (1837)
Taney and Civil War Courts (1836–1888)	Roger Taney (1836–1864) Salmon Chase (1864–1873) Morrison Waite (1874–1888)	Continued assertion of federal power over states (with some accommodation for state police powers) Growing North–South splits on the Court Court showdowns with Congress at the onset and conclusion of the Civil War Growth of Court's caseload, with the majority of post–Civil War cases involving private law issues and war litigation Congress fixes Court size at nine	*United States v. Libellants and Claimants of the Schooner Amistad* (1841) *Luther v. Borden* (1849) *Dred Scott v. Sandford* (1857) *Ableman v. Booth* (1859) *Ex parte Vallandigham* (1864) *Ex parte Milligan* (1866) *Cherokee Tobacco Case* (1871) *The Butchers' Benevolent Association of New Orleans v. The Crescent City Livestock Landing and Slaughterhouse Co.* (1873) *Esteben v. Louisiana* (1873)

Court Era	Chief Justices	Defining Characteristics	Major Court Cases
			Bradwell v. Illinois (1873) *Minor v. Happersett* (1875) *Reynolds v. United States* (1879) *United States v. Stanley* (1883) *United States v. Ryan* (1883) *United States v. Nichols* (1883) *United States v. Singleton* (1883) *Robinson and Wife v. Memphis and Charleston Railroad Co.* (1883) *Yick Wo v. Hopkins* (1886)
Conservative Court Eras (1889–1937)	Melville Fuller (1888–1910) Edward White (1910–1921) William Howard Taft (1921–1930) Charles Evans Hughes (1930–1937)	But for a brief period reflecting progressivism, the Courts of this era tended to protect business interests over governmental police powers Court sets "civil rights" policy of "separate but equal" Congress relieves justices of circuit-riding duty Congress, in 1925 Judiciary Act, gives Court greater discretion over its docket Despite Judiciary Act, Court's docket continues to grow, with many cases reflecting economic issues (for example, congressional power under the Commerce Clause) Some important construction of Bill of Rights guarantees (protection of rights increases after WW I) Showdown with FDR over New Deal legislation: Court continues to strike down New Deal, leading the president to propose a Court-packing plan	*In re Neagle* (1890) *Fong Yue Ting v. United States* (1893) *Pollock v. Farmer's Loan and Trust Co. I* (1895) *Pollock v. Farmer's Loan and Trust Co. II* (1895) *In re Debs* (1895) *Plessy v. Ferguson* (1896) *Williams v. Fears* (1900) *De Lima v. Bidwell* (1901) *Downes v. Bidwell* (1901) *Lone Wolf v. Hitchcock* (1903) *Lochner v. New York* (1905) *Patterson v. Colorado* (1907) *Loewe v. Lawlor* (1908) *Berea College v. Kentucky* (1908) *Muller v. Oregon* (1908) *Standard Oil Co. of New Jersey v. United States* (1911) *Lawlor v. Loewe* (1915) *Frank v. Magnum* (1915) *Caminetti v. United States* (1917) *Buchanan v. Warley* (1917) *Goldman v. United States* (1918) *Hammer v. Dagenhart* (1918) *Schenck v. United States* (1919) *Debs v. United States* (1919) *Abrams v. United States* (1919)

Court Era	Chief Justices	Defining Characteristics	Major Court Cases
			Adkins v. Children's Hospital (1923)
			Pierce v. Society of Sisters (1925)
			Gitlow v. New York (1925)
			Village of Euclid v. Ambler Realty Co. (1926)
			Nixon v. Herndon (1927)
			Buck v. Bell (1927)
			Whitney v. California (1927)
			United States v. Macintosh (1931)
			Near v. Minnesota (1931)
			Nixon v. Condon (1932)
			Powell v. Alabama (1932)
			Nebbia v. New York (1934)
			Norris v. Alabama (1935)
			Humphrey's Executor v. United States (1935)
			Schechter Poultry Corp. v. United States (1935)
			United States v. Butler (1936)
			National Labor Relations Board v. Jones and Laughlin Steel Corp. (1937)
The Roosevelt and World War II Court Eras (1937–1953)	Charles Evans Hughes (1937–1941) Harlan Fiske Stone (1941–1946) Fred Vinson (1946–1953)	With the "switch in time that saved nine" the Court begins to uphold federal regulations under the Commerce Clause, as well as state use of police powers Expansion of rights and liberties, until WW II and ensuing cold war Increases in nonconsensual behavior (dissents and concurrences) among the justices	*Cantwell v. Connecticut* (1940) *Minersville School District v. Gobitis* (1940) *Bridges v. California* (1941) *Chaplinsky v. New Hampshire* (1942) *Ex Parte Quirin* (1942) *Parker v. Brown* (1943) *West Virginia State Board of Education v. Barnette* (1943) *Hirabayashi v. United States* (1943) *Smith v. Allwright* (1944) *Korematsu v. United States* (1944) *Screws v. United States* (1945) *Bridges v. Wixon* (1945) *In re Yamashita* (1946) *Louisiana ex rel. Francis v. Resweber* (1947) *Sipuel v. Oklahoma State Board of Regents* (1948)

Court Era	Chief Justices	Defining Characteristics	Major Court Cases
			Shelley v. Kraemer (1948) *Dennis v. United States* (1951) *Youngstown Sheet and Tube Co. v. Sawyer* (1952)
The Warren Court Era (1953–1969)	Earl Warren (1953–1969)	Expansion of rights, liberties, and criminal justice Establishment of the right to privacy Emergence of Court as national policy maker Continued increase in Court's docket, with steady growth in the number of *in forma pauperis* petitions Growth in the percentage of constitutional cases on Court's plenary docket First black justice (Marshall) appointed to the Court	*Rosenberg v. United States* (1953) *Brown v. Board of Education of Topeka* (1954) *Bates v. City of Little Rock* (1960) *Mapp v. Ohio* (1961) *Baker v. Carr* (1962) *Engel v. Vitale* (1962) *NAACP v. Button* (1963) *Gideon v. Wainwright* (1963) *School District of Abingdon Township v. Schempp* (1963) *New York Times Co. v. Sullivan* (1964) *Bell v. Maryland* (1964) *Reynolds v. Sims* (1964) *Heart Of Atlanta Motel v. United States* (1964) *United States v. Seeger* (1965) *Griswold v. Connecticut* (1965) *United States v. Price* (1966) *Miranda v. Arizona* (1966) *Time, Inc. v. Hill* (1967) *Loving v. Virginia* (1967) *In re Gault* (1967) *Katz v. United States* (1967) *Epperson v. Arkansas* (1968) *Terry v. Ohio* (1968) *Tinker v. Des Moines Independent Community School District* (1969) *Red Lion Broadcasting Co. v. Federal Communications Commission* (1969) *Brandenburg v. Ohio* (1969) *Powell v. McCormack* (1969) *Goldberg v. Kelly* (1970) *Oregon v. Mitchell* (1970)
Republican Court Eras (1969–)	Warren Burger (1969–1986) William Rehnquist (1986–2005)	Attempts in some areas (for example, criminal law) to limit or rescind Warren Court rulings	*Griggs v. Duke Power Co.* (1971) *Swann v. Charlotte-Mecklenburg County Board of Education* (1971)

Court Era	Chief Justices	Defining Characteristics	Major Court Cases
	John G. Roberts Jr. (2005–)	Expansion of women's rights, including right to abortion Some attempt to increase state power Legitimation of affirmative action policies Court increasingly called on to resolve intergovernmental disputes involving separation of powers or the authority of one branch of government over another Appointment of first woman (O'Connor) to the Court Rejection of race-based legislative districting Increased recognition of gay rights Intervention in the 2000 presidential election Further definition of reasonable accommodation under Americans with Disability Act Recognition of legal limits on technology to investigate crimes Continued focus on political campaign finance Reviews of due process rights for enemy combatants in terrorism-related cases Rulings on public displays of religious symbols	*Lemon v. Kurtzman* (1971) *New York Times Co. v. United States* (1971) *Reed v. Reed* (1971) *Sierra Club v. Morton* (1972) *Wisconsin v. Yoder* (1972) *Flood v. Kuhn* (1972) *Furman v. Georgia* (1972) *Branzburg v. Hayes* (1972) *Roe v. Wade* (1973) *San Antonio Independent School District v. Rodriguez* (1973) *Frontiero v. Richardson* (1973) *Miller v. California* (1973) *Cleveland Board of Education v. LaFleur* (1974) *Gertz v. Robert Welch* (1974) *Miami Herald v. Tornillo* (1974) *United States v. Nixon* (1974) *Buckley v. Valeo* (1976) *Dothard v. Rawlinson* (1977) *Regents of the University of California v. Bakke* (1978) *Richmond Newspapers, Inc. v. Virginia* (1980) *Chandler v. Florida* (1981) *Kissinger v. Halperin* (1981) *Plyler v. Doe* (1982) *Nixon v. Fitzgerald* (1982) *Bob Jones University v. United States* (1983) *Immigration and Naturalization Service v. Chadha* (1983) *Roberts v. United States Jaycees* (1984) *New Jersey v. T.L.O.* (1985) *Wallace v. Jaffree* (1985) *Meritor Savings Bank v. Vinson* (1986) *Bowers v. Hardwick* (1986) *Johnson v. Transportation Agency, Santa Clara County* (1987) *Edwards v. Aguillard* (1987) *Hazelwood School District v. Kuhlmeier* (1988)

Court Era	Chief Justices	Defining Characteristics	Major Court Cases
			Hustler Magazine, Inc. v. Falwell (1988)
			Thompson v. Oklahoma (1988)
			DeShaney v. Winnebago County Department of Social Services (1989)
			Price Waterhouse v. Hopkins (1989)
			Texas v. Johnson (1989)
			Employment Division, Dept. of Human Resources of Oregon v. Smith (1990)
			Cruzan v. Director, Missouri Department of Health (1990)
			Hodgson v. Minnesota (1990)
			Lee v. Weisman (1992)
			Church of the Lukumi Babalu Aye, Inc. and Ernesto Pichardo v. City of Hialeah (1993)
			Shaw v. Reno (1993)
			United States v. Lopez (1995)
			Vernonia School District 47J v. Acton (1995)
			Shaw v. Hunt (1996)
			Romer v. Evans (1996)
			United States v. Virginia (1996)
			Clinton v. Jones (1997)
			Agostini v. Felton (1997)
			City of Boerne v. Flores (1997)
			Vacco v. Quill (1997)
			Reno v. American Civil Liberties Union (1997)
			Davis v. Monroe County Board of Education (1999)
			Hunt v. Cromartie (1999)
			United States v. Playboy Entertainment Group, Inc. (2000)
			Santa Fe Independent School District v. Doe (2000)
			Apprendi v. New Jersey (2000)
			Boy Scouts of America v. Dale (2000)
			Bush v. Gore (2000)
			Easley v. Cromartie (2001)
			PGA Tour v. Martin (2001)
			Kyllo v. United States (2001)

Court Era	Chief Justices	Defining Characteristics	Major Court Cases
			Good News Club v. Milford Central School (2001)
			Zelman v. Simmons-Harris (2002)
			Republican Party of Minnesota v. White (2002)
			Lawrence v. Texas (2003)
			Grutter v. Bollinger (2003)
			McConnell v. Federal Election Commission (2003)
			Elk Grove Unified School District v. Newdow (2004)
			Al Odah v. United States (2004)
			Hamdi v. Rumsfeld (2004)
			Rasul v. Bush (2004)
			Rumsfeld v. Padilla (2004)
			Roper v. Simmons (2005)
			Gonzalez v. Raich (2005)
			Kelo v. City of New London (2005)
			McCreary County, Kentucky v. American Civil Liberties Union of Kentucky (2005)
			MGM v. Grokster (2005)
			Van Orden v. Perry (2005)

SOURCE: Adapted from Lee Epstein and Thomas G. Walker, *Constitutional Law for a Changing America: Rights, Liberties, and Justice,* 5th ed. (Washington, D.C.: CQ Press, 2004).

ONLINE SOURCES OF DECISIONS

By using the Internet, one can read the full text of Supreme Court decisions and listen to oral arguments from historic cases. The following sites are some of the best.

U.S. Supreme Court Web site

supremecourtus.gov

The U.S. Supreme Court's Web site opened April 17, 2000. Opinions are available the day they are handed down, although the Cornell University or FindLaw sites are often quicker. In addition to opinions, the site contains basic information about the Court and its operations: rules, argument calendars, bar admission forms, visitors' guides, and a small number of photographs and historical materials.

Cornell Legal Information Institute

supct.law.cornell.edu/supct/index.html

Although several Internet sites provide Supreme Court opinions, the Cornell Legal Information Institute is a popular choice because it is so easy to use.

Cornell offers the full text of all Supreme Court decisions from May 1990 to the present. Decisions are posted the same day the Court releases them and can be accessed by using the name of the first party, the name of the second party, keyword, date, and other variables.

The site also provides nearly 600 historic Supreme Court decisions dating back to the Court's beginnings on such topics as school prayer, abortion, administrative law, copyright, patent law, and trademarks. Cases can be accessed by topic, party name, or opinion author.

The site also has the full text of the Supreme Court Rules, the Court calendar for the current term, the schedule of oral arguments, biographical data about current and former justices, and a glossary of legal terms.

liibulletin

Send an email message to listserv@listserv.law.cornell.edu

The liibulletin is a free mailing list that alerts subscribers when new Supreme Court decisions are placed on the Internet. The list provides syllabi of new decisions, in addition to instructions about how to obtain the full text. Cornell Law School's Legal Information Institute operates the site.

To subscribe, send an email message to listserv@listserv.law.cornell.edu and leave the subject line blank. In the message area type: subscribe liibulletin *firstname lastname*, where *firstname* and *lastname* are replaced by your first and last names.

Oyez Oyez Oyez: A U.S. Supreme Court Database

oyez.org

This site offers recordings of oral arguments from about 1,000 Supreme Court cases. The site is operated by Northwestern University, and the recordings are digitized from tapes in the National Archives.

Listening to the cases requires RealAudio software. Oyez offers a link to another Internet site where the software can be downloaded for free.

The database can be searched by title, citation, subject, and date. For each case, the site provides recordings of oral arguments and text listing the facts of the case, the constitutional question involved, and the Court's conclusion.

Oyez also provides brief biographies of all current and former justices and a virtual tour of the Supreme Court building.

FindLaw

findlaw.com/casecode/supreme.html

This site provides the full text of all Supreme Court decisions from 1893 to the present. The database can be browsed by year and *U.S. Reports* volume number, and it also can be searched by citation, case title, and keywords. The decisions are in HTML format, and many have hyperlinks to citations from previous decisions.

The site also offers the full text of the U.S. Constitution, with annotations by the Congressional Research Service, and links to cited Supreme Court cases. FindLaw, a legal publisher, operates the site.

FedWorld/FLITE Supreme Court Decisions

fedworld.gov/supcourt/index.htm

FedWorld's database contains the full text of all Supreme Court decisions issued between 1937 and 1975. The database was originally compiled by the U.S. Air Force and has been placed online by the National Technical Information Service.

The more than 7,000 decisions are from volumes 300 to 422 of *U.S. Reports*. They can be searched by case name and keyword. The decisions are provided in ASCII text format.

SOURCE: Bruce Maxwell, *How to Access the Federal Government on the Internet: Washington Online,* 4th ed. (Washington, D.C.: Congressional Quarterly, 1999); Kenneth Jost, ed. *The Supreme Court A to Z,* 3d ed. (Washington, D.C.: CQ Press, 2003), 545–546. Updated by the author.

HOW TO READ A COURT CITATION

The official version of each Supreme Court decision and opinion is contained in a series of volumes entitled *United States Reports,* published by the U.S. Government Printing Office.

Although there are several unofficial compilations of Court opinions, including *United States Law Week,* published by the Bureau of National Affairs; *Supreme Court Reporter,* published by West Publishing Company; and *United States Supreme Court Reports, Lawyers' Edition,* published by Lawyers Cooperative Publishing Company, it is the official record that is generally cited. An unofficial version or the official slip opinion might be cited if a decision has not yet been officially reported.

A citation to a case includes, in order, the name of the parties to the case, the volume of *United States Reports* in which the decision appears, the page in the volume on which the opinion begins, the page from which any quoted material is taken, and the year of the decision.

For example, *Griswold v. Connecticut,* 381 U.S. 479, 482 (1965) means that the Supreme Court decision in the case of Griswold against the state of Connecticut can be found in volume 381 of *United States Reports* beginning on page 479. The number 482 refers to the page where the specific quotation in question can be found. The date is the year the opinion was issued.

All of the cases in this book use the official U.S. cite, even though early cases were cited in a different way. Until 1875 the official reports of the Court were published under the names of the Court reporters, and it is their names, or abbreviated versions, that appear in cites for those years; U.S. volume numbers have been assigned to them retroactively. A citation such as *Marbury v. Madison,* 1 Cranch 137 (1803) means that the opinion in the case of Marbury against Madison is in the first volume of reporter Cranch beginning on page 137. (Between 1875 and 1883 a Court reporter named William T. Otto compiled the decisions and opinions; his name appears on the volumes for those years as well as the *United States Reports* volume number, but Otto is seldom cited.)

The titles of the volumes to 1875, the full names of the reporters, and the corresponding *United States Reports* volumes are:

1–4	Dall.Dallas	1–4 U.S.
1–9 Cranch or Cr.	Cranch	5–13 U.S.
1–12 Wheat.	Wheaton	14–25 U.S.
1–16 Pet.	Peters	26–41 U.S.
1–24 How.	Howard	42–65 U.S.
1–2 Black	Black	66–67 U.S.
1–23 Wall.	Wallace	68–90 U.S.

SOURCE: Adapted from Kenneth Jost, ed., *The Supreme Court A to Z,* 3d ed. (Washington, D.C.: CQ Press, 2003), 534.

GLOSSARY OF COMMON LEGAL TERMS

Accessory. In criminal law, a person not present at the commission of an offense who commands, advises, instigates, or conceals the offense.

Acquittal. Discharge of a person from a charge of guilt. A person is acquitted when a jury returns a verdict of not guilty. A person may also be acquitted when a judge determines that there is insufficient evidence to convict him or that a violation of due process precludes a fair trial.

Adjudicate. To determine finally by the exercise of judicial authority to decide a case.

Affidavit. A voluntary written statement of facts or charges affirmed under oath.

A fortiori. With stronger force, with more reason.

Amicus curiae. A friend of the court, a person not a party to litigation, who volunteers or is invited by the court to give his views on a case.

Appeal. To take a case to a higher court for review. Generally, a party losing in a trial court may appeal once to an appellate court as a matter of right. If he loses in the appellate court, appeal to a higher court is within the discretion of the higher court. Most appeals to the U.S. Supreme Court are within the Court's discretion. However, when the highest court in a state rules that a U.S. statute is unconstitutional or upholds a state statute against the claim that it is unconstitutional, appeal to the Supreme Court is a matter of right.

Appellant. The party that appeals a lower court decision to a higher court.

Appellee. One who has an interest in upholding the decision of a lower court and is compelled to respond when the case is appealed to a higher court by the appellant.

Arraignment. The formal process of charging a person with a crime, reading him the charge,

asking whether he pleads guilty or not guilty, and entering his plea.

Attainder, Bill of. A legislative act pronouncing a particular individual guilty of a crime without trial or conviction and imposing a sentence upon him.

Bail. The security, usually money, given as assurance of a prisoner's due appearance at a designated time and place (as in court) to procure in the interim his release from jail.

Bailiff. A minor officer of a court usually serving as an usher or a messenger.

Brief. A document prepared by counsel to serve as the basis for an argument in court, setting out the facts of and the legal arguments in support of his case.

Burden of proof. The need or duty of affirmatively proving a fact or facts that are disputed.

Case Law. The law as defined by previously decided cases, distinct from statutes and other sources of law.

Cause. A case, suit, litigation, or action, civil or criminal.

Certiorari, Writ of. A writ issued from the Supreme Court, at its discretion, to order a lower court to prepare the record of a case and send it to the Supreme Court for review.

Civil law. Body of law dealing with the private rights of individuals, as distinguished from criminal law.

Class action. A lawsuit brought by one person or group on behalf of all persons similarly situated.

Code. A collection of laws, arranged systematically.

Comity. Courtesy, respect; usually used in the legal sense to refer to the proper relationship between state and federal courts.

Common law. Collection of principles and rules of action, particularly from unwritten English law, that derive their authority from longstanding usage and custom or from courts recognizing and enforcing these customs. Sometimes used synonymously with case law.

Consent decree. A court-sanctioned agreement settling a legal dispute and entered into by the consent of the parties.

Contempt (civil and criminal). Civil contempt consists in the failure to do something that the party is ordered by the court to do for the benefit of another party. Criminal contempt occurs when a person willfully exhibits disrespect for the court or obstructs the administration of justice.

Conviction. Final judgment or sentence that the defendant is guilty as charged.

Criminal law. That branch of law which deals with the enforcement of laws and the punishment of persons who, by breaking laws, commit crimes.

Declaratory judgment. A court pronouncement declaring a legal right or interpretation but not ordering a specific action.

De facto. In fact, in reality.

Defendant. In a civil action, the party denying or defending itself against charges brought by a plaintiff. In a criminal action, the person indicted for commission of an offense.

De jure. As a result of law, as a result of official action.

Deposition. Oral testimony from a witness taken out of court in response to written or oral questions, committed to writing, and intended to be used in the preparation of a case.

Dicta. See Obiter dictum.

Dismissal. Order disposing of a case without a trial.

Docket. See Trial docket.

Due process. Fair and regular procedure. The Fifth and Fourteenth Amendments guarantee persons that they will not be deprived of life, liberty, or property by the government until fair and usual procedures have been followed.

Error, Writ of. A writ issued from an appeals court to a lower court requiring it to send to the appeals court the record of a case in which it has entered a final judgment and which the appeals court will now review for error.

Ex parte. Only from, or on, one side. Application to a court for some ruling or action on behalf of only one party.

Ex post facto. After the fact; an ex post facto law makes an action a crime after it has already been committed, or otherwise changes the legal consequences of some past action.

Ex rel. Upon information from; usually used to describe legal proceedings begun by an official in the name of the state, but at the instigation of, and with information from, a private individual interested in the matter.

Grand jury. Group of twelve to twenty-three persons impaneled to hear in private evidence presented by the state against persons accused of crime and to issue indictments when a majority of the jurors find probable cause to believe that the accused has committed a crime. Called a "grand" jury because it comprises a greater number of persons than a "petit" jury.

Grand jury report. A public report released by a grand jury after an investigation into activities of public officials that fall short of criminal actions. Grand jury reports are often called "presentments."

Guilty. A word used by a defendant in entering a plea or by a jury in returning a verdict, indicating that the defendant is legally responsible as charged for a crime or other wrongdoing.

Habeas corpus. Literally, "you have the body"; a writ issued to inquire whether a person is lawfully imprisoned or detained. The writ demands that the persons holding the prisoner justify his detention or release him.

Immunity. A grant of exemption from prosecution in return for evidence or testimony.

In camera. "In chambers." Refers to court hearings in private without spectators.

In forma pauperis. In the manner of a pauper, without liability for court costs.

In personam. Done or directed against a particular person.

In re. In the affair of, concerning. Frequent title of judicial proceedings in which there are no adversaries, but rather where the matter itself—as a bankrupt estate—requires judicial action.

In rem. Done or directed against the thing, not the person.

Indictment. A formal written statement based on evidence presented by the prosecutor from a grand jury decided by a majority vote, charging one or more persons with specified offenses.

Information. A written set of accusations, similar to an indictment, but filed directly by a prosecutor.

Injunction. A court order prohibiting the person to whom it is directed from performing a particular act.

Interlocutory decree. A provisional decision of the court that temporarily settles an intervening matter before completion of a legal action.

Judgment. Official decision of a court based on the rights and claims of the parties to a case that was submitted for determination.

Jurisdiction. The power of a court to hear a case in question, which exists when the proper parties are present, and when the point to be decided is within the issues authorized to be handled by the particular court.

Juries. See Grand jury and Petit jury.

Magistrate. A judicial officer having jurisdiction to try minor criminal cases and conduct preliminary examinations of persons charged with serious crimes.

Mandamus. "We command." An order issued from a superior court directing a lower court or other authority to perform a particular act.

Moot. Unsettled, undecided. A moot question is also one that is no longer material; a moot case is one that has become hypothetical.

Motion. Written or oral application to a court or a judge to obtain a rule or an order.

Nolo contendere. "I will not contest it." A plea entered by a defendant at the discretion of the judge with the same legal effect as a plea of guilty, but it may not be cited in other proceedings as an admission of guilt.

Obiter dictum. Statement by a judge or justice expressing an opinion and included with, but not essential to, an opinion resolving a case before the court. Dicta are not necessarily binding in future cases.

Parole. A conditional release from imprisonment under conditions that if the prisoner abides by the law and other restrictions that may be placed upon him, he will not have to serve the remainder of his sentence. But if he does not abide by specified rules, he will be returned to prison.

Per curiam. "By the court." An unsigned opinion of the court or an opinion written by the whole court.

Petit jury. A trial jury, originally a panel of twelve persons who tried to reach a unanimous verdict on questions of fact in criminal and civil proceedings. Since 1970 the Supreme Court has upheld the legality of state juries with fewer than twelve persons. Because these small juries comprise fewer persons than "grand" juries, they are called "petit" juries.

Petitioner. One who files a petition with a court seeking action or relief, including a plaintiff or an appellant. But a petitioner is also a person who files for other court action where charges are not necessarily made; for example, a party may petition the court for an order requiring another person or party to produce documents. The opposite party is called the respondent. When a writ of certiorari is granted by the Supreme Court, the parties to the case are called petitioner and respondent in contrast to the appellant and appellee terms used in an appeal.

Plaintiff. A party who brings a civil action or sues to obtain a remedy for injury to his rights. The party against whom action is brought is termed the defendant.

Plea Bargaining. Negotiations between prosecutors and the defendant aimed at exchanging a plea of guilty from the defendant for concessions by the prosecutors, such as reduction of charges or a request for leniency.

Pleas. See Guilty and Nolo contendere.

Presentment. See Grand jury report.

Prima facie. At first sight; referring to a fact or other evidence presumably sufficient to establish a defense or a claim unless otherwise contradicted.

Probation. Process under which a person convicted of an offense, usually a first offense, receives a suspended sentence and is given his freedom, usually under the guardianship of a probation officer.

Quash. To overthrow, annul, or vacate; as to quash a subpoena.

Recognizance. An obligation entered into before a court or magistrate requiring the performance of a specified act—usually to appear in court at a later date. It is an alternative to bail for pretrial release.

Remand. To send back. In the event of a decision being remanded, it is sent back by a higher court to the court from which it came for further action.

Respondent. One who is compelled to answer the claims or questions posed in court by a petitioner. A defendant and an appellee may be called respondents, but the term also includes those parties who answer in court during actions in which charges are not necessarily brought or in which the Supreme Court has granted a writ of certiorari.

Seriatim. Separately, individually, one by one.

Stare decisis. "Let the decision stand." The principle of adherence to settled cases, the doctrine that principles of law established in earlier judicial decisions should be accepted as authoritative in similar subsequent cases.

Statute. A written law enacted by a legislature. A collection of statutes for a particular governmental division is called a code.

Stay. To halt or suspend further judicial proceedings.

Subpoena. An order to present one's self before a grand jury, court, or legislative hearing.

Subpoena duces tecum. An order to produce specified documents or papers.

Tort. An injury or wrong to the person or property of another.

Transactional immunity. Protects a witness from prosecution for any offense mentioned in or related to his testimony, regardless of independent evidence against him.

Trial docket. A calendar prepared by the clerks of the court listing the cases set to be tried.

Use immunity. Protects a witness against the use of his own testimony against him in prosecution.

Vacate. To make void, annul, or rescind.

Writ. A written court order commanding the designated recipient to perform or not perform acts specified in the order.

CASE NAME INDEX

Page numbers in **bold** indicate primary cases.

SUBJECT INDEX

AAA (Agricultural Adjustment Act), 132–144
Abolition, 2
Abortion, 236, 241, 299–308, 345
Abrams, Floyd, 383
Ackerman, Bruce, 365
Ackerman, Gary, 325
ACLU. *See* American Civil Liberties Union
Adams, John Quincy, 11
Adkins, Jesse, 121
Advertiser (New Jersey)
    on Cherokee cases, 22
Advocacy of violence, 174–183
Affirmative action programs, 309–318
AFL-CIO, 378
African Americans
    affirmative action programs, 309–318
    capital punishment, public opinion of, 297
    civil liberties, protection of, 34–43
    civil rights movement, 309
    interracial marriage, 252–261
    legislative apportionment issues, 226–234
    married women's right to practice law, analogy to, 46
    NIRA and, 138
    school segregation, 197–205
Afrique Nouvelle
    on *Brown v. Board of Education,* 198
Agricultural Adjustment Act (AAA), 132–144
Alabama
    moment-of-silence laws, 319–328
    reapportionment, 226–234
    school prayer, 223
Alabama Journal
    on Cherokee cases, 21–22
Alameda Times-Star
    on *McConnell v. FEC,* 382
Alaska, 85, 89, 93
Aleinikoff, Alexander, 93
Alexander, Nanci, 354
Alexandre, Maurice, 167
Alger, George, 124–125
Alien Land Law, 162
Allen, Lafon, 64
Allott, Gordon, 232

Almond, J. Lindsay, 202
Altgeld, John P., 72–73
Amar, Akhil, 363
A.M.E. Church Review
    on *Plessy v. Ferguson,* 77–78
America
    on *Engel v. Vitale,* 222–223
    on *Wisconsin v. Yoder,* 279
American Bar Association, 145, 213, 371
American Center for Law and Justice, 223, 372, 374
American Civil Liberties Union (ACLU)
    Amish children and compulsory school attendance, 277
    BCRA, 378, 382–383
    capital punishment, 294
    exclusionary rule, 206–207
    flag salute requirement, 145, 147–148
    freedom of speech and advocating violence, 180–181
    Miranda rights, 246, 247
    moment-of-silence laws, 323
    peyote use in religious ceremonies, 343
    ritual animal sacrifices, 352, 356
    sodomy laws, 371, 372
American Civil Rights Coalition, 316
American Coalition for Traditional Values, 322
American Economic Association, 64
American Family Association, 372
American Farm Bureau Federation, 140
American Federation of Labor, 96, 138
American Indian Religious Freedom Act of 1978, 346
American Jewish Committee, 222, 352
American Jewish Congress, 222, 343, 351
American Jewish World
    on *Engel v. Vitale,* 222
American Law Review
    on *Bradwell v. Illinois,* 49
    on Income Tax Cases, 64
    on Insular Cases, 93
    on *Milligan,* 39
    on *Plessy v. Ferguson,* 79, 82
American Liberty League, 141
American Psychological Association, 371